Trade Commission Act §5	Trade Commission Act §6	Trade Commission Act §§7-18	Trade Commission Act §§1-5	McCarran-Ferguson (Insurance ... Moratorium Act) §§1-5	... (Fair Trade) Act	... Act	...dia Act §§1-10	...dia Act §11	...dia Act §§13-15	...man Act §1	...man Act §2	Robinson-Patman Act §§3-4	Sherman Act §1	Sherman Act §§2-6	Sherman Act §8	Webb-Pomerene Act §§1-5
					•							•				
														•		
															•	
										•						
												•				
•				•												
	•															
		•														
			•													•
								•								
							•									
									•							

ANTITRUST
ADVISER

ANTITRUST ADVISER

CARLA ANDERSON HILLS, *Editor*

McGraw-Hill Book Company / Shepard's Citations, Inc.

New York · St. Louis · San Francisco · Colorado Springs
Düsseldorf · Johannesburg · Kuala Lumpur · London
Mexico · Montreal · New Delhi · Panama
Rio de Janeiro · Singapore · Sydney · Toronto

ANTITRUST ADVISER

Preface

The genesis of *Antitrust Adviser* occurred in 1964 in Los Angeles at an informal luncheon of attorneys who practice in the antitrust area. The conversation was of the "would you believe" variety, enumerating a long parade of instances known to those present of *per se* violations that had been written into documents prepared or reviewed by lawyers without antitrust experience. The implications of these serious oversights caused the group to ask "What could be done to help prevent such professional disasters?" The consensus was that the busy general practitioner is not aided greatly by available treatises or case books, because of his lack of time and the fact that most of the books are statute oriented, which means that he must know at the outset that he has a Clayton Act problem, for instance. It was suggested at that meeting that a volume on antitrust that was problem oriented might be of real use to such a lawyer whose client asked him to comment on his new pricing policy, to revise a proposed distribution agreement, or to review his contracts with suppliers or customers.

The California Continuing Education of the Bar, particularly Felix F. Stumpf, took an interest in the project and provided encouragement. Subsequently McGraw-Hill became convinced that the project had value beyond the boundaries of California and provided the catalysis for this work.

Thus, *Antitrust Adviser* was written especially for the practitioner who represents business to assist him to circumvent antitrust problems in preparing typical business documents and to handle antitrust controversy for his client when it arises. The *Adviser* deals with the areas believed to be the most frequently transgressed, including arrangements among competitors, distribution of products, acquisitions and mergers, pricing problems, unfair competition, problems with trade associations, and the antitrust implications of the patent system and of labor law. With respect to handling controversies, the *Adviser* analyzes the problems of prosecution and defense, and perhaps most importantly, it sets forth guidelines for compliance.

This has been a lengthy, time-consuming project. We hope it has contributed to the practice of law.

Contents

1

Orientation

Carla Anderson Hills

Mrs. Hills received the AB degree from Stanford University in 1955 and the LLB degree from Yale Law School in 1958. She is a member of the Los Angeles County, Federal, and American Bar Associations, the State Bar of California, and the Los Angeles firm of Munger, Tolles, Hills and Rickershauser.

I. Organization

I. Organization

A. [§1.1] Sensitive Antitrust Areas

The *Adviser* strives to delineate for the lawyer the areas in business and in litigation believed to be the most sensitive. Being problem oriented, the *Adviser* discusses the provisions of the Sherman Act, the Clayton Act, the Robinson-Patman Act, and the Federal Trade Commission Act in context

1

of these business or litigation problems in the hopes that the practitioner can find his type of problem in the discussion and thereby obtain help in its solution.

Relationships with competitors probably generate most antitrust problems. Horizontal restraints of trade that result from agreements or arrangements between competitors are discussed in Chapter 2. Trade associations, a legitimate combination of competitors *per se*, may provide an irresistible setting for improper activities between competitors. Controversial association activities and preventive measures available to trade associations as well as company counsel are discussed in Chapter 8.

Problems that germinate from relationships with persons up and down the distribution chain, be they suppliers or customers, are discussed in Chapter 3.

Pricing problems, in particular the requirement for price uniformity, are discussed in Chapter 5.

Mergers and acquisitions may occur horizontally between competitors or vertically up and down the chain of distribution. Those having anti-competitive effects are prohibited and are discussed in Chapter 4.

Patent and labor law are distinct specialities that embody important policies which at times collide with the pro-competitive policy of the antitrust laws. These points of potential collision are discussed in Chapter 7 and in Chapter 14, respectively.

B. [§1.2] Controversy

If controversy erupts, counsel should know how to react. If the government is involved, counsel's reaction may differ depending on whether the acting agency is the Federal Trade Commission, discussed in Chapter 6, or the Department of Justice, discussed in Chapter 11, or whether the investigation is being conducted through the Federal Bureau of Investigation or the grand jury, discussed in Chapter 10. Defense of an antitrust action, government or private, is discussed in Chapter 13.

A fact of business life is the private treble-damage action, which is discussed in Chapter 12.

C. [§1.3] Compliance

Counsel's most important contribution to his client may be to review his client's proposed course of conduct before controversy erupts and to recommend changes in those activities that are likely to cause problems. Compliance is discussed in Chapter 6.

D. [§1.4] Exclusions and Inclusions

Many aspects of the antitrust laws are not covered. There is little discussion of state antitrust statutes, of various federal regulatory statutes applicable to specific industries, or of the application of the federal antitrust laws to foreign commerce. The emphasis throughout the *Adviser* is on those areas having federal antitrust implications that are most frequently encountered by the business lawyer.

The authors have each approached their subject matters individually. As a result there are instances in which the same topic is discussed from different points of view by different authors. It is believed that this treatment adds a helpful dimension to the volume.

To facilitate the *Adviser*'s use, each chapter is preceded by an outline for initial broad referencing and extensive cross-referencing is employed throughout. In addition there is a detailed index, a table of cases, and on the inside of the book's cover a reprint of the most relevant provisions of the Sherman Act, the Clayton Act, the Robinson-Patman Act, and the Federal Trade Commission Act. Checklists and forms are provided wherever possible.

II. [§1.5] Acknowledgments

This has been a lengthy and time-consuming project. To list all of those whom the authors would like publicly to thank is not feasible. However, special thanks are owing to William L. Blaine, Lawbook Editor of McGraw-Hill, for holding the faith to the end.

2

Horizontal Restraints of Trade–The Sherman Act

Gordon F. Hampton and Don T. Hibner, Jr.

Mr. Hampton received the AB degree from Stanford University in 1935 and the JD degree from Harvard Law School in 1938. Mr. Hibner received the BA degree from Stanford University in 1955 and the LLB degree from Stanford Law School in 1962. Mr. Hampton and Mr. Hibner are members of the Los Angeles County Bar Association, the State Bar of California, and are members of the Los Angeles firm of Sheppard, Mullin, Richter and Hampton.

I. Introduction: The Sherman Act

A. [§2.1] Scope of Chapter

The general objective of the antitrust laws has been declared to be the promotion of competition in open markets, a primary feature of our private enterprise system. *1955 Report of the Attorney General's National Committee to Study the Antitrust Laws* 1 (hereafter *Attorney General's*

Report, 1955). A key guardian of this fundamental principle has been the Sherman Antitrust Act of 1890, 15 USC §§1–7. This chapter will analyze horizontal restraints of trade, concentrating on two of the key sections of the Sherman Act—Sections 1 and 2. These two sections have resulted in the bulk of all criminal cases prosecuted by the Department of Justice and the great majority of the treble-damage actions authorized by Section 4 of the Clayton Act (15 USC §45) to be brought by private parties "injured in their business or property."

Because of the great variety of factual situations in which cases under Section 1 may arise, the treatment given here will deal primarily with horizontal arrangements between competitors rather than with so-called "vertical" problems between suppliers and distributors. Vertical arrangements will be treated in Chapter 3. Monopolization, and attempts and conspiracy to monopolize, all declared unlawful by Section 2 of the Sherman Act, will be treated in this chapter because of their increasing importance to practitioners and their close relationship to Section 1. Other horizontal relationships are dealt with in Chapter 4.

B. [§2.2] Common-Law Background

The history of the common law of restraints of trade has been carefully documented by legal scholars. See, *e.g.*, Sanderson, *Restraint of Trade in English Law* (1926); Hedges, *The Law Relating to Restraint of Trade* (1932); Peppin, *Price-Fixing Agreements Under the Sherman Antitrust Law* (1940) 28 *Calif L Rev* 297, 677.

This common-law background is important to practitioners because the Supreme Court in interpreting the Sherman Act has ruled that it codified existing common law, which thereby became the cornerstone upon which our present-day interpretation of the Sherman Act is based. See *United States v Addyston Pipe & Steel Co.* (6th Cir 1898) 85 F 271, *aff'd* (1899) 175 US 211; *Standard Oil Co. of New Jersey v United States* (1911) 221 US 1.

Restraints of trade at common law were generally associated with contracts creating voluntary restraints of an individual's engaging in the business or profession of another. Originally, all such agreements were considered contrary to public policy. In time, however, the English courts upheld such contracts if the restraint was reasonable, and limited temporally and territorially. See *Mitchell v Reynolds* (K.B. 1711) 1 P. Williams 181, 24 Eng Rep 347. These distinctions gave rise to the terms "ancillary" and "nonancillary" restraints. See *United States v Addyston Pipe & Steel Co., supra.* An ancillary restraint, which was valid, was one that was subordinate to a main lawful purpose of a transaction it was designed to effectuate. An example of an ancillary covenant is a limited agreement not to compete entered into on the sale of a business. A nonancillary restraint, which was invalid, was one whose main purpose was to restrain trade. A key test in determining the "reasonableness" of an ancillary restraint was whether it imposed a restraint greater than was required to protect the person exacting the restraining covenant. See 2 *Restatement, Contracts* §514. Although this distinction has lost some of its vitality, it is with us today as the "rule of reason." The rule of reason is basic not only to the Sherman Act (15 USC §§1-7) but also to other sections of the antitrust laws, such as Section 3 of the Clayton Act (15 USC §14).

While common-law influence has affected the development of the Sherman Act, it must be emphasized that before the Sherman Act, the common law was inconsistent with itself and was developing in several directions at once. Compare Handler, *A Study of the Construction and Enforcement of the Federal Antitrust Laws* (1941) TNEC Monograph no. 38 at 4-5 with Peppin, *Price-Fixing Agreements under the Sherman Antitrust Law* (1940) 28 *Calif L Rev* 297, 350. The Sherman Antitrust Act channeled this development under a broad congressional mandate.

C. [§2.3] Legislative History

The end of the American Civil War heralded a period of accelerated industrial growth and increasing concentration of economic power in certain key industries. For example, by 1880 the Standard Oil Company controlled the major share of the petroleum-refining industry, and the tobacco industry was rigidly controlled by a few large producers who could regulate prices and control production. By 1890, loose-knit confederations, commonly referred to as "trusts," existed in the petroleum, tobacco, cotton oil, linseed oil, sugar, whiskey, envelope, salt, cordage, oilcloth, paving pitch, school-slate, cast-iron pipe, and paper industries. Agitation against the trusts began in earnest with the Granger Movement of 1870. The 1888 Republican Party platform condemned all combinations organized to control the conditions of trade arbitrarily and recommended legislation to prevent such activities. On December 4, 1889, Senator John Sherman introduced an antitrust bill, which was redrafted in the Senate Judiciary Committee, passed by Congress, and signed into law by President Harrison on July 2, 1890.

There are some excellent works on the legislative history of the Sherman Act. See Letwin, *Congress and the Sherman Antitrust Law; 1887-1890* (1956) 23 *U Chi L Rev* 221; Clark, *The Federal Trust Policy* (1931); Thorelli, *The Federal Antitrust Policy* (1955). A reading of the legislative history discloses that the Sherman Act was primarily concerned with combinations of industry and capital that had monopolized major segments of the economy. Because of the almost constitutional broadness of the language of the act, however, it has been applied to a multitude of factual situations, large and small, and probably to many situations not within the initial contemplation of Congress.

D. [§2.4] Summary of Provisions

The key section of the Sherman Act, directed against concerted action, is Section 1. The basic part of Section 1 has remained unchanged from the day it was passed and provides simply (15 USC §1):

Every contract, combination in the form of trust or otherwise, or conspiracy, in restraint of trade or commerce among the several States, or with foreign nations, is declared to be illegal.

Section 1 also provides that:

Every person who shall make any contract or engage in any combination or conspiracy declared by sections 1-7 of this title to be illegal shall be deemed guilty of a misdemeanor, and, on conviction thereof, shall be punished by fine not exceeding fifty thousand dollars, or by imprisonment not exceeding one year, or by both said punishments, in the discretion of the court.

Section 2 (15 USC §2) defines the three separate crimes of monopolization, combination and conspiracy to monopolize, and attempts to monopolize. Section 3 (15 USC §3) applies the general language of Section 1 to territories of the United States and the District of Columbia. Section 4 (15 USC §4) vests authority in the Department of Justice to institute equity proceedings to restrain violations of the Sherman Act. Section 5 (15 USC §5) provides for extraterritorial service of process in a government equity proceeding, and Section 6 (15 USC §6) provides for the forfeiture of goods in transit owned under a combination in violation of Section 1. Section 7 originally granted private persons the right to sue for treble damages. However, with the passage of the Clayton Act in 1914, Section 7 was superseded by Section 4 of the Clayton Act (15 USC §15). Section 7 was repealed in 1955, thus eliminating duplicative coverage. 69 Stat 283 (1955).

There are five basic types of actions that may be brought charging violations of Section 1 of the Sherman Act: (a) government criminal proceedings; (b) government proceedings in equity under Section 15 of the Clayton Act (15 USC §25); (c) private injunctive actions under Section 16 of the Clayton Act (15 USC §26); (d) private treble-damage actions under

Section 4 of the Clayton Act (15 USC §15); and (e) government action for single damages under Section 4A of the Clayton Act (15 USC §15a). Before 1958, only private persons could maintain damage suits.

In addition, the FTC may attack acts violative of Section 1 and many acts violative of Section 2 under Section 5 of the Federal Trade Commission Act (15 USC §45) as "unfair methods of competition." See *FTC v Cement Institute* (1948) 333 US 683, 689-693. Section 5 does not require the existence of a conspiracy and hence can be used when a Sherman Act suit might fail. However, only the FTC may bring a Section 5 action; it does so through its institution of cease and desist proceedings. See discussion of the Federal Trade Commission Act in Chapter 6.

II. Concerted Action: Section 1 of the Sherman Act

A. [§2.5] Meaning of Key Terms

It is impossible to understand an act as broadly written as Section 1 (15 USC §1) without first giving some attention to the meaning of certain key terms, upon which the legal issues raised by the cases so often turn.

1. [§2.6] Every

Obviously, if "every" were to be given literal effect, all partnerships, mergers, and output and requirement contracts would have to be held illegal, because they all involve, in varying degrees, some restraint of trade. Since the landmark case, *Standard Oil Co. of New Jersey v United States* (1911) 221 US 1, the Sherman Act has been interpreted as requiring application consistent with current economic and social values. Consequently, "every" has been qualified to mean every *unreasonable* contract, combination, or conspiracy in restraint of trade. See, *e.g., Chicago Board of Trade v United States* (1918) 246 US 231, 238 and *Lawson v Woodmere* (4th Cir 1954) 217 F2d 148, 151.

2. [§2.7] Contract, Combination, or Conspiracy

Underlying the entire thrust of Section 1 are the terms "contract, combination . . ., or conspiracy." These dictate a concert of action between two or more persons and thus distinguish Section 1 from Section 2 (15 USC §2) which is applicable to individual as well as concerted activity. The terms are susceptible to parallel construction and are sometimes used interchangeably. However, each has a distinctive connotation.

a. [§2.8] Contract and Combination

"Contract," most often used, has its familiar legal meaning of a formal bargain. In addition to its use in specifying a nonancillary restraint of trade, "combination" has a supplemental meaning. In *Northern Securities Co. v United States* (1904) 193 US 197, for example, the term is used to refer to mergers, acquisitions, and consolidations. It has often been used interchangeable with "conspiracy" and has not developed a separate existence of its own.

In *United States v Parke, Davis & Co.* (1960) 362 US 29, the Supreme Court found an unlawful "combination" when a manufacturer of drugs, seeking compliance with announced resale prices, went beyond mere customer selection and conferred with drug retailers concerning their willingness to cooperate with the manufacturer's accouncements.

More recently, in *Albrecht v Herald Co.* (1968) 390 US 145, the Supreme Court held that a newspaper publishing company was engaged in an unlawful combination when it hired a circulation sales company and set up a rival to force a distributor to lower his prices. "Combination" connotes a loose-knit association as opposed to the "agreement" contemplated by a "conspiracy."

b. [§2.9] Conspiracy

"Conspiracy" is by far the most important of the three terms. Its essence is an agreement to achieve either an unlawful object, or a lawful object by unlawful means. The complicity standards are similar to those relied on in other areas of criminal law. For example, in *Esco Corp. v United States* (9th Cir 1965) 340 F2d 1000, 1008, the Court held that a company's participation in but two of ten conspiratorial meetings alleged would be sufficient to find participation in the entire conspiracy if its involvement in the two was unlawful and knowing. Furthermore, evidence not relating directly to a particular defendant's participation may be admitted to prove the existence of the conspiracy, consequently allowing proof of the defendant's relation to the entire agreement. See *Continental Ore Co. v Union Carbide & Carbon Corp.* (1962) 370 US 690, 710.

Direct evidence of an express agreement is not essential; circumstantial evidence may be sufficient. See *American Tobacco Co. v United States* (1946) 328 US 781, at 810: "Where the circumstances are such as to warrant a jury in finding that the conspirators had a unity of purpose or a common design and understanding, or a meeting of the minds in an unlawful arrangement, the conclusion that a conspiracy is established is justified." See also *United States v Paramount Pictures, Inc.* (1947) 334 US 131, 142. The agreement may be established by admissions contained in correspondence among the principals (see, *e.g., Jerrold Electronics Corp. v*

Westcoast Broadcasting Co., Inc. (9th Cir 1965) 341 F2d 653, 662, *cert den* (1965) 382 US 817), or formalized in the bylaws of a trade association. (See, *e.g.*, *Associated Press v United States* (1945) 326 US 1; *United States v Insurance Board of Cleveland* (ND Ohio 1960) 188 F Supp 949.

(1) [§2.10] Conspiracy Inferred from Uniform Action: Conscious Parallelism

What kind of circumstantial evidence will establish a conspiracy is a difficult problem in Sherman Act cases. *Interstate Circuit, Inc. v United States* (1939) 306 US 208 is credited with the creation of the doctrine of "conscious parallelism." Interstate, an exhibitor of motion pictures, requested eight film distributors to exact agreements for minimum admission prices from exhibitors to whom they distributed films. In upholding the conviction of the participants in the arrangement, the Court said (306 US at 227):

[A]cceptance by competitors, without previous agreement, of an invitation to participate in a plan, the necessary consequence of which, if carried out, is restraint of interstate commerce, is sufficient to establish an unlawful conspiracy under the Sherman Act.

The *Interstate Circuit* case gave rise to speculation that such conscious parallelism of action may have supplanted the necessity for proof of an agreement. This notion was laid to rest in *Theatre Enterprises, Inc. v Paramount Film Distrib. Corp.* (1954) 346 US 537, 541, in which the majority declared:

[T]his Court has never held that proof of parallel business behavior conclusively establishes agreement or, . . . that such behavior itself constitutes a Sherman Act offense.

In short, conscious parallelism "is admissible circumstantial evidence from which the fact finder may infer agreement" (346 US 540) and thus may help support a finding of conspiracy, but standing alone it is not enough. In *Joseph E. Seagram and Sons, Inc. v Hawaiian Oke and Liquors* (9th Cir 1969) 416 F2d 71, *cert den* (1970) 396 US 1062, *reh den* (1970) 397 US 1003, the appellate court held that an instruction to the effect that "proof of parallel business behavior does not of itself necessarily establish an agreement," constituted reversible error on the ground that it permitted the jury to find a conspiracy on the basis of conscious parallel action alone, stating (at 84):

We think that the court erred. . . . We know of no case holding that conscious parallel action, standing alone, is sufficient to support a finding of conspiracy, in the absence of "circumstances which logically suggest joint agreement, as distinguished from individual action."

To the same effect, see *Klein v American Luggage Works, Inc.* (3d Cir 1963) 323 F2d 787, 791, a private action in which the Third Circuit reversed a finding of conspiracy when the evidence showed only that the retailers adhered to the manufacturer's suggested retail prices with knowledge that the manufacturer expected all retailers to conform.

Conspiracy may be inferred from proof of substantially similar business behavior, unrebutted by defendants in a position to do so. Naturally, the significance of uniform action varies depending on "the particular business setting in which it occurs." *Attorney General's Report, 1955,* 40. Compare, for example, *C-O TWO Fire Equipment Co. v United States* (9th Cir 1952) 197 F2d 489, *cert den* (1952) 344 US 892, which held that price uniformity with respect to fire extinguishers not naturally standardized was a factor in finding a violation of the Sherman Act, with *Pevely Dairy Co. v United States* (8th Cir 1949) 178 F2d 363, *cert den* (1950) 339 US 942, which dismissed a government complaint charging violation of the Sherman Act on the ground that the product involved was milk, a naturally standardized product, and therefore uniform price did not prove conspiratorial action.

The *Attorney General's Report, 1955* sets out (at page 39) a number of criteria that should be examined in determining whether the uniformity of action is sufficient to permit an inference of conspiratorial action. These include:

a. How pervasive is the uniformity?

b. Does it extend to price alone or to all other terms and conditions of sale?

c. How nearly identical is the uniformity?

d. What is the time lag, if any, between a change by one competitor and that of the other or others?

e. Is the product involved homogeneous or differentiated?

f. In the case of price uniformity, have the defendants raised as well as lowered prices in parallel fashion?

g. Can the conduct, no matter how uniform, be adequately explained by independent business justifications?

For further discussion of conspiracy in the context of uniform action see *Norfolk Monument Co. & Woodlawn Memorial Gardens, Inc.* (1969) 394 US 700; *United States v General Motors Corp.* (1966) 384 US 127; *United States v United States Gypsum Co.* (1948) 333 US 364; *Morton Salt Co. v United States* (10th Cir 1956) 235 F2d 573, *aff'd* (1959) 360 US 395; *Independent Iron Works, Inc. v United States Steel Corp.* (9th Cir 1963) 322 F2d 656, 661, *cert den* (1963) 375 US 922. See also Rahl,

Conspiracy and the Antitrust Laws (1950) 44 *Ill L Rev* 743; Turner, *The Definition of Agreement under the Sherman Act: Conscious Parallelism & Refusals to Deal* (1962) 75 *Harv L Rev* 655, 703–705; Note, *Conscious Parallelism—Fact or Fancy?* (1951) 3 *Stan L Rev* 679.

(2) [§2.11] Intracorporate Conspiracy Doctrine

It has long been the law that when a corporation commits a crime the officers and directors who participated in the unlawful act are guilty of criminal conspiracy. *Barron v United States* (1st Cir 1925) 5 F2d 799. This doctrine applies when a corporation engages in a scheme to monopolize in violation of Section 2 of the Sherman Act (15 USC §2). See discussion of combinations and conspiracies to monopolize at §2.65.

In contrast, Section 1 of the Sherman Act (15 USC §1) does not prohibit restraints of trade as such, but only contracts, combinations, and conspiracies in restraint of trade. Since a corporation cannot conspire with itself and can act only through its officers and employees, no conspiracy results when a corporation's personnel confer with each other, even about restraints of trade.

But separate corporate subsidiaries or a parent corporation and a subsidiary, even one wholly owned, can conspire. The law was aptly summarized in *Nelson Radio & Supply Co. v Motorola* (5th Cir 1952) 200 F2d 911, 914, *cert den* (1953) 345 US 925:

It is basic in the law of conspiracy that you must have two persons or entities to have a conspiracy. A corporation cannot conspire with itself any more than a private individual can, and it is the general rule that the acts of the agent are the acts of the corporation. . . . [A] corporation and its subsidiaries can be guilty of a conspiracy in restraint of trade but that involves separate corporate entities.

See also *United States v Yellow Cab Co.* (1947) 332 US 218, 227; *Timken Roller Bearing Co. v United States* (1951) 341 US 593, 598.

Exemplifying a conspiracy between a parent corporation and its wholly owned subsidiary is *United States v General Motors Corp.* (7th Cir 1941) 121 F2d 376, 404, *cert den* (1941) 314 US 618, in which the court held that an auto manufacturer, its wholly owned sales subsidiary, and its wholly owned finance subsidiary could conspire to restrain trade in violation of Section 1 of the Sherman Act.

Exemplifying a conspiracy between two subsidiaries is *Kiefer-Stewart Co. v Joseph E. Seagram & Sons, Inc.* (1951) 340 US 211, 215, in which the Court held that a refusal to deal and an agreement between subsidiary corporations to fix prices violated Section 1 of the Sherman Act.

The *Attorney General's Report, 1955*, at page 34, reviewed several of the pre-1955 Supreme Court cases and concluded:

The use of subsidiaries is generally induced by normal prudent business considerations. No social objective would be attained were subsidiaries enjoined from agreeing not to compete with each other or with their parent. To demand internal competition within and between the members of a single business unit is to invite chaos without promotion of the public welfare.

The substance of the Supreme Court decisions is that concerted action between a parent and subsidiary or between subsidiaries which has for its purpose or effect coercion or unreasonable restraint on the trade of strangers to those acting in concert is prohibited by Section 1. . . . Where such concerted action restrains no trade and is designed to restrain no trade other than that of the parent and its subsidiaries, Section 1 is not violated.

The analysis of the *Attorney General's Report* was seemingly borne out in *Sunkist Growers, Inc. v Winckler & Smith Citrus Products, Co.* (1962) 370 US 19. The Court reversed the Ninth Circuit's finding in a treble-damage action that there was a conspiracy violating Sections 1 and 2 of the Sherman Act between Sunkist, the parent cooperative, Exchange Orange, a wholly owned subsidiary, and Exchange Lemon, a separate cooperative belonging to Sunkist. The Court stated (320 US at 29):

There is no indication that the use of separate corporations had economic significance in itself or that outsiders considered and dealt with the three entities as independent organizations.

The question then arises whether divisions within the same corporation can conspire. The courts have held that divisions of a single corporation, not being separate legal entities, cannot conspire. See, *e.g., Poller v Columbia Broadcasting System, Inc.* (DC Cir 1960) 284 F2d 599, 603, rev'd on other grounds (1962) 368 US 464: "We conclude that CBS, its unincorporated division, and its employees were incapable of conspiring to restrain trade or commerce." Complaints were dismissed in: *Deterjet Corp. v United Aircraft Corp.* (D Del 1962) 211 F Supp 348 (It was alleged that United Aircraft combined with Pratt & Whitney, its division, and others, to preclude plaintiff from marketing its product in competition with defendant's product); *Kemwel Automotive Corp. v Ford Motor Co.* (SD NY 1966) 1966 Trade Cases ¶71,882 (It was alleged that Ford and Ford International, an unincorporated division, conspired to monopolize the export of Ford automotive parts and accessories); *Johnny Maddox Motor Co. v Ford Motor Co.* (WD Tex 1960) 202 F Supp 103 (It was alleged that Ford, its divisions, and others, conspired to discriminate against plaintiff-distributor in price and merchandise and services provided). In *Alpha Distributing Co. v Jack Daniels Distillery* (ND Calif 1961) 207 F Supp 136, *aff'd* (9th Cir 1962) 304 F2d 451, the court refused to enjoin a manufacturer and its corporate affiliate from marketing its product except through the plaintiff, finding no legal support for the conspiracy allegation.

The commentators are in accord with the decisions (See *e.g.*, Areeda, *Antitrust Analysis* 238 (1967)) and so is the *Attorney General's Report, 1955*, at page 35. More recently the Ninth Circuit, reversing, held similarly. *Joseph E. Seagram and Sons, Inc. v Hawaiian Oke and Liquors, Ltd.* (9th Cir 1969) 416 F2d 71, *cert den* (1970) 396 US 1062, *reh den* (1970) 397 US 1003. The court stated (at 83):

Once the theory that "divisions" or other internal administrative units of a single corporation can "conspire" with each other is accepted, we can see no sensible basis upon which it can be decided that, in one case, there has been a conspiracy and that, in another, there has not. No corporation of any size can operate without an internal division of labor between various of its officers and agents. The larger the enterprise, the more necessary such internal units become. Moreover, sound management demands extensive delegation of authority within [an] organization. Yet, under the trial court's ruling, the more delegation there is, the more danger there will be that the holders of such delegated authority will be found by a court to be capable of conspiring with each other in carrying on the corporation's business, as in this case, where the trial court so held as a matter of law.

For commentaries on the intracorporate conspiracy doctrine, see McQuade, *Conspiracy, Multicorporate Enterprises, and Section 1 of the Sherman Act* (1955) 41 *Va L Rev* 183; Rahl, *Conspiracy and the Antitrust Laws* (1950) 44 *Ill L Rev* 743; Willis and Pitofsky, *Antitrust Consequences of Using Corporate Subsidiaries* (1968) 43 *NYU L Rev* 20; Barndt, *Two Trees or One? The Problem of Intra-Enterprise Conspiracy* (1962) 23 *Mont L Rev* 158.

To date, the intracorporate doctrine has only been applied to intracorporate conduct that can be characterized as predatory or coercive vis-a-vis outsiders. As stated by Donald F. Turner, former Assistant Attorney General in charge of the Antitrust Division, in 34 ABA Antitrust LJ 122, 123 (1967):

It seems to us that as the law has developed in this area it has been thought appropriate to apply the conspiracy concept to the activities of a group of closely related corporations where the conduct involved is beyond defense and involves coercion of outsiders.

3. Trade or Commerce

a. [§2.12] Interstate Commerce

The scope of commercial activity to which the Sherman Act applies is as broad as the commerce clause is in other areas of the law. *United*

States v Southeastern Underwriters Ass'n. (1944) 322 US 533, 558. As stated in *Mandeville Island Farms, Inc. v American Crystal Sugar Co.* (1948) 334 US 219, 234:

[T]he inquiry whether the restraint occurs in one phase or another, interstate or intrastate, of the total economic process is now merely a preliminary step, except for those situations in which no aspect of or substantial effect upon interstate commerce can be found in the sum of the facts presented. For, given a restraint of the type forbidden by the Act, though arising in the course of intrastate or local activities, and a showing of actual or threatened effect upon interstate commerce, the vital question becomes whether the effect is sufficiently substantial and adverse to Congress' paramount policy declared in the Act's terms to constitute a forbidden consequence.

This test has been adapted to the "flow of commerce" concept, so that the restraint can be at the beginning or end of a continuum of activity in question. See *United States v Employing Plasterers' Ass'n.* (1954) 347 US 186, holding that restraints on plastering work in Chicago adversely affected the flow of plastering materials from out-of-state sources. Thus, even if the challenged activity is entirely intrastate, it is sufficient for purposes of the Sherman Act if it substantially affects interstate commerce under the "flow of commerce" theory. In *Burke v Ford* (1967) 389 US 320, 321–322, a private plaintiff charged that a statewide division of the liquor market by wholesalers violated Section 1 of the Sherman Act (15 USC §1). The lower courts ruled that the liquor, which was shipped from out-of-state to the wholesalers' warehouses, "came to rest" in the local warehouses, and the division of markets therefore did not occur in interstate commerce. The Supreme Court reversed *per curiam*, holding that the interstate commerce requirement of the Sherman Act was satisfied:

[F]or it is well established that an activity which does not itself occur *in* interstate commerce comes within the scope of the Sherman Act if it substantially *affects* interstate commerce. . . . Horizontal territorial divisions [albeit intrastate] almost invariably reduce competition among the participants. [citations] When competition is reduced, prices increase and unit sales decrease. The wholesalers' territorial division here almost surely resulted in fewer sales to retailers—hence fewer purchases from out-of-state distillers than would have occurred had free competition prevailed among the wholesalers. . . . Thus the statewide wholesalers' market division inevitably affected interstate commerce.

To the same effect is *United States v Yellow Cab Co.* (1947) 332 US 218, in which the Court said (at 225) that "it is enough if some appreciable part of interstate commerce is [affected]." See also *United States v Penn-*

sylvania Refuse Removal Ass'n. (3d Cir 1966) 357 F2d 806, 808–809, *cert den* (1966) 384 US 961; *Washington State Bowling Proprietors Ass'n. v Pacific Lanes, Inc.* (9th Cir 1966) 356 F2d 371, 380, *cert den* (1966) 384 US 963.

If the challenged activity occurs *in* or *in the flow of* interstate commerce, as distinguished from merely having an *effect upon* the flow of commerce, the Court has generally held that the amount of commerce affected is immaterial. See, *e.g., United States v Socony-Vacuum Oil Co.* (1940) 310 US 150, 225: "[T]he amount of interstate or foreign trade involved is not material [citation], since § 1 of the Act brands as illegal the character of the restraint not the amount of commerce affected." However, purchasing equipment from out of state "does not turn what was really a local activity into an interstate one." *Sun Valley Disposal Co. v Silver State Disposal Co.* (9th Cir 1969) 420 F2d 341 at 343.

For a discussion of the commerce issue in general, see Eiger, *The Commerce Element in Federal Antitrust Litigation* (1965) 25 Fed BJ 282.

b. [§2.13] Trade

The term "trade" has been defined by the Supreme Court as any "occupation, employment, or business whether manual or mercantile," carried on for the purpose of profit or gain. *United States v National Ass'n. of Real Estate Bds.* (1950) 339 US 485, 490–91. Under this broad rationale, the Sherman Act (15 USC §§1) has been held applicable to the sale of various services as well as goods:

a. Transportation services. *United States v Trans-Missouri Freight Ass'n.* (1897) 166 US 290; *United States v Joint Traffic Ass'n.* (1898) 171 US 505.

b. Cleaning, dying, and renovating wearing apparel. *Atlantic Cleaners & Dyers v United States* (1932) 286 US 427.

c. Procurement of medical and hospital services. *American Medical Ass'n. v United States* (1943) 317 US 519.

d. Furnishing of news. *Associated Press v United States* (1945) 326 US 1.

e. Providing stock exchange wire service. *Silver v New York Stock Exchange* (1963) 373 US 341.

f. Advertising services. *Indiana Farmer's Guide Pub. Co. v Prairie Farmer Pub. Co.* (1934) 293 US 268.

g. Fire and burglar-alarm central-station services. *United States v Grinnell Corp.* (1966) 384 US 563.

h. Producing theatrical attractions. *Hart v B. F. Keith Vaudeville Exch.* (1923) 262 US 271; *United States v Shubert* (1955) 348 US 222.

i. Taxicab service. *United States v Yellow Cab Co.* (1947) 332 US 218.

j. Collecting garbage. *United States v Penn Refuse Removal Ass'n.* (ED Pa 1965) 242 F Supp 794, *aff'd* (3d Cir 1966) 357 F2d 806, *cert den* (1966) 384 US 961. But see *Sun Valley Disposal Co. v Silver State Disposal Co.* (9th Cir 1969) 420 F2d 341.

k. Producing, distributing, and exhibiting motion pictures. *United States v Paramount Pictures, Inc.* (1948) 334 US 131; *Schine Chain Theatres v United States* (1948) 334 US 110.

l. Circulating price lists. *United States v Utah Pharmaceutical Assn.* (D Utah 1962) 201 F Supp 29, *appeal dismissed* (10th Cir 1962) 306 F2d 493, *aff'd* (1962) 371 US 24.

m. Real estate brokerage. *United States v National Ass'n. of Real Estate Boards* (1950) 339 US 485.

n. Professional football. *Radovich v National Football League* (1957) 352 US 445.

o. Professional boxing. *United States v International Boxing Club* (1955) 348 US 236.

Professional baseball, in contrast to professional football and boxing, has been accorded an exemption from the Sherman Act. For this and other areas in which the Sherman Act does not apply, see §§2.14–2.22.

The Clayton Act, which contains overlapping prohibitions, does not apply to services; hence, the Sherman Act, at times, has broader coverage. Illustrative of this fact is the application of Section 3 of the Clayton Act (15 USC §14) to various business arrangements, discussed in Chapter 3. For example, see the discussion of tying arrangements at §§3.9–3.18.

B. [§2.14] Antitrust Exemption Areas

Even before the Sherman Act was passed, lobbyists were seeking exemptions from its proposed provisions. In the years since its passage, Congress has granted numerous complete or partial exemptions from the antitrust laws. Some industries, such as professional baseball, are for all practical purposes free from any type of regulation under the antitrust laws. Other industries have been exempted from the antitrust laws merely to be put under the direct supervision of a federal agency.

If an antitrust exemption is unclear or partial, and an industry is subject to a degree of federal regulation, "primary jurisdiction" problems often arise, which are complex and require extensive analysis. Also, the mere fact that an industry has been exempted from the antitrust laws and is subjected, perhaps, to agency or executive regulation does not necessarily guarantee exemption from penalties or sanctions of an antitrust nature provided by separate statute or regulation. For example, in *Silver v New York Stock Exchange* (1963) 373 US 341, the Court held that the fact that the New York Stock Exchange is regulated by the Securities Exchange Act of 1934 and authorized to regulate itself did not exempt it from the antitrust laws. Anticompetitive action outside the scope of the act was subject to the proscription of the Sherman Act.

The key antitrust exemption areas are discussed in §§2.15–2.22.

1. [§2.15] Professional Baseball

Professional baseball has been held to be exempt from the Sherman Act. *Federal Baseball Club v National League* (1922) 259 US 200; *Toolson v New York Yankees, Inc.* (1953) 346 US 356. This exemption is anachronistic and is limited to the facts of the decided cases. A recent case criticizing it is *Salerno v American League of Professional Baseball Clubs* (2d Cir 1970) 1970 Trade Cases ¶73,276.

2. [§2.16] Fair-Trade Laws

Under the Miller-Tydings (15 USC §1) and McGuire (15 USC §45) Fair-Trade Acts, fair-trade agreements and enforcement activities pursuant to state fair-trade laws are exempt from Sherman Act proscription. Such resale price-maintenance agreements would otherwise constitute *per se* violations.

3. [§2.17] Labor Unions

Labor organizations are given partial exemption under three interdependent statutory sections. Section 6 of the Clayton Act (15 USC §17) states that the labor of a human being is not a commodity or article of commerce. Labor organizations not having capital stock are exempt in the same manner as agricultural corporations. Section 20 of the Clayton Act (29 USC §52) supplemented by Section 4 of the Norris-La Guardia Act (29 USC §105), denies federal courts jurisdiction to grant injunctions against concerted activity relating to a dispute concerning terms or conditions of employment.

A labor organization, however, has no exemption when it acts in concert with an employer in a way prohibited by the Sherman Act. In *United Mine Workers v Pennington* (1965) 381 US 657, the union was found in violation of Section 1 (15 USC §1) when it entered into a collective bargaining agreement with a multiemployer association imposing wage scales on employees outside the association. Cf. *Carroll v American Fed'n. of Musicians* (2d Cir 1967) 372 F2d 155, *rev'd on other grounds*, (1968) 391 US 99. See also Meltzer, *Labor Unions, Collective Bargaining and the Antitrust Laws* (1965) 32 *U Chi L Rev* 659.

4. [§2.18] Agricultural and Horticultural Associations

Section 6 of the Clayton Act (15 USC §17) grants broad exemptions to agricultural and horticultural organizations that are nonstock or not conducted for profit. Farmers, ranchers, dairymen, and nut or fruit growers are authorized by the Capper-Volstead Act (7 USC §§291–292) to combine in associations to process, prepare, and market their products collectively. Antitrust liability will result, however, if an exempt organization combines or conspires with nonproducers, who are not exempted. See *Case-Swayne v Sunkist Growers, Inc.* (1967) 389 US 384; *United States v Borden Co.* (1939) 308 US 188; *Sunkist Growers, Inc. v Winkler & Smith Citrus Prods. Co.* (1962) 370 US 19.

5. [§2.19] Air Carriers

The Federal Aviation Act (49 USC §§1301 et seq) exempts air carriers from antitrust sanction if the carrier is acting under an approval order of the Civil Aeronautics Board. See *Pan American World Airways, Inc. v United States* (1963) 371 US 296, 309.

6. [§2.20] Export Trade Associations

Export trade associations are exempt from Sherman Act prohibitions under Section 2 of the Webb-Pomerene Act (15 USC §62). The purpose of the act was to encourage Americans to enter the world-trade area on more equal terms with foreign cartels, which are often aided by their governments.

To come within the exemption of the act, the association must have been entered "for the sole purpose of engaging in export trade and actually engaged solely in such export trade" as defined in the act. 15 USC §§61, 62. The association itself, however, may be composed of "any corporation or combination, by contract or otherwise, of two or more persons, partnerships, or corporations." 15 USC §61. Thus, a corporation may be a member of an export trade association under the act even though it also is engaged in trade within the United States. Cf. *United States v Concentrated Phosphate Export Ass'n.* (SD NY 1967) 273 F Supp 263, *rev'd* (1968) 393 US 199; *United States Alkali Export Ass'n. v United States* (1945) 325 US 196.

7. [§2.21] Insurance

In *United States v Southeastern Underwriters Ass'n.* (1944) 322 US 533, insurance transactions were held to be "commerce" and subject to federal law. Congress thereafter passed the Insurance Antitrust Moratorium

(McCarran-Ferguson) Act, 15 USC §§1011-1015, declaring that continued state regulation was in the public interest, and that silence by Congress was not to bar regulation by the states. After June 30, 1948, the Sherman Act and the Clayton Act applied to insurance only to the extent that state regulation was not present. Boycotts, however, are not exempted.

8. [§2.22] Motor, Rail, and Interstate Water Carriers

Under the Interstate Commerce Act, as amended by the Reed-Bulwinkle Act (49 USC §5), any carrier participating in an agreement approved by the Interstate Commerce Commission is protected from Sherman Act sanctions.

C. Interpretation of the Act

1. [§2.23] General Attitudes of the Courts

In *Appalachian Coals, Inc. v United States* (1933) 288 US 344, 359, the Court said of the Sherman Act:

As a charter of freedom, the act has a generality and adaptability comparable to that found to be desirable in constitutional provisions. It does not go into detailed definitions which might either work injury to legitimate enterprise or through particularization defeat its purposes by providing loopholes for escape. The restrictions the act imposes are not mechanical or artificial.

The cases decided under the Sherman Act disclose that there is one predominate policy goal: the preservation of competition and the open market. This policy is predicated on the assumption that competition is the best means of achieving the most efficient utilization of resources, thereby accomplishing a maximization of wealth. *Standard Oil Co. of New Jersey v United States* (1911) 221 US 1, 50. See also Kaysen and Turner, *Antitrust Policy: An Economic and Legal Analysis* (1959) Harv Univ Press; Bork, *The Rule of Reason and the Per Se Concept; Price Fixing and Market Division* (1965) 74 *Yale LJ* 775; but see Blake, Bork, Bowman, and Jones, *Goals of Antitrust: A Dialogue on Policy* (1965) 65 *Col L Rev* 363.

2. [§2.24] Competition under the Sherman Act

An important principle in the application of the Sherman Act is that "competition" is used in a legal rather than economic sense. Courts may not inquire whether prices are fixed at a reasonable level or whether a monopoly is good or bad; the question is whether an agreement restrains competition or whether a monopoly exists.

Obviously this principle cannot be extended to its ultimate conclusion, or the Sherman Act would have outlawed all mergers, partnerships, and other business vehicles. Consequently, economic considerations are important in determining what types of activities are inherently anticompetitive or unreasonably restrictive and what degree of market power is to be used in establishing various legal definitions.

A secondary theme in litigation under the Sherman Act is a concern for social and noneconomic values, exemplified by *Appalachian Coals, Inc. v United States* (1933) 288 US 344, 374. In this and other cases, the Court has gone beyond the question whether there is actually a restraint of trade to determine whether the restraint has any redeeming qualities. See Blake, Bork, Bowman, and Jones, *Goals of Antitrust: A Dialogue on Policy* (1965) 65 *Col L Rev* 363. More than anything, these cases represent the difficulty in establishing legal doctrine responsive to the myriad demands of our modern economic environment.

3. [§2.25] The Rule of Reason

The basic standard of interpretation is the rule of reason. Although an argument can be made that the rule originated in Mr. Justice Peckman's opinion in *United States v Trans-Missouri Freight Association* (1897) 166 US 290 holding illegal an agreement by railroad companies concerning rates, the consensus is that it was first articulated by Mr. Chief Justice White in *Standard Oil Co. of New Jersey v United States* (1911) 221 US 1, 62:

[T]he criteria to be resorted to in any given case for the purpose of ascertaining whether violations of the section have been committed, is the rule of reason guided by the established law and by the plain duty to enforce the prohibitions of the act and thus the public policy which its restrictions were obviously enacted to subserve.

This rule, founded on the policy favoring free competition, enables courts to judge whether a restraint or monopoly is unreasonably anticompetitive and avoid deciding whether the arrangements are socially preferable in a particular industry.

Agreements may restrain trade in some respect and still not be inherently anticompetitive. At common law this fact was recognized in the concepts of ancillary and nonancillary restraints of trade. A nonancillary restraint of trade has as its predominant purpose the limitation of competition. In contrast, an ancillary or indirect restraint of trade is the by-product of a larger, entirely legitimate agreement. Some mergers constitute ancillary restraints; although the competition between the merging parties may be reduced, the overall aim is to achieve greater efficiency in operation. A predecessor to the rule of reason, the ancillary concept enables courts to inquire into the purpose of the agreement and evaluate both the market power of the parties and the effect on competition in order to determine whether the Sherman Act has been violated.

4. [§2.26] The Per Se Rule and Exceptions

Some forms of restraint are conclusively presumed to be unreasonable restraints of trade and are termed *per se* violations. Included are price fixing, customer allocations, geographic market divisions, and group boycotts. For discussion of *per se* violations, see §§2.27–2.33. In these areas, once the existence of the condemned activity is established, there is no need for further investigation into the power of the conspiring parties or the effect of the agreement on the market to establish the illegality of the conduct.

Acts that would normally be *per se* violations may not be if the industries are federally regulated. For example, in *Silver v New York Stock Exchange* (1963) 373 US 341, the discontinuance of wire service to nonmembers was attacked. The Supreme Court held that no exemption from antitrust liability could be inferred from the Securities Exchange Act of 1934 (48 Stat 881; codified in scattered sections of 15 USC) if none was needed to make the act work. The Court held that the discontinuance of wire service without notice or hearing was not necessary to the regulatory scheme and was so lacking in procedural fairness that it was outside the self-policing contemplated by the Exchange Act. Under the *Silver* analysis, no action taken by an exchange pursuant to its "federally mandated duty of self-policing" (373 US at 352) can be a *per se* violation of the antitrust laws. To decide whether an action in a regulated industry is immune from the antitrust laws, the courts must apply the rule of reason to determine first whether the action is necessary to the overall regulatory scheme and second whether the necessary procedural safeguards have been afforded. (373 US at 364). See also *United States v Borden* (1939) 308 US 188, in which the government charged a combination in violation of the Sherman Act and Borden claimed exemption from the antitrust laws under Section 6 of the Clayton Act (15 USC §17) and Sections 1 and 2 of the Capper-Volstead Act (7 USC §§291, 292), exempting certain agreements. The Court concluded that the conduct challenged was not taken pursuant to either statute and constituted a violation of the Sherman Act. To the same effect see *Maryland and Virginia Milk Producers Association, Inc. v United States* (1960) 362 US 458.

25

III. Horizontal Restraints of Trade under the Sherman Act

A. Agreements Concerning Price

1. [§2.27] Price-Fixing Agreements

Price fixing is a commonly used but not always fully understood term. The price-fixing concept is broad, and any arrangement (not only the fixing of prices) tampering with price structures is illegal *per se* under Section 1 of the Sherman Act (15 USC §1). Illustrative of the breadth of the doctrine is the often quoted statement from *United States v Socony-Vacuum Oil Co.* (1940) 310 US 150, 223, which held that an agreement to stabilize market prices by indirect means constituted a *per se* violation of Section 1 of the Sherman Act, notwithstanding that no prices were actually fixed:

Under the Sherman Act a combination formed for the purpose and with the effect of raising, depressing, fixing, pegging, or stabilizing the price of a commodity in interstate or foreign commerce is illegal *per se*.

The rationale for applying the *per se* rule to price-fixing agreements is that such agreements can have no purpose except the elimination or reduction of price competition. To allow the fixing of "reasonable" prices would turn the courts into regulatory agencies, thereby violating the spirit of the Sherman Act, which is designed to allow the market, not the courts, to determine prices. Also, the *per se* concept provides swift adjudication in cases that would otherwise demand extraordinarily time-consuming inquiries into the economic power of the participants and the effect of the agreement on the market.

Consequently, in criminal cases, all the prosecution need establish is the presence of the price-fixing agreement and an overt act in its furtherance. In civil treble-damage suits, the plaintiff must in addition prove that an overt act in furtherance of the conspiracy was the proximate cause of his damage. See *Radiant Burners, Inc. v Peoples Gas Light & Coke Co.* (1961) 364 US 656, holding a complaint sufficient alleging that defendant association's refusal to certify plaintiff's technically sound gas burner and defendant gas company's refusal to sell gas for use in plaintiff's burner were part of an unlawful conspiracy to restrain trade to plaintiff's substantial damage. The Court states (at 660):

[T]o state a claim upon which relief can be granted under [Section 1 of the Sherman Act] allegations adequate to show a violation, and in a private treble damage action, that plaintiff was damaged thereby are all the law requires.

See also *Seattle First Nat'l. Bank v Hilltop Realty* (9th Cir 1967) 383 F2d 309, 313, *cert den* (1968) 390 US 1025.

In *Socony-Vacuum, supra,* defendant gasoline refiners attempted to stem the flow of "distress" gasoline in their markets by establishing implied quotas for its purchase at a "fair going market price." The Supreme Court ruled that such an indirect stabilization of market prices is a *per se* violation, even though no prices were actually fixed, and further that lack of power to fix prices in a particular market is no defense to a charge of price fixing. It did not matter whether or not the aim was total elimination of price competition, nor did it matter whether the parties had "power to control the market." In applying the *per se* concept to price fixing, the Court concluded (at 226, n. 59):

Whatever economic justification particular price-fixing agreements may be thought to have, the law does not permit an inquiry into their reasonableness. They are all banned because of their actual or potential threat to the central nervous system of the economy.

There must be, however, some conscious commitment to a scheme to affect prices. As stated in *United States v Standard Oil Co.* (7th Cir 1963) 316 F2d 884, 890: "There is no such thing as an 'unwitting conspirator.'"

The commitment to the scheme may be shown by activity that falls short of a formal agreement. *Esco Corp. v United States* (9th Cir 1965) 340 F2d 1000, 1007 held evidence of meetings among competitors at which prices were discussed followed by uniform pricing activities sufficient to support a finding of illegal price fixing. The court said, "A knowing wink can mean more than words."

Illegal price-fixing arrangements can occur in agency relationships. In *Simpson v Union Oil Co.* (1964) 377 US 13, the Court found a price-fixing agreement to exist between Union and its retail dealers even though Union retained title to the gasoline and the retailers sold it on a consignment basis. The facts the Court deemed crucial were the following:

Dealers, like Simpson, are independent businessmen; and they have all or most of the indicia of entrepreneurs, except for price fixing. The risk of loss of the gasoline is on them, apart from acts of God. Their return is affected by the rise and fall in the market price, their commissions declining as retail prices drop. Practically the only power they have to be wholly independent businessmen, whose service depends upon their own initiative and enterprise, is taken from them by the proviso that they must sell their gasoline at prices fixed by Union Oil. [377 US at 20] By reason of the lease and "consignment" agreement dealers are coercively laced into an arrangement under which their supplier is able to impose non-competitive prices on thousands of persons whose prices otherwise might be competitive. ... The evil of this resale price maintenance program, like that of

27

the requirements contracts held illegal by *Standard Oil Co. v. United States,* supra, is its inexorable potentiality for and even certainty in destroying competition in retail sales of gasoline by these nominal "consignees" who are in reality small struggling competitors seeking retail gas customers. [377 US at 21] To allow Union Oil to achieve price fixing in this vast distribution system through this "consignment" device would be to make legality for antitrust purposes turn on clever draftsmanship. [377 US at 24]

Compare *United States v Arnold, Schwinn & Co.* (1967) 388 US 365, 378–379 in which the Court found the consignment plan to have a legitimate business purpose and noted that the "manufacturer completely retains ownership and risk of loss." It held that the territorial and customer restrictions placed by Schwinn on its consignees were lawful, but suggested that the distinction between outright sale and agency might be obliterated had there been evidence of price fixing. See discussion of *Schwinn* at §3.21.

The proponents of the rule of reason, citing cases of considerable age, have argued that the *per se* concept is not ironclad even in the area of price fixing, and that in some instances the Court will examine the effect of the agreement. Some support for the argument may be found in *Chicago Board of Trade v United States* (1918) 246 US 231 in which a rule was established that no wheat, corn, oats, or rye could be traded after the exchange closed except at the closing bid price on the last business day. The Court held that the primary purpose of the agreement was to regulate the hours of trading and that any price fixing was merely ancillary to the primary and proper purpose of regulating the exchange. See also *Appalachian Coals, Inc. v United States* (1933) 288 US 344 in which the Court held that the creation of a corporation by 137 producers of coal to act as their joint selling agent was not price fixing in view of the depressed condition of the industry.

The view that price-fixing agreements may be ancillary to a lawful agreement has very little current vitality. *United States v Columbia Pictures Corp.* (SD NY 1959) 169 F Supp 888 dealt with an agreement between two companies to distribute films and divide the profits pro rata. The court, relying on *Chicago Board of Trade,* refused to grant the government's motion for summary judgment so that the market and the effect of the agreement on the market could be analyzed at a full hearing. Although the court implied that there was no intent to fix prices and any resulting price uniformity was merely ancillary to the primary purposes of the distribution agreement, the denial of the summary judgment is a long way from holding that price-fixing agreements should be assessed under the rule of reason. In view of the fact that the courts have repeatedly and clearly held that price-fixing arrangements are illegal *per se*, reliance upon the rule of reason in this area is not justified.

2. [§2.28] Examples of Price-Fixing Arrangements

Price-fixing violations have been found in a broad spectrum of activities, some of which do not immediately appear to concern prices. Following are examples of illegal price-fixing arrangements:

a. Agreements among competitors to depress prices at which they will buy essential raw material for end product. *National Macaroni Mfrs. Ass'n. v Federal Trade Commission* (7th Cir 1965) 345 F2d 421.

b. Agreements to establish a maximum price for products. *Kiefer-Stewart Co. v Joseph E. Seagram & Sons, Inc.* (1951) 340 US 211; *Albrecht v Herald Co.* (1968) 390 US 145.

c. Agreements to establish uniform discounts, or to eliminate discounts. *United States v United Liquors Corp.* (WD Tenn 1956) 149 F Supp 609, *aff'd per curiam* (1957) 352 US 991; *United States v Olympia Provision & Baking Co.* (SD NY 1968) 282 F Supp 819, *aff'd sub nom Local 627, AMC & BW v United States* (1969) 393 US 480.

d. Implicit agreement between manufacturers to price a premium commodity a specified amount above inferior commodities. *United States v American Smelting & Ref. Co.* (SD NY 1960) 182 F Supp 834; and agreements not to sell below cost. *Food & Grocery Bureau, Inc. v United States* (9th Cir 1943) 139 F2d 973.

e. Uniform trade-in allowances. *Plymouth Dealers Ass'n. v United States* (9th Cir 1960) 279 F2d 128.

f. Establishment of uniform costs and minimum markup percentages. *California Retail Grocers & Merchants Ass'n. v United States* (9th Cir 1943) 139 F2d 978.

g. Agreements not to give trading stamps, though the agreement may arise from the terms of a collective bargaining agreement. *United States v Gasoline Retailers Ass'n.* (7th Cir 1961) 285 F2d 688.

h. Establishment of multiple basing-point system for determining delivered price. *FTC v Cement Institute* (1948) 333 US 683; see *Price Systems and Competition: The Basing Point Issues* (1949) 58 *Yale LJ* 426.

i. Agreements not to advertise prices. *United States v Gasoline Retailers Ass'n.* (7th Cir 1961) 285 F2d 688.

j. Agreements to use list prices as a place to start bargaining. *Plymouth Dealers Ass'n., supra,* e.

k. Marketing agreements between competitors, *e.g.,* one in which a manufacturer agrees to market his product and the product of a competitor, resulting in price uniformity. *American Smelting & Ref. Co., supra,* d; but see *United States v Columbia Pictures Corp.* (SD NY 1960) 189 F Supp 153, upholding a substantially similar agreement on the ground that resultant price uniformity was merely the ancillary result of arms-length negotiations.

l. Bid rigging, an activity that may involve the misuse of bid depositories, foreclosures of competitive activity for a period of time, rotation of jobs among competitors, and submission of complementary bids not intended to secure acceptance by the customer; see *Addyston Pipe & Steel Co. v United States* (1899) 175 US 211; *Las Vegas Merchant Plumbers Ass'n. v United States* (9th Cir 1954) 210 F2d 732, *cert den* (1954) 348 US 817; *Mechanical Contractors Bid Depository v Christiansen* (10th Cir 1965) 352 F2d 817, *cert den* (1966) 384 US 918; *United States v Bakersfield Associated Plumbing Contractors, Inc.* (SD Calif 1958) 1958 Trade Cases ¶69.087, *modified* (SD Calif 1958) 1959 Trade Cases ¶69,266. For example, a complementary bid may simply be too high, or perhaps specify a competitive price on terms that are unacceptable to the prospective customer.

m. Agreements to discontinue a product. Numerous consent decrees prohibit a manufacturer from agreeing with anyone engaged in the manufacture of competitive lines to limit size, styles or quantities of items comprising such lines. See, *e.g., United States v Cincinnati Milling Machine Co.* (ED Mich 1954) 1954 Trade Cases ¶67,733; *United States v General Electric* (D NJ 1954) 1954 Trade Cases ¶67,714, 67,794, 67,795, 67,796. In *United States v Roll Mfg. Institute* (D Pa 1955) 1955 Trade Cases ¶68,110 a consent decree enjoined an association from adopting standards for case steel rolls that might have the effect of preventing manufacturers from refraining from conforming to those standards.

n. Agreements to restrict volume of production. *Hartford-Empire Co. v United States* (1945) 323 US 386, 406–407. Numerous consent decrees prohibit a manufacturer from limiting production or setting quotas. See, *e.g., United States v Chemical Specialties Co., Inc.* (SD NY 1958) 1958 Trade Cases ¶69,186, prohibiting agreements limiting the production of certain drugs; *United States v United Fruit Co.* (ED La 1958) 1958 Trade Cases ¶68,941, prohibiting agreements limiting the production of bananas; *United States v Sperry Rand Corp.* (WD NY 1962) 1962 Trade Cases ¶70,491, prohibiting agreements limiting numbers of colors for filing cabinets.

o. Agreements to channel production. These are forms of agreements to divide markets or allocate customers, which are discussed at §§2.29 and

2.30. These agreements also are reprehensible because of their effects on price but are carved out for special treatment because they are quite common. An old case that talks in terms of channeling distribution rather than market division, the far more common terminology, is *Ellis v Inman Paulsen & Co.* (9th Cir 1904) 131 Fed 182, holding that an agreement between Oregon and Washington mills that the latter would not sell in the Portland area was unlawful.

p. Certain agreements to exchange price information. For example, in *United States v Container Corporation of America* (1969) 393 US 333, the Court found an agreement illegal in an industry, dominated by relatively few sellers, with a fungible product and an inelastic demand. The Court reasoned that exchange of price data in an oligopolistic market promoted price uniformity and had an anticompetitive effect.

See generally, Rahl, *Price Competition & the Price-Fixing Rule—Preface & Perspective, Symposium on Price Competition & Antitrust Policy* (1962) 57 *Nw UL Rev* 137; *Per Se Illegality of Price Fixing—Sans Power, Purpose or Effect* (1952) 19 *U Chi L Rev* 837. See also Chapter 8, particularly §8.23.

B. Division of Markets or Customers Among Competitors

1. [§2.29] Division of Markets

Like price-fixing agreements, horizontal agreements to divide territories or allocate customers are illegal *per se.* In *Addyston Pipe & Steel Co. v United States* (1899) 175 US 211 involving a classic market division, the Court held unlawful agreements among companies controlling two-thirds of the relevant markets to submit noncompetitive bids for jobs in areas reserved to members of the agreement.

Similarly, an agreement between the nation's two largest lead producers was held illegal in *United States v American Smelting & Refining Co.* (SD NY 1960) 182 F Supp 834. The eastern manufacturer agreed to be the exclusive distributor in the East of the western manufacturer's lead, thereby effectively dividing the national lead market.

A trademark licensing system will not effectively camouflage what is in fact a division of territories by potential competitors. In *United States v Sealy, Inc.* (1967) 388 US 350 a company substantially owned by a group of manufacturers of bedding products licensed the manufacturers to make and sell bedding products under the company name and trademarks. The Court found that the licensor-company was in effect engaged in a joint venture with and was an instrumentality of the licensees and that the licensor-company and the licensees-manufacturers were engaged in a horizontal division of market territories.

Agreements to divide international markets are also illegal. In *Timken Roller Bearing Co. v United States* (1951) 341 US 593 an allocation of markets among an American firm and two of its foreign subsidiaries was held unlawful. To the same effect see *United States v National Lead Co.* (1947) 332 US 319; *United States v General Dyestuff Corp.* (SD NY 1944) 57 F Supp 642; *United States v United States Alkali Export Ass'n.* (SD NY 1949) 86 F Supp 59.

2. [§2.30] Allocation of Customers

Very similar to agreements to divide territories and to refrain from soliciting or selling in certain areas are agreements not to sell to specified customers of a competitor. The effect is the same; in both cases competitors are agreeing to divide the available business. Illegal arrangements may also result from an agreement with a potential competitor not to sell a particular product or product line to specified customers. All these types of arrangements constitute *per se* violations of the Sherman Act. *Johnson v Joseph Schlitz Brewing Co.* (ED Tenn 1940) 33 F Supp 176, *aff'd per curiam* (6th Cir 1941) 123 F2d 1016.

C. [§2.31] Concerted Refusals to Deal

A unilateral refusal to deal without more and "in the absence of any purpose to create or maintain a monopoly" is generally speaking lawful under the Sherman Act. *United States v Colgate & Co.* (1919) 250 US 300, 307. The right to choose the persons with whom one is willing to deal is fundamental to commerce and repeatedly recognized by the Court. *United States v Colgate Co., supra; Times-Picayune Publishing Co. v United States* (1953) 345 US 594, 625; *United States v Parke, Davis & Co.* (1960) 362 US 29. Even unilateral conduct may be unlawful on other grounds, for example if the refusal to deal is intended to create a monopoly (*Lorain Journal Co. v United States* (1951) 342 US 143, holding unlawful a newspaper's refusal to deal with persons who placed advertisements with the local radio station), or aims at preventing customers from selling to discounters (*United States v General Motors Corp.* (1966) 384 US 127), or aims at preventing customers from handling a competing line of products (*Lessig v Tidewater Oil Co.* (9th Cir 1964) 327 F2d 459, *cert den* (1964) 377 US 993).

Absent an unlawful purpose, a sole trader may decide not to deal with another or to cease dealing with another for any number of reasons, including poor credit rating, unsatisfactory prior business relationships, or purely personal reasons. For an excellent analysis of the right of a manufacturer to cut off a distributor, see *Joseph E. Seagram and Sons, Inc. v Hawaiian Oke and Liquors, Ltd.* (9th Cir 1969) 416 F2d 71, *cert den* (1970) 396 US 1062, *reh den* (1970) 397 US 1003, and the cases and commentary cited. *Seagram* held that an understanding between two suppliers to transfer their business from one distributor to another was not a *per se* violation of Section 1 of the Sherman Act (15 USC §1). The court pointed out that there was no evidence of any anticompetitive motive but only of mutual dissatisfaction with the first distributor. In short, the court viewed the manufacturers' refusals as unilateral refusals to deal based on good business reasons, which had to be assessed under the rule of reason.

In sharp contrast, a group boycott, often called a concerted refusal to deal, almost always constitutes a *per se* violation of the Sherman Act. In *Eastern States Lumber Ass'n. v United States* (1914) 234 US 600, 614 the Court held that retailers' concerted refusals to deal with wholesalers who sold directly to consumers violated the Sherman Act. It noted the difference between unilateral and group boycotts:

An act harmless when done by one may become a public wrong when done by many acting in concert, for it then takes on the form of a conspiracy.

The *per se* rule applies to group boycotts because they are deemed "naked restraints of trade with no purpose except stifling of competition." *White Motor Co. v United States* (1963) 372 US 253, 263. A concerted refusal to deal is a *per se* violation of Section 1 of the Sherman Act, and it does not matter whether it is directed toward customers (*Kiefer-Stewart v Joseph E. Seagram & Sons, Inc.* (1951) 340 US 211; *Fashion Originators' Guild v FTC* (1941) 312 US 457; *Klor's Inc. v Broadway-Hale Stores, Inc.* (1959) 359 US 207; *United States v General Motors Corp., supra; Binderup v Pathe Exchange, Inc.* (1923) 263 US 291) or toward competitors (*Radiant Burners, Inc. v Peoples Gas Light & Coke* (1961) 364 US 656; *Associated Press v United States* (1945) 326 US 1). Vertical or horizontal, a concerted refusal constitutes a *per se* violation of the Sherman Act. Even when the refusal to deal appears to be unilateral, if it is utilized to destroy competition the Court has gone very far in finding the element of concerted action, which calls in the *per se* rule in lieu of the analysis required by the rule of reason. See, for example, *United States v General Motors Corp., supra; Albrecht v Herald Co.* (1968) 390 US 145. For further discussion of refusals to deal, see §§3.37–3.40.

Examples of concerted refusals to deal:

a. Denying competitors entry to trade associations through exclusive membership clauses. See *Associated Press v United States, supra; United States v Insurance Bd. of Cleveland* (ND Ohio 1956) 144 F Supp 684; (ND Ohio 1960) 188 F Supp 949. These clauses are *per se* illegal even if they do not affect competition.

b. Agreements between manufacturers and dealers to refuse to deal with price-cutting distributors. See *United States v General Motors Corp., supra.*

c. Agreements to boycott competitors or distributors who are engaged in the unethical practice of style piracy. *Fashion Originators' Guild v FTC, supra.*

d. Agreements between manufacturer and distributor to sell to a competing distributor at discriminatorily high prices. *Klor's Inc. v Broadway-Hale Stores, Inc., supra.*

D. [§2.32] Tying Arrangements

Tying arrangements are contracts in which a seller or lessor conditions the sale or lease of goods or services on the purchase of another product. For example, *International Business Machines Corp. v United States* (1936) 298 US 131 forbade IBM from leasing machines only on the condition that lessees bought IBM punch cards. *United States v Loew's Inc.* (1962) 371 US 38 dealt with defendant motion picture distributors' practice of conditioning the sale of feature films to television stations on the purchase of unwanted or inferior films.

Although numerous tying cases have been brought under the more specific language of Section 3 of the Clayton Act (15 USC §14), such arrangements are also subject to the general prohibition of Section 1 of the Sherman Act (15 USC §1). See *United States v Loew's Inc., supra.* The Sherman Act, unlike Section 3 of the Clayton Act, may be used to reach tie-ins involving services. See, *e.g., Northern Pacific Ry. Co. v United States* (1958) 356 US 1 dealing with the tying of the railroad's freight service to the sale or lease of valuable land.

Tying arrangements are frequently treated as *per se* violations of Section 1 of the Sherman Act on reasoning similar to that used in price-fixing cases. "Tying arrangements serve hardly any purpose beyond the suppression of competition." *Standard Oil Co. of California v United States* (1949) 337 US 293, 305–306. As stated by the Court in the *Loew's* case, *supra,* "[Tying arrangements] are a concern for two reasons—they may force buyers into giving up the purchase of substitutes for the tied product [citations] and they may destroy the free access of competing suppliers of the tied product to the consuming market [citation]." 371 US at 44–45.

There is a threefold difficulty in unequivocally classifying tying arrangements as *per se* violations. First, the courts require, in addition to establishing the tie-in arrangement, a showing that the seller possesses sufficient economic leverage to force the buyer to accept the tied product. See, *e.g., United States v Loew's Inc., supra.* However, the ease with which courts find "sufficient economic power" once a tie-in arrangement has been established makes this requirement more theoretical than real.

Second, there is a so-called "goodwill exemption." According to the cases recognizing this exemption, a seller may tie in an additional product if that product is necessary to maintain the goodwill of the principal product. *Susser v Carvel Corp.* (2d Cir 1964) 332 F2d 505, 519–520, *cert dismissed* (1965) 381 US 125, concurring opinion. The goodwill exemption was applied in *Baker v Simmons Co.* (1st Cir 1962) 307 F2d 458, 468–469, holding that motels displaying the Simmons sign must have its mattresses in its rooms; and *Dehydrating Process Co. v A.O. Smith Corp.* (1st Cir 1961) 292 F2d 653, *cert den* (1961) 368 US 931, holding that the sale of a silo unloading device may be tied to the sale or ownership of a silo made by the same manufacturer. (Evidence showed the unloader did not work properly with silos of different makes.) In *Standard Oil Co. of California v United States, supra,* 306 the Court said of the goodwill exemption: 1618997

The only situation, indeed, in which the protection of goodwill may necessitate the use of tying clauses is where specifications for a substitute would be so detailed that they could not practically be supplied.

Third, there is an exemption sometimes made for the "small company [trying] to break into a market." *Brown Shoe Co. v United States* (1962) 370 US 294, 330. See, for example, *United States v Jerrold Electronics Corp.* (ED Pa 1960) 187 F Supp 545, *aff'd* (1961) 356 US 567, *reh den* 356 US 810, permitting tying of services to sale of community antenna equipment while the industry was new and its success uncertain, but rejecting continuation of the tie-in after the industry became established.

See discussion of tying arrangements in §§3.9–3.18.

E. [§2.33] Mergers under Section 1 of the Sherman Act

Although Section 7 of the Clayton Act (15 USC §18) is the most popular weapon for attacking mergers, Section 1 of the Sherman Act (15 USC §1) may also be employed under the rationale that mergers are "combinations." *Northern Securities Co. v United States* (1904) 193 US 197. The coverage of the two sections is nearly coextensive since the application of Section 7 to bank mergers in *United States v Philadelphia Nat'l. Bank* (1963) 374 US 321. Most actions are instituted under Section 7 of the Clayton Act because the burden of proof under Section 1 of the Sherman Act is heavier. While an *actual* restraint must be proved under the Sherman Act, the *incipiency* standard of the Clayton Act requires only proof that a merger may substantially lessen competition. Compare *United States v Von's Grocery Co.* (1966) 384 US 270, 278, finding a violation of Section 7 of the Clayton Act, with *United States v Columbia Steel Co.* (1948) 334 US 495, 527–529, finding no violation of Section 1 of the Sherman Act; but see *United States v First Nat'l. Bank* (1964) 376 US 665.

A Section 1 count is of value to the government in the initial stages of an antitrust action. For example, if a corporation disposes of a division and an action under Section 7 is brought against the acquirer, interrogatories and motions to produce cannot be directed against the disposing corporation. To gain discovery, the government generally charges violation of both Section 7 of the Clayton Act and of Section 1 of the Sherman Act. See, *e.g., United States v Philadelphia Nat'l. Bank, supra.*

For more complete discussion of mergers, see Chapter 4.

F. [§2.34] Joint Ventures under Section 1 of the Sherman Act

A horizontal combination in the form of a joint venture is, like a merger, subject to attack under Section 1 of the Sherman Act (15 USC §1). As with mergers, Section 7 of the Clayton Act (15 USC §18) is the most popular weapon for attacking joint ventures because of the reduced burden of proof.

United States v Penn-Olin Chemical Company (1964) 378 US 158 dealt with a joint venture agreement under which Pennsalt Chemical and Olin Mathieson each acquired 50% of a new Penn-Olin Chemical Company, which commenced producing sodium chlorate for distribution in the Southeast. The Justice Department attacked the joint venture under both Section 1 of the Sherman Act and Section 7 of the Clayton Act. The district court dismissed the complaint on the ground that there was no proof that the parent corporations would have entered the market had Penn-Olin not been formed. The Supreme Court reversed, concluding that while the requisite showing under the Sherman Act had not been made, it had been made under the Clayton Act. The Court considered the following factors pertinent to the application of Section 1 of the Sherman Act (at 176–177):

We note generally the following criteria which the trial court might take into account in assessing the probability of a substantial lessening of competition: the number and power of the competitors in the relevant market; the background of their growth; the power of the joint venturers; the relationship of their lines of commerce; the competition existing between them and the power of each in dealing with the competitors of the other; the setting in which the joint venture was created; the reasons and necessities for its existence; the joint venture's line of commerce and the relationship thereof to that of its parents; the adaptability of its line of commerce to non-competitive practices; the potential power of the joint venture in the relevant market; an appraisal of what the competition in the relevant market would have been if one of the joint venturers had entered it alone instead of through Penn-Olin; the effect, in the event of this occurrence, of the other joint venturer's potential competition; and such other factors as might indicate potential risk to competition in the relevant market. In weighing these factors the court should remember that the mandate of the Congress is in terms of the probability of a lessening of substantial competition, not in terms of tangible present restraint.

After retrial, the legality of the joint venture was upheld by the equally-divided Court (1967) 389 US 308.

G. [§2.35] Reciprocal Practices

Reciprocal practices, both coercive and consensual, whereby sellers trading on their buying power obtain purchase commitments from their suppliers, have been attacked under Section 5 of the Federal Trade Commission Act (15 USC §45) (*Waugh Equipment Co.* (1931) 15 FTC 232; *California Packing Corp.* (1937) 25 FTC 379) and under Section 7 of the Clayton Act (15 USC §18) (*FTC v Consolidated Foods Corp.* (1965) 380 US 592) as well as under Section 1 of the Sherman Act (15 USC §1). In *United States v General Dynamics Corp.* (SD NY 1966) 258 F Supp 36, the Department of Justice challenged General Dynamics' acquisition of Liquid Carbonic Corporation under Section 1 of the Sherman Act and Section 7 of the Clayton Act and demonstrated that General Dynamics had a "special sales program" to develop reciprocal relations with its suppliers who also purchased from Liquid Carbonics. The district court held that the merger agreement violated Section 1 of the Sherman Act, stating (258 F Supp at 59):

When a sufficient volume of trade is concerned, a balancing of interests requires that the businessman's freedom of operation must be curtailed to prevent concentrations of economic power inimical to the public interest.

This court finds that reciprocity, whether coercive in nature or based on mutual patronage, is an anti-competitive practice.

In *United States v United States Steel Corp.* (WD Pa 1969) 1969 Trade Cases ¶72,826, in which the government had charged that defendant's reciprocal practices violated the Sherman Act, the district court entered a final consent decree prohibiting for 10 years reciprocal arrangements between defendant and its suppliers. See also complaint filed in *United States v General Tire & Rubber Co.* (3/7/67) 295 ATRR p A-1, in which the government charged, outside the merger context, that General Tire & Rubber Co. and its subsidiaries violated the Sherman Act by using their combined purchasing power to increase sales.

In a speech (reported in 426 ATRR p X-1 (9/9/69)) before the Antitrust Committee of the Federal Bar Association, Baddia J. Rashid, Director of Operations, Antitrust Division, stated:

Elaborate proof of particular contracts should not be required [to support a Section 1 violation when there is a] conscious pursuit of a systematic reciprocity program, which includes the maintenance of trade balance records comparing sales and purchase information, which favors one's own customers when purchasing, and which is communicated to customers and suppliers in the expectation that they will act upon it.

For further discussion of reciprocity in the context of mergers, see §4.31.

IV. Sherman Act Defenses

A. [§2.36] Introduction

There are relatively few affirmative defenses to a Sherman Act charge. Among them the statute of limitations, lack of interstate commerce, the statutory exemptions discussed at §§2.14-2.22, release, prior adjudication, and the "constitutional" exemption of the *Noerr-Pennington* rule (see §2.47). Many other "defenses," while often pleaded affirmatively, are in reality raised by a denial contained in the answer. These include lack of standing to sue or indirectness of injury. The latter is available only in private treble-damage actions, and is not a bar in a government criminal or civil injunctive action. Other defenses, such as in pari delicto (see §2.46) and "pass-on" (see §2.49) have been severely curtailed by recent Supreme Court decisions.

Because of shifting trends, each defense should be carefully researched before use. Some of the defenses, such as release, are common to all litigation and will be mentioned only in the context of choice of law. Others, such as interstate commerce and statutory exemption, have been considered previously at §§2.12 and 2.14-2.22 respectively. The defenses peculiar to Sherman Act litigation are treated briefly in §§2.37-2.50.

B. Statute of Limitations

1. [§2.37] Statute of Limitations Governing Criminal Actions

A criminal action under the Sherman Act must be brought "within five years next after such offense shall have been committed." 18 USC §3282. If the offense is a single act, the statute runs from the date of the act. If the offense is a series of acts, as is almost always the case, the statute runs from the date of the last act necessary to constitute the offense; that is to say, the statute commences to run when all the elements of the crime have occurred. Where the offense is continuing, such as a continuing conspiracy to restrain trade under the Sherman Act, the statute runs from the last act in furtherance of the conspiracy. In *United States v Kissel* (1910) 218 US 601, 607-608, Mr. Justice Holmes rejected the argument that a conspiracy is an unlawful agreement that constitutes a completed crime when formed and thus starts the statute running, saying:

It is true that the unlawful agreement satisfies the definition of the crime, but it does not exhaust it. . . . A conspiracy to restrain trade or monopolize trade by improperly excluding a competitor from business contemplates that the conspirators will remain in business and will continue their combined efforts to drive the competitor out until they succeed.

The last act in furtherance of the unlawful conspiracy, from which the statute will run, need not be itself unlawful. See *United States v Atlantic Co.* (MD Ga 1950) 1950-1951 Trade Cases ¶62,717 for a jury instruction concerning the running of the statute.

2. [§2.38] Statute of Limitations Governing Civil Actions

Section 4B of the Clayton Act (15 USC §15b) was amended effective January 7, 1956, to provide for a four-year period of limitations for all civil antitrust actions to recover damages commenced after that date, whether brought by the government pursuant to Section 4A of the Clayton Act (15 USC §15a) or by a private party pursuant to Section 4 of the Clayton Act (15 USC §15). Injunctive actions brought under Sections 15 and 16 of the Clayton Act (15 USC §§25, 26), which authorize injunctive relief for the United States and private parties respectively, are concerned with preventing threatened violations and are subject to no statute of limitations.

Generally a civil cause of action under the Sherman Act accrues when all the elements of Sections 4 or 4A of the Clayton Act have occurred—in the statutory language, when a prospective private plaintiff or the United States has been "injured in his business or property by reason of anything forbidden in the antitrust laws." Therefore, the statute begins to run when plaintiff can sue—when a Sherman Act violation has had an "impact" on the plaintiff's business or property—when, for example, he orders goods and has been refused. In *Garelick v Goerlich's, Inc.* (6th Cir 1963) 323 F2d 854, plaintiff sued defendant for terminating his distributorship five years earlier. He argued that his right of action was kept alive because a salesman of defendant had solicited an order from plaintiff (which the home office refused to fill) within the four-year period. The court affirmed a summary judgment for defendant, stating (at 855–856):

All the authorities are in accord that a right of action for a civil conspiracy under the antitrust laws accrues from the commission of the last overt act causing injury or damage. [citations] If the statute of limitations were tolled or an accrual of a suit set up by an overt act which did not cause damage, . . . it would effectively destroy the statute of limitations as a statute of peace.

If damages continue to accrue from a single injurious act, the period of limitations is not extended; of course, the amount of damages is increased. *Fleischer v A.A.P. Inc.* (SD NY 1959) 180 F Supp 717, *cert den* (1959) 359 US 1002. In *Steiner v Twentieth Century-Fox Corporation* (9th Cir 1956) 232 F2d 190, the court states (at 194–195):

In a civil conspiracy, the statute of limitations runs from the commission of the last overt act alleged to have caused damage. . . . [T]o start the running of the statute of limitations there must be damage occasioned by an overt act. In a continuing conspiracy causing continuing damage without further overt acts, the statute of limitation runs, as we have noted, from the time the blow which caused the damage was struck.

To the same effect *Laitram Corp. v Deepsouth Packing Co., Inc.* (ED La 1968) 279 F Supp 883 at 887.

Of course if the defendant's conduct causes injuries amounting to several causes of action, the statute will begin running as to each when it first accrues. *Emich Motors Corp. v General Motors Corp.* (7th Cir 1956) 229 F2d 714. "[A] conspiracy itself is not actionable." *Charles Rubenstein, Inc. v Columbia Pictures Corp.* (D Minn 1957) 154 F Supp 216, *aff'd* (8th Cir 1961) 289 F2d 418. The fact that a conspiracy is continuous does not prevent accrual of a claim, if the prior overt acts have had an impact. As stated in *Rubenstein, supra:*

A continuing conspiracy as such is not actionable. It is the impact of the conspiracy which gives rise to a claim for damages, and it is the date of such impact of the wrong engendered by the conspiracy from which this statute of limitations begins to run.

Thus, the statute will move along barring recovery for injuries sustained more than four years before. *Ellingson Timber v Great Northern Ry. Co.*

(D Ore 1968) 1968 Trade Cases ¶72,506, at 85,713; *Highland Supply Corporation v Reynolds Metal Company* (8th Cir 1964) 327 F2d 725; *Suckow Borax Mines Consol. v Borax Consol.* (9th Cir 1950) 185 F2d 196, *cert den* (1951) 340 US 943. Similarly, as a latecomer to a conspiracy is liable for the prior acts done by the conspirators in furtherance of the conspiracy, he may take advantage of the statute of limitations barring suit for those early acts. *Rubenstein, supra.*

3. [§2.39] Statute Tolled Pending Government Proceeding

Section 5(b) of the Clayton Act (15 USC §16(b)) provides that "[w]henever any civil or criminal proceeding is instituted by the United States to prevent, restrain, or punish violations of any of the antitrust laws," the running of the statute of limitations shall be suspended "in respect of every private right of action arising under said laws and based in whole or in part on any matter complained of in said proceeding" during the pendency of the government suit and for one year after, but that an action shall be barred unless commenced either within one year after the government suit is terminated or within four years after the cause of action accrued.

Key questions are: What is a government proceeding? When is a private action based in whole or in part on any matter complained of in the government proceeding? Can there be more than one suspension period if more than one government action is pending? and When is a government proceeding terminated? Recent decisions have given partial answers to these questions. See §§2.40–2.43.

a. [§2.40] What is a Government Proceeding?

Section 5(b) of the Clayton Act (15 USC §16(b)) provides that the statute of limitations will be tolled by a government civil or criminal proceeding to prevent, restrain, or punish violations of the antitrust laws. A damage claim brought by the government under Section 4A of the Clayton Act (15 USC §15a) is expressly excluded by Section 5(b). Section 1 of the Clayton Act (15 USC §12) lists the "antitrust laws" as the Sherman Act, the Clayton Act, and Sections 73–77 of the Wilson Tariff Act (15 USC §§8–11). In *Nashville Milk Co. v Carnation Co.* (1958) 355 US 373, 376, the Court held this listing to be exclusive. Since the Robinson-Patman Act is not one of the "antitrust laws" (except for Section 1, prohibiting price discriminations, which amends Section 2 of the Clayton Act (15 USC §13)), a government suit brought to punish or restrain discriminatory or predatory acts under Section 3 of the Robinson-Patman Act (15 USC §13a) would not toll the statute.

In *Minnesota Mining & Mfg. Co. v New Jersey Wood Finishing Co.* (1965) 381 US 311, the Court held that an action brought by the FTC to enforce Section 7 of the Clayton Act, an antitrust law, tolled the statute "to the same extent and in the same circumstances as it is by the Justice Department actions." 381 US at 321-322. Subsequent district court cases have distinguished between the FTC's actions to enforce the Clayton Act, an "antitrust law," and actions to attack unfair methods of competition brought under Section 5 of the Federal Trade Commission Act (15 USC §45). not an "antitrust law." It has been held that Section 5 actions are not brought under the antitrust laws, even though the unfair competition could have been challenged under an "antitrust law." See *Y & Y Popcorn Supply Co. v ABC Vending Corp.* (ED Pa 1967) 263 F Supp 709, 711-712; *Rader v Balfour* (ND Ill 1968) 1969 Trade Cases ¶72,209; *Laitram Corp. v Deepsouth Packing Co.* (ED La 1968) 279 F Supp 883 at 890. At least one court has ruled that since Section 5 can restrain "in their incipiency, practices which, if allowed to continue, would grow into antitrust law violations," all FTC proceedings brought under Section 5, except against deceptive practices, are sufficient to toll the statute of limitations. *Lippa's, Inc. v Lenox, Inc.* (D Vt 1969) 305 F Supp 185. It should be noted that the FTC has no independent jurisdiction to attack Sherman Act violations, but must do so through the "unfair methods of competition" language of Section 5 of the Federal Trade Commission Act. See Chapter 6. Cf. *FTC v Cement Institute* (1948) 333 US 683, at 708. Whether the distinctions noted here will stand must await future development.

b. [§2.41] When is a Private Action Based in Whole or in Part on Any Matter Complained of in the Government Proceeding?

The statute (15 USC §16(b)) requires as a condition of tolling that the private action be based "in whole or in part on any matter complained of in [the government] proceeding." The degree of subject matter identity that must exist is far from clear. In *Leh v General Petroleum Corp.* (1965) 382 US 54, a private plaintiff named some but not all defendants named in the government suit. The Court stated that broad effect is to be given the terms "based in whole or in part on any matter complained of" and held that it is not necessary that the conspiracies alleged by the private party have the same breadth and scope as that alleged by the government or that the participants be identical. In *Lippa's, Inc. v Lenox, Inc.* (D Vt 1969) 305 F Supp 185, the district court found sufficient overlap between the public and private suit notwithstanding the time period and the purpose of the conspiracy alleged differed. However, the government suit must bear a "real relation to the private plaintiff's claim for relief." (382

US at 59.) Thus, in *Peto v Madison Square Garden Corp.* (2d Cir 1967) 384 F2d 682, *cert den* (1968) 390 US 989, the court affirmed a summary judgment for defendant because the government action concerned different sports activities and different periods of time.

If there is sufficient identity of subject matter and parties to toll the statute it is tolled not only against the defendants named in the prior government proceeding but also against alleged coconspirators. *Michigan v Morton Salt Co.* (D Minn 1966) 259 F Supp 35, 54, *aff'd sub nom Hardy Salt Co. v Illinois* (8th Cir 1967) 377 F2d 768, 775, *cert den* (1967) 389 US 912; *Vermont v Cayuga Rock Salt Co.* (D Me 1967) 276 F Supp 970; *New Jersey v Morton Salt Co.* (3d Cir 1967) 387 F2d 94, *cert den sub nom International Salt Co. v New Jersey* (1968) 391 US 967.

c. [§2.42] Can There Be More Than One Suspension Period?

Normally the government criminal and civil actions are concurrent, and the statute of limitations is suspended until both actions are concluded. If the criminal action is concluded before the civil action is filed, the question arises as to whether there can be more than one period of suspension under Section 5(b) of the Clayton Act (15 USC §16(b)). The language of that provision speaks of suspension by a civil *or* criminal proceeding and also refers to *the* period of suspension, suggesting that there can be only one period of suspension. The court in *Dickinson, Inc. v Kansas City Star Co.* (WD Mo 1959) 173 F Supp 423, 425, suggested that if the criminal case was terminated before the related civil case was filed, there would be only one period of suspension, running from the termination of the first action. If the civil and criminal actions are pending concurrently, the reported cases have held that the period of suspension will continue until both of the actions are terminated. See, *e.g., Michigan v Morton Salt Co.* (D Minn 1966) 259 F Supp 35, 51, *aff'd on other grounds sub nom Hardy Salt Co. v Illinois* (8th Cir 1967) 377 F2d 768, *cert den* (1968) 389 US 912; *Dickinson, Inc. v Kansas City Star Co., supra.* However, in *Maricopa County v American Pipe and Construction Co.* (D Ariz 1969) 303 F Supp 77, the court ruled that a plaintiff may use successive, noncontemporaneous government actions to extend the suspension of the statute of limitations.

d. [§2.43] When is the Government Proceeding Terminated?

The statute provides that the statute of limitations will be tolled during the pendency of the government action and for one year after the government suit is terminated. It has been held that the government suit terminates when a final judgment or decree is disposed of on appeal, or if no appeal is taken, when the time for appeal has expired. *Electric Theater Co. v Twentieth Century-Fox Film Corp.* (WD Mo 1953) 113 F Supp 937. A judgment or decree is final notwithstanding a provision reserving power to the court to modify its judgment or decree. *Alex Theatre Corp. v Balaban and Katz Corp.* (ND Ill 1952) 1952 Trade Cases ¶67,357. *Russ Togs, Inc. v Grinnell Corp.* (SD NY 1969) 304 F Supp 279, *aff'd* (2d Cir 1970) 426 F2d 850, dealt with a situation in which the Supreme Court, affirming a district court judgment for the government, remanded for further hearings on the question of relief. The court held that the action would not be terminated until final resolution of the remedy issue.

New Jersey v Morton Salt Co. (3d Cir 1967) 387 F2d 94, *cert den sub nom International Salt Co. v New Jersey* (1968) 391 US 967, held that the entry of a consent decree does not necessarily "terminate" the government's action with respect to the consenting party; the consenting party was one of several alleged coconspirators, and the statute of limitations remained tolled until the termination of the government's action against the group as a whole. This holding is contrary to earlier cases, including *Gordon v Loew's, Inc.* (D NJ 1956) 147 F Supp 398, *aff'd on other grounds* (3d Cir 1957) 247 F2d 451; *Sun Theatre Corp. v RKO Radio Pictures, Inc.* (7th Cir 1954) 213 F2d 284; *Charles Rubenstein, Inc. v Columbia Pictures Corp.* (D Minn 1957) 154 F Supp 216, *aff'd* (8th Cir 1961) 289 F2d 418; *Court Degraw Theatre, Inc. v Loew's Inc.* (ED NY 1959) 172 F Supp 198.

4. [§2.44] Fraudulent Concealment

The federal judicial doctrine that the statute of limitations is tolled during the period that a conspiracy is "fraudulently concealed" was first formulated in *Bailey v Glover* (1874) 88 US (21 Wall) 342 in the context of the bankruptcy laws and has since been "read into every federal statute of limitations," even though the statute itself contains no such provision. *Holmberg v Armbrecht* (1946) 327 US 392, 397. This doctrine applies to the antitrust laws (*Winkler-Koch Eng'r. Co. v Universal Oil Prods. Co.* (SD NY 1951) 100 F Supp 15; *Atlantic City Electric Co. v General Electric Co.* (2d Cir 1962) 312 F2d 236, *cert den* (1963) 373 US 909) and has been used in Sherman Act cases with increasing frequency. The issue is often of prime importance in a case.

The burden of proof on the issue of fraudulent concealment is on the plaintiff, who must establish that he neither knew of the illegal acts nor had reason to believe or suspect their existence. Further, plaintiff must generally show affirmative acts by the defendant that successfully concealed the existence of the illegal acts despite due diligence on the part of the plaintiff. *Baker v F & F Investment* (7th Cir 1970) 420 F2d 1191, *cert den sub nom Action Realty Co. v Baker* (1970) 400 US 821; *Picoult v Ralston Purina Co.* (SD NY 1969) 1969 Trade Cases ¶72,681, at 86,432–86,433; *Moviecolor Ltd. v Eastman Kodak Co.* (2d Cir 1961) 288 F2d 80; *Laundry Equipment Sales Co. v Borg Warner Corp.* (7th Cir 1964) 334 F2d 788. See also *Suckow Borax Mines Consol. v Borax Consol.* (9th Cir 1950) 185 F2d 196, *cert den* (1951) 340 US 943, holding that plaintiff's knowledge of the illegal activity precluded reliance on the fraudulent concealment doctrine; *Crummer Company v E.I. duPont de Nemours* (5th Cir 1958) 255 F2d 425, holding that the issue should go to the jury; *Philco Corp. v Radio Corp. of America* (ED Pa 1960) 186 F Supp 155, holding that plaintiff-corporation's top official's knowledge of the illegal activity precluded reliance on the fraudulent concealment doctrine. When fraudulent concealment is established, the statute begins to run when the plaintiff discovers the violation. *Moviecolor Ltd. v Eastman Kodak Co., supra.*

C. [§2.45] Release

The execution of a release as to one defendant or potential defendant may effectively bar a subsequent action against others. The distinction between a release and a covenant not to sue is crucial. Conspirators are joint tortfeasors. It has been held that federal rather than state law governs the effect of a release in federal antitrust actions and that a release of one joint tortfeasor releases all unless a contrary intention is demonstrated. *Twentieth Century-Fox Film Corp. v Winchester Drive-In Theatre, Inc.* (9th Cir 1965) 351 F2d 925, 928, *cert den* (1966) 382 US 1011. See also *Miami Parts & Spring, Inc. v Champion Spark Plug Co.* (5th Cir 1968) 402 F2d 83. In contrast, a covenant not to sue executed in favor of one joint tortfeasor is merely a contract between the parties and will not discharge other joint tortfeasors. For forms of releases and covenants, see §§12.76–12.79.

D. [§2.46] In Pari Delicto and Unclean Hands

The common law defense of in pari delicto is applied if the plaintiff participated in the asserted wrongful acts of the defendant. Literally, the term means "of equal fault," but the actual involvement required for its application is unclear. See, *e.g., Davidson v Kansas City Star Co.* (WD Mo 1962) 202 F Supp 613, *rev'd on other grounds sub nom Bales v Kansas City Star Co.* (8th Cir 1964) 336 F2d 439. The defense of unclean hands, although frequently confused by the courts and commentators with the in pari delicto doctrine, is distinct in that it asserts that the plaintiff is guilty of an independent wrongful act that should bar recovery. Plaintiff's unclean hands is no defense in an antitrust action. *Kiefer-Stewart Co. v Joseph E. Seagram & Sons, Inc.* (1951) 340 US 211; *Union Leader Corp. v Newspapers of New England, Inc.* (1st Cir 1960) 284 F2d 582, *cert den* (1960) 365 US 833; *Magna Pictures Corp. v Paramount Pictures Corp.* (CD Cal 1967) 265 F Supp 144.

The in pari delicto defense was considerably weakened but apparently not absolutely precluded by the Supreme Court in *Perma Life Mufflers, Inc. v International Parts Corp.* (1968) 392 US 134. Plaintiffs claimed that franchise agreements containing unlawful provisions on resale price maintenance, exclusive dealing, and exclusive territorial restrictions caused them injury. Defendant countered that the franchisees had enjoyed the benefits flowing from the franchise agreements and were thus precluded from attacking them.

The Seventh Circuit regarded the facts as a classic case for the application of the in pari delicto doctrine and dismissed the complaint (376 F2d 699). The Supreme Court, in a divided opinion, viewed the facts quite differently and reversed the appellate court. The majority observed that the franchisees "did not actively seek each and every clause" and that their "participation was not voluntary in any meaningful way" (392 US at 139). The Court concluded that public policy required encouraging plaintiffs' suits even if they were "no less morally reprehensible than defendant." The Court held that "the doctrine of in pari delicto, with its complex scope, is not to be recognized as a defense to an antitrust action," but it acknowledged that a plaintiff's "complete involvement and participation in a monopolistic scheme" might bar recovery. (392 US at 140) The Court may have been thinking of participation in a horizontal conspiracy as distinguished from the vertical arrangement before it. The separate opinions of five of the justices indicate that some degree of involvement by the plaintiff may still raise a defense in antitrust actions. Only future developments will reveal what degree of involvement will be necessary, but it appears that the defense is not quite dead yet. See Ellis, *In Defense of Pari Delicto* (1970) 56 ABAJ 346.

E. [§2.47] Efforts to Influence Government Action: The Noerr-Pennington Exemption

Concerted efforts to disparage a competitor or to induce others not to deal with him have been traditionally within the ambit of Section 1 of the Sherman Act (15 USC §1). See, *e.g., Klor's, Inc. v Broadway-Hale Stores,*

Inc. (1959) 359 US 207; *Professional & Business Men's Life Ins. Co. v Bankers Life Co.* (D Mont 1958) 163 F Supp 274.

The situation is different, however, when concerted efforts are directed to influence the action of a public official. Regardless of purpose, such activities are protected as an exercise of free speech and of the right to petition the government and are not subject to Sherman Act sanctions. *Eastern R.R. Presidents Conference v Noerr Motor Freight, Inc.* (1961) 365 US 127 dealt with a publicity campaign by defendant railroads against long-haul truckers designed to foster law-enforcement practices and regulations destructive of the trucking business. To give their campaign the appearance of spontaneity, a "third-party" technique was used. This involved using "independent groups" as vehicles for propaganda. The Court held that the Sherman Act was not applicable to the conduct, even though its sole purpose was to destroy the truckers as competitors. The Court reasoned that a contrary result would substantially impair governmental action.

The principle of *Noerr* was reaffirmed and strengthened by *United Mine Workers v Pennington* (1965) 381 US 657. A union and an employer group conspiring to eliminate smaller coal companies jointly approached the Secretary of Labor to secure establishment of a high minimum wage for employees of contractors selling coal to the TVA. The Court reversed a jury verdict against the union and held that it was reversible error not to instruct the jury that approaches to the Secretary of Labor, or to TVA, were legal regardless of purpose. The Court states (at 381 US 669–670):

In *Eastern R.R. Presidents Conf. v. Noerr Motors* [cite] the Court rejected an attempt to base a Sherman Act conspiracy on evidence consisting entirely of activities of competitors seeking to influence public officials. The Sherman Act, it was held, was not intended to bar concerted action of this kind even though the resulting official action damaged other competitors at whom the campaign was aimed. . . . Nothing could be clearer from the Court's opinion than that anti-competitive purpose did not illegalize the conduct there involved. . . . Joint efforts to influence public officials do not violate the antitrust laws even though intended to eliminate competition. Such conduct is not illegal, either standing alone or as part of a broader scheme itself violative of the Sherman Act.

The scope of the *Noerr-Pennington* exemption is further illustrated by the case of *United States v Johns-Manville Corp.* (ED Pa 1965) 245 F Supp 74. The government contended that asbestos-cement pipe manufacturers, in furtherance of a conspiracy to monopolize the market, promoted specifications designed to limit the use of foreign-made asbestos-cement pipe. In promoting the restrictive specifications, contacts were made with purchasing authorities of municipalities and the American Society for Testing and Materials, a nonprofit public-service organization. In granting a motion for summary judgment by one defendant, the court noted (at 81,392) that *Noerr*, as stated in *Pennington*, "shields from the Sherman Act a concerted effort to influence public officials regardless of intent or motive." The contacts with ASTM are illustrative of the "third-party technique" immunized in *Noerr*.

The *Noerr* exemption given to anticompetitive action taken to influence legislative or executive decisions does not extend to such action taken to influence the judiciary or a non-discretionary administrative agency, on the theory that the latter, being interpreters rather than initiators, do not need to be free from antitrust restrictions to perform their functions. See, e.g., *Trucking Unlimited v California Motor Transport Co.* (9th Cir 1970) 432 F2d 755 at 757–759; *George R. Whitten, Jr., Inc. v Paddock Pool Builders, Inc.* (1st Cir 1970) 424 F2d 25 at 31, *cert den* (1970) 400 US 850; *Sun Valley Disposal Co. v Silver State Disposal Co.* (9th Cir 1969) 420 F2d 341 at 342. For further discussion, see §§12.67, 13.31.

F. [§2.48] Standing to Sue

Section 4 of the Clayton Act (15 USC §15) provides that any person "injured in his business or property" may maintain a private action for treble damages. There must be proof with certainty of the legal fact of injury; however, the assessment of damages after "impact" has been proved need not be precise. See *Bigelow v RKO Radio Pictures, Inc.* (1946) 327 US 251, 164; *Story Parchment Co. v Paterson Parchment Paper Co.* (1931) 282 US 555, 562.

The courts have created conclusive legal presumptions that certain categories of plaintiffs have no standing to sue because their injuries are too remote. Examples of these—sometimes seemingly arbitrary—categories follow:

☐ Shareholders, officers, employees, and creditors of corporations injured by antitrust violations. *Walker Distributing Company v Lucky Lager Brewing Co.* (9th Cir 1963) 323 F2d 1, 10 (shareholder); *Bookout v Schine Chain Theatres, Inc.* (2d Cir 1958) 253 F2d 292 (shareholder); *Martens v Barrett* (5th Cir 1957) 245 F2d 844 (creditor); *Peter v Western Newspaper Union* (5th Cir 1953) 200 F2d 867, 872 (shareholder); *Walder v Paramount Publix Corp.* (SD NY 1955) 132 F Supp 912 (shareholder); *Centanni v T. Smith & Son, Inc.* (ED La 1963) 216 F Supp 330, 338, *aff'd* (5th Cir 1963) 323 F2d 363 (employees); *Westmoreland Asbestos Co. v Johns-Manville Corp.* (SD NY 1939) 30 F Supp 389, 391, *aff'd per curiam,* (2d Cir 1940) 113 F2d 114 (shareholder); *Gerli v Silk Ass'n. of America* (SD NY 1929) 36 F2d 959 (shareholder). But cf. *Dailey v Quality School Plan, Inc.* (5th Cir 1967) 380 F2d 484, in which a corporate officer was permitted to sue; *Data Digests, Inc. v Standard & Poors Corp.* (SD NY 1967) 1967 Trade Cases ¶72,323 at 84,850, which permitted the addition of a corporate president as a party plaintiff.

☐ A partner if, under state law, the cause of action belongs to the partnership entity. *Coast v Hunt Oil Co.* (5th Cir 1952) 195 F2d 870, *cert den* (1952) 344 US 836. Cf. *Leh v General Petroleum Corp.* (1965) 382 US 54.

☐ Landlords suing for loss of rents from injured tenants. *Melrose Realty Co. v Loew's, Inc.* (3d Cir 1956) 234 F2d 518, *cert den* (1956) 352 US 890; *Skouras Theatres Corp. v Radio-Keith-Orpheum Corp.* (SD NY 1961) 193 F Supp 401; *Harrison v Paramount Pictures, Inc.* (ED Pa 1953) 115 F Supp 312, *aff'd per curiam* (3d Cir 1954) 211 F2d 405, *cert den* (1954) 348 US 828; *Westmoreland Asbestos Co. v Johns-Manville Corp., supra.* But cf. *Congress Building Corp. v Loew's, Inc.* (7th Cir 1957) 246 F2d 587; *Steiner v Twentieth Century-Fox Film Corp.* (9th Cir 1956) 232 F2d 190. See also *Erone Corp. v Skouras Theatres Corp.* (SD NY 1957) 166 F Supp 621.

☐ Supplier suing for loss of sales to injured customer. *Volasco Prods. Co. v Lloyd A. Fry Roofing Co.* (6th Cir 1962) 308 F2d 383, 395, *cert den* (1963) 372 US 907. But see *Karseal Corp. v Richfield Oil Corp.* (9th Cir 1955) 221 F2d 358; *South Carolina Council of Milk Producers, Inc. v Newton* (4th Cir 1966) 360 F2d 414, 418, *cert den* (1966) 385 US 934; *Sanitary Milk Producers v Bergjans Farm Dairy, Inc.* (8th Cir 1966) 368 F2d 679, 688–689.

☐ Patent owner suing for loss of royalties from injured licensee. *Productive Inventions, Inc. v Trico Prods. Corp.* (2d Cir 1955) 224 F2d 678, *cert den* (1956) 350 US 936.

☐ Insurance broker suing for loss of commissions. *Miley v John Hancock Mut. Life Ins. Co.* (D Mass 1957) 148 F Supp, *aff'd per curiam* (1st Cir 1957) 242 F2d 758, *cert den* (1957) 355 US 828.

☐ Music composers suing for loss of royalties resulting from injury to ASCAP. *Schwartz v Broadcast Music, Inc.* (SD NY 1959) 180 F Supp 322.

☐ Franchiser suing for loss of revenue from injured franchise holders. *Nationwide Auto Appraiser Serv., Inc. v Association of Cas. & Sur. Cos.* (10th Cir 1967) 382 F2d 925.

☐ A state suing as *parens patriae* for damages to its citizens. One court has recognized standing to assert such a claim when the alleged injury was to the state's economy generally. *Hawaii v Standard Oil Co.* (D Haw 1969) 1969 Trade Cases ¶72,916, *rev'd* (9th Cir 1970) 431 F2d 1282, *cert filed* 12-5-70. Another has declined to recognize standing when damages were sought for individual citizens, and in addition, when administration of such a suit was unworkable. *Philadelphia Housing Authority v American Radiator & Standard Sanitary Corp.* (ED Pa 1969) 309 F Supp 1057.

On the other hand, sales agents suing to recover lost commissions have somewhat anomalously, but without exception, been found to have standing. *Dailey v Quality School Plan, Inc.* (5th Cir 1967) 380 F2d 484; *Nichols v Spencer Int'l. Press, Inc.* (7th Cir 1967) 371 F2d 332; *Vines v General Outdoor Advertising Co.* (2d Cir 1948) 171 F2d 487; *Roseland v Phister Mfg. Co.* (7th Cir 1942) 125 F2d 417; *McWhirter v Monroe Calculating Mach. Co.* (WD Mo 1948) 76 F Supp 456; *Klein v Sales Builders, Inc.* (ND Ill 1950) 1950 Trade Cases ¶62,600.

The lack-of-standing defense has been weakened by *Karseal Corp. v Richfield Oil Corp.* (9th Cir 1955) 221 F2d 358. A manufacturer of auto polish claimed that a producer of petroleum products violated Section 3 of the Clayton Act (15 USC §14) and Section 1 of the Sherman Act (15 USC §1) by entering into exclusive dealing contracts with independent service-station operators covering not only petroleum products but also polishes. The Ninth Circuit reversed a judgment dismissing the amended complaint, holding that Karseal "was within the target area" of the illegal practices and "was not only hit," but "was aimed at." 221 F2d at 365. The court recognized that persons injured "incidentally" cannot recover. The test of whether a plaintiff is within the "target area" is whether its "business . . . is 'within that area of the economy which is endangered by a breakdown of competitive conditions in a particular industry' " (quoting *Conference of Studio Unions v Loew's Inc.* (9th Cir 1951) 193 F2d 51, *cert den* (1952) 342 US 919. Since exclusive dealing contracts would naturally foreclose competitive access, Karseal was within the "target area." 221 F2d at 363–364.

The increasing reluctance of courts to presume that a plaintiff was not directly injured has resulted in a breakdown of the lack-of-standing defense. Except in actions traditionally regarded as derivative to a corporation, its usefulness as a defense is uncertain. More common today is the attitude of the court in *Hoopes v Union Oil Co.* (9th Cir 1967) 374 F2d 480, quoting the Supreme Court in *Mandeville Island Farms v American Crystal Sugar Co.* (1948) 334 US 219, 236:

The statute does not confine its protection to consumers, or to purchasers, or to competitors, or to sellers. Nor does it immunize the outlawed acts because they are done by any of these. . . . The Act is comprehensive in its terms and coverage, protecting all who are made victims of the forbidden practices by whomever they may be perpetrated.

G. [§2.49] "Pass-On" or "Pass Through"

Section 4 of the Clayton Act (15 USC §15) provides for the recovery of treble damages only if the plaintiff has been "injured in his business or property" by antitrust violations. If plaintiff claims he has been damaged by higher prices resulting from illegal price fixing, but defendant can show that plaintiff has "passed on" to his customers any overcharge, it would seem that the plaintiff has not been "injured in his business or property" by the alleged violation.

In *Keogh v Chicago & Northwestern Ry.* (1922) 260 US 156 the Supreme Court upheld the pass-on defense, although it had been rejected in a different context in *Southern Pacific Co. v Darnell-Taenzar Co.* (1918) 245 US 531.

In *Hanover Shoe, Inc. v United Shoe Mach. Corp.* (1968) 392 US 481 the Supreme Court, dismissing *Keogh* as dicta, said (at 489):

> If in the face of the overcharge the buyer does nothing and absorbs the loss, he is entitled to treble damages. This much seems conceded. The reason is that he has paid more than he should and his property has been illegally diminished, for had the price paid been lower his profits would have been higher. It is also clear that if the buyer, responding to the illegal price, maintains his own price but takes steps to increase his volume or to decrease other costs, his right to damages is not destroyed. Though he may manage to maintain his profit level, he would have made more if his purchases from the defendant had cost him less. We hold that the buyer is equally entitled to damages if he raises the price for his own product. As long as the seller continues to charge the illegal price, he takes from the buyer more than the law allows. At whatever price the buyer sells, the price he pays the seller remains illegally high, and his profits would be greater were his costs lower.

The Court stressed that because pricing decisions are based on many factors, it would normally be impossible for a defendant to show that a rise in the plaintiff's prices would not have occurred in the absence of an overcharge by the defendant. Nonetheless, it recognized that many defendants would attempt the impossible if permitted to do so. This added complication in already complex proceedings would unnecessarily impede the effectiveness of enforcing the antitrust laws through private treble-damage actions, and consequently the Court held that pass-on was not to be generally recognized as a defense.

The Court admitted that there might be limited situations in which the pass-on defense could succeed, citing as an example "cost-plus" contracts on which absence of damage would be easy to establish. This exception is probably broad enough to sustain the result in the so-called "oil jobber cases" in which the jobber was given a guaranteed margin between his purchase and selling prices. See *Clark Oil Co. v Phillips Petroleum Co.* (8th Cir 1945) 148 F2d 580, *cert den* (1945) 326 US 734; *Northwestern Oil Co. v Socony-Vacuum Oil Co.* (7th Cir 1943) 138 F2d 967, *cert den* (1944) 321 US 792; *Twin Ports Oil Co. v Pure Oil Co.* (8th Cir 1941) 119 F2d 747, *cert den* (1941) 314 US 644.

One important problem raised by the *Hanover* case is the measure of aggregate recovery in suits by a series of successive buyers. If a buyer on the second level of distribution can recover for the amount his costs were increased by the passed-on overcharge, the defendant might be liable to him as well as to the direct buyer, for a total of six times the actual overcharge. If there is a buyer with standing on the third level of distribution, total recovery might be nine times the overcharge. As a practical matter, the danger might be removed by the consolidation of all cases before a single judge for trial.

H. [§2.50] Lack of Authority to Bind Principal

It is hornbook law that in order to hold a principal for the acts of its purported agent, the fact and extent of the agency must be proved. The application of this rule to the field of antitrust was reaffirmed in *United States v Ward Baking Co.* (ED Pa 1965) 243 F Supp 713; in entering a judgment for the defendant in a government civil suit, the court stated (at 717):

> The plaintiff has not sustained its burden of showing that an agent of defendant who had authority to bind it participated in any way in the conspiracy initiated by representatives of the Schulz Baking Company or ratified such participation.
>
> The uncontroverted evidence establishes that Mr. Doyle had no authority to fix the prices of defendant's products. . . .

The court pointed out that *Restatement of Agency*, 2d. §34, Comment (g) states that the authority to commit criminal or tortious acts is not to be readily inferred. See also, *Flintkote Co. v Lysfjord* (9th Cir 1957) 246 F2d 368, 386, *cert den* (1957) 355 US 835.

V. Monopolization

A. Introduction

1. [§2.51] Basic Principles

While Section 2 of the Sherman Act (15 USC §2) deals with the concept of monopolization, three separate and distinct crimes are delineated.

Section 2 provides that every person who shall (1) monopolize, (2) attempt to monopolize, or (3) conspire to monopolize any part of trade or commerce shall be subject to fines not exceeding $50,000 or imprisonment not exceeding one year or both. The three crimes are not mutually exclusive and a defendant may be found in violation of each of the offenses. In *American Tobacco Co. v United States* (1946) 328 US 781 the defendants were found guilty of violating each of the three crimes of Section 2 as well as the crime of conspiracy in restraint of trade in violation of Section 1 of the Sherman Act. Of course, any person injured in his business or property by reason of the three acts specified in Section 2 can bring a private treble-damage action pursuant to Section 4 of the Clayton Act (15 USC §15).

Section 2 of the Sherman Act contemplates a more complete and severe restraint on competition than those condemned under Section 1 of the Sherman Act (see §§2.1-2.35). The greatest distinction, however, is that while Section 1 requires *concerted* action, a single firm, through *unilateral* action, may be found guilty of violating Section 2. Because unilateral action is reached by Section 2 and because the three offenses under Section 2 are essentially economic in character, they may trap the aggressive but unwary business firm.

Because monopolization is power in a *relevant market* that is any part of trade or commerce, the definition of the market will determine how much power is necessary to constitute monopolization. If the market is narrow, a small corporation may possess the required monopoly power. This is particularly true if the company manufactures a unique product for which there are limited substitutes.

The courts have tended to narrow the relevant market in which monopoly power is measured, thus increasing the chance that a smaller company may be guilty of monopolization. In *United States v Grinnell Corp.* (1966) 384 US 563, 573 the United States Supreme Court equated the phrase "any part of trade or commerce" contained in Section 2 of the Sherman Act with "any line of commerce in any section of the country" contained in Section 7 of the Clayton Act (15 USC §18). The effect of this equation is to apply to monopolization cases the more restrictive standards of relevant markets that have been traditionally applicable to mergers under the Clayton Act. See discussion of relevant market for purposes of the Sherman Act at §§2.55-2.57; for purposes of the Clayton Act at §§4.24-4.26.

The law of monopolization and attempts to monopolize under Section 2 of the Sherman Act is vague in comparison with the detailed development of Section 1 in a large number of district and appellate court cases.

The reason for the lack of development is the very nature of monopolization itself. Because monopolization is an economic concept, it requires expert analysis and proof, which is expensive and time-consuming in both preparation and proof. Few actions warrant such treatment. Even when Section 2 crimes are alleged, the violations are usually discussed in the context of other violations and are rarely given careful individual analysis. It is possible to allege a Section 2 violation in many breach-of-contract or unfair-competition cases; but in the vast majority of cases, doing so raises so many issues that it is unwise.

2. [§2.52] Types of Action

As in cases under Section 1 of the Sherman Act (15 USC §1), activity constituting a violation of Section 2 of the Sherman Act (15 USC §2) may be subject to a government criminal prosecution, a government civil action for injunctive relief, a private treble-damage action under Section 4 of the Clayton Act (15 USC §15), or an action by the FTC for an order to cease and desist from "unfair methods of competition."

Monopolization and attempt-to-monopolize counts are being joined with increasing frequency with counts alleging violations under Section 3 of the Clayton Act (15 USC §14) brought by franchisees against their franchisors challenging exclusive dealing contracts. See, *e.g.*, *Campbell Dist. Co. v Jos. Schlitz Brewing Co.* (D Md 1962) 208 F Supp 523; see also *United States v Jerrold Electronics Corp.* (ED Pa 1960) 187 F Supp 545, *aff'd per curiam* (1961) 365 US 567; Buxbaum, *Boycotts and Restrictive Marketing Arrangements* (1966) 64 *Mich L Rev* 671, 684 n. 70.

It is also common to allege all three offenses under Section 2 of the Sherman Act in connection with allegations of the conspiracy or combination in restraint of trade under Section 1 of the Sherman Act. Even if the plaintiff fails to prove the concerted action required by Section 1, he may still prevail under a Section 2 unilateral monopolization or attempt-to-monopolize theory. A plaintiff who alleges a conspiracy to restrain trade in violation of Section 1 of the Sherman Act and also monopolization and attempted monopolization in violation of Section 2 is entitled to an instruction on unilateral action. *Continental Ore Co. v Union Carbide and Carbon Corp.* (1962) 370 US 690, 709.

B. [§2.53] Monopolization Defined in Terms of Monopoly Power

Monopolization under Section 2 of the Sherman Act (15 USC §2) consists of two elements. These are (1) the possession of monopoly power in the relevant market *and* (2) the "purposeful" acquisition or maintenance of monopoly power. See *United States v Grinnell Corp.* (1966) 384 US 563, 570-571; *United States v E. I. du Pont de Nemours & Co.* (1957) 353 US 586, 592; *American Tobacco Co. v United States* (1946) 328 US 781, 811. Thus, it is not economic "monopoly" that constitutes the offense of monopolization, but the possession of a degree of economic power with an "intent" or "purpose" to acquire monopoly power or to use it once acquired. The monopoly power may be possessed by a number of firms, acting in concert or by one firm unilaterally. Compare *American Tobacco Co. v United States, supra,* with *United States v Aluminum Co. of America* (2d Cir 1945) 148 F2d 416.

1. [§2.54] Monopoly Power

The Supreme Court in *American Tobacco Co. v United States* (1946) 328 US 781 defined monopoly power as "the power to control prices or exclude competition." See also *United States v Grinnell Corp.* (1966) 384 US 563 at 571. Monopoly power over price may derive from control of a sufficiently large portion of the supply of a product in a particular locality, from control of advertising media, or from control of related but separate product markets. The power to exclude competition may derive from any number of "unfair" practices that make it difficult for a new competitor to enter the market and become or remain viable.

As "the power to control prices or exclude competitors" is an elusive concept at best, the courts have sought to develop more concrete indicia. The courts have held that the existence of monopoly power may be inferred from the predominance of the business done in a relevant market by a particular defendant, *i.e.,* percentage of total market held by defendant measured by gross sales. See *United States v Grinnell Corp., supra,* 570-571; *American Tobacco Co. v United States, supra; United States v Aluminum Co. of America* (2d Cir 1945) 148 F2d 416.

The percentage of a given market that supports the inference of monopoly power has never been precisely defined, because each market differs considerably. Factors to be analyzed in deciding whether a firm has power to control prices or exclude competition include the defendant's role in the market, the increase or decrease of a defendant's share of the market, the ease of market entry by newcomers, and the effects of price changes on consumer behavior. In *United States v Aluminum Co. of America, supra,* monopoly power was found; the defendant had 90% of the ingot aluminum market. In *United States v United Shoe Machinery Corp.* (D Mass 1953) 110 F Supp 295, *aff'd per curiam* (1954) 347 US 521, it was held that a 75% share of the shoe machinery market showed monopoly power, while a 50% share in certain supply markets was insufficient to support such an inference. In *United States v Grinnell Corp.*, *supra*, 87% of the national market for insurance company-accredited central-station burglary and fire-protection services was held sufficient to establish monopoly power. Cf. *Amplex of Maryland, Inc. v Outboard Marine Corp.* (4th Cir 1967) 380 F2d 112, *cert den* (1968) 389 US 1026, leaving open the question whether monopoly power could be inferred from the manufacture and sale of "nearly 60%" of the outboard motors in the United States and Canada.

2. [§2.55] The Relevant Market

In order to measure the market share that may point to monopoly power, the courts have developed a yardstick in the concept of "relevant market," which has two dimensions: the product market and the geographic market. See *Indiana Farmer's Guide Publishing Co. v Prairie Farmer Publishing Co.* (1934) 293 US 268, 279.

The importance of a proper definition of the relevant market, product and geographic, cannot be overemphasized. The definition of the market will expand or contract the universe in which the defendant's "power" is to be measured. In the famous 1956 *Cellophane* case, for example, the court found that, although defendant du Pont controlled 75% of the nation's moisture-proof cellophane industry, other products were "reasonably interchangeable," and that the proper relevant product market was that of flexible packaging materials on a national basis. As du Pont had only 20% of this broader market, monopoly power was found to be lacking. *United States v E. I. du Pont de Nemours & Co.* (1956) 351 US 377. While the cases are difficult to reconcile, the analysis of the *Cellophane* case illustrates the importance of careful market definition. See §§2.56–2.57.

a. [§2.56] Determining the Relevant Product Market

Determining the relevant product market is an exercise in factual analysis in which the courts are directed to look at "market realities." *United States v Grinnell Corp.* (1966) 384 US 563. The reported cases, however, make it difficult to conclude that "market realities" have always been recognized. In *Times-Picayune Publishing Co. v United States* (1953) 345 US 594, the Court refused to consider newspaper, radio, and television advertising as part of the same market, despite the fact that some competition between them existed. In *United States v Aluminum Co. of America* (2d Cir 1945) 148 F2d 416, 424–426, the fact that Alcoa was the sole supplier of aluminum ingot caused the Court to exclude scrap aluminum from the relevant product market. However, in other cases, the uniqueness of a service or product readily explains the narrower market definition. Thus, in *United States v Paramount Pictures, Inc.* (1948) 334 US 131, the Court held that the relevant market should be first-run theatres in 92 major cities, not all theatres. Similarly, in *International Boxing Club v United States* (1959) 358 US 242, championship boxing was held to constitute the relevant product market.

What factors determine the scope of the product market? If there are substitute products to which more than a limited number of buyers will turn within reasonable variations in price, the relevant product market should include these substitutes. See *United States v Grinnell Corp.*, *supra*, 570–571; *United States v E. I. du Pont de Nemours & Co.* (D Del 1953) 118 F Supp 41, 215–217, *aff'd on other grounds* (1956) 351 US 377. It is clear that the substitutes include only products that are actually competitive, and for which there is cross-elasticity of demand. The key question is how close the substitutes must be to be "reasonably interchangeable" and thus included in the product market.

The *Cellophane* case made it clear that the substitutes need not be "fungible" or have a general similarity in appearance. What was important was interchangeability in end use. Of course, the more similar a product is in appearance or use, the better the chance of its being included as a substitute. While the principles of the *Cellophane* case were reiterated in *United States v Grinnell Corp.*, *supra*, the Supreme Court upheld the district court's narrow product-market definition, excluding from the product market of insurance-accredited central-station fire-and burglar-alarm protection systems such substitutes as watchman service and noninsurance-approved systems, although evidence showed that price would determine consumer preferences, and that the end-user was the same. In *Brown Shoe Co. v United States* (1962) 370 US 294, 325, the Court listed the facts that should be considered in defining a product market. *Brown Shoe* was a suit under Section 7 of the Clayton Act (15 USC §18) to enjoin a merger, but in *Grinnell, supra*, 384 US at 573, the Court equated the standards for relevant market under Section 2 of the Sherman Act (15 USC §2) and Section 7 of the Clayton Act. The list:

1. [Lack of] reasonable interchangeability of use [between] . . . the product itself and substitutes for it.

2. Industry or public recognition of the . . . market as a separate economic entity.

3. The product's peculiar characteristics and uses.

4. Unique production facilities.

5. Distinct customers.

6. Distinct prices.

7. Sensitivity to price changes.

8. Specialized vendors.

Therefore, substitutes, while they need not be fungible, should be as fungible as possible. Similarities should be carefully pointed out. If a defendant is successful in defining the market in the trial court, carefully tailored findings of fact are essential. Under the Federal Rules findings of fact will not be overturned unless "clearly erroneous." FRCP 52(a).

b. [§2.57] Determining the Relevant Geographic Market

Just as important, and just as difficult, is the determination of the geographic market in which the product is to be measured. Generally, a defendant will argue for a broader geographic market, since the market-share percentage will usually be smaller, and the likelihood of monopoly power, less. But the choice may be difficult. If a broader geographic market is established, any resulting injunctive decree will be broader, and the scope of potential treble-damage suits greater. Analysis is required in each case. In *Standard Oil Co. of California v United States* (1949) 337 US 293, 299, the appropriate market was defined as the "area of effective competition" within which the defendant operates. To the same effect, see *United States v Addyston Pipe & Steel Co.* (6th Cir 1898) 85 Fed 271, 291-292, *aff'd* (1899) 175 US 211 (four-state area); and *Indiana Farmer's Guide Publishing Co. v Prairie Farmer Publishing Co.* (1934) 293 US 268 (eight-state area where plaintiff and defendant newspapers principally circulated). In *Becker v Safelite Glass Corp.* (D Kan 1965) 244 F Supp 625, 637, however, the court held that in an "attempt" case, the relevant geographic market was the "area in which the attempt occurred." This is unsound, because it dispenses with the economic realities of the geographic market and prejudges the defendant's guilt.

The geographic markets found by the courts vary from a single city to the entire country. The *Merger Guidelines* issued by the Justice Department define geographic market as "any commercially significant section of the country (even as small as a single community)," unless the seller can demonstrate that competitors outside the proposed geographic market suffer no competitive disadvantage in selling within the market. A seller thus attempting to stretch the bounds of the relevant geographic market might show absence of any appreciable difference in transportation costs, distribution facilities, customer inconvenience, or established customer preference for local products. *Merger Guidelines*, Trade Reg Rep ¶4430, at 6683.

Compare *Beacon Fruit & Produce Co. v H. Harris & Co.* (D Mass 1958) 160 F Supp 95, *aff'd per curiam* (1st Cir 1958) 260 F2d 958, *cert den* (1959) 359 US 984 (Greater Boston), with *United States v Grinnell Corp.* (1966) 384 US 563 (the entire country). In between are many combinations. See *United States v Columbia Steel Co.* (1948) 334 US 495, 508 (eleven-state area); *United States v Jerrold Electronics Corp.* (ED Pa 1960) 187 F Supp 545, *aff'd per curiam* (1961) 365 US 567 (four-state area). If a defendant engages in local business in many areas, advertises nationally, and plans local activities on a national level, the chances are greatly increased that the court will find the relevant geographic market to be the entire country. See *United States v Grinnell Corp., supra*, at 575-576.

3. [§2.58] The Requirement of Intent

In order for monopoly power to become "monopolization," it is necessary that an intent be found to exercise the power. *United States v Griffith* (1948) 334 US 100, 107; *Volasco Prods. Co. v Lloyd A. Fry Roofing Co.* (6th Cir 1962) 308 F2d 383, 389, *cert den* (1963) 372 US 907. However, the nature of the requisite intent is obscure; it appears to be nothing more than the intent to do the act—a general rather than a specific intent. See *United States v Aluminum Co. of America* (2d Cir 1945) 148 F2d 416, 432 ("no monopolist monopolizes unconscious of what he is doing"). Thus, the intent required to constitute the crime of monopolization is much different from the specific intent prerequisite to a finding of attempt to monopolize or conspiracy to monopolize. See *Times-Picayune Publishing Co. v United States* (1953) 345 US 594; *Campbell Dist. Co. v Jos. Schlitz Brewing Co.* (D Md 1962) 208 F Supp 523. The uncertainty over the nature of the requisite intent and the question whether any intent at all, in the traditional sense, is required, caused the Attorney General's National Committee to designate it as "deliberateness, the purpose or intent to exercise that power." See *Attorney General's Report, 1968,* at 34.

As stated by the district court in the *Grinnell* case affirmed by the Supreme Court, *supra* (236 F Supp 244, 248, *aff'd* (1966) 384 US 563):

Once the [plaintiff] has borne the burden of proving what is the relevant market and how predominant a share of that market defendant has, it follows that there are rebuttable presumptions that defendant has monopoly power and has monopolized in violation of Section 2.

C. [§2.59] The "Thrust Upon" Defense

In the *Alcoa* case, it was suggested that if monopoly power were innocently acquired through superior skill, foresight, or industry, or if a change in cost or taste had destroyed all but one firm, Section 2 (15 USC §2) would not be violated. This was because, as Judge Learned Hand wrote, the power had been "thrust upon it." *United States v Aluminum Co. of America* (2d Cir 1945) 148 F2d 416, 429. In *American Tobacco Co. v United States* (1946) 328 US 781, 786, the Supreme Court suggested that Section 2 would not be violated if monopoly power were necessarily acquired because a defendant was the original entrant into a new market, or had made a new discovery that carried the power with it.

From these examples, the affirmative defense of "thrust upon" was developed. Almost from its inception, the defense fell upon hard times, because although monopoly power may be legally obtained, the intent to maintain it by calculated acts directed against potential market entrants transforms the legally obtained power into illegal monopolization. See *United States v Aluminum Co. of America, supra,* 432. As the requisite intent or "deliberateness" is so easily found, the defense is somewhat tenuous. See *United States v United Shoe Machinery Corp.* (D Mass 1953) 110 F Supp 295, 344, *aff'd per curiam* (1954) 347 US 521.

However, the Supreme Court has not decided whether acts legal in themselves taken to maintain monopoly power will transform it into unlawful monopolization. The lower courts seem to indicate that lawfully acquired monopoly power maintained by active underpricing and dynamic but lawful business acumen does not constitute unlawful monopolization. *American Football League v National Football League* (4th Cir 1963) 323 F2d 124, 131: "When one has acquired a national monopoly by means which are neither exclusionary, unfair, or predatory, he is not disempowered to defend his position fairly." To the same effect see *Union Leader Corp. v Newspapers of New England, Inc.* (1st Cir 1960) 284 F2d 582, *cert den* (1961) 365 US 833; *John Wright & Associates v Ulrich* (8th Cir 1964) 328 F2d 474, 480.

The "thrust-upon" defense is a valuable trial tool for any defendant, however. Because it puts skill and industry in issue, a defendant has a useful vehicle to explain its good works to the jury. The burden of proof of the defense is, of course, on the defendant. *United States v United Shoe Machinery Corp., supra,* at 342.

D. Attempts to Monopolize

1. [§2.60] Introduction

"Attempt to monopolize" is a separate crime under Section 2 (15 USC §2), differing materially from the crime of monopolization and from the crime of combination or conspiracy to monopolize. The attempt may be unilateral or concerted. See *Continental Ore Co. v Union Carbide & Carbon Corp.* (1962) 370 US 690, 710. There have not been numerous cases on attempts to monopolize, and in many the allegation of attempt is a makeweight in a Section 1 case. Therefore, little clear analysis is to be found on the crime. However, the cases are on the increase, and the practitioner should be aware of the pitfalls of an attempt-to-monopolize case. As in many areas of the law, one of the earliest cases is the best reasoned, with a gradual disintegration following. See *Swift & Co. v United States* (1905) 196 US 375. See also *Kansas City Star Co. v United States* (8th Cir 1957) 240 F2d 643, *cert den* (1957) 354 US 923; *North Texas Producers Ass'n. v Metzger Dairies, Inc.* (5th Cir 1965) 348 F2d 189, *cert den* (1966) 382 US 977; *Bergjans Farm Dairy Co. v Sanitary Milk Producers* (ED Mo 1965) 241 F Supp 476, *aff'd* (8th Cir 1966) 368 F2d 679.

2. [§2.61] The Criminal Law of Attempt

As murder has attempted murder, so monopolization has attempted to monopolize. To be guilty of an attempt to commit a crime, the actor must do an overt act that if successful would bring about the consummation of the substantive crime itself. See Skilton, *The Requisite Act in a Criminal Attempt* (1937) 3 *U Pitt L Rev* 308; Note (1958) 27 *Geo Wash L Rev* 227, 230. The crime "attempt to monopolize" is committed if acts are performed with specific intent which, if successful, would result in actual monopolization, and in falling short produce a dangerous probability of monopolization. See *Swift & Co. v United States* (1905) 196 US 375, 396; *United States v Winslow* (1913) 227 US 202, 218; *American Tobacco Co. v United States* (1946) 328 US 781, 785.

3. [§2.62] The Requirement of Dangerous Probability

"Dangerous probability" was declared in *Swift & Co. v United States* (1905) 196 US 375 to be an essential element of attempt to monopolize along with an intent to achieve actual monopolization. *Swift* has been followed and cited with approval frequently. See, *e.g.*, *United States v Winslow* (1913) 227 US 202, 218; *American Tobacco Co. v United States* (1946) 328 US 781, 785; *Lorain Journal Co. v United States* (1951) 342 US 143; *United States v Socony-Vacuum Oil Co.* (1940) 310 US 150, 226, n. 59.

Since "dangerous probability" refers to the power to achieve monopolization if the overt acts are successful, it is necessary to measure monopoly power in the proper market by the same means as in a monopolization case. *Walker Process Equipment, Inc. v Food Mach. & Chem. Corp.* (1965)

382 US 172; Hibner, *Attempts to Monopolize: A Concept in Search of Analysis* (1967) 34 ABA Antitrust LJ 165; Johnston, *Monopolize or Attempt to Monopolize, Proceedings, ABA Section of Antitrust Law* (1953) 72, 76; Note (1959) 27 *Geo Wash L Rev* 227, 233. On relevant market, see §§2.55–2.57.

4. [§2.63] The Requirement of Specific Intent

Specific, rather than general, intent must be established in an attempt-to-monopolize case. See *Campbell Dist. Co. v Jos. Schlitz Brewing Co.* (D Md 1962) 208 F Supp 523; *United States v Griffith* (1948) 334 US 100, 105; *Kansas City Star Co. v United States* (8th Cir 1957) 240 F2d 643, 663, *cert den* (1957) 354 US 923 (holding that the requisite specific intent could be inferred from coercive conduct forcing advertisers to use the *Star* and not competitive papers plus purchase of another newspaper); *Independent Iron Works, Inc. v United States Steel Corp.* (9th Cir 1963) 322 F2d 656, 667, *cert den* (1963) 375 US 922, (holding that refusal to fill orders of customer did not establish requisite intent because there was a shortage and defendant had attempted to ration the product among all its customers). Even the *Alcoa* case recognized that the requisite intent must go beyond the mere intent to do the act. *United States v Aluminum Co. of America* (2d Cir 1945) 184 F2d 416, 432. In *Mackey v Sears, Roebuck & Co.* (7th Cir 1956) 237 F2d 869, 873, *cert dismissed* (1957) 355 US 865, the complaint was dismissed because the only intent alleged was to destroy one competitor. The specific intent may be established by contemporaneous documents, and from the history of the defendants' business conduct. See *United States v Jerrold Electronics Corp.* (ED Pa 1960) 187 F Supp 545, 567, *aff'd per curiam* (1961) 365 US 567; Note (1959) 27 *Geo Wash L Rev* 227, 231–232.

5. [§2.64] A Cautionary Note—The Lessig Case

In *Lessig v Tidewater Oil Co.* (9th Cir 1964) 327 F2d 459, *cert den* (1064) 377 US 993, the proper analysis of attempt-to-monopolize was thrown into confusion. The court stated that when the charge is attempt (or conspiracy) to monopolize, relevant market is not an issue, and that probability of actual monopolization is not an essential element of proof of attempt to monopolize. 327 F2d at 464. On rehearing, the court limited itself to the facts before it, and stated that the opinion should be read "in the light of the anti-competitive purposes" and conduct dealt with by the case. See also Turner, *Antitrust Policy and the Cellophane Case* (1956) 70 *Harv L Rev* 281, 294.

While it is unclear what the court meant in the *Lessig* case, it apparently means that specific intent plus an overt act is all that would be necessary to make a prima facie case. As intent may be inferred from the business conduct of a defendant, every unfair trade practice or business tort may potentially be an attempt to monopolize. The case is unsupported by any of the authorities it cites, and thus far has not been followed by any district court, even in the Ninth Circuit. See *Hiland Dairy, Inc. v Kroger Co.* (8th Cir 1968) 402 F2d 968, *cert den* (1969) 395 US 961; *Bernard Food Industries, Inc. v Dietene Co.* (7th Cir 1969) 415 F2d 1279, *cert den* (1970) 397 US 912; *Becker v Safelite Glass Corp.* (D Kan 1965) 244 F Supp 625, 637; *United States v Chas. Pfizer & Co.* (ED NY 1965) 245 F Supp 737, 738–739; *United States v Johns-Manville Corp.* (ED Pa 1964) 231 F Supp 690, 699–700; *Bailey's Bakery, Ltd. v Continental Baking Co.* (D Haw 1964) 235 F Supp 705 (jury instruction no. 27). Language contradicting the *Lessig* holding also appears in contemporaneous cases heard by other panels of the Ninth Circuit. See *Walker Distrib. Co. v Lucky Lager Brewing Co.* (9th Cir 1963) 323 F2d 1; *Independent Iron Works, Inc. v United States Steel Corp.* (9th Cir 1963) 322 F2d 656, 667, *cert den* (1963) 375 US 922. Finally, the case is at variance with pronouncements by the Supreme Court. See *Walker Process Equip., Inc. v Food Mach. & Chem. Corp.* (1965) 382 US 172, 177–178; *United States v Grinnell Corp.* (1966) 384 US 563, 586–587 (Fortas, J., dissenting). But cf. *McCormack v Theo. Hamm Brewing Co.* (D Minn 1968) 284 F Supp 158, in which the court asserted that a "[s]ubstantial probability of success" need no longer be shown in an attempt case, failing to distinguish plaintiff's claims of attempted monopolization and conspiracy to monopolize and relying solely on *United States v Consolidated Laundries Corp.* (2d Cir 1961) 291 F2d 563, a conspiracy case.

E. [§2.65] Combinations and Conspiracies to Monopolize

While monopolization and attempted monopolization may be either unilateral or concerted, combinations and conspiracies to monopolize by definition require plural action. Any violation of this part of Section 2 (15 USC §2) will also be a combination or conspiracy in restraint of trade under Section 1 (15 USC §1). As attempted monopolization must be analyzed by the law of criminal attempt, combination and conspiracy to monopolize must be analyzed by the law of conspiracy. It is not necessary that actual monopolization be approached; all that is needed in a criminal case is a finding of conspiracy, with the specific intent to achieve monopolization, plus an overt act in furtherance of the conspiracy. *United*

States v Consolidated Laundries Corp. (2d Cir 1961) 291 F2d 563, 572–573; cf. *Hyde v United States* (1912) 225 US 347, 384 (Holmes, J., dissenting). For discussion of the elements of combination and conspiracy, see §§2.7–2.11. In a treble-damage action, of course, impact and damage must be proved as well as a violation of Section 2. See Chapter 12.

BIBLIOGRAPHY

1. Outstanding works on antitrust policy in general:

   Blake, Bork, Bowman, and Jones: *Goals of Antitrust: A Dialogue on Policy* (1965) 65 *Col L Rev* 363;

   Dewey: *Monopoly in Economics and Law* (1959) Rand;

   Edwards: *Big Business and the Policy of Competition* (1956);

   Kahn: *Standards of Antitrust Policy* (1954) 67 *Harv L Rev* 28;

   Kaysen and Turner: *Antitrust Policy: An Economic and Legal Analysis* (1959) Harvard University Press;

   Massell: *Competition and Monopoly; Legal and Economic Issues* (1962) Brookings;

   Neale: *The Antitrust Laws of the United States of America* (1960) Cambridge;

   Prettyman: *Functioning of the Economist for Antitrust Litigation* (1962) 20 ABA Antitrust Section 10;

   Report of the Attorney General's National Committee to Study the Antitrust Laws (1955).

2. Practically-oriented works:

   Anderson: *Effective Antitrust Compliance Programs and Procedures (An Outline)* (1963) 18 *Bus Law* 739;

   Kintner: *Counselling Small Business under the Antitrust Laws and the Robinson-Patman Act* (1963) 23 *Fed BJ* 309.

3. Periodic publications helpful in keeping up with antitrust developments:

   Antitrust and Trade Regulation Report;
   Antitrust Bulletin;
   Antitrust Law Journal;
   Handler: *Annual Antitrust Review, Association of the Bar of the City of New York Record.*

4. Common-Law Background:

Handler: *A Study of the Construction and Enforcement of the Federal Antitrust Laws*, TNEC Monograph no. 38 at 4–5 (1941);

Hedges: *The Law Relating to Restraint of Trade* (1932);

Letwin: *Law and Economic Policy in America; The Evolution of the Sherman Antitrust Act* (1965);

Letwin: *The English Common Law Concerning Monopolies* (1954) 21 *U Chi L Rev* 355;

Peppin: *Price-Fixing Agreements under the Sherman Antitrust Law* (1940) 28 *Calif L Rev* 297, 677;

Sanderson: *Restraint of Trade in English Law* (1926);

Thorelli: *The Federal Antitrust Policy* (1955) Johns Hopkins.

5. Legislative History:

Clark: *The Federal Antitrust Policy* (1954);

Letwin: *Congress and the Sherman Antitrust Law: 1887–1890* (1956) 23 *U Chi L Rev* 221;

Letwin: *Law and Economic Policy in America, supra;*

Thorelli: *supra.*

6. Terms:

Barndt: *Two Trees or One?—The Problem of Intra-Enterprise Conspiracy* (1962) 23 *Mont L Rev* 158;

Comment: *Evidentiary Value of Conscious Parallelism* (1962) 45 *Marq L Rev* 633;

Handler: *Contract, Combination or Conspiracy, An Antitrust Handbook* (1958);

Note: *"Combinations" in Restraint of Trade: A New Approach to Section 1 of the Sherman Act* (1966) 1966 *Utah L Rev* 75;

Note: *The Nature of Sherman Act Conspiracy* (1954) 54 *Col L Rev* 1108;

Rahl: *Conspiracy and the Antitrust Laws* (1950) 44 *Ill L Rev* 743;

Stengel: *Intra-Enterprise Conspiracy under Section 1 of the Sherman Act* (1963) 35 *Miss LJ* 5;

Turner: *Definition of Agreement under the Sherman Act: Conscious Parallelism and Refusals to Deal* (1962) 75 *Harv L Rev* 655;

Willis and Pitofsky: *Antitrust Consequences of Using Corporate Subsidiaries* (1968) 43 *NYU L Rev* 20.

7. The Rule of Reason and *Per Se* Violations:

Adams: *The "Rule of Reason": Workable Competition or Workable Monopoly* (1954) 63 *Yale LJ* 348;

Attorney General's Report, supra;

Blake, Bork, Bowman, and Jones, *supra;*

Bork: *Ancillary Restraints and the Sherman Act* (1959) 15 ABA Antitrust Section 211;

Bork: *The Rule of Reason and the Per Se Concept: Price Fixing and Market Division* (1965) 74 *Yale LJ* 775 and (1966) 75 *Yale LJ* 375;

Comment: *The Per Se Illegality of Price Fixing—Sans Power, Purpose or Effect* (1952) 19 *U Chi L Rev* 837.

8. Exemption Areas:

a. *Generally*

Orrick: *The Recent Erosion of Certain Antitrust Exemptions* (1965) 10 *Antitrust Bulletin* 667;

Symposium: *Antitrust Exemptions* (1967) 33 ABA Antitrust LJ 1.

b. *Agricultural Cooperatives*

Agricultural Cooperatives and the Antitrust Laws: A New Departure (1961) 36 *Ind L Rev* 497;

Note: *The Antitrust Impact of Vertical Integration in Agricultural Cooperatives* (1966) 51 *Iowa L Rev* 971.

c. *The Regulated Industries*

Asch: *The Antitrust Laws and the Regulated Securities Markets* (1966) 11 *Antitrust Bulletin* 209;

Comment: *Exemptions for Regulated Industries* (1961) 60 *Mich L Rev* 213;

Hale and Hale: *Competition or Control, I–VI* (a series)

  I. *Chaos in the Cases* (1958) 106 *U Pa L Rev* 641

  II. *Radio and Television Broadcasting* (1959) 107 *U Pa L Rev* 585

  III. *Motor Carriers* (1960) 108 *U Pa L Rev* 775

  IV. *Airlines* (1961) 109 *U Pa L Rev* 311

  V. *Production and Distribution of Electric Energy* (1962) 110 *U Pa L Rev* 57

  VI. *Application of Antitrust Laws to Regulated Industries* (1962) 111 *U Pa L Rev* 46;

Latta: *Primary Jurisdiction for the Regulated Industries and the Antitrust Laws* (1961) 30 *U Chi L Rev* 261;

Mervin: *Antitrust Immunity of "Public Utilities" Regulated by the FPC* (1968) 54 ABAJ 687;

Note: *Antitrust and the Stock Exchange: Minimum Commission or Free Competition?* (1965) 18 *Stan L Rev* 213;

Symposium: *Antitrust and Monopoly Policy in the Communications Industries* (1968) 13 *Antitrust Bulletin* 871.

d. *Labor*

Comment: *Labor's Antitrust Exemption* (1967) 55 *Calif L Rev* 254;

Comment: *Labor's Antitrust Exemption after Pennington and Jewel Tea* (1966) 66 *Col L Rev* 742;

Cox: *Labor and the Antitrust Laws: Pennington and Jewel Tea* (1966) 46 *Boston UL Rev* 317;

Farmer: *Association Bargaining: Pennington and Jewel Revisited* (1967) 12 *Antitrust Bulletin* 555;

Note: *Impact of the Antitrust Laws on Labor Organizations in the Light—or Shadow—of Pennington and Jewel Tea* (1966) 46 *Boston UL Rev* 83;

Note: *Labor Law and Antitrust: "So Deceptive and Opaque are the Elements of These Problems"* (1966) 1966 *Duke LJ* 191;

Zimmer and Silberman: *Pennington and Jewel Tea: Antitrust Impact on Collective Bargaining* (1966) 11 *Antitrust Bulletin* 857.

e. *Professional Sports*

Anderson: *The Sherman Act and Professional Sports Associations' Use of Eligibility Rules* (1968) 47 *Neb L Rev* 82;

Note: *Constitutional Law—Pre-emption—Baseball's Immunity from State Antitrust Law* (1967) 13 *Wayne L Rev* 417;

Note: *The Super Bowl and the Sherman Act: Professional Team Sports and the Antitrust Laws* (1967) 81 *Harv L Rev* 418.

9. The *Per Se* Violations:

See articles cited under 7, *supra,* for discussion of price fixing and market division.

10. Newly emerging areas of *per se* violations:

a. *Boycotts*

Barber: *Refusals to Deal under the Federal Antitrust Laws* (1955) 103 *U Pa L Rev* 847;

Buxbaum: *Boycotts and Restrictive Marketing Arrangements* (1966) 64 *Mich L Rev* 671;

Coons: *Non-Commercial Purpose As a Sherman Act Defense* (1962) 56 *Nw UL Rev* 705;

Kelley: *John Won't Sell—Bill Won't Buy. Does It Matter What the Reason Why? Antitrust Refusals to Deal* (1967) 4 *San Diego L Rev* 1;

Note: *Concerted Refusals to Deal under the Federal Antitrust Laws* (1958) 71 *Harv L Rev* 1531;

Rahl: *Per Se Rules and Boycotts under the Sherman Act—Some Reflections on the Klors Case* (1959) 45 *Va L Rev* 1165.

b. *Tying Arrangements*

Bowman: *Tying Arrangements and the Leverage Problem* (1959) 67 *Yale LJ* 19;

Pearson: *Tying Arrangements and Antitrust Policy* (1965) 60 *Nw UL Rev* 626;

Turner: *The Validity of Tying Arrangements under the Antitrust Laws* (1958) 72 *Harv L Rev* 50.

c. *Mergers and Joint Ventures*

Bock: *Mergers and Markets* (3d ed 1964) National Industrial Conference Board;

Comment: *Joint Ventures and Antitrust Policy* (1965) 26 *Ohio State LJ* 439;

Hale: *Joint Ventures, Collaborative Subsidiaries and the Antitrust Laws* (1956) 42 *Va L Rev* 927;

Sproul: *United States Antitrust Laws and Foreign Joint Ventures* (1968) 54 ABAJ 889;

Whipple: *Problems of Combinations—Integration, Intracorporate Conspiracy and Joint Ventures* (1958) 1958 Antitrust Law Symp 34.

11. Defenses:

a. *Statute of Limitations*

Comment: *Fraudulent Concealment as Tolling the Antitrust Statute of Limitations* (1967) 36 *Fordham L Rev* 328;

Comment: *Private Antitrust Suits: Tolling the Statute of Limitations as to Defendants Not Named in a Prior Government Suit* (1967) 1 *USF L Rev* 348;

Hale and Hale: *Delimiting the Geographical Market: A Problem in Merger Cases* (1966) 61 *Nw UL Rev* 538;

Hogan and Koelke: *Determination of the Market for Antitrust Purposes: Difficulties and Problems* (1962) 39 *U Det LJ* 519;

Holl: *Market Definition and Antitrust Policy* (1963) 20 *Wash & Lee L Rev* 47;

Houghton: *The Role of an Economist in Delineating the Relevant Market for an Antitrust Proceeding* (1962) 6 *Antitrust Bulletin* 125;

Lanzillotti: *Market Structure and Antitrust Vulnerability* (1963) 8 *Antitrust Bulletin* 853;

Note: *Product Market Definition under the Sherman and Clayton Acts* (1962) 110 *U Pa L Rev* 861;

Upshaw: *The Relevant Market in Merger Decisions: Antitrust Concept or Antitrust Device?* (1965) 60 *Nw UL Rev* 424.

c. *Attempts and conspiracies to monopolize*

Hibner: *Attempts to Monopolize: A Concept in Search of Analysis* (1967) 33 ABA Antitrust LJ 165;

Note: *Prosecutions for Attempts to Monopolize: The Relevance of the Relevant Market* (1967) 42 *NYU L Rev* 110;

Smith: *Attempts to Monopolize: Its Elements and Their Definition* (1950) 27 *Geo Wash L Rev* 227.

3

Product Distribution

Robert E. Cooper, Paul G. Bower, and Don J. Belcher

Mr. Cooper received the AB degree from Northwestern University in 1961 and the LLB degree from Yale Law School in 1964. He is a member of the Los Angeles County and American Bar Associations. Mr. Bower received the BS degree from Rice University in 1955 and the LLB degree from Stanford University in 1963. He is a member of the Los Angeles County and American Bar Associations. Mr. Belcher received the AB degree from the University of California at Los Angeles in 1962 and the LLB degree from the University of California at Los Angeles Law School in 1965. He is a member of the Los Angeles County Bar Association. Mr. Cooper, Mr. Bower and Mr. Belcher are members of the Los Angeles firm of Gibson, Dunn and Crutcher.

D. **Refusal to Deal**
  1. *[§3.37] The Colgate Doctrine*
  2. *[§3.38] Subsequent Limitations to the Colgate Doctrine*
  3. *[§3.39] Present Status of the Colgate Doctrine*
  4. *[§3.40] Using Refusal to Sell to Enforce Restraints Other Than Resale Price*

I. [§3.1] Introduction

Every manufacturer has a vital interest in the successful distribution and marketing of his product. In the context of the modern industrial economy, even a product of the highest inherent quality is likely to be a commercial failure without an effective distribution program.

Some manufacturers perform the distribution function themselves. Integration of the manufacturing and distribution operations does not ensure an efficient and profitable sales program, of course. However, it does permit the manufacturer to exercise full control and to employ whatever practices he believes will work best. The principal drawback to such integration, however, is that the establishment of a distribution system ordinarily is very expensive—so expensive that relatively few manufacturers are able or willing to afford it. See generally, Jordan, *Exclusive and Restricted Sales Areas under the Antitrust Laws* (1962) 9 *UCLA L Rev* 111.

Because of the sizeable investment that manufacturers must make to distribute their own products, most prefer to leave distribution to others. Consequently, an almost infinite variety of arrangements are entered into involving such independent entities as distributors, jobbers, wholesalers, and retailers (here sometimes referred to generically as "distributors"). Many of the antitrust problems in the area of product distribution result from attempts on the part of manufacturers to control the activities of the independent entities that perform the distribution function.

This chapter is concerned with four basic types of controls (and their variations) that manufacturers have commonly attempted to exercise over the behavior of distributors: (1) exclusive-dealing arrangements (see §§3.2–3.8), which preclude the distributor from dealing in competing products; (2) tying arrangements (see §§3.9–3.18), which condition the sale of one product on the purchase of another; (3) territorial and customer restrictions (§§3.19–3.24), which limit the geographic area in which the distributor may sell, or the class of customers to which he may sell; and (4) resale price maintenance (§§3.25–3.39), whereby the manufacturer sets the price at which the distributor will resell.

Under some circumstances, each of these practices may constitute a violation of the broad proscriptions of Section 1 of the Sherman Act (15 USC §1), relating to combinations or contracts in restraint of trade, or Section 2 of the Sherman Act (15 USC §2), which is concerned with monopolization and attempts to monopolize. See Chapter 2. But the statute that most specifically governs product-distribution arrangements is Section 3 of the Clayton Act (15 USC §14), which provides as follows:

It shall be unlawful for any person engaged in commerce, in the course of such commerce, to lease or make a sale or contract for sale of goods, wares, merchandise, machinery, supplies, or other commodities, whether patented or unpatented, for use, consumption, or resale . . . or fix a price charged therefor, or discount from, or rebate upon, such price, on the condition, agreement, or understanding that the lessee or purchaser thereof shall not use or deal in the goods, wares, merchandise, machinery, supplies, or other commodities of a competitor or competitors of the lessor or seller, where the effect of such lease, sale, or contract for sale or such condition, agreement, or understanding may be to substantially lessen competition or tend to create a monopoly in any line of commerce.

Of late these practices frequently have been found to fall within Section 5 of the Federal Trade Commission Act (15 USC §45), which prohibits in a broad and general fashion "unfair methods of competition in commerce."

II. Exclusive-Dealing Arrangements

A. [§3.2] Introduction

The term "exclusive dealing" usually refers to a contract or understanding between a supplier and a purchaser that forbids the latter from handling competitive products. Another prevalent form of the exclusive-dealing arrangement is found in requirements contracts, which typically obligate the purchaser to obtain all or a percentage of his "requirements" of a certain product from a sole supplier. ("Exclusive dealing" may also refer to output contracts, which obligate a manufacturer to sell all or part of his production to one buyer.) Finally, a manufacturer may simply announce and enforce a policy of refusing to deal with distributors who handle competitive products. For discussion of the opportunities and difficulties of refusal to deal as a device for enforcing exclusive dealing arrangements, see §3.40.

These points may be helpful in deciding whether an exclusive dealing arrangement is vulnerable under the antitrust laws:

☐ If the arrangement clearly affects a significant amount of commerce, it is probably vulnerable. See §§3.4, 3.6.

☐ If the arrangement affects relatively little commerce, it may nevertheless be vulnerable if similar arrangements are used by competitors and the arrangements taken together are significant (see §§3.4, 3.6), or if one party to the transaction is at a significant bargaining disadvantage, or if the courts conclude that the arrangement is inimical to competition even though it affects little commerce. See §§3.5–3.6.

☐ If the arrangement is reasonably short, it is less likely to be vulnerable. See §3.7.

☐ Enforcement of an exclusive dealing arrangement through refusals to deal may or may not be valid. See §3.40.

☐ The arrangement may be justifiable as protecting goodwill or, possibly, as affording economic advantages. See §3.8.

B. [§3.3] The Tests of Illegality

Exclusive-dealing agreements and requirements contracts have been attacked both under Section 1 of the Sherman Act (15 USC §1) as contracts in restraint of trade and under the more specific provisions of Section 3 of the Clayton Act (15 USC §14), quoted in §3.1. In determining whether the requisite probability of competitive injury is present under Section 3 of the Clayton Act, two quite different tests have been employed by the courts and the FTC: "quantitative substantiality" and "qualitative substantiality."

1. [§3.4] Quantitative Substantiality

The so-called "quantitative substantiality" test was born in the *Standard Stations* case, *Standard Oil Co. of California v United States* (1949) 337 US 293. There, the Supreme Court held that Standard's contracts with retail gasoline stations obligating the stations to purchase their requirements of gasoline (and, in some cases, tires, batteries, and accessories) from Standard were unlawful under Section 3 of the Clayton Act (15 USC §14). Standard had executed such contracts with 16% of all retail gasoline outlets in the western states, covering 6.7% of the total volume of gasoline sold in the West. Standard's six major competitors generally operated under similar exclusive-dealing arrangements with their dealers. Together, the seven majors controlled 76% of all stations in the West and accounted for at least 65% of the total gallonage sold. The Court held that under these circumstances, it was not necessary for the plaintiff to prove that the exclusive-dealing contracts were actually anticompetitive, expressing doubt that the courts are qualified to embark on an elaborate economic analysis of the actual and probable injury to competition that exclusive-dealing arrangements may cause. For the same reason, the Court rejected evidence offered by Standard to justify its use of exclusive-dealing contracts. The Court held that to establish a violation it was sufficient to prove that "a substantial portion of commerce is affected" by the contracts. The Court thereby proposed a simple test to assess the legality of exclusive arrangements, an approach that has been described as essentially a "power" test. Kessler and Stern, *Competition, Contract and Vertical Integration* (1959) 69 *Yale LJ* 1, 27.

The rule of *Standard Stations*, then, is that Section 3 of the Clayton Act is violated whenever exclusive-dealing arrangements foreclose competition "in a substantial share of the line of commerce affected." 337 US at 314. This approach has been labeled the "quantitative substantiality" test, since it postulates that exclusive-dealing arrangements that cover a "substantial" quantity of the market necessarily tend substantially to lessen competition.

Since Standard's contracts affected only 6.7% of the relevant market, *Standard Stations* can be read as a warning that exclusive-dealing contracts that foreclose more than a *de minimis* share of the market from other suppliers automatically violate Section 3 of the Clayton Act. However, the Court emphasized that an important factor in its decision was the widespread use of similar exclusive-dealing contracts by all the other major suppliers which, together, insulated the vast bulk of the total gasoline market. Thus, *Standard Stations* is of almost no help in determining what share of the market will be deemed "substantial" when there is only individual and not collective foreclosure. Nor does *Standard Stations* offer any hint whether the substantiality of the market share may vary according to the nature of the industry.

In the aftermath of *Standard Stations*, the lower courts, and initially the FTC, declined to consider the economic effect of exclusive-dealing contracts; instead, they merely inquired whether the arrangements affected a substantial portion of the relevant market. Thus, in *Dictograph Corp. v FTC* (2d Cir 1954) 217 F2d 821, *cert den* (1955) 349 US 940, the exclusive-dealing contracts of a hearing-aid manufacturer that affected 22% of the more desirable retail distributors and accounted for 2 million dollars in annual sales were held illegal. The FTC and the court of appeals considered irrelevant Dictograph's evidence demonstrating that its competitors had increased and flourished during the life of the contracts and that new retail outlets were easily established. Again, however, the court alluded to similar exclusive-dealing practices on the part of other major manufacturers in the hearing-aid industry. Other cases that applied the "quantitative substantiality" test include *Pennsylvania Water & Power Co. v Consolidated Gas Electric Light & Power Co.* (4th Cir 1950) 184 F2d 552, *cert den* (1950) 340 US 906; *Red Rock Bottlers v Red Rock Cola* (ND Ga 1952) 1952 Trade Cases ¶67,375; *Automatic Canteen v FTC* (7th Cir 1952) 194 F2d 433, *rev'd on other grounds* (1953) 346 US 61; *Mytinger & Casselberry Inc.* (1960) FTC Dkt 6962, 57 FTC 717, *aff'd* (DC Cir 1962) 301 F2d 534.

2. [§3.5] Qualitative Substantiality

"Qualitative" or "comparative" substantiality refers to the approach pioneered by the FTC in *Maico Co., Inc.* (1953) FTC Dkt 5822, 50 FTC 485, and apparently adopted in the most recent Supreme Court decision dealing with an exclusive-dealing arrangement, *Tampa Electric Co. v Nashville Coal Co.* (1961) 365 US 320, as well as in dicta in *United States v Brown Shoe* (1962) 370 US 294. See also, *FTC v Motion Picture Advertising Service Company* (1953) 344 US 392, in which the Supreme Court first hinted that it might approve a test of qualitative substantiality.

In *Maico*, the FTC announced that it would not adhere to the *Standard Stations* test of "quantitative substantiality" in evaluating exclusive-dealing arrangements, but rather would evaluate evidence of the actual or probable economic effects of such arrangements in order to perform "the very services" that agency was created to provide. Presumably operating under this broader approach, the FTC found the probability of a substantial lessening of competition in several cases, although on appeal its decisions were tested and affirmed by the courts on the basis of *Standard Stations*. See *Dictograph Products v FTC* (1953) FTC Dkt 5655, 50 FTC 281, *aff'd* (2d Cir 1954) 217 F2d 821, *cert den* (1955) 349 US 940; *Anchor Serum Co. v FTC* (1954) FTC Dkt 5965, 50 FTC 681, *aff'd* (7th Cir 1954) 217 F2d 867; *Revlon Products Corp.* (1954) FTC Dkt 5685, 51 FTC 260; *Outboard Marine & Mfg. Co.* (1956) FTC Dkt 5882, 52 FTC 1553.

In an ironic twist, six years after *Maico*, the FTC retreated, in *Mytinger & Casselberry Inc.* (1960) FTC Dkt 6962, 57 FTC 717, *aff'd* (DC Cir 1962) 301 F2d 534, to the simpler *Standard Stations* quantitative test, only to see the Supreme Court a few months later, in *Tampa Electric Co. v Nashville Coal Co.* (1961) 365 US 320, adopt the qualitative approach by considering evidence of the probable effect on competition of an exclusive-dealing arrangement. Several coal producers had sought to invalidate under the antitrust laws a contract requiring them to supply a public utility with all its requirements of coal, about 128 million dollars worth, for a term of twenty years. The Court upheld the validity of the contract, establishing guidelines for determining whether an exclusive-dealing contract is unlawful (365 US at 329): The probable effect of the contract on the relevant area of effective competition must be weighed, "taking into account the relative strength of the parties, the proportionate volume of commerce involved in relation to the total volume of commerce in the relevant market area, and the probable immediate and future effects which pre-emption of that share of the market might have on effective competition. . . ."

Although this language on its face certainly signals a rejection of the rule of "quantitative substantiality" (at least as that rule evolved in subsequent application by the lower courts), the Court in *Tampa Electric* did not expressly overrule *Standard Stations*, but tried to harmonize *Standard Stations* with the new approach by pointing out that the exclusive contracts in that case—covering 16% of the retail outlets in the relevant market, some 6,000 stations, and a large dollar volume of gasoline sales—involved just the type of "potential clog" on competition that Section 3 of the Clayton Act (15 USC §14) was designed to remove. By contrast, after the Court had defined the relevant geographic market very broadly in *Tampa Electric*, the exclusive-dealing arrangement in question foreclosed less than one percent of the market.

3. The Uneasy Synthesis of Qualitative and Quantitative Substantiality

a. [§3.6] Which Rule Applies?

That the absolute arithmetical "quantitative substantiality" test was a casualty of *Tampa Electric* (see §3.5) is clear; yet, at least on the surface, *Standard Stations* (see §3.4) and *Tampa Electric* have been left by the Supreme Court to coexist as best they can. And later dicta in *United States v Brown Shoe* (1962) 370 US 294, to the effect that under Section 3 of the Clayton Act (15 USC §14) factors in exclusive-dealing cases other than the portion of the market foreclosed must be considered, are similarly inconclusive as to the extent to which the evaluation of economic factors is now necessary in judging the legality of an exclusive-dealing contract.

Subsequent to the dicta in the *Brown Shoe* case there have been no pronouncements by the Supreme Court on whether the quantitative or qualitative test governs exclusive-dealing cases. The Court has utilized the quantitative substantiality test in a number of merger cases under Section 7 of the Clayton Act (15 USC §18) and Section 1 of the Sherman Act (15 USC §1). See, *e.g.*, *United States v Philadelphia Nat'l. Bank* (1963) 374

US 321. Also, the Court has long employed the quantitative substantiality approach in judging the legality of tying arrangements under Section 3 of the Clayton Act. See, *e.g., United States v Loew's Inc.* (1962) 371 US 38. For discussion, see §§3.9–3.18. The FTC in *In Re Columbia Broadcasting System* (1967) FTC Dkt 8512, 3 Trade Reg Rep ¶18,037 at 20,456, *modified, Columbia Broadcasting System, Inc. v FTC* (7th Cir 1969) 414 F2d 974, *cert den* (1970) 397 US 907, applied the Supreme Court's standards on horizontal mergers to hold an exclusive-dealing arrangement illegal.

The recent lower-court decisions likewise provide relatively little guidance on what rule governs exclusive-dealing contracts. *Susser v Carvel Corporation* (2d Cir 1964) 332 F2d 505 concerned the legality of trademark-based franchise contracts between a manufacturer of soft ice cream and related supplies and its 340 franchised dealers. These contracts prohibited the franchisees from selling anything except Carvel products and required them to purchase from Carvel or Carvel-approved sources all the necessary ingredients including ice cream mix, cones, toppings, nuts, and flavors. In a designated market area, Carvel sold 37% of the soft ice cream and 4.5% of all ice cream. Carvel's sales of equipment and supplies approximated 5 million dollars annually.

The court noted that *Tampa Electric* deviated from the inflexible quantitative rule of *Standard Stations* and established criteria requiring scrutiny of the economic factors present in an exclusive-dealing arrangement. 332 F2d at 516. But the court focussed primarily on the extent to which a seller has a legitimate business interest in imposing an exclusive-dealing arrangement on his customers. The court held that Carvel's exclusive-dealing agreements were not illegal because the franchisor had a legitimate business need to control the quality of the products sold at outlets bearing its trademark and trade name.

Other decisions adopting the qualitative test for determining the legality of exclusive-dealing contracts include *Englander Motors, Inc. v Ford Motor Co.* (6th Cir 1959) 267 F2d 11; *Fargo Glass & Paint Co. v Globe America Corp.* (7th Cir 1953) 201 F2d 534, *cert den* (1953) 345 US 942; *Preformed Lime Products Co. v Fanner Mfg. Co.* (6th Cir 1964) 328 F2d 265, *cert den* (1964) 379 US 846; *2361 State Corporation v Sealy, Inc.* (ND Ill 1967) 263 F Supp 845; *Denison Mattress Factory v Spring-Air Co.* (5th Cir 1962) 308 F2d 403; *United States v Chas. Pfizer & Co.* (ED NY 1965) 246 F Supp 464; *Curley's Dairy, Inc. v Dairy Co-op Ass'n.* (D Ore 1962) 202 F Supp 481.

However, other decisions subsequent to *Tampa Electric* seem to hark back to the *Standard Stations* quantitative test, particularly when the degree of market foreclosure is great. *FTC v Brown Shoe Co.* (1965) 384

US 316 considered the validity of a program under which some 650 retail shoe outlets agreed, in return for special benefits, to purchase only one complete line of shoes—Brown Shoe's. They were permitted to handle other manufacturers' individual models, but not their complete lines. The FTC held that this program was an unfair method of competition under Section 5 of the Federal Trade Commission Act (15 USC §45). Brown was the second largest shoe manufacturer, and sales by Brown retailers constituted about 1% of the shoe sales in the United States. On an average, Brown retailers purchased 75% of their requirements from Brown and 25% from competitors.

The Eighth Circuit reversed on the grounds that the program was not an unfair method of competition (reasoning that it served the legitimate business purpose of promoting "loyalty" to Brown Shoes), that the program was not a tying arrangement, and that there was no proof that an exclusive-dealing arrangement existed. *Brown Shoe Co. v FTC* (8th Cir 1964) 339 F2d 45, 56. The tenor of the circuit court's opinion is that the Brown program was a reasonable business arrangement.

The Supreme Court reinstated the decision of the FTC, noting that the result of the program was to foreclose Brown Shoe's competitors from selling to a "substantial number of retail shoe dealers." 384 US at 319. This, the Court stated, was sufficient to justify the decision of the FTC. Although the case was decided under Section 5 of the Federal Trade Commission Act, the Court stated that the Brown Shoe program "obviously conflicts with the central policy of both §1 of the Sherman Act and §3 of the Clayton Act against contracts which take away freedom of purchasers to buy in an open market." 384 US at 321.

In *Atlantic Refining Co. v FTC* (1965) 381 US 357, the Court affirmed a decision of the FTC holding that Goodyear Tire & Rubber Company's payment of a commission to Atlantic for encouraging the sale of Goodyear's tires, batteries, and accessories by Atlantic's wholesale dealers and retail service stations violated Section 5 of the Federal Trade Commission Act. Atlantic argued that business reasons required it to maintain tires, batteries, and accessories at its dealers' stations and that its sales commission offset its cost of giving its dealers sales promotional assistance. (On business needs as a justification, see §3.8.) The Court noted the economic leverage that Atlantic had over its dealers, citing *Simpson v Union Oil Co.* (1964) 377 US 13, and stated (381 US at 371):

Just as the effect of this plan is similar to that of a tie-in, so is it unnecessary to embark upon a full scale economic analysis of competitive effect. We think it enough that the Commission found that a not insubstantial portion of commerce is affected.

To the same effect see *FTC v Texaco, Inc.* (1968) 393 US 223.

In *Mytinger & Casselberry, Inc. v FTC* (DC Cir 1962) 301 F2d 534, the court affirmed an FTC decision, holding that defendant's exclusive-dealing contracts entered into with 80,700 door-to-door independent salesmen of vitamin concentrates accounting for 61.5% of all house-to-house sales, 34.6% of all retail and wholesale sales, and 8.6% of total retail sales of the products, violated Section 3 of the Clayton Act. The court held, in agreement with the FTC, that foreclosure of 61.5%, 34.6%, *or* 8.6% of the market by exclusive-dealing contracts was sufficient proof that competition had been substantially lessened. In reaching its conclusion, the court relied entirely on the quantitative test of *Standard Stations* and interpreted *Tampa Electric* as applicable only in *de minimis* foreclosure situations.

The *Mytinger & Casselberry* decision, in particular, and the trend of the various cases following *Tampa Electric*, suggest that the two tests will continue to coexist. It may be fairly concluded that the simple—almost *per se*—quantitative test will be applied if exclusive-dealing contracts are imposed on numerous outlets by a seller with a dominant market position, or if the seller has significant economic leverage over the buyer, whereas the qualitative test of *Tampa Electric* will be applied if the seller is small and not dominant in its industry and the number of outlets affected are few.

b. [§3.7] Duration of Exclusive-Dealing Contracts

If the standards of the qualitative test are applied to an exclusive-dealing arrangement, the period of time during which distributors are foreclosed from dealing in competitive goods may be an important factor bearing on its legality. If the terms are reasonably short in duration, the arrangement is less susceptible to attack since other sellers will be permitted to compete for the business of the distributors relatively often. In *FTC v Motion Picture Advertising Service Co.* (1953) 344 US 392, the Supreme Court dealt with an FTC attack on five-year exclusive contracts between defendant producer-distributor and theater owners foreclosing about 75% of the theater outlets for advertising films. The Court affirmed a cease-and-desist order against defendant prohibiting exclusive contracts with motion picture exhibitors having terms of more than one year. In *ABC Consolidated Corp.* (1964) FTC Dkt 7652, Trade Reg Rep ¶17,109, the FTC settled by consent decree an action in which it charged that defendant and its affiliates entered into unreasonably long exclusive contracts for concessionary rights in motion picture theaters. The consent decree permitted five-year contracts with provisions for termination by theaters at the end of the third and fourth years. But see *Tampa Electric Co. v Nashville Coal Co.* (1961) 365 US 320, in which the Court upheld a twenty-year requirements contract.

c. [§3.8] Legitimate Business Need as Justification

Exclusive-dealing contracts, particularly requirements contracts, assure the buyer of a continuing source of supply and afford protection against price fluctuations, permitting meaningful long-term cost programming. In addition, such contracts reduce the buyer's "shopping" expenses. They may also substantially reduce the seller's marketing expenses, allow him to enjoy a reasonably predictable market for his product, and insulate him against a price decline.

Generally speaking, the courts have refused to consider economic justifications for exclusive-dealing arrangements. See, *e.g.*, *Standard Oil Co. of California v United States* (1949) 337 US 293; *Anchor Serum Co. v FTC* 50 FTC 681, *aff'd* (7th Cir 1954) 217 F2d 867; *Dictograph Products v FTC* (1953) FTC Dkt 5055, 50 FTC 281, *aff'd* (2d Cir 1954) 217 F2d 821, *cert den* (1955) 349 US 940; *Fashion Originators' Guild v FTC* (1941) 312 US 457. However, the Court in *Tampa Electric Co. v Nashville Coal Co.* (1961) 365 US 320 took note of the fact that the requirements contract was of economic advantage to both buyer and seller by assuring the buyer a supply while affording the seller a certain market and reduced selling expenses. And in both *Susser v Carvel* (2d Cir 1964) 332 F2d 505 and *Coca-Cola Bottling Co. v Coca-Cola Co.* (D Del 1920) 269 F 796, franchisors were permitted to continue exclusive-dealing arrangements that served to protect the goodwill of the franchisor's trademark or trade name. See also, *Standard Oil Co. of New York v FTC* (2d Cir 1921) 273 F 478; *FTC v Sinclair Refining Co.* (1923) 261 US 463; and *Denison Mattress Factory v Spring-Air Co.* (5th Cir 1962) 308 F2d 403.

III. Tying Arrangements

A. [§3.9] Introduction

A tying arrangement (or "tie-in") exists when the seller requires his buyer or lessee to take a product he does not want (the tied item) as a condition to obtaining a product he does want (the tying item). Section 3 of the Clayton Act (15 USC §14) prohibits such arrangements if they have a substantially anticompetitive effect and if the tying and tied items constitute "goods, wares, merchandise, machinery, supplies, or other commodities," whether patented or unpatented. Tying arrangements also may be illegal under Section 1 of the Sherman Act (15 USC §1), which condemns contracts, combinations, or conspiracies in restraint of trade, and Section 2 of the Sherman Act (15 USC §2), which condemns monopolies, attempts to monopolize, and combinations or conspiracies to monopolize. Tying arrangements that include services, which are not covered by Section 3 of the Clayton Act, may be illegal under the broader language of the Sherman Act and the Federal Trade Commission Act, both of which cover services as well as goods.

The following points may be helpful in deciding whether a tying arrangement is vulnerable under the antitrust laws:

- ☐ If an insubstantial amount of interstate commerce is affected, the tie-in will not fall within the prohibitions of the Sherman or Clayton Acts. See §3.10.
- ☐ There can be no tie-in if there is only one product. For discussion of whether the product should be classed as one or two, see §3.15.
- ☐ Assuming that there are two products and a not insubstantial amount of commerce is affected, a tie-in may be justified if the seller is a small company trying to break into a market or is only trying to protect goodwill. See §§3.17, 3.18.
- ☐ If none of the above applies, the tie-in is unreasonable "whenever a party has sufficient economic power with respect to the tying product to appreciably restrain free competition in the market for the tied product . . ." *Northern Pacific Ry. Co. v United States* (1958) 356 US 1, 11. See §§3.10–3.14.
- ☐ Sufficient economic power is presumed if the tying product is patented or copyrighted, but the presumption does not extend to trademarks. See §§3.12, 3.13.
- ☐ Absent a patent or copyright, sufficient economic power can be found from market dominance or from the desirability or uniqueness of the tying product. The existence of the tying arrangements is itself evidence of sufficient economic power. See §3.11.
- ☐ Full line forcing, a kind of tying arrangement, may be lawful if properly limited. See §3.16.
- ☐ On the use of refusals to sell to enforce tying arrangements, see §3.40.

B. [§3.10] Per Se Illegality

The Supreme Court has dealt harshly with the numerous tying arrangements it has reviewed, once describing the species as serving "hardly any purpose beyond the suppression of competition." *Standard Oil Co. of*

California v United States (1949) 337 US 293, 305. From a series of cases has evolved the rule that tying agreements are "unreasonable in and of themselves whenever a party has sufficient economic power with respect to the tying product to appreciably restrain free competition in the market for the tied product and a not insubstantial amount of interstate commerce is affected." *Northern Pacific Ry. Co. v United States* (1958) 356 US 1, 11. This near-*per se* rule of illegality is apparently the applicable test under both the Sherman and Clayton Acts, and the Supreme Court in *Times-Picayune Publishing Co. v United States* (1953) 345 US 594, 609 stated that Section 5 of the Federal Trade Commission Act (15 USC §45) "minimally . . . registers violations of the Clayton Act and the Sherman Act." Accordingly all three enactments should be considered in reviewing a tie-in.

The genesis of the rule of the pseudo-*per se* illegality of tying arrangements is found in *International Salt Co. v United States* (1947) 332 US 392. On appeal, International Salt argued that a summary judgment deprived it of a trial at which it could show the reasonableness of its agreements. The Supreme Court held that the lease of patented machinery on condition that the lessee use only the lessor's salt with the machinery was a violation of both Section 1 of the Sherman Act (15 USC §1) and Section 3 of the Clayton Act (15 USC §14). After noting that the volume of salt sold for use in the leased machines was about $500,000 annually, the Court concluded as follows (332 US at 396):

Not only is price-fixing unreasonable, *per se*, . . . but also it is unreasonable, *per se*, to foreclose competitors from any substantial market. . . . The volume of business affected by these contracts cannot be said to be insignificant or insubstantial and the tendency of the arrangement to accomplishment of monopoly seems obvious.

However, in *Times-Picayune Publishing Co. v United States, supra,* an action brought *only* under Section 1 of the Sherman Act, the Supreme Court held that the defendant newspaper company's practice of selling advertising space in its morning newspaper on the condition that the advertiser also purchase space in the defendant's evening paper did *not* amount to an illegal tying arrangement. The Court emphasized that "the essence of illegality in tying agreements is the wielding of monopolistic leverage . . ." (345 US at 611) and described the rules for assessing tying arrangements with some specificity (345 US 608-609):

When the seller enjoys a monopolistic position in the market for the "tying" product, *or* if a substantial volume of commerce in the "tied" product is restrained, a tying arrangement violates the narrower standards expressed in §3 of the Clayton Act because from either factor the requisite potential lessening of competition is inferred. And because for even a lawful monopolist it is "unreasonable, *per se*, to foreclose competitors from any substantial market," a tying arrangement is banned by §1 of the Sherman Act whenever *both* conditions are met.

The Court noted that since the government had "elected to proceed not under the Clayton but the Sherman Act," a violation could be found only if *both* elements were established. The Court, relying upon comparative marketing data which demonstrated that the morning paper's sale of advertising lineage constituted only about 40% of the total advertising market, found that the morning newspaper did not occupy a dominant position in the newspaper advertising market in New Orleans. The Court also noted that the case in question was "unlike other 'tying' cases where patents or copyrights supplied the requisite market control." 345 US at 611.

The *Times-Picayune* rule was substantially revised by the Supreme Court five years later in *Northern Pacific Ry. Co. v United States, supra,* in which the Court held unlawful *per se* preferential routing clauses in contracts under which the railroad sold or leased land only if purchasers and lessees of the land would ship on defendant's railroad all the commodities or products produced or manufactured on the land so long as defendant's rates and services were at least as favorable as those of competing carriers. Because the tied item was a service rather than a commodity, the government proceeded against Northern Pacific only under the Sherman Act. The Court first stated unequivocally that tying arrangements are among the practices which, because of "their pernicious effect on competition and lack of any redeeming virtue," are illegal *per se*. 356 US at 5. The Court defined its rule of *per se* illegality in one brief sentence: Tying agreements "are unreasonable in and of themselves whenever a party has sufficient economic power with respect to the tying product to appreciably restrain free competition in the market for the tied product and a 'not insubstantial' amount of interstate commerce is affected" 356 US at 6. The requirement that a tie-in affect a substantial amount of commerce in the tied product is not a significant loophole. In *United States v Loew's Inc.* (1962) 371 US 38, defendant Screen Gems had done only $60,800 in relevant business. And in *Fortner Enterprises, Inc. v United States Steel Corp.* (1969) 394 US 495, the Court held that annual purchases under the tying arrangement amounting to $190,000 could not be regarded as insubstantial. In *Siegel v Chicken Delight, Inc.* (ND Calif 1970) 311 F Supp 847, 850, the court (citing *Fortner Enterprises*) held that "this test is fulfilled if the dollar amount is not *de minimis* or not 'paltry.' "

Accordingly, "sufficient economic power" replaced "monopoly power" as the test for assessing power over the tying product, *i.e.*, the product sought after, thus reducing the power needed to find a violation. If a seller has "sufficient economic power" with respect to the market for one product, and if a not insignificant amount of commerce would be affected by tying to it the sale of another product, the tying device may not be used. However, "sufficient economic power" is by no means a concept whose application is self-evident, and in order to make it meaningful it is necessary to examine the various cases in which it has been found to exist.

C. Sufficiency of Economic Power

1. [§3.11] Uniqueness and Customer Appeal

The question of the sufficiency of economic power in *Northern Pacific Ry. Co. v United States* (1958) 356 US 1, was resolved by the finding that the railroad's extensive landholdings gave it the leverage to induce large numbers of purchasers and lessees of that land to agree to use its railroad to ship goods produced on the land. The Court emphasized that any power sufficient to impose an appreciable restraint upon competition in the tied product would meet the test, and even stated that the existence of the series of tying arrangements was itself compelling evidence of the defendant's economic power, since there was no other explanation offered for the existence of the agreements. 356 US at 7–8.

In *United States v Loew's Inc.* (1962) 371 US 38, the government challenged the practice of block-booking in the movie industry, a practice under which distributors refused to license or to sell exhibition rights to popular films unless the exhibitor also took less popular films. Reaffirming that "market dominance" ("some power to control price and exclude competition") was not the only or necessary test for determining whether a seller has "sufficient economic power," the Court stated that such power "may be inferred from the tying product's desirability to consumers or from uniqueness in its attributes." 371 US at 45. Indeed, the Court suggested in a footnote that "it should seldom be necessary in a tie-in sale case to embark upon a full-scale factual inquiry into the scope of the relevant market for the tying product and into the corollary problem of the seller's percentage share in that market." 371 US at 45 n. 4.

In *Fortner Enterprises, Inc. v United States Steel Corp.* (1969) 394 US 495, a subsidiary of U.S. Steel had offered developers 100% financing for subdivisions, but only on condition that they purchase U.S. Steel's prefabricated homes. In an action challenging the arrangement as an unlawful tie-in, the district court granted defendant's motion for summary judgment, in part on the premise that U.S. Steel does not have sufficient economic power with respect to the "tying product", financing. The Supreme Court reversed, holding that it is an issue of fact whether or not 100% financing is sufficiently unique or desirable to permit U.S. Steel to "raise prices, or impose other burdensome terms such as a tie-in, with respect to any appreciable number of buyers within the market." 394 US at 504.

2. [§3.12] Patents and Copyrights

The first half of the test of illegality stated in *Northern Pacific Ry. Co. v United States* (1958) 356 US 1—"sufficient economic power with respect to the tying product to appreciably restrain free competition in the market for the tied product"—is automatically presumed to have been met when the tying product is patented or copyrighted. See, *e.g.*, *International Salt v United States* (1947) 332 US 392; *United States v Loew's Inc.* (1962) 371 US 38; *United States v Paramount Pictures, Inc.* (1948) 334 US 131.

International Salt first held illegal the lease of patented machines for utilization of salt on the condition that the lessee purchase from the lessor all salt consumed in the leased machines. See discussion at §3.10. The *Paramount* and the *Loew's* cases extended the principle of *International Salt* to arrangements under which copyrighted feature films were sold to motion picture theaters and television stations only in groups. Both decisions held that the tying of poor-quality films to high-quality films constituted an illegal tie-in under Section 1 of the Sherman Act (15 USC §1). The basis of the decisions was that defendants by reason of their copyrights enjoyed a monopolistic position with respect to each group of tying films and thus had sufficient economic power to impose an appreciable restraint on free competition in the tied products. The Court's pronouncement in the *Loew's* case left little hope for arrangements involving patented or copyrighted tying items (371 US at 49–50):

There may be rare circumstances in which the doctrine we have enunciated under §1 of the Sherman Act prohibiting tying arrangements involving patented or copyrighted tying products is inapplicable. However, we find it difficult to conceive of such a case, and the present case is clearly not one.

The requirement that a not insubstantial amount of commerce in the tied product be affected is not a significant loophole. In the *Loew's* case defendant Screen Gems had done only $60,800 in relevant business.

3. [§3.13] Trademarks

The presumption that sufficient economic power is present whenever the tying product is patented or copyrighted has recently been extended to include trademarks. *Susser v Carvel Corp.* (SD NY 1962) 206 F Supp 636, *aff'd* (2d Cir 1962) 332 F2d 505 dealt with a franchise arrangement pursuant to which Carvel obligated its franchisees to purchase either from Carvel or from Carvel-approved sources various supplies including ice cream mix, cones, toppings, and nuts, which would become part of the end product, soft ice cream, sold to the public. The district court held that the arrangement was illegal *per se*, but the Second Circuit reversed on the ground, among others, that the plaintiffs had failed to establish that Carvel had sufficient market power to effect an appreciable restraint on competition. The court thereby implicitly recognized that the existence of a trademark on the tying item *alone* does not necessarily establish sufficient economic power.

However, in the recent case of *Siegel v Chicken Delight, Inc.* (ND Calif 1970) 311 F Supp 847, the court held that, *as a matter of law*, the defendant's "admittedly unique, registered trademark combined with its power to impose the tie-in demonstrates the existence of sufficient market power to bring the case within the Sherman Act." 311 F Supp at 849. If this decision is upheld on appeal, it will, of course, have a dramatic impact on the entire franchising industry.

4. [§3.14] Incipient Economic Power

Sufficient economic power was found to be lacking by the court of appeals in *Brown Shoe Company v FTC* (8th Cir 1964) 339 F2d 45, in a decision later reversed by the Supreme Court (*FTC v Brown Shoe Co.* (1965) 384 US 316). The appellate court held that a shoe manufacturer-distributor's practice of offering valuable services (such as architectural plans, signs, business forms, accounting assistance, etc.) to retailers who bought their shoes under the manufacturer's franchise program did not constitute an illegal tie-in, finding "no evidence that Brown's 'power or leverage' in the tying product was such as to force the purchase of the 'tied product' (shoes)." The court stressed the fact that Brown had no monopoly or other control or dominance over the tying product (franchise services) and expressly distinguished *Loew's* with the comment that, unlike a copyrighted movie, more than one source exists from which to obtain the services that Brown offered under the franchise agreement. The FTC insisted that the franchise agreements also constituted requirements contracts, but the court concluded that the FTC had failed to establish their illegality on that basis. See §3.6.

The opinion of the Supreme Court did not specifically discuss the appellate court's analysis of the legality of the tie-in aspects of the distributor arrangements; nor did it expressly decide whether the arrangement resulted in illegal requirements contracts. Rather, the unanimous Court, in a simple opinion, asserted that the FTC had the "broad power" under Section 5 of the Federal Trade Commission Act (15 USC §45) to declare "unfair" trade practices that "conflict with the basic policies of the Sherman and Clayton Acts even though such practices may not actually violate these laws." The Court rejected Brown Shoe's argument that the FTC had failed to show that the franchises might substantially lessen competition or tend to create a monopoly, noting that the FTC may arrest trade restraints in their incipiency without proof that the challenged practices constitute an outright violation of Section 3 of the Clayton Act (15 USC §14). The impact of this remark, which confirms a similar remark in the earlier *FTC v Motion Picture Advertising Service Co.* (1953) 344 US 392, 394–395, is that the FTC may declare illegal an *incipient* violation in its *incipiency*, since Section 3 of the Clayton Act is designed on its face to arrest prospectively anticompetitive conduct.

The Court did find that Brown Shoe's franchise agreements substantially limited the availability of retail outlets to its competitors. It may be that the foreclosure of 75% of the business done by 659 shoe retailers throughout the country would have been sufficient to establish a violation of Section 3 of the Clayton Act under the standards ordinarily applicable to requirements contracts. (See §3.4.) Or, had the Court approached the case differently, it may have regarded the arrangement as falling within the broad proscriptions of Section 2 of the Sherman Act (15 USC §2). In any event, the Court made it clear that the practices in question could be declared illegal under Section 5 of the Federal Trade Commission Act even though they did not necessarily rise to the level of a violation of the other antitrust laws.

It may be safely concluded that very little is required to establish that a seller who employs a tying arrangement has "sufficient economic power" with respect to the tying product to restrain a "substantial" amount of commerce in the market for the tied product. Indeed, in view of the recent cases, one may reasonably doubt that an effective tying arrangement could exist in which "sufficient economic power" is lacking, even absent a patent or copyright. See *e.g., Fortner Enterprises, Inc. v United States Steel Corp.* (1969) 394 US 495; *SCM Corp. v Advance Business Systems & Supply Co.* (4th Cir 1969) 415 F2d 55, *cert den* (1970) 397 US 920.

D. [§3.15] One Product or Two

There can be no tying arrangement, of course, unless the tying and tied items are two separate and distinct units. However, it is not always simple to determine whether there is one product or two; although the courts have articulated some of the factors to be considered in making that determination, the only safe conclusion is that each case will be decided on an ad hoc basis.

In *Times-Picayune Publishing Co. v United States* (1953) 345 US 594, the defendant had required that advertisements be placed in its evening newspaper as a condition of accepting advertising in its more popular morning paper. The Supreme Court reversed the district court's decision that this practice constituted an unlawful tying arrangement, relying in part on the ground that the morning and evening papers, although separate and distinct in the minds of the reading public, were but a single medium to advertisers (345 US at 614):

The common core of the adjudicated unlawful tying arrangements is the forced purchase of a second distinct commodity with the desired purchase of a dominant "tying" product, resulting in economic harm to competition in the "tied" market. Here, however, two newspapers under single ownership at the same place, time, and terms sell indistinguishable products to advertisers; no dominant "tying" product exists (in fact, since space in neither the [morning paper] nor the [evening paper] can be bought alone, one may be viewed as "tying" as the other); no leverage in one market excludes sellers in the second, because for present purposes the products are identical and the market the same. . . . In short, neither the rationale nor the doctrines evolved by the "tying" cases can dispose of the Publishing Company's arrangements challenged here.

Fortner Enterprises, Inc. v United States Steel Corp. (1969) 394 US 495 was initiated by a real estate developer seeking treble damages pursuant to Sections 1 and 2 of the Sherman Act (15 USC §§1-2) on the ground that defendants, a steel company and its wholly owned subsidiary, used an unlawful tie-in; the subsidiary extended credit for purchasing land on condition that the steel company's prefabricated homes be purchased for use on the land. The Court, reversing a grant of summary judgment for defendants, rejected defendants' argument that "every sale on credit in effect involves a tie" (394 US at 506-507):

In the usual sale on credit the seller, a single individual or corporation, simply makes an agreement determining when and how much he will be paid for his product. In such a sale the credit may constitute such an inseparable part of the purchase price for the item that the entire transaction could be considered to involve only a single product. . . . Sales such as that are a far cry from the arrangement involved here, where the credit is provided by one corporation on condition that a product be purchased from a separate corporation, and where the borrower contracts to obtain a large sum of money over and above that needed to pay the seller for the physical products purchased. Whatever the standards for determining exactly when a transaction involves only a "single product," we cannot see how an arrangement such as that present in this case could ever be said to involve only a single product.

At least one court seems to have held that when there are sound economic reasons for a challenged tying arrangement, the product may be treated as one rather than several. In *United States v Jerrold Electronics Corp.* (ED Pa 1960) 187 F Supp 545, *aff'd per curiam* (1961) 365 US 567, the district court held that it was unlawful at that time for the defendant to market the several components of its community antenna system as a single product and to tie a servicing contract to the sale of the system. The district court indicated that when the complex antenna system was first developed, defendant was justified in tying the components of the system together and tying a service contract to the system, because "a wave of system failures at the start would have greatly retarded, if not destroyed, this new industry. . . ." 187 F Supp at 557. It was only after the new industry "took root and grew" that the tying aspects of defendant's contracts became unlawful. Because the service contract would not have been very effective except in conjunction with a fully integrated system, the court concluded "that Jerrold's policy of full system sales was a necessary adjunct to its policy of compulsory service and was reasonably regarded as a [single] product as long as the conditions which dictated the use of the service contract continued to exist." 187 F Supp at 560.

Despite its holding, the district court listed a series of factors that, it said, tended to establish that the components of the antenna system were separate and distinct products: others in the industry did not insist on selling the parts as a single unit; the number of components in each system varied, so that the overall "products" were not uniform; and customers were charged separately for each of the component parts.

It would probably have been analytically sounder if the court had held that tying was justified on economic grounds rather than holding that because the alleged tying arrangement is economically justified the several products may be treated as one. But the result is the same under either approach, and the court was undoubtedly inhibited by the *per se* rule that the Supreme Court has put forth.

The fact that two or more units are physically separate and are ordinarily priced separately seems to be important in determining whether they constitute one product or more than one. In *Susser v Carvel Corp.* (2d Cir

1964) 332 F2d 505, the defendant had insisted that its franchised soft ice cream retailers purchase all their supplies from defendant or sources approved by defendant. The defendant argued that there was only one product since all the supplies and ingredients were ultimately formed into the single item sold to the consumer. The court responded to this contention by pointing out that the defendant itself purchased the various items separately. The court also made it clear that the determination whether there is one product or more than one is to be made at the time of the *defendant's* sale rather than at some subsequent time (332 F2d at 514):

[The defendant] sells supplies as distinct items in large quantities—for example, ten gallons of mix, ten gallons of chocolate syrup, and so forth. [Defendant] itself purchases these supplies as distinct items from a wide variety of suppliers who in turn make individual deliveries to the franchise outlets. By their very nature it seems clear that there is no reason to treat these separate products as one unified product although to the ultimate consumer of an ice cream cone or a sundae they would seem to be one.

The court held, however, that the tying arrangement was necessary to protect the seller's goodwill, and was therefore lawful. See §3.18.

E. [§3.16] Full-line Forcing

"Full-line forcing" refers to a requirement by a supplier or manufacturer that its dealers handle the supplier's full line of products. Two cases have held that full-line forcing does not constitute a violation of the antitrust laws if the supplier has not coerced its distributor to overstock or to sell only the supplier's line of products. *Miller Motors, Inc. v Ford Motor Co.* (4th Cir 1958) 252 F2d 441, 449-50; *United States v J. I. Case Co.* (D Minn 1951) 101 F Supp 856, 867-68.

Osborn v Sinclair Refining Company (4th Cir 1960) 286 F2d 832, *cert den* (1962) 366 US 963 concerned Sinclair's cancellation of a local gas station operator's lease because of the lessee's failure to purchase enough Goodyear tires, batteries, and accessories (TBA). Sinclair had entered into an agreement with Goodyear under which Sinclair received commissions on Goodyear's TBA sales to Sinclair dealers. The court found that the purchase of substantial quantities of Goodyear TBA was tied to the lease and the sale of Sinclair gasoline. The court considered it decisive that Sinclair supplied more than 10% of the gasoline sold in Maryland and that "a not unsubstantial amount of commerce" was therefore affected.

The court flatly rejected the argument, based on the *Miller* and *J.I. Case*, that the tie-in was not *per se* unreasonable since the buyer was not obligated to obtain all his requirements of the tied product from the seller. But it is significant that Sinclair had not merely required its dealers to purchase substantial amounts of its full line of products, but had also forced its dealers to handle the products of another supplier. The court made the pointed observation that the "perniciousness of the imposed tie-in" was "aggravated by the fact that the defendant is not even in the business of selling the tied products. . . ." The *Osborn* decision also differs markedly from the decision in *J.I. Case* in the court's finding that the tying arrangement was "solely for the defendant's economic benefit and not justified by the nature of the products." 286 F2d at 840. See also, *Osborn v Sinclair Refining Co.* (4th Cir 1963) 324 F2d 566; *Atlantic Refining Co. v FTC* (1965) 381 US 357; *FTC v Texaco Inc.* (1968) 393 US 223.

It may be concluded that it is not unlawful for a manufacturer to require its dealers to carry the full line of the manufacturer's products, so long as the dealers are not required to purchase more than a reasonable inventory of such products and are not precluded from dealing also in products made by the manufacturer's competitors.

F. Justifications

1. [§3.17] Small Newcomer in the Market

There are apparently only two justifications for tying arrangements that will stand against the *per se* rule. The first is available to the small newcomer. The Supreme Court commented in *Brown Shoe Co. v United States* (1962) 370 US 294, 330, that "unless the tying device is employed by a small company in an attempt to break into a market, cf. Harley-Davidson Motor Co., 50 F.T.C. 1047, 1066, the use of a tying device can rarely be harmonized with the strictures of the antitrust laws. . . ."

In *United States v Jerrold Electronics* (ED Pa 1960) 187 F Supp 545, *aff'd* (1961) 356 US 567, the court concluded that Jerrold's practice of selling its community antenna equipment only in conjunction with a service contract did not violate the Sherman Act when Jerrold was launching a new business with a highly uncertain future. However, Jerrold failed to convince the court that this practice remained reasonable throughout the entire period of its use, and the court held that a violation of Section 1 (15 USC §1) had occurred in the continuation of the practice. The court reached the same decision on Jerrold's policy of selling only full antenna systems, and not individual component parts.

2. [§3.18] Necessary Protection of Product Goodwill

Another justification of an otherwise illegal tying arrangement is predicated on the necessity that the tying and tied products be sold and used together, lest the buyer use a substandard product that might affect or detract from the performance of the tying product. In *IBM v United States* (1936) 298 US 131, the Supreme Court expressly considered and rejected IBM's goodwill defense. IBM contended that it was justified in leasing its machines on the condition that the lessees use only IBM tabulating cards because the use of poor quality cards would foul the machines. The Court found that other manufacturers made cards of adequate quality, and that IBM could protect its goodwill by stating in its leases the specifications to which cards used in the machine must conform.

In *Pick Mfg. Co. v General Motors Corp.* (1936) 299 US 3, the Supreme Court affirmed *per curiam* a judgment that an arrangement tying sales of authorized parts to the granting of a new-car dealer franchise did not violate the antitrust laws. One of the grounds for the decision of the Seventh Circuit was that the tying arrangement was necessary to protect the seller's goodwill. *Pick Mfg. Co. v General Motors Corp.* (7th Cir 1935) 80 F2d 641.

In *United States v Jerrold Electronics Corp.* (ED Pa 1960) 187 F Supp 545, *aff'd per curiam* (1961) 365 US 567, a new firm with a new product was held to have been initially justified in employing a tie-in contract on the ground that it was necessary to protect the goodwill of the new company and its fledgling product. The district court emphasized the sensitivity and complexity of the systems and the need for expert servicing and compatible component parts. See also, *General Talking Pictures Corp. v American Tel. & Tel. Co.* (D Del 1937) 18 F Supp 650.

Dehydrating Process Co. v A. O. Smith Corp. (1st Cir 1961) 292 F2d 653, *cert den* (1961) 368 US 931, a private treble-damage suit, is significant because it held that the protection of goodwill justified the use of a tying arrangement by an established seller in an established industry. The defendant had tied the sale of its patented unloading machine to its patented silo, but only after it had received many complaints about the malfunctioning of the unloader when used with silos manufactured by other companies.

Similarly, in *Susser v Carvel Corp.* (2d Cir 1964) 332 F2d 505, the court held that a franchisor, to protect the quality of its end product and the validity of its trademark, was justified in requiring its franchised trademark licensees to purchase from the franchisor all the ingredients of the trademarked product, soft ice cream. The court acknowledged that (332 F2d at 520):

[I]nstances of impossibility of control through specification may indeed be rare in cases involving proper functioning of mechanical elements of a machine, [citing, *inter alia, International Business Machines Corp. and International Salt Co., supra*].

The Court distinguished the case at hand:

[S]uch cases are scarcely relevant to the problem of controlling something so insusceptible of precise verbalization as the desired texture and taste of an ice cream cone or sundae. . . .

In *Siegel v Chicken Delight, Inc.* (ND Calif 1970) 311 F Supp 847, the district court held as a matter of law that the franchisor's interest in protecting its trademark and goodwill could not justify its insistence that franchisees purchase from it all their paper food and drink containers. 311 F Supp at 851. The court noted that the franchisor's concern for quality and goodwill could easily be satisfied by permitting the franchisees to purchase paper products from others under specifications provided by the franchisor. The court submitted to the jury the question whether the tie-in of chicken fryers and the defendant's "secret" dip and spice mix was necessary to protect the franchisor's goodwill. On the basis of contradictory evidence, the jury found that these tie-ins were also unjustified. 311 F Supp at 853.

There are several ways to protect product integrity and goodwill without the antitrust risk of a tying arrangement. For example, a supplier may require in the contract for the sale or lease of a product that only products that conform to prescribed specifications may be used with it. Or the contract may contain a performance guarantee effective only if certain conditions are met, for example the use of the seller's complementary products. A third possibility is a cost-justified price differential (see §§5.44–5.48) in service or repair contracts permitting the seller to charge more for service if another manufacturer's equipment is used with the seller's product. See generally, Kaysen & Turner, *Antitrust Policy* 158–159 (1959).

One must conclude from the foregoing that protection of goodwill is a defense to an unlawful tying arrangement only if the seller is not a dominant power in the market; if the seller and buyer are not of such disparate economic size that there is an inference of coercion; if there is clear business reason for the restriction (*e.g.*, complaints received or the difficulty of specifying standards or other demonstrable facts proving clear and present danger to goodwill); and if alternative restrictions are not reasonably available or are inadequate to protect the seller's goodwill. See *IBM v United States, supra*.

IV. Territorial and Customer Restrictions

A. [§3.19] Introduction

In an effort to ensure that its products will be energetically promoted, a manufacturer sometimes assigns specific geographic areas to its distributors. Often the distributor is prohibited from selling outside his own territory and is assured that the manufacturer will sell to no other distributors within the territory. Related to this system of territorial restrictions is the practice of prohibiting distributors from selling to certain classes of customers, either because the manufacturer wants to sell to them directly or wants to sell to them through other distributors. The antitrust problems inherent in each of these practices are similar.

The following points may be helpful in analyzing territorial or customer restrictions:

☐ Restrictions may be accomplished with true agency or consignment arrangements in some limited and qualified circumstances. See §§3.21–3.22.

☐ If the arrangement only requires a distributor to devote his best efforts to a prescribed area (an "area-of-primary-responsibility" clause) even though it prohibits the distributor from setting up sales offices or agencies outside the area, it is probably valid. See §3.23.

☐ If the arrangement limits the *supplier's* sales to a single distributor in a territory, with or without an area-of-primary-responsibility clause, it is probably valid unless it was coerced by the buyer. See §3.24.

☐ Vertically imposed territorial or customer restrictions may be valid under limited circumstances if the manufacturer is either a newcomer in the market or is a "failing company." See §3.21 for discussion and qualifications.

☐ Vertically imposed territorial or customer restrictions by a company or in a form not described above are *per se* illegal. See §3.21.

☐ Customer or territorial restrictions agreed upon among competitors are *per se* illegal. See §3.20.

☐ On the use of refusal to deal to enforce territorial or customer restrictions, see §§3.23, 3.40.

B. [§3.20] Horizontal Territorial or Customer Allocation Illegal Per Se

It is important at the outset to draw a distinction between vertical territorial and customer restrictions—those imposed upon distributors by the manufacturer—and horizontal restrictions—those agreed to among the distributors themselves. Agreements by a group of distributors to allocate customers or territories constitute *per se* violations of Section 1 of the Sherman Act (15 USC §1) because they are "naked restraints of trade with no purpose except stifling of competition." *White Motor Co. v United States* (1963) 372 US 253, 263. In *Burke v Ford* (1967) 389 US 320, 321, the Court reversed a Tenth Circuit decision holding that division of local markets by wholesale liquor companies did not injure competition, stating "Horizontal territorial divisions almost invariably reduce competition among the participants." See also *Timken Roller Bearing Company v United States* (1951) 341 US 593. Similarly, if a group of distributors jointly cause a manufacturer to allocate territories or customers among them, the arrangement is treated as horizontal. *United States v Sealy* (1967) 388 US 350.

Accordingly, it is important to determine the origin and purpose behind a manufacturer's proposed distribution program. If in fact the contemplated territorial or customer restrictions are imposed unilaterally by the manufacturer upon each distributor, and are not extracted from it as a result of an agreement among its distributors, there is no need for concern that the plan constitutes a horizontal allocation of customers and markets.

C. [§3.21] Vertical Territorial or Customer Consignment

The Supreme Court in *United States v Arnold, Schwinn & Co.* (1967) 388 US 365, held that it is illegal *per se* for a manufacturer (and presumably any other seller) to impose territorial or customer restrictions on its distributors or retailers if the purchasers buy the product it seeks to restrict, but that such restrictions on distributors who are *bona fide* consignees or agents are not illegal *per se* and must be assessed under the so-called rule of reason. For discussion of the rule of reason, see §2.25.

In 1952, after obtaining a clearance from the FTC, Schwinn franchised some 5,500 retailers to sell Schwinn bicycles, restricting each to a specified location or locations, and requiring each to purchase from the Schwinn distributor authorized to serve his particular area. Furthermore, the retailers were authorized to sell only to consumers and not to other unfranchised retailers.

Schwinn also sold its bicycles outright or transferred its bicycles to 22 distributors under a consignment or agency arrangement for sale to Schwinn retailers. The distributors, purchasers and agents alike, were permitted to sell only to the franchised Schwinn retailers within their territory.

The government charged that Schwinn's distribution system constituted a conspiracy to restrain trade in violation of Section 1 of the Sherman Act

(15 USC §1), in that it utilized resale price fixing, allocation of territories, and unlawful boycott of retailers who were not franchised by Schwinn, all of which it claimed were unlawful *per se.*

The district court rejected the government's charge of price fixing but held that the territorial limitations on distributors who actually purchased the bicycles were illegal *per se.* However the court approved the basic franchising system employed by Schwinn, finding that it was "the only solution remaining in order to enable [it] to remain in the business of manufacturing a quality product, . . . and instead of restraining trade . . . has actually made for genuine competition in the bicycle manufacturing industry." (*United States v Arnold, Schwinn & Co.* (ND Ill 1965) 237 F Supp 323, 337–338.) No appeal was taken by the government on the issue of price fixing nor by the defendants on the issue of territorial restrictions.

The government took a direct appeal pursuant to the Expediting Act, 15 USC §29, challenging the validity of the Schwinn franchising system, which imposed vertical restrictions upon both distributors and retailers. The government contended that the territorial restrictions placed on distributors who sold as agents for Schwinn should be held unlawful and that the requirement that distributors selling as agents sell only to franchised retailers be held unlawful. The government did not urge, as it had at the trial level, that these practices were unlawful *per se,* but conceded that they should be assessed under the rule of reason.

The Supreme Court held (388 US at 379) that customer and territorial restrictions placed on distributors who actually purchased the bicycles were illegal *per se* under the ancient rule against "restraints on alienation." Cf. *Dr. Miles Medical Co. v Park & Sons Co.* (1911) 220 US 373; *United States v Bausch & Lomb Optical Co.* (1944) 321 US 707.

The meaning the Court gives to the concept of *per se* illegality in the *Schwinn* opinion is something different from the meaning usually given: The majority opinion suggests that such vertical restrictions upon customers who purchase outright may not be illegal if the manufacturer is a "newcomer" or a "failing company." In short, the Court suggested that there may be narrow exceptions to the *per se* concept. For discussion of the "newcomer" rationale in tying arrangements, see §3.17; for further discussion of the failing company doctrine, see §4.38.

The territorial and customer restrictions on the distributors acting as the manufacturer's agents were treated differently: "[W]here the manufacturer retains title, dominion and risk with respect to the product and the position and function of the dealer in question are, in fact, indistinguishable from those of an agent or a salesman of the manufacturer" (388 US at 380). The Court held that these restrictions must be assessed under the rule of reason. In holding that Schwinn's restrictions on agent-distributors were valid, the Court indicated that four factors were critical to its decision: (1) the availability of competitive and substantially similar bicycles throughout the marketplace; (2) the freedom of the Schwinn distributors and retailers to handle other brands of bicycles in addition to the Schwinn line; (3) the absence of any price-fixing arrangements; and (4) the finding of the district court that competition from such mass merchandising concerns as Sears and Montgomery Ward made the Schwinn restrictions necessary.

The Court also emphasized the district court's finding that the Schwinn restrictions were not only justified by competition, but went no further than required to meet that competition.

Subsequent to *Schwinn*, the Third Circuit in *Tripoli Co. v Wella Corp.* (3d Cir 1970) 425 F2d 932, *cert den* (1970) 400 US 831 applied a "rule of reason" in upholding a manufacturer's restraints on the class of customers to whom one of its distributors could sell, despite the fact that the distributor acquired title to the products. The court sidestepped *Schwinn's per se* language by emphasizing that the restraint in question had a "lawful main purpose"—the protection of the general public from potentially dangerous products. However, in another case dealing with restrictions on resale, *United States v Glaxo Group Ltd.* (D DC 1969) 302 F Supp 1, the court declared the restrictions *per se* illegal, citing *Schwinn* as foreclosing resort to a rule of reason at least in the case of restraints on customers and territories.

Prior to *Schwinn*, in *White Motor Company v United States* (1963) 372 US 253, the Supreme Court had expressly considered but declined to rule on the question whether vertical territorial confinement and customer allocation clauses are unlawful. White, a manufacturer and seller of trucks, imposed territorial and customer restrictions on its distributors and dealers. If a distributor or dealer sold outside his designated area he was required to return all or part of his profit to the distributor or dealer in whose territory the sale was made. The district court granted the government's motion for summary judgment, holding that such restrictions were illegal *per se*.

The Supreme Court reversed, noting that although horizontal agreements among competitors to divide territories constitute a *per se* violation of Section 1 of the Sherman Act (15 USC §1), vertical agreements between a manufacturer and its distributors and dealers required an evaluation at a trial of the impact of the restrictions on competition.

Justice Brennan, in a concurring opinion, suggested that when the trial court inquired into the reasonableness of territorial restrictions, he would be interested in learning whether: (1) Such clauses foster vigorous inter-brand competition that might otherwise be absent; (2) a manufacturer starting out in business or marketing a new product might find it essential to guarantee distributors territorial insulation in order to acquire and attain outlets; and (3) a manufacturer might have to employ such clauses to ensure full advertisement and promotion of his product in the various sales territories. If such justifications were present, Justice Brennan indicated, the district court should then inquire whether or not the territorial restrictions were more onerous and anticompetitive than necessary.

After the *White Motor* decision, but before the *Schwinn* opinion, the Sixth Circuit court of appeals, relying upon *White Motor*, reversed a decision of the FTC holding that a vinyl floor-covering manufacturer violated Section 5 of the Federal Trade Commission Act (15 USC §45) by entering into territorial and customer confinement agreements with its distributors. *Sandura Company v FTC* (6th Cir 1964) 339 F2d 847. The system the FTC had condemned required Sandura's distributors to resell Sandura floor covering only within their assigned territories, and only to retail dealers. Since Sandura actually sold its floor coverings to its distributors, who then resold the product, under *Schwinn* the Sandura arrangements presumably would now be illegal *per se*. Although the Sixth Circuit ignored the fact that Sandura actually sold its product to the distributors upon whom it imposed the restrictions, the reasoning of the court in validating the Sandura agreements may provide guidelines for situations where agency or consignment arrangements are involved.

The court examined the impact of the restrictions on competition as developed before the FTC hearing examiner. It was against the background of near bankruptcy and the loss of its distributors that Sandura, a relatively small concern, had adopted the closed territorial system in an effort to attract distributors willing to invest in the advertising and promotional campaigns necessary for the revival of Sandura's vinyl floor-covering product. Sandura supported its claim that the closed distributor system was essential to its survival with an "impressive array of testimony," including virtually unanimous testimony from its distributors that such a program was essential to their decision to handle the product and to the competitive position of the product. 339 F2d at 851. Further, the court found that Sandura's need for closed territories continued in light of Sandura's evidence that it was facing renewed competitive difficulties at the time of the FTC hearing as a result of the development of similar vinyl floor products by larger manufacturers, and consequently that its percentage of sales was declining.

If agency or consignment arrangements are utilized, *Snap-On Tools Corporation v FTC* (7th Cir 1963) 321 F2d 825, also decided shortly after the *White Motor* case and before the *Schwinn* case, may further assist in formulating guidelines when read in conjunction with *Sandura.* The FTC found that Snap-On's territorial restrictions, which required dealers who *purchased* the manufacturer's products to resell only within specifically described territories, violated Section 5 of the Federal Trade Commission Act. 321 F2d at 830. The Seventh Circuit concluded that Snap-On's vertical territorial restrictions were prompted by justifiable business reasons and therefore were not significantly anticompetitive, stressing the fact that Snap-On was not in a monopolistic position vis-a-vis its competitors. In fact, the evidence demonstrated that there were over 80 competing firms in the hand-tool industry, resulting in a competitive situation the court characterized as "bitter and bloody."

D. Permissible Territorial and Customer Restrictions

1. [§3.22] Agency Arrangements

The cases discussed in §3.21 indicate that a manufacturer may impose territorial and customer restrictions on its distributors only under bona fide consignment or agency arrangements, and then only when the manufacturer is a small concern facing severe competition, either from large concerns or a mass of competitors. The distributor must be free to handle competitive brands, and there must be neither horizontal price-fixing arrangements among the distributors nor vertical resale price maintenance by the manufacturer.

2. [§3.23] Areas of Primary Responsibility

A manufacturer would be well advised to avoid the grave risk that accompanies the imposition of territorial confinement clauses even under consignment arrangements and to consider instead an "area of primary responsibility" provision. This will most likely accomplish everything the manufacturer wants to accomplish. Such a provision does not confine a distributor to sales in a specified area but does require him to devote his best efforts to the promotion and sale of the product in a prescribed territory. The distributor might also be prohibited from setting up any sales offices or agencies outside his assigned area. The arrangement may be subject to termination if the distributor does not "adequately" represent the manufacturer in his area of primary responsibility. See, *e.g., Frank Chevrolet Co. v General Motors Corp.* (6th Cir 1969) 419 F2d 1054. Provided there is no conduct by the manufacturer or distributor evidencing an agreement between them (or between the manufacturer and other distributors) to restrict the distributor's sales to his area of responsibility, the courts have upheld the manufacturer's right to refuse to deal with a distributor who, because he is pursuing customers outside his area, is not devoting his best efforts or "adequately" representing the manufacturer in his assigned area.

Both the FTC and the courts have suggested an "area of primary responsibility" clause as a reasonable alternative to a territorial confinement clause. *Boro Hall Corp. v General Motors Corp.* (2d Cir 1942) 124 F2d 822, *cert den* (1943) 317 US 695; *White Motor Company v United States* (1963) 372 US 253, 271 (Brennan, J., concurring); *United States v Bostitch, Inc.* (D RI 1958) 1958 Trade Cases ¶69,207; *Snap-On Tools Corp.* (1961) FTC Dkt 7116, 59 FTC 1035, 1963 Trade Cases ¶70,861, *rev'd* (7th Cir 1963) 321 F2d 825. Many consent decrees permit area of primary responsibility clauses as a substitute for territorial confinement provisions. *United States v American Type Founders Co.* (D NJ 1958) 1958 Trade Cases ¶69,065; *United States v Rudolph Wurlitzer Co.* (WD NY 1958) 1958 Trade Cases ¶69,011; *United States v J. P. Seeburg Corp.* (ND Ill 1957) 1957 Trade Cases ¶68,613; *United States v Philco Corp.* (ED Pa 1956) 1956 Trade Cases ¶68,409.

The recent *Schwinn* decision (*United States v Arnold, Schwinn & Co.* (1967) 388 US 365) might seem to cast some doubt on the propriety of areas of primary responsibility, in view of the mandate directing entry of a decree against *any limitation* effective after title passes. However, Justice Fortas, for the majority, said nothing to repudiate the district court's statement that a manufacturer "has a right to assign primary responsibility to a distributor in an area or territory," and to terminate for cause. Further, the district court on remand specified that Schwinn could continue to designate territories of prime responsibility for its distributors and could terminate any distributor who failed adequately to represent Schwinn and promote Schwinn sales in its area of primary responsibility. 1968 Trade Cases ¶72,480 (ND Ill 1968).

3. [§3.24] Exclusive Distributorships

Another alternative to strict territorial confinement is the simple exclusive distributorship under which the manufacturer or seller promises not to appoint any other distributors or to sell to any other buyers in the exclusive distributor's specified area. Such a restriction logically complements an area of primary responsibility agreement.

Since an exclusive distributorship as defined above does not involve an agreement not to deal in the goods of a competitor, by itself it is outside the reach of Section 3 of the Clayton Act (15 USC §14). However, such arrangements have been attacked under the Sherman Act. In *United States v Bausch & Lomb Optical Co.* (SD NY 1942) 45 F Supp 387, 398–399, a manufacturer's commitment to its distributor not to compete and not to sell to any other distributors was held not to violate the Sherman Act. The arrangement in question was held reasonable, since its main purpose was to give a source of supply to the distributor, who was spending "large sums to develop his good will and enlarge the public patronage of a relatively new article of commerce." 45 F Supp at 398. This portion of the ruling of the district court was affirmed by the Supreme Court in *United States v Bausch & Lomb Optical Co.* (1943) 321 US 707.

In *United States v Arnold, Schwinn & Co.* (1967) 388 US 365, 376, the Supreme Court noted in dictum:

[A] manufacturer of a product other and equivalent brands of which are readily available in the market may select his customers, and for this purpose he may "franchise" certain dealers to whom, alone, he will sell his goods. Cf. *United States v. Colgate & Co.*, 250 U.S. 300 (1919). If the restraint stops at that point—if nothing more is involved than vertical "confinement" of the manufacturer's own sales of the merchandise to selected dealers, and if competitive products are readily available to others, the restriction, on these facts alone, would not violate the Sherman Act.

See, *e.g., Top-All Varieties, Inc. v Hallmark Cards, Inc.* (SD NY 1969) 301 F Supp 703. If a concern is in operation, the establishment of an exclusive distributorship will require termination of other distributors in the area. *Packard Motor Car Co. v Webster Motor Car Co.* (DC Cir 1957) 243 F2d 418, *cert den* (1957) 355 US 822 dealt with Packard's decision to cancel all but its largest dealer in Baltimore. The Court approved the exclusive dealership, notwithstanding it was established at the behest of the dealer who received the exclusive right of sale. See also *Schwing Motor Car Co. v Hudson Sales Corp.* (D Md 1956) 138 F Supp 899, *aff'd per curiam* (4th Cir 1956) 239 F2d 176, *cert den* (1957) 355 US 823.

It should be noted that *Packard* (described by Justice Brennan as of "necessarily limited scope" in *White Motor Company v United States* (1963) 372 US 253) and *Schwing* were both cases in which manufacturers were minor competitors to whom the exclusive-dealing arrangements appeared reasonably necessary because they were experiencing sharp sales setbacks.

By contrast, if exclusive distributorships are demanded and obtained by a major buyer with substantial bargaining power to augment his market position and cripple his competitors, the arrangement may well violate the antitrust laws. For example, it was held illegal for the manufacturers of the most popular solid chocolate bars to sell to only the three largest theater vending-machine companies. *Hershey Chocolate Corp. v FTC* (3d Cir 1941) 212 F2d 968. Similarly, the accumulation of exclusive distributorships by a single wholesaler from all or most sellers of a product line has been condemned as monopolization. *United States v Blitz* (SD NY 1959) 179 F Supp 80, *rev'd in part on other grounds* (2d Cir 1960) 282 F2d 465.

To summarize, if exclusive distributorships are utilized, and more particularly if existing distributors must be discontinued, it is helpful if (1) the manufacturer is smaller than its competitors, (2) there are many competitors, and (3) there is proof of economic necessity.

Frequently, the distributor may be satisfied with a unilateral statement by the manufacturer that it is its policy not to appoint a second distributor in any area in which a distributor is already "primarily responsible," particularly if that policy has always been followed in the past. There being no agreement, the antitrust risk is virtually removed.

Sometimes, because a new distributor assumes considerable risk, he will insist on an exclusive distributorship. The exclusive agreement should be limited in duration, for example, to two years, and should not be renewed unless the economic necessity is clear and convincing. It is wise to add to such an exclusive agreement a preamble reciting the economic necessity for such a limitation, *e.g.*, that the establishment of the distributorship requires a substantial capital investment and competition is keen.

V. Resale Price Maintenance

A. [§3.25] Introduction

As part of its distribution plan the manufacturer or its distributors may want to establish a uniform resale price. The manufacturer may seek to maximize profit for all persons in the chain, whereas the distributor may seek to prevent price competition, and to provide a stable and predictable profit margin.

"Vertical" resale price maintenance can be achieved by (1) direct contractual relationships between the supplier and the dealer outside the so-called fair-trade laws (see §§3.26–3.27); (2) a contractual arrangement sanctioned by the fair-trade laws, which binds not only the dealer who is a party to the price-maintenance agreement, but also, in some states, those dealers who have knowledge of the agreement (see §§3.28–3.36); or (3) a refusal on the part of the supplier to sell to those dealers who do not adhere to his suggested resale prices (see §§3.37–3.39). This portion of the chapter is concerned with the antitrust problems presented by these various forms of resale price maintenance.

The following points may be helpful in analyzing price maintenance problems:

☐ Price-fixing agreements between a supplier and independent dealers covering trademarked or brand-name goods are legitimate if the supplier complies with the fair-trade laws. In some states, the supplier can bind not only contracting parties, but noncontracting parties with notice. See §§3.28–3.36.

☐ Absent compliance with the fair-trade laws, price fixing may be achieved if the supplier resells through his own employees or agents (including independent sales representatives). The arrangement apparently must be genuine; the manufacturer must retain title and risk. Even then, the arrangements will be vulnerable if they "unreasonably" restrict competition. See §3.27.

☐ On the use of refusals to deal to enforce a price-maintenance program, see §§3.37–3.39.

B. Contractual Arrangements outside the Fair-trade Laws

1. [§3.26] Vertical Price Maintenance Agreements

In the absence of the protection of fair-trade statutes, vertical resale price maintenance agreements are *per se* violations of the Sherman Act, and an unfair method of competition under Section 5 of the Federal Trade Commission Act (15 USC §45). *Dr. Miles Medical Co. v John D. Park & Sons* (1911) 220 US 373 established that an express agreement between a supplier and a dealer designed to maintain resale prices was an unlawful restraint of trade under the common law and under the Sherman Act. Later cases have extended this rule to encompass both express and implied agreements. See *FTC v Beech-Nut Packing Co.* (1922) 257 US 441. But see §§3.28–3.36.

2. [§3.27] Agency Arrangements

If a manufacturer or supplier resells through his own employees or agents, he can set the resale price of the goods without any danger of violating the antitrust laws. But if the agency arrangement is a sham, the so-called "agent" will be treated as an independent dealer and the resale price maintenance arrangement will be unlawful. *Dr. Miles Medical Co. v John D. Park & Sons* (1911) 220 US 373.

A type of relationship often used in the distribution of goods is the consignment. Although a consignment arrangement may take many forms, essentially it is the transfer of a product to a dealer for resale with title remaining in the transferor until the resale is effected. In *United States v General Electric Co.* (1926) 272 US 476, the Supreme Court held there was no violation of the Sherman Act when General Electric consigned patented electric light bulbs to wholesale and retail dealers and set the price at which the dealers were to resell. The Court held that the consignees were genuine agents and that there was no violation of the antitrust laws when an owner fixed the price at which his agents sold for him directly to the consumer.

However, in the recent *Simpson v Union Oil Co.* (1964) 377 US 13, the Court, although not expressly overruling *General Electric*, seriously undermined its authority. The defendant had a distribution system under which gasoline was consigned to a large number of retail dealers. The consignment agreements fixed the price at which the gasoline was to be sold to the public. Simpson, a consignment dealer with a one-year lease on his station, requested permission to reduce his selling price in order to meet prices charged by competitors. When defendant rejected the request, Simpson reduced the price anyway. Union then refused to renew Simpson's lease because of his failure to adhere to the price set by Union. In a treble-damage action brought by Simpson against Union, the district court dismissed the complaint on the ground that a consignor has the right to set retail prices, and the Ninth Circuit affirmed.

The Supreme Court reversed and held that Union's consignment plan, coupled with its control of the resale price, violated Section 1 of the Sherman Act (15 USC §1). It also held that neither Simpson's consent to the agreement nor the fact that he had only a one-year terminable lease prevented him from properly stating a claim for damages. (In subsequent proceedings the Supreme Court reversed the appellate court's affirmance that the doctrine had only prospective application to the plaintiff. 396 US 13.) Although the Court did not hold that all price-setting consignment agreements are unlawful under the antitrust laws, it apparently narrowed the scope of permissible activity substantially. The significance of the *Simpson* case has been discussed in a number of subsequent cases and law-review articles, but the exact scope of the prohibition against resale price fixing by means of consignment agreements cannot presently be ascertained. See, for example, *Sun Oil Co. v FTC* (7th Cir 1965) 350 F2d 624, *cert den* (1966) 382 US 982 (limited application of *Simpson* in case under Section 5 of the Federal Trade Commission Act (15 USC §45); *Atlantic Refining Co. v FTC* (6th Cir 1965) 344 F2d 599, *cert den* 382 US 939 (applying *Simpson*); *Lyons v Westinghouse Electric Co.* (SD NY 1964) 235 F Supp 526 (*Simpson* doctrine not retroactive); *United States v General Electric Co.* (SD NY 1969) 303 F Supp 1121; Rahl, *The Demise of Vertical Price Fixing Through Consignment Arrangements: The Simpson Case* (1965) 29 ABA Antitrust Law Section 216.

It seems clear that the Court in the *Simpson* case was greatly influenced by the consignor's coercive use of its dominant economic power and by its view that the principal purpose of the consignment arrangement was to fix prices rather than to implement any legitimate business end. As the Court stated (377 US at 20):

Dealers, like Simpson, are independent businessmen; and they have all or most of the indicia of entrepreneurs, except for price fixing. The risk of loss of the gasoline is on them, apart from acts of God. Their return is affected by the rise and fall in the market price, their commissions declining as retail prices drop. Practically the only power they have to be wholly independent businessmen, whose service depends on their own initiative and enterprise, is taken from them by the proviso that they must sell their gasoline at prices fixed by Union Oil. By reason of the lease and "consignment" agreement dealers are coercively laced into an arrangement under which their supplier is able to impose noncompetitive prices on thousands of persons whose prices otherwise might be competitive.

See also *FTC v Texaco Inc.* (1968) 393 US 223, 229, holding illegal under Section 5 of the Federal Trade Commission Act (15 USC §45) the acceptance of commissions by the franchisor from a third-party supplier on sales made to the franchisee and utilizing a similar rationale based on the "inherent coercion" in such a marketing system.

In *United States v Arnold, Schwinn & Co.* (1967) 388 US 365, the Court was careful to state what it meant by an agency arrangement and how it read the *Simpson* case (388 US at 380):

Where the manufacturer retains title, dominion, and risk with respect to the product and the position and function of the dealer in question are, in fact, indistinguishable from those of an agent or salesman of the manufacturer, it is only if the impact of the confinement is "unreasonably" restrictive of competition that a violation of §1 results from such confinement unencumbered by culpable price fixing. *Simpson v Union Oil Co.* . . . .

Although the Court tested the legality of territorial restraints imposed by agency or consignment under the "rule of reason," the references to such restraints "unencumbered by" or "absent" price fixing leads to the conclusion that price fixing, even in a valid consignment arrangement would be *per se* unlawful. See *United States v General Electric Co., supra.* At the least, price restrictions attending a consignment arrangement will be found unreasonably restrictive of competition if it is imposed by a coercion or by one possessing dominant economic power.

A manufacturer or supplier may also utilize so-called "sales representatives" to resell products. Although these sales representatives are often established as independent contractors, they have many of the characteristics of an agent and perform generally the same functions as sales employees. It has been held that sales representatives are agents for purposes of determining whether there has been a violation of the antitrust laws. *Loren Specialty Mfg. Co. v Clark Mfg. Co.* (ND Ill 1965) 241 F Supp 493, *aff'd* (7th Cir 1966) 360 F2d 913, *cert den* (1966) 385 US 957. A manufacturer or supplier, then, should be able to establish by express contract the resale price of products sold by bona fide sales representatives.

C. Contractual Arrangements under the Fair-trade Laws

1. [§3.28] Introduction

The fair-trade laws provide a legislatively created exception to the general rule that express agreements between a supplier and independent dealers fixing the price at which products are resold are a *per se* violation of the Sherman and the Federal Trade Commission Acts. If the supplier or manufacturer complies with the provisions of these acts, he may fix and maintain resale prices of trademarked goods not only as against those dealers with whom he has contracts but also, in some states, as against dealers who have notice of the agreements.

2. [§3.29] History and Present Status of Fair-trade Laws

The fair-trade laws provide an exemption from antitrust liability by an interlacing of federal and state legislation. During the early 1930s many states enacted legislation permitting manufacturers to set resale prices in order to allow trademark owners to protect their goodwill, prevent the use of loss leaders to the detriment of the consumer, and guard against destructive price wars. For favorable discussion of the purpose of these laws see Adams, *Resale Price Maintenance; Fact or Fancy* (1955) 64 *Yale LJ* 755. For critical discussion see Rahl, *The Case against Fair Trade* (1959) 44 *Ill BJ* 754; Herman, *A Note in Fair Trade* (1955) 65 *Yale LJ* 23.

Because of the supremacy of federal law (and the illegality of vertical price-fixing arrangements under *Dr. Miles Medical Co. v John D. Park & Sons* (1911) 220 US 373), state laws could not protect trademarked goods in interstate commerce. To meet the demand for exempting fair-trade agreements from application of the federal antitrust laws, Congress enacted the Miller-Tydings Act in 1937.

In *Schwegmann Bros. v Calvert Distillers Corp.* (1951) 341 US 384, the Supreme Court held that the Miller-Tydings Act did not sanction application of state laws to nonsigners, but merely permitted enforcement of the vertical arrangements against the dealers who had entered into them.

In 1952, Congress responded by enacting the McGuire Act, which amended Section 5(a) of the Federal Trade Commission Act (15 USC §45(a)) to permit the enforcement of vertical price-fixing agreements on trademarked goods both against parties to the contract and those having knowledge of the contract. The act provides (15 USC §45(a)(3)):

> Nothing contained in this section or in any of the Antitrust Acts shall render unlawful the exercise or the enforcement of any right or right of action created by any statute, law, or public policy now or hereafter in effect in any State, Territory, or the District of Columbia, which in substance provides that willfully and knowingly advertising, offering for sale, or selling any commodity at less than the price or prices prescribed in such contracts or agreements whether the person so advertising, offering for sale, or selling is or is not a party to such a contract or agreement, is unfair competition and is actionable at the suit of any person damaged thereby.

Most of the states have enacted legislation of the kind authorized by the McGuire Act.

The validity of these fair-trade statutes under the federal constitution has been upheld both by the United States Supreme Court (see *Old Dearborn Distributing Co. v Seagram Distillers Corp.* (1936) 299 US 183) and by the highest courts of some of the states, but several state courts have declared the acts unconstitutional under the state constitutions. As of 1970, all states except Alaska, Missouri, Texas, and Vermont had enacted fair-trade legislation and Hawaii, Kansas, Mississippi, Nebraska, Nevada, and Rhode Island had repealed their statutes. Alabama, Montana, Utah, and Wyoming had held their laws unconstitutional, and twenty state courts have held the nonsigner provisions unconstitutional. See Trade Reg Rep ¶6041 and Conant, *Resale Price Maintenance: Constitutionality of Nonsigner Clauses* (1961) 109 *U Pa L Rev* 539. Fair-trade programs are enforceable against noncontracting dealers with notice in sixteen states and against contracting parties in thirty-six states. *Antitrust Developments 1955-1968, Supplement to Report of Attorney General's National Committee to Study the Antitrust Laws,* 112. See tabulation, Trade Reg Rep ¶6041. Note, *Counter-revolution in State Constitutional Law* (1963) 15 *Stan L Rev* 309.

3. Requirements of a Valid Fair-trade Program

a. [§3.30] Only Vertical Agreements Are Covered

Both Section 5(a)(5) of the McGuire Act (15 USC §45(a)(5)) and the related state statutes specifically provide that the exemption from the prohibition of the antitrust laws applies only to vertical agreements between a manufacturer or supplier and his dealers. In short, although a manufacturer or supplier can establish a system whereby the resale prices of all his dealers are set, the dealers by joint action themselves cannot achieve that result.

The restriction of the McGuire Act to vertical agreements has been construed by the Supreme Court to prohibit an integrated manufacturer from entering into horizontal fair-trade agreements with independent dealers who are in competition with the manufacturer's own sales outlets. For example, in *United States v McKesson & Robbins, Inc.* (1956) 351 US 305, the Supreme Court held a drug manufacturer/wholesaler's fair-trade agreements with independent wholesalers to be *per se* violations of Section 1 of the Sherman Act (15 USC §1) unprotected by the McGuire Act.

For a discussion of problems not solved by the *McKesson* case—for example, what happens if there is only limited competition between the integrated seller and dealers—see Weston, *Fair Trade, Alias Quality Stabilization, Status, Problems, and Prospects* (1963) 22 ABA Antitrust LJ 78, 83–87.

b. [§3.31] Need for Trademark or Brand Name

The McGuire Act (15 USC §45) applies only to a "commodity which bears, or the label or container of which bears, the trade-mark, brand, or name of the producer or distributor of such commodity. . . ." Many of the related state statutes contain the same limitation. However, enforcement of the act is not limited to the owner of the trademark: "[A]ny person damaged" by reason of sales below the stipulated price is entitled to enforce the act by a suit for unfair competition. 15 USC §45(a)(3).

c. [§3.32] Commodity in Free and Open Competition

The exemption created by the McGuire Act applies only to commodities in "free and open competition with commodities of the same general class produced or distributed by others." 15 USC §45(a)(2). The state statutes generally contain similar language. Interpreting this provision of the McGuire Act, a lower federal court has held that a manufacturer of color film could not maintain resale prices on such film when the other suppliers sold only black and white film. Since Kodak color film was at that time the only product of its kind, it was not in free and open competition with other commodities of the same general class. *Eastman Kodak Co. v FTC* (2d Cir 1946) 158 F2d 592, *cert den* (1947) 330 US 828. But the introduction of one competitive product apparently satisfies the requirements. *Eastman Kodak Co.* (1947) FTC Dkt 4322, Trade Reg Rep ¶24,357. For a discussion of the requirement, see Herman, *Free and Open Competition* (1957) 9 *Stan L Rev* 323.

d. [§3.33] Nonsigner Provisions

The most controversial provisions of the fair-trade laws are those that bind resellers of the product who are not parties to a fair-trade agreement, but who have notice of the agreement. These sections, generally referred to as the "nonsigner provisions," typically provide that it is unfair competition for any person willfully and knowingly to advertise, offer for sale, or sell any fair-traded commodity at a price less than the price stipulated in a fair-trade agreement. As noted in §3.29, twenty state courts have held these provisions unconstitutional.

e. [§3.34] Establishment and Enforcement of a Fair-trade Program

A manufacturer or producer of a commodity, and even any "vendor" of the commodity, can establish a fair-trade program by entering into an agreement with a dealer stipulating the resale price of a commodity and notifying all other dealers selling the commodity of the existence of the agreement and the prices stipulated.

Once a fair-trade program has been established, there are a number of means of enforcing the program, and a number of persons have standing to enforce it. The manufacturer or vendor can of course enforce the fair-trade agreements by a suit for breach of contract against those dealers who are parties to the agreements. Further, if authorized by state law, a manufacturer or vendor can bring an action against nonsigners for unfair competition under the state statutes as a person who has been damaged by willfull and knowing sale, or advertisement for sale, below the price stipulated in a fair-trade agreement. For a list of states enforcing agreements against nonsigners, see §3.29.

Whether a trade association of retailers can enforce fair-trade agreements is not clear. Compare *Winfield Drug Stores, Inc. v Warshaw* (NY Sup Ct 1956) 1956 Trade Cases ¶68,447, with *De Candido v Wagonfeld* (NY Sup Ct 1959) 190 NYS2d 858. Some state legislation expressly permits an association to enforce fair-trade prices (NH Rev Stat Ann 1966, §357.4), and at least one federal court has assumed that the federal legislation permitted it. *Chattanooga Pharmaceutical Ass'n. v United States* (ED Tenn 1964) 1965 Trade Cases ¶71,524, *aff'd on other grounds* (6th

Cir 1966) 358 F2d 864. See Note, *The Enforcement of Resale Price Maintenance* (1959) 69 *Yale LJ* 168, 174–177.

In any of these actions, the usual remedies for unfair competition are available, including injunctive relief (see, *e.g., Glaser Bros. v 21st Sales Co.* (1964) 224 Cal App 2d 197), and exemplary damages (*Sterling Drug, Inc. v Benatar* (1950) 99 Cal App 2d 393).

f. [§3.35] Exemptions and Defenses to Fair-trade Programs

The state statutes commonly provide certain exemptions from the application of the fair-trade laws. "Closing out" sales for discontinuing a commodity are typically exempted, as are sales of damaged or deteriorated goods and sales by officers acting under orders of any court, as for example in foreclosure or bankruptcy sales. For a tabulation see Trade Reg Rep ¶¶6043–6045.

The enforcement of a fair-trade program has been affected by a number of judicially created defenses to fair-trade actions. In particular, several New York cases have considered the extent to which a manufacturer's failure to enforce fair-trade prices constitutes a defense for dealers who do not maintain the prices. A recent case has significantly lightened the burden of a manufacturer who is seeking to enforce fair-trade prices by holding that once a fair-trade agreement and a violation have been established, the only bar to enforcement is a showing that the manufacturer deliberately abandoned the contract or is using the fair-trade contract inequitably to favor some retailers against others. *National Distillers & Chem. Corp. v R. H. Macy & Co., Inc.* (NY Sup Ct App Div 1965) 258 NYS2d 298, 1965 Trade Cases ¶71,423.

Other enforcement problems may arise when a supplier markets combination packages with components that are fair traded separately (*Upjohn Co. v Vineland Discount Center* (D NJ 1964) 235 F Supp 191; compare *Upjohn Co. v Carlton Drug Co.* (SD NY 1966) 1966 Trade Cases ¶71,775); when a firm carrying on intrastate business has not qualified to do business in the state (*Champion Spark Plug Co. v T.G. Stores, Inc.* (4th Cir 1966) 356 F2d 462); when retailers give discounts below fair-trade prices by means of trading stamps (*Jantzen, Inc. v E.J. Korvette, Inc.* (SD NY 1963) 219 F Supp 604; *Vornado v Corning Glass Works* (3d Cir 1968) 388 F2d 11; *Shulton v Hogue and Knott* (6th Cir 1966) 364 F2d 765); and when retailers give allowances for trade-ins (compare *Schwanhaussa* (1955) FTC Dkt 6328, Trade Reg Rep ¶24,500 in which the FTC prohibited use of fair-trade agreements to restrict amount of trade-ins, with provision in Ohio statute limiting trade-in allowance on fair-traded items to "actual market value thereof." Ohio Rev Code Ann ¶1333.32). For a tabular presentation of some of these problems, see Trade Reg Rep ¶¶6043–6047.

4. [§3.36] Current Use of Fair-trade Agreements

Although accurate statistics are difficult to develop, it is the general consensus that fair-trade enforcement of resale prices is of limited present vitality. The difficulties and expenses of effective enforcement of a fair-trade program have led many firms to abandon such programs; litigation is expensive and no customer likes to be sued. These difficulties, plus the tendency of many state courts to declare fair-trade laws unconstitutional, have undoubtedly contributed to a general demise of well-enforced fair-trade programs.

D. Refusal to Deal

1. [§3.37] The Colgate Doctrine

The decision in *United States v Colgate & Co.* (1919) 250 US 300 provides a potential method for a supplier to set the resale prices of his distributors in a state that has not enacted fair-trade legislation. In that case, the Court dismissed an indictment under the Sherman Act (15 USC §1), and held as follows (250 US at 307):

In the absence of any purpose to create or maintain a monopoly, the act does not restrict the long recognized right of trader or manufacturer engaged in an entirely private business, freely to exercise his own independent discretion as to parties with whom he will deal. And, of course, he may announce in advance the circumstances under which he will refuse to sell.

Thus, in theory at least, a supplier may establish a resale price maintenance program simply by "suggesting" the price at which his products are to be resold by his distributors and by announcing that he will sell to only those distributors who adhere to the suggested resale prices. If enforced by refusals to deal, the practical result of such a policy will be the same as though the supplier had express resale price agreements with the distributors. But see §§3.38–3.39.

2. [§3.38] Subsequent Limitations to the Colgate Doctrine

The full scope of the *Colgate* (*United States v Colgate & Co.* (1919) 250 US 300) doctrine was short-lived, for a series of subsequent Supreme Court cases has severely eroded it. The major cases include: *United States v Schrader's Son, Inc.* (1920) 252 US 85; *Frey & Son, Inc. v Cudahy*

Packing Co. (1921) 256 US 208; *FTC v Beech-Nut Packing Co.* (1922) 257 US 441; *United States v Bausch & Lomb Optical Co.* (1944) 321 US 707; and *United States v Parke, Davis & Co.* (1960) 362 US 29.

The thrust of these cases has been to limit the protection of the *Colgate* doctrine to a unilateral announcement of prices and a unilateral refusal to deal with those not adhering to the prices. "Something more" than this subjects the activities to a finding of illegality under the antitrust laws.

The fatal "something more" often consists of soliciting or permitting the assistance of customers in enforcing resale prices. Such cooperative activity between the manufacturer and its customers may constitute an unlawful agreement under Section 1 of the Sherman Act (15 USC §1) and Section 3 of the Clayton Act (15 USC §14). For example, in *United States v General Motors Co.* (1966) 384 US 127, dealers' insistence on enforcement of resale prices and assistance in policing a competing dealer's sale to discount houses was held to be a violation of Section 1 of the Sherman Act (15 USC §1).

In *United States v Parke, Davis & Co., supra,* a manufacturer's threats to refuse to deal with wholesalers who sold to price-cutting retailers resulted in an unlawful combination violating Section 1 of the Sherman Act. The manufacturer sought and obtained assurances from its retailers of compliance with its resale price schedule; a price-maintenance conspiracy resulted, in violation of the Sherman Act. For similar holdings, see *FTC v Beechnut Packing Co., supra; Girarde v Gates Rubber Co. Sales Division* (9th Cir 1963) 325 F2d 196.

Alternatively, the fatal "something more" may consist of the assistance of persons other than customers. For example, *Albrecht v Herald Co.* (1968) 390 US 145 was a suit by a newspaper carrier who charged his subscribers more than the newspaper's specified maximum price. The newspaper advised his subscribers that it would deliver at a lower rate, hired a circulation company to solicit the offending carrier's subscribers, assigned the subscribers to another carrier for servicing on a temporary basis, and informed the offending carrier that the customers would be returned if he would not exceed the suggested prices. The Court found a combination in violation of Section 1 of the Sherman Act.

Finally, the fatal "something more" may be supplied by coercive use of a refusal to deal. For example, in *Simpson v Union Oil Co.* (1964) 377 US 13, the defendant oil company was held to violate Section 1 of the Sherman Act when it refused to renew a service-station lease because the lessee sold the gasoline consigned to him below the agreed resale price.

In *Beech-Nut, supra,* the Court declared unlawful under Section 5 of the Federal Trade Commission Act (15 USC §45) a policy of refusing to sell to retailers who would not adhere to a schedule of resale prices. The policy was implemented by a refusal to sell to wholesalers who sold to price-cutting retailers, the use of code numbers on products to detect price cuts, and a system of reporting price cutters to the supplier. See also *United States v Parke, Davis & Co., supra.*

3. [§3.39] Present Status of the Colgate Doctrine

In private litigation, the *Colgate* doctrine may still be viable as a defense against a treble-damage action brought by a terminated dealer if there has been a strictly unilateral refusal to deal. For example, in *Klein v American Luggage Works, Inc.* (3d Cir 1963) 323 F2d 787, the court found no violation of the Sherman Act: A manufacturer suggested retail prices in catalogs and attached preprinted price tickets to luggage. Its sales representatives told retailers that full compliance with these prices was mandatory and that sales below the prices would result in a refusal to deal with the price cutter. Klein was cut off by the manufacturer after the latter's agents discovered that Klein had been making sales below the suggested prices. Klein sued under the Sherman Act, claiming that the activity of the manufacturer was an unlawful price-fixing scheme. The district court agreed. The Third Circuit reversed, however, holding that the activities of the manufacturer in inducing adherence to suggested resale prices were the type of conduct sanctioned by *Colgate*. Other cases to the same effect are: *Dart Drug Co. v Parke, Davis & Co.* (D DC 1963) 221 F Supp 948, *aff'd* (3d Cir 1965) 344 F2d 173; *Graham v Triangle Publications, Inc.* (ED Pa 1964) 233 F Supp 825, *aff'd* (3d Cir 1965) 344 F2d 775; *Southend Oil Co. v Texaco, Inc.* (ND Ill 1965) 237 F Supp 650. But compare *Simpson v Union Oil Co.* (1964) 377 US 13.

Reliance on the doctrine as an effective means of establishing and maintaining resale prices presents serious hazards. First, if the supplier enlists the aid of wholesalers or retailers to enforce the retail prices, he may lose *Colgate* protection under the rule set out in *United States v Parke, Davis & Co.* (1960) 362 US 29. See §3.38.

Second, by enlisting the aid of customers to cut off a price-cutting competitor of retailers who maintain the suggested prices, the supplier runs the risk of being a party to a boycott, another *per se* violation of the Sherman Act. See *United States v General Motors Corp.* (1966) 384 US 127.

Third, if the supplier induces a dealer to continue to adhere to the suggested resale prices by threats to cut off the dealer if he does not do so (a "communicated danger of termination"), the supplier runs the risk that the continuation of the business relationship and the maintenance of the prices will be held an implied price-fixing agreement, found in *Dr. Miles Medical Co. v John D. Park & Sons* (1911) 220 US 373 to violate the Sherman Act. *United States v Arnold, Schwinn & Co.* (1967) 388 US 365, 372; *Albrecht v Herald Co.* (1968) 390 US 145, 150 n. 6; *Perma Life Mufflers, Inc. v International Parts Corp.* (1968) 392 US 134, 142.

Fourth, if the supplier suggests the resale prices by preticketing his products but cannot or will not enforce these prices, it may amount to aiding and abetting a deceptive practice in violation of the Federal Trade Commission Act. See *Regina Corp.* (1961) FTC Dkt 8323, *aff'd* (3d Cir 1963) 322 F2d 765.

Fifth, if the supplier is in a superior bargaining position, coercing adherence to resale prices by refusing to deal may violate the Sherman Act. See *Simpson v Union Oil Co., supra.*

In any event, the *Colgate* doctrine will not protect the supplier who is a monopolist even though the monopoly power may have been lawfully acquired. Under these circumstances a refusal to deal with those who do not adhere to suggested resale prices, or an attempt to impose other unlawful restraints of trade by refusal to deal, may amount to a violation of Section 2 of the Sherman Act (15 USC §2). *Times-Picayune Pub. Co. v United States* (1953) 345 US 594, 625; *Lorain Journal Co. v United States* (1951) 342 US 143.

It must be concluded that the *Colgate* doctrine has only limited usefulness as a means of enforcing a resale price maintenance program. For various discussions of its present status, see: Fulda, *Individual Refusals to Deal: When Does Single Firm Conduct Become Vertical Restraint?* (1965) 30 *Law & Cont Probs* 590; Turner, *The Definition of Agreement under the Sherman Act: Conscious Parallelism and Refusals to Deal* (1962) 75 *Harv L Rev* 655; Halpern, *Individual Refusals to Deal: Customer Selection or Dealer Protection?* (1963) 22 ABA Antitrust LJ 49; Pitofsky & Dam, *Is The Colgate Doctrine Dead?* (1968) 37 ABA Antitrust LJ 772.

4. [§3.40] Using Refusal to Sell to Enforce Restraints Other Than Resale Price

Although the refusal-to-deal doctrine was developed primarily from efforts to maintain resale prices, it can also be used to impose other restraints. For example, a manufacturer may announce that he will refuse to sell to dealers who handle competitive products. On exclusive dealing generally, see §§3.2–3.8. If such a restraint were imposed by means of an agreement with the dealer, it could violate Section 3 of the Clayton Act (15 USC §14) as well as Section 1 of the Sherman Act (15 USC §1). But if the manufacturer unilaterally terminates a dealer for failure to comply with an announced policy, such as exclusive dealing, the courts have generally held that the dealer has no cause of action against the manufacturer under the antitrust laws, reasoning that an agreement, an essential element of a violation of both Section 3 of the Clayton Act and of Section 1 of the Sherman Act, cannot be established since the dealer is actually complaining about the *lack* of a sale or lease agreement. See, *e.g.*, *Amplex of Maryland, Inc. v Outboard Marine Corp.* (4th Cir 1967) 380 F2d 112, *cert den* (1968) 389 US 1036; *Associated Beverages Co. v Ballantine & Sons* (5th Cir 1961) 287 F2d 261; *Walker Distributing Co. v Lucky Lager Brewing Co.* (9th Cir 1963) 323 F2d 1, 9; *Leo J. Meyberg Co. v Eureka Williams Corp.* (9th Cir 1954) 215 F2d 100, *cert den* (1954) 348 US 875; *Nelson Radio & Supply Co. v Motorola, Inc.* (5th Cir 1952) 200 F2d 911, *cert den* (1953) 345 US 925. But compare *Albrecht v Herald Co.* (1968) 390 US 145, 150, 156; *Simpson v Union Oil Co.* (1964) 377 US 13; and *Lessig v Tidewater Oil Co.* (9th Cir 1964) 327 F2d 459, *cert den* (1964) 377 US 993.

In contrast, in suits brought by the government, a manufacturer's announced policy of refusing to deal to enforce exclusive dealing by its dealers may establish a violation of Section 3 of the Clayton Act. *United States v Sun Oil Co.* (ED Pa 1959) 176 F Supp 715, 727, 739. *Outboard Marine & Mfg. Co.* (1956) 52 FTC 1553.

A supplier who attempts to use the *Colgate* doctrine (*United States v Colgate & Co.* (1919) 250 US 300) as a means of enforcing exclusive-dealing arrangements or tie-in agreements, or imposing requirements contracts or other territorial or customer restrictions, would be faced with many of the same problems attendant on enforcing resale price maintenance. See §§3.37–3.39. Because of the narrow scope of permissible conduct, the doctrine is a weak enforcement device and it is difficult to see that it would be of significant help as a defense to suits brought by the government, or even by private parties, if there is a pattern of restrictive practices imposed upon dealers by threats of refusal to deal. See *United States v Arnold, Schwinn & Co.* (1967) 388 US 365; *Lessig v Tidewater Oil Co.*, *supra*, 472–473.

On the other hand, a supplier is entitled to deal only with those distributors who properly apply themselves to the sale of his products, and the *Colgate* doctrine may be of value in defending suits brought by dealers who have been cut off for failure to meet the standards imposed by the manufacturer. Furthermore the *Colgate* doctrine will still justify termination of a dealer based on bona fide business reasons. See, *e.g.*, *Packard Motor Co. v Webster Motor Co.* (DC Cir 1957) 243 F2d 418, *cert den* (1957) 355 US 822.

4

Mergers and Acquisitions

Robert K. Johnson

Mr. Johnson received the BA degree from Harvard University in 1961 and the JD degree from Stanford University in 1964. He is a member of the Los Angeles County and American Bar Associations and the State Bar of California, and is a member of the Los Angeles firm of Munger, Tolles, Hills and Rickershauser. Mr. Johnson was a Special Assistant to the Assistant Attorney General in the Antitrust Division, U.S. Department of Justice from 1965 to 1968.

V.   Advising Client Opposing Acquisition

A. [§4.77] Introduction
B. [§4.78] Complaint to Government
C. [§4.79] Intervention in Government Suit
D. [§4.80] Remedies Available in a Private Suit
E. [§4.81] Opposing Tender Offer or Attempted Take-Over

VI.   [§4.82]   Government Investigations of Mergers

A. [§4.83] Merger Investigations by the Department of Justice
B. [§4.84] Merger Investigations by the Federal Trade Commission

I. Introduction

A. [§4.1] Scope of Chapter

Merger activity has recently been at an all-time high. Between 1966 and 1968, the number of annual corporate mergers more than doubled, reaching a total of over 4,000 in 1968. The value of the assets of acquired firms with total assets exceeding $10 million rose from $4 billion in 1966 to more than $12 billion in 1968. A record-breaking 4,550 corporate mergers were recorded in 1969.

The sharp rise in the number of acquisition and merger proposals makes it imperative that counsel at least be cognizant of the various legal problems that may arise in a merger. Many of the questions relate to requirements of the Securities and Exchange Commission, seller's liabilities, accounting treatment, and tax considerations in planning a taxable or tax-free arrangement, to name only a few of the more obvious areas of potential legal problems. This chapter will examine the antitrust considerations.

Most frequently antitrust advice will be sought on a particular acquisition or joint venture, but a client may also seek advice in connection with planning an overall program of acquisitions. Occasionally, and with increasing frequency, a client may want to oppose a merger or acquisition involving one of its competitors, or it may be the target of a take-over attempt that it seeks to oppose. This chapter attempts to assist the attorney who is asked to advise a client in these situations.

For antitrust purposes it will be irrelevant whether a corporate union is accomplished by means of an acquisition of stock, an acquisition of assets, or a statutory merger. The terms "acquisition" and "merger" will, therefore, be used interchangeably to refer to all transactions that bring under single control enterprises previously independent, whether the transaction takes the form of a technical merger of one corporate entity into another, a consolidation by which a new corporation supplants two or more predecessors, an acquisition by one corporation of the stock or assets of another corporation, an acquisition by a holding company of effective control over previously independent businesses, or a simple purchase of physical assets.

B. [§4.2] Definition of Horizontal, Vertical, and Conglomerate Mergers

It is common to classify mergers as horizontal, vertical, or conglomerate.

Horizontal mergers are mergers between companies that sell one or more competing products in the same geographic market—for example, a merger between two soft drink bottlers in the city of Los Angeles. *Vertical* mergers are mergers between companies that have a buyer-seller relationship—for example, a merger between an aluminum ingot manufacturer and an aluminum product fabricator. *Conglomerate* mergers are all others; the class may be further separated into three subcategories: product extension, market extension, and pure conglomerate mergers. A *product extension* conglomerate merger is one between companies that sell noncompetitive products that are related in production or distribution—for example, a merger between a soap manufacturer and a bleach manufacturer. A *market extension* conglomerate merger is one between companies that manufacture the same product but sell it in different geographic markets—for example, a merger between a soft drink bottler in Los Angeles and a soft drink bottler in New York. *Pure* conglomerate mergers are those that do not fall into any of the foregoing categories. Examples of pure conglomerate mergers in 1969 were Ling-Temco-Vought's (highly diversified company with no steel operations) acquisition of Jones and Laughlin (a steel company) and International Telephone and Telegraph's (a communication and electronics company) acquisitions of Canteen (a vending machine operator and distributor), Grinnell (a manufacturer of automatic sprinkler fire protection systems), and Hartford Fire Insurance (an insurance company).

II. [§4.3] Assessing a Merger

It is not enough to advise a client that his merger may be challenged; management will want answers to specific questions. What are the chances that a suit will be brought to challenge the acquisition? If a suit is brought, will it be filed before or after the acquisition is consummated? Will a preliminary injunction be sought, and, if so, what is the likelihood that it will be granted? What possibility is there of successfully defending the merger if a suit is brought, and how long would it take to have the matter resolved? What antitrust risks will there be in making the acquisition?

An acquisition may be so clearly safe from antitrust attack or so likely to be subject to suit that it will not be difficult to advise a client. In other situations, however, the answers to the foregoing questions will not be so clear, and counsel may want to associate special antitrust counsel.

In almost every instance, management of the purchaser and seller will be well advised to seek independent advice on the application of the antitrust laws. The seller should resist the temptation to rely on the acquiring company for antitrust advice since the potential risks to the purchaser and seller will be different.

Counsel will need a substantial amount of information to be able to advise his client intelligently about an acquisition. Management will usually want an antitrust opinion promptly, and this will make it essential for counsel to obtain as much of this factual information as he can from his client. There may be too little time for counsel to make an independent investigation of the other company's business, and he may have to rely on the materials his client gives him. A checklist of information counsel should request from his client as soon as he is asked to advise on a proposed merger appears at §4.5.

A. [§4.4] Steps in Assessing a Merger

1. Get information from client. See §4.5.

2. Determine whether any government agency must approve or be notified about the acquisition. See §§4.71–4.73.

3. Determine what laws may apply. See §§4.7–4.13.

4. Check for possible corporate interlocks. See §4.13.

5. Determine whether the acquisition complies with the guidelines issued by the Federal Trade Commission or Department of Justice. See §§4.22–4.23.

6. Analyze theories on which the acquisition might be challenged. See §§4.21–4.37.

7. Predict likelihood of suit to challenge acquisition. See §§4.42–4.50.

8. Consider steps to minimize likelihood of suit. See §§4.51–4.53.

9. Explore possible defenses and assess chances of successfully defending merger if suit is brought. See §§4.38–4.41.

10. Examine risks to client in making acquisition deemed unsafe. See §§4.54–4.68.

11. Consider steps to minimize risks of potential merger remedies. See §§4.69–4.70.

12. Decide whether to seek advance clearance. See §§4.74–4.76.

On advising a client opposing an acquisition or resisting a take-over attempt, see §§4.77–4.81. On government investigations of mergers, see §§4.82–4.84.

1. [§4.5] Get Factual Data from Client

Much basic data will be needed in order to undertake an antitrust analysis of a prospective merger. Most of this information will have to be furnished by the client, although some of it may be available in published sources. Some of the information will be difficult to obtain, particularly sales statistics of competitors, needed in order to make market share determinations.

Counsel may be required to give an opinion on a proposed merger before definitive data can be obtained. Counsel and both parties should work together to locate the most reliable data that can be obtained within the time available. Normally counsel should not accept responsibility for the reliability of the data, and counsel's opinion should be based solely on the data that is available.

When counsel is asked for an antitrust opinion on a proposed merger, he should ask the client to begin immediately to assemble the following information for use in reviewing the acquisition:

A. Existing Documents

1. Copy of merger agreement. Determine whether any contingent shares are involved. See §4.70.

2. Copies of any minutes, memoranda, or other written materials relating to the proposed acquisition and reasons for it. These materials will be particularly important in connection with conglomerate mergers on issues such as potential competition and reciprocity. See §§4.29–4.36.

3. Copies of any proxy statement or press releases relating to the acquisition. Be aware of possibility of minimizing risk of suit. See §4.51.

4. Copies of most recent annual reports and subsequent interim financial statements for both companies, and sales projections for both companies for the current year.

5. Copies of any prior consent decrees entered into by either company in antitrust actions brought by the Department of Justice or the Federal Trade Commission. See §4.73.

B. Documents to be Prepared

6. A list of the products or services sold by each company and the geographic markets in which each product or service is sold, including a breakdown of annual dollar volume of sales (for the most recent year for which data is available) for each significant product and each distinct geographic market. (Preliminary analysis may be required to determine what product and geographic markets will be considered relevant for antitrust purposes. See §§4.24–4.26.) Approximate sales figures should also be obtained for at least two other years within the past ten years, one of which should be at least five years before the merger, in order to determine whether any markets display a trend toward increased concentration. A trend is especially important in horizontal mergers (§4.27) and certain conglomerate mergers (§§4.29–4.36). See also items 7 and 9.

7. A list of any markets and submarkets (§4.25), in which the two companies have been or are competitors (§4.27) or potential competitors or have occupied a supplier-purchaser relationship (§4.28), including a breakdown of annual dollar volume of sales or purchases (for the most recent year for which data is available) for both companies in each market. See the comment on trends in item 6.

8. A list of any markets in which one of the merging firms is a supplier and the other a purchaser, with the annual dollar volume of sales and purchases, respectively, for the two firms in the markets. This data will be necessary to evaluate possible opportunities for reciprocal dealing. See §4.31.

9. An exhibit (based on published data or the client's estimate) showing the annual dollar volume of sales (a) by each of the top ten firms and (b) by all firms combined in each market identified under 7 and 8 above and any other market in which the company to be acquired is an important seller. This data will be essential to determine the market shares of the merging firms and the market structure, i.e., concentrated or unconcentrated. See the comment on trends in item 6.

10. A list of all prior acquisitions made by both companies since 1950 with total dollar sales for each acquired company for the year preceding its acquisition showing separately all mergers in the markets identified under items 7 and 8. See §4.47.

11. A list of all significant mergers during the past ten years by other firms in the markets identified under items 7 and 8. See §4.47.

12. A list of prior government antitrust cases or investigations of which the client is aware dealing with (a) prior acquisitions made by either of the merging firms, (b) any mergers made by other firms operating in any

of the markets identified under items 7 or 8, (c) any other matters involving either of the merging firms, or (d) any other matters involving other firms operating in any of the markets identified under items 7 and 8.

2. [§4.6] Determinations of Law or Fact to Make

Some of the following items require information from the client; others require legal or sophisticated factual decisions by the lawyer.

1. Form of organization of both companies (corporation, partnership, sole proprietorship). See §4.8.

2. If the company to be acquired is in serious financial difficulty, full information on financial status and efforts to find other buyers; the failing-company defense may be available. See §4.38.

3. Plans, if any, to close down or dispose of plants or other assets of either company. See §4.52.

4. Whether other acquisitions under consideration will be postponed or dropped as a result of this one.

5. What problems will be created if the acquisition has to be abandoned. See §4.54.

6. What purchasers there may be for the acquired company if it must be divested See §4.62.

7. What effect a ban on future acquisitions would have on the acquiring firm. See §4.61.

8. Patents, trademarks, or trade names that the company might be forced to license. See §4.65.

9. Likelihood that someone will complain to the government about the acquisition or file a private suit. See §4.48.

10. Finally, any information that will help in estimating the client's exposure to treble-damage claims. See §4.66.

B. [§4.7] Applicable Statutes

A number of different antitrust statutes may apply to make a merger or joint venture unlawful. Acquisitions are challenged most frequently under Section 7 of the Clayton Act (15 USC §18), which makes unlawful any corporate acquisition whose effect "in any line of commerce in any section of the country . . . may be substantially to lessen competition, or to tend to create a monopoly." See §4.8. Acquisitions may also be condemned under Sections 1 or 2 of the Sherman Act (15 USC §§1-2) as a restraint of trade or as a monopoly (see §§4.9-4.10), under Section 5 of the Federal Trade Commission Act (15 USC §45; see §4.11) as an unfair method of competition, or under state antitrust laws. See §4.12. While these statutes establish somewhat different standards for determining the legality of a merger, the differences will not be important in most cases. In addition, a merger may result in a violation of Section 8 of the Clayton Act (15 USC §19; see §4.13) if any directors of the acquiring corporation serve as directors of companies that compete with the acquired corporation.

The Department of Justice and the Federal Trade Commission may both bring suit to challenge a merger under Section 7 of the Clayton Act. The Department of Justice may also challenge mergers under Sections 1 or 2 of the Sherman Act; the Federal Trade Commission may use Section 5 of the Federal Trade Commission Act.

In order to coordinate enforcement efforts and to avoid duplication of investigations, the Department of Justice and the Federal Trade Commission have adopted procedures for notifying each other and obtaining "clearance" from the other agency when one of them proposes to conduct an investigation of a merger. After an investigation has been "cleared" to one agency, the other agency normally will not participate or undertake an independent investigation of the same merger.

Private parties may challenge a merger claiming a violation of Section 7 of the Clayton Act or Sections 1 or 2 of the Sherman Act. Section 4 of the Clayton Act (15 USC §15) creates a private right of action for treble damages (discussed at §4.66), and Section 16 of the Clayton Act (15 USC §26) gives private parties the right to seek a preliminary injunction (discussed at §4.58) and, perhaps, divestiture (discussed at §4.62). For discussion of plaintiff's prosecution, see Chapter 12.

1. [§4.8] Section 7 of the Clayton Act

Section 7 of the Clayton Act (15 USC §18) was substantially amended by the Celler-Kefauver Act of 1950. Among other changes, this act made it clear that Section 7 applies to acquisitions of assets as well as to acquisitions of stock and to vertical and conglomerate mergers as well as to horizontal mergers. Congress also rejected the standards adopted by the courts for judging the legality of mergers under the Sherman Act as inappropriate and made it clear that Section 7 was intended to prevent mergers when a trend to a lessening of competition in any line of commerce was still in its incipiency. For a comprehensive discussion of the legislative history of the 1950 amendment, see *Brown Shoe Co. v United States* (1962) 370 US 294, 311-323. As a result of these changes, cases decided under Section 7 prior to 1950 have very limited utility today.

In its present form Section 7 prohibits a *corporation* from acquiring stock or assets of another *corporation* in some circumstances. Specifically, the first paragraph of Section 7 now reads:

No corporation engaged in commerce shall acquire, directly or indirectly, the whole or any part of the stock or other share capital and no corporation subject to the jurisdiction of the Federal Trade Commission shall acquire the whole or any part of the assets of another corporation engaged also in commerce, where in any line of commerce in any section of the country, the effect of such acquisition may be substantially to lessen competition, or to tend to create a monopoly.

To come within the scope of Section 7 of the Clayton Act, the acquisition must involve the stock or assets of a "corporation" which is "engaged in commerce." Thus, a corporation's acquisition of all the assets of an unincorporated business was held not to violate Section 7. *Bender v Hearst Corp.* (D Conn 1957) 152 F Supp 569, *aff'd* (2d Cir 1959) 263 F2d 360. However, Section 7 applies to the formation of a new corporation as a joint venture between existing corporations. *United States v Penn-Olin Chemical Co.* (1964) 378 US 158.

Section 7 applies equally to stock and asset acquisitions since the enactment of the Celler-Kefauver Act in 1950, despite differences in the wording of the applicable provisions. The Supreme Court has held that the objective of Congress in including the language "corporation subject to the jurisdiction of the Federal Trade Commission" in relation to asset acquisitions was not to limit the scope of Section 7, but rather was to counteract earlier court decisions limiting the scope of the Federal Trade Commission's divestiture power under Section 7. See *United States v Philadelphia Nat'l. Bank* (1963) 374 US 321, 346, 347.

Section 7 *may not* apply to: (1) asset acquisitions in industries, such as banking, not subject to Federal Trade Commission jurisdiction; (2) asset acquisitions completed before 1950, when the Clayton Act was amended to cover asset purchases; and (3) stock acquisitions made before enactment of the Clayton Act in 1914.

2. [§4.9] Section 1 of the Sherman Act

Section 1 of the Sherman Act (15 USC §1), which prohibits contracts, combinations, or conspiracies in restraint of trade, may also be used to invalidate mergers. Indeed, when the Sherman Act was enacted in 1890, corporate consolidations and mergers were one of its primary targets. While only a handful of antimerger cases have been brought under Section 1 of the Sherman Act since the enactment of the Clayton Act in 1914, the 1964 decision of the Supreme Court in *Lexington Bank (United States v First Nat'l. Bank and Trust Co.* (1964) 376 US 665) indicates that Section 1 will present a formidable hurdle to a merger whenever there may be a technical or procedural obstacle to applying Section 7 of the

Clayton Act (15 USC §18; see §4.8) and formulated a very strict test for judging mergers under Section 1 (376 US at 671-672):

. . . where merging companies are major competitive factors in a relevant market, the elimination of significant competition between them, by merger or consolidation, itself constitutes a violation of §1 of the Sherman Act.

See also *United States v Philadelphia Nat'l. Bank* (1963) 374 US 321. The Sherman Act applies to acquisitions or mergers of entities other than corporations, unlike Section 7 of the Clayton Act. Compare *Western Laundry and Linen Rental Co. v United States* (9th Cir 1970) 1970 Trade Cases ¶73,128. It may apply to any acquisition that results in the elimination of significant competition. See discussion of Section 1 of the Sherman Act in Chapter 2.

3. [§4.10] Section 2 of the Sherman Act

An acquisition may also result in a monopoly and therefore violate Section 2 of the Sherman Act (15 USC §2), which makes it unlawful for anyone to "monopolize, or attempt to monopolize, or combine or conspire with any other person or persons, to monopolize any part of" the interstate or foreign commerce of the United States. See discussion of monopolization at §§2.51-2.59.

4. [§4.11] Section 5 of the Federal Trade Commission Act

An acquisition or a series of acquisitions may be challenged by the Federal Trade Commission under Section 5 of the Federal Trade Commission Act (15 USC §45) as an unfair method of competition. A substantial number of FTC merger complaints include a charge under Section 5 as well as a charge under Section 7 of the Clayton Act (15 USC §18), and on a few occasions the Commission has filed a complaint under Section 5 alone. There is at least one important difference in scope between Section 7 of the Clayton Act and Section 5 of the Federal Trade Commission Act. While Section 7 applies only to corporate acquisitions, Section 5 expressly forbids unfair methods of competition on the part of persons and partnerships as well as corporations.

The Federal Trade Commission has indicated that acquisitions involving sole proprietorships or partnerships will be governed by the same standards under Section 5 as would be applicable under Section 7. *Beatrice Foods Co.* (1965) [1965-1967 Transfer Binder] Trade Reg Rep ¶17,244 at 22,335-22,336. And see *Foremost Dairies, Inc.* (1962) [1961-1963 Transfer Binder] Trade Reg Rep ¶15,877. In *Dean Foods Co.* (1966) [1965-1967 Transfer Binder] Trade Reg Rep ¶17,765, the Commission indicated that whether or not the acquired company would be a proper defendant in a charge brought under Section 7 of the Clayton Act, the purchaser and seller may both be charged with a violation of Section 5 of the Federal Trade Commission Act since the purchase agreement itself constitutes an unfair method of competition. For discussion of the Federal Trade Commission Act see Chapter 6.

5. [§4.12] State Antitrust Laws

The antitrust laws of Louisiana, Mississippi, New Jersey, and Washington have specific provisions relating to stock acquisitions. The test of legality in each instance is whether or not the acquisition will cause a substantial lessening of competition or have a tendency to create a monopoly. The Washington law also covers asset acquisitions, and the Mississippi law covers the acquisition of certain assets. In the other states, the legality of acquisitions or mergers is governed by the general provisions of their antitrust laws.

6. [§4.13] Section 8 of the Clayton Act—Corporate Interlocks

Section 8 of the Clayton Act (15 USC §19), in general, prohibits any person from serving at the same time as a director of two or more corporations which are or have been competitors in any market. The potential application of Section 8 must be considered in connection with every merger. Counsel for the acquiring corporation should review the directorates its board members hold in other corporations to determine whether any of these other corporations compete in any market with the company being acquired. Director posts on competing corporations should be resigned.

There have been relatively few reported cases under Section 8. However, it has been held that Section 8 applies only to horizontal relationships, those "between companies performing similar functions in the production or sale of comparable goods or services," and not to future or potential competition, and that "[d]e minimis competition is not encompassed by the proscription of §8." *Paramount Pictures Corp. v Baldwin-Montrose Chemical Co.* (SD NY 1966) 1966 Trade Cases ¶71,678 at 82,065. See also *United States v W. T. Grant Co.* (1953) 345 US 629; *United States v Sears, Roebuck & Co.* (SD NY 1953) 111 F Supp 614; *Treves v Servel, Inc.* (SD NY 1965) 244 F Supp 773; and *United States v Newmont Mining Corp.* (SD NY 1964) 1964 Trade Cases ¶71,030. In 1968 the Department of Justice announced that eight cases it was prepared to file challenging eleven interlocking directorates had been settled through agreement by the parties to resign from one or more directorates.

A number of consent judgments in merger cases contain provisions prohibiting the corporations involved from having any common directors. See, *e.g., United States v Third Nat'l. Bank* (MD Tenn 1968) 1968 Trade Cases ¶72,556; *United States v American Smelting and Refining Co.* (SD NY 1967) 1967 Trade Cases ¶72,003; *United States v Newmont Mining Corp.* (SD NY 1966) 1966 Trade Cases ¶71,709; *United States v Valley Nat'l. Bank* (D Ariz 1966) 1966 Trade Cases ¶71,901; and *United States v General Motors Corp.* (ED Mich 1965) 1965 Trade Cases ¶71,624.

C. [§4.14] Business Transactions Affected

The laws discussed in §§4.7-4.13 have broad possible application to mergers, stock acquisitions (including tender offers and take-overs), asset acquisitions, joint ventures, and even to partial stock acquisitions and to acquisitions of single important assets. It probably makes no difference whether the parties to an acquisition are corporations, partnerships, or sole proprietors. While Section 7 of the Clayton Act (15 USC §18) by its terms applies only if both the acquiring company and the acquired company are corporations, Section 1 of the Sherman Act (15 USC §1) and Section 5 of the Federal Trade Commission Act (15 USC §45) should cover *any* combination whether of corporations, partnerships, sole proprietorships, or any other entities. Some applications:

☐ Section 7 specifically covers the acquisition of the "whole or any part" of the assets of a corporation. While there is no definition of the term "assets" in the Clayton Act, assets have been defined as "anything of value" (*United States v Columbia Pictures Corp.* (SD NY 1960) 1960 Trade Cases ¶69,766 at 77,006) and as "property or property rights, real or personal, tangible or intangible, which is subject to transfer and which has been used by the seller and could be used by the buyer competitively." (*Farm Journal, Inc.* (1956) 53 FTC 26, 48-49, opinion of hearing examiner adopted by the Federal Trade Commission without opinion.) Patents, trademarks, registered trade names, current lists of subscribers, lists of advertisers, exclusive patent licenses, exclusive licenses to distribute copyrighted feature films, and exclusive rights to publish syndicated features have all been regarded as "assets" within the meaning of Section 7. See *United States v Lever Bros. Co.* (SD NY 1963) 216 F Supp 887; *Farm Journal Inc., supra; United States v Columbia Pictures Corp., supra; Western Geophysical Co. of America v Bolt Associates, Inc.* (D Conn 1969) 1969 Trade Cases ¶72,838;

United States v World Journal Tribune, Inc. (SD NY 1966) 1966 Trade Cases ¶71,925; and *United States v Scott Paper Co.* (ED Mich 1969) 1969 Trade Cases ¶72,919 (consent decree).

☐ Partial stock acquisitions are subject to Section 7 whether or not control has been achieved. *Vanadium Corp. of America v Susquehanna Corp.* (D Del 1962) 203 F Supp 686. Subsequent use of the stock, as well as initial acquisition, may violate Section 7. For example, voting stock to obtain minority representation on the board of directors has been prohibited under Section 7. See *Hamilton Watch Co. v Benrus Watch Co.* (D Conn 1953) 114 F Supp 307, *aff'd* (2d Cir 1953) 206 F2d 738; *American Crystal Sugar Co. v Cuban-American Sugar Co.* (2d Cir 1958) 259 F2d 524. An additional acquisition of stock in a company in which the acquiring company already owns a stock interest may also violate Section 7.

☐ Section 7 may also cover the acquisition or retention of promissory notes or other deferred obligations in another corporation. See *United States v Gould Inc.* (ND Ohio 1969) 1969 Trade Cases ¶72,863.

☐ Acquisitions of stock or assets may be indirect and still be prohibited by Section 7; the section applies whether an acquisition is accomplished by purchase, assignment, lease, license, or other means. See *United States v Columbia Pictures Corp., supra.* An acquisition may violate Section 7 because of its possible effects on competition between the acquired company and the owner of a substantial stock interest in the acquiring company. *Swingline Inc.* (1968) 3 Trade Reg Rep ¶¶18,305, 18,948. The source of funds used to finance an acquisition may also result in a violation of Section 7. *Metro-Goldwyn Mayer Inc. v Transamerica Corp.* (SD NY 1969) 303 F Supp 1344.

☐ Joint ventures involving joint control, operation, or ownership of a business may violate Section 7 of the Clayton Act or constitute a restraint of trade in violation of Section 1 of the Sherman Act (15 USC §1), or may be an unfair method of competition in violation of Section 5 of the Federal Trade Commission Act (15 USC §45), or constitute a monopolization, an attempt to monopolize, or a combination or conspiracy to monopolize trade in violation of Section 2 of the Sherman Act (15 USC §2). Furthermore, the acquisition by one partner in a joint venture of the remaining half interest in the joint venture may be unlawful. *Allied Chemical Corp.* (1968) 3 Trade Reg Rep ¶18,496 (complaint); ¶18,654 (discovery denied).

☐ An agreement between two competitors or potential competitors under which one of the partners agrees to market or distribute products of the other may likewise violate Section 7. See *United States v F.&M. Schaefer Brewing Co.* (ED NY 1969) 1969 Trade Cases ¶72,902 and 1967 Trade Cases ¶72,253. It is also possible for two firms to be charged with conspiring to acquire a third company. *OKC Corp.* (File No. 691 0637, 1969) 3 Trade Reg Rep ¶18,809.

☐ Termination of a merger agreement may not preclude the filing of a suit under Section 7. In *United States v Allied Chemical Corp.* (SD NY 1964) 1964 Trade Cases ¶71,193, the court denied a motion for summary judgment dismissing the government's complaint after the parties had terminated the merger agreement. In response to the contention that the case was rendered moot by the termination, the government claimed that the exchange of records, processes, and know-how by the parties in preparation for the planned merger might amount to a "partial acquisition of assets within the meaning of §7" (at 79,757). The case was subsequently settled by entry of a consent judgment which enjoined the defendants from utilizing any tangible or intangible assets acquired from each other during the course of merger negotiations, including know-how, secret processes, methods of operation, customer lists, and other trade secrets or proprietary data. See *United States v Allied Chemical Corp.* (SD NY 1965) 1964 Trade Cases ¶71,311.

☐ It is doubtful whether the act of offering employment contracts to management personnel of a competitor would ever be held an acquisition of "assets" in violation of Section 7 or any other antitrust statute; the strong public policy in favor of permitting an individual wide latitude in seeking employment, illustrated by the severe limitations in employment contracts on covenants not to compete, would inhibit such a holding. Analogously, in *United States v Wilson Sporting Goods Co.* (ND Ill 1968) 288 F Supp 543, 569, granting a preliminary injunction against a merger in part because divestiture might prove difficult, the court suggested (at 569) that, "Certainly no court order of divestiture would compel George Nissen to follow the assets of his former company."

☐ Internal expansion will almost always be lawful. Government spokesmen and the courts in merger cases have repeatedly emphasized that when growth through acquisition may be barred, nevertheless the same growth may be achieved through internal expansion, limited only by the antimonopoly provisions of Section 2 of the Sherman Act (15 USC §2). See *Hiland Dairy, Inc. v Kroger Co.* (8th Cir 1968) 402 F2d 968, *cert den* (1969) 395 US 961.

1. [§4.15] Interstate Commerce Requirement

Section 7 of the Clayton Act (15 USC §18) technically applies only when both the acquiring corporation and the acquired corporation are "engaged in commerce." This limitation, however, does not apply to the acquiring corporation in the case of stock acquisitions by holding companies, since the requirement does not appear in the second paragraph of Section 7. For purposes of Section 7, "commerce" is defined in Section 1 of the Clayton Act (15 USC §12) as trade or commerce among the several states and with foreign nations, or within the District of Columbia and other places under federal jurisdiction.

The Sherman Act applies to "trade or commerce among the several States, or with foreign nations," (15 USC §1) a phrase interpreted as going "to the utmost extent of its Constitutional power in restraining trust and monopoly agreements." *United States v South-Eastern Underwriters Ass'n.* (1944) 322 US 533, 558. See discussion of the commerce requirement of the Sherman Act at §2.12.

Section 5 of the Federal Trade Commission Act (15 USC §45) applies to unfair methods of competition "in commerce," the definition of which (at 15 USC §44) is similar to the definition in the Clayton Act. But unlike the situation under the Clayton Act, it is sufficient under Section 5 if only the acquiring company is engaged "in commerce"; the acquired firm may be engaged solely in intrastate operations.

Although the differences in jurisdictional requirements among the various statutes may become significant in litigation, they will have little practical significance for planning purposes. Because even minimal acts can amount to engaging in interstate commerce, it must be considered extremely unlikely for planning purposes that any acquisition that might substantially lessen competition or tend to create a monopoly will escape the antitrust laws for failure to satisfy the commerce requirement.

2. [§4.16] Effect of Foreign Commerce

Acquisitions and joint ventures between American and foreign corporations may be subject to Section 7 of the Clayton Act (15 USC §18), Sections 1 and 2 of the Sherman Act (15 USC §§1 and 2), and Section 5 of the Federal Trade Commission Act (15 USC §45).

An acquisition of a foreign company will violate Section 7 if the acquired firm is "engaged" in the foreign commerce of the United States and the effect of the acquisition is to lessen competition "in any line of commerce in any section of the country." In *United States v Jos. Schlitz Brewing Co.* (ND Calif 1966) 253 F Supp 129, *aff'd per curiam* (1966) 385 US 37, the first case challenging a foreign acquisition, Labatt, a Canadian brewer, was treated as "engaged in commerce" for purposes of Section 7 because it produced and sold a product that flowed continually into the United States. Schlitz's acquisition of 39.3% of the stock of Labatt, which in turn controlled General Brewing Co. of California, was held unlawful primarily because it would eliminate actual and potential competition between Schlitz and General Brewing Co., and also in part, because Labatt was a potential competitor in the United States. See also *United States v Standard Oil Co.* (D NJ 1966) 253 F Supp 196; *United States v Aluminium Ltd.* (D NJ 1965) 1965 Trade Cases ¶71,366.

A foreign firm will probably also be regarded as "engaged in commerce" if it buys products flowing continuously out of the United States. The "engaged in commerce" requirement may also be satisfied (1) if the acquired company is doing some business in the United States, even though not in the field in which competition may be lessened, (2) if it has granted licenses in this country from which it derives royalties, and, (3) perhaps, even if it is simply a potential competitor in the United States. See *An Interview with the Honorable Donald F. Turner* (1968) 37 ABA Antitrust LJ 290, 304.

There have also been numerous cases under both Sections 1 and 2 of the Sherman Act in which foreign acquisitions and joint ventures have played a prominent role. See, *e.g., Timken Roller Bearing Co. v United States* (1951) 341 US 593; *United States v National Lead Co.* (SD NY 1945) 63 F Supp 513, *modified and aff'd* (1947) 332 US 319; *United States v Imperial Chemical Industries, Ltd.* (SD NY 1951) 100 F Supp 504, *supp opinion on remedies* (SD NY 1952) 105 F Supp 215; *United States v Minnesota Mining & Mfg. Co.* (D Mass 1950) 92 F Supp 947, *modified* (D Mass 1951) 96 F Supp 356.

It is too early to know what standards will ultimately develop for evaluating acquisitions and joint ventures with foreign firms. It is probable that the same standards applied in judging domestic mergers and joint ventures will be applied to foreign mergers and joint ventures that have a direct effect on the domestic commerce of the United States. If the only effects of a merger or joint venture are on the foreign commerce of the United States, it is possible that more lenient standards will be established. Additional guidance may come from a handful of cases that have been filed within the past few years. See, *e.g., United States v Monsanto Chemical Co.* (WD Pa 1967) 1967 Trade Cases ¶72,001; *United States v Gillette Co.* (D Mass 1968) 5 CCH Trade Reg Rep ¶45,068 (case 1988); *Litton Industries, Inc.* (1969) 3 Trade Reg Rep ¶18,729 and 18,828.

For further discussion, see Brewster, *Antitrust and American Business Abroad* (1958); Fugate, *Foreign Commerce and the Antitrust Laws* (1958);

and Surrey and Shaw, *A Lawyer's Guide to International Business Transactions* 619–637.

Problems of extraterritorial jurisdiction, jurisdiction in personam, and difficulties of enforcement are beyond the scope of this chapter.

3. [§4.17] Exemption for Purchasing Stock for Investment

Section 7 of the Clayton Act (15 USC §18) does not "apply to corporations purchasing . . . stock solely for investment and not using the same by voting or otherwise to bring about, or in attempting to bring about, the substantial lessening of competition." This so-called exemption for the purchase of stock "solely for investment" has been severely limited and has been of little practical significance.

The intentions of the acquirer's present management in making the stock investment will not necessarily be determinative; the decision will probably turn on whether, objectively, the company whose stock is acquired is likely to be influenced in its dealings with the acquirer. The courts have considered such factors as the absence of an investment portfolio, the liquidity normally desirable in an ordinary investment, the relationship between the amount of stock acquired and the amount of stock normally traded, and the amount paid for the stock. See, *e.g.*, *American Crystal Sugar Co. v Cuban-American Sugar Co.* (SD NY 1957) 152 F Supp 387, *aff'd* (2d Cir 1958) 259 F2d 524; *Hamilton Watch Co. v Benrus Watch Co.* (D Conn 1953) 114 F Supp 307, *aff'd* (2d Cir 1953) 206 F2d 738.

The exemption may not be relied on as the basis for acquiring a controlling interest or any substantial minority interest in a company if the outright acquisition of the company might be in violation of Section 7. Nor will the exemption protect an acquisition of a minority stock interest if the acquiring company has actually exerted its influence to become or to entrench itself as a primary supplier or customer of the company whose stock was acquired or to achieve a closer relationship with a competitor. See *United States v E.I. du Pont de Nemours & Co.* (1957) 353 US 586; *United States v Jerrold Electronics Corp.* (ED Pa 1960) 187 F Supp 545, *aff'd per curiam* (1961) 365 US 567; *Briggs Mfg. Co. v Crane Co.* (ED Mich 1960) 185 F Supp 177, *aff'd* (6th Cir 1960) 280 F2d 747; *Hamilton Watch Co. v Benrus Watch Co., supra.*

An acquisition of a minority stock interest may also be vulnerable if it is reasonably likely to result in representation on the company's board of directors. In a number of the cases cited in this section, it has been suggested that board representation is inconsistent with unrestrained competition between the firms or that it would be likely to limit the effectiveness of competition.

The investment exemption is more likely to be available to protect an acquisition of a minority stock interest in a company if some other single shareholder owns a majority interest in the company. See *Golden Grain Macaroni Co.* (1969) 3 Trade Reg Rep ¶18,768 (initial opinion of hearing examiner). Noncontrolling interests ranging from 22% to 25% have been successfully challenged in at least three cases. See *Briggs Mfg. Co. v Crane Co., supra; American Crystal Sugar Co. v Cuban-American Sugar Co., supra;* and *Hamilton Watch Co. v Benrus Watch Co., supra.* In *United States v Newmont Mining Corp.* (SD NY 1966) 1966 Trade Cases ¶71,709, which was settled by the entry of a consent judgment, the government challenged a stock acquisition resulting in an ownership interest of less than 3%.

In general, almost any corporate purchase of stock for investment may be challenged under Section 7 of the Clayton Act if the corporation acquiring the minority stock interest is likely to exert some influence on the corporation in whose stock it has invested. The investment exemption will probably be available, if at all, for relatively insubstantial stock investments when the acquiring firm is seeking solely passive financial participation, and there appears to be no danger whatsoever that management of the acquired firm will be influenced as a result of the investment or that the firm making the investment will gain access to any confidential information.

While the investment exemption may not normally be relied on for purposes of planning a stock acquisition, there will be no harm in pleading the exemption as an affirmative defense if a suit is brought. Indeed, in a number of conglomerate merger cases, including Ling-Temco-Vought-Jones & Laughlin (5 Trade Reg Rep ¶45,069 at 52,712 (case 2045)) the defense has been pleaded even when the acquired stock was a majority interest in the acquired company.

4. [§4.18] Exemption for Forming Subsidiary Corporations

Section 7 of the Clayton Act (15 USC §18) expressly does not "prevent a corporation engaged in commerce from causing the formation of subsidiary corporations for the actual carrying on of their immediate lawful business, or the natural and legitimate branches or extensions thereof, or from owning and holding all or a part of the stock of such subsidiary corporations, when the effect of such formation is not to substantially lessen competition." While the language of this exemption contains the restriction that the effect of such formation is not to substantially lessen competition, no significance has been attached to this limitation. A corporation has virtually complete immunity in establishing subsidiary corporations to conduct its business.

5. [§4.19] Partial Exemption for Certain Regulated Industries

Section 7 (15 USC §18) does not apply to

transactions duly consummated pursuant to authority given by the Civil Aeronautics Board, Federal Communications Commission, Federal Power Commission, Interstate Commerce Commission, the Securities and Exchange Commission in the exercise of its jurisdiction under [§10 of the Public Utility Holding Company Act of 1935, 15 USC § 79], the United States Maritime Commission, or the Secretary of Agriculture under any statutory provision vesting such power in such Commission, Secretary, or Board.

A merger with or acquisition by a corporation subject to regulation by one of the listed agencies will be exempt from Section 7 only if it is "duly consummated pursuant to authority given" by the agency "under any statutory provision vesting such power" in the agency. A detailed discussion of the various regulatory statutes these agencies enforce is beyond the scope of this chapter. For further discussion of the application of Section 7 to regulated industries, see *Antitrust and the Regulated and Exempt Industries* (1961) 19 ABA Antitrust Section 261; *Antitrust Exemptions* (1967) 33 ABA Antitrust LJ 1.

6. [§4.20] Exemption for Approved Bank Mergers

Each year the Department of Justice files a number of complaints challenging bank mergers. *United States v Philadelphia Nat'l. Bank* (1963) 374 US 321 held that Section 7 of the Clayton Act (15 USC §18) applied to the merger of two commercial banks; a district court recently held that it is equally applicable to nonstock mutual savings banks. *United States v Chelsea Savings Bank* (D Conn 1969) 300 F Supp 721. Mergers between even relatively small banks may be subject to attack. See *United States v Phillipsburg Nat'l. Bank* (1970) 399 US 350.

Every merger or acquisition by a bank must be approved by one of the three bank regulatory agencies. Before approving an acquisition (except in certain emergency conditions) the responsible agency is required to request reports on the competitive factors from the Attorney General and the other two banking agencies. These reports must be furnished within thirty days from the date on which they are requested. Anyone wanting to oppose a bank merger may submit comments to the responsible agency or one of the other banking agencies or may complain to the Department of Justice.

Under the terms of the Bank Merger Act of 1966 (12 USC §1828(c)), no bank merger may be consummated (except in certain emergency situations) until thirty days after the merger has been approved by the responsible agency. Any action under the antitrust laws to challenge the merger must be commenced within this period, and the commencement of the action will automatically stay the consummation of the merger unless the court otherwise specifically orders.

Under the act, no bank merger whose effect "may be substantially to lessen competition" may be approved unless the agency finds the anticompetitive effects to be "clearly outweighed in the public interest by the probable effect of the transaction in meeting the convenience and needs of the community to be served." (12 USC §1828(c)(5)(B)) While the precise scope of this so-called "convenience and needs" defense has not yet been determined, the Supreme Court has held that the merging banks have the burden of proving that a merger which may substantially lessen competition should nevertheless be permitted under this defense. *United States v First City Nat'l. Bank* (1967) 386 US 361. On the scope of the "convenience and needs" defense, see, also, *United States v Third Nat'l. Bank* (1968) 390 US 171; *United States v Provident Nat'l. Bank* (ED Pa 1968) 280 F Supp 1; and *United States v Crocker-Anglo Nat'l. Bank* (ND Calif 1967) 277 F Supp 133. A full discussion of bank mergers is beyond the scope of this chapter.

D. Standards for Evaluating Legality of Mergers

1. [§4.21] Introduction

The evaluation of a proposed acquisition for antitrust purposes should begin with the "policy statements," if relevant, issued by the Federal Trade Commission for certain industries (see §4.22) and the merger guidelines issued by the Department of Justice (§4.23). To apply the Commission's industry guidelines or the department's general guidelines, counsel will need to determine the relevant markets and the degree of concentration in the market. Standards are set out in the guidelines and the case law. See §§4.24-4.26.

After analyzing the proposed acquisition in relation to the guidelines, counsel should review the cases that relate to the type of acquisition. See §§4.27-4.37. He should consider whether any judicial trends indicate that the courts, particularly the Supreme Court, may now view the acquisition differently. See §4.50.

After reviewing the possible bases for suit, counsel should also consider whether any defenses may be available. See §§4.38-4.41. Finally, counsel should attempt to assess the likelihood of suit (see §§4.42–4.50) and seek to minimize the possibility. See §§4.51–4.53.

2. [§4.22] FTC Industry Guidelines

To date the Federal Trade Commission has issued four formal statements of enforcement policy, or "industry" guidelines. They apply to:

1. Vertical mergers in the cement industry. Federal Trade Commission, *Commission Enforcement Policy with Respect to Vertical Mergers in the Cement Industry* (January 3, 1967) 1 Trade Reg Rep ¶4510. See Liekeler, *Toward a Consumer's Antitrust Law: The Federal Trade Commission and Vertical Mergers in the Cement Industry* (1968) 15 *UCLA L Rev* 1153; Peck and McGowan, *Vertical Integration in Cement: A Critical Examination of the FTC Staff Report* (1967) 12 *Antitrust Bulletin* 505.

2. Mergers in the food distribution industries. *Commission Enforcement Policy with Respect to Mergers in the Food Distribution Industries* (January 3, 1967) 1 Trade Reg Rep ¶4520.

3. Product extension mergers in grocery products manufacturing. Federal Trade Commission, *Commission Enforcement Policy with Respect to Product Extension Mergers in Grocery Products Manufacturing* (May 15, 1968) 1 Trade Reg Rep ¶4530.

4. Mergers in the textile mill products industry. Federal Trade Commission, *Commission Enforcement Policy with Respect to Mergers in the Textile Mill Products Industry* (November 22, 1968) 1 Trade Reg Rep ¶4540.

In 1965 the Commission established informal guidelines for mergers in the dairy products industry in an opinion in *Beatrice Foods Co.* (1965) Trade Reg Rep ¶17,244. The Commission's staff, in a 1966 report, proposed guidelines for mergers by automotive tire producers, but these guidelines have not been adopted by the Commission. Staff Report to the Federal Trade Commission, *Economic Report on the Manufacture and Distribution of Automotive Tires* (Government Printing Office, 1966). The Commission's staff has also published an economic report on the baking industry. Staff Report to the Federal Trade Commission, *Economic Report on the Baking Industry* (Government Printing Office, 1967); see 3 Trade Reg Rep ¶10,370. The Commission has also announced that it is conducting an investigation of acquisitions of independent gasoline marketers and refiner-marketers by major oil companies. FTC Release (July 29, 1969) 3 Trade Reg Rep ¶10,120. .

The legal status and effect of the four formal statements of enforcement policy are unclear. In issuing each policy statement the Commission has emphasized that firms subject to its policy statement are not required to seek Commission approval (advance notice must be given of certain mergers or acquisitions in the cement and food industries) before consummating a prospective merger or acquisition, but that it would continue to provide advisory opinions on the legality of particular mergers for firms that want them.

In reaffirming its enforcement policy on mergers in the textile mill products industry, the Commission has stated that the policy statements do not attempt to draw precise legal boundaries for every prospective merger, but that their purpose is to identify the types of future mergers "which appear to require the Commission's attention in the discharge of its statutory responsibilities." Federal Trade Commission, *Statement Reaffirming and Clarifying its Enforcement Policy with Respect to Mergers in the Textile Mill Products Industry* (FTC News Release, August 18, 1969) 1 Trade Reg Rep ¶4540.10. In a dissenting statement Commissioner Jones contended that "the Commission's clarification statement furnishes what to me is a new interpretation of guidelines which so far as I know has never before been the basis for issuing merger guidelines in a given industry," and she criticized "the ambiguity now interjected by the Commission into exactly what it intends these guidelines to mean for the industry." In her view, "If guidelines were simply an indication of what industries were to be examined by the Commission and no more, then their issuance would constitute a real deception on the business community since in fact the Commission staff screens most mergers involving companies whose assets are in excess of $10 million." According to Commissioner Jones, the "publication of guidelines for a given industry was intended as a statement on the part of the Commission that mergers in these industries of the type covered by the guidelines would in all probability be *challenged* by the Commission."

At a minimum, the Commission's statements of enforcement policy tell firms in covered industries what kinds of mergers the Commission is concerned about. As a practical matter, it is unlikely that a merger failing to satisfy the guidelines will be allowed unless there are clearly mitigating circumstances.

The publication of a statement of enforcement policy has been held not to establish prejudgment on the part of the Commission of the issues raised in a particular case, and motions to transfer a merger proceeding to the Department of Justice and to dismiss a merger complaint on this basis have been denied. See *Lehigh Portland Cement Co. v FTC* (ED Va 1968) 291 F Supp 628, *aff'd* (4th Cir 1969) 416 F2d 971, and *Missouri Portland Cement Co.* (1969) 3 Trade Reg Rep ¶18,805.

For a discussion of the overall purpose of the FTC merger guidelines, see Elman, *Rulemaking Procedures in the F.T.C.'s Enforcement of the Merger Law* (1964) 78 *Harv L Rev* 385. See also Friendly, *The Federal Administrative Agencies: The Need for Better Definition of Standards* (Harvard, 1962).

3. [§4.23] Department of Justice Merger Guidelines

On May 30, 1968, during the tenure of former Assistant Attorney General Donald F. Turner, the Department of Justice issued "merger guidelines" describing the standards used in determining whether to challenge corporate acquisitions and mergers under Section 7 of the Clayton Act (15 USC §18). See 1 Trade Reg Rep ¶4430. The guidelines are framed in general terms and apply to all mergers and acquisitions.

In a press release announcing the merger guidelines, former Attorney General Ramsey Clark indicated that the Department of Justice expected to amend the guidelines from time to time to reflect changes in enforcement policy that might result from subsequent court decisions, comments of interested parties, or department reevaluations. He said that changes in enforcement policy would be made as the occasion demanded and would usually precede the issuance of amended guidelines. Therefore, "the existence of unamended guidelines should not be regarded as barring [the Department] from taking any action it deems necessary to achieve the purposes of Section 7." It was further stated that the guidelines should not be treated as a substitute for the department's business review procedures, under which businessmen may obtain a statement of the department's present enforcement intentions concerning a particular proposed merger or acquisition. (Department of Justice Press Release, May 30, 1968.)

In an address given March 6, 1969, before the National Industrial Conference Board, the present Assistant Attorney General, Richard W. McLaren, stated:

The Guidelines furnish an excellent checklist for analyzing mergers in terms of Section 7. They pinpoint clearly *bad* mergers, but they do not necessarily identify *all* mergers that will be attacked. I hope soon to be able to indicate, at least in a general way, additional signs or factors which will give warning of likely prosecution of mergers which presently appear not to violate the Guidelines.

On March 27, 1969, he said to the Antitrust Section of the American Bar Association:

As a final point—and again I am repeating what I have said in other forums— the Merger Guidelines issued last May provide an excellent framework for analysis, and they will provide a pretty firm "no" answer in many cases. But in the conglomerate field; in industries with large capital requirements and difficult conditions of entry; and in cases where there are borderline situations horizontally and/or vertically and/or on reciprocity grounds, let me again urge you to take advantage of the Business Review Procedure.

Assistant Attorney General McLaren has further cautioned that he is "not persuaded that Section 7 will not reach purer types of conglomerate mergers than have been dealt with by the courts thus far." In this spirit he has "tried to warn businessmen and their lawyers that they cannot rely on the Merger Guidelines issued by my predecessors in this area—that we may sue even though particular mergers appear to satisfy those Guidelines—and that, to be safe, firms desiring to merge should learn our enforcement intentions by applying for a Business Review letter." (Statement by Richard W. McLaren, Assistant Attorney General, Antitrust Division, before the House Ways and Means Committee, March 12, 1969. See 5 Trade Reg Rep ¶50,233 at 55,465.)

On June 6, 1969, Attorney General Mitchell announced in an address to the Georgia Bar Association that the Department of Justice will probably challenge mergers in three situations that "some may regard . . . as something of an expansion of the published antimerger Guidelines of the Department," stating (6 Ga St BJ 92, 96 (1969):

The Department of Justice may very well oppose any merger among the top 200 manufacturing firms or firms of comparable size in other industries.

The Department of Justice will probably oppose any merger [sic] by one of the top 200 manufacturing firms of any leading producer in any concentrated industry.

And, of course, the Department will continue to challenge mergers which may substantially lessen potential competition or develop a substantial potential for reciprocity.

See §§4.29–4.36.

The courts have agreed with the Department's statement of the legal effect of the merger guidelines. In *United States v Atlantic Richfield Co.* (SD NY 1969) 297 F Supp 1061, 1073, the defendants opposed the government's motion for a preliminary injunction against the proposed merger of Sinclair Oil Company and Atlantic Richfield Company in part on the ground that the Department's merger guidelines suggested that a merger resulting in market shares of this size would ordinarily not be challenged. The court held:

The purpose of the Guidelines is "to insure that the business community, the legal profession and other interested persons are informed of the Department's policy of enforcing Section 7 of the Clayton Act." However, they are in no way binding on the Department in a particular case and the Department is entitled to evaluate each case on the basis of its own facts and the varied factors that must be taken into consideration. Indeed, the Department has available a business review procedure which, as the Guidelines point out, "make available statements of the Department's present enforcement intentions with regard to particular proposed mergers or acquisitions." The defendants did not avail themselves of the review procedure here.

It will not be a defense, therefore, when the Department challenges a merger, that the merger is permissible under the Department's guidelines. But this circumstance may be influential in helping to persuade a court that a particular merger is not anticompetitive.

The legal effect of the merger guidelines was discussed in *Allis-Chalmers Mfg. Co. v White Consolidated Industries, Inc.* (3d Cir 1969) 1969 Trade Cases ¶72,856, at 87,200–87,201; *United States v Northwest Industries, Inc.* (ND Ill 1969) 301 F Supp 1066, 1084; *United States v International Telephone and Telegraph Corp.* (D Conn 1969) 306 F Supp 766, 1969 Trade Cases ¶72,943; and *United States v Wilson Sporting Goods Co.* (ND Ill 1968) 288 F Supp 543, 550 n. 14.

4. [§4.24] Sources for Defining Relevant Market

Section 7 of the Clayton Act (15 USC §18) prohibits mergers "in any line of commerce in any section of the country" if the effect of the merger is a substantial lessening of competition. It was clear, at least before *United States v Pabst Brewing Co.* (1966) 384 US 546, that a determination of the relevant product and geographic market was necessary before it could be known whether an acquisition substantially lessened competition. Thus, in *Brown Shoe Co. v United States* (1962) 370 US 294, 324, the Supreme Court, quoting from *United States v E.I. du Pont de Nemours & Co.* (1957) 353 US 586, 593, reiterated that:

[D]etermination of the relevant market is a necessary predicate to a finding of a violation of the Clayton Act because the threatened monopoly must be one which will substantially lessen competition "within the area of effective competition." Substantiality can be determined only in terms of the market affected. The "area of effective competition" must be determined by reference to a product market (the "line of commerce") and a geographic market (the "section of the country").

Language in *Pabst* suggests that the Court's position may be changing. For discussion, see §4.25–4.26. But market definition has been and will probably continue to be a major battleground in most merger cases. The government has almost invariably been successful in gaining Supreme

Court acceptance of its market definition, so much so that on one occasion Mr. Justice Fortas accused the Court of approving a "strange, red-haired, bearded, one-eyed man-with-a-limp classification" (*United States v Grinnell Corp.* (1966) 384 US 563, 591 (dissenting opinion). But with changes in membership, it would not be surprising to see the Court begin to insist on a more precise delineation of the relevant market than it has in the past. This is an area in which the facts in each case will be crucial. In many cases it will be advisable at the outset to retain one or more well-qualified economists to aid in defining the relevant markets.

After determining the relevant market, it will be necessary to obtain data on the size of the market and the market shares of the leading firms. Paragraph 3 of the merger guidelines (see §4.23) states that a market should ordinarily be measured primarily by "the dollar value of the sales or other transactions (*e.g.*, shipments, leases) for the most recent twelve-month period for which the necessary figures for the merging firms and their competitors are generally available." 1 Trade Reg Rep ¶4430 at 6683. In some markets, the guidelines indicate that it may be more appropriate to measure the market by other indicia, such as total deposits in commercial banking.

It may be difficult to obtain market data. The Federal Trade Commission's premerger notification special report form asks for information on the value of shipments broken down according to 4-digit SIC code and 7-digit Census product code. Statistics published by the government showing market data broken down on this basis may provide one source of information, particularly in determining the degree of concentration of the market, although it may be several years old. *Concentration Ratios in Manufacturing Industry* (1963), Subcommittee on Antitrust and Monopoly of the Committee on the Judiciary, U.S. Senate, 89th Cong., 2d Sess. Industry trade journals may also contain market data. Finally, the client may have made some market surveys. These sources should be consulted first, and the client should also be asked to furnish his estimates of the total size of the market and the share occupied by each of the 8 to 10 largest sellers.

a. [§4.25] Definition of Relevant Product Market

The Department's guidelines (1 Trade Reg Rep ¶4430 at 6682) establish the following criteria for identifying the relevant product market or the "line of commerce" (par. 3(i)):

The sales of any product or service which is distinguishable as a matter of commercial practice from other products or services will ordinarily constitute a relevant product market, even though, from the standpoint of most purchasers, other products may be reasonably, but not perfectly, interchangeable with it in terms of price, quality, and use. On the other hand, the sales of two distinct products to a particular group of purchasers can also appropriately be grouped into a single market where the two products are reasonably interchangeable for that group in terms of price, quality, and use. In this latter case, however, it may be necessary also to include in that market the sales of one or more other products which are equally interchangeable with the two products in terms of price, quality, and use from the standpoint of that group of purchasers for whom the two products are interchangeable.

The "reasonably interchangeable" test for determining broad product markets is traceable to *United States v E.I. du Pont de Nemours & Co.* (1956) 351 US 377. This test has been utilized by the government to expand the product market in order to find a competitive overlap. For example, in *United States v Continental Can Co.* (1964) 378 US 441, the district court dismissed the complaint on the ground that glass and metal containers constituted separate lines of commerce and hence a merger between a producer of metal containers and a producer of glass containers could have no significant effect upon competition in either line of commerce. The Supreme Court reversed, holding that although metal containers and glass containers were from separate industries, interindustry competition made them part of one combined product market for the purposes of evaluating the merger.

However, reasonable interchangeability alone has not been a sufficient basis for including two or more products in the same submarket. In *Brown Shoe Co. v United States* (1962) 370 US 294, 325, the Supreme Court ruled that there may be both broad markets whose outer boundaries "are determined by the reasonable interchangeability of use or the cross-elasticity of demand between the products it sells and substitutes for it," and, within such broad markets, "well defined sub-markets . . . which in themselves, constitute the product markets for antitrust purposes." According to *Brown Shoe*, a narrow market or a separate submarket may be identified by applying seven tests:

[1] industry or public recognition of the sub-market as a separate economic entity, [2] the product's peculiar characteristics and uses, [3] unique production facilities, [4] distinct customers, [5] distinct prices, [6] sensitivity to price changes, and [7] specialized vendors.

To date these tests for determining a submarket have been rather strictly applied. For example, in *United States v Aluminum Co. of America* (1964) 377 US 271, the Court held that aluminum conductor constituted a separate line of commerce, although aluminum and copper conductor were functionally interchangeable, since there were significant price differentials between aluminum and copper conductor, their prices did not respond to one another, and one was regularly used for overhead wiring whereas the other was regularly used for underground wiring. See also *FTC v Proctor & Gamble Co.* (1967) 386 US 568, 571, in which the Court held that household liquid bleach is "a distinctive product with no close substitutes."

The only case in which the government's attempt to invalidate a merger was defeated by the existence of reasonably interchangeable substitute products is *United States v Columbia Pictures Corp.* (SD NY 1960) 189 F Supp 153; that case was not appealed and was decided before the Supreme Court ruled in the *Brown Shoe* case.

b. [§4.26] Definition of Relevant Geographic Market

The merger guidelines of the Department of Justice state (1 Trade Reg Rep ¶4430 at 6683) the following criteria for identifying the relevant geographic market or appropriate "section of the country" (Par. 3(ii)):

The total sales of a product or service in any commercially significant section of the country (even as small as a single community), or aggregate of such sections, will ordinarily constitute a geographic market if firms engaged in selling the product make significant sales of the product to purchasers in the section or sections. The market need not be enlarged beyond any section meeting the foregoing test unless it clearly appears that there is no economic barrier (*e.g.*, significant transportation costs, lack of distribution facilities, customer inconvenience, or established consumer preference for existing products) that hinders the sale from outside the section to purchasers within the section; nor need the market be contracted to exclude some portion of the product sales made inside any section meeting the foregoing test unless it clearly appears that the portion of sales in question is made to a group of purchasers separated by a substantial economic barrier from the purchasers to whom the rest of the sales are made.

These criteria follow closely the government's argument in the Supreme Court in *United States v Pabst Brewing Co.* (1966) 384 US 546; the Justice Department argued that in order to establish an appropriate section of the country, "it need show only (1) that both the acquired and acquiring firm made substantial sales to customers located in that section, and (2) that there is reason to believe that sellers whose sales were not included in the market suffer from some disadvantages in competing with those whose sales were included." (Brief for the Department of Justice, pages 15-16.) According to the government, disadvantages that may prevent sellers from competing on equal terms include high freight costs, unavailability of adequate distribution facilities, area brand preferences that would be expensive and time-consuming to overcome, and other obstacles of a similar character.

In its brief in *Pabst*, the Department stated (at 14) that the purpose of defining a market is to make possible an intelligent appraisal of the competitive significance of a merger's effects. In its decision, the Court stated (384 US at 549-50):

> Certainly the failure of the Government to prove by an army of expert witnesses what constitutes a relevant "economic" or "geographic" market is not an adequate ground on which to dismiss a §7 case. . . . Congress did not seem to be troubled about the exact spot where competition might be lessened; it simply intended to outlaw mergers which threatened competition in *any* or all parts of the country. Proof of the section of the country where the anticompetitive effect exists is entirely subsidiary to the crucial question in this and every §7 case which is whether a merger may substantially lessen competition *anywhere* in the United States. (Emphasis added)

The Court's approach to geographic market definition in *Pabst* appears to be a departure from the approach it had previously followed. See, *e.g.*, *Brown Shoe Co. v United States* (1962) 370 US 294, at 336; *United States v Philadelphia Nat'l. Bank* (1963) 374 US 321, 359.

Its merger guidelines seem to indicate that the Department of Justice will not accept the Court's invitation in *Pabst* to dispense with proof of a relevant geographic market, and it is not clear what effect will be given to the Supreme Court's holding. A definitive resolution will probably have to await a further test in the Supreme Court. The lower courts have interpreted *Pabst* differently. In *United States v Provident Nat'l. Bank* (ED Pa 1968) 280 F Supp 1, 6, the district court ruled that *Pabst* "did away with the requirement that Courts . . . had to decide upon an appropriate geographic market as a preliminary step in discovering whether a merger was anticompetitive." On the other hand, in *United States v Crocker-Anglo Nat'l. Bank* (ND Calif 1967) 277 F Supp 133, the district court held (at 170-171, n. 29) that *Pabst* should be limited to its facts and undertook a detailed analysis of the geographic market.

The Department in its merger guidelines makes it clear that it believes it proper to challenge "any merger which appears to be illegal in any reasonable geographic market, even though in another reasonable market it would not appear to be illegal."

In past merger cases, national, regional, and local markets have been selected as appropriate sections of the country. In *Brown Shoe* the relevant geographic market at the manufacturing level was held to be the entire nation, while at the retail level the relevant geographic market was found to be cities "with a population exceeding 10,000 and its immediate contiguous surrounding territory in which both Brown and Kinney sold shoes at retail through stores they either owned or controlled" (370 US at 337).

Counsel will often have to rely primarily on his client for the information necessary to determine the relevant market or markets and for market-share data. There may be no time for independent investigation and no available published statistics. In discussions with his client counsel should stress the obvious fact that his advice on the legality of a proposed merger can be no better than the market data on which it is based. Therefore, it will be in the client's best interest to furnish the most reliable possible market information, and the client should be prepared to accept responsibility for the accuracy of this information.

5. [§4.27] Criteria for Horizontal Mergers

Horizontal mergers are mergers between direct competitors. According to paragraph 4 of the Merger Guidelines of the Department of Justice (1 Trade Reg Rep ¶4430 at 6683; see §4.23) the government's enforcement of Section 7 of the Clayton Act (15 USC §18) against horizontal mergers has the following purposes: (1) preventing elimination as an independent business entity of any company likely to have been a substantial competitive influence in a market; (2) preventing any company or small group of companies from obtaining a position of dominance in a market; (3) preventing significant increases in concentration in a market; and (4) preserving significant possibilities for eventual deconcentration in a concentrated market.

In appraising horizontal mergers, the Department accords primary significance to the size of the market share held by both the acquiring and the acquired firms. Market-share statistics are appraised in light of the concentration and concentration trends in the market.

In a "highly concentrated" market, defined as one in which the shares of the four largest firms amount to 75% or more of the market, the Department of Justice will ordinarily challenge mergers between concerns that account for the following percentages of the market:

Acquiring Firm	Acquired Firm
4%	4% or more
10%	2% or more
15% or more	1% or more

In a "less highly concentrated" market, defined as one in which the shares of the four largest firms amount to less than 75% of the market, the Department will ordinarily challenge mergers between concerns that account for the following percentages of the market:

Acquiring Firm	Acquired Firm
5%	5% or more
10%	4% or more
15%	3% or more
20%	2% or more
25% or more	1% or more

According to the guidelines, percentages not shown in the above tables should be interpolated proportionately to the percentages that are shown. Merger Guidelines, pars. 5 and 6, *supra* at 6683–6684.

In a "market with a trend toward concentration," the Department of Justice applies stricter standards than those applicable to "less highly concentrated" markets. A trend toward increased concentration will be considered to be present "when the aggregate market share of any grouping of the largest firms in the market from the two largest to the eight largest has increased by approximately 7% or more of the market over a period of time extending from any base year 5–10 years prior to the merger (excluding any year in which some abnormal fluctuation in market shares occurred) up to the time of the merger." If a trend toward increased concentration is present, the merger guidelines indicate that "The Department will ordinarily challenge any acquisition, by any firm in a grouping of such largest firms showing the requisite increase in market share, of any firm whose market share amounts to approximately 2% or more." Merger Guidelines, paragraph 7, *supra* at 6684.

In addition, the merger guidelines describe two nonmarket-share standards for challenging horizontal mergers. These are: (a) an acquisition of a competitor who is a particularly "disturbing," "disruptive," or otherwise unusually competitive factor in the market; and (b) a merger between a substantial firm and a firm which, despite an insubstantial market share, possesses an unusual competitive potential or has an asset that confers an unusual competitive advantage (for example, the acquisition by a leading firm of a newcomer having a patent on a significantly improved product or production process). Merger Guidelines, paragraph 8, *supra* at 6684.

The standards established for horizontal mergers in the merger guidelines are pretty much in line with the market shares that the Supreme Court and lower courts have held to be illegal. Indeed, some decisions have gone beyond the guidelines in invalidating mergers.

Like the merger guidelines, the Supreme Court has stressed market-share statistics, concentration ratios, and industry concentration trends in its decisions on horizontal mergers. The Court has given little consideration to other elements of market structure and performance, such as ease of entry, the strength of the remaining competitors, the character of supply and demand in the market, the vigor of competition in the industry, and "other characteristics" of the industry—factors that it had considered in its pre-1950 decision in *United States v Columbia Steel Co.* (1948) 334 US 495 and referred to in *Brown Shoe Co. v United States* (1962) 370 US 294.

Even in *Brown Shoe*, the Court relied primarily on market-share data in appraising the merger's effects, suggesting that even relatively small combined shares could violate Section 7; the Court said that even in a highly fragmented industry, a merger of competing retailers occupying as little as 5% of a market might be unlawful (370 US at 343–344).

In *United States v Philadelphia Nat'l. Bank* (1963) 374 US 321, 363, the Court announced a simplified test, relying principally upon market shares and market concentration, for judging the legality of horizontal mergers:

> . . . a merger which produces a firm controlling an undue percentage share of the relevant market, and results in a significant increase in the concentration of firms in that market, is so inherently likely to lessen competition substantially that it must be enjoined in the absence of evidence clearly showing that the merger is not likely to have such anticompetitive effects.

While the Court did not fix precise numerical standards for applying this test, it cited the writings of economists who had recommended a 20 to 25% combined share and a 7 to 8% increase in concentration as lines of prima facie illegality (374 US at 364 n. 41), and held presumptively unlawful a merger that would have resulted in a bank with over 30% of the market, with the four largest banks occupying 75% of the market. 334 US at 331.

The simplified test announced in *Philadelphia Bank* has been followed in a number of subsequent cases. *United States v Continental Can Co.* (1964) 378 US 441 held illegal prima facie a merger in which the acquiring firm had 21.9% and the acquired firm 3.1% of a market in which the six largest firms had 70.1% of the business.

In *United States v Aluminum Co. of America* (1964) 377 US 271, acquisition of Rome Cable, a firm occupying only 1.3% of a concentrated market, by a firm occupying 27.8% was held to be illegal. In response to the objection that the acquisition increased Alcoa's share of the market by only a small amount, the Court stressed the importance of small but significant competitors in preventing the development of "parallel policies of mutual advantage" or oligopolistic behavior. The Court found that Rome Cable was an "aggressive competitor" and a "pioneer" in aluminum insulation and that it had a "special aptitude and skill" in insulation and an "active and efficient research and sales organization." The Court concluded (377 US at 281):

> Preservation of Rome, rather than its absorption by one of the giants, will keep it "as an important competitive factor," . . . Rome seems to us the prototype of the small independent that Congress aimed to preserve by §7.

In *United States v Von's Grocery Co.* (1966) 384 US 270, the Court found a trend toward concentration on the basis of a reduction of the number of firms competing in the market, and held that a merger between the third and sixth largest retail grocery chains in the Los Angeles metropolitan area, resulting in a firm with approximately 7.5% of the market, was illegal.

In *United States v Pabst Brewing Co.* (1966) 384 US 546, the Court held that the government had established a prima facie case of illegality in each of the three distinct geographic markets, where the acquisition by Pabst of Blatz resulted in combined beer sales of 23.95% in Wisconsin, 11.32% in the three-state Wisconsin-Illinois-Michigan area, and 4.49% of nationwide sales. The Court found that concentration was increasing and indicated that it was irrelevant that the trend to concentration was not shown to have been due to mergers, stating: "a trend toward concentration in an industry, whatever its causes, is a highly relevant factor in deciding how substantial the anti-competitive effect of a merger may be." (384 US at 552–553.)

The above decisions signify that almost any merger between viable competitors occurring in an industry already marked by a trend toward concentration may be unlawful. In *United States v Atlantic Richfield Co.* (SD NY 1969) 297 F Supp 1061, a preliminary injunction was granted to restrain a proposed merger between firms with market shares of approximately 5% and 2.3%. Although the top four firms accounted for only 43.4% of the market, the court found that there was a trend toward industry concentration. In *H.C. Bohack Co.* (1968) 3 Trade Reg Rep ¶18,443, the Federal Trade Commission challenged the acquisition by one New York grocery chain of another; the two chains had market shares in the New York area of 2.92% and .88%, respectively. The Commission has also recently refused to grant clearance for a proposed merger between grocery retailing corporations with 18% or 20% and 1.5% of the same metropolitan market; the four leading firms accounted for 57% of the market. (FTC Advisory Opinion Digest No. 344 (May 2, 1969) 3 Trade Reg Rep ¶18,570.)

Any advice on a prospective horizontal acquisition must recognize that virtually every horizontal merger *may* be held to be unlawful *if* challenged. Even compliance with the guidelines issued by the Federal Trade Commission or the Department of Justice will not provide immunity from attack, although the likelihood of attack will be relatively slight unless the firms are large, or there is potential competition.

6. [§4.28] Criteria for Vertical Mergers

Vertical mergers are mergers between firms in a supplier-purchaser relationship. A vertical acquisition may be "backward" into a supplying market or "forward" into a purchasing market.

The merger guidelines of the Department of Justice indicate that an appraisal of a vertical merger requires consideration of the probable competitive consequences of the merger in both the market in which the supplying firm sells and the market in which the purchasing firm sells. A significant adverse effect in either market will ordinarily result in a challenge by the Department. According to the guidelines (1 Trade Reg Rep ¶4430 at 6685), vertical mergers may lessen competition by raising the barriers to entry in the market of the supplying firm or the purchasing firm, or both, or by artificially inhibiting the expansion of presently competing sellers in either or both markets, in the following ways, among others (par. 11):

(i) by foreclosing equal access to potential customers, thus reducing the ability of non-integrated firms to capture competitively the market share needed to achieve an efficient level of production, or imposing the burden of entry on an integrated basis (*i.e.,* at both the supplying and purchasing levels) even though entry at a single level would permit efficient operation; (ii) by foreclosing equal access to potential suppliers, thus either increasing the risk of a price or supply squeeze on the new entrant or imposing the additional burden of entry as an integrated firm; or (iii) by facilitating promotional product differentiation, when the merger involves a manufacturing firm's acquisition of firms at the retail level.

A vertical merger (or series of mergers) will ordinarily be challenged because of adverse effects in the *supplying* firm's market when a supplying firm with 10% or more of the sales in its market acquires one or more purchasing firms accounting in the aggregate for approximately 6% or more of the purchases in that market, "unless it clearly appears that there are no significant barriers to entry into the business of the purchasing firm or firms." (Merger Guidelines par. 12, *supra* at 6686.) Barriers to entry are defined to mean relatively stable market conditions which tend to increase the difficulty of potential competitors' entering the market as new sellers (par. 11, *supra* at 6685). The guidelines indicate that the foregoing test will also normally identify most vertical mergers that may have an adverse effect in the *purchasing* firm's market.

In addition, vertical mergers that are not subject to challenge under the above test may be challenged "on the ground that they raise entry barriers in the purchasing firm's market, or disadvantage the purchasing firm's competitors, by conferring upon the purchasing firm a significant supply advantage over unintegrated or partly integrated existing competitors or over potential competitors." The most common of these situations is said to be that in which the supplying firm and its competitors sell a complex product in which innovating changes have been taking place or a scarce raw material or other product whose supply cannot be readily expanded to meet increased demand. In this situation it is claimed that the merged firms may have the power to use any temporary superiority, or any shortage, in the product of the supplying firm to put competitors of the purchasing firm at a disadvantage. Accordingly, the guidelines provide that if such a product is a significant feature or ingredient in the end-product manufactured by the purchasing firm and its competitors, the Department will ordinarily challenge "a merger or series of mergers between a supplying firm, accounting for approximately 20% or more of the sales in its market, and a purchasing firm or firms, accounting *in toto* for approximately 10% or more of the sales in the market in which it sells the product whose manufacture requires the supplying firm's product." Merger Guidelines, par. 13, *supra* at 6686.

Finally, the merger guidelines state that the Department will occasionally challenge "acquisitions of suppliers or customers by major firms in an industry in which (i) there has been, or is developing, a significant trend toward vertical integration by merger such that the trend, if unchallenged, would probably raise barriers to entry or impose a competitive disadvantage on unintegrated or partly integrated firms, and (ii) it does not clearly appear that the particular acquisition will result in significant economies of production or distribution unrelated to advertising or other promotional economies." (Par. 14(a) *supra* at 6686-6687.) The Department will also ordinarily challenge an "acquisition by a firm of a customer or supplier for the purpose of increasing the difficulty of potential competitors in entering the market of either the acquiring or acquired firm, or for the purpose of putting competitors of either the acquiring or acquired firm at an unwarranted disadvantage." Merger Guidelines par. 14(b) *supra* at 6687.

155

There have been relatively few cases dealing with vertical mergers. In general the courts have recognized the same possible anticompetitive consequences described in the Department's merger guidelines. In *Brown Shoe Co. v United States* (1962) 370 US 294, the Supreme Court stated (370 US at 323–324):

The primary vice of a vertical merger or other arrangement tying a customer to a supplier is that, by foreclosing the competitors of either party from a segment of the market otherwise open to them, the arrangement may act as a "clog on competition" which "deprive[s] . . . rivals of a fair opportunity to compete."

In *Brown Shoe* the merger between Brown Shoe (a shoe manufacturer) and Kinney (a national retail chain) was declared illegal based on its vertical aspects, although Kinney's national market share was only 1% of men's shoes, 1.5% of women's shoes, and 2% of children's shoes (370 US at 303). The Supreme Court found that (1) the avowed purpose of the merger was to force Brown's shoes into Kinney's outlets and (2) there was a strong trend toward vertical integration in the shoe industry (370 US at 334).

Considering only the market shares in *Brown Shoe*, the result was quite strict. But it is important to note the Supreme Court's expression of the view that while the share of the market foreclosed is an "important consideration" in determining whether a vertical merger violates Section 7 (15 USC §18), this factor "will seldom be determinative" (370 US at 328). The Court suggested that unless the share of the market foreclosed is very large or *de minimis*, it is "necessary to undertake an examination of various economic and historical factors in order to determine whether the arrangement under review is of the type Congress sought to proscribe" (370 US at 329). One of the most important factors to examine is "the very nature and purpose of the arrangement."

In *Brown Shoe*, the Supreme Court noted that the criteria for judging vertical mergers should be similar to those applied in determining the legality of requirements contracts under Section 3 of the Clayton Act (15 USC §14). Requirements contracts covering 6% of total sales and 16% of the number of outlets in a market were held to be illegal in *Standard Oil Co. of California v United States* (1949) 337 US 293. For discussion, see §§3.2–3.8.

The Supreme Court has written no opinions in vertical merger cases since *Brown Shoe*. Previously, in *United States v E.I. du Pont de Nemours & Co.* (1957) 353 US 586, the Court held that Section 7 as originally enacted applied to vertical mergers. The Court has affirmed *per curiam* two district court decisions holding mergers with vertical aspects unlawful. *United States v Kennecott Copper Corp.* (SD NY 1964) 231 F Supp 95, *aff'd per curiam* (1965) 381 US 414; *United States v Aluminum Co. of America* (ED Mo 1964) 233 F Supp 718, *aff'd per curiam* (1965) 382 US 12.

In *United States v Ford Motor Co.* (ED Mich 1968) 286 F Supp 407, the district court held that Section 7 was violated by Ford's acquisition of a company with a sparkplug manufacturing plant and an automotive battery plant. Ford accounted for approximately 9.6% of the total sparkplug market and 6.2% of the total market for automotive batteries. See also *United States v Kimberly-Clark Corp.* (ND Calif 1967) 264 F Supp 439.

In *Marquette Cement Mfg. Co.* (1969) 3 Trade Reg Rep ¶18,657, the Federal Trade Commission held a vertical merger illegal between a supplying firm accounting for 3.5% or 4.8% of its market and a customer with 1.6% or 1.8% of its market, but stated that not every vertical merger involving comparable market shares would be unlawful, but rather "whether a particular vertical merger is illegal depends on the facts and the market setting in which it occurs." See also *Reynolds Metals Co. v FTC* (DC Cir 1962) 309 F2d 223.

Based on its decisions in horizontal merger cases subsequent to *Brown Shoe*, the Supreme Court might have been expected to develop simplified tests for determining the legality of vertical mergers, but it may well be that as a result of changes in its membership the Court will continue to view each vertical merger separately "in the context of its particular industry." Vertical mergers may be motivated by an attempt to achieve economies through integrated production, and there is respectable support for the view that vertical mergers should, therefore, be judged more precisely than horizontal mergers on a case-by-case approach.

While in *Brown Shoe* the Supreme Court emphasized the importance of the *purpose* of a vertical acquisition in determining its legality, it remains to be seen what purposes, if any, the Court will regard favorably. Possibly, a combination of minor companies permitting more effective competition with larger competitors will be viewed more favorably in a vertical merger than in a horizontal merger. A new company may be able to justify a small vertical merger on the basis of its need for vertical integration with customers or suppliers in order to establish itself in the market. Acquisitions of sources of supply may be viewed more favorably than customer acquisitions. However, these possibilities are only speculation and must await developments in future cases. On the other hand, if the demonstrable purpose of an acquisition is to tie up the business of suppliers or customers, a vertical merger will almost certainly be declared illegal.

It will be more difficult to forecast the outcome in a vertical merger case than in a horizontal case, and it will also be more difficult to predict whether a vertical merger will be challenged. In evaluating a vertical merger counsel should determine whether the merger is in one of the industries in which the Federal Trade Commission has issued a statement of enforcement policy on mergers or in which it has challenged vertical mergers in the past, since the Commission has adopted more stringent standards for and has been more active in challenging vertical mergers than has the Department of Justice. The numerical criteria established in the few decided cases are also more restrictive than those contained in the merger guidelines issued by the Department of Justice. Accordingly, while the Department's guidelines provide criteria that may normally be used for planning purposes, not every vertical merger meeting those guidelines will be safe. Vertical acquisitions of significant customers by large companies are especially likely to provoke investigation and attack. An industry trend to vertical mergers may also stimulate attack. Vertical mergers that do not satisfy the numerical standards in the Department's merger guidelines will probably have a chance to succeed only if both firms are relatively small.

7. Criteria for Conglomerate Mergers

a. [§4.29] Introduction

Conglomerate mergers have been defined as all those mergers that are not horizontal (see §4.27) or vertical (see §4.28). The Department of Justice Merger Guidelines state (par. 17, 1 Trade Reg Rep ¶4430 at 6687) that "the purpose of the Department's enforcement activity regarding conglomerate mergers is to prevent changes in market structure that appear likely over the course of time to cause a substantial lessening of the competition that would otherwise exist or to create a tendency toward monopoly."

As of the date of issuance, the guidelines described three categories of conglomerate mergers as having identifiable anticompetitive effects: (1) mergers involving a potential entrant into the market (§4.30); (2) mergers creating a danger of reciprocal buying (§4.31); and (3) mergers resulting in an entrenchment of market power (§§4.32–4.35). In 1969, Attorney General Mitchell identified mergers among large firms that contribute to "aggregate concentration" as a fourth category of conglomerate mergers that might be subject to challenge. See §4.36.

In considering whether a conglomerate merger is likely to be challenged, it is extremely important to bear in mind that the present Assistant Attorney General in charge of the Antitrust Division, Richard W.

McLaren, has frequently stated his disagreement with the prior administration over the extent to which "pure" forms of conglomerate mergers (see §4.2) could be reached under Section 7 (15 USC §18). He has warned businessmen not to rely on the merger guidelines for conglomerate mergers and announced before the National Industrial Conference Board on March 6, 1969, an intention to indicate additional factors that will give warning of likely prosecution of mergers that presently appear not to violate the guidelines.

As a rough guide, the conglomerate mergers most likely to be attacked are those between large firms (e.g., those among the 200–300 largest manufacturing firms) or those in which the acquiring company is very large and the acquired company is one of the three or four leading firms in a concentrated market, with a market share in excess of 10 or 20%. In the latter case, a merger will be particularly vulnerable if (1) the acquired company manufactures a product that is closely related to or competes with a product sold by the acquiring company; (2) the merger creates a substantial opportunity for reciprocal dealing; (3) the merger will give the acquired company significant promotional or marketing advantages over its competitors, for example, in advertising rates or by augmenting its product line; or (4) all the firms in the acquired company's market are much smaller than the acquiring company. See generally, Turner, *Conglomerate Mergers and Section 7 of the Clayton Act* (1965) 78 *Harv L Rev* 1313; Davidow, *Conglomerate Concentration, Section 7: The Limitations of the Anti-Merger Act* (1968) 68 *Col L Rev* 1231; and Kestenbaum, *Potential Competition: Trends and Developments* (1969) 38 Antitrust Law Journal 652.

b. [§4.30] Conglomerate Mergers Involving a Potential Market Entrant

According to the merger guidelines issued by the Department of Justice, potential competition is important in many situations because it "may often be the most significant competitive limitation on the exercise of market power by the leading firms, as well as the most likely source of additional actual competition. The guidelines state (par. 18(a), 1 Trade Reg Rep ¶4430 at 6687–6688) that the Department will ordinarily challenge any merger between "one of the most likely entrants" into a market and:

(i) any firm with approximately 25% or more of the market;

(ii) one of the two largest firms in a market in which the shares of the two largest firms amount to approximately 50% or more;

(iii) one of the four largest firms in a market in which the shares of the eight largest firms amount to approximately 75% or more, provided the merging firm's share of the market amounts to approximately 10% or more; or

159

(iv) one of the eight largest firms in a market in which the shares of these firms amount to approximately 75% or more, provided either (A) the merging firm's share of the market is not insubstantial and there are no more than one or two likely entrants into the market, or (B) the merging firm is a rapidly growing firm.

The guidelines also state (par. 18(b) *supra* at 6688) that the Department will ordinarily challenge a merger between an existing competitor in a market and a likely entrant which is undertaken to prevent the competitive "disturbance" or "disruption" that an entry might create.

In determining whether a firm is one of the most likely potential entrants into a market, the guidelines state that "the Department accords primary significance to the firm's capability of entering on a competitively significant scale relative to the capability of other firms (*i.e.*, the technological and financial resources available to it) and to the firm's economic incentive to enter" the market. This incentive may be evidenced by "the general attractiveness of the market in terms of risk and profit; or any special relationship of the firm to the market; or the firm's manifested interest in entry; or the natural expansion pattern of the firm; or the like." (Par. 18(a) *supra* at 6688.)

While the few decided cases have not established any numerical standards for determining when a merger may be illegal due to the elimination of potential competition, they appear to impose at least three general requirements: *first*, the market must be relatively highly concentrated so that potential competition is an important factor checking "oligopoly" behavior; *second*, the acquired firm must be one of the leading firms in this relatively concentrated market; and *third*, the acquiring firm must be one of relatively few, or demonstrably one of the few most likely, potential entrants into the market.

To date, the leading case holding a conglomerate merger unlawful because of the elimination of potential competition is *FTC v Procter & Gamble Co.* (1967) 386 US 568. The Court held that Procter & Gamble's acquisition of Clorox Chemical Company violated section 7 of the Clayton Act (15 USC §18). The acquisition was characterized as a product-extension conglomerate merger. See definitions at §4.2. P & G was the nation's leading manufacturer of household soaps and detergents. Clorox was the nation's leading manufacturer of household liquid bleach and the only national seller, with almost 50% of total industry sales and even larger percentages in some regions of the country. The market for household liquid bleach was a highly concentrated one. The Court found that P & G was the leading, and perhaps only likely, potential entrant. See also the discussion of potential competition in *United States v El Paso Natural Gas Co.* (1964) 376 US 651; *United States v Penn-Olin Chemical Co.*

(1964) 378 US 158, *decision on remand* (D Del 1965) 246 F Supp 917, *aff'd per curiam by an equally divided Court* (1967) 389 US 308.

There has been one opinion of a three-judge district court rejecting a challenge to a conglomerate merger based on the elimination of potential competition. In *United States v Crocker-Anglo Nat'l. Bank* (ND Calif 1967) 277 F Supp 133, which was not appealed by the government, the court upheld a market-extension conglomerate merger between the fifth and eighth largest banks in California, Crocker and Citizens, which prior to the merger had operated exclusively in Northern California and Southern California, respectively. The court rejected the contention that the merger would eliminate potential competition in the Los Angeles area on two grounds: *First*, elimination of one potential competitor "could have no material effect upon the conduct of those competing in the market" since "there were at least two applications for new banking offices for each permit that became available"; and, *second*, no recommendation to enter the Los Angeles market *de novo* had ever been made by any Crocker official and all Crocker officials rejected this possibility. (277 F Supp at 184.)

One question that has not yet been fully resolved is the extent to which objective or subjective tests will be applied in determining the likelihood of entry. In *United States v Penn-Olin Chemical Co.*, *supra*, dealing with a joint venture formed by two companies, the Court stated that (at 174), "Potential competition cannot be put to a subjective test." To require subjective evidence, it said, would convert the "statutory requirement of reasonable probability into a requirement of certainty." (378 US at 174–175.) The government subsequently appealed from an adverse decision on remand (*supra*), claiming that the lower court had failed to heed the Court's direction to accord primary weight to "objective" rather than "subjective" evidence, and an equally divided court affirmed the lower court's decision (*supra*).

In *Clorox, supra*, the Supreme Court relied on objective evidence to find that P & G was the most likely entrant into the liquid bleach market. It observed that (386 US at 580):

Procter was engaged in a vigorous program of diversifying into product lines closely related to its basic products. Liquid bleach was a natural avenue of diversification since it is complementary to Procter's products, is sold to the same customers through the same channels, and is advertised and merchandised in the same manner.

These objective factors indicating P & G's capability and incentive to enter the market were sufficient to overcome the fact that the only evidence of P & G's interest in entering the liquid bleach market independently was a memorandum rejecting this possibility and concluding that the only practical means of entering the market was to acquire Clorox. The memorandum's failure to state any reasons to explain why independent entry would not be practical resulted in its receiving little weight. See also *United States v Wilson Sporting Goods Co.* (ND Ill 1968) 288 F Supp 543; *Foremost Dairies, Inc.* (1962) 60 FTC 944; *Beatrice Foods Co.* (1965) [1965-1967 Transfer Binder] Trade Reg Rep ¶17,244; and *National Tea Co.* (1966) [1965-1967 Transfer Binder] Trade Reg Rep ¶17,463.

At the same time, a few district court decisions, including the decision in *Penn-Olin, supra,* on remand, have refused to find a likelihood of independent entry, relying on expressions of intent by corporate management. See, *e.g., United States v Crocker-Anglo Nat'l. Bank, supra; United States v Atlantic Richfield Co.* (SD NY 1969) 297 F Supp 1061, 1069-1070.

Evidence that management had not or would not have considered entering a market apart from the acquisition under challenge may or may not be given weight by the courts. But it is certain that evidence indicating that the acquiring firm had favorably considered entering the market through internal expansion or through acquisition of a smaller firm, or that, in fact, it would have entered the market but for the merger, will be accorded great weight. Compare *Bendix Corp.* (1970) 3 Trade Reg Rep ¶19,288. Counsel should therefore make certain, whenever his client is planning an acquisition in a market it had previously studied and decided not to enter independently, that there is some company memorandum or statement in the corporate minutes reciting the company's conclusion that independent entry would not be practical and giving the reasons for this conclusion.

Instead of claiming that the acquiring company is a potential entrant into the acquired firm's market, the government may allege that existing products manufactured by the two firms are in potential competition with one another. In *United States v Continental Can Co.* (1964) 378 US 441, Continental, the second largest producer of tin cans, sought to acquire Hazel-Atlas, the third largest manufacturer of glass jars. The Court invalidated the merger on two grounds. First, it defined the relevant market to include both cans and bottles so that the acquisition was illegal under the standards applicable to horizontal mergers. Second, the Court indicated that the merger might eliminate potential competition between glass containers sold by Hazel-Atlas and metal containers sold by Continental in the markets for baby food and soft drink containers. See also *United*

States v Amfac (D Haw 1966) 5 Trade Reg Rep ¶45,066 at 52,639-3 (case 1923) and *United States v Eversharp, Inc.* (ED Pa 1967) 1967 Trade Cases ¶72,221. In these cases the government has alleged that mergers would tend to decrease competition between concrete and wood for use as material for floors and home sidewalks, and between blade razors and electric razors.

c. [§4.31] Conglomerate Mergers Creating a Danger of Reciprocal Buying

Reciprocal buying is defined by the Merger Guidelines (par. 19(a), 1 Trade Reg Rep ¶4430 at 6688) as "favoring one's customer when making purchases of a product which is sold by the customer." In other words, it is the use of buying power to secure an advantage in the sale of one's products. Not only may a merger be invalidated if it creates an opportunity for reciprocity, but the practice of reciprocity, itself, may violate sections 1 and 2 of the Sherman Act (15 USC §§1 and 2) or section 5 of the Federal Trade Commission Act (15 USC §45). See, *e.g., United States v General Dynamics Corp.* (SD NY 1966) 258 F Supp 36; *United States v United States Steel Corp.* (WD Pa 1969) 1969 Trade Cases ¶72,826; *United States v General Tire & Rubber Co.* (ND Ohio 1967) 5 Trade Reg Rep ¶45,067 at 52,643 (case 1929); and *Union Camp Corp.* (Affidavit, 1969) 3 Trade Reg Rep ¶18,669. See also McLaren, *Recent Cases, Current Enforcement Views, and Possible New Antitrust Legislation* (1969) 38 ABA Antitrust LJ 211, 213-214.

The merger guidelines state that since reciprocal buying is "an economically unjustified business practice which confers a competitive advantage on the favored firm unrelated to the merits of its products, the Department will ordinarily challenge any merger which creates a significant danger of reciprocal buying." A significant danger of reciprocal buying is deemed to be present whenever approximately 15% or more of the total purchases in a market in which one of the merging firms (the selling firm) sells are accounted for by firms which also make substantial sales in markets where the other merging firm (the buying firm) is both a substantial buyer and a more substantial buyer than all or most of the competitors of the selling firm.

In addition, the guidelines state that the department will ordinarily challenge "(i) any merger undertaken for the purpose of facilitating the creation of reciprocal buying arrangements, *and* (ii) any merger creating the possibility of any substantial reciprocal buying where one (or both) of the merging firms has within the recent past, or . . . after consummation of the merger, actually engaged in reciprocal buying, or attempted direct-

163

ly or indirectly to induce firms with which it deals to engage in reciprocal buying." Merger Guidelines, par. 19(a), (b), 1 Trade Reg Rep ¶4430 at 6688.

No numerical standards have been adopted in any of the cases decided to date. In *FTC v Consolidated Foods Corp.* (1965) 380 US 592, 600, the Supreme Court sustained an FTC order overturning Consolidated Food's acquisition of Gentry, Inc., stating:

> We do not go so far as to say that any acquisition, no matter how small, violates §7 if there is a probability of reciprocal buying. Some situations may amount only to *de minimis.* But where, as here, the acquisition is of a company that commands a substantial share of a market, a finding of probability of reciprocal buying by the Commission, whose expertise the Congress trusts, should be honored, if there is substantial evidence to support it.

Consolidated Foods does not establish any definite criteria for examining conglomerate mergers creating the possibility of reciprocal buying. It dealt with the acquisition by a large producer of food products of one of two dominant producers of dehydrated onion and garlic (a concentrated industry), whose competitors were all relatively small companies, and there was evidence that the acquiring company had attempted to practice reciprocity following the acquisition.

In *United States v Penick & Ford, Ltd.* (D NJ 1965) 242 F Supp 518, the acquired firm had only about 13% of a market not highly concentrated and there was evidence that the acquiring company had a firm policy against reciprocity. A district court refused to enjoin a merger on reciprocity grounds. However, this case has since been settled by a consent decree requiring divestiture of the acquired firm. See 1969 Trade Cases ¶72,886.

In *United States v Northwest Industries, Inc.* (ND Ill 1969) 301 F Supp 1066, a preliminary injunction was likewise denied, in part, because there was evidence of a strong (if recent) policy of the acquiring company against reciprocity. The court may have been impressed by evidence that the acquiring company treated its divisions and subsidiaries as separate profit centers, with management in each center having a financial stake in its profits. The defendants argued that this form of corporate structure would negate any incentive to engage in reciprocity. Although the court refused to grant an injunction, its interim order included terms prohibiting Northwest from practicing reciprocity and contained provisions designed to carry out this prohibition. See *United States v International Telephone & Telegraph Corp.* (D Conn 1969) 306 F Supp 766.

The Department's recent complaints typically allege that the merged firm will have increased power to practice "reciprocity" and ability to benefit from "reciprocity effect" in the sale of the leading product or products of the acquired company because of the greater purchasing capacity and product diversity of the acquiring firm. See, e.g., *United States v Ling-Temco-Vought, Inc.* (WD Pa 1969) 5 Trade Reg Rep ¶45,069 at 52,712 (case 2045) (LTV-Jones & Laughlin); *United States v International Telephone and Telegraph Corp.* (ND Ill 1969) 5 Trade Reg Rep ¶45,069 at 52,715 (case 2047) (ITT-Canteen); *United States v Northwest Industries, Inc.* (ND Ill 1969) 5 Trade Reg Rep ¶45,069 at 52,719 (case 2052) (Northwest-B.F. Goodrich); *United States v International Telephone and Telegraph Corp., supra* (ITT-Hartford Fire) and (ITT-Grinnell).

It is too early to tell whether the courts will ultimately accept the Department's view that a conglomerate merger may be found unlawful on a showing that it will create a situation in which firms selling to the acquiring company will be likely to buy from the acquired firm, whether coerced to do so or not, in the belief that it may help them in making sales. There is some support for this argument in *United States v Ingersoll-Rand Co.* (3d Cir 1963) 320 F2d 509, 524:

[T]he mere existence of this purchasing power might make its conscious employment toward this end unnecessary; the possession of the power is frequently sufficient, as sophisticated businessmen are quick to see the advantages in securing the good will of the possessor.

See also *Allis-Chalmers Mfg. Co. v White Consolidated Industries, Inc.* (3d Cir 1969) 414 F2d 506, 518, *cert den* (1970) 396 US 1009, in which the court issued a preliminary injunction in part because it found that the merger would create a market structure in the rolling mill market conducive to reciprocity since the major purchasers of rolling mills were steel companies and the company resulting from the merger would purchase a far larger amount of steel than any of its competitors in the rolling mill market. But compare *United States v International Telephone and Telegraph Corp., supra.*

Pending further court clarification of the law on reciprocity, this may be an area in which the parties to a proposed merger will be justified in taking substantial risks of noncompliance with the Department's merger guidelines, particularly if there is only a possibility of reciprocity and there is affirmative evidence that the parties are not likely to engage in it.

d. [§4.32] Conglomerate Mergers Resulting in an Entrenchment of Market Power

The merger guidelines state (par. 20, 1 Trade Reg Rep ¶4430 at 6688-6689) that the Department of Justice will "ordinarily investigate the possibility of anticompetitive consequences . . . where an acquisition of a leading firm in a relatively concentrated or rapidly concentrating market may serve to entrench or increase the market power of that firm or raise barriers to entry in that market," and cites the following examples:

(i) a merger which produces a very large disparity in absolute size between the merged firm and the largest remaining firms in the relevant markets, (ii) a merger of firms producing related products which may induce purchasers, concerned about the merged firm's possible use of leverage, to buy products of the merged firm rather than those of competitors, and (iii) a merger which may enhance the ability of the merged firm to increase product differentiation in the relevant markets.

No specific market share or other standards for determining when a merger may entrench market power are given in the merger guidelines because of the "novel problems" presented and the need for further analysis.

(1) [§4.33] Entrenchment by Increasing Product Differentiation

The leading cases on entrenchment through enhanced ability of the merged firm to increase product differentiation, the third category listed in paragraph 20 of the merger guidelines (1 Trade Reg Rep ¶4430 at 6688-6689), are *FTC v Procter & Gamble Co.* (1967) 386 US 568 and *General Foods Corp. v FTC* (3d Cir 1969) 386 F2d 936, *cert den* (1968) 391 US 919.

In both the *Procter & Gamble-Clorox* and the *General Foods-SOS* attempted mergers, the acquiring companies were giant producers of a variety of heavily advertised household items, and the acquired companies sold related products functionally identical to competitors' products and dependent on extensive advertising and promotional expenditures. Before its merger with P & G, Clorox was the leading manufacturer in the highly concentrated household liquid bleach industry. Before its merger with General Foods, SOS, a manufacturer of steel-wool pads, was the largest competitor in an almost perfectly balanced duopoly.

In *Procter & Gamble Co.* (1963) [1963-1965 Transfer Binder] Trade Reg Rep ¶16,673, the FTC concluded (at 21,579) that

Procter, by increasing the Clorox advertising budget, by engaging in sales promotions far beyond the capacity of Clorox's rivals, and by obtaining for Clorox the advertising savings to which Procter, as a large national advertiser, is entitled, is in a position to entrench still further the already settled consumer preference for the Clorox brand, and thereby make new entry even more forbidding than it was prior to the merger.

A unanimous Supreme Court agreed that the substitution of P & G, with its huge assets and advertising budget and its ability to obtain preferred shelf space in markets, for the already dominant Clorox would reduce competition in the household liquid bleach industry by raising already high entry barriers and dissuading smaller competitors from competing aggressively.

In *General Foods, supra,* advertising and sales promotion were similarly vital; the court of appeals held that the substitution of General Foods for SOS in the already concentrated steel-wool soap pad market would lessen competition by confronting "existing competitors and such potential competitors as existed [with] an even more formidable opponent," thereby substantially raising "the factual and psychological barriers to entry" and tending to make the market "an even more rigid oligopoly." (386 F2d at 945-946).

The major distinction between *Clorox* and *General Foods* is that in the latter case there was no finding that General Foods was a potential competitor on the fringe of the market exerting an influence upon existing competition. However, the court of appeals concluded, "We do not read *Clorox* as holding that 'product extension' mergers must involve the elimination of this type of potential competition to run afoul of the Clayton Act." (386 F2d at 946).

(2) [§4.34] Entrenchment by Creating Sales Leverage

The leading case on entrenchment through increased selling leverage (the second category listed in paragraph 20 of the merger guidelines) is *United States v Wilson Sporting Goods Co.* (ND Ill 968) 288 F Supp 543. The leading seller of sporting goods (Wilson) sought to acquire the leading seller of gymnastic equipment (Nissen).

The court found that, unlike the situation in *Clorox* and *General Foods* (see §4.33), mass advertising played no significant role in the sale of gymnastic equipment. However, the district court found that the Wilson-Nissen merger "would certainly change the character of the [gymnastic equipment] industry by casting a relative colossus . . . into the midst of a group of small competitors." "One danger that may be introduced into a market by a disproportionately sized firm which sells other related products," it indicated, "is that the product involved in the merger may tend to receive favored treatment from distributors." (288 F Supp at 554). Significant marketing advantages in the sale of Nissen's products might result from the merger because of Wilson's influence over a large number of dealers who also carried its numerous products and were dependent on it for credit and other forms of cooperation and assistance. Concluding that the merger would entrench the market power of Nissen and raise the barriers to entry in the market for gymnastic equipment, and that it would entrench Wilson in its leading position as a maker of a broad line of sporting goods, the court granted the first preliminary injunction in a conglomerate merger case. See also *Ekco Products Co. v FTC* (7th Cir 1965) 347 F2d 745; *United States v Amfac* (D Haw 1966) 5 Trade Reg Rep ¶45,066 at 52,639-3.

Support for the *Wilson* rationale may be found in *United States v Aluminum Co. of America* (ED Mo 1964) 233 F Supp 718, *aff'd per curiam* (1965) 382 US 12, in which the district court invalidated a vertical acquisition by Alcoa of an aluminum curtain-wall fabricator (Cupples), in part on the ground that Cupples would gain an unfair advantage over its competitors as a result of its relationship with Alcoa. For example, the court suggested that Alcoa's prestige among architects and builders might lead them to prefer Cupples in the future, and that the customary 5- to 20-year guarantee on aluminum curtain walls might be more attractive when backed by Alcoa's wealth and its reputation for solving engineering problems. Compare *United States v Continental Can Co.* (1964) 378 US 441, 463-464.

In *United States v International Telephone and Telegraph Corp.* (D Conn 1969) 306 F Supp 766, 776 the court stated:

. . . when a company which is the dominant competitor in a relatively oligopolistic market is acquired by a much larger company, such acquisition violates Section 7 if the acquired company gains marketing or promotional advantages which will entrench or increase its dominant market position.

However, while the district court found that Grinnell (the acquired company) was the leading manufacturer in the market for the manufacture and installation of sprinkler systems with approximately 25% of both markets, it held that this was insufficient to support a finding of dominance in either market, where there were two or three other sizeable competitors and a number of smaller ones. This holding may be overturned on appeal, and it would be premature to rely on it yet in planning mergers.

In addition, the district court indicated that even assuming that Grinnell could be characterized as the dominant competitor in any relevant market, the government had failed to establish how Grinnell would gain competitive marketing or promotional advantages as a result of the merger. The court rejected the government's contention as lacking factual support that Grinnell would be able to engage in "package" or "system" selling after the merger; but the fact that a merger would enable the acquired firm to offer a "complete line of equipment" has been used in other cases to support a finding that it would gain competitive marketing advantages from the merger. See, *e.g., United States v Ingersoll-Rand Co.* (3d Cir 1963) 320 F2d 509, 524.

The ability of a merged firm to entrench its market power by increasing its sales leverage is explored in the sharply conflicting opinions of Judge Stahl and Judge Aldisert in *Allis-Chalmers Mfg. Co. v White Consolidated Industries, Inc.* (3d Cir 1969) 414 F2d 506, *cert den* (1970) 396 US 1009. Allis-Chalmers challenged White's acquisition of 31.2% of its outstanding stock, in part on the ground that it might entrench the position of Blaw-Knox (a subsidiary of White) in the metal-rolling mill market.

In granting the preliminary injunction to enjoin the White takeover of Allis-Chalmers, Judge Stahl stated (414 F2d at 518):

Blaw-Knox's design and construction capabilities and its position as a leading manufacturer of rolling mills, when coupled with Allis' position as the third largest supplier of the electrical drive components for such mills, would result in Blaw-Knox becoming the only company capable of designing, producing and installing a complete metal rolling mill. The emergence of a company offering such a complete product would raise higher the already significant barriers to the entry of others into the various segments of the metal rolling mill market.

Judge Aldisert disagreed completely, finding the rationale of *Clorox, General Foods* and *Wilson* (see §4.33) to be wholly inapplicable to the facts presented (414 F2d at 536–537):

I do not consider the facts in *Clorox, General Foods* or *Wilson Sporting* comparable to the case at bar. In all of these cases, the corporations involved, both the acquiring firm and the acquired, were dominant in their respective industries. . . .

In contrast to the giants represented in these cases, the present appeal involves midgets. If Blaw-Knox controls between 11 to 20 per cent of the rolling mill market, it is by no means the industry's dominant figure. Allis-Chalmers has none of it. And even if we are to consider Allis' share of the market for electrical equipment for rolling mills, its share is only 6 per cent, a feeble percentage when compared to the 45 per cent and 40 per cent share commanded by General Electric and Westinghouse.

Another illustration of the potential limits of *Wilson* may be found in the initial decision in *Bendix Corp.* (1969) 3 Trade Reg Rep ¶18,896, *rev'd on other grounds* (1970) 3 Trade Reg Rep ¶19,288 (opinion of full Commission). An FTC hearing examiner dismissed a complaint challenging Bendix's acquisition of the Fram Corporation and, in so doing, distinguished *Clorox*, in part on the grounds (1) that Fram, unlike Clorox, was not the dominant company in its industry and a number of its competitors were subsidiaries of strong national companies such as General Motors, Textron, and Tenneco and (2) that, while both Bendix and Fram manufactured what might loosely be called automotive parts, there was no close relationship between their products and no possibility for integration at the marketing and distribution levels, such as existed in *Clorox*.

(3) [§4.35] Entrenchment by Creating a Size Disparity

The merger guidelines (1 Trade Reg Rep ¶4430 at 6688–6689) state that the Department of Justice will ordinarily investigate any acquisition of a leading firm in a relatively concentrated or rapidly concentrating market that produces a very large disparity in absolute size between the merged firm and the largest remaining firms in the relevant markets. (The first category of mergers listed in paragraph 20 of the merger guidelines.)

On June 6, 1969, Attorney General Mitchell announced in an address before the Georgia Bar Association (6 *Ga St BJ* 92, 96) an even more extreme version of the Department's position on conglomerate mergers that create a size disparity:

> The Department of Justice will probably oppose any merger [*sic*] by one of the top 200 manufacturing firms of any leading producer in any concentrated industry.

Compare the rules, which also go further than the formal guidelines, proposed by Campbell and Shepherd in *Leading-Firm Conglomerate Mergers* (1968) 13 Antitrust Bulletin 1361. See also address by Edwin M. Zimmerman, Assistant Attorney General, before the Association of the Bar of the City of New York, December 12, 1968, pp. 24–25.

There is little if any direct support for the Department's formal guideline on size disparity, much less the more extreme informal guideline announced by Attorney General Mitchell, and it is too early to tell whether either will be accepted by the Supreme Court. It is interesting to note that Chief Justice Burger, in ruling as a circuit judge in *Reynolds Metals Co. v FTC* (DC Cir 1962) 309 F2d 223, 230, stated:

> . . . we do not, nor could we intimate that the mere intrusion of "bigness" into a competitive economic community otherwise populated by commercial "pygmies" will *per se* invoke the Clayton Act.

A few courts have suggested, in passing, that the policy expressed in Section 7 (15 USC §18) will be promoted by permitting large firms to enter concentrated markets only through internal expansion or acquisition of one of the smaller firms in the market. See, *e.g., United States v Wilson Sporting Goods Co.* (ND Ill 1968) 288 F Supp 543, 563, 565–566 (the court suggested that anything else Wilson might do "would be more pro-competitive than the path it has chosen." If Wilson were to enter through internal expansion, that obviously would increase competition by adding another competitor to the market. If instead it entered by buying one of the small companies in the field, "it would have the effect of increasing the strength of a small company at the expense of the leading companies, and that would be more pro-competitive.") See also *Beatrice Foods Co.* (1965) [1965-1967 Transfer Binder] Trade Reg Rep ¶17,244 at 22,337.

In addition, a number of courts have cited as one of the grounds for invalidating a conglomerate merger the possibility that a merger may trigger mergers by competitors of the acquired firm. Thus, in *United States v Wilson Sporting Goods, supra,* the court found that competitors of Nissen had become "seriously worried about their ultimate survival and [were] considering the possibility of merger with larger firms" and that other large firms that were considering entering the market through internal expansion would be more likely to consider entry through an acquisition. See also *United States v Continental Can Co.* (1964) 378 US 441, 464; and *General Foods Corp. v FTC* (3d Cir 1967) 386 F2d 936, 946, *cert den* (1968) 391 US 919.

Some support for the Justice Department's guideline may also be derived from cases decided under the so-called "deep pocket" or "rich parent" theory. The "deep pocket" theory was first elaborated in *Reynolds Metals Co. v FTC, supra,* by Chief Justice Burger, then a member of the court of appeals for the District of Columbia circuit. In affirming the decision of the FTC holding the merger invalid, the court stated (309 F2d at 229-230):

Arrow's assimilation into Reynolds' enormous capital structure and resources gave Arrow an immediate advantage over its competitors who were contending for a share of the market for florist foil. The power of the "deep pocket" or "rich parent" for one of the florist foil suppliers in a competitive group where previously no company was very large and all were relatively small opened the possibility and power to sell at prices approximating cost or below and thus to undercut and ravage the less affluent competition.

See also *National Tea Co.* (1966) [1965-1967 Transfer Binder] Trade Reg Rep ¶17,463; *United States v Aluminum Co. of America* (ED Mo 1964) 233 F Supp 718, 727-728, *aff'd per curiam* (1965) 382 US 12. For decisions rejecting the "deep pocket" theory, see *Smith-Victor Corp. v Sylvania Electric Products, Inc.* (ND Ill 1965) 242 F Supp 315; and *New Grant-Patten Milk Co. v Happy Valley Farms, Inc.* (ED Tenn 1963) 222 F Supp 319.

It will be essential for counsel advising a client on a merger that runs afoul the informal guideline announced by Attorney General Mitchell to review the status of the significant conglomerate merger cases filed by the Department of Justice in 1969 and later. At the present time, if a merger would not be subject to challenge on potential competition (see §4.30), reciprocity (see §4.31), or the more traditional entrenchment grounds (see

§§4.32–4.34), the parties will have an excellent chance of defeating a motion for a preliminary injunction and a good chance to prevail ultimately.

e. [§4.36] Aggregate Concentration

In several recent complaints (including Northwest-B.F. Goodrich (*United States v Northwest Industries, Inc.* (ND Ill 1969) 301 F Supp 1066), LTV-Jones & Laughlin (*United States v Ling-Temco-Vought, Inc.* (WD Pa 1969) 5 Trade Reg Rep ¶45,069 at 52,712 (case 2045)), and IT&T-Hartford Fire Ins. (*United States v International Telephone and Telegraph* (D Conn 1969) 306 F Supp 766)), the Department of Justice has alleged that one of the ways in which a merger violated Section 7 (15 USC §18) was by furthering the current trend of mergers among large firms, thereby (i) concentrating control of manufacturing assets, (ii) reducing the number of firms capable of entering concentrated markets, (iii) reducing the number of firms with the capability and incentive for competitive innovation, (iv) increasing the barriers to entry in concentrated markets, and (v) diminishing the vigor of competition by increasing actual and potential customer-supplier relationships among leading firms in concentrated markets.

A similar theory appeared in the proposed FTC complaint challenging the White–Allis-Chalmers acquisition; it alleged (1) a lessening of competition in machinery manufacturing generally and (2) in the manufacturing segment of the community. *White Consolidated Industries, Inc.* (1969) 3 Trade Reg Rep ¶18,688.

Apparently in reliance on this "aggregate concentration" theory, Attorney General Mitchell announced in a speech cited at §4.35 that "the Department of Justice may very well oppose any merger among the top 200 manufacturing firms or firms of comparable size in their industries."

The "aggregate concentration" theory represents a sharp departure from former policy. It has been decisively rejected by the first court to consider it, in *United States v Northwest Industries, Inc., supra*, at 1096:

> The issue of concentration raises a special question, for the Government is here urging that given a trend to economic concentration, the consolidation of two of the country's one hundred largest corporations constitutes a violation of Section 7 without any specific demonstration of a substantial lessening of competition in any section of the country. We do not so read Section 7. While it is certainly more probable that the consolidation of two of the country's corporate giants may have anti-competitive results in one or more lines of commerce, the Government contends that they are inherent in such mergers because of the great economic power resulting therefrom even though there is no competitive relationship between

them. Presumably if United States Steel and A. & P. were to consider consolidating, this would be challenged as a violation of Section 7.

There may be very good reasons indeed to limit the growth of this country's largest corporations, particularly through mergers and acquisitions. . . . The law as it now stands, however, makes the adverse effect on competition the test of validity and until Congress broadens the criteria, the Court must judge proposed transactions on that standard.

See also *United States v International Telephone & Telegraph Corp.*, *supra*; and the theory of the proposed FTC complaint quoted in *Allis-Chalmers Mfg. Co. v White Consolidated Industries, Inc.* (3d Cir 1969) 1969 Trade Cases ¶72,856, at 87,200.

8. [§4.37] Criteria for Joint Ventures

The term "joint venture" encompasses a wide variety of business arrangements. As used here, a joint venture refers to the joint participation by two or more separate "parent" companies in the organization or construction of a new producing or servicing organization.

Participation in a joint venture may result in a violation of Section 7 of the Clayton Act (15 USC §18), Section 5 of the Federal Trade Commission Act (15 USC §45), or Sections 1 or 2 of the Sherman Act (15 USC §§1-2). In *United States v Penn-Olin Chemical Corp.* (1964) 378 US 158, *decision on remand* (D Del 1965) 246 F Supp 917, *aff'd per curiam* (1967) 389 US 308, discussed below, the Supreme Court held for the first time that Section 7 of the Clayton Act applies to joint ventures. In *Citizen Publishing Co. v United States* (1969) 394 US 131, the Court held a joint venture agreement unlawful *per se* under Section 1 of the Sherman Act and violative of Section 2 of the Sherman Act. The agreement, between the only two daily newspapers of general circulation in Tucson, Arizona, provided for common production facilities, joint setting of advertising and circulation rates, and pooling of profits. See also *Timken Roller Bearing Co. v United States* (1951) 341 US 593; *United States v Minnesota Mining & Mfg. Co.* (D Mass 1950) 92 F Supp 947; *United States v Imperial Chemical Industries, Ltd.* (SD NY 1951) 100 F Supp 504; cf. *Northern Natural Gas Co. v Federal Power Comm'n.* (DC Cir 1968) 399 F2d 953.

While the general standards for mergers will no doubt apply to joint ventures, it is reasonable to expect the courts to adopt a somewhat more favorable attitude toward joint ventures. Unlike a merger with an existing firm, a joint venture formed for the purpose of entering a market in which neither party was previously a competitor introduces a new competitive force into the market.

The potential anticompetitive effects of a joint venture are the same as those that may result from a merger. A joint venture formed by horizontal competitors to engage in some phase of their present business will normally eliminate competition between them in the activities of the joint venture. Joint network coverage of presidential election results or joint research and development of auto safety devices are examples of such joint ventures. A joint venture that stands in a vertical relationship to one or more of its parents may foreclose competitors of the parent from doing business with the joint venture. For example, oil companies that participate in a joint venture to construct a pipeline are likely to use the pipeline facilities for their own use to the competitive disadvantage of independent pipeline competitors. Joint ventures that have neither a horizontal nor a vertical relationship to the parent firms pose the same dangers as conglomerate mergers.

The *Penn-Olin* case, *supra*, illustrates a conglomerate-type joint venture that may eliminate potential competition (see discussion at §4.30). In *Penn-Olin*, the Olin-Matheison Chemical Corporation and Pennsalt Chemical Corporation formed a joint venture to manufacture and sell sodium chlorate in the Southeastern United States, where neither of them had sold previously. After the district court dismissed the case on the ground that the government had failed to show that both companies would have entered the market independently absent the joint venture, the Supreme Court reversed on the ground that competition might be substantially lessened even if only one company would have entered the market while the other company would have remained an important potential competitor on the edge of the market. The Court listed a number of factors as being relevant in appraising potential competition (378 US at 177):

. . . the number and power of the competitors in the relevant market; the background of their growth; the power of the joint venturers; the relationship of their lines of commerce; the competition existing between them and the power of each in dealing with the competitors of the other; the setting in which the joint venture was created; the reasons and necessities for its existence; the joint venture's line of commerce and the relationship thereof to that of its parents; the adaptability of its line of commerce to non-competitive practices; the potential power of the joint venture in the relevant market; an appraisal of what the competition in the relevant market would have been if one of the joint venturers had entered it alone instead of through Penn-Olin; the effect, in the event of this occurrence, of the other joint venturer's potential competition; and such other factors as might indicate potential risk to competition in the relevant market.

On remand, the district court held that neither company was reasonably likely to have entered the market absent the joint venture. The government appealed primarily on the ground that the district court had failed to apply a proper standard for determining the likelihood of independent entry, but an equally divided Supreme Court affirmed the judgment in favor of the defendants in a *per curiam* opinion.

Some useful guidelines have been formulated by former Assistant Attorney General Edwin M. Zimmerman to guide those who contemplate forming a joint venture (*Adventures in Jointness* (1968) 37 ABA Antitrust LJ 125).

1. If the joint venture will have some adverse competitive effects on actual or potential relationships among the participants in the joint venture, then every effort should be made to limit the scope of the joint venture both to the minimum number of firms essential and to the smallest possible range of economic activity.

2. The participants contemplating a joint venture should consider whether useful alternatives to the joint venture exist. If joint action is not necessary because individual action would be feasible, it will be difficult to justify any significant restraints. It may be that a series of separate, less inclusive joint ventures would be possible.

3. There should be no restraints associated with the joint venture that are not absolutely essential to its operation. In general, the parent firms should not be precluded from competing with the joint venture. Likewise, the participants should receive no guarantee against possible future competition from the joint venture.

4. If the scale requirements permit only one or, at most, very few joint ventures, the usual rule that encourages a limitation on the number of firms participating in the joint venture should be reversed. In this situation every effort should be made to maximize access to the advantages of the joint venture for all firms. On this point, see, *e.g., Associated Press v United States* (1945) 326 US 1; and *United States v Terminal R.R. Ass'n.* (1912) 224 US 383. See also Pitofsky, *Joint Ventures Under the Antitrust Laws: Some Reflections on the Significance of Penn-Olin* (1969) 82 *Harv L Rev* 1007.

Citizen Publishing, supra, furnishes support for the suggestion that a joint venture should not be more restrictive than necessary; the decree of the district court required modification of the joint operating agreement to eliminate price fixing, market control, and profit-pooling provisions, but it did not prohibit the use of common production facilities.

The relief sought by the government in a joint venture case may differ depending upon whether the Department of Justice or the Federal Trade Commission files suit. To date, the Department of Justice has simply required one party to the joint venture to dispose of its interest. The Federal Trade Commission may seek to require both participants to dispose of their interests in certain facilities of the joint venture and may even ask that one or both participants construct new facilities to compete with those operated by the joint venture. See, e.g., *Continental Oil Co.* (1967) Trade Reg Rep ¶18,079. See Bicks, *Relief in Joint Venture Cases* (1968) 37 ABA Antitrust LJ 223.

E. Defenses

1. [§4.38] Failing Company

The merger guidelines of the Department of Justice state (pars. 9, 15, 21; 1 Trade Reg Rep ¶4430 at 6684):

> A merger which the Department would otherwise challenge will ordinarily not be challenged if (i) the resources of one of the merging firms are so depleted and its prospects for rehabilitation so remote that the firm faces the clear probability of a business failure, and (ii) good faith efforts by the failing firm have failed to elicit a reasonable offer of acquisition more consistent with the purposes of Section 7 by a firm which intends to keep the failing firm in the market. The Department regards as failing only those firms with no reasonable prospect of remaining viable; it does not regard a firm as failing merely because the firm has been unprofitable for a period of time, has lost market position or failed to maintain its competitive position in some other respect, has poor management, or has not fully explored the possibility of overcoming its difficulties through self-help.

In addition to the requirements (1) that the acquired company be in a failing condition and (2) that there be no available alternative purchasers whose merger with the failing company would have a less anticompetitive effect, the Federal Trade Commission may apply a third requirement for meeting the "failing company" defense. The parties may have to show that the anticompetitive effects of the merger are outweighed by the probable harm to innocent individuals. Such a requirement was first stated in *United States Steel Corp.* (1968) 3 Trade Reg Rep ¶18,626 at 20,981–20,982. But compare *Occidental Petroleum Corp.* (1969) 3 Trade Reg Rep ¶18,864.

The requirements for meeting the "failing company" defense stated in the merger guidelines of the Department of Justice have ample support in the decided cases. The third requirement suggested by the Federal Trade Commission faces an uncertain future and, to date, has not been adopted by any appellate court.

The merger guidelines also permit a "failing division" defense, although this defense will be even more difficult to sustain than the "failing company" defense. The guidelines state (par. 9, *supra*):

> In determining the applicability of the above standard to the acquisition of a failing division of a multi-market company, such factors as the difficulty in assessing the viability of a portion of a company, the possibility of arbitrary accounting practices, and the likelihood that an otherwise healthy company can rehabilitate one of its parts, will lead the Department to apply this standard only in the clearest of circumstances.

There have been no appellate decisions determining whether the defense would be available in a failing division situation, although a district court, in *United States v Reed Roller Bit Co.* (WD Okla 1967) 274 F Supp 573, 584, has stated that the doctrine "would seem" to extend to the sale of an unprofitable subsidiary by a prosperous parent.

The Federal Trade Commission has ruled that the failing company doctrine may not be invoked with respect to the acquisition of the failing parts of a profitable company. See *Farm Journal Inc.* (1956) 53 FTC 26; *Dean Foods Co.* (1966) [1965–1967 Transfer Binder] Trade Reg Rep ¶17,765.

The failing company defense originated in *International Shoe Co. v FTC* (1930) 280 US 291, 302–303. The most recent expression of this defense by the Supreme Court occurred in *Citizen Publishing Co. v United States* (1969) 394 US 131, which held that defendants have the burden of proof in establishing that a company was "failing" and that there was "no alternative purchaser." See also *United States v Diebold, Inc.* (1962) 369 US 654; *United States v Philadelphia Nat'l. Bank* (1963) 374 US 321, 372 n. 76. For discussion of the defense in the lower courts, see *Erie Sand and Gravel Co. v FTC* (3d Cir 1961) 291 F2d 279; *Crown Zellerbach Corp. v FTC* (9th Cir 1961) 296 F2d 800.

The two material elements of the "failing company" defense were restated by the district court on remand in *United States v Pabst Brewing Co.* (ED Wis 1969) 1969 Trade Cases ¶72,723 at 86,582:

> . . . the defendants must establish two material elements to their defense: that at the time of the merger, the firm was indeed "failing" in the same sense that the firm was heading inevitably in the direction of bankruptcy, with the grave probability that failure would ensue—that is, that the trend was irreversible; and that in respect of the merger, there were available no reasonable, possible, or feasible alternatives which would have permitted the acquiring firm to remain an independent, competitive factor within the brewing industry.

Under the criteria established to date, it is extremely difficult to sustain an acquisition on the basis of the failing company defense. Indeed, the only cases in which this defense has ultimately been upheld are *United States v Maryland & Virginia Milk Producers Ass'n.* (D DC 1958) 167 F Supp 799, 808, *aff'd in part and rev'd in part,* (1960) 362 US 458; *Union Leader Corp. v Newspapers of New England, Inc.* (1st Cir 1960) 284 F2d 582; and *Granader v Public Bank* (ED Mich 1967) 281 F Supp 120.

On the other hand, evidence that one of the parties to a proposed acquisition is in serious danger of failing and that reasonable efforts have been made to find an alternative purchaser without success will carry substantial weight with the Department of Justice and the Federal Trade Commission in deciding whether to bring a legal action. For example, the Federal Trade Commission has never sustained the failing company defense in any of its litigated cases, but in 14 of 26 merger-clearance advisory opinions announced on February 13, 1968, it relied on the acquired company's "failing" (or sometimes "unprofitable," "poor," or "distressed") condition as a major reason for its failure to oppose acquisitions. In general, the Commission also indicated that reasonable efforts had been made to find other buyers but had been unsuccessful.

On occasion, merging parties seeking to rely upon the failing company defense may have to accept certain conditions in order to gain approval for their merger. For example, a merger of competing newspapers was permitted on the basis of the defense in *United States v World Journal Tribune, Inc.* (SD NY 1966) 1966 Trade Cases ¶71,925, but the surviving newspaper was required to waive the exclusive rights to publication of certain syndicated features.

The acquisition of a company in serious financial difficulties is one situation in which it may often be advisable to seek advance clearance, formal or informal, before consummating an acquisition. Difficulties the surviving firm may encounter if it is forced to divest itself of the acquired firm, particularly if it is required to restore it as a viable competitor, may make it a very costly gamble to proceed without clearance.

2. [§4.39] Economies of Production or Distribution

The merger guidelines of the Department of Justice state that unless there are "exceptional circumstances" the Department will not accept as a justification for an acquisition subject to challenge under the guidelines the claim that the merger will produce economies (*i.e.,* improvements in efficiency). (Pars. 10, 10, 18(c), 19(c), 1 Trade Reg Rep ¶4430 at 6684-6688.) An exception is stated (par. 14(a), *supra*) for certain vertical mergers if it appears that the particular acquisition "will result in significant economies of production or distribution unrelated to advertising or other promotional economies."

One of the principal reasons stated for the Department's refusal to recognize economies as a defense is the view that if substantial economies are potentially available, they can normally be realized through internal expansion. It is further stated that there usually will be severe difficulties in establishing accurately the existence and magnitude of economies claimed for a merger.

In *FTC v Procter & Gamble Co.* (1967) 386 US 568, 580, the Supreme Court apparently rejected economies as a defense, stating:

> Possible economies cannot be used as a defense to illegality. Congress was aware that some mergers which lessen competition may also result in economies but it struck the balance in favor of protecting competition.

However, in *United States v Wilson Sporting Goods Co.* (ND Ill 1968) 288 F Supp 543, 566 n 38, the district court went out of its way to suggest that economies may be used to defend a merger at least in some cases. Also, former Commissioner Elman of the FTC has suggested a basis on which the statement quoted above may be distinguished. See Elman, *Clorox and Conglomerate Mergers* (1967) 36 ABA Antitrust LJ 23, 26. Finally, a former Special Economic Assistant to the Assistant Attorney General in charge of the Antitrust Division has presented a strong argument for allowing efficiencies to be treated as a defense. See Williamson, *Economies as an Antitrust Defense* (1968) 58 *Amer Econ Rev* 18; Williamson, *Allocative Efficiency and the Limits of Antitrust* (1969) 59 *Amer Econ Rev*, Papers & Proceedings 105.

Nevertheless, under the present state of the law parties planning a merger should not rely on economies or efficiencies that a merger will produce to sustain it against a claim of illegality. But in litigation it will be worthwhile to raise this defense and to attempt to prove the extent of the economies through expert economic and technical witnesses. If very large economies may be demonstrated, it would probably be advisable to bring these economies to the attention of the government if it has initiated an investigation of the acquisition. The Department may be reluctant to press its position that economies may not be used as a defense, particularly in an extreme case. If advance clearance is being sought, for example, because of the failing or poor financial condition of the acquired company, it would also be advisable to seek to establish that economies would result from the acquisition.

3. [§4.40] Merger of Small Companies to Compete More Efficiently

Another defense the parties to a merger may want to raise in litigation, but on which it would be unsafe to rely in planning an acquisition, is that the merger occurred "between two small companies to enable the combination to compete more effectively with larger corporations dominating the relevant market." *Brown Shoe Co. v United States* (1962) 370 US 294, 319.

This line of defense, first suggested by the Court in *Brown Shoe*, has met with no success to date. Moreover, it may have been restricted in *United States v Von's Grocery Co.* (1966) 384 US 270, 277, in which the Court characterized the *Brown Shoe* defense as based "on the ground that one of the companies was about to fail or that the two had to merge to save themselves from destruction by some larger and more powerful competitor." In a dissenting opinion Mr. Justice Stewart observed that this "gratuitous dictum" undercuts the principle outlined in *Brown Shoe* "by confining it to cases in which competitors are obliged to merge to save themselves from *destruction* by a larger and more powerful competitor." 384 US at 298 n. 28.

4. [§4.41] Ease of Entry

Still another defense that is appropriate for litigation but not for planning a merger is the so-called "ease of entry" defense which is also traced to *Brown Shoe Co. v United States* (1962) 370 US 294. The Court stated that it would be proper to take into account whether the industry "had witnessed the ready entry of new competition or the erection of barriers to prospective entrants . . . [and whether it] experienced easy access to markets by suppliers and easy access to suppliers by buyers." 370 US at 322. See Low, *Ease of Entry: A Fundamental Economic Defense in Merger Cases* (1968) 36 *Geo Wash L Rev* 515.

While it is clear that the government will challenge a merger on the ground that it will increase the barriers to entry in a given market, neither the government nor the courts have accepted "ease of entry" as an affirmative defense. The Federal Trade Commission expressly repudiated the defense in *Ekco Products Co.* (1964) [1963–1965 Transfer Binder] Trade Reg Rep ¶16,879, at 21,900. But compare *Crown Zellerbach Corp. v FTC* (9th Cir 1961) 296 F2d 800, 830 and *American Crystal Sugar Co. v Cuban-American Sugar Co.* (SD NY 1957) 152 F Supp 387, 400, *aff'd on other grounds* (2d Cir 1958) 259 F2d 524.

F. [§4.42] Predicting Likelihood of Suit

In assessing the likelihood that an acquisition will be challenged, the starting point and most important single consideration is the status of the acquisition under the guidelines issued by the Federal Trade Commission (see §4.22) and the Department of Justice (see §4.23) and, to a lesser extent, under the decided cases. If a merger clearly violates the guidelines, it is reasonably likely to be challenged *if* the government learns of the acquisition *and* discovers the potential violation.

Obviously, not all mergers, and not even all large mergers, are challenged. In 1968 there were more than 4,000 mergers in the United States, and only 35 complaints were filed by the government. On the average, only one out of every ten large mergers (acquired companies with assets of $10 million or more) are challenged. The Department of Justice and the Federal Trade Commission together probably conduct no more than 200 full-scale investigations in a year, if that many. While the element of chance may not be totally discounted, various factors play a part in determining which mergers are subject to investigation and suit. Most of the statistics that follow come from Bock, *Mergers and Markets: 7, An Economic Analysis of Developments in 1967-1968 Under the Merger Act of 1950*, Studies in Business Economics, No. 105: National Industrial Conference Board, Inc., New York (1969), and Mueller, *The Celler-Kefauver Act: 16 Years of Enforcement* (1969) 1 Journal of Reprints for Antitrust Law and Economics 113.

1. [§4.43] Type of Merger Challenged in the Past

There has been a marked change in the relative number of horizontal, vertical, and conglomerate mergers during the period from 1948 to 1968. Horizontal and vertical mergers represented 48% of all mergers from 1952 to 1959; 39% of all mergers from 1960 to 1963; 22% from 1964 to 1967; and only 9% in 1968. Conversely, conglomerate mergers increased sharply from 38.1% of all mergers from 1948 to 1951 to 91% of all mergers in 1968.

Over half the large mergers challenged between 1951 and 1966 included some horizontal relationship between the merging companies; another 26% included vertical relationships; and the remainder were so-called conglomerate mergers. Of the large conglomerate mergers challenged, half were market extension and half were product extension mergers. No "pure" conglomerate mergers were challenged. (For definitions, see §4.2.) This pattern may be changing; five of the six merger cases (other than bank merger cases) instituted under the new administration

181

and the leadership of Assistant Attorney General McLaren through August 1, 1969, were aimed at conglomerate mergers, most of which might be termed "pure" conglomerate mergers.

2. [§4.44] Size of Merging Companies

The size of the merging companies will be important in determining the likelihood of investigation and suit. If the combined assets of the two firms equals $250 million or more and the acquired firm has assets of $10 million or more, the merger will have to be reported in advance to the Federal Trade Commission under its premerger notification program announced in 1969. This will ensure close scrutiny of the merger. See discussion at §4.72.

In general, the larger the acquiring firm the more likely an acquisition is to be subject to challenge. In more than 62% of the cases filed in recent years the total sales of the acquiring company have exceeded $100 million. In contrast, the total sales of the acquiring company have been under $50 million in less than 15% of the cases, although there have been cases in which the sales of the acquiring company were as low as $6 million and $7 million. In more than half the recent cases the total assets of the acquiring company have exceeded $100 million; in less than one case out of five has the acquiring company had assets of less than $50 million. Only eight companies with assets between $5 million and $10 million have been challenged, and only two companies with assets of less than $5 million have been sued.

The acquired company's total sales have been between $1 million and $50 million in almost three-fourths of the cases in recent years. In only four cases were the total sales of the acquired company less than $4 million. The acquired company's total assets have been less than $50 million in from one-half to two-thirds of the cases in recent years. A total of four cases have been brought in which the acquired firm had assets of less than $1 million. In the last few years the lowest total assets of an acquired firm were $3 million.

3. [§4.45] Market Rank of Merging Companies

A case is more likely to be instituted if either the acquiring firm or the acquired firm, or both, are among the leaders in their markets. Mergers in which one of the companies is a leading firm in an industry are not only more likely to violate the standards established in the merger guidelines and the decided cases, but also are more likely to come to the attention of the government or be the subject of a complaint by a private party. Leading firms in relatively concentrated "small-firm" markets are particularly likely to experience difficulty in selling to larger firms. See §§4.32–4.35. Statistically, the acquiring firm has ranked from first to fourth in its market in approximately 77% of the most recent cases. The acquired firm has ranked either first or second in its market in approximately one-half of the recent cases.

4. [§4.46] Market Concentration

Mergers are more likely to be challenged if the market in which there are possible anticompetitive effects is relatively highly concentrated or experiencing a trend toward concentration. Concentrated markets are more likely to receive close attention from the government, and the standards for permissible mergers are also far more difficult to satisfy.

The degree of market concentration is usually expressed as the share of industry sales accounted for by the four largest or eight largest firms. The merger guidelines of the Department of Justice define a highly concentrated market to mean a market in which the shares of the four largest firms amount to 75% or more. See discussion at §4.27. The standards traditionally used for measuring economic concentration have been criticized in Finkelstein and Friedberg, *The Application of an Entropy Theory of Concentration to the Clayton Act* (1967) 76 *Yale LJ* 677.

While it may frequently be difficult or impossible to obtain precise concentration data, it should be possible to obtain a fairly accurate indication of market concentration from data supplied by the client estimating the market shares of the ten leading firms. Among the industries that are highly concentrated are automobiles, computers, telephone equipment, steel, aluminum, certain electrical equipment sectors, flat glass, certain chemicals, copying equipment, photographic supplies, metal containers, tires and tubes, tobacco, and synthetic detergents. A substantially larger number of more narrowly defined relevant product and geographic markets would be regarded as highly concentrated under the Department's definition.

5. [§4.47] History of Prior Acquisitions

An acquisition will be more likely to come to the attention of someone in the government and receive a full investigation if (1) the acquiring company has been investigated in connection with previous acquisitions or attempted acquisitions, (2) the government has investigated a previous attempt to purchase the acquired company, (3) previous acquisitions by other companies in the industry were investigated by the government, or (4) one of the merging companies or other companies in the industry have recently been investigated or sued under the antitrust laws in connection with other activities unrelated to mergers. Acquiring companies with a history of past acquisitions that have been investigated by the government, such as IT&T and LTV, are almost certain to have future acquisitions thoroughly investigated.

It will be important for the company to be acquired to consider the likelihood of a government investigation. If the merger is not consummated, either because of government action or otherwise, information the government obtains during an investigation and its increased familiarity with the business of the company to be acquired may make it more difficult for that company to merge with other firms in the future.

6. [§4.48] Complaints by Private Parties

Complaints by private parties are an important source of government information in antitrust matters. While private complaints concerning mergers are relatively infrequent, an effort should be made to determine whether any private party may have a strong objection to the acquisition and therefore be a potential complainant to the government. Competitors who feel that their existing market share is directly threatened or customers who feel that there is a serious risk of foreclosure are the most likely potential complainants. In the case of an attempted "take-over" of a company against the wishes of management, a complaint to the government is almost certain.

7. [§4.49] Specific Industries

Mergers in industries covered by "policy statements" issued by the Federal Trade Commission are subject to precise guidelines and are almost certain to be reviewed and challenged when the guidelines are not met. These industries include cement, food distribution, textiles, and grocery products. See §4.22.

There are also a number of other areas in which either the Federal Trade Commission or the Department of Justice have been active in filing complaints challenging mergers. Among the industries in which the Department of Justice has been active are alcoholic beverages, banks, petroleum products, primary metals, motion pictures, newspapers, and other publications. Industries in which the Federal Trade Commission has been active include cement, concrete, containers, dairy products, bakery products, chain department stores, grocery chains, and vending machines. Both agencies have been active in steel and paper products.

A merger occurring in an industry in which the Department of Justice or the Federal Trade Commission have been active or have recently investigated an acquisition is likely to receive a careful review. Moreover, the government's knowledge of market structure and market conditions acquired during a previous investigation may enable it to spot potential anticompetitive effects that otherwise might have been overlooked.

8. [§4.50] Trends and Predictions

Mr. Justice Stewart has observed that the "sole consistency" in the Supreme Court's merger decisions since the passage of the Celler-Kefauver amendment in 1950 is that "in litigation under §7 [15 USC §18] the Government always wins." *United States v Von's Grocery Co.* (1966) 384 US 270, 301 (dissenting opinion). In fact, the government's record in the Supreme Court in cases under amended Section 7 is almost perfect; only once has the Court left standing a lower court decision that an acquisition was not in violation of the antitrust laws. In *United States v Penn-Olin Chemical Co.* (D Del 1965) 246 F Supp 917, *aff'd per curiam* (1967) 389 US 308, a decision adverse to the government on remand was affirmed *per curiam* by an equally divided Court. In a handful of government cases under amended section 7 in which lower courts have upheld a merger or have denied a preliminary injunction, the government has not appealed or has taken no further action. These cases include: *United States v Columbia Pictures Corp.* (SD NY 1960) 189 F Supp 153; *United States v Ling-Temco Electronics, Inc.* (ND Tex 1961) 1961 Trade Cases ¶70,160; *United States v Bliss & Laughlin, Inc.* (SD Calif 1963) 1963 Trade Cases ¶70,734; *United States v Lever Bros. Co.* (SD NY 1963) 216 F Supp 887; *United States v FMC Corp.* (ND Calif 1963) 218 F Supp 817, *appeal dismissed* (9th Cir 1963) 321 F2d 534, *application for preliminary injunction denied* (1963) 84 S Ct 4 (Opinion of Mr. Justice Goldberg in chambers); *United States v Crocker-Anglo Nat'l. Bank* (ND Calif 1967) 277 F Supp 133; and *United States v Tidewater Marine Service, Inc.* (ED La 1968) 284 F Supp 324.

However, very few of the Supreme Court's decisions in merger cases under amended Section 7 have been unanimous, and the Court has often been sharply divided. While it is too early to reach any conclusions, it is possible that recent and prospective changes in the membership of the Supreme Court may bring some changes in the direction of the Court's merger decisions. Robert L. Stern, former Acting Solicitor General and First Assistant to the Solicitor General of the United States, recently analyzed all the antitrust decisions rendered by the Warren Court and calculated that retired Chief Justice Warren voted for the government or plaintiff in 59 out of 60 antitrust cases. Likewise, Justices Black, Douglas, and Brennan voted virtually 100% for the government or plaintiff. On the other hand, Chief Justice Burger, while sitting on the court of appeals for

185

the District of Columbia, participated in nine antitrust cases and voted six times for the defendant and only three times for the government.

Recognizing the intrinsic unreliability of making predictions from a count of cases pro and con, it would nevertheless appear that the parties to a merger may have a greater chance to prevail in the Supreme Court in the future than in the past. At least, the future decisions of the Supreme Court are less predictable than previously. The next few decisions by the Supreme Court in difficult merger cases may be helpful in predicting the direction the Court will take.

It is unlikely that changes in membership of the Supreme Court will result in a reversal of the standards established in the Court's past merger decisions. It will probably never again be possible for the second and sixth largest companies in the steel industry or any other substantial industry to contemplate a merger. Cf. *United States v Bethlehem Steel Corp.* (SD NY 1958) 168 F Supp 576. It is also unlikely that a court will ever again express the view that preliminary injunctions are not available in conglomerate merger cases. Cf. *United States v FMC Corp.* (ND Calif 1963) 218 F Supp 817. But the formulation of standards in areas yet to be resolved, particularly with respect to conglomerate mergers and to a lesser extent with respect to vertical mergers, is less predictable.

Finally, it should be noted that repeal of the Expediting Act of 1903 (15 USC §§28–29, 49 USC §45) would have a significant effect in merger cases. The Expediting Act currently provides that any appeal by either party to a civil antitrust suit brought by the Department of Justice must be taken directly to the Supreme Court. Under a bill the administration has introduced, appeals would ordinarily be taken to the federal courts of appeals subject to further review by the Supreme Court in its discretion. The bill also provides that in cases that the attorney general or the district court determines to be of general public importance, a direct appeal may be taken to the Supreme Court. If government civil antitrust cases were normally first subject to review by a court of appeals, it is likely that the Supreme Court would ultimately decide fewer merger cases than it has in the past. It is unlikely that the government would enjoy as much success in the various courts of appeals as it has in the past in the Supreme Court.

G. Steps to Minimize Likelihood of Suit

1. [§4.51] Careful Drafting of Proxy Statement or Press Release

In borderline cases it will be extremely difficult to predict whether or not a merger will be challenged. Much may depend on the extent and nature of the publicity given to an acquisition. For example, any publicity emphasizing possible horizontal aspects of an acquisition, possible elimination of potential competition, or other possible anticompetitive effect, will increase the likelihood of a suit challenging the acquisition. The parties to a merger should assume that either the Department of Justice or the Federal Trade Commission, or both, will read any article about the merger in the *Wall Street Journal*, industry trade publications, or local newspapers in cities in which field offices of either agency are located.

The "visibility" of an acquisition may also depend on whether the companies are public or private. It is more likely that a suit will be brought if it is necessary to file a proxy statement with the Securities and Exchange Commission in order to obtain shareholder approval. The information required in a proxy statement will be far more detailed than what might be included in a press release.

This is an area where the antitrust adviser may play an important role in the ultimate success or failure of the acquisition. He should review all press releases issued by the client. Within limits set by requirements for disclosure under the securities law, he should attempt to ensure that news releases do not themselves invite antitrust attack.

2. [§4.52] Sale of Certain Assets or Closing of Plant before Acquisition

The parties to a merger may be able to eliminate possible grounds on which the merger might be held to be unlawful by arranging for the sale of those assets of either firm that create a competitive overlap or produce an anticompetitive effect. Such a sale would have to be made to a viable and effective competitor and could occur before or simultaneous with consummation of the merger.

In *United States v Atlantic Richfield Co.* (SD NY 1969) 297 F Supp 1061, Atlantic Richfield agreed to merge with Sinclair Oil. After the merger agreement had been entered into but before it had received stockholder approval, Atlantic agreed to sell all the marketing properties of Sinclair in the Northeastern United States and various other properties to a wholly owned subsidiary of British Petroleum Corporation. The sale was made for the express purpose of eliminating potential anticompetitive consequences of the merger in the Northeast.

The government argued that the sale to British Petroleum should be completely ignored in determining the legality of the acquisition. The court rejected this contention, stating (297 F Supp at 1069):

> The Government seems to take the position that the parties to a merger should not be able to cure possible anti-competitive effects by a sale of a portion of the assets to a third party. No cases are cited to support this position, and I know of

none. I see no reason why merging companies cannot eliminate probable anticompetitive effects by such a disposition of assets as will be made here.

The court found that the sale to British Petroleum "would substitute a new and viable competitor for Sinclair in the Northeast" and that there was no doubt that British Petroluem would "actively and vigorously market gasoline in that area" (297 F Supp at 1068). Accordingly, it held that the government had failed to show any potential anticompetitive effect of the merger in the northeastern section of the country. However, the court granted a preliminary injunction to enjoin the merger due to probable anticompetitive consequences in the southeastern states.

The court subsequently granted defendant's motion to vacate the preliminary injunction after Atlantic Richfield agreed to sell the Sinclair marketing properties in the southeastern as well as the northeastern states to British Petroleum. The court indicated (at 1076) that this action "eliminates the probability that the Government will succeed at trial on the issue of probable lessening of competition in that section as a result of the merger." The government did not oppose the defendants' motion, and the defendants entered into a stipulation that included an agreement by Atlantic Richfield to "act in good faith to preserve its ability to comply with an ultimate divestiture order in this case." *United States v Atlantic Richfield Co.* (SD NY 1969) 297 F Supp 1075.

If the merging firms seek to avoid antitrust challenge by arranging to have one of them sell its competing product lines to a third company, the surviving corporation in the merger probably should relinquish all interest in the third party. It should certainly own no stock in the third party, and probably should not even retain promissory notes or other deferred obligations. Illustrating this is *United States v Gould Inc.* (ND Ohio 1969) 1969 Trade Cases ¶72,863. Gould and Clevite Corporation entered into a merger and simultaneously transferred certain assets of both companies to Business Funds, Inc. to eliminate possible antitrust problems. In exchange Gould received cash and a substantial amount of promissory notes issued by Business Funds. The Department of Justice filed a complaint alleging that the effect of Gould's acquisition of promissory notes from Business Funds would be to restrain competition between Gould and Business Funds. Under the terms of a simultaneous consent judgment Gould agreed to sell all promissory notes and other deferred obligations received from Business Funds within 12 months. But compare *United States v Atlantic Richfield Co., supra,* 1068.

Closing down plants creating a competitive overlap will not be viewed as favorably as a sale of those assets to a viable competitor. In *Diamond*

Alkali Co. (1967) 3 Trade Reg Rep ¶18,078, the Federal Trade Commission had to decide for the first time what remedy it would impose "where the acquiring firm has divested itself of the preacquisition assets corresponding to the particular assets whose acquisition gave the merger its anticompetitive character" (at 20,524). Although Diamond Alkali expressed its intention to withdraw from the cement industry if it were required to divest the cement production facilities that it had acquired and was using in place of facilities it had dismantled, the Commission nevertheless ordered divestiture, largely on the basis that Diamond Alkali would nevertheless remain "a credible potential competitor in the eyes of those in the industry" (at 20,528). Divestiture, therefore, promised "beneficial competitive results" since it would create one or more additional competitors and would leave Diamond Alkali as a potential competitor.

In *United States v Continental Oil Co.* (D NM 1967) 1967 Trade Cases ¶72,292, *aff'd per curiam* (1968) 393 US 79, Continental was required to divest a plant acquired from Malco, notwithstanding the fact that it had closed down its own competing plant subsequent to the acquisition. In *United States v Pabst Brewing Co.* (1966) 384 US 546, Pabst absorbed Blatz's management and equipment into its own operations and completely dismantled the Blatz brewery so that there was no identifiable separate operation. This circumstance was not even mentioned in the opinions of the District Court or the Supreme Court.

However, in one case, the respondent requested approval for the acquisition of a *vacant* plant, indicating that after the acquisition it would close down its own plant operating in the same market. No transfer of customer lists or goodwill would be made. The acquisition was approved by the Federal Trade Commission. *Continental Baking Co.* (1969) 3 Trade Reg Rep ¶18,708. See also *Brillo Mfg. Co., Inc.* (1969) 3 Trade Reg Rep ¶18,716.

It is possible that different standards will be applied if the parties can establish that they were not considering the acquisition at the time when one of them closed down its plant and that the firm that closed its plant was not planning to and would not have replaced it. Normally this will require that the plant have been shut down a substantial time before the acquisition. In this situation the parties may be able to succeed in having the merger treated as a conglomerate acquisition and examined under the standards used in evaluating potential competition. See §4.30. On the other hand, if the merger was contemplated when the plant was closed or if the plant would have been replaced in any event, the standards applicable to horizontal mergers will undoubtedly be applied as if the parties were competitors.

3. [§4.53] Acquisition of Smaller Firm in Market—"Foothold Acquisition"

The present Assistant Attorney General in charge of the Antitrust Division, Richard W. McLaren, has frequently stated that the government would welcome "foothold" acquisitions (the purchase of one of the smaller firms in an industry) by large conglomerate firms in concentrated industries. See, e.g., Address by Richard W. McLaren, Assistant Attorney General, Antitrust Division, before the Town Hall of California, May 27, 1969, p.12. This invitation represents the other side of the Department's effort to prohibit the nation's largest companies from acquiring any leading firm in a concentrated industry. See discussion at §§4.32–4.35. It is based on the premise that when a very large firm buys a small firm in a concentrated industry, it has the resources to expand the firm's capacity and to try to increase its share of the market. Therefore, the merger can infuse new vigor and ideas into that market. The FTC has unanimously voiced approval of "toehold" acquisitions in *Bendix Corp.* (1970) 3 Trade Reg Rep ¶19,288.

Any large firm contemplating an acquisition should at least be aware of this relatively safe method of entering an industry by acquisition. Litton Industries has made more than seventy multi-million dollar acquisitions during the past ten years with only one challenge, apparently by avoiding any significant horizontal or vertical overlaps and by not purchasing a firm that ranks higher than fourth or fifth in its market. See Davidow, *Conglomerate Concentration and Section 7: The Limitations of the Anti-Merger Act* (1968) 68 *Col L Rev* 1231, 1270.

To date, no precise standards for a "foothold" acquisition have been established. However, the market share and position and the absolute size of the acquired firm will apparently be considered. For example, the Department of Justice challenged LTV's acquisition of Jones & Laughlin, the fifth largest steel company. In an interview with *Forbes* magazine (June 1, 1969, p.23), Assistant Attorney General McLaren characterized Jones & Laughlin as "fabulously large" and termed this acquisition as "a lot more than a foothold."

H. Risks of Making Acquisition Deemed Unsafe

1. [§4.54] Introduction

Assuming the proposed acquisition appears to fall within the danger areas (see §§4.42–4.50), the client will want to know what the actual risks are if he proceeds. The risks will be different for the acquired and acquiring companies and will be different before and after the acquisition.

In general, shareholders of the acquired company will be "safe" after the acquisition is consummated except in unusual circumstances. If the government seeks to enjoin the acquisition, the hearing on the motion for a preliminary injunction will be the watershed event for the shareholders. See §4.60.

The potential costs of a suit enjoining the merger will frequently be greater for the acquired company itself. Employee and executive morale may drop after the announcement of plans to sell the company and there may consequently be difficulties in retaining or replacing key people. Problems may develop in sales of the company's products because customers will be uncertain of the company's future. Other opportunities to sell the company may be lost. Furthermore, information the government may acquire about the selling company in the course of its investigation and its increased familiarity with its business may make a future sale of the company more difficult.

On the other hand, the acquiring company will remain subject to suit. There is no statute of limitations on a government suit challenging a merger, and a suit may not be filed until several years after the acquisition. The acquiring company may ultimately be forced to divest itself of the acquired business; hence it is important to consider the potential cost of divestiture. Divestiture can be either extremely profitable or extremely costly, to some extent depending on how successfully the acquiring firm conducts the business of the acquired firm. For example, Brown Shoe is reported to have made a pre-tax profit of over $14 million on its sale of Kinney, whereas Schlitz is reported to have lost as much as $21 million as a result of the forced divestiture of John Labatt Ltd., General Brewing Corporation, and Burgermeister. 421 ATRR A-7 (August 5, 1969).

Even if it is eventually successful in defending against a suit, the acquiring firm's operation of the acquired business may be adversely affected during the prolonged period that suit is pending. Management probably will be unwilling to make new investments that may be necessary to realize maximum earnings from the acquired business, and it may be unwilling to reassign existing managerial personnel or to recruit new employees to manage the acquired business. As a result it may not be able to realize its projected earnings from the acquisition.

In addition to divestiture, the purchaser may also be forced to license patents, trademarks, or trade names, perhaps on a royalty-free basis, or to render assistance to the divested or spun-off company. A ban may be placed on future acquisitions for a lengthy period of time, and prior acquisitions may be investigated. Treble-damage actions may be brought by private parties. Finally, substantial legal fees may be incurred. It is essential that the antitrust adviser point out all these risks to a company contemplating an acquisition that falls within the area of potential challenge.

2. [§4.55] Risk of Suit for Preliminary Injunction

Both the acquired and the acquiring firms are exposed to risks of a government or private suit before consummation of an acquisition. So far, no acquisition has ever been consummated after a preliminary injunction was granted. While the Department of Justice, the Federal Trade Commission, and private parties all may obtain a preliminary injunction, each must proceed under a separate statute.

a. [§4.56] Department of Justice

The Department of Justice is authorized to bring suit in the district courts "to prevent and restrain . . . violations" of Section 7 (15 USC §18) under Section 15 of the Clayton Act (15 USC § 25). To obtain a preliminary injunction, the Department must establish to the satisfaction of the court that there is a reasonable probability that it will prevail in a trial on the merits. See Note, *Preliminary Relief for the Government Under Section 7 of the Clayton Act* (1965) 79 *Harv L Rev* 391. While it is not required to show that the merger will cause probable injury to the public, a number of courts have considered the probable injury to the defendants that might ensue from the issuance of an injunction. See, *e.g.*, *Allis-Chalmers Mfg. Co. v White Consolidated Industries, Inc.* (3d Cir 1969) 414 F2d 506; *United States v Ingersoll-Rand Co.* (3d Cir 1963) 320 F2d 509; *United States v Atlantic Richfield Co.* (SD NY 1969) 297 F Supp 1061; *United States v Wilson Sporting Goods Co.* (ND Ill 1968) 288 F Supp 543; *United States v Chrysler Corp.* (D NJ 1964) 232 F Supp 651; *United States v Crocker-Anglo Nat'l. Bank* (ND Calif 1963) 223 F Supp 849.

From the defendant's standpoint, the most favorable statement of the requirements for granting a preliminary injunction appears in the recent ITT case, *United States v International Telephone and Telegraph Corp.* (D Conn 1969) 306 F Supp 766, 769. The court indicated that a motion for a preliminary injunction presents the following basic questions:

(1) Whether the government has sustained its burden of establishing a reasonable probability of success in proving its case on the merits upon final hearing.

(2) Whether the alleged injury to the public interest resulting from denial of a preliminary injunction outweighs the alleged injury to defendants resulting from the granting of a preliminary injunction.

(3) Whether, under all the circumstances here present, the interests of the respective parties, as well as the public interest, would be best served by the entry of a hold separate order to preserve the status quo pending hearing and decision of the case on the merits.

The parties to a merger typically make three arguments in opposing the government's motion for a preliminary injunction. First, they argue that the government has not adequately demonstrated a probability that the merger will ultimately be held unlawful under Section 7; second, that a greater injury will be inflicted on the merging firms if the injunction is granted than would be borne by the government or the public if the injunction is denied, usually claiming that the merger will be terminated unless it can be consummated immediately, whereas divestiture will always be available if the government should prevail in proving a violation of Section 7; and, finally, they normally agree to stipulate that the two companies will be operated separately during the litigation so that divestiture will pose no problem if the merger is found to violate the law.

Preliminary injunctions have been denied almost twice as often as they have been granted in cases instituted by the Department of Justice, but the frequency of granting has been increasing recently. Denial of a preliminary injunction has usually been on condition that the two companies be operated under "hold separate" orders pending the outcome of the suit. See, *e.g., United States v Brown Shoe Co.* (ED Mo 1956) 1956 Trade Cases ¶68,244 and *United States v Northwest Industries, Inc.* (ND Ill 1969) 301 F Supp 1066, 1097–1100.

It may be possible to negotiate the terms of a "hold separate" order in advance. In *United States v Ling-Temco-Vought, Inc.* (WD Pa April 14, 1969) 5 Trade Reg Rep ¶45,069 at 52,712, the government entered into an agreement with Ling-Temco-Vought and Jones & Laughlin before filing its complaint under which the parties consented to the entry of an interim order pending final adjudication, permitting LTV to retain up to 81% of the outstanding common stock of Jones & Laughlin on condition that the stock be held in a voting trust and the business and financial operations of the two companies be maintained completely separate. The parties also stipulated that divestiture would be appropriate if the acquisition was ultimately held to violate Section 7.

b. [§4.57] Federal Trade Commission

The Federal Trade Commission was widely believed not to be empowered to seek preliminary relief prior to the Supreme Court's decision in *FTC v Dean Foods Co.* (1966) 384 US 597. Despite the absence of any explicit statutory authority giving the Commission power to seek preliminary injunctive relief, the Court held, five to four, that the All Writs Act (28 USC §1651(a)) authorizes the courts of appeals to issue preliminary injunctions preventing the consummation of a merger on a motion by the Commission.

The Commission has rarely used the power to seek preliminary injunctions. FTC complaint counsel must obtain authorization from the Commission before seeking a preliminary injunction, and permission is not always granted. See, *e.g.*, *Litton Industries, Inc.* (1969) 3 Trade Reg Rep ¶18,828.

One reason why the Commission may be reluctant to seek more preliminary injunctions is the severe procedural problems posed for the courts of appeals. Since preliminary hearings on injunctive relief in merger cases require complex fact finding, amounting to miniature trials on the merits, the task is not one that courts of appeals are accustomed to performing and may interfere with their other duties.

It is not yet certain what standard will be applied by the courts of appeals in deciding whether to issue preliminary injunctions in cases initiated by the FTC. While there is language in the Supreme Court's opinion in *Dean Foods* that might support a more stringent standard than that applied in cases instituted in the district court by the Department of Justice, on remand the court of appeals apparently applied the same standard—reasonable probability that the merger would be found to violate Section 7—normally applied in cases brought by the Department of Justice. Resolution of this question will have to await future cases. For further discussion of the power of the Federal Trade Commission to seek preliminary injunctions, see Comment, *The FTC's Power to Seek Preliminary Injunctions in Anti-Merger Cases* (1967) 66 *Mich L Rev* 142.

c. [§4.58] Private Parties

Private parties may also seek to enjoin consummation of a merger under Section 16 of the Clayton Act (15 USC §26). This statute differs from Section 15 of the Clayton Act, which authorizes the Department of Justice to obtain a preliminary injunction, in that it requires the private party to make "a showing that the danger of irreparable loss or damage is immediate." In deciding whether a showing of irreparable harm has been made, the courts may also consider prospective harm to the public, such as a showing that divestiture will not be possible or that the restored company will not be as strong a competitor as the acquired firm. In addition, of course, the plaintiff must also establish that there is a reasonable probability that it will ultimately prevail on the merits.

Most of the private actions for preliminary injunctions have been brought by corporations seeking to prevent further acquisitions of their own stock or the voting of their stock by firms attempting to gain control or obtain representation on the board of directors against management's wishes. See, *e.g.*, *Allis-Chalmers Mfg. Co. v White Consolidated Indus-*

tries, Inc. (3d Cir 1969) 414 F2d 506. There would appear to be no reason why preliminary relief should not be available to competitors or customers of either of the merging firms, assuming they are able to show that the merger will cause irreparable injury to their business.

In cases of attempted "take-overs," the courts have sometimes weighed the potential harm to both firms that would result from granting or denying preliminary relief. In two recent cases preliminary injunctions were granted on findings of irreparable harm based on factors including the adverse effects a "take-over" would have on employee recruitment, morale, and performance; possible withholding of orders by customers uncertain about the attempted "take-over"; and the possibility that the acquiring firm would gain access to trade secrets or other secret information about the acquired firm's business. See *Allis-Chalmers Mfg. Co. v White Consolidated Industries, Inc., supra;* and *American Smelting and Refining Co. v Pennzoil United, Inc.* (D Del 1969) 1969 Trade Cases ¶72,776. See also *Hamilton Watch Co. v Benrus Watch Co.* (2d Cir 1953) 206 F2d 738, 742; and *Crane Co. v Briggs Mfg. Co.* (6th Cir 1960) 280 F2d 747.

d. [§4.59] Appealability of Orders Granting or Denying Preliminary Relief

An order granting or denying a preliminary injunction in a private suit clearly may be appealed (28 USC §1292(a)(1)). See, *e.g., Crane Co. v Briggs Mfg. Co.* (6th Cir 1960) 280 F2d 747; *Allis-Chalmers Mfg. Co. v White Consolidated Industries, Inc.* (3d Cir 1969) 414 F2d 506. The authorities are divided on the appealability of orders granting or denying preliminary relief in a government suit. This difference arises because Section 2 of the Expediting Act of 1903 (15 USC §29) makes final judgments in government civil antitrust suits appealable directly to the Supreme Court, but says nothing about interlocutory orders. Compare *United States v Ingersoll-Rand Co.* (3d Cir 1963) 320 F2d 509, with *United States v FMC Corp.* (9th Cir 1963) 321 F2d 534.

3. [§4.60] Risks to Shareholders of Acquired Company after Consummation of Acquisition: Rescission

In the past it has been assumed that if a selling company can escape a preliminary injunction and the sale is consummated, then it is "home free." This assumption may still be substantially accurate, but it cannot be accepted without reservation.

When a company sells all its stock or assets to another corporation and ceases to exist after the merger, the antitrust laws will almost never continue to be a *direct* threat to the former shareholders of the acquired firm after the merger has been consummated. At the same time, the shareholders will often receive stock of the acquiring company, and the principal shareholders will frequently receive investment letter stock which they must hold for a substantial time. As a result, the former shareholders of the acquired firm may be affected indirectly by a government suit against the acquiring firm. There may be a more direct effect on the former management of the acquired firm if they continue to work for the acquiring company if divestiture is ultimately decreed.

If the selling company remains in existence after the sale is consummated, it is possible that rescission of the transaction may be sought by the government. To date this drastic form of relief has never been granted. In *United States v Reed Roller Bit Co.* (WD Okla 1967) 274 F Supp 573, 590, the government sought rescission and return of the acquired assets to the seller as its "preferred remedy." The defendants argued that there was no congressional authority for this form of relief. The court found it unnecessary to make a choice between these positions, since it found that rescission of the merger would not be the most effective form of relief. See also *Dean Foods Co.* (1966) [1965-1967 Transfer Binder] Trade Reg Rep ¶17,765 at 23,117-23,128. If rescission is granted at all, it is most likely to occur when the government has filed suit before consummation of the acquisition, has requested but failed to obtain a preliminary injunction, and when the selling company has remained in existence as a viable business. Also, rescission probably would be granted more readily when the acquired company is privately owned than when it is a widely held public company.

To date no other form of relief has been requested or granted against the acquired firm or its shareholders after an acquisition has been consummated.

4. [§4.61] Ban on Future Acquisitions

Future-merger bans have been included in a large majority of both consent decrees and litigated judgments in cases brought recently against the acquiring firm by both the Department of Justice and the Federal Trade Commission. This ban may prohibit certain types of mergers for a specified period or require that the defendant obtain permission from or notify the Department of Justice or the Federal Trade Commission before making any acquisitions.

The most common time limit in consent decrees negotiated by both government agencies is ten years, although a few decrees specify a longer or shorter period. In litigated cases the time period has varied widely, but frequently has been for less than ten years. In *United States v Joseph Schlitz Brewing Co.* (ND Calif 1966) 253 F Supp 129, *aff'd per curiam* (1966) 385 US 37, the court entered an order permanently enjoining Schlitz from making any acquisitions in the brewing industry elsewhere in the United States for a period of ten years without the consent of the Department of Justice. On the other hand, in *United States v Times Mirror Co.* (CD Calif 1967) 274 F Supp 606, 623, the court denied the government's request for a permanent merger ban.

Counsel is well advised to obtain a time limit if a ban is imposed lest an unlimited ban against acquisitions haunt the client in the distant future. See, *e.g.,* Justice Department challenges of General Host's 1969 acquisition and Greyhound's 1970 acquisition of Armour & Co. as violating a 1920 consent decree. The former case was ordered dismissed as moot after General Host sold its Armour stock to Greyhound. *United States v Armour & Co.* (1970) 398 US 268.

Most bans are limited to a particular industry, but Procter & Gamble has consented to a decree that prohibits it from acquiring "any company which manufactures, produces, sells or distributes any household consumer product." *Procter & Gamble Co.* (1967) [1965–1967 Transfer Binder] Trade Reg Rep ¶17,858 at 23,215. Frito-Lay, Inc. has agreed not to acquire any manufacturer of soft drinks, coffee, tea, milk, sugar, potato chips, corn chips, nuts, or pretzels. *Frito-Lay, Inc.* (1968) 3 Trade Reg Rep ¶18,437. See also *Occidental Petroleum Corp.* (1968) 3 Trade Reg Rep ¶18,527.

Usually the ban is not limited to any specific geographic area. But see *United States v First Nat'l. Bank* (1967) 1967 Trade Cases ¶72,180; *United States v Peabody Coal Co.* (1967) 1967 Trade Cases ¶72,213; *United States v Gulf & Western Industries, Inc.* (1967) 1967 Trade Cases ¶72,166; *United States v Joseph Schlitz Brewing Co., supra,* all cases with geographic limits written into consent decrees negotiated with the Justice Department.

Some future-merger bans specifically exclude from their prohibition acquisitions of firms with gross annual sales below a certain dollar amount or acquisitions of firms that are unable to pay their current obligations when due. For example, in *United States v Continental Oil Co.* (D NM 1968) 1968 Trade Cases ¶72,374, *aff'd per curiam* (1968) 393 US 79, the Supreme Court affirmed a district court judgment that imposed a ten-year ban on future acquisitions of any oil refinery or wholesale distributor of gasoline, except for acquisitions in any twelve-month period of distributors having combined annual sales of not more than $250,000. See also *H.C. Bohack Co.* (1968) 3 Trade Reg Rep ¶18,443 and *Chemetron Corp.*

(1969) 3 Trade Reg Rep ¶18,794. In the latter case, only temporary acquisitions were permitted.

Future-merger bans are commonly imposed whether or not divestiture or partial divestiture is also required and may be imposed when the government obtains a preliminary injunction against a merger. After the court granted a preliminary injunction against the proposed merger between Wilson Sporting Goods Co. and Nissen Corporation in *United States v Wilson Sporting Goods Co.* (ND Ill 1968) 288 F Supp 543, a consent judgment was subsequently entered permanently enjoining the acquisition and prohibiting Wilson for a period of five years from acquiring any interest in any manufacturer of gymnastic equipment in the United States without notifying the government 60 days before the consummation of such acquisition. See *United States v Wilson Sporting Goods Co.* (ND Ill 1968) 1968 Trade Cases ¶72.585.

It may be possible in negotiating a consent decree to provide that a ban on future mergers will be subject to modification if less restrictive orders are subsequently accepted from firms competing in the same industry as the acquiring firm. To protect the ability to modify a consent order, counsel should attempt to get a provision in the original order enabling the proceeding to be reopened to permit modification. Compare *Grand Union Co.* (1968) 3 Trade Reg Rep ¶18,414 and *Winn-Dixie Stores, Inc.* (1968) 3 Trade Reg Rep ¶18,415 with *National Tea Co.* (1969) 3 Trade Reg Rep ¶18,782.

In at least one FTC proceeding, a voluntary undertaking not to make mergers within a certain class for a period of ten years has been required from the purchaser of property being divested as a condition of the Commission's approval of the proposed divestiture. See *Lucky Stores, Inc.* (Assurance of Voluntary Compliance, January 2, 1968) 3 Trade Reg Rep ¶18,145. In another case a firm subject to a consent order precluding it from making acquisitions for a five-year period without prior approval of the FTC was able to obtain the Commission's approval for a proposed merger only by agreeing to extend the ban on future acquisitions for three additional years. See *Broadway-Hale Stores, Inc.* (1969) 3 Trade Reg Rep ¶18,692.

The power of the FTC to impose a ban on future mergers has been questioned, particularly when the Commission is acting solely under Section 7 of the Clayton Act (15 USC §18) and not under Section 5 of the Federal Trade Commission Act (15 USC §45) as well. However, no decisions to date have denied the authority to the Commission. See *Ekco Products Co. v FTC* (7th Cir 1965) 347 F2d 745, affirming a twenty-year ban on mergers. See also *American Brake Shoe Co.* (1968) 3 Trade Reg

Rep ¶18,339 at 20,717; and *Foremost Dairies, Inc.* (1962) 60 FTC 944, 1092. In *Luria Bros. & Co. v FTC* (3d Cir 1968) 389 F2d 847, 865, the court stated, "Beyond all doubt the Commission has the power to enjoin future acquisitions."

5. [§4.62] Divestiture

Divestiture of the acquired assets is the most common form of relief sought by the government in merger cases. While partial divestiture has been required more frequently than total divestiture, total divestiture is becoming increasingly common.

The leading case on divestiture is the Supreme Court's decision in *United States v E.I. du Pont de Nemours & Co.* (1962) 366 US 316, in which the Court ordered complete divestiture by duPont of its General Motors stock over a ten-year period. After observing that "complete divestiture is peculiarly appropriate in cases of stock acquisitions which violate §7" (366 US at 328), the Court stated (366 US at 330–331):

> Divestiture has been called the most important of antitrust remedies. It is simple, relatively easy to administer, and sure. It should always be in the forefront of a court's mind when a violation of §7 has been found.

While the Court agreed that relief must not be punitive, it held that "economic hardship can influence choice only as among two or more effective remedies." If "complete divestiture is a necessary element of effective relief, the Government cannot be denied [this] remedy because economic hardship, however severe, may result" (366 US at 327).

In *United States v El Paso Natural Gas Co.* (1964) 376 US 651, the Supreme Court held that the acquisition by El Paso Natural Gas Company of Pacific Northwest Pipeline Corporation violated Section 7 of the Clayton Act (15 USC §18) and ordered divestiture "without delay." Subsequently the Supreme Court set aside a settlement without divestiture as not complying with the mandate of the Court. *Cascade Natural Gas Corp. v El Paso Natural Gas Co.* (1967) 386 US 129. On remand, the district court refused to permit El Paso to select a buyer from a list of qualified applicants the court might have chosen but decided that the court should choose from among the various potential purchasers the one that is "best qualified to make New Company a serious competitor" in the California market. *United States v El Paso Natural Gas Co.* (D Utah 1968) 1968 Trade Cases ¶72,533 at 85,840. After the district court selected Colorado Interstate Corporation, the Utah Public Service Commission appealed to the Supreme Court, but moved to dismiss its appeal before oral argument. The Supreme Court refused to grant the motion to dismiss the appeal and after oral argument, in a four-to-two decision, vacated the judgment and remanded the case for further proceedings. *Utah Public Service Comm'n. v El Paso Natural Gas Co.* (1969) 395 US 464.

Of particular significance were the Court's determinations (at 470–472) that (1) the allocation of gas reserves between El Paso and the company purchasing the former property of Pacific Northwest (New Company) must be done in a way "to rectify, if possible, the manner in which El Paso has used the illegal merger to strengthen its position in the California market" (at 470) and must "place New Company in the same relative competitive position *vis-a-vis* El Paso in the California market as that which Pacific Northwest enjoyed immediately prior to the illegal merger"; (2) the selection of the applicant to acquire New Company should take into account "whether an award to a particular applicant will have any anti-competitive effects either in the California market or in other markets"; and (3) El Paso should not be permitted to retain any stock in New Company notwithstanding the enlarged income-tax burden that would result to it by requiring a cash sale.

In *United States v Aluminum Co. of America* (1967) 389 US 49, the Department of Justice appealed from a decree of divestiture on the ground that new anticompetitive consequences would be posed by a sale to the purchaser approved by the court. The judgment of the district court was vacated as moot after another purchaser satisfactory to the government was found.

Companies planning a merger must assume that divestiture may be required to a purchaser selected or approved by the government and/or the court, which may not necessarily be the purchaser who offers the highest price, that a sale for cash may be required, and that various forms of assistance may have to be rendered to the firm that purchases the divested assets.

Normally the divesting company is required to notify potential purchasers of and to advertise the availability of the property. Some orders specify classes of ineligible purchasers or specify whether the assets may be split up or whether they must be sold as a single unit.

Provisions specifying a minimum price to be charged for the assets to be divested appear in a few orders. However, the Department of Justice will almost never agree to include such an "upset" price in a consent decree and will oppose the use of such a provision in a court decree.

Most divestiture orders establish a time limit within which the sale must be made. Some decrees permit the acquiring company to retain the acquired assets if divestiture cannot be accomplished within the specified period, and there have been some instances in which divestiture was not achieved and the acquiring company ultimately retained the acquired assets. This has occurred most often when the acquired business was not being operated profitably. Other decrees contain a provision allowing the Federal Trade Commission or the district court to modify the order if divestiture cannot be accomplished.

Some orders, especially in vertical mergers, have given the acquiring firm some flexibility in determining which outlets to divest. For example, under the terms of two consent judgments, manufacturers of dental products were required to divest dental supply houses accounting for 50% of the acquiring company's total retail volume of dental products in one case and for a specified dollar volume of retail sales in another case. See *United States v Dentists' Supply Co. of New York* (ED Pa 1968) 1967 Trade Cases ¶72,321, and *United States v Pennsalt Chemicals Corp.* (ED Pa 1968) 1967 Trade Cases ¶72,322. See also *United States v Aluminium Ltd.* (D NJ 1966) 1966 Trade Cases ¶71,895; *United States v National Cleaning Contractors, Inc.* (SD NY 1966) 1966 Trade Cases ¶71,814; and *United States v Gannett Co.* (ND Ill 1969) 1968 Trade Cases ¶72,644.

Similarly, in conglomerate mergers, the Department of Justice has sometimes negotiated the question of what interests must be divested. See, *e.g.*, settlement proposal in suit challenging Ling-Temco-Vought, Inc.'s acquisition of 81% of the stock of Jones & Laughlin Steel Corp. Within three years LTV could divest all its interests in Braniff Airways, Inc. and the Okonite Co., retaining its interests in Jones & Laughlin *or* divest all its interest in Jones & Laughlin, retaining its interest in the other companies. See *United States v Ling-Temco-Vought, Inc.* (WD Pa 1970) 1970 Trade Cases ¶73,105.

Most orders provide that the capacity of the acquired unit must be maintained between the time when an order is issued and the date of divestiture. Accordingly, the acquiring firm may be prevented from closing down or dismantling acquired facilities. See, *e.g.*, *United States v Cities Service Co.* (D Mass 1968) 289 F Supp 133, and *United States v Crown Textile Mfg. Co.* (ED Pa 1967) 1967 Trade Cases ¶72,188. But compare *United States v Aluminium Ltd., supra.*

The government also takes the position that any divestiture order should require divestiture of adequate working capital for the divested company plus sufficient funds to finance any needed capital improvements or other modernization of the facilities to be divested.

If a merger may have adverse effects in only a few markets, it remains an open question whether the courts will require complete divestiture or only partial divestiture encompassing the lines of commerce that raise competitive problems. For the last several years the Department of Justice has normally refused to negotiate consent decrees permitting partial divestiture, arguing that complete divestiture is essential in order to find the strongest possible purchaser for the offending lines. While the Supreme Court has usually ordered complete divestiture, it has at least left open the door for the use of partial divestiture in some situations. In *Brown Shoe Co. v United States* (1962) 370 US 294, 337 n. 65, after indicating that the fact that two merging firms competed with each other in only a fraction of the markets in which they were engaged would not be a bar to finding a violation of Section 7, the Court stated: "[T]hat fact would, of course, be properly considered in determining the equitable relief to be decreed." In contrast, the Federal Trade Commission and the district courts have frequently ordered only partial divestiture, sometimes finding that complete divestiture would be unwarranted or unsuitable. For example, in *United States v Reed Roller Bit Co.* (WD Okla 1967) 274 F Supp 573, 586, the district court held that when a merger may have anticompetitive effects in some markets but not in others, divestiture "may be confined to the operations in the markets adversely affected" if this form of limited divestiture "is at least equally effective as any other form of relief." The district court also noted that partial divestiture would have the further advantage of decreasing the size of the purchase that must be made by another firm and would thereby be likely to increase the number of potential buyers (274 F Supp at 590). In addition, it found that the merger would have pro-competitive effects in other markets and observed (274 F Supp at 589):

> This Court recognizes that pro-competitive consequences in one market cannot be considered so as to outweigh the anticompetitive consequences in another market. . . . At the same time the fact that a merger has beneficial effects on competition in some markets is material to the type of relief to be decreed where permitting the acquiring company to keep the assets relating to the market where competition has been increased will at least be as effective in restoring competition in the other markets that have been adversely affected by the merger.

See also, *Occidental Petroleum Corp.* (1968) 3 Trade Reg Rep ¶18,527 and ¶18,599, and *Foremost Dairies, Inc.* (1967) [1965-1967 Transfer Binder] Trade Reg Rep ¶17,835.

It is not yet clear whether or in what circumstances an acquiring firm will be required to divest itself of assets in some way related to the acquired assets but acquired or constructed after the challenged acquisition. The government frequently insists on divestiture of after-acquired assets in negotiating a consent decree and seeks such relief in litigation. In *Reynolds Metals Co. v FTC* (DC Cir 1962) 309 F2d 223, 231, the court, in an opinion written by Chief Justice Burger while he was a circuit judge, modified an order of the FTC to delete the requirement for divestiture of a plant constructed after the acquisition. After indicating that "after-acquired properties are not relevant, except in the case where they represent reinvestment of capital realized from the sale of property included in a forbidden acquisition and replacement of that property," the court stated that if after-acquired property may ever be subject to divestiture, there would have to be a strong demonstration of (1) a nexus between continued possession of the after-acquired property and the violation of Section 7 and (2) a necessity for divestiture of such property in order to restore the competitive status quo. In contrast, in *United States v Aluminum Co. of America* (ED Mo 1964) 247 F Supp 308, *aff'd per curiam* (1965) 382 US 12, the Supreme Court approved *per curiam* a district court decree requiring Alcoa to divest itself of a plant it had built after an illegal acquisition.

In order to minimize the possibility that new facilities constructed to replace older acquired facilities will have to be divested, the new facilities should be constructed so that they are completely separate and independent from the acquired facilities. Compare *United States v Ford Motor Co.* (ED Mich 1970) 1970 Trade Cases ¶73,254 at 89,018.

The authority of the FTC to order divestiture was questioned and upheld in *Luria Bros. & Co. v FTC* (3d Cir 1968) 389 F2d 847, 865. The government may bring an action for civil penalties against a defendant who fails to comply with the Commission's divestiture order. In *United States v ABC Consolidated Corp.* (ED NY 1968) 1968 Trade Cases ¶72,621, the first civil action seeking penalties for failure to complete divestiture as ordered by the FTC, damages of $1,000 per day, totaling $319,000, were sought. The court denied the government's motion for summary judgment and held that a trial on the issue of proper compliance would be required.

The authorities are divided on whether divestiture is available in a private suit. To date, no court has granted this relief in a private action. Compare *Julius M. Ames Co. v Bostitch, Inc.* (SD NY 1965) 240 F Supp 521 and *Bailey's Bakery, Ltd. v Continental Baking Co.* (D Haw 1964) 235 F Supp 705, 717, with *American Commercial Barge Line Co. v Eastern Gas & Fuel Associates* (SD Ohio 1962) 204 F Supp 451, 453 and *Fanchon & Marco, Inc. v Paramount Pictures, Inc.* (SD NY 1952) 107 F Supp 532, 542, *rev'd on other grounds* (2d Cir 1953) 202 F2d 731. See also *Allis-Chalmers Mfg. Co. v White Consolidated Industries, Inc.* (3d Cir 1969) 414 F2d 506. See Note (1965) 40 *NYU L Rev* 771, 776, and Note (1964) 49 *Minn L Rev* 267.

6. [§4.63] Spin-Off

An alternative form of relief closely related to divestiture is a spin-off of the acquired assets or stock either in a distribution to the shareholders of the acquiring company or in a public offering. This alternative requires that management for the "spun-off" business be found. Accordingly, this form of relief is more likely to be possible in the case of a partial stock acquisition than in the case of an acquisition of the entire stock or assets of a business. A distribution to shareholders will only be feasible if the stock of the acquiring company is widely held by the public.

Under present tax laws the acquiring firm will normally oppose a spin-off since the distribution of shares of the new company to its shareholders will be taxed as a dividend if the divesting company has accumulated earnings and profits.

There have been few instances of spin-offs as the form of relief in merger cases, apart from the DuPont-General Motors case, *United States v E.I. duPont de Nemours & Co.* (1961) 366 US 316, after which DuPont distributed its 23 percent stock interest in General Motors to its shareholders. In that instance a special statute was enacted to avoid the harsh tax treatment that otherwise would have applied.

In *FTC v Consolidated Foods Corp.* (1965) 380 US 592, the Federal Trade Commission order (*Consolidated Foods Corp.* (1963) 62 FTC 929, 964) gave Consolidated Foods a choice between selling an acquired company to a third party or organizing a new corporation and distributing its shares pro-rata to Consolidated's stockholders. Likewise, a number of consent judgments have given the acquiring company the "option" of electing a form of spin-off. To date, however, no company has elected voluntarily to utilize a spin-off.

7. [§4.64] Establishing a New Company

When it is impossible to identify the acquired assets, or as an alternative to divestiture, the government may seek to require the acquiring firm to establish a new competitor to enter the market affected by the original acquisition and to sever connections with it. This form of relief has been imposed under several recent consent judgments.

Under the terms of the consent judgment entered in *United States v Third Nat'l. Bank* (MD Tenn 1968) 1968 Trade Cases ¶72,556, Third Nat'l. Bank was ordered "to organize a viable new banking organization" (at 85,929) and, for that purpose, to provide a specified minimum sum as initial capital, to transfer certain designated assets to the new firm, and to "exercise its best efforts to obtain qualified management" (at 85,930) for the new organization. It was also required to sell the stock of the new company to a purchaser approved by the government as promptly as possible.

In *United States v Eversharp, Inc.* (ED Pa 1967) 1967 Trade Cases ¶72,221, a consent judgment permitted the merger of an electric shaver manufacturer with a wet-shave instrument manufacturer on condition that the resulting firm would form separate electric and wet-shave subsidiaries and sell one of them within five years. See also *United States v Peabody Coal Co.* (ND Ill 1967) 1967 Trade Cases ¶72,213; *United States v Mercantile Trust Co. Nat'l. Association* (ED Mo 1968) 1968 Trade Cases ¶72,379; and *Swingline Inc.* (1969) 3 Trade Reg Rep ¶18,867 and ¶18,948.

8. [§4.65] Assistance to Purchaser of Divested Property

To aid the company acquiring the divested assets to establish itself as a viable competitor, the company required to divest itself of acquired assets may be ordered to assist the purchaser of the divested assets in one or more ways or to refrain from competing with it for a specified time. Such provisions are becoming increasingly common in consent judgments.

Various consent judgments have required the divesting firm to provide the purchaser of the divested assets with technical or engineering assistance, assistance in the selection and acquisition of appropriate locations for conducting the business, cooperation and assistance in the employment of management and other personnel, including an agreement to release from employment contracts anyone who desires to accept employment with the purchaser, and a list of all customers who made any purchases of the divested enterprise's products. Some orders require the acquiring company to grant licenses on patent rights and know-how to the purchaser of the divested assets. Other orders require divestiture of acquired trademarks, trade names, and related rights.

Many orders in vertical merger cases require the divesting company to make specified purchases from the company purchasing the divested assets or to sell specified supplies to the purchaser of divested assets for a certain period of time. In the case of horizontal acquisitions some orders prohibit the divesting firm from competing with the divested unit, as for example barring the sale, for a period, of its competing products to distributors that previously purchased products manufactured by the divested unit.

This brief description of various forms of assistance the divesting company may be required to render to the purchaser of the divested assets is illustrative, and by no means complete.

9. [§4.66] Treble-Damage Claims Challenging Mergers

In order to have standing to sue, a private plaintiff must bring himself within Section 4 of the Clayton Act (15 USC §15), which states:

> Any person who shall be injured in his business or property by reason of anything forbidden in the antitrust laws may sue therefor . . . and shall recover threefold the damages by him sustained. . . .

For a number of years, the authorities were divided on whether Section 7 (15 USC §18) could be the basis for a treble-damage recovery. While the Supreme Court has not yet ruled on the question, it is fairly well established in the lower courts that a private damage action will lie for a violation of Section 7. See *Gottesman v General Motors Corp.* (2d Cir 1969) 414 F2d 956; *Dailey v Quality School Plan, Inc.* (5th Cir 1967) 380 F2d 484; *Sam S. Goldstein Industries, Inc. v Botany Industries, Inc.* (SD NY 1969) 1969 Trade Cases ¶72,858; *Kirihara v Bendix Corp.* (D Haw 1969) 1969 Trade Cases ¶72,941; *Metropolitan Liquor Co., Inc. v Heublein, Inc.* (ED Wis 1969) 1970 Trade Cases ¶72,990; *Julius M. Ames v Bostitch, Inc.* (SD NY 1965) 240 F Supp 521. But see *Highland Supply Corp. v Reynolds Metals Co.* (8th Cir 1964) 327 F2d 725; *Bailey's Bakery Ltd. v Continental Baking Co.* (D Haw 1964) 235 F Supp 705; *Dairy Foods Inc. v Farmers Cooperative Creamery* (D Minn 1969) 298 F Supp 774; *Isidor Weinstein Investment Co. v Hearst Corp.* (ND Calif 1969) 303 F Supp 646. Cf. *Highland Supply Corp. v Reynolds Metals Co.* (ED Mo 1965) 245 F Supp 510. See generally, Stein, *Section 7 of the Clayton Act as the Basis for the Treble-Damage Action: When May the Private Litigant Bring His Suit?* (1968) 56 *Calif L Rev* 968. As a protective measure, it would be advisable to file any damage action based on a merger under Sections 1 and 2 of the Sherman Act (15 USC §§1–2) as well as Section 7 of the Clayton Act.

In the few private treble-damage actions based on mergers filed to date, no recovery of damages has yet occurred. However, it would not be surprising to see the number of private treble-damage actions based on violations of Section 7 increase dramatically, particularly if any of the actions now pending results in large recoveries for the plaintiffs. Pending are *Gottesman v General Motors Corp., supra,* decision on remand, *Gottesman v General Motors Corp.* (SD NY 1970) 310 F Supp 1257, a shareholder derivative action brought by minority stockholders of General Motors immediately after the Supreme Court's decision in the *DuPont-General Motors* case (*United States v E.I. duPont deNemours & Co.* (1961) 366 US 316); *Purex v Procter & Gamble Co.* (CD Calif 1970) 308 F Supp 584; and *Purex Corp. v General Foods Corp.* (CD Calif) Civil Action No. 69-965-IH.

Both of the cases brought by Purex were filed subsequent to litigated judgments favorable to the government in cases instituted by the Federal Trade Commission. In its action against Procter & Gamble based on the acquisition of Clorox, Purex is seeking actual damages in the amount of $174,500,000 (or $523,500,000 after trebling). In its action against General Foods based on the acquisition of SOS Company, Purex is seeking actual damages of $32,186,000 (or $96,558,000 after trebling). On whether the Commission's order in an FTC action will be admitted as prima facie evidence of an antitrust violation in a private action, see *Farmington Dowel Products Co. v Forster Mfg. Co.* (1st Cir 1969) 421 F2d 61, and *Purex Corp. v Procter & Gamble Co., supra.* See discussion at §6.10.

As these cases illustrate, the acquiring firm may be exposed to very large damage claims. A plaintiff who is a competitor or customer of one of the merging firms may encounter substantial problems in establishing its damages and that any damages are directly attributable to the acquisition. However, if there has already been a finding in the government's suit that the merger would produce an injury to competition, it may not be too difficult for a court to conclude that at least some competitors or customers have in fact been injured as a result of the merger. But compare *Gottesman v General Motors Corp., supra,* and *Dole Valve Co. v Perfection Bar Equipment, Inc.* (ND Ill 1970) 311 F Supp 459.

There is still some uncertainty whether a private damage claim under Section 7 may be asserted against both the purchaser and seller of the acquired assets or only against the purchasing firm. See *Dailey v Quality School Plan, Inc., supra,* 488, holding that a private treble-damage action against the seller based on Section 7 would not lie. But see *Metropolitan Liquor Co. Inc. v Heublein, Inc., supra,* holding that a terminated exclusive distributor can sue the seller and the buyer for violation of Section 7 of the Clayton Act. Of course, an action under Sections 1 or 2 of the Sherman Act will lie against both the purchaser and seller.

10. [§4.67] Attacks on Past Acquisitions: Statute of Limitations

There is no statute of limitations on government suits challenging mergers that seek a preliminary injunction, divestiture, or other equitable relief. In the *DuPont-General Motors* case, the Supreme Court held that "the Government may proceed at any time that an acquisition may be said with reasonable probability to contain a threat that it may lead to a restraint of commerce or tend to create a monopoly of a line of commerce," regardless of the time the acquisition was made. The Court further stated that "the test of a violation of §7 is whether, at the time of the suit, there is a reasonable probability that the acquisition is likely to result in the condemned restraints." See *United States v E.I. duPont deNemours & Co.* (1957) 353 US 586, 597, 607. This doctrine has been reaffirmed by the Supreme Court in *United States v Penn-Olin Chemical Co.* (1964) 378 US 158, 168, and *FTC v Consolidated Foods Corp.* (1965) 380 US 592, 598.

It has not been uncommon for the government, following the investigation of a pending or recent acquisition, to file a suit challenging not only that acquisition but also other acquisitions made by the acquiring firm over a period of years. Acquisitions dating back as long as fifteen years and numbering as many as 175 separate acquisitions have been challenged. See, *e.g., Beatrice Foods Co.* (1967) [1965-1967 Transfer Binder] Trade Reg Rep ¶17,244; *Maremont Corp.* (1968) 3 Trade Reg Rep ¶18,431; and *United States v Hart Schaffner & Marx* (ND Ill 1968) 5 Trade Reg Rep ¶45,068 at 52,697 (case 2026). Obviously any firm contemplating an acquisition must consider the possibility that the government will challenge not only the current acquisition but past acquisitions as well. The penalty may be severe for a firm that takes one bite too many.

It is also not uncommon for the government to file a suit challenging a merger two or three years after it has occurred. Occasionally, an acquisition may come to the attention of the government after it is consummated. In other cases a series of mergers may occur in an industry over a period of a few years, and the government may challenge all mergers posing the same problem in order to avoid discriminatory treatment. It has been much less common for the government to challenge an acquisition that occurred many years earlier when there are no recent acquisitions that are also being challenged. Compare Orrick, *The Clayton Act: Then and Now* (1964) 24 ABA Antitrust Section 44, 52, with Subcommittee on Section 7 of the Clayton Act of the ABA Antitrust Section, *The Backward Sweep Theory and the Oligopoly Problem* (1966) 32 ABA Antitrust LJ 306.

There is likewise no statute of limitations on private suits seeking injunctive or other equitable relief. However, the doctrine of laches may apply, although in *International Telephone & Telegraph Corp. v General Telephone & Electronics Corp.* (D Haw 1969) 1969 Trade Cases ¶72,691 at 86,463, the court stated:

> The private litigant, no less than the government, is entitled to the opportunity to ponder and evaluate the effect of acquisitions, and need not bull ahead indiscriminately to avoid the proscriptive doctrine of laches.

But see *Burkhead v Phillips Petroleum Co.* (ND Calif 1970) 308 F Supp 120, 125, which holds that a private suit under Section 7 of the Clayton

Act may be brought only at the time the acquisition is actually consummated and not thereafter.

A four-year statute of limitations applies to claims for monetary damages in government actions under Section 4A of the Clayton Act (15 USC §15a) and to private damage claims under Section 4B of the Clayton Act (15 USC §15b). The statute begins to run when plaintiff first suffers injury, not necessarily when the merger is consummated. Hence in *Metropolitan Liquor Co. Inc. v Heublein Inc.* (ED Wis 1969) 1970 Trade Cases ¶72,990, a damage suit by a terminated exclusive distributor against the acquired and acquiring supplier, the court held that the statute ran from the time the acquiring company terminated plaintiff's exclusive status, not from the time the merger occurred. Section 5(b) of the Clayton Act (15 USC §16(b)) suspends the running of the four-year statute of limitations on private actions during the pendency of parallel government actions and for one year thereafter. Also, section 5(a) of the Clayton Act (15 USC §16(a)) provides that judgments or decrees obtained by the government in such suits may be used as "prima facie evidence" in a private action.

11. [§4.68] Litigation Costs

The cost of litigation is one of the most obvious expenses that may be incurred if an acquisition is challenged. In a complex merger case the attorney's fees have been known to exceed $100,000 in a single year during litigation. While the annual fees will normally be considerably less than this, a vast amount of preparation will be required to try a merger case, and a protracted trial followed by lengthy appeals is not uncommon. While most cases will ultimately be settled, the legal fees incurred in negotiating acceptable terms of settlement may also be substantial. If the acquisition has been consummated before suit, these costs will be borne solely by the acquiring firm. However, if a suit is brought prior to consummation, both firms will incur legal costs. Litigation will also divert the time and energy of executives from other management tasks.

I. Steps to Minimize Risk of Possible Merger Remedies

1. [§4.69] Provision Permitting Withdrawal from Merger in Event of Challenge

In order to protect both firms, the acquisition agreement should provide that either party can withdraw in the event of litigation or threatened litigation against the merger before its consummation. This will avoid the possibility of having to hold the transaction in suspension during prolonged litigation, when the parties fail to agree on their course of action. The possible duration of litigation under Section 7 (15 USC §18) is illustrated by the length of time between the filing of the government complaint and the ultimate disposition of the case in some of the cases that have reached the United States Supreme Court: Times have ranged from 12 years in *El Paso Natural Gas* and 10 years in *Procter and Gamble* and *Pabst Brewing Co.*, to more than 2 years in *Philadelphia Nat'l. Bank*.

2. [§4.70] Provision For Contingent Shares

It is becoming increasingly common in merger agreements to provide for the issuance of additional shares to the former shareholders of the acquired firm contingent on the future earnings of the acquired business. These so-called "contingent stock pay-outs" often continue for a period as long as five years.

In any agreement providing for contingent shares it will be important for the parties to include some provision to cover the possibility of a suit challenging the acquisition. A pay-out of additional shares based on the future earnings of the acquired business will become unworkable if the acquiring firm is forced to divest the acquired business. Counsel for the acquiring company should seek to have the earnings pay-out terminate in the event of a suit attacking the merger, or at least in the event of divestiture of the acquired business. Counsel for the acquired company will want to have the maximum number of shares that could have been received under the merger agreement become payable if the acquired business is sold for any reason, including an antitrust suit.

III. Pre-Merger Notification Requirements

A. [§4.71] Introduction

There is no general requirement for advance notification with respect to mergers and acquisitions, but parties to some acquisitions may be required to notify the Federal Trade Commission or the Department of Justice in advance, either under the FTC pre-merger notification requirements or the requirements of a prior consent decree. See §§4.72–4.73. See discussion of ban on future mergers at §4.61.

B. [§4.72] FTC Pre-Merger Notification Requirement

On April 8, 1969, the Federal Trade Commission adopted a resolution requiring advance notification of and the submission of "Special Reports" on certain large corporate mergers and acquisitions. See 1 Trade Reg Rep ¶4455. O'Brien, *The Federal Trade Commission's Pre-Merger Notification Requirements* (1969) 14 *Antitrust Bulletin* 557.

The pre-merger notification requirements apply to any merger or acquisition of firms which (1) are subject to the Federal Trade Commission's jurisdiction, (2) have assets of $10 million or more, and (3) have *combined* assets of $250 million of more (at 6703). Mergers, acquisitions of assets, and acquisitions of 10 percent or more of the voting stock of another corporation are all covered. In general, notification is required within 10 days after any agreement or understanding in principle is reached and, when possible, no less than 60 days before the consummation of the transaction. However, the Commission has announced that it will not attempt to impose a strict 60-day waiting period before consummation of a merger or acquisition. If the time schedule does not permit, a letter must be submitted to the Commission's Division of Mergers within 10 days after agreement or understanding in principle is reached, stating the reasons why the deadline cannot be met and when the Special Report will be filed. The Special Report, itself, must be submitted "as promptly as possible." 1 Trade Reg Rep ¶4455.25 at 6706-6707.

The specific notification and reporting requirements, with the 60-day period subject to modification as indicated above, can be paraphrased as follows:

1. Within 10 days after any agreement or understanding in principle is reached to merge or to acquire assets of $10 million or more, and no less than 60 days prior to the consummation of the merger or acquisition, the parties to the agreement must notify the Commission of the proposed merger or acquisition, and a party with assets of $250 million or more must file a Special Report;

2. Upon becoming a party to an agreement or understanding as defined in Item 1, any corporation with assets of less than $250 million must file a Special Report if directed to do so by the Commission;

3. Within 10 days after amassing 10 percent or more of the voting stock of another corporation with assets of $10 million or more, any acquiring corporation with assets of $250 million or more must notify the Commission of the stock holdings and must file a Special Report, and any acquiring corporation with assets of less than $250 million, if the combined assets of the acquiring and acquired corporations are $250 million or more, must notify the Commission and, if directed to do so by the Commission, file a Special Report.

4. At least 60 days before effecting a stock acquisition that will give the acquiring corporation 50 percent or more of the voting stock of another corporation with assets of $10 million or more, any acquiring corporation with assets of $250 million or more must notify the Commission of the proposed acquisition and file a Special Report, and any acquiring corporation with assets of less than $250 million, if the combined assets of the acquiring and acquired are $250 million or more, must notify the Commission and, if directed to do so by the Commission, file a Special Report;

THIS REPORT IS REQUIRED BY LAW. It is mandatory under the authority of the Federal Trade Commission Act (15 U.S.C. 46). On or before the Reporting Date, complete and return one notarized copy of this Special Report to: Chief, Division of Mergers, Bureau of Restraint of Trade, Federal Trade Commission, Washington, D. C. 20580. Phone (202) 393-6800.

NOTICE OF DEFAULT. Failure to file this Special Report on or before the Reporting Date constitutes default and subjects the reporting company to penalties authorized by law.

REPORTING DATE. (1) The tenth (10th) day following the reporting company's entering into any agreement or understanding in principle to merge or to acquire assets of $10 million or more, and no later than the sixtieth (60th) day prior to the consummation of the merger or acquisition. (2) The tenth (10th) day following the reporting company's amassing of 10 percent or more of the voting stock of another corporation with assets of $10 million or more. (3) No later than the sixtieth (60th) day prior to the reporting company's effecting a stock acquisition which will result in the reporting company's holding 50 percent or more of the voting stock of another corporation with assets of $10 million or more.

FTC Form 6-21(4-69)	Federal Trade Commission	Budget Bureau No. 056-R-0026
	Washington, D. C. 20580	
	SPECIAL REPORT	Approval expires April 15, 1972
	MERGERS AND ACQUISITIONS	

INSTRUCTIONS

For purposes of this Special Report, the "reporting company" includes your company and all companies in which your company has an ownership interest through either (1) holding a majority of the outstanding voting stock, or (2) holding the power to formulate, determine, or veto basic business decisions through the use of dominant minority stockholding rights, proxy voting, contractual arrangements, agents, or other means.

Each answer should identify the question to which it is addressed. If you are unable to answer any question fully, give such information as is available to you, explain why your answer is incomplete, and indicate the source from which a complete answer may be obtained. If books and records which provide accurate answers are not available, enter your best estimates and indicate the sources or bases of your estimates. Estimated data should be followed by the notation "est."

Except where stated otherwise, all inquiries refer to the reporting company's domestic operations. All references to "year" refer to calendar year. If the reporting company does not maintain its records on a calendar year basis, supply the requested data for the company's fiscal year reporting period which most nearly corresponds to the calendar year specified.

INFORMATION TO BE PROVIDED

1. State the correct corporate name, mailing address, and state and date of incorporation for (1) the reporting company, and (2) all active companies included within the reporting company.

2. Provide the following information on the (proposed) merger or acquisition:

(a) the corporate names, mailing addresses, and principal business activities of the parties involved;
(b) if applicable, the date on which the acquiring company had amassed 10 percent of the voting stock of the acquired company;
(c) if applicable, the scheduled consummation date of the proposed merger or acquisition, a description of the manner in which the transaction is to be carried out, a description of all stocks or assets to be transferred, and the consideration to be paid.

3. Furnish copies of all annual, quarterly, or other reports (including annual balance sheets and profit and loss statements) and proxy statements made by the reporting company to its stockholders during the most recent three-year period.

4. Submit a tabulation(s) which will provide the following information for the most recent calendar year:

(a)   the reporting company's total domestic commercial sales in each of the following areas: manufacturing; mining; contract construction; wholesale and retail trade; finance, insurance, and real estate; agriculture, forestry, and fisheries; transportation, communication, electric, gas, and sanitary services; housing, repair and personal services; other industries (describe);

(b)   the total sales of all foreign subsidiaries and divisions of the reporting company.

5. List and describe by its 4-digit SIC code and short title each industry listed in the 1967 <u>Standard Industrial Classification Manual</u> (Bureau of the Budget) in which the reporting company operated establishments in 1967 or currently operates establishments, and provide the following information for each such industry:

(a)   the number of establishments operated by the reporting company in 1967;

(b)   the number of establishments currently operated by the reporting company;

(c)   the reporting company's 1967 value of shipments (sales, revenues received or other unit of value used in reports to the Bureau of the Census; for 4-digit industries in which value is not reported, show employment for payroll period which included March 12, 1967);

(d)   for each merger or acquisition which the reporting company has made in the industry since January 1, 1961, indicate the name(s) of the merged or acquired company(s) and the date that the merger or acquisition was consummated. If the transaction represented the initiation of the reporting company's operation in the industry, so indicate.

6. Describe and list by its 7-digit Census product code each product produced in manufacturing establishments of the reporting company in 1967 and report value of shipments in calendar year 1967 for each such product. In addition, provide the following information:

(a)   for each product manufactured in 1967 which has subsequently been dropped indicate the date upon which the product was dropped;

(b)   for each product which was added in 1968 indicate the value of shipments in 1968 (give period covered by shipment figure);

(c)   for each product which has been added since January 1, 1969, give the date upon which the product was added.

CERTIFICATION

This SPECIAL REPORT was prepared under my supervision and is true and correct to the best of my knowledge.

_____   _____
(Signature and title of company official)   (Date)

Subscribed and sworn to before me at the City of _____, State of _____

this _____ day of _____, 19 __. _____
                                          Notary Public

My Commission Expires _____

Print or type the name, address, and telephone number of the person to contact regarding this SPECIAL REPORT

_____   _____   _____
(Name)   (Business address)   (Business telephone no.)

5. Any corporation whose voting stock has been acquired in the amount described in Item 3, or whose voting stock is the subject of a proposed acquisition as described in Item 4, must file a Special Report if directed to do so by the Commission.

Notification of a merger or acquisition may be made in a letter indicating (1) the names and mailing addresses of the corporations involved, (2) the type of proposed transaction, (3) the date of the agreement, and (4) the consummation date of the proposed merger or acquisition.

The Special Report (FTC Form 6-21 (4-69)—see page 212) requires more detailed information. Notification and Special Reports should be addressed to: Chief, Division of Mergers, Bureau of Restraints of Trade, Federal Trade Commission, Washington, D.C. 20580.

Information supplied in response to the notification requirements will be made public by the Commission, but Special Reports become a part of the Commission's confidential records. They will be made available to the Commission's staff and, on a request complying with the Commission's Rules of Practice and Procedure, may be made available to other government agencies. Information is shared with the Department of Justice on a regular basis.

The Commission based its authority to require pre-merger notification on Sections 3, 6, 9, and 10 of the Federal Trade Commission Act, 15 USC §§43, 46, 49 and 50. It is generally accepted that the Commission has authority under Section 6(b) to require notification and the filing of Special Reports. *United States v Morton Salt Co.* (1950) 338 US 632. It is doubtful whether the Commission would have the authority to insist that all mergers and acquisitions subject to its pre-merger notification requirement be held up for a sixty-day period following notification of the Commission, but the question is unlikely to be litigated in view of the Commission's decision to require 60 days advance notification only when the time schedule of a particular acquisition permits.

Indications are that corporations are complying with the FTC pre-merger notification requirement. It is unclear what penalties would be imposed for failure to comply. Under 15 USC §50, a corporation failing to file a required report is subject to a civil forfeiture action to recover $100 per day of noncompliance. But the Commission must first serve a notice of default and 30 days must elapse after notice. It is possible that a corporation could purge itself of any default by filing within 30 days of receipt of a notice of default. Failure to comply might also be viewed as a willful disregard of the Commission's lawful process, which could result in criminal penalties under Section 10 and, if discovered, would almost certainly result in an investigation of a proposed merger or acquisition.

Special pre-merger notification requirements apply to mergers in the food distribution industry and to vertical mergers in the cement industry. These requirements are described in §4.22.

C. [§4.73] Prior Judgment or Consent Decrees

A prior judgment or consent decree may require a party to an acquisition to notify the Federal Trade Commission, the Department of Justice, or a court before consummation of an acquisition, or it may prohibit an acquisition completely unless permission of the Antitrust Division, the FTC, or a court is obtained. It will, therefore, be essential to examine any judgments or consent decrees entered at any time in antitrust actions concerning either of the parties to an acquisition.

As discussed at §4.61, a ban or restriction on future acquisitions is a common form of ancillary relief in merger cases. The restrictions frequently will apply for a ten-year period, but may last longer. For example, the Department of Justice challenged the attempted take-over of Armour and Co. by General Host as violating a 1920 consent decree enjoining Armour from acquiring any interest in a company engaged in handling certain food products. The Department acted under Section 5 of the Sherman Act (15 USC §5), which provides a jurisdictional basis for bringing a non-party before the court when the ends of justice so require. See *United States v Swift and Co.* (ND Ill 1969) 1969 Trade Cases ¶72,701, dismissed as moot, *United States v Armour & Co.* (1970) 398 US 268.

The Federal Trade Commission has brought a penalty suit under Section 5 of the Federal Trade Commission Act (15 USC §45) charging that Continental Baking made three acquisitions in violation of a 1962 FTC consent order (*Continental Baking Co.* (1962) 60 FTC 1183).

The procedure for applying for approval of an acquisition under an outstanding order of the Federal Trade Commission is the same as its procedure for requesting an advance clearance for a merger (described at §4.75).

If notification or prior approval of the Department of Justice or a court is required before making an acquisition, the terms of the judgment will dictate the procedure to be followed.

IV. Advance Clearance

A. [§4.74] Advisability

Both the Federal Trade Commission and the Department of Justice have pre-merger clearance procedures under which a party to a prospective merger or acquisition may seek advance clearance. See §§4.75 and 4.76.

In general, unless there is some compelling business necessity for obtaining an advance clearance, there is probably little purpose in applying for one. In borderline cases, when a clearance would be most helpful, neither agency is likely to grant a clearance. While the refusal of a clearance does not necessarily indicate that the government will sue, it increases the uncertainty of the merging parties. Moreover, a request for clearance insures a careful examination of the transaction that might not otherwise take place.

Only a limited number of requests for formal clearances of mergers and acquisitions are submitted each year. A majority of the requests for formal clearances are directed to the Federal Trade Commission, possibly because there are more companies subject to outstanding orders requiring its approval of acquisitions and perhaps, also, because the Commission may be more likely to approve a merger when the acquired company qualifies as a "failing company" or has serious financial problems. See discussion at §4.38.

Formal clearance is most commonly sought when one of the parties is subject to an existing order requiring it to obtain approval from the Department of Justice or Federal Trade Commission in order to make an acquisition. Another common situation is that in which the acquired company is failing or has serious financial problems. In 1968 the Federal Trade Commission released digests of 26 advisory opinions given since the inception of its pre-merger clearance program in 1962. (FTC Advisory Opinion Digest Nos. 164–189 (1968) 3 Trade Reg Rep ¶¶18,186–18,211. In 17 out of 19 cases in which clearances were granted, the acquired company was experiencing financial difficulties at least to some degree.

It may be advisable to seek advance clearance before acquiring a company experiencing serious financial difficulty because of the possible difficulty of selling it pursuant to an order requiring divestiture. Another situation in which it may sometimes be advisable to seek an advance clearance would be for a "foothold acquisition" by a major company as a means of entry into a highly concentrated market (see §4.53). An advance clearance might also be sought in some cases prior to entering into a joint venture, particularly if there is some public benefit from the joint venture that cannot be achieved in any other way. See §4.37.

A clearance is less likely to be given if one of the parties to the acquisition is a very large corporation. Compare FTC Advisory Opinion Digest Nos. 192 (1968) 3 Trade Reg Rep ¶18,216 and 238 (1968) 3 Trade Reg Rep ¶18,326 with FTC Advisory Opinion Digest Nos. 259 (1968) 3 Trade Reg Rep ¶18,410 and 308 (1968) 3 Trade Reg Rep ¶18,586. A clearance is also more likely to be granted if the firm being acquired is a small company. In over two-thirds of the cases in which the Commission has given a clearance, the acquired company had sales of less than $5 million.

B. Procedures

1. [§4.75] Federal Trade Commission Clearance Procedure

The FTC clearance procedure appears in Sections 1.2-1.4 of the Commission's Rules of Practice. See 3 Trade Reg Rep ¶9801.02-9801.04.

The request for clearance, including complete information on the proposed transaction, must be submitted in writing to the Secretary of the Commission. Conferences with members of the Commission's staff may be held before or after submission of the request. Additional information may be requested.

As a result of a modification of its pre-merger clearance procedure announced on May 23, 1969, and further revision in August and October, 1969, all applications for approval, together with supporting materials, are made public when they are received by the Commission, except for information the application has requested (with justification) to be classified as confidential, "and which the Commission, with due regard to statutory restrictions, its rules, and the public interest, has determined should not be made public." Within 30 days, "any person" may file written objections or comments with the secretary, and these comments are also placed on the public record. If substantial questions of fact are involved, the Commission may take appropriate action to resolve these issues before finally acting on the request, and in this connection it may convene a public hearing.

The Commission's disposition of the application, together with a statement of supporting reasons, will be made public in a press release. The Commission may refuse to rule on a request for clearance if it believes that an extensive investigation would be necessary before giving clearance. FTC Advisory Opinion Digest 173 (1968) 3 Trade Reg Rep ¶18,195.

Any advice given is without prejudice to the right of the Commission to reconsider the questions and, if the public interest requires, to rescind or revoke the clearance.

These same procedures apply to applications for approval of divestitures, acquisitions, or similar transactions subject to Commission review under outstanding orders.

2. [§4.76] Department of Justice Business Review Procedure

The "business review procedure" of the Department of Justice appears in Title 28, Code of Federal Regulations, Section 50.6. See 2 Trade Reg Rep ¶8559.10.

A request for a business review letter must be submitted in writing to the Assistant Attorney General, Antitrust Division, Department of Justice, Washington, D.C. 20530. The requesting parties are under an affirmative obligation to make full and true disclosure with respect to the business conduct for which review is requested. "Each request must be accompanied by all relevant data including background information, complete copies of all operative documents and detailed statements of all collateral oral understandings, if any." The requesting parties must supply any additional information requested by the Antitrust Division, and the Division will also conduct whatever independent investigation it believes is appropriate.

The Department of Justice at one time would not consider a review request for conduct subject to approval by a regulatory agency until after agency approval had been obtained; it now will, except for bank mergers or acquisitions, in circumstances "where it appears that exceptional and unnecessary burdens might otherwise be imposed on the party or parties requesting review." Any business review letter issued in these circumstances may not be taken to indicate the Department's views on the legal or factual issues that may be raised before the regulatory agency or in an appeal from a regulatory agency's decision. Furthermore, the issuance of a business review letter in these circumstances may not be represented to mean that the Department believes that there are no anticompetitive consequences warranting agency consideration.

In response to a request, the Antitrust Division may (1) state its present enforcement intentions with respect to the proposed business conduct, (2) decline to pass on the request, or (3) take such other position or action as it considers appropriate. A business review letter will have no application to any party that does not join in the request therefor. In 1969 the Antitrust Division formally adopted a policy of advising the press at the same time it advises counsel of its enforcement intentions with respect to a merger or acquisition. Normally the information will be released after the close of the stock market.

A business review letter states only the enforcement intention of the Antitrust Division as of the date of the letter, and the Department of Justice remains completely free to bring whatever action or proceeding it subsequently comes to believe is required by the public interest. See *United States v Grinnell Corp.* (D RI 1962) 30 FRD 358, 363, which upholds the Department's right to bring an action after issuing a favorable business review letter. It is extremely unlikely that the Department will challenge an acquisition after issuing a favorable business review letter absent unusual circumstances.

Any requesting party may withdraw a request for review at any time. The Antitrust Division remains free to comment anyway.

The business review procedure states that no oral clearance, release, or other statement may be given purporting to bind the enforcement discretion of the Antitrust Division. A requesting party may rely only on a written business review letter signed by the attorney general, deputy attorney general, or assistant attorney general in charge of the Antitrust Division. Notwithstanding this statement, it is fairly common for counsel to seek an informal indication from the assistant attorney general in charge of the Antitrust Division to the effect that he will not bring suit to challenge a particular merger or acquisition. This procedure is not formalized, but is probably used more frequently than the formal business review procedure. The availability of such an informal clearance may vary somewhat from time to time depending on who is the assistant attorney general in charge of the Antitrust Division.

V. Advising Client Opposing Acquisition

A. [§4.77] Introduction

There is a wide variety of situations in which a client may wish to oppose an acquisition. Management of a company may wish to oppose an unsolicited tender offer. See, e.g., *Allis Chalmers Mfg. Co. v White Consolidated Industries, Inc.* (3d Cir 1969) 414 F2d 506. A competitor or a customer or supplier of one of the parties to a proposed merger may feel threatened with a loss of market share or foreclosure from a market or source of supplies. See, e.g., *Metropolitan Liquor Co. Inc. v Heublein Inc.* (ED Wis 1969) 1970 Trade Cases ¶72,990. Conceivably a labor union fearing a potential lay-off of employees as a result of a merger may wish to stop an acquisition. A recent decision even holds that an employee who loses his job as a result of a merger may bring an action for treble damages. *Dailey v Quality School Plan, Inc.* (5th Cir 1967) 380 F2d 484.

In each of these situations the party threatened by the proposed merger may seek to induce the government to file suit (§4.78) or, if a government suit has already been filed, attempt to intervene in it (§4.79). In addition, the threatened party may file a private action seeking to enjoin the merger (§4.80). If the merger has already occurred, an action may be brought for treble damages and possibly to compel divestiture.

B. [§4.78] Complaint to Government

A party opposing a merger may seek to induce the government to commence an investigation and file suit to enjoin the merger. A government *investigation* of a prospective merger will often be more effective than a private *suit* in preventing an acquisition. It will also be less costly to the party opposing the acquisition. Before making a complaint, a company with its own plans for future mergers should take into account the possibility that it may encounter more difficulty in connection with future acquisitions because of the government's increased awareness of its existence and the nature of its business.

If a complaint is to be made, it will be necessary to decide whether to notify the Department of Justice or the Federal Trade Commission, or both. Since both agencies will almost never investigate the same acquisition, an effort should be made to ascertain the prior experience of the two agencies in the given markets and their current enforcement policies concerning the type of merger in question. Responsibility for investigating a particular merger will not necessarily be assigned to the agency that receives the initial complaint, but the chances that this agency will conduct the investigation will be increased significantly.

Knowledge of the personnel and pending cases at the Antitrust Division and the Federal Trade Commission will help to determine which individual or individuals to notify within either agency. Absent such information, notification may be made to the Director of the Bureau of Competition or the Director of the Office of Policy Planning and Evaluation in the Federal Trade Commission or the Director of Operations or the Director of Policy Planning in the Antitrust Division. Section 2.2(b) of the FTC Procedures and Rules of Practice (3 Trade Reg Rep ¶9807.02) indicates that a request to the Commission to institute an investigation should be in the form of a signed statement of the alleged violation of law, enclosing any available supporting information. The Commission will not divulge the name of the complaining party. §2.2(d).

If a merger requires the approval of a regulatory agency, it may be possible to intervene in the proceeding before the regulatory agency or to induce the Department of Justice to intervene in opposition to the proposed acquisition. The Department of Justice is required to submit comments on every bank merger to the responsible banking agency.

It will also do no harm, and it may help, for the client to notify its representatives in Congress of its objections to a proposed merger and to ask them to bring the matter to the attention of the Department of Justice or the Federal Trade Commission.

C. [§4.79] Intervention in Government Suit

There are few, if any, reasons for a private party to seek to intervene in a contested government case during the liability phase of the litigation. Any knowledge or evidence that a private party has can be presented to the government for its use in the trial of the case. The intangible advantage on the side of the government in most antitrust cases may be lost through intervention of a private party as an additional plaintiff. Moreover, a private party who intervenes in a government case is subject to extensive discovery that otherwise may be avoided.

A private party will normally seek to intervene in a government suit only if the government proposes to accept a consent decree terminating a case or in the relief phase of a litigated case. It may feel that the relief in a proposed consent judgment provides inadequate protection against the adverse consequences of a merger or it may oppose any consent judgment because it seeks a government adjudication for use in a private treble-damage action. See discussion of the use of government judgment decrees as prima facie evidence in a private suit at §4.66. Another unrelated situation in which a private party may seek to intervene is to enforce compliance with a prior government judgment. Compare *United States v Western Electric Co.* (D NJ 1968) 1968 Trade Cases ¶72,415, *aff'd per curiam sub nom Clark Walter & Sons, Inc. v United States* (1968) 392 US 659 with *New Jersey Communications Corp. v American Telephone and Telegraph Co.* (SD NY 1967) 1968 Trade Cases ¶72,455.

Intervention rights will depend on whether a merger is challenged by the Federal Trade Commission or the Department of Justice. A decision by the Federal Trade Commission to accept a consent order is not appealable. There appears to be no recourse for a private party in such a case except to file a private suit. Compare *Kennecott Copper Corp.* (1970) 3 Trade Reg Rep ¶19,281.

Private parties may be able to intervene in the district court to seek additional relief in suits brought by the Department of Justice. While the government has invariably opposed efforts at formal intervention, it has regularly acquiesced when private parties have sought to file statements or briefs with the district court as amicus curiae or have requested an opportunity for oral argument. Since 1961, the Department has followed a policy of filing proposed consent judgments with the court thirty days before they are to become final under a stipulation giving it an unqualified right to withdraw its consent any time during the thirty-day period. When the stipulation and proposed judgment are filed, the Department issues a press release describing the terms of the proposed decree. The information made available in the press release is usually given wide circulation in newspapers and trade journals serving the industry, as well as in antitrust professional trade publications. In addition, the Department usually sends copies of the proposed judgment to known complainants. During this thirty-day period, interested parties have often filed amicus curiae briefs opposing entry of the judgment. In several instances the thirty-day waiting period has been extended to permit the Department to investigate information brought to its attention, and in some instances additional information or problems brought to the Department's attention by private parties have led to revisions in negotiated decrees. *United States v Blue Chip Stamp Co.* (CD Calif 1967) 272 F Supp 432, *aff'd per curiam sub nom Thrifty Shoppers Scrip Co. v United States* (1968) 389 US 580, is the most notable example of this.

The government has opposed formal intervention, fearing that it might be held to carry with it full rights to present evidence and to appeal, thus eliminating one of the major motivating factors that leads both the government and defendants to attempt to work out an appropriate consent judgment. Since the Department is committed to a formal policy of opposing all efforts by private parties to intervene in its cases, it is advisable to seek to persuade the Department to modify a proposed consent judgment first before filing a motion to intervene.

Intervention should be considered in three situations: (1) when the Department of Justice indicates that it will not make the suggested changes in the form of relief, in order to preserve a right of appeal, (2) whenever any difficulty is encountered in obtaining a full hearing and presenting all relevant evidence to the district court or (3) when it is in the best interest of the party to seek to make the government litigate the issue of liability in order to make use of the judgment in a private treble-damage action.

The standards for intervention of right and permissive intervention are set forth in Rules 24(a) and (b), respectively, of the Federal Rules of Civil Procedure. For discussion, see Lavine and Horning, *Manual of Federal Practice* §§3.148–3.155.

In opposing a motion to intervene, the government will invariably claim that it is adequately representing the applicant's interest, a sufficient ground for denying intervention; that the disposition of the action will not as a practical matter impair or impede the applicant's ability to protect its interest in the property or transaction which is the subject of the action; and that to admit a number of third parties as intervenors, each with a right to make objections, to cross-examine witnesses, to produce its own witnesses, and to take an appeal, would inevitably delay effective relief.

The leading case permitting intervention of right is *Cascade Natural Gas Corp. v El Paso Natural Gas Co.* (1967) 386 US 129, which failed to provide any general guidance on when intervention would be warranted. As a result, the government has been largely successful in its policy of seeking to limit the holding in *El Paso* to its facts. One of the principal grounds for distinguishing *El Paso* has been that intervention was sought to ensure compliance with an earlier Supreme Court mandate. Thus, in *United States v Blue Chip Stamp Co., supra,* the court even suggested that *El Paso* furnishes a basis for denying intervention if a prior mandate of the courts is not involved, noting (at 272 F Supp 438):

> Obviously, a ruling by a court that intervention is proper to insure compliance with its earlier mandate is no authority for asserting that a court which has issued a mandate should permit intervention for the purpose of attacking the mandate. In this respect, *El Paso* is actually authority for the denial of the instant motions to intervene, because the present court has power to interpret and enforce the mandate which it has issued.

Intervention has been denied in a number of other cases subsequent to *El Paso.* See, *e.g., United States v Aluminum Co. of America* (ED Mo 1967) 41 FRD 342, *appeal dismissed sub nom Lupton Mfg. Co. v United States* (1967) 388 US 457; *United States v Harper & Row Publishers, Inc.* (ND Ill), *aff'd sub nom City of New York v United States* (1968) 390 US 715. Cf. *United States v Shubert* (SD NY 1969) 1969 Trade Cases ¶72,859.

Although the Department of Justice in opposing intervention in *El Paso* argued that a successful intervenor having the rights of a party could block a consent judgment and require a litigated proceeding, the court, in *United States v First Nat'l. Bank & Trust Co.* (ED Ky 1967) 280 F Supp 260, *aff'd per curiam sub nom Central Bank & Trust Co. v United States* (1968) 391 US 469, allowed intervention but entered a proposed consent judgment over the objections of the persons allowed to intervene, and the Supreme Court affirmed the judgment *per curiam,* despite the assertion of the intervenors that the district court could not enter the order without their consent.

In the *Blue Chip* case, *supra,* the court also held that applicant's petition to intervene was not "timely" since it was not filed until after the decree had been entered by the court following a hearing at which the applicant had appeared as amicus curiae. Accordingly, if a motion to intervene is to be filed, it should be filed before the date set for hearing on the proposed consent judgment.

In sum, it is extremely difficult to intervene in a government case, and even if intervention is granted, it may not accomplish anything. Normally it will be advisable for a private party to expend his efforts in marshalling evidence to support its basis for objecting to entry of the judgment and to present this evidence as amicus curiae rather than to attempt to intervene over the government's objections.

D. [§4.80] Remedies Available in a Private Suit

A private party may obtain a preliminary injunction to bar consummation of a proposed merger (see §4.58) and may bring an action for treble damages (see §4.66). The authorities are divided on whether divestiture is available in a private suit (see §4.62). A shareholder derivative suit for treble damages may also be maintained. See *Gottesman v General Motors Corp.* (2d Cir 1968) 401 F2d 510; *Rogers v American Can Co.* (3d Cir 1962) 305 F2d 297; and *Fanchon & Marco, Inc. v Paramount Pictures, Inc.* (2d Cir 1953) 202 F2d 731. For discussion of the elements of a private cause of action, see *Private Antitrust Enforcement* (1966) 32 ABA Antitrust LJ 1-148. For discussion of the statute of limitations in private actions, see §4.67. On standing, see §4.66.

The Publicity In Taking Evidence Act (15 USC §30) may also be useful in developing a case. This provision requires generally that depositions and hearings before any examiner or a special master be open to the public as freely as trials in open court and that no order excluding the public from attendance at any such proceedings shall be valid or enforceable.

It is not yet settled whether third parties are automatically entitled to see progress reports that a defendant may be required to file under a divestiture order. The district court's authority to enter a protective order prohibiting disclosure of divestiture plans was upheld in *United States v United Fruit Co.* (5th Cir 1969) 410 F2d 553, *cert den* (1969) 396 US 820. At the same time, the court acknowledged that if the information had been sought for use in another pending case, a different question might have been presented. See also Commission Rules §4.9(g).

Against the potential benefits from a private suit for injunctive relief or damages must be weighed the cost in legal fees and executive time and the possibility of a counterclaim challenging acquisitions made by the complainant. In this connection it should be noted that while the court, in *International Telephone & Telegraph Corp. v General Telephone & Electronics Corp.* (D Haw 1969) 296 F Supp 920, refused to recognize a defense of unclean hands based on prior illegal mergers made by the plaintiff, it did state at 927: "If plaintiff is also a violator of the antitrust laws, defendant's remedy lies in recourse to a separate proceeding (as is set forth in defendant's counterclaim)."

E. [§4.81] Opposing Tender Offer or Attempted Take-Over

According to a prominent financial consulting firm there were 249 tender offers in the United States in 1968. During the first quarter of 1969, there were 70 such offers, compared with only 28 in the similar period in 1968. The filing of a private suit under Section 7 (15 USC §18) seeking a preliminary injunction (see §4.58) may be an effective tactic in preventing an unwelcome tender offer or attempted take-over bid. For an excellent discussion of this subject, see Bradner, *Use of Section 7 of the Clayton Act in Corporate Control Struggles* (1967) 12 *Antitrust Bulletin* 401. In addition to the cases cited in §4.58, see *Muskegon Piston Ring Co. v Gulf & Western Industries, Inc.* (6th Cir 1964) 328 F2d 830; *American Crystal Sugar Co. v Cuban-American Sugar Co.* (2d Cir 1958) 259 F2d 524; *Maryland Cas. Co. v American Gen. Ins. Co.* (D DC 1964) 232 F Supp 620; *Vanadium Corp. v Susquehanna Corp.* (D Del 1962) 203 F Supp 686; and *General Outdoor Adv. Co. v Gamble* (D Minn 1961) 1961 Trade Cases ¶70,137.

One of the most spectacular take-over attempts during the last few years was the $1 billion tender offer by Northwest Industries to acquire B. F. Goodrich. Goodrich's efforts to ward off Northwest's take-over attempt are described in the July, 1969 issue of *Fortune* magazine. This was the first case in which the government filed suit to enjoin a tender offer. Although the government's motion for a preliminary injunction was denied, Northwest subsequently withdrew its tender offer. See *United States v Northwest Industries, Inc.* (ND Ill 1969) 301 F Supp 1066.

A company that is the target of a take-over attempt may seek to strengthen its case under Section 7 by acquiring a smaller company that competes with the company seeking to acquire it. However, it must be careful to ensure that such a defensive merger does not, itself, create antitrust problems. The recent *Atlantic Richfield-Sinclair Oil* case illustrates this problem. There Gulf & Western Industries had made a tender offer to the Sinclair shareholders, and Sinclair thereafter arranged a merger with Atlantic Richfield. In *United States v Atlantic Richfield Co.* (SD NY 1969) 297 F Supp 1061, 1075, the government obtained a preliminary injunction prohibiting consummation of the Sinclair-Atlantic Richfield merger. However, after a spin-off of certain assets by Atlantic Richfield, the court allowed the merger to be consummated under a hold-separate order while continuing the litigation.

It may also be possible to combat a tender offer on the basis of possible anticompetitive effects flowing from the proposed source of financing of the tender offer. See *Metro-Goldwyn-Mayer Inc. v Transamerica Corp.* (SD NY 1969) 1969 Trade Cases ¶72,890.

VI. [§4.82] Government Investigations of Mergers

The Department of Justice and Federal Trade Commission learn of prospective mergers from FTC pre-merger notification reports, private complaints concerning a prospective merger, and articles appearing in newspapers and trade journals. If a public company is a party, they will be able to obtain information from proxy statements on file with the Securities and Exchange Commission.

A. [§4.83] Merger Investigations by the Department of Justice

The Department of Justice will almost always commence a merger investigation by sending an informal request for information to the parties. At this point the parties should carefully assess the prospects of satisfying the Department of the legality of the merger or prevailing in litigation. If the prospects of success are very slight, the parties may want to abandon the merger at this stage in order to avoid the possibilities of eventually having to accept a decree that may include a ban on future acquisitions and of inviting an investigation and possible challenge of prior acquisitions.

If the prospects of establishing the legality of the merger appear to be good, or the parties wish to proceed with the merger plans in any event, it will normally be advisable to cooperate with the Department of Justice and to supply whatever information is requested. The Department will otherwise seek to obtain the same information by means of a civil investigative demand pursuant to the Antitrust Civil Process Act (15 USC §§1311–1314; 18 USC §1505). See discussion at §§10.24–10.27. Although *Petition of Union Oil Co.* (SD Calif 1963) 225 F Supp 486, *aff'd* (9th Cir 1965) 343 F2d 29 held that the act does not authorize the use of a civil investigative demand to obtain information relating to a "proposed acquisition," since an acquisition that is merely proposed cannot constitute a past or present violation of the antitrust laws, there is some question whether the same decision would be reached by another court. There is no question concerning the government's ability to obtain the information once the merger has been consummated.

The Department of Justice will sometimes ask the parties to delay consummation of a proposed merger so that it can complete its investigation. Normally the parties will have no choice but to comply with this request, since the Department will probably otherwise seek a preliminary injunction.

The parties to a prospective merger invariably have knowledge of any investigation being conducted by the Department of Justice. Counsel should ask to be notified of the Department's intentions after it has completed its investigation. It may be advantageous to seek a meeting with the trial attorney who is conducting the investigation and, if the trial attorney recommends suit, either with his section chief, the chief of the evaluation section, the director of operations, the director of policy planning, or the first assistant to the assistant attorney general, depending on the circumstances. Ultimately a meeting may be requested with the assistant attorney general and, in some instances, with the attorney general. The Department will normally disclose whether or not it intends to file a suit, and the parties can usually abandon the merger at that point without being subject to any further penalty unless the Department has determined as a result of its investigation to challenge prior mergers made by either party.

If the Department indicates that it intends to file suit because of potential anticompetitive effects limited to a small segment of the parties' activities, it may be possible to negotiate the simultaneous filing of a complaint and consent decree. At present, the Department's policy is to conduct prefiling negotiations only in selected cases, and usually only after the complaint has been signed and is ready for filing.

Once a civil complaint is filed, defense counsel may initiate negotiations for settlement of the case. The Antitrust Division does not initiate settlement negotiations but holds itself out to engage in them. Negotiations take place initially at the staff level. If it is thought that a particular matter presents policy considerations that merit or require the personal attention of the assistant attorney general or, in an exceptional situation, of the attorney general, the proper procedure is to request the chief attorney in charge of the case to arrange an interview at an appropriate time with the assistant attorney general.

When a consent judgment is negotiated, whether before or after the filing of the complaint, the usual practice is for the defendant to submit the first draft of the judgment. If the trial staff and their respective section or field office chief approve the proposed consent judgment, the matter is referred to the judgments and judgment enforcement section for review. If the proposed judgment is approved by the chief of the judgments and judgment enforcement section, it is submitted to the director of operations and the director of policy planning who, in turn, forward their recommendations to the first assistant and the assistant attorney general. The staff is not authorized to agree to any provisions of a proposed consent judgment before its submission to the assistant attorney general. After the proposed consent judgment is approved by the assistant attorney general, it is filed with the court.

Under the terms of an order issued by the attorney general in 1961, persons who "may be affected by such judgment" are given an opportunity to submit written comments concerning it to the Department of Justice. The Department reserves the right to "withdraw or withhold its consent to the proposed judgment if the comments, views or allegations submitted disclose facts or considerations which indicate that the proposed judgment is inappropriate, improper or inadequate." Order No. 246-61, Office of the Attorney General (June 29, 1961) 26 Fed Reg 6026.

Even when it is impossible to reach an agreement allowing a merger to proceed or on the terms of a consent judgment, it may be possible to negotiate the terms of a hold-separate order so that the government will not seek a preliminary injunction. See *United States v Ling-Temco-Vought* (WD Pa, April 14, 1969) Civil Action No. 69-438; *United States v Atlantic Richfield Co.* (SD NY 1969) 297 F Supp 1075.

B. [§4.84] Merger Investigations by the Federal Trade Commission

The principal investigatory powers of the Commission are based on Sections 6(b) and 9 of the Federal Trade Commission Act (15 USC §§46(b), 49). See generally, *St. Regis Paper Co. v United States* (1961) 368 US 208. See discussion of FTC investigating powers at §§10.29–10.34.

The FTC Procedures and Rules of Practice, §§3.31–3.37 (3 Trade Reg Rep ¶9815.31–9815.37) provide for comprehensive precomplaint *investigation* and for postcomplaint *discovery*, but not for postcomplaint *investigation*. The rules governing FTC discovery are discussed at §§10.28–10.35.

The Federal Trade Commission has established formal procedures for the negotiation and entry of consent orders, set out in FTC Procedures and Rules of Practice §§2.31–2.35 (3 Trade Reg Rep ¶9807.31–9807.35) and discussed at §13.2.

BIBLIOGRAPHY

ABA Section of Antitrust Developments—1955-1968: A Supplement to the Report of the Attorney General's National Committee to Study the Antitrust Laws, 1955, Chapter 3;

Bock: *Mergers and Markets* (7th ed 1969) National Industrial Conference Board;

Bok: *Section 7 of the Clayton Act and the Merging of Law and Economics* (1960) 74 *Harv L Rev* 226;

Bradner: *Use of Section 7 of the Clayton Act in Corporate Control Struggles* (1967) 12 *Antitrust Bulletin* 401;

Brodley: *Oligopoly Power Under the Sherman and Clayton Acts—From Economic Theory to Legal Policy* (1967) 19 *Stan L Rev* 285;

Campbell and Shepherd: *Leading-Firm Conglomerate Mergers* (1968) 13 *Antitrust Bulletin* 1361;

Davidow: *Conglomerate Concentration and Section Seven: The Limitations of the Anti-Merger Act* (1968) 68 *Col L Rev* 1231;

Donovan: *Legality of Acquisitions and Mergers Involving American and Foreign Corporations Under the United States Antitrust Laws* (1966) 39 *So Calif L Rev* 526 and (1967) 40 *So Calif L Rev* 38;

Elman: *Clorox and Conglomerate Mergers* (1967) 36 ABA Antitrust LJ 23;

Kaysen and Turner: *Antitrust Policy: An Economic and Legal Analysis* (1959) Harvard University Press;

Kestenbaum: *Potential Competition: Trends and Developments* (1969) 38 *Antitrust Bulletin* 652;

Turner: *Conglomerate Mergers and Section 7 of the Clayton Act* (1965) 78 *Harv L Rev* 1313;

Williamson: *Economies as an Antitrust Defense* (June 1968) *American Economic Review*;

Zimmerman: *Adventures in Jointness* (1968) 37 ABA Antitrust LJ 125.

5

Pricing the Product

Carla Anderson Hills

Mrs. Hills received the AB degree from Stanford University in 1955 and the LLB degree from Yale Law School in 1958. She is a member of the Los Angeles County, Federal, and American Bar Associations, the State Bar of California, and the Los Angeles firm of Munger, Tolles, Hills, and Rickershauser.

I. Introduction

A. [§5.1] Scope of Chapter

Pricing is perhaps the most important activity of a business enterprise. It may spell success or failure; it also raises more antitrust problems than any other single activity. The Robinson-Patman Act, generally speaking, prohibits discriminatory or unreasonably low pricing practices.

The provisions of this Act, unlike those of the Sherman Antitrust Act, are directed at individual rather than collective action. Their application is pervasive, for the pricing of commodities affects almost every type of business at every level of production and distribution process, be it manufacturing, processing, distributing, wholesaling, jobbing, or retailing. Hence, a practitioner who advises any business should be at least familiar with its prescriptions. Yet, in the opinion of many, Robinson-Patman is the least understood and appreciated of any of the antitrust enactments. It has been called "a hodge-podge of confusion and inconsistency that any competent, order-loving lawyer must find offensive. . . ." (Stedman, *Twenty-Four Years of the Robinson-Patman Act,* 1960 *Wis L Rev* 197,

218); and "an extremely poorly drafted statute . . . muddled rather than clarified by court decisions . . . [comprising a] melange of generalities, qualified by proviso upon proviso" (Landis, *Report on Regulatory Agencies to the President-Elect, Sub-Committee on Administrative Practice and Procedure of the Senate Committee on Judiciary*, 86th Cong., 2d Sess. 50-51 (Comm. Print 1960).

There is no question but that comprehension of only a portion of the antitrust laws is insufficient—and may be dangerous. Because of the overlap among the various enactments, the practitioner advising business clients should be aware of at least the major pieces of antitrust legislation, *viz.*, the Sherman Act, the Clayton Act, the Robinson-Patman Act, the Federal Trade Commission Act, and the applicable state laws.

This chapter is limited to a discussion of the potential antitrust problems in pricing commodities, a subject dealt with principally by the Robinson-Patman Act.

B. [§5.2] Legislative History

Because the language of the Robinson-Patman Act is not as clear as one might hope, ("precision of expression is not an outstanding characteristic of the Robinson-Patman Act" *Automatic Canteen Co. v FTC* (1953) 346 US 61, 65.) its legislative history is important in understanding its purpose.

It should be kept in mind that the civil provisions of the Robinson-Patman Act, enacted on June 19, 1936, 49 Stat 1526, 15 USC §13 were not an independent enactment, but by their terms constituted "an Act to amend section 2" of the Clayton Act which Congress passed October 15, 1914, 38 Stat 730.

The Clayton Act sought to eliminate discriminatory pricing practices used in certain localities for the purpose of destroying a local competitor and "acquiring a monopoly in the particular locality." H.R. Rep. No. 627, 63d Cong., 2d Sess. 8 (1914). In short, the Clayton Act was concerned with protecting competition among sellers, not competition among the seller's customers. *National Biscuit Co. v FTC* (2d Cir 1924) 299 F 733, *cert den* (1924) 266 US 613.

Furthermore, the Clayton Act expressly exempted price differences based on the "quantity" of the commodity sold, thus giving large concerns a distinct purchasing advantage. *Goodyear Tire and Rubber Co. v FTC* (6th Cir 1939) 101 F2d 620, *cert den* (1939) 308 US 557.

The Robinson-Patman Act came into being following the chain-store inquiry of 1934 (S. Doc. No. 4, 74th Cong., 1st Sess.), which reinforced the view that the Clayton Act had failed to stop the monopolistic growth in distribution, particularly of chain stores, with the attending decline of independents. Its provisions sought to declare unlawful those devices by which "large buyers gained discriminatory preferences over smaller ones by virtue of their greater purchasing power." *FTC v Henry Broch & Co.* (1960) 363 US 166, 168.

C. [§5.3] Summary of Provisions

The amendatory Robinson-Patman Act contains the basic prohibition against discriminatory pricing practices that adversely affect competition. In discussing the pricing prohibition, most courts and commentators speak of "Section 2 violations," referring to the Clayton Act section numbers. Hence, we shall use the more common reference to the Clayton Act.

Section 2(a) (15 USC §13(a)) embodies the Act's basic prohibition, forbidding sellers to discriminate in price between customers engaged in interstate commerce, unless the seller can cost justify the price differential or prove changing market conditions. Section 2(b) (15 USC §13(b)) provides a third defense—that the price differential was granted in good faith to meet the price of a competitor.

Section 2(f) (15 USC §13(f)), aimed at powerful buyers, prohibits knowing receipt by a buyer of a price discrimination forbidden by Section 2(a).

Section 2(c) (15 USC §13(c)) forbids the grant to or a receipt by a buyer or a buyer's agent of brokerage payments or an equivalent.

Sections 2(d) and 2(e) (15 USC §13(d) and (e)) respectively forbid the granting of discriminatory allowances or payments for promotional services or facilities furnished by the customer, and the discriminatory furnishing of promotional service or facilities to a customer.

Section 3 of the Robinson-Patman Act (15 USC §13a), which is an independent, not an amendatory, enactment, makes it a criminal offense for a seller to charge different prices or unreasonably low prices for his products in different geographic areas "for the purpose of destroying competition or eliminating a competitor." It also declares it a criminal offense "to be a party to or assist in" enumerated discriminatory treatment of competing buyers.

D. Enforcement and Sanctions of the Robinson-Patman Act

1. [§5.4] Government Enforcement

The Robinson-Patman Act is enforced primarily by the Federal Trade Commission, which has broad powers to issue sweeping cease-and-desist orders that will be upset only if unwarranted by the record. See, *e.g., FTC v Henry Broch & Co.* (1962) 368 US 360, 366–368. These orders may prescribe conditions for future pricing. For discussion of the difficulty of upsetting FTC orders, see §§13.14–13.15.

Before issuing a complaint, the Commission will dispose of a proceeding on the basis of an assurance of voluntary compliance. Section 2.21, FTC Rules of Practice, 3 Trade Reg Rep ¶9807.21. After the complaint issues, the Commission will not accept an assurance of voluntary compliance but will require a formal consent order. See *Suburban Propane Gas Corp.* (1967) [1967–1970 Transfer Binder] FTC Dkt 8672, Trade Reg Rep ¶17,965. For discussion of the Commission's informal enforcement procedures, see §§6.16–6.19; for discussion of consent orders, see §13.2.

Severe sanctions result from obstructing a Federal Trade Commission investigation into possible price discriminations. See, *e.g., United States v Fruchtman* (ND Ohio 1968) 282 F Supp 534, *aff'd* (6th Cir 1970) 421 F2d 1019, *cert den* (1970) 400 US 849 (company's executive vice-president sentenced to one year and one day in prison, plus $10,000 fine).

The court of appeals of the circuit within which the violation occurred or within which the person restrained by the Commission's order resides or carries on business has the power, on petition filed within 60 days, to review the Commission's orders. 15 USC §21(c). After the 60-day period, the orders automatically become final. Each violation of a final order is subject to a $5,000 fine, and each day of violation is deemed a separate offense. The United States may recover the penalty in a civil suit filed in the district court.

The Department of Justice has concurrent authority with the Federal Trade Commission to enforce the Robinson-Patman Act. For discussion of criminal offenses, see §5.53. It may also file civil suits for damages in an appropriate district court (15 USC §15(a)), or enjoin violations (15 USC §25). The Department of Justice rarely acts to enforce Section 2 of the Clayton Act, as amended by the Robinson-Patman Act (15 USC §13), but will do so when violations are combined with violations of other antitrust provisions, *e.g.,* the Sherman Act.

2. [§5.5] Private Enforcement

A private party who has been injured by "anything forbidden in the antitrust laws" may bring an action in "any district court of the United States in the district in which the defendant resides or is found or has an agent, without respect to the amount in controversy, and shall recover threefold the damages by him sustained, and the cost of suit, including a reasonable attorney's fee" (15 USC §15). By the terms of Section 1 of the Clayton Act, 15 USC §12, §2 of the Robinson-Patman Act (15 USC §13) is one of the antitrust laws, but the Supreme Court in *Nashville Milk Co. v Carnation Co.* (1958) 355 US 373 held that §3 (15 USC §13a) is not. Private persons may also seek injunctive relief. Suits filed by private parties claiming injury from violations of the Robinson-Patman Act are increasing sharply.

II. Pricing the Product

A. [§5.6] Introduction

The basic purpose of the Robinson-Patman Act is to require sellers to treat buyers fairly and equally and to prohibit large buyers from improperly using their enormous buying powers to induce preferential treatment so that small independents will not be foreclosed from, or driven out of, the market. The small independents within the statute's intended scope of protection are competing sellers, competing nonfavored buyers, and the buyers' customers.

The prohibitions against below-cost pricing and discriminatory pricing raise the questions of how low can prices go and how uniform prices must be. Minimum prices are discussed at §5.7; price uniformity, at §§5.10–5.26.

B. Minimum Prices

1. [§5.7] Prohibition against Below-Cost Pricing

Section 3 of the Robinson-Patman Act (15 USC §13a) declares it a crime, *inter alia*, for "any person engaged in commerce, in the course of such commerce . . . to sell, or contract to sell goods at unreasonably low prices for the purpose of destroying competition or eliminating a competitor." See discussion at §5.53.

This criminal prohibition, enforceable only by the government, not by private parties, is directed primarily at below-cost pricing with a predatory intent. See, *e.g., Balian Ice Cream Co. v Arden Farms Co.* (SD Calif 1952) 104 F Supp 796, 807, *aff'd* (9th Cir 1955) 231 F2d 356, *cert den* (1956) 350 US 991. See §5.53. See also discussion of state and federal prohibitions on below-cost pricing in La Rue, *Pitfalls for Price Competitors: State and Federal Restrictions on Below Cost or Unreasonably Low Prices* (1965) 15 *W Res L Rev* 35.

2. [§5.8] Definition of Cost

The prohibition against below-cost pricing with a predatory intent, discussed above, was held constitutional by the Supreme Court in 1963.

However, the Court did not decide whether cost meant direct cost or fully distributed cost, or whether it should be defined some other way. *United States v National Dairy Products Corp.* (1963) 372 US 29.

3. [§5.9] Justifications

The Supreme Court has recognized a number of potential defenses to the charge of below-cost pricing with a predatory intent. These have been called, variously, "acceptable business exigency," "legitimate commercial objective," or "justifying business reason." See, *e.g., United States v National Dairy Products Corp.* (1963) 372 US 29, 33, 37.

The defenses mentioned in §§2(a) and (b) (15 USC §§13(a) and (b))— cost justification; liquidation of excess, obsolete, or perishable merchandise under certain changing market conditions; or meeting competition— are recognized as valid against a charge of below-cost pricing. See §§5.43–5.52.

C. Uniformity of Prices

1. [§5.10] Reviewing Clients' Pricing Policies

Section 2(a) of the Clayton Act, as amended by the Robinson-Patman Act (15 USC §13(a)), prohibits price discrimination between customers engaged in interstate commerce if the effect may be to injure competition, whether with other sellers or between favored and nonfavored buyers.

How does the lawyer commence to advise his client concerning prices?

First, the lawyer should carefully analyze and thoroughly understand (1) his client's business, recognizing the customers to whom he sells, their size, and the persons to whom they sell; (2) his client's "basic" prices, discounts, rebates, and special services, to whom they are given, and under what circumstances; and (3) his client's position in each product and geographic market, and the relative market positions of his client's competitors.

Second, after carefully analyzing his client's business, the lawyer should determine whether his client's pricing falls within the scope of the Robinson-Patman Act. Some discriminatory pricing policies fall outside the act's prohibitions because of its numerous jurisdictional requirements. The requirements for finding a prima facie violation, are a direct or indirect price discrimination

1. By the same seller
2. On contemporaneous sales
3. To different purchasers
4. Of commodities

5. Of like grade and quality
6. In interstate commerce
7. Within the United States, producing
8. Injury to competition

For example, the act applies only to sales, not to leases or refusals to deal (see §5.14); it applies only to sales in interstate, not intrastate, commerce (see §5.17). The act applies only to sales that are contemporaneous, not those separated by an unreasonable period of time (see §5.16). It applies only to sales of comparable goods (see §§5.20–5.22). Any one of these jurisdictional requirements may exempt the client's pricing policy from the standards of the Robinson-Patman Act.

Finally, if the client's activities are found to be covered by the act, the lawyer should next ascertain whether it is financially feasible to alter the client's pricing policies so that they fall outside its scope. For example, since the act applies only to sales in interstate commerce, it should be considered whether plant territories could be reallocated so that all sales from a single plant are intrastate. See, *e.g., Hiram Walker, Inc. v A & S Tropical, Inc.* (5th Cir 1969) 407 F2d 4, *cert den* (1969) 396 US 901, and discussion at §5.17. Perhaps the client could incorporate separate sales divisions for separate classes of customers, thereby taking advantage of the provision that the prohibited discriminatory sales must be made by the same seller. See §5.11. The client may be able to use consignments rather than sales, thereby avoiding Robinson-Patman. See §5.14. Perhaps the client can develop special product specifications suitable to his large customers that would justify a price difference between sales of these products and sales to his other customers. See §§5.20–5.21. The client might also consider relinquishing control over the sales of his independent distributors, so that the pricing policies of his distributors will not be attributed to him. See §5.12.

The most practical defense to a charge of price discrimination in violation of the Robinson-Patman Act is proof that the lower price was set to meet a competitive price. See §§5.49–5.51. The best proof of the defense is a contemporaneous and thorough written report by a salesman on the scene. For a form of report, see §9.61, based on a form suggested by Richard A. Whiting in *Compliance with the Federal Price Discrimination Law* in ABA *Law Notes*, July, 1966.

From information reported by salesmen in the field, sales personnel can decide whether basic prices should be altered or a discount granted.

Large orders tempt special prices; if meeting competition is not a possible defense for granting a lower than usual price, it may be that the price differential can be justified by the cost savings generated by the large order. See §§5.44–5.48.

Discounts purportedly based on cost savings occasioned by one or more transactions of sizeable proportions should be based on a contemporaneous cost analysis. Cost studies prepared after the price differential is challenged have far less chance of succeeding.

2. [§5.11] Identification of Seller

Section 2(a) of the Clayton Act as amended by the Robinson-Patman Act (15 USC §13(a)) prohibits discriminatory pricing practices only when they are engaged in by the same seller selling to different buyers. See, e.g., Advisory Opinion Digest 48 (1966) [1965–1967 Transfer Binder] Trade Reg Rep ¶70,541. Questions of identification generally come up in the context of parent and subsidiary corporate entities.

A sale by a subsidiary corporation generally will not be attributed to its parent even though the parent owns 100 percent of the subsidiary's stock and the directors and officers of the two corporations are identical. Accordingly, the subsidiary corporation may charge higher or lower prices than its parent corporation for the same goods without violating the Robinson-Patman Act. An exception to this general rule occurs if it can be shown that one corporation so completely dominates the other that their separate existence is more a matter of form than of fact.

For example, in *National Lead Co. v FTC* (7th Cir 1955) 227 F2d 825, 829, *rev'd on other grounds* (1957) 352 US 419, the Court dismissed price discrimination charges against a corporation that had two wholly owned subsidiaries with interlocking boards of directors, stating: "[T]here must be evidence of such complete control of the subsidiary by the parent as to render the former a mere tool of the latter, and to compel the conclusion that the corporate identity of the subsidiary is a mere fiction." See also *Baim & Blank, Inc. v Philco Corp.* (ED NY 1957) 148 F Supp 541.

The separate corporate identity of a subsidiary corporation has further Robinson-Patman repercussions: If the parent sells goods to its subsidiary as well as to buyers in competition with its subsidiary, the parent corporation may not give its subsidiary preferential prices. See *Reines Distributors, Inc. v Admiral Corp.* (SD NY 1965) 257 F Supp 619, 621 and (SD NY 1966) 256 F Supp 581, 585–586. *Reines* held that a sale from parent to subsidiary would be unlawfully discriminatory if plaintiff could prove damage arising from discrimination by defendant in price and services as between distributors who competed for the same customers. See also *Dean Milk Co.* (1965) [1965–1967 Transfer Binder] FTC Dkt 8032, Trade Reg Rep ¶17,357, *rev'd in part, aff'd in part* (7th Cir 1968) 395 F2d 696.

3. [§5.12] Identification of Buyer

Section 2(a) of the Clayton Act, as amended by the Robinson-Patman Act (15 USC §13(a)), is not violated unless there are two purchasers; there is no prohibition against charging the same buyer different prices for different orders.

As with the requirement that the discrimination be effected by the same seller, questions as to whether there are two purchasers typically arise in the corporate area. Again, substance rather than form governs, and the same legal concepts govern. See §5.11.

A distributing division of a corporation is not a separate entity under general legal principles; hence, unless it has been treated as a separate, autonomous entity by its parent, it will not be treated as a separate entity to make it one of the two required purchasers under the Robinson-Patman Act. See, *e.g., Reines Distributors, Inc. v Admiral Corp.* (SD NY 1966) 256 F Supp 581, 583-584. See also *Joseph E. Seagram and Sons, Inc. v Hawaiian Oke and Liquors, Ltd.* (9th Cir 1969) 416 F2d 71, *cert den* (1970) 396 US 1062, *reh den* (1970) 397 US 1003; *Cliff Food Stores Inc. v Kroger, Inc.* (5th Cir 1969) 417 F2d 203, holding (in the context of an alleged Sherman Act violation) that a corporation cannot conspire with its unincorporated division. See discussion of the intracorporate conspiracy doctrine at §2.11.

If a seller sidesteps its regular lines of distribution, directly soliciting buyers of its goods and negotiating the terms of sale, the buyers may be deemed "indirect purchasers" of the seller although they ultimately purchase from an intermediate source, whether it be an independent jobber, wholesaler, or sales subsidiary. The "indirect purchaser" doctrine was early stated by the Commission in *Kraft-Phoenix Cheese Corp.* (1937) 25 FTC 537, 546:

> A retailer is none the less a purchaser because he buys indirectly if, as here, the manufacturer deals with him directly in promoting the sale of his products and exercises control over the terms upon which he buys.

See also *Dean Milk Co.* (1965) [1965-1967 Transfer Binder] FTC Dkt 8032, Trade Reg Rep ¶17,357, *rev'd in part and aff'd in part* (7th Cir 1968) 395 F2d 696.

The courts have approved and applied this doctrine. See *e.g., Hiram Walker Inc. v A & S Tropical, Inc.* (5th Cir 1969) 407 F2d 4, *cert den* (1969) 396 US 901; *Purolator Products, Inc. v FTC* (7th Cir 1965) 352 F2d 874, 883, *cert den* (1968) 389 US 1045; *Baim & Blank, Inc. v Philco Corp.* (ED NY 1957) 148 F Supp 541; *Western Fruit Growers Sales Co. v FTC* (9th Cir 1963) 322 F2d 67, *cert den* (1964) 376 US 907; *Whitaker Cable Corp. v FTC* (7th Cir 1956) 239 F2d 253, *cert den* (1957) 353 US 938.

The doctrine has been held to apply to consumer purchasers as well as to purchasers buying for resale. See *Checker Motors Corp. v Chrysler Corp.* (SD NY 1968) 283 F Supp 876. However, the Third Circuit rejected the doctrine in private suits on the ground that the plaintiff must be an actual purchaser to bring suit. See *Klein v Lionel Corp.* (3d Cir 1956) 237 F2d 13. See discussion of standing to sue at §5.35.

The doctrine has also been applied when the seller grants promotional payments to an "indirect customer" for services and facilities furnished by the "indirect customer" in violation of §2(d) of the Clayton Act, as amended by the Robinson-Patman Act (15 USC §13(d)). See, *e.g., American News Co. v FTC* (2d Cir 1962) 300 F2d 104, 109, *cert den* (1962) 371 US 824; *K.S. Corp. v Chemstrand Corp.* (SD NY 1961) 198 F Supp 310, 312–313. However, the significance of the indirect customer doctrine in the context of promotional payments was greatly reduced by the Supreme Court's ruling in *FTC v Fred Meyer, Inc.* (1968) 390 US 341 that a seller must regard as its "customers" all the retail customers of its wholesalers who compete with direct-buying retailers to whom the seller gives promotional assistance. See discussion of *Fred Meyer* at §§5.31, 5.33.

4. Necessity for Comparable Sale of Commodities

a. [§5.13] Lack of Sale from Refusal to Deal

The Robinson-Patman Act is not violated by a refusal to deal. The right to select one's customers is based on express statute language as well as Commission and judicial interpretation.

The statute provides that "nothing herein contained shall prevent persons engaged in selling goods, wares, or merchandise in commerce from selecting their own customers in bona fide transactions and not in restraint of trade." (15 USC §13(a)).

The Commission early recognized, in *Bird & Son, Inc.* (1937) 25 FTC 548, 553, that a seller "may discriminate in the choice of his customers" because "not until there is a discrimination in price among those chosen does section 2(a) of the Act have any application." The courts have upheld this construction. See *FTC v Simplicity Pattern Co.* (1959) 360 US 55; *Klein v Lionel Corp.* (3d Cir 1956) 237 F2d 13; *Naifeh v Ronson Art Metal Works, Inc.* (10th Cir 1954) 218 F2d 202; *Becker v Safelite Glass Corp.* (D Kan 1965) 244 F Supp 625; *Peter Satori of California, Inc. v Studebaker-Packard Corp.* (SD Calif 1964) 1964 Trade Cases ¶71,309.

b. [§5.14] Non-Sales Transactions

Section 2(a) of the amended Clayton Act (15 USC §13(a)) has been interpreted to apply only when there are at least two sales during a reasonably contemporaneous period of time. *Bruce's Juices, Inc. v American Can Co.* (1947) 330 US 743, 755. A complaint alleging discriminatory sales will be dismissed if only one sale can be established. See, *e.g., Becker v Safelite Glass Corp., Inc.* (D Kan 1965) 244 F Supp 625.

The sales requirement removes such commercial transactions as leases (*Gaylord Shops, Inc. v Pittsburgh Miracle Mile Town and Country Shopping Center, Inc.* (WD Pa 1963) 219 F Supp 400); consignments (*Loren Specialty Mfg. Co. v The Clark Mfg. Co.* (ND Ill 1965) 1965 Trade Cases ¶71,454, *aff'd* (7th Cir 1966) 360 F2d 913; *Students Book Co. v Washington Law Book Co.* (DC Cir 1955) 232 F2d 49, *cert den* (1956) 350 US 988); licenses (*County Theatre Co. v Paramount Film Distributing Corp.* (ED Pa 1956) 1956 Trade Cases ¶68,500); or loans (*United States v Investors Diversified Services* (D Minn 1951) 102 F Supp 645, 647 [dealing with Section 3 of the Clayton Act, 15 USC §14]).

The sale must be actual, not potential; a mere quotation of a discriminatory price will not suffice. See *Robinson v Stanley Home Products* (D Mass 1959) 178 F Supp 230, *aff'd on other grounds* (1st Cir 1959) 272 F2d 601; *Wholesale Auto Supply Co. v Hickok Manufacturing Co.* (D NJ 1963) 221 F Supp 935, 939–940; cf. *American Can Co. v Bruce's Juices, Inc.* (5th Cir 1951) 187 F2d 919, 924, *pet for rehearing den* (5th Cir 1951) 190 F2d 73, 74, *cert dismissed* (1951) 342 US 875. Nor will a comparison of a seller's published price list with sales on better terms to a favored customer demonstrate that there has been a violation of the act, absent an actual sale. See *Castlegate, Inc. v National Tea Co.* (D Col 1963) 34 FRD 221, 229.

But once the buyer and seller have executed a contract for the transfer of goods, a "sale" is effected for the purpose of the statute, even though delivery and payment have not yet occurred. See *Aluminum Co. of America v Tandet* (D Conn 1964) 1964 Trade Cases ¶71,281.

c. [§5.15] What are Commodities?

Section 2(a) of the Clayton Act, as amended by the Robinson-Patman Act (15 USC §13(a)), prohibits price discrimination between "different purchasers of commodities." Sales of services and intangibles are excluded, except sales of insurance to the extent that they are not regulated by state law. (15 USC §1012). The circuit court in *Amana Refrigeration, Inc. v Columbia Broadcasting System* (7th Cir 1961) 295 F2d 375, 378 concluded that the word "commodity" in the Robinson-Patman Act meant goods, wares, merchandise, machinery, and supplies.

Mr. Patman agreed with this definition in his *Complete Guide to the Robinson-Patman Act* 33 (1963):

In its broadest sense the word "commodity" might possibly include terms of trade other than those in tangible form—for example, advertising, insurance, brokerage service and similar items. However, the word is ordinarily used in the commercial sense to designate any movable or tangible thing that is produced or used as the subject of barter. This is the definition for the word "commodity" in the application of the Robinson-Patman Act.

See also Rowe, *Price Discrimination under the Robinson-Patman Act* 61–62 (1962).

Even the sale of intangibles usually entails some tangible evidence. For example, there is often a written contract. But the "dominant nature of the transaction" governs. In *Tri-State Broadcasting Co. v United Press International, Inc.* (5th Cir 1966) 369 F2d 268, 270, holding that a news report service does not constitute a commodity within the contemplation of the Robinson-Patman Act, the court stated:

Virtually no transfer of an intangible in the nature of a service, right, or privilege can be accomplished without the incidental involvement of tangibles, and we conclude that in such circumstances the dominant nature of the transaction must control in determining whether it falls within the provisions of the Act. [citations] Here, the dominant purpose of the transaction was not merely the purchase by appellant of tangible written news reports, but rather the valuable right and privilege of broadcasting to its listeners news supplied by a reputable news information service. In substance, the contract contemplates the sale of a service together with the privilege of vocally passing on the information supplied by that service to a radio audience. The news items in their printed form at best represent tangible incidents of appellant's contractual right to utilize UPI's services.

Thus, the definition of "commodity" has been held to exclude from coverage by the Robinson-Patman Act the sale of television time (*Amana Refrigeration, Inc. v Columbia Broadcasting System, supra*); the sale of news report service (*Tri-State Broadcasting Co. v United Press International, Inc., supra*); the sale of radio advertising (*Syracuse Broadcasting Corp. v Newhouse* (2d Cir 1963) 319 F2d 683; the district court had held "radio advertising is not a commodity under the terms of the Clayton Act." Plaintiff dropped the price discrimination charge on appeal, so the Court of Appeals noted but did not pass on the matter); leasing of real estate (*Gaylord Shop, Inc. v Pittsburgh Miracle Mile Town and Country Shopping Center, Inc.* (WD Pa 1963) 219 F Supp 400); and the sale of material and labor pursuant to a construction contract (*General Shale Products Corp. v Struck Const. Co.* (6th Cir 1942) 132 F2d 425, cert den (1943) 318 US 780). See also *United States v Investors Diversified Services, Inc.* (D Minn 1951) 102 F Supp 645, holding that a contract for the loan of money secured by real estate mortgages did not entail a "commodity" within the meaning of Section 3 of the Clayton Act, 15 USC §14.

d. [§5.16] What Is a Contemporaneous Sale?

Even if two actual sales can be proved, they must also be proved to be reasonably contemporaneous. Whether two sales are sufficiently close in time depends on the industry involved. In one business the passage of one day between two sales might find the market situation completely changed. In another industry several months might pass between sales and make no appreciable difference. See *Fred Meyer, Inc. v FTC* (9th Cir 1966) 359 F2d 351, 357, *rev'd in part on other grounds and remanded* (1968) 390 US 341.

When a charge of unlawful price discrimination is made in an industry with fluctuating prices, such as grain, metals, and perishable foods, the defense is often raised that market conditions changed between the sales in question. Changing market conditions can clearly be the cause of pricing differences, but just as clearly one can discriminate in a fluctuating market. Only the proof becomes more difficult.

Illustrative of the few court decisions in this area are, on the one hand, *Fred Meyer, Inc.*, *supra* (sales six months apart were sufficiently contemporaneous in the retail food industry) and, on the other hand, *Atalanta Trading Corp. v FTC* (2d Cir 1958) 258 F2d 365 (sales six and eight months apart were not sufficiently contemporaneous in the meat products industry) and *Valley Plymouth v Studebaker-Packard Corp.* (SD Calif 1963) 219 F Supp 608 (sales six months apart were not sufficiently contemporaneous in the automotive industry). In each instance it is a question of fact.

e. [§5.17] Interstate Requirement

Antitrust legislation is enacted by Congress under its constitutional authority "to regulate commerce with foreign nations and among the several states." (US Const, Art I, §8.)

The three cumulative commerce requirements specified in §2(a) of the Clayton Act as amended by the Robinson-Patman Act (15 USC §13(a)) limit its application to a "person [1] engaged in commerce," who [2] "in the course of such commerce" discriminates in price between different purchasers [3] "where either or any of the purchases involved in such discrimination are in commerce." Section 1 of the Clayton Act (15 USC §12) defines "person" to include corporations and associations, and "commerce" generally speaking as "trade or commerce among the several States and with foreign nations". The Senate Committee Report No. 1502, February 3, 1936, makes it clear that "the specific definitions of Section 1 of the Clayton Act will apply without repetition to the terms concerned where they appear in this [Robinson-Patman] bill. . . ."

It is generally recognized that the commerce definition in the Clayton Act is less broad than in the Sherman Act. "In an action brought under the Robinson-Patman Act it is necessary to allege and prove that the transactions complained of are actually in interstate commerce, while in actions brought under the Sherman Antitrust Act it is sufficient if the transactions complained of are shown to have affected interstate commerce." *Willard Dairy Corp. v National Dairy Products Corp.* (6th Cir 1962) 309 F2d 943, 946, *cert den* (1963) 373 US 934. See discussion at §2.12.

Nonetheless the three commerce requirements are jurisdictional and must be satisfied. The first requirement, that the seller be engaged in commerce, generally is apparent from the facts and has caused few, if any, problems.

The second and third requirements, that the discrimination occur in the course of commerce and that at least one of the purchases be in commerce, have been interpreted together to require that at least one discriminatory transaction cross a state line. It does not matter whether that sale is to the favored or the disfavored customer. See, *e.g., Moore v Mead's Fine Bread Co.* (1954) 348 US 115, 120; *Food Basket, Inc. v Albertson's, Inc.* (10th Cir 1967) 383 F2d 785.

But, "where a manufacturer sells only to customers within the State, his business is beyond the reach of Federal authority and is not included within the provisions of [the Robinson-Patman] bill." 80 Cong. Rec. 9416 (1936).

Even if the seller is engaged in interstate commerce, the Clayton Act is not violated if the sales on which plaintiff bases his complaint are all intrastate. Thus, in *Willard Dairy Corp. v National Dairy Products Corp.*, *supra*, an interstate seller of milk processed in Ohio cut prices in Willard, Ohio, where it was in competition with the plaintiff, but did not cut its prices in any other area in Ohio. The court, affirming summary judgment for defendants, ruled that "It is not enough under the Clayton Act, as amended by the Robinson-Patman Act, that the defendant be engaged in interstate commerce but it must also be shown that the sale complained of was one occurring in interstate commerce." See also *Abramson v Colonial Oil Co.* (5th Cir 1968) 390 F2d 873, *cert den* (1968) 393 US 831; *Universal-Rundle Corp. v FTC* (7th Cir 1967) 382 F2d 285; *Jones v Metzger Dairies, Inc.* (5th Cir 1964) 334 F2d 919; *Food Basket, Inc. v Albertson's, Inc., supra; Cream Crest-Blanding Dairies, Inc. v National Dairy Products Corp.* (WD Mich 1965) 243 F Supp 331, *aff'd* (6th Cir 1967) 370 F2d 332, *cert den* (1967) 387 US 930.

A transaction will be deemed "in commerce" if it is part of a larger transaction in which there has been a crossing of state lines, under the so-called "stream-of-commerce" doctrine. *Foremost Dairies, Inc. v FTC* (5th Cir 1965) 348 F2d 674, 675-676, *cert den* (1965) 382 US 959, dealt with an interstate seller of milk who granted a discount to one retail chain in Albuquerque, New Mexico, but not to its other customers in that area. The seller contended that there was no Robinson-Patman violation because the compared discriminatory sales were intrastate. The court rejected this argument, holding the commerce requirement satisfied because 20 percent of the milk supplied to Albuquerque came from Colorado and was processed in Santa Fe. "[U]nder the stream of commerce doctrine, milk produced in one state and processed and distributed in another state does not lose its interstate character because of standardization and pasteurization." The court characterized this processing as "a rather negligible . . . operation, which did not change its character appreciably" and noted evidence that the process usually took less than an hour. See also *Standard Oil Co. v FTC* (1951) 340 US 231, 238; *Corn Products Refining Co. v FTC* (1945) 324 US 726; *Dean Milk v FTC* (7th Cir 1968) 395 F2d 696.

On the other hand, if raw materials are transformed into a finished or substantially different product after interstate shipment, the stream of commerce is destroyed. Thus, a seller manufactured in California and sold to California buyers wallboard made from Colorado gypsum rock. The court found the stream-of-commerce doctrine inapplicable because the ingredients from out of state had undergone substantial physical change in the course of their transformation into wallboard. Therefore, the wallboard sold to plaintiff and its competitors originated in California. *Baldwin Hills Building Material Co. v Fibreboard Paper Products Corp.* (CD Calif 1968) 283 F Supp 202.

The Tenth Circuit has gone further in finding interruption in the stream of commerce. In *Food Basket, Inc. v Albertson's, Inc., supra*, at 788, the court acknowledged that the interstate commerce requirement is satisfied "if goods originating out of the state are shipped to the wholesalers in anticipation of orders from the retailers, or if a substantial part of the goods were shipped directly out of state to the retailers as drop shipments." However, the court held that the necessary continuity or stream was destroyed where the goods, after being shipped from outside the state, came to rest in the hands of wholesalers within the state before being shipped to retailers on order within the same state.

f. Sales Not Subject to Comparison

(1) [§5.18] Sales to Government or Eleemosynary Institutions

Sales to the federal government and its agencies are not subject to the provisions of §2 of the Clayton Act as amended by the Robinson-Patman Act (15 USC §13) or §3 of the Robinson-Patman Act (15 USC §13a). Hearings before House Committee on the Judiciary on Bills to Amend the Clayton Act, 74th Cong., 1st Sess. 250 (1935); Opinion of the Attorney General of the United States (1936) 38 Op Att'y Gen 539; *General Shale Products Corp. v Struck Const. Co.* (WD Pa 1941) 37 F Supp 598, 602–603, *aff'd* (6th Cir 1942) 132 F2d 425, *cert den* (1943) 318 US 780; Rowe, *Price Discrimination under the Robinson-Patman Act* 84 (1962).

Sales to states, their agencies, and municipalities have also been held exempt from the act's coverage. *Sachs v Brown-Forman Distillers Corp.* (SD NY 1955) 134 F Supp 9, 16, *aff'd* (2d Cir 1956) 234 F2d 959, *cert den* (1956) 352 US 925. See Patman, *Complete Guide to the Robinson-Patman Act* 30 (1963); Rowe, *Price Discrimination under the Robinson-Patman Act* 83–85 (1962).

Sales to eleemosynary institutions are expressly made exempt from the provisions of the act. Nonprofit Institutions Act passed May, 1938, amending the Robinson-Patman Act, 15 USC §13(c). See *Logan Lanes, Inc. v Brunswick Corp.* (9th Cir 1967) 378 F2d 212, *cert den* (1967) 389 US 898. However, the exemption is inapplicable if the institution resells the goods for profit. See, *e.g., Students Book Co. v Washington Law Book Co.* (DC Cir 1955) 232 F2d 49 at 50–51 n. 5, *cert den* (1956) 350 US 988.

Although §4 of the Robinson-Patman Act (15 USC §13b) permits a cooperative association to distribute its earnings to its members without violating §2 of the Clayton Act as amended, that section does not insulate the cooperative association from prosecution for any illegal activity that may have produced the earnings. See, *e.g., Mid-South Distributors v FTC* (5th Cir 1956) 287 F2d 512, *cert den* (1961) 368 US 838.

(2) [§5.19] Sales Outside the United States

The price discrimination provisions of the Robinson-Patman Act are expressly limited to "commodities . . . sold for use, consumption, or resale within the United States or any territory thereof or the District of Columbia or any insular possession or other place under the jurisdiction of the United States." (15 USC §13(a).) Export sales are thus excluded in accordance with Congress' intention to enable domestic sellers to dispose of their surplus products abroad at lower than domestic prices. 80 Cong Rec 6333 (1936).

Although no language in the act prevents it from applying to import sales, the problem of obtaining jurisdiction over foreign sellers is a fairly effective block to its enforcement. However, the act has been applied to discriminatory import sales by a foreign corporation within the United States. See Rowe, *Price Discrimination under the Robinson-Patman Act* 83 (1962) ns. 160 and 161 (1963).

5. [§5.20] Discrimination Based on Product Differences

Section 2(a) of the Clayton Act as amended (15 USC §13(a)) declares it unlawful to discriminate in price between purchasers of commodities of "like grade and quality." Obviously, if the items of merchandise in question are entirely distinct as to ingredients, appearance, and utility, there is no reason why they should be sold for the same price. Thus, in *United Banana Co., Inc. v United Fruit Co.* (2d Cir 1966) 362 F2d 849, a seller who sold bananas to plaintiff's competitors at lower prices showed that the bananas in question were less valuable or in poorer condition than those sold to plaintiff. The court held that the sales did not violate the Robinson-Patman Act because they were not of "like grade and quality."

Conversely, "[C]ommodities having actual, genuine physical sameness with respect to ingredients, appearance, utility, and acceptance would be regarded as being of like grade and quality under the Robinson-Patman Act." Patman, *Complete Guide to the Robinson-Patman Act* 34 (1963). See also Rowe, *Price Discrimination under the Robinson-Patman Act* 63-76 (1962).

Physical sameness may be inferred from identical style numbers on the invoices sent to the favored and disfavored customers. See, *e.g.*, *Fred Meyer, Inc. v FTC* (9th Cir 1966) 359 F2d 351, 358, *rev'd on other grounds* (1968) 390 US 341.

But, as discussed in §5.21, a finding of like grade and quality does not necessarily imply physical identity.

a. [§5.21] Physical Differences

A general line of products of similar quality may be deemed of like grade and quality notwithstanding they are not interchangeable. In *Moog Industries, Inc. v FTC* (8th Cir 1956) 238 F2d 43, 49, *aff'd on other grounds* (1958) 355 US 411, a manufacturer of automobile replacement parts argued that the Commission had failed to prove that the competing purchasers bought the same or even interchangeable parts at different prices. The court ruled that it is not necessary to "identify, item by item, the exact parts in any line sold by petitioner to particular purchasers, but only [deal] with them by same lines as they were sold by petitioner." See also *Joseph A. Kaplan & Sons, Inc.* (1963) [1963-1965 Transfer Binder] FTC Dkt 7813, Trade Reg Rep ¶16,666, *aff'd and modified on other grounds* (DC Cir 1965) 347 F2d 785.

Similarly, a finding of like grade and quality may be made despite differences in size. In a treble-damage action against a can manufacturer, the court found that cans of different sizes were of like grade and quality since they "were all of commercial grade and quality and gave substantially identical performance . . . [and] were adapted for the function for which they were sold and purchased, to wit, as containers of juice, and they were 'the same kind of goods'." *Bruce's Juices, Inc. v American Can Co.* (SD Fla 1949) 87 F Supp 985, 987, *aff'd* (5th Cir 1951) 187 F2d 919, *mod* (5th Cir 1951) 190 F2d 73, *cert dismissed* (1951) 342 US 875.

Nor may differences in physical appearance and lack of commercial fungibility be sufficient to avoid a finding of like grade and quality. In *General Foods Corp.* (1956) 52 FTC 798, the court found like grade and quality when a seller of coffee, selling to both institutions and markets, added a particular bean to coffee for institutions, to give longer freshness, and packed the coffee in larger containers.

On the other hand, differences in size, design, styling, or features *that affect the marketability of a product* support a conclusion that the merchandise in question is not of like grade and quality. As stated in *Antitrust Developments 1955-1968* 122:

[T]he current position of the FTC [seems] to be that bona fide physical differences affecting marketability—even though small and having no effect on the seller's costs—cause products to be deemed not of "like grade and quality."

In *Universal-Rundle* (1964) [1963-1965 Transfer Binder] FTC Dkt 8070, Trade Reg Rep ¶16,948, *rev'd on other grounds* (7th Cir 1965) 352 F2d 831, *rev'd on other grounds and remanded* (1967) 378 US 244, it appeared that Universal had sold bathtubs to Sears Roebuck for less money than it charged its distributors for its brand of bathtubs. The Sears bathtubs were one inch lower in height in addition to other slight design and size differentials. The Commission concluded that the physical differences affected marketability and hence precluded finding the two bathtubs of "like grade and quality." See also Advisory Opinion Digest 43 (1966) [1965-1967 Transfer Binder] Trade Reg Rep ¶17,528; *Quaker Oats Co.* (1964) [1963-1965 Transfer Binder] FTC Dkt 8112, Trade Reg Rep ¶17,134.

Similarly in *Checker Motors Corp. v Chrysler Corp.* (SD NY 1968) 283 F Supp 876, 888-889, *aff'd* (2d Cir 1969) 405 F2d 319, *cert den* (1969) 394 US 999, a taxicab manufacturer charged a competitor with selling its taxis at a lower price than its passenger cars, claiming that the cars were of "like grade and quality" despite slight differences in mechanical devices, seat cover, paint, and exterior trim. The court denied the plaintiff's motion for summary judgment, stating that "[C]ross-elasticity of demand, substitutability, physical appearance, and identity of performance, are factors to be considered. . . . Although it seems clear that denominating one vehicle a 'taxicab' and an identical one a 'passenger car' will not preclude a finding of 'like grade and quality,' . . . *if there are substantial physical differences in products affecting consumer use, preference or marketability, such products are not of 'like grade and quality,' regardless of manufacturing costs.*" (emphasis added).

Also, the fact that the commodity is made to order to a customer's specifications and is different from the manufacturer's usual product has been held sufficient to preclude a finding of like grade and quality. See, *e.g.*, *Central Ice Cream Co. v Golden Rod Ice Cream Co.* (ND Ill 1960) 184 F Supp 312, *aff'd* (7th Cir 1961) 287 F2d 265, *cert den* (1961) 368 US 829; Advisory Opinion Digest 43, *supra.* See also, *1955 Report of the Attorney General's National Committee to Study the Antitrust Laws* 158 (hereafter *Attorney General's Report, 1955*).

b. [§5.22] Brand Differences

Prior to March 23, 1966, a debate raged concerning the effect of different brand names on physically identical goods. The FTC's position was that such goods were of like grade and quality for purposes of the Robinson-Patman Act. See, *e.g.*, *Goodyear Tire and Rubber Co.* (1936) 22 FTC 232, *rev'd* (6th Cir 1939) 101 F2d 620; *Hansen Innoculator Co.* (1950) 46 FTC 998; *Page Dairy Co.* (1953) 50 FTC 395; *Whitaker Cable Corp.* (1955) 51 FTC 958. However, the commentators were divided. See *FTC v Borden Co.* (1966) 383 US 637, 640–641 n. 3.

FTC v Borden put the controversy to rest. Borden had marketed evaporated milk under various brand names owned by its customers at lower prices than it marketed identical evaporated milk under its own brand name. The Fifth Circuit held that whereas a difference in brand name alone would not support a finding of difference in grade, such a finding was justified when there was a decided customer preference for one brand over another and a willingness to pay more for the premium brand. The Supreme Court reversed, holding that the milk in question was of "like grade and quality" in spite of the brand-name differences, thereby adopting the "longstanding interpretation" of the Commission to the effect that "labels do not differentiate products for the purpose of determining grade or quality, even though the one label may have more customer appeal and command a higher price in the marketplace from a substantial segment of the public." 383 US at 640.

The opinion concluded by quoting the rationale expressed in the *Attorney General's Report, 1955,* 159:

[T]angible consumer preferences as between branded and unbranded commodities should receive due legal recognition in the more flexible "injury" and "cost justification" provisions of the statute.

Thus the manufacturer of a nationally advertised premium brand cannot sell its product for more than it sells an identical product carrying its customer's less valuable brand unless it is prepared to prove no injury to competition, or to justify the price differential by showing that the price difference reflects the cost of promoting its products, or one of the other defenses discussed below. See §§5.43–5.52.

The *Borden* doctrine was applied in *Perma Life Mufflers, Inc. v International Parts Corp.* (7th Cir 1967) 376 F2d 692, *rev'd and remanded on other grounds* (1968) 392 US 134. A manufacturer of two brands of automobile mufflers which were physically identical priced them differently because one brand carried a lifetime guarantee. The circuit court, reversing, held that the lifetime guarantee did not constitute a dissimilarity or justify "a difference in price. . . .[T]he Midas trade name or trademark does not differentiate its mufflers for the purpose of determining grade or quality, even though its guarantee may have more customer appeal and command a higher price in the market place." 376 F2d at 703.

If a manufacturer of both a nationally advertised premium brand and a private brand can point to some physical difference between the commodities, a price difference may be justifiable. A physical difference that affects customer preference will justify a price difference even if the manufacturer's costs are the same; but *Borden* held that a brand difference that affects customer preference will not support such a price difference.

On the remand of *Borden v FTC* (5th Cir 1967) 381 F2d 175, the court found no evidence to support a finding of injury to competition at the seller's level (the primary level). The only evidence presented was testimony of Borden's competitors that they were not successful in competing with Borden for business. This testimony would be relevant to the charge that Borden sold its brand of milk at discriminatory prices but not to the charge in issue, that Borden sold its customers' private brand of milk at lower prices than its own premium brand of milk.

The Fifth Circuit also found no injury to competition at Borden's customers' level (the secondary level) stating (381 F2d at 181):

We are of the firm view that where a price differential between a premium and nonpremium brand reflects no more than a customer preference for the premium brand, the price difference creates no competitive advantage to the recipient of the cheaper private brand product on which injury could be predicated. "[R]ather it represents merely a rough equivalent of the benefit by way of the seller's national advertising and promotion which the purchaser of the more expensive branded product enjoys." The record discloses no evidence tending to show that Borden's price differential exceeds the recognized consumer appeal of the Borden label. Nor has it been suggested that the prices are unreasonably high for Borden brand milk on the one hand, or unrealistically low for the private label milk on the other.

The Commission disagreed with the holding of the Fifth Circuit, which placed the burden on the Commission to prove that the private-brand price differential exceeds the premium-brand consumer appeal, as evidenced by its unsuccessful efforts to persuade the Solicitor General to bring the *Borden* case before the Supreme Court a second time. ATRR No. 341 (Jan 23, 1968) B–2. Accordingly, one can anticipate further action by the Commission dealing with private brands, particularly those allegedly causing injury at the secondary level.

Of course, by making private brands and their usually lower prices available to all customers, the manufacturer would destroy the casual connection required for the finding of competitive injury. See discussion at §§5.34, 5.39, and 5.40. In fact, many manufacturers could not offer a lower price for private brands if the number handled were large and thereby required them to spend the advertising savings on managing private labels.

6. [§5.23] Discrimination Based on Buyer's Function

The Robinson-Patman Act contains no language authorizing functional discounts. The act makes it a prima facie violation to grant a price differential that will probably adversely affect competition. Functional discounts are justified on the basis of their lack of injury to competition.

Traditionally, a functional discount is based on the classification of the purchaser with respect to how he disposes of the seller's product. Usual groupings include warehouse distributor, wholesaler, jobber, fleet operator, and retailer. These purchasers relieve the seller of the task of performing their functions, and the functional discounts granted to each group "reflect rough and long-range estimates by the supplier of the economic advantage of dealing with broad customer classes performing characteristic marketing functions." *Attorney General's Report, 1955,* 203. Perhaps the most common functional discount is granted to wholesalers who perform the functions of warehousing, distributing, marketing, and promoting the seller's product.

The functional discount need not reflect the cost or the value of the function either to the buyer or the seller. Its legality does not rest on cost justification but rather on the fact that different classes of customers performing different functions do not compete, and thus price differentials between these different classes can have no harmful effect upon competition. See discussion at §5.40.

The classification of customer groups must be reasonable. The general rule is to look to the customers to whom the buyer resells to form the classification. If, for example, a discount is given to a stocking jobber but not to a non-stocking jobber, and the facts show that the so-called stocking jobber received a discount even on merchandise shipped directly to its customers, the class is arbitrarily formed. *Mueller Co. v FTC* (7th Cir 1963) 323 F2d 44, 46, *cert den* (1964) 377 US 923.

In *William H. Rorer, Inc.* (1966) [1965-1967 Transfer Binder] FTC Dkt 8599, Trade Reg Rep ¶17,535, *modified on other grounds* (2d Cir 1967) 374 F2d 622, a manufacturer of pharmaceutical products was held to have improperly segregated "chain drugstores" (which it defined as five or more registered pharmacies under single ownership) and independent drugstores performing in the same fashion and selling to the same customers. See also Advisory Opinion Digest 41 (1966) [1965-1967 Transfer Binder] Trade Reg Rep ¶17,526.

So long as the traditional functions in the distribution process are segregated and the classes of customers are reasonably formed, there is no competition between the classes to be adversely affected. But complex problems arise with the ever-increasing integration of functions within the distribution process. In the present economy many larger retailers buy directly from manufacturers and perform wholesaling services. Smaller retailers have attempted without great success to organize group buying associations to perform wholesaler functions and thereby obtain the wholesaler's discount. See discussion in §§5.30 and 5.42.

Where a buyer acts both as wholesaler and retailer, the Commission and the courts take the view that such a mixed-function buyer is entitled to the wholesaler's discount only on the merchandise purchased for wholesale and that it is unlawful to grant a wholesale discount on the merchandise purchased for retail. See, *e.g.*, *Champion Spark Plug* (1953) 50 FTC 30; *E. Edelmann & Co. v FTC* (1955) 51 FTC 978, *aff'd* (7th Cir 1956) 239 F2d 152, *cert den* (1958) 355 US 941; Advisory Opinion Digest 67 (1966) [1965-1967 Transfer Binder] Trade Reg Rep ¶17,586; *Knoll Associates, Inc.* (1966) [1965-1967 Transfer Binder] FTC Dkt 8549, Trade Reg Rep ¶17,668.

In short, a method-of-resale test governs, *i.e.*, to whom does the buyer resell, and with whom is the buyer in competition? See, *e.g.*, Advisory Opinion Digest 202 (1968) 3 Trade Reg Rep ¶18,248: "The controlling element . . . is whether or not resale competition actually exists as between and among these various resellers rather than the names they use to describe themselves."

FTC v Ruberoid Co. (1952) 343 US 470 dealt with a manufacturer of asbestos and asphalt roofing materials who sold to wholesalers, applicators, and retailers and gave decreasing discounts to each group. Some of the wholesalers did applicating work, and it was argued that the retailers in fact competed with the applicators in that both resold the materials to the public. The Commission enjoined the manufacturer from selling to any customer at prices lower than those granted competing customers, regardless of their functional labels, reasoning that the grant to a wholesaler-applicator of a wholesaler's discount injured ordinary applicators and that the grant of an applicator discount to the applicator injured the retailer. The Supreme Court agreed.

This position has been criticized as thwarting competition and efficiency in the distribution process. There has been some agitation for a more liberal test to be applied to the mixed-function buyer emphasizing the function performed by the buyer rather than how the buyer disposes of the goods. See *Attorney General's Report, 1955,* 207–208.

In this view, if the wholesaler-retailer performs a wholesaler's function (*i.e.*, warehousing, distributing, marketing, and promoting) on all his purchases, he should obtain a functional discount on all of them, regardless of how he disposes of them. This analysis raises problems with respect to competing retailers who are put at a disadvantage with the wholesaler-retailer if the discount exceeds the cost of whatever function the wholesaler-retailer performs. Requiring cost justification of the functional discount to remedy this problem would eliminate the functional discount for all practical purposes. See discussion of cost justification in §§5.44–5.48. But the discount could approximately equal the average value of the service without requiring the precision of cost justification.

Some commentators have suggested that the broader test of permitting a functional discount based on the buying function of the buyer rather than on how the buyer disposes of the merchandise would work "if the [wholesaler-retailer] does not take advantage of his wholesale status to undersell and thus unfairly compete with retailers of the same product who have bought through him or through some other wholesale customer of the manufacturer." Patman, *Complete Guide to the Robinson-Patman Act* (1963) 29–30.

However, the courts have found that maintenance of identical retail prices by the favored and disfavored purchaser does not eliminate a violation. For example, in *E. Edelmann & Co. v FTC* (7th Cir 1956) 239 F2d 152, 155, *cert den* (1958) 355 US 941, a manufacturer of automotive products sold to warehouse distributors, who in turn sold to automotive jobbers and to cooperative buying groups sometimes composed of jobbers, and to jobbers direct. The manufacturer gave varying discounts to the distributors and to the buying groups without attempting to justify these discounts on the basis of cost savings. The court affirmed the Commission's order finding unlawful price discrimination, stating:

Petitioner suggested resale prices at all levels of distribution and it was found that these suggested prices were regularly adhered to. . . . It is not necessary that a price advantage be used to lower the resale price and thereby attract business away from the unfavored competitors. Sales are not the sole indicium that reflects the health of the competitive scene.

It has also been suggested that the validity of payments for services rendered by a customer should be determined by the standards of §2(d) (15 USC §13(d)), which requires that an offer of such payments for services be made to all customers on proportionally equal terms. See, *e.g.*, dicta in *Alhambra Motor Parts v FTC* (9th Cir 1962) 309 F2d 213, 216; Patman, *Complete Guide to the Robinson-Patman Act* (1963) 23–24; Advisory Opinion Digest 263 (1968) 3 Trade Reg Rep ¶18,425.

The present status of the law would seem to make it very risky for a manufacturer to grant a functional discount on all its sales to a mixed-function buyer. See, *e.g.*, *Monroe Auto Equipment v FTC* (7th Cir 1965) 347 F2d 401, *cert den* (1966) 382 US 1009. The manufacturer must apportion the functional discount to those goods purchased for resale in the given function. And it is the manufacturer's responsibility to require some evidence of how the customer is disposing of the merchandise. Generally this is easier to accomplish at the end of a period with appropriate price adjustments.

What evidence is required to prove a lawful functional discount by a seller? The strongest evidence would be the customer's own sales invoices. However, a demand for invoices may well be refused by the customer, who may suspect that the supplier is seeking to sell direct, particularly if the seller already engages in direct selling. A demand for invoices might also subject the seller to a charge of attempting to police resale prices.

Probably the best solution from the seller's point of view is to request a periodic written statement from his buyer stating what percentage of his purchases were resold at retail and what percentage of his purchases were resold at wholesale. As long as the seller is not reasonably in possession of information refuting the accuracy of the buyer's written statement, it would seem that he could rely on it. Analogies are liability for *knowing* inducement of favorable prices under §2(f) (15 USC §13(f); see §5.42) and the defense that a seller met what he *believed* to be lawful competitive prices (15 USC §13(b); see §§5.49-5.51)

7. [§5.24] Discrimination Based on Geography

In order to compete in distant markets, sellers may be forced to quote "delivered" prices, which means that the seller quotes prices to his buyers at their place of business, regardless of the buyer's location, so that the quoted price necessarily includes a freight factor to offset some portion of the transportation costs, as opposed to a quote f.o.b. factory, *i.e.*, a price excluding transportation.

The reason for this is aptly stated in the *Attorney General's Report, 1955*, 214:

To compete successfully for sales in a distant area, sellers must quote prices to prospective customers which *after* taking into account the element of freight cannot exceed the offer of a more favorably situated rival. A disadvantageously situated seller might, of course, neutralize a rival's transportation by initiating a corresponding cut in price at the mill only applicable to distant customers in the competitor's marketing territory [which assumes that the territories are clearly defined with no customers situated on the fringes]. Or he could reduce his mill price to *all* customers in order to tempt those located in remote areas [risking losing money on the majority of sales in his territory in an effort to induce purchases from a few customers in a distant territory]. (Bracketed phrases added.)

There is a variety of descriptive labels given the different schemes of "delivered" prices, all of which have encountered a stormy judicial assessment. A "uniform delivered" price means that the seller averages his freight costs to all customers and includes within his quoted price for his goods the average freight cost. The result of utilizing uniform delivered prices is that buyers far from the seller's plant get more transportation than buyers close to the seller's plant, without paying more.

One of the most common "delivered" price schemes is called "basing point prices," which means the seller takes the price at a selected geographic point, usually one of the seller's plants, rather than from the plant of purchase, and adds the actual freight cost from the selected point to the buyer to reach the price quoted the buyer. The result is that buyers who buy from a plant located nearer to them than the seller's selected basing point will pay a price that reflects more than the actual freight

257

charge attributable to their orders. Conversely, buyers who buy from a plant located farther from them than the selected basing point pay a price that reflects less than the actual freight costs attributed to their orders.

In *Corn Products Refining Co. v FTC* (1945) 324 US 726, the Court held a basing-point system invalid; the seller quoted glucose prices f.o.b. Chicago regardless of the location of the plant from which a sale was made. Buyers located near the seller's Kansas plants were forced to pay prices that included the equivalent of transportation costs from Chicago. See also *FTC v Staley Mfg. Co.* (1945) 324 US 746.

In a variation of the basing-point system, sometimes called "freight equalization," the seller charges customers no more for freight than they would have to pay for transportation from competing sellers. In effect the basing point is the seller's competitor located nearest to the customer.

"Zone pricing" is similar. The total geographic area serviced by the seller is divided into zones, and buyers within each zone pay the same delivered price regardless of their distance from the plant.

Although all delivered prices were initially regarded as suspect, the *Attorney General's Report, 1955* recommended (at 219) that "sellers [be] free to meet competition in distant markets by quoting delivered prices to equalize the freight advantages of more favorably situated competitors."

In 1957 the Supreme Court construed a Commission order as not prohibiting "the practice of the absorption of actual freight as such in order to foster competition." *FTC v National Lead Co.* (1957) 352 US 419, 431.

In *United States v Pennsalt Chemicals Corp.* (ED Pa 1967) 1967 Trade Cases ¶71,982 at 83,476, a consent judgment entered in a case under the Sherman Act prohibited defendant's use of "any pricing system having an f.o.b. factory price with freight equalization adjustment *unless.* . . [defendant offers] the customer the option to purchase . . . at the factory . . . at not more than its f.o.b. factory price, when the customer furnishes . . . or arranges . . . transportation compatible with loading facilities and schedules of [defendant]" (emphasis added).

It is now clear that if the delivered price to each buyer is the same, there is no violation even though some buyers get more transportation with their purchase than others. Advisory Opinion Digest 194 (1968) 3 Trade Reg Rep ¶18,224 dealt with these facts: A West Coast manufacturer charged an f.o.b. factory price of $99.50 for an item of merchandise. Actual freight costs to West Coast customers was $.50, making their total price $100.00. Actual freight to Denver customers was $1.00. The manufacturer granted a freight allowance of $.50 to his Denver customers with the result that the latter paid freight of $1.00 and a purchase price of $99.00, but the same $100.00 total as the West Coast customers. This practice was ruled valid.

Absent uniform prices, it is difficult to advise a client with any degree of certainty. *Guyott Co. v Texaco, Inc.* (D Conn 1966) 261 F Supp 942 was a treble-damage action by a plaintiff who paid a lower f.o.b. plant price but charged that a higher delivered price paid by a competitor was discriminatory because it was not sufficiently higher to take into account the actual freight charges, a portion of which the seller absorbed. The seller moved for a summary judgment on the ground that the price subject to comparison was "the total delivered price . . . regardless of the place or method of delivery." The court denied the motion, stating that "discriminatory use of freight or delivery terms of sale having the proscribed adverse effect on competition constitutes unlawful indirect price discrimination under Section 2(a)." 261 F Supp at 948, 949.

The Commission's position in this area is confusing. In one advisory opinion it cautioned the seller against granting a freight allowance to buyers picking up their goods f.o.b. factory equal to the actual cost of the freight from the factory to the buyer, because by using a delivered price system with respect to other buyers the seller incorporated a "freight factor included within the price [which] is not the actual freight to any given point, but an average of the freight costs for all customers." In rendering this decision the Commission acknowledged that "this conclusion may seem unreasonable . . . since the allowance would be for no more than the actual freight saved. . . ." Advisory Opinion Digest 147 (1967) 3 Trade Reg Rep ¶18,089.

Nor, according to the Commission, can the average freight factor be allowed when the buyer does his own hauling because the allowance would be too generous to buyers living close to the basing point and too parsimonious to those living distant from the basing point. Advisory Opinion Digest 198 (1968) 3 Trade Reg Rep ¶18,237.

The confusion is aptly pointed out in the *Antitrust Developments 1955-1968* 165:

[T]he seller may grant to customers freight allowances equal to the seller's actual common carrier freight cost savings to enable such customers to pay the applicable freight directly to a common carrier performing the transportation service, and yet the seller may not grant to customers pick-up allowances equal to the outbound common carrier freight cost even though such customers perform the same transportation service as a common carrier would perform.

The opinions of the Commission lead inexplicably to the conclusion that the practitioner will have difficulty in advising his client with any degree of certainty unless the seller offers the same price to all buyers. Only time will tell whether the Commission will develop more meaningful guidelines in this area.

8. [§5.25] Discrimination Based on Quantity Purchased

In 1936 Congress deleted the proviso in §2 of the Clayton Act (15 USC §13) that permitted discriminations in price "on account of differences in . . . quantity," a proviso the courts had interpreted as permitting quantity discounts. *Goodyear Tire and Rubber Co. v FTC* (6th Cir 1939) 101 F2d 620. Congress did so in the view that the proviso "render[ed] [section 2] inadequate if not almost a nullity." H. Rep. No. 2281, 74th Cong. 2d Sess. 7 (1936). See also, *Morton Salt Co. v FTC* (1948) 334 US 37, 43. The purpose of the amendment was to limit "the use of quantity price differentials to the sphere of actual cost differences." H. Rep. No. 2281, 74th Cong. 2d Sess. 9 (1936); Rep. No. 1502, 74th Cong. 2d Sess. 4-6 (1936); *Morton Salt Co. v FTC, supra,* at 49.

The practitioner must recognize that the *only* justification for granting a purchaser a quantity discount is that the size of the order generated a cost savings to the seller. The defense based upon cost justification is not easily established. See discussion at §5.44-5.48.

It is much more difficult to justify a cumulative quantity discount (*i.e.,* a discount based on the amount of merchandise purchased over a period of time) than it is to justify a discount granted on the basis of a single order. This is because the most obvious cost savings generated by a single large order are savings of handling and freight, both of which are sizeable and relatively easy to document. Several small orders do not generate such savings. See, *e.g., Standard Motor Products, Inc. v FTC* (2d Cir 1959) 265 F2d 674, *cert den* (1959) 361 US 826, holding a retroactive rebate on annual purchases unlawful. To the same effect, see *C. E. Niehoff & Co. v FTC* (7th Cir 1957) *vacated on other grounds* (1958) 355 US 941; *P. & D. Manufacturing Co. v FTC* (7th Cir 1957) 245 F2d 281, *cert den* (1957) 355 US 884; *E. Edelmann & Co. v FTC* (7th Cir 1956) 239 F2d 152, *cert den* (1958) 355 US 941; *Whitaker Cable Corp. v FTC* (7th Cir 1956) 239 F2d 253, *cert den* (1957) 353 US 938; *P. Sorensen Manufacturing Co. v FTC* (DC Cir 1957) 246 F2d 687. See also Advisory Opinion Digest 151 (1967) 3 Trade Reg Rep ¶18,121 (a 10 percent discount to customers with over $15,000 of purchases within calendar year probably would constitute unlawful price discrimination under §2(a) (15 USC §2(a))); Advisory Opinion Digest 153 (1967) 3 Trade Reg Rep ¶18,130 (supplier's discount to jobbers based on increase in amounts of purchases during year over total purchases during preceding year would violate §2(a)); Advisory Opinion

Digest 274 (1968) 3 Trade Reg Rep ¶18,473 (merchandising plan under which customers with annual purchases below a fixed amount would obtain a lesser discount than those whose annual purchases exceed the amount would violate §2(a)).

Even cost justification of quantity discounts, as distinguished from cumulative discounts, is not easy. If a seller offers his merchandise at $10 per item for 1 to 50 items and $9 per item for 51 to 100 items, it may be difficult to justify, on the basis of the cost savings to the seller, the 10 percent price differential between an order for 50 items and one for 51 items. But if the seller offers his merchandise at a 5 percent discount for a carload order, a 2 percent discount for a half-car order, and no discount for smaller orders, the differences in handling and transportation costs may well justify the price differential.

When quantity discounts are offered to all customers placing orders of a specified size, such as a carload lot, the Supreme Court has approved grouping the customers for purposes of analyzing the cost savings rather than conducting what may be an exhaustive customer-by-customer cost analysis. *United States v Borden Co.* (1962) 370 US 460. See discussion of customer grouping at §5.46.

The Commission reads the *Borden* rule permitting customer grouping more narrowly than do the courts. Illustrating the dichotomy is *FTC v Standard Motor Products, Inc.* (2d Cir 1967) 371 F2d 613, 619, in which the court refused to enforce a cease-and-desist order issued when the Commission rejected a cost defense for a volume rebate discount. The court concluded that "[t]he Commission has not suggested any administrable alternative means of classifying customers," and that the Commission's insistence on detail constituted a customer-by-customer analysis of costs.

In pricing orders of various sizes, it must be kept in mind that price differentials between each grouping of orders must be cost justified and that the pricing schedule must be made known to all customers so that they can increase the size of their purchases and enjoy the cost savings that a larger order generates.

9. [§5.26] Discrimination Based on Terms of Sale

Section 2(a) of the Clayton Act as amended by the Robinson-Patman Act (15 USC §13(a)) makes it illegal for "any person engaged in commerce . . . either directly or indirectly, to discriminate in price between different purchasers. . . ."

The accepted definition of "price" is the seller's invoice price, including prepaid freight, and deducting discounts and allowances against the invoice price. See Rowe, *Price Discrimination under the Robinson-Patman Act* (1962) 87. Discrimination has been defined by the Supreme Court as "merely a price difference." *FTC v Anheuser-Busch, Inc.* (1960) 363 US 536, 549.

By the "direct or indirect" clause, Congress extended the act's prohibition to discrimination in the sale terms resulting in a price advantage to the favored customer. Common sale terms that may be easily translated into price advantages include freight allowances (*American Can Co. v Russellville Canning Co.* (8th Cir 1951) 191 F2d 38; *Guyott Co. v Texaco, Inc.* (D Conn 1966) 261 F Supp 942; *Chicago Spring Products Co. v U.S. Steel* (ND Ill 1966) 254 F Supp 83, *aff'd* (7th Cir 1966) 371 F2d 428; *Viviano Macaroni Co.* (1968) FTC Dkt 8666, 3 Trade Reg Rep ¶18,246); free goods (*Matter of Curtiss Candy Co.* (1947) 44 FTC 237; Advisory Opinion Digest 132 (1967) 3 Trade Reg Rep ¶17,981; Advisory Opinion Digest 131 (1967) 3 Trade Reg Rep ¶17,980); option or return privileges (*Corn Products Refining Co. v FTC* (1945) 324 US 726); advertising allowances (*United States v Borden Co.* (ND Ill 1953) 111 F Supp 562); cash discounts (*Hudson House, Inc.* (1959) 55 FTC 1225); or free merchandise equipment (*United States v Borden, supra*).

In *Corn Products Refining Co. v FTC, supra*, the Court struck down the practice of a glucose manufacturer, when it changed prices, of permitting favored customers to order goods at old prices for a longer time and for later delivery. Section 2(a) proscribes discrimination in the terms and conditions of sale as an "indirect" price discrimination.

Clausen & Sons, Inc. v Theo. Hamm Brewing Co. (D Minn 1967) 284 F Supp 148, *rev'd on other grounds*, (8th Cir 1968) 395 F2d 388, indicated that offering more advantageous credit terms to favored purchasers might constitute unlawful price discrimination under §2(a) but does not violate §2(d) or 2(e) (15 USC §13(d)-(e)) as an unlawful grant of promotional services or facilities because credit does not constitute "services" or "facilities" within the meaning of these subsections. See discussion of promotional allowances and services at §§5.31–5.33.

III. Dealing with Brokers

A. [§5.27] General Analysis

Section 2(c) of the Clayton Act as amended by the Robinson-Patman Act (15 USC §13(c)) declares it illegal for any person engaged in commerce in the course of such commerce to pay or grant, or to receive or accept, anything of value as a commission, brokerage, or other compensation, . . . except for services rendered in connection with the sale or purchase of goods, wares, or merchandise, either to the other party to such transaction or to an agent, representative, or other intermediary therein where such intermediary is acting in fact for or in behalf, or is subject to the direct or indirect control, of any party to such transaction other than the person by whom such compensation is so granted or paid.

In short, neither the seller or the buyer may pay a fee to the other or to the other's agent.

Section 2(c) was enacted because

'large chain buyers were obtaining competitive advantages in several ways other than direct price concessions and were thus avoiding the impact of the Clayton Act. One of the favorite means of obtaining an indirect price concession was by setting up "dummy" brokers who were employed by the buyer and who, in many cases, rendered no services. The large buyers demanded that the seller pay "brokerage" to these fictitious brokers who then turned it over to their employer. This practice was one of the chief targets of §2(c) of the Act.'

FTC v Henry Broch & Co. (1960) 363 US 166, 168–169.

Section 2(c) lacks several of the express limitations written into §2(a) (15 USC §13(a)). For example, its application is not restricted to goods sold for use, consumption, or resale within the United States or its territories, and hence a purchase made for export could be covered. See, *e.g., Canadian Ingersoll-Rand Co. v D. Loveman & Sons, Inc.* (ND Ohio 1964) 227 F Supp 829; *Baysoy v Jessop Steel Co.* (ND Pa 1950) 90 F Supp 303. Nor is its application limited to instances "where the effect . . . may be substantially to lessen competition" (*Oliver Bros., Inc. v FTC* (4th Cir 1939) 102 F2d 763) or to instances in which the brokerage payment results in discrimination. By its terms, §2(c) makes it unlawful to pay a brokerage fee to the other party to the transaction or to his agent, and the courts have construed this prohibition to be absolute, unprotected by any defenses, and requiring no showing of discrimination to establish a violation. *FTC v Simplicity Pattern Co.* (1959) 360 US 55.

The §2(c) prohibition does not affect a bona fide broker serving either as a "representative of the seller to find him market outlets or as a representative of the buyer to find him sources of supply." H.R. Rep. No. 2287, 74th Cong. 2d Sess., p. 14 (1936). But prior to 1960 the courts interpreted §2(c) to prohibit "a buying and selling service . . . combined in one person" (*Great Atlantic & Pacific Tea Co. v FTC* (3d Cir 1939) 106 F2d 667, *cert den* (1940) 308 US 625) regardless of whether the services were actually rendered or the parties acted in good faith. See, *e.g., Modern Marketing Service, Inc. v FTC* (7th Cir 1945) 149 F2d 970.

In 1960, in a 5 to 4 decision in *FTC v Henry Broch & Co.*, *supra*, the Supreme Court made substantial inroads into this heretofore *per se* concept. In that case an independent broker accepted a cut in his commission to induce a price lower than that given to other buyers. The Court held that the seller had violated §2(c) by granting the buyer a discount in lieu of paying the full brokerage fee.

Notwithstanding the Court's finding of a violation, the Court made it clear that it was not applying a *per se* rule, indicating that the result might have been different in circumstances "[in which] the buyer rendered any services to the seller or to the [broker] [or in which] anything in its method of dealing justified its getting a discriminatory price by means of a reduced brokerage charge." 363 US at 173. The Court indicated a relaxation of the heretofore absolute rule in three particulars:

First, the Court ruled that the 2(c) prohibition was not absolute, stating (363 US at 175-176):

[Not] every reduction in price, coupled with a reduction in brokerage, automatically compels the conclusion that an allowance "in lieu" of brokerage has been granted. . . . [W]hether such a reduction is tantamount to a discriminatory payment of brokerage depends on the circumstances of each case.

Second, it suggested that cost justification would be a defense against a §2(c) charge.

Third, the Court indicated that discrimination was usually an essential in establishing a violation of the section when the seller's broker reduces his commission in order to make the sale to the buyer. 363 US at 176.

This relaxation of the absolute concept is consistent with the criticism leveled at the former judicial interpretation of §2(c). See, *e.g.*, *Attorney General's Report, 1955*, 188, 190-193, disapproving of "the disparity in statutory consequences which attach to economically equivalent business practices", depending on whether the concession is classified as an indirect price discrimination under §2(a) or an allowance in lieu of brokerage under §2(c), and recommending that the exception for services rendered be revitalized to correct this legal incongruity.

The incongruity is well illustrated in *Empire Rayon Yarn Co. v American Viscose Corp.* (SD NY 1965) 238 F Supp 556, *rev'd* (2d Cir 1965) 354 F2d 182, *vacated in rehearing en banc* (2d Cir 1966) 364 F2d 491. A defendant producer of yarn entered into contracts with defendant jobbers who purchased the producer's yarn and undertook to resell it to fabric manufacturers at the producer's list price in exchange for a 5 percent discount. Defendant producer refused to enter into such a contract with plaintiff jobber but sold to it at its list price. Plaintiff then sued the producer and the jobbers for treble damages, claiming that the discount to its competitors was a payment in lieu of brokerage.

The district court granted a summary judgment for the defendants, relying upon language in the *Broch* case. The court of appeals reversed on the ground that the jobbers were retailers, not brokers, and that the absolute rule against buyer-brokers applied. Over a strong dissent, the majority opinion found §2(a) inapplicable, stating (354 F2d at 187) "discrimination in price, as such, is governed by Section 2(a). Where the price discrimination is effected by a discount which is related to the sale by the person receiving the discount (*i.e.* a commission or brokerage or such similar compensation), Section 2(c) is applicable."

Subsequently, the court of appeals, granting a rehearing *en banc*, vacated its former decision and affirmed the district court's summary judgment for the defendants, adopting the dissent's statutory interpretation for the reasons that (1) the jobbers were not dummy brokers but rather were independent businessmen who satisfied a definite economic need in moving yarn from the manufacturer to small units in the textile trade; (2) the 5% discount bears all the characteristics of a functional discount, the validity of which should be judged under §2(a); and (3) reliance upon §2(c) might well render all functional discounts illegal *per se* and prevent the recognition of price differentials at non-competing business levels. 364 F2d at 492–493.

The case dramatically illustrates the tremendous difference in result that can flow from labeling (sometimes in apparently arbitrary fashion) a payment, from seller to buyer performing some distribution function, a discount in lieu of brokerage or a functional discount. See discussion at §5.30.

In other cases, identical trade practices are sometimes labeled brokerage allowances in violation of §2(c), and other times labeled an indirect price discrimination under §2(a), the latter requiring proof of injury to competition and being subject to a number of statutory defenses. Compare, for example, *Champion Spark Plug Co.* (1953) 50 FTC 30 and *Lambert Pharmacal Co.* (1940) 31 FTC 734. These decisions point up the legal incongruity and lack of certainty in this area.

B. [§5.28] Circumstances under Which Brokerage May Be Paid

Brokerage may be paid to those persons, including the principals to the transaction, who render services in connection with the sale or purchase in the amount of the value of the services rendered. In *FTC v Washington Fish & Oyster Co.* (9th Cir 1960) 282 F2d 595, a cease-and-desist order issued against a salmon packer who sold through brokers, paying them 5 percent commission except in one instance where it paid the brokers a 2 percent commission and gave the buyer a 3 percent deduction designated as a promotional allowance. The court of appeals agreed that the 3 percent deduction was prohibited under §2(c) (15 USC §13(c)), but stated (282 F2d at 597):

Excepted from this prohibition [of §2(c)] are allowances or discounts given in lieu of compensation for services rendered in connection with such sale and purchase.

The court found that the seller had failed to discharge the burden of showing that the deductions were for genuine services rendered.

If a buyer renders services in connection with the transaction, a reduced brokerage or commission on the transaction may be justified to the extent of the cost savings engendered by the services rendered.

In *Thomasville Chair Co. v FTC* (5th Cir 1962) 306 F2d 541, a furniture manufacturer sold furniture to 200 jobber customers (its largest volume accounts) at 5 percent below the price charged to its 4,500 carload customers, and it paid its salesmen a 3 percent commission on the jobber accounts and a 6 percent commission on its carload accounts. The manufacturer could cost justify the price differential between the two types of accounts only if it were permitted to include the salesmen's commission as a selling cost. The Commission held that in passing on the savings in salesmen's commissions to its jobbers, the manufacturer was violating §2(c) by giving a discount in lieu of brokerage.

The court of appeals set aside the Commission's order on the ground that the Commission erred in holding that the passing of a salesmen's commissions was *per se* unlawful in view of language in *FTC v Henry Broch & Co.* (1960) 363 US 166, 175-176, that "[Not] every reduction in price, coupled with a reduction in brokerage" was unlawful. The court interpreted the *Broch* case as prohibiting a simultaneous reduction in price and brokerage "only if such reduction in price is 'discriminatory' [and] . . . without justification," but rejected the theory that a §2(c) violation would be established when "the entire price reduction cannot be justified on a cost basis exclusive of the commission differential." (306 F2d at 545). The appellate court remanded the case to the Commission for a determination of the propriety of the manufacturer's segregating jobber's accounts from the carload accounts and the legality of its compensating its salesmen at a lesser rate for sales to the larger volume jobber accounts, in effect holding that the Commission should investigate to determine whether the jobbers deserved favored treatment because of possible cost savings to the manufacturer in dealing with them. The Commission subsequently dismissed the case but stated that "the Commission does not, however, acquiesce in the opinion of the Court of Appeals . . ." *Thomasville Chair Co.* (1963) [1963–1965 Transfer Binder] FTC Dkt 7273, Trade Reg Rep ¶16,624 at 21,515.

Subsequently other appellate courts have refused to find §2(c) violations when the discount was given for services actually rendered, and when the discount approximated the cost savings to the seller and was indistinguishable from the traditional functional discount, notwithstanding the discount was equal to the usual brokerage given in the industry. See, *e.g., Central Retailer-Owned Grocers, Inc. v FTC* (7th Cir 1963) 319 F2d 410, discussed at §5.30; *Empire Rayon Yarn Co., Inc. v American Viscose Corp.* (2d Cir 1966) 364 F2d 491, discussed at §5.27. See discussion of functional discounts at §5.23.

Whether the Commission in the future will regard discounts given for actual services rendered as permissible functional discounts rather than unlawful brokerage is impossible to predict at this juncture, but cannot be viewed with great optimism. See, *e.g.,* Advisory Opinion Digest 243 (1968) 3 Trade Reg Rep ¶18,334 cautioning a wholesale food distributor against accepting a 5 percent discount from its supplier for rendering "special services," noting that the supplier paid a 5 percent commission to brokers and that special services, not discussed in the opinion, were normally performed by brokers. See also *Modern Marketing Serv.* (1967) [1967–1970 Transfer Binder] FTC Dkt 3783, Trade Reg Rep ¶17,945, refusing to reopen a 1945 proceeding resulting in a cease and desist order.

C. [§5.29] Prohibited Payments

As discussed above, brokerage or discounts may not be paid to or received by one of the principals to the transaction if no services are rendered to justify the payment. *FTC v Henry Broch & Co.* (1960) 363 US 166; *FTC v Washington Fish & Oyster Co.* (9th Cir 1960) 282 F2d 595; Advisory Opinion Digest 243 (1968) 3 Trade Reg Rep ¶18,334.

The Commission has obtained a number of consent orders prohibiting discounts in lieu of brokerage in violation of §2(c) (15 USC §13(c)). For example, consent orders were entered in a series of cases dealing with railroad parts such as train stairs (*Morton Mfg. Co.* (1968) FTC Dkt C-1381, Trade Reg Rep ¶18,387); couplers (*Armstead Industries* (1968) FTC Dkt C-1382, Trade Reg Rep ¶18,388); shock-cushioning devices (*Standard Car Truck Co.* (1968) FTC Dkt C-1383, Trade Reg Rep ¶18,389); roller side bearings (*William S. Hansen, dba A. Stucki Co.* (1968) FTC Dkt C-1384, Trade Reg Rep ¶18,390). Each order prohibited payment of unlawful or secret rebates through an intermediary to the railroad to induce the purchase of products.

However, Congress purposely did not limit the prohibition of §2(c) to instances in which the brokerage payment results in price discrimination. "The debates on the bill show clearly that §2(c) was intended to proscribe other practices such as the 'bribing' of a seller's broker by the buyer. See 80 Cong. Rec. 7759-7760, 8111-8112." *FTC v Henry Broch & Co., supra* at 169, n. 6.

Rangen, Inc. v Sterling Nelson & Sons (9th Cir 1965) 351 F2d 851, *cert den* (1966) 383 US 936, held that the §2(c) prohibition permitted recovery in a private treble-damage action brought by a fish-food manufacturer who complained that its competitor bribed a state official to ensure that the state bought only the defendant's product. The court was of the opinion that nothing in the statutory context limited the application of §2(c) to cases of price discrimination. In its words (351 F2d at 857):

Where commercial bribery is associated with evils which a particular provision of the antitrust laws was designed to prevent, the fact that it was bribery rather than a more defensible arrangement ought not to preclude application of the statute.

D. [§5.30] Dealing with Buying Associations

Practitioners representing small businesses should be particularly interested in the application of §2(c) (15 USC §13(c)) to group buying associations, usually composed of small businesses banding together in an effort to reduce their costs. (See also the discussion of functional discounts at §5.23 and buyer's liability under §2(f) at §5.42.)

In *Central Retailer-Owned Grocers, Inc. v FTC* (7th Cir 1963) 319 F2d 410, it appeared that suppliers granted price concessions to Central, a corporation owned by 35 member grocers. Each year the members submitted an estimate of their needs to Central, which negotiated for prices on the basis of these total quantities. During the year the members ordered groceries from Central as they needed them, and the supplier shipped directly to the members but billed Central. Central paid the supplier and billed the member at a higher rate. At the end of the year Central distributed any surplus to its members.

The Commission, over Commissioner Elman's dissent, found that the supplier's price concession to Central correlated mathematically with brokerage commissions that the supplier paid on other sales and that the services rendered by Central, taking orders from members and eliminating the need for suppliers to solicit, constituted a brokerage service. The

Commission entered a cease-and-desist order on the ground that the brokerage payment violated §2(c).

The Seventh Circuit set aside the cease-and-desist order, rejecting the finding that Central was a broker, stating (319 F2d at 414–415):

The fact that Central, because of its strong purchasing power, was able to buy at favorable prices, or on discounts and allowances by its suppliers, is not proof that Central was rendering a broker service. It bought on its own order and on its own credit. It was billed by the suppliers and it paid the bills. A broker does not purchase for his own account, is not billed by the seller, and does not make payment to the seller. Central was able to secure favorable prices from its suppliers, because of (1) their assured volume of business, (2) their lack of any credit risk, (3) a reduction in their billing work, and (4) Central's advance commitments for later requirements. . . . [T]he suppliers knew that, in selling to Central, they were for these reasons realizing savings in their business operations, which enabled Central's members, in turn, to benefit when they purchased from Central. Reason does not permit our ignoring these facts in order to declare illegal a worthy effort by a number of wholesale grocers, owned by retailers, to reduce the ultimate sale prices to the consumer, by entering into the arrangement with Central, which made them stronger in their competition with large chain stores.

The appellate court concluded that the rule against reduced brokerage stated in *FTC v Henry Broch & Co.* (1960) 363 US 166 did not apply since this was not a brokerage case.

In contrast to *Central,* in cases concerning group buying associations, the Commission has usually proceeded under the basic pricing provisions, §2(a) and 2(f) (15 USC §13(a) and (f)), rather than the brokerage provision §2(c). Hence that case uniquely points up the vastly different result that can occur from labeling a price concession "brokerage" or a "discount." The former is governed by §2(c) and constitutes, at least in the Commission's view, a *per se* violation. The latter is governed by §2(a) and 2(f) and requires proof, *inter alia*, of discrimination and injury to competition. Contrast the court's ruling in *Central* to *Western Fruit Growers Sales Co. v FTC* (9th Cir 1963) *cert den* (1964) 376 US 907, in which the court ruled that "[If a seller-buyer] relationship did exist [between Western and its purchasers, Western] violated §2(c)."

See also Advisory Opinion Digest 23 (1966) [1965–1967 Transfer Binder] Trade Reg Rep ¶17,481 ("grave risk" of violating §2(c) would be presented by corporation serving as exclusive buyer for a purchaser for resale, with corporation buying and being billed in its own name, and purchaser for resale owning stock of corporation and participating in brokerage received by corporation).

IV. Promotional Allowances and Services

A. [§5.31] General Analysis

Section 2(d) (15 USC §13(d)), which governs payment for services and facilities furnished by the customer, provides:

It shall be unlawful for any person engaged in commerce to pay or contract for the payment of anything of value to or for the benefit of a customer of such person in the course of such commerce as compensation or in consideration for any services or facilities furnished by or through such customer in connection with the processing, handling, sale, or offering for sale of any products or commodities manufactured, sold, or offered for sale by such person, unless such payment or consideration is available on proportionally equal terms to all other customers competing in the distribution of such products or commodities.

Section 2(e) (15 USC §13(e)), which governs the furnishing of services or facilities to customers, provides:

It shall be unlawful for any person to discriminate in favor of one purchaser against another purchaser or purchasers of a commodity bought for resale, with or without processing, by contracting to furnish or furnishing, or by contributing to the furnishing of, any services or facilities connected with the processing, handling, sale, or offering for sale of such commodity so purchased upon terms not accorded to all purchasers on proportionally equal terms.

In spite of the minor language variations in the two sections quoted above (*e.g.*, "customer" versus "purchaser"), they are generally given the same interpretation, and requirements omitted from one have been read into the other (*e.g.*, the requirement in §2(d) that there be competing customers in commerce has been read into §2(e)) *Elizabeth Arden, Inc. v FTC* (2d Cir 1946) 156 F2d 132, *cert den* (1947) 331 US 806.

The legislative purpose of these sections is clear (80 Cong. Rec. 9418 (1936)):

The existing evil at which this part of the Bill is aimed is, of course, the grant of discriminations under the guise of payments for advertising and promotional services which, whether or not the services are actually rendered as agreed, results in an advantage to the customer so favored as compared with others who have to bear the cost of such services themselves.

Tri-Valley Packing Association v FTC (9th Cir 1964) 329 F2d 694 illustrated a §2(d) violation. A supplier gave one wholesaler $150 per year for advertising the wholesaler's private-label canned fruit but did not promote its label purchased by competing wholesalers. By comparison, §2(e) is violated if, for example, a manufacturer furnishes free display and storage cabinets only to its larger customers. See *FTC v Simplicity Pattern Co.* (1959) 360 US 55.

Although the proscriptions of §2(d) and 2(e) are deemed absolute and apply regardless of whether they adversely affect competition or can be cost justified (*FTC v Simplicity Pattern Co., Inc., supra*), the courts have suggested, although rarely have held, that a seller who deviates from a "proportionally equal" advertising program may defend on the ground that he was meeting *a particular* competitive situation. See *Surprise Brassiere Co., Inc. v FTC* (5th Cir 1969) 406 F2d 711; *Exquisite Form Brassiere Inc. v FTC* (DC Cir 1965) 360 F2d 492, *cert den* (1966) 384 US 959; *Rabiner & Jontow, Inc. v FTC* (2d Cir 1967) 386 F2d 667, *cert den* (1968) 390 US 1004. In spite of the absolute nature of these provisions, the elements necessary to establish a violation provide some limiting factors.

The sections prohibit a seller from giving an allowance or service to its "customer" or "purchaser." Therefore no violation occurs unless there has been a sales transaction, and the same analysis of sales, purchasers, and indirect purchasers applicable to §2(a) (15 USC §13(a)) applies here. See discussion at §§5.11–5.19. Thus, the furnishing of price lists and catalogs are merely invitations to deal and do not constitute a service to a purchaser that can be basis of complaint by one who was refused them. *Chicago Seating Co. v S. Karpen & Bros.* (7th Cir 1949) 177 F2d 863.

Also, for §2(d) or §2(e) to apply, the supplier's payment or service must be connected with the buyer's resale of the goods involved. Other payments or services granted to the buyer may constitute indirect price discrimination under §2(a), but do not violate §2(d) or (e). See *Vanity Fair Paper Mills, Inc. v FTC* (2d Cir 1962) 311 F2d 480. Hence preferential terms of sale are assessed as indirect price discriminations under §2(a) rather than under §2(d) or 2(e). See discussion of discrimination based on terms of sale at §5.26.

In *Chicago Spring Products Co. v United States Steel* (ND Ill 1966) 254 F Supp 83, *aff'd per curiam* (7th Cir 1966) 371 F2d 428, in dismissing a private treble-damage action brought under §2(d) by a buyer against his supplier alleging discriminatory freight allowances and rebates to plaintiff's competitors, the court stated (254 F Supp at 84–85):

[T]he better view is to limit actions on price differentials, including freight rebates, to Section 2(a), and to consider Section 2(d) and 2(e) applicable only to unlawful promotional arrangements connected with *resale*, *i.e.*, services unrelated to price. . . .

When plaintiff herein dropped its charges of Section 2(a) violations by filing its Second Amended Complaint, it did so to avoid the necessity of proving competitive injury, and to escape from meeting a cost justification defense. In the opinion

271

of this Court, plaintiff did not have the opportunity to make such a choice. Its remedy, if any, for freight allowance discriminations must fall under Section 2(a). Sections 2(d) and 2(e) . . . are not applicable.

Similarly, a supplier's grant of credit and payment for storage and delivery to a distributor who delivered to a customer of the supplier from the distributor's inventory did not violate §2(d), since the service was not made in connection with a resale of goods that the distributor had bought from the supplier. *General Foods Corporation* (1956) 52 FTC 798.

Also, the furnishing of services by a supplier to a consumer but not to the supplier's distributor does not violate §2(e), since the consumer is not a purchaser for resale. *Sano Petroleum Corporation v American Oil Co.* (ED NY 1960) 187 F Supp 345.

However, the sale of hair-coloring products to beauty salons and the salon's subsequent use of the products constitutes a resale for purposes of §2(d) and 2(e), notwithstanding the fact that substantial services are sold with the product. *Clairol, Inc.* (1966) [1965-1967 Transfer Binder] FTC Dkt 8647, Trade Reg Rep ¶17,594, *aff'd* (9th Cir 1969) 410 F2d 647.

Both sections specify that the prohibited payment for services or furnishing of services by the supplier to his customer be connected with "the processing, handling, sale, or offering for sale" of the commodity the supplier has sold the customer.

Examples of services held not to be connected with the "processing, handling, sale, or offering for sale" of a specific commodity include (1) the withholding of wages from seller's employees in payment for goods purchased from a retailer (seller's subsidiary corporation) but refusing to do the same for a competing retailer (*I. M. Skinner v United States Steel Corp.* (5th Cir 1956) 233 F2d 762); (2) the grant of 30-day credit terms to one retailer while requiring payment on delivery from another (*Secatore's, Inc. v Esso Standard Oil Co.* (D Mass 1959) 171 F Supp 665); (3) the furnishing of repair services (*George W. Warner & Co. v Black & Decker Mfg. Co.* (ED NY 1959) 172 F Supp 221, *rev'd on other grounds* (2d Cir 1960) 277 F2d 787); (4) the payment of a freight allowance (*Chicago Springs Products Co. v United States Steel, supra*). However, such services may constitute an indirect price discrimination under §2(a), discussed at §5.26.

Section 2(d) expressly prohibits payments "to or for the benefit of a customer." When the payment is made directly to the customer, the "benefit" is generally obvious. But payments to third parties that benefit customers may also violate §2(d) and are not so obvious. For example, a supplier's payments of prize moneys to one customer's sales employees violated §2(d) (*Exquisite Form Brassiere, Inc. v FTC* (DC Cir 1961) 301

F2d 499, *cert den*   (1962) 369 US 888). Also, a food manufacturer's payment to a radio broadcasting company that benefited certain chains (*P. Lorillard Co. v FTC* (3d Cir 1959) 267 F2d 439, *cert den* (1959) 361 US 923); and a manufacturer's payment for an advertising sign to benefit a particular customer were held to violate §2(d) (*Swanee Paper Corp. v FTC* (2d Cir 1961) 291 F2d 833, *cert den*   (1962) 368 US 987).

A supplier who, paying the same rates as other advertisers, advertises in a medium owned, controlled, and operated by a customer, is generally held not to violate §2(d) or (e) if there is no "showing that some benefit accrued to, or was intended to accrue to, the customer." See *Nuarc Co. v FTC* (7th Cir 1963) 316 F2d 576. However, such advertisement will violate §2(d) if the court finds a "benefit" to the customer. It is sometimes difficult to discern a meaningful distinction in the facts to warrant the difference in result. See, *e.g.*, *State Wholesale Grocer v Great Atlantic & Pacific Tea Co.* (7th Cir 1958) 258 F2d 831, *cert den*   (1959) 358 US 947; *Individualized Catalogues, Inc.* (1964) [1963–1965 Transfer Binder Trade Reg Rep ¶16,873.

The prohibitions of both sections have been limited to allowances and services granted to "competing customers." For example, the Commission has advised a manufacturer that it could properly grant advertising allowances to all customers in a specified trading area, so long as the customers offered the allowance do not compete with those not offered the allowance. See Advisory Opinion Digest 157 (1968) 3 Trade Reg Rep ¶18,147.

The "competing customer" requirement has been interpreted to mean competition at the same functional level. See *FTC v Simplicity Pattern Co., Inc.* (1959) 360 US 55; *Tri-Valley Packing Association v FTC* (9th Cir 1964) 329 F2d 694, 708–710.

Prior to March 1968, however, there was a difference of view among the courts and the Commission as to whether a violation occurred if the supplier granted the promotional payment or service to a direct-buying retailer but not to a wholesaler whose customers compete with the favored direct-buying retailer.

The Ninth Circuit, in *Fred Meyer, Inc. v FTC* (9th Cir 1966) 359 F2d 351, 359, *rev'd* (1968) 390 US 341, held that absent a showing that the customers of the disfavored wholesaler were "indirect purchasers" of the supplier, it was not unlawful for a supplier to grant a promotional payment to a direct-buying retailer but not to a wholesaler, because the favored retailer and the disfavored wholesaler "do not compete at the same functional level." The Supreme Court reversed, ruling that retailers buying through a disfavored wholesaler who sold in competition with the favored direct-buying retailer were "customers" of the supplier for purposes of §2(d) and were legally entitled to proportionally equal payments for services rendered. See also *Krug v International Telephone and Telegraph Corp.* (D NJ 1956) 142 F Supp 230, holding that a wholesaler can maintain a treble-damage action against his supplier for granting promotional allowances only to direct-buying retailers.

The effects of the *Fred Meyer* decision, coupled with the new Guides for Advertising Allowances and Other Merchandising Payments and Services issued by the Commission on May 29, 1969 (see discussion at §5.33), cannot yet be predicted. Obviously the program proposed, the number of retailers involved, the geographic scope of the market, as well as the nature of the industry (e.g., perishability of goods, inventory turnover rate) will affect the number and severity of the seller's "supervising" problems. Too much supervision by a supplier of his wholesaler may cause the customers of the latter to become the former's "indirect customers" and raise problems under §2(a). See discussion of indirect-purchase doctrine at §5.12. If the administrative problems to the wholesaler are great, should he be recompensed? If so, must the supplier cost-justify the compensation? See discussion of cost justification §§5.44–5.48.

It is almost impossible at this juncture to advise a client with both direct-buying and indirect-buying retailers who wishes to initiate a cooperative seller-buyer advertising program. Most suppliers would find it very difficult to ascertain the number and names of all indirect-buying retailers who compete with direct-buying retailers in order to notify them of their promotional program. It has been suggested that the notice required to unknown retailers purchasing the seller's product from an intermediary be printed on the shipping carton. Depending on the program envisioned and the time between sale to the intermediary and resale to the indirect-buying retailer, such a proposal may not be practicable.

The problem of satisfying the "proportional equality" requirement in this context also poses tough questions to the supplier who has no way of computing the purchase volume of each unknown retailer. Hence the favorite method of allowing a percentage of dollar volume probably would not be available to the supplier.

Because of these problems some suppliers may terminate all advertising programs. Other suppliers may seek to limit sales to direct-buying retailers. It is too early to make any meaningful predictions.

B. [§5.32] Requirements for Compliance

When the supplier offers a promotional program, he must be careful to inform all his competing customers about the program and make it available to them on proportionally equal terms. The supplier is obliged to ascertain whether his customers do in fact compete. See, e.g., *Flotill Products, Inc. v FTC* (9th Cir 1966) 358 F2d 224 *rev'd on other grounds* (1967) 389 US 179.

The customers must be given adequate notice. Mere instructions to the supplier's salesmen to tell the customers is insufficient without a showing that the customers were in fact informed. *Vanity Fair Paper Mills v FTC* (2d Cir 1962) 311 F2d 480; *House of Lord's, Inc.* (1966) [1965–1967 Transfer Binder] FTC Dkt 8631, Trade Reg Rep ¶17,437. The Commission has approved the notice feature in a promotional allowance program offered by a publisher who alerted all newsstand operators handling its publication by a conspicuous notice on the outside cover (Advisory Opinion Digest 66 (1966) [1965–1967 Transfer Binder] Trade Reg Rep ¶17,584) and has advised a seller that it may notify its retailers of a display-allowance plan by means of an advertisement published in a trade journal of general circulation among dealers *so long as all dealers receive notice* (Advisory Opinion Digest 195 (1968) 3 Trade Reg Rep ¶18,225).

In short, although the statute does not specifically require that all competing customers be given individual notice, the Commission has stated in its Guides (discussed at §5.33) that the seller must take formal action to inform his customers of any advertising allowance. The Commission leaves to the seller's discretion what means of notification to use, but warns that if actual notice is not directed to each customer, the seller bears the burden of ensuring that the customer received notice. If the variety of customers makes notification difficult and some discrimination unavoidable, the view seems to be that promotional plans in that context are unacceptable rather than excused from compliance. *Clairol Inc. v FTC* (9th Cir 1969) 410 F2d 647.

The promotional program must be "accorded" or made "available" to "all" customers on "proportionally equal terms." Obviously a program suitable for a large retailer may not be suitable for a small retailer. To the extent that the program is impossible to adapt to a given customer's business, it is not available to "all" customers. Thus, in *State Wholesale Grocers v Great Atlantic & Pacific Tea Co.* (7th Cir 1958) 258 F2d 831, cert den (1959) 358 US 947, it was held that §2(d) (15 USC §13(d)) was violated when suppliers purchased advertisements in a customer-owned publication without providing an alternative for customers not having such a publication. See also *House of Lord's, Inc., supra.*

To avoid the act's prohibition, the supplier must fashion and offer suitable alternatives which the customer, not the supplier, selects for himself. *Exquisite Form Brassiere, Inc. v FTC* (DC Cir 1961) 301 F2d 499, *cert den* (1962) 369 US 888. As long as such alternatives are available, the customer has no claim under §2(e) (15 USC §13(e)) merely because, for its own convenience, it elects the more expensive alternative. *United Banana Co. v United Fruit Co.* (D Conn 1965) 245 F Supp 161, *aff'd* (2d Cir 1966) 362 F2d 849.

The Commission strictly construes the term "proportionally equal terms." For example, in Advisory Opinion Digest 52 (1966) [1965–1967 Transfer Binder] Trade Reg Rep ¶17,556, a promotional concern proposed an advertising program whereby twelve food manufacturers would jointly finance promotional kits, divided into twelve segments containing aisle-end displays promoting products of the manufacturers, for use by their retailers free of charge but upon their agreement to stock the manufacturer's products near the display and to place the displays at ends of aisles. The Commission advised that

1. notice must be given to all competing retailers of all twelve manufacturers even if the retailer were only a small customer of any one manufacturer;

2. retailers must not be required to take the entire kit or nothing. They must be permitted to use the segment that suits them, and customers whose space is too small to accommodate aisle-end displays must be offered an alternative program;

3. retailers cannot demand cash in lieu of the kit; and

4. manufacturers may limit the program to one product, even though customers buy more than one, and limit kits to the customers who buy and resell that one product.

To the same effect, see Advisory Opinion Digest 53 (1966) [1965–1967 Transfer Binder] Trade Reg Rep ¶17,557 (dealing with self-locating shopping guides to be furnished by a sales promotion company to wholesalers for distribution to retail customers).

The Commission tends to test proportionally equal terms by basing the payments made or the services furnished on the dollar volume or the quantity of goods purchased during a specified time. Advisory Opinion Digest 26 (1966) [1965–1967 Transfer Binder] Trade Reg Rep ¶17,490. Specifically, if a supplier gives a customer purchasing $100,000 worth of merchandise a promotional allowance or services worth $1,000, then the supplier must give the small customer purchasing $1,000 worth of merchandise an allowance or services worth $10. In short, all competing customers would be entitled to an advertising allowance or service worth 1 percent of their purchases. See, *e.g.*, Advisory Opinion Digest 10 (1965) [1965–1967 Transfer Binder] Trade Reg Rep ¶17,390.

In Advisory Opinion Digest 261 (1968) [1967–1970 Transfer Binder] Trade Reg Rep ¶18,416, the Commission approved a plan offering payments computed at 7 percent of each customer's net purchases over a six-month period to be applied to three categories of promotional activity: (1) point-of-sale materials delivered by the supplier to the customer and charged against the latter's allowance unless returned in ten days; (2) up to two-thirds the cost of cooperative advertising in newspapers listed in *Standard Rate and Data*; and (3) other promotions including advertising in newspapers not listed in *Standard Rate and Data*, catalog and local radio and television advertising, envelope stuffers, and sales-incentive programs and contests. Allowances earned but not used in a six-month period could not be carried forward.

The supplier must take care that the allowances for services are not excessive for the service rendered and that the customer is performing the service envisioned by the promotional plan.

Once discrimination has been shown, the seller has the burden of proving proportionally equal treatment for all his customers. See, *e.g.*, *Vanity Fair Paper Mills v FTC* (2d Cir 1962) 311 F2d 480.

The only defense that has been recognized, though not approved, to a charge of violating the absolute provisions of §2(d) or (e) is that of meeting competition, discussed at §§5.49–5.51 and §5.31. See *Exquisite Form Brassiere, Inc. v FTC, supra*, in which the court of appeals remanded to permit the raising of the meeting-competition defense; *Ludwig v American Greetings Corporation* (6th Cir 1960) 282 F2d 917; *Surprise Brassiere Co., Inc. v FTC* (5th Cir 1969) 406 F2d 711; *Exquisite Form Brassiere, Inc. v FTC* (DC Cir 1965) 360 F2d 492, *cert den* (1966) 389 US 959; *Rabiner & Jontow, Inc. v FTC* (2d Cir 1967) 386 F2d 667, *cert den* (1968) 390 US 1004, suggesting but not holding that a seller may defend a charge that his promotional program was not proportionally equal on the ground that he was meeting a specific competitive situation.

The Commission has stated in its 1969 Guides, discussed in §5.33, that the meeting-competition defense, although applicable to a §2(d) or 2(e) violation, "is subject to important limitations."

C. [§5.33] FTC Guides

On May 19, 1960, the Federal Trade Commission issued *Guides for Allowances and Services* (1 Trade Reg Rep ¶3980), which is quite helpful in setting out the Commission's position in this area of the law. See discussion at §6.13.

Following the Supreme Court's decision in *FTC v Fred Meyer, Inc.* (1968) 390 US 341, requiring a seller to make available to retailers who buy the seller's product through a wholesaler the same promotional allowances offered to direct-buying retailers, the Commission issued *Guides for Advertising Allowances and Other Merchandising Payments and Services* (May 29, 1969) 34 Fed Reg 8285, 16 CFR Part 240, 1 Trade Reg Rep ¶4003. These expanded certain concepts, including who is a customer, seller's duty to inform, availability to all competing customers, meeting competition in good faith, and checking customers' use of payments.

The new Guides, issued over Commissioner Elman's strong dissent, go further than *Fred Meyer* and indicate that even the supplier who sells only to wholesalers and who offers promotional allowances for passing further down the line of distribution must make certain that the allowances are passed on in a proportionally equal fashion. See Guides 8 and 13.

In addition the Commission has formulated a number of Trade Practice Conference Rules in cooperation with specific industries, running the gamut from air-conditioning contracting to yeast, which serve as guides to the members of the industry covered. See 4 Trade Reg Rep ¶41,018-41,227. For the more recent examples see proposed Guides for the toy industry (1968) 1 Trade Reg Rep ¶4001; Guides for the greeting card industry (1968) 1 Trade Reg Rep ¶4002.

V. Robinson-Patman Litigation

A. Civil Litigation

1. Plaintiff's Problems

a. [§5.34] Burdens of Proof

Section 2 of the Clayton Act as amended (15 USC §13) does not apply without proof that "the effect of such discrimination may be [1] substantially to lessen competition or [2] tend to create a monopoly in any line of commerce, or [3] to injure, destroy, or prevent competition with any person who either grants or knowingly receives the benefits of such discrimination, or with the customers of either of them."

In almost every instance §2 has been applied in the third situation— when it is shown that competition may be injured at the seller's level (primary-line competition), the buyer's level (secondary-line competition), or the buyer's customers' level (tertiary-line competition).

The accepted rule is that the plaintiff, whether the government or a private party, carries the burden of alleging and proving as part of its case that defendant's discriminatory pricing practices may substantially interfere with competition at the seller's level, the buyer's level, or the buyer's customers' level. *Anheuser-Busch, Inc. v FTC* (1960) 363 US 536, 543, 549–550, *remanded* (7th Cir 1961) 289 F2d 835, 843; *Dayco Corp. v FTC* (6th Cir 1966) 362 F2d 180; *Elgin Corp. v Atlas Building Products Co.* (10th Cir 1958) 251 F2d 7, 11, *cert den* (1958) 357 US 926; *Balian Ice Cream Co. v Arden Farms Co.* (9th Cir 1955) 231 F2d 356, *cert den* (1956) 350 US 991.

The courts construe the term "substantially" to require proof of "substantial, not trivial or sporadic, interference with competition to establish violation of its mandate." *Minneapolis-Honeywell Reg Co. v FTC* (7th Cir 1951) 191 F2d 786, 790, *cert dismissed* (1952) 344 US 206. See also *Whitaker Cable Corp. v FTC* (7th Cir 1956) 239 F2d 253, 256, *cert den* (1957) 353 US 938 ("The Act was not intended to reach every remote, adverse effect upon competition. The effect must be substantial.").

The plaintiff must allege and prove that defendant's price differentials are the proximate cause of probable injury to one or more levels of competition. See, *e.g., Balian Ice Cream Co. v Arden Farms, supra,* at 367 ("there was no causal connection between the different prices of ice cream sold by Arden in Arizona, Washington and Oregon and any damage sustained by plaintiffs as a result of the lowering of prices in the Los Angeles area."); *American Oil Co. v FTC* (7th Cir 1963) 325 F2d 101, 106, *cert den* (1964) 377 US 954 ("[P]robative analysis must reveal a causal relation between the price discrimination and an actual or reasonably probable injury to competition in the context of the factual situation involved.").

Once the plaintiff alleges and proves a prima facie case that includes the necessary causal connection between the discriminatory pricing and the competitive injury, "the burden shifts to the defendant, if it can do so, to show that the damage, if any, was otherwise caused." *American Co-op Serum Association v Anchor Serum Co.* (7th Cir 1946) 153 F2d 907, 912, *cert den* (1946) 329 US 721. For example, the defendant might establish that the damage was caused by the plaintiff's inefficiencies or a deterioration of the general condition of the market, or that the price discrimination was in effect for so short a time that no damage could have resulted. See, *e.g., Balian Ice Cream Co. v Arden Farms Co., supra,* at 367; *Tri-Valley Packing Association v FTC* (9th Cir 1964) 329 F2d 694, 703–704; *opinion on remand Tri-Valley Packing Association* (1966) [1965–1967 Transfer Binder] Trade Reg Rep ¶17,657. See further discussion of proving causation in cases involving competing sellers at §5.39, and in cases involving competing buyers at §5.40.

The Second Circuit has ruled that plaintiff establishes a prima facie case upon proving discriminatory prices and that the burden then shifts to defendant to show that its prices are not injurious to competition. See *Enterprise Industries, Inc. v Texas Co.* (2d Cir 1957) 240 F2d 457, 460, cert den (1957) 353 US 965. Cf. *Albert H. Cayne Equipment Corp. v Union Asbestos & Rubber Co.* (SD NY 1963) 220 F Supp 784, 789.

As a general rule, plaintiff must allege probable injury to competition, not simply to him; or in case of the government as plaintiff, not simply to one competitor. As stated in *Atlas Building Products v Diamond Block and Gravel Co.* (10th Cir 1959) 269 F2d 950, 954, cert den (1960) 363 US 843:

Antitrust legislation is concerned primarily with the health of the competitive process, not with the individual competitor who must sink or swim in competitive enterprise.

In some instances injury to one competitor will establish injury to competition in general. Thus, in *Moore v Mead's Fine Bread Co.* (1954) 348 US 115, the Court held that defendant injured competition within the meaning of the Robinson-Patman Act by destroying its only competitor in a defined geographic area. See also *H.J. Heinz Co. v Beech-Nut Lifesavers, Inc.* (SD NY 1960) 181 F Supp 452, 463, 464 (possible elimination of one of three major competitors in the baby food industry might constitute injury to competition).

b. [§5.35] Standing to Sue

A private plaintiff, in addition to proving that injury to competition may flow from the discrimination, must also show standing by proving that he is within the competitive level in question. Thus, in a primary-line injury case only a competitor of the discriminator may sue, and in a secondary-line injury case only a customer of the discriminator may sue. See, *e.g., Boysen, Inc. v H.P. Hood & Sons, Inc.* (D Conn 1964) 1964 Trade Cases ¶71,167; *Bolick-Gillman Co. v Continental Baking Co.* (D Nev 1961) 206 F Supp 151.

c. [§5.36] Standard of Proof

The courts are in agreement that the standard of proof is only a probability that there "may" be an injury to competition. As stated by the Supreme Court in *Corn Products Refining Co. v FTC* (1945) 324 US 726:

The statute is designed to reach such discriminations "in their incipiency," before harm to competition is effected. It is enough that they "may" have the prescribed effect . . . (324 US at 738).

[T]he statute does not require that the discriminations must in fact have harmed competition, but only that there is a reasonable possibility that they "may" have such an effect (342 US at 742).

See also *Morton Salt Co. v FTC* (1948) 334 US 37; *American Motors Corp. v FTC* (6th Cir 1967) 384 F2d 247, *cert den* (1968) 390 US 1012.

The Commission and the courts subsequently have used the term "probability" with no apparent change intended in the proof standard. See e.g., *Whitaker Cable Corp. v FTC* (7th Cir 1956) 239 F2d 253, *cert den* (1957) 353 US 938; *Moog Industries, Inc. v FTC* (8th Cir 1956) 238 F2d 43, *aff'd* (1958) 355 US 411.

d. [§5.37] Amount of Damages Recoverable

The Eighth and Ninth Circuits have held that a plaintiff can recover damages in the amount of the price discrimination proved unless the evidence establishes a greater consequential or special injury flowing from the discrimination. *Elizabeth Arden Sales Corporation v Gus Blass Co.* (8th Cir 1945) 150 F2d 988, *cert den* (1945) 326 US 773; *Fowler Mfg. Co. v Gorlick* (9th Cir 1969) 415 F2d 1248, *cert den* (1970) 396 US 1012.

In contrast, the Second and Sixth Circuits have held that a plaintiff cannot recover damages in the amount of the discrimination but must prove consequential injury to his business in loss of customers or profits before he can recover. *Enterprise Industries, Inc. v Texas Co.* (2d Cir 1957) 240 F2d 457, *cert den* (1957) 353 US 965; *Kidd v Esso Standard Oil Co.* (6th Cir 1961) 295 F2d 497. See also *Youngson v Tidewater Oil Co.* (D Ore 1958) 166 F Supp 146, following this rule.

This divergence in view has not been resolved by the Supreme Court.

e. [§5.38] Sample Form of Complaint

(Title of District Court)

(Title of Cause)

No. _____

Complaint for Damages for Violation of the Robinson-Patman Act

_____ (Jury Demanded) _____

Plaintiff alleges:

Jurisdiction and Venue

1. This action is brought under the Robinson-Patman Act, 49 Stat 1526, 15 USC § 13(a). This Court has jurisdiction of this action under §4 of the Clayton Act, 38 Stat 731, 15 USC § 15. Venue is proper in this district, wherein defendant resides, under §4 of the Clayton Act, supra.

Parties

2. Plaintiff A is a corporation organized and existing under the laws of the State of California, and at all times material to this action maintained its principal place of business in Los Angeles, California. Between January, 1960, and February, 1969, plaintiff was engaged in the business of selling throughout Southern California, Arizona, and New Mexico widgets manufactured by defendant.

3. Defendant B is a corporation organized and existing under the laws of the State of Delaware and at all times material to this action maintained its principal place of business in Los Angeles, California. Defendant B is now and has been since 1955, the leading manufacturer of widgets in the western United States. Defendant B sells its widgets through interstate commerce to dealers located in California, Oregon, Washington, Idaho, New Mexico, Arizona, Nevada, and Texas, for resale to users and consumers.

Offense

4. Between January, 1965 and February, 1969, plaintiff purchased more than $400,000 worth of widgets from defendant. During this period of time plaintiff is informed and believes that defendant discriminated against plaintiff in that it sold widgets of like grade and quality to dealers located in Southern California, Arizona, and New Mexico, who sell widgets in competition with plaintiff, at prices below those defendant charged plaintiff, with the result that plaintiff was unable to compete with dealers receiving favorable price concessions from defendant, and competition in widgets in Southern California, Arizona, and New Mexico was substantially lessened.

Plaintiff's Damage

5. As a direct result of the aforementioned price discrimination practiced by defendant, plaintiff suffered serious damage in the form of:

(a) Loss of profits, which but for the defendant's unlawful price discrimination plaintiff would have made on sales between 1965 and February, 1969, in the amount of $100,000.

(b) Gradual loss of customers between 1965 and 1969 and finally in February, 1969, the loss of its business having a value of at least $400,000.

WHEREFORE, plaintiff prays that:

1. The court adjudge and decree that defendant has engaged in price discrimination in violation of the provisions of §2(a) of the Clayton Act as amended by the Robinson-Patman Act, 15 USC § 13(a).

2. Plaintiff recover from defendant its actual damages specified in paragraph 5 in the amount of $500,000.

3. Plaintiff have judgment for its actual damages trebled, reasonable attorneys' fees, and the cost of suit, all as provided by section 4 of the Clayton Act, 15 USC § 15.

4. This Court award such other and further relief as it may deem just and proper under the circumstances.

DATED: _____

_____ (signature) _____
Attorney for Plaintiff

COMMENT: For discussion of amount of damages recoverable, see §5.37. Note that the demand for jury is optional. Federal Rule of Civil Procedure 38 provides that demand for a jury may be made "at any time after the commencement of the action and not later than 10 days after the service of the last pleading directed to such issue."

Filing and service requirements are the same as in other civil actions in federal courts.

f. [§5.39] Proving Competitive Injury at the Seller's Level

The Robinson-Patman amendatory legislation protects competition at three levels: (1) the primary, or seller's, level; (2) the secondary, or buyer's, level; and (3) the tertiary, or buyer's customers', level. These various levels are discussed separately below.

Most primary-line cases deal with territorial price discriminations, *i.e.*, the discriminator charges a low price in one geographic area and a high price in another geographic area. See, *e.g.*, *Utah Pie Co. v Continental Baking Co.* (1967) 386 US 685; *Moore v Mead's Fine Bread Co.* (1954) 348 US 115.

Injury to competition at the seller's level is in general more difficult to prove than injury at the buyer's level. See, *e.g.*, *FTC v Anheuser-Busch, Inc.* (1960) 363 US 536, 552; *Shore Gas and Oil Co. v Humble Oil and Refining Co.* (D NJ 1963) 1964 Trade Cases ¶70,990. First, in a primary line case, plaintiff must prove a competitive relationship between the discriminating seller and the sellers allegedly injured by the discriminator's pricing practices. In short, the injured sellers must sell the same product in the same general geographic area as the alleged offender. See, *e.g.*, *Guyott Co. v Texaco, Inc.* (D Conn 1966) 261 F Supp 942, quoting Rowe, *Price Discrimination under the Robinson-Patman Act* (1963) 142. Thus, in *Volasco Products Co. v Lloyd A. Fry Roofing Co.* (6th Cir 1965) 346 F2d 661, *cert den* (1965) 382 US 904, a local manufacturer of asphalt-saturated felt with headquarters in Knoxville, Tennessee, proved competitive injury at the primary level by showing that a national manufacturer of the same product charged lower prices in the Knoxville area than it charged in the area of Brookville, Indiana, the site of defendant's closest competing plant.

283

Second, plaintiff must prove a causal connection between the discriminatory price and the alleged injury. As a general rule, causation is more carefully scrutinized in seller's-level cases than in buyer's-level cases. See, e.g., *Dean Milk Co. v FTC* (1965) [1965-1967 Transfer Binder] FTC Dkt 8032, Trade Reg Rep ¶17,357, *rev'd in part and aff'd in part* (7th Cir 1968) 395 F2d 696, which reversed for lack of substantial evidence a Commission finding that defendant's quantity discount system caused injury to competing sellers.

The easiest situation in which to prove that the discrimination caused injury to competition at the seller's level is that in which the discriminator manifests a predatory intent to eliminate a competitor. Since the plaintiff must show that the discrimination "may" injure competition, it must establish a factual basis from which that projection reasonably can be made. "If [the discriminator] is using its competitive power fairly in the market place and respecting the rights of its competitors, then no forecast of future adverse effects on competition based on those facts is valid. If, on the other hand, the projection is based upon predatoriness or buccaneering, it can reasonably be forecast that an adverse effect on competition *may* occur. In that event, the discriminations in their incipiency are such that they *may* have the prescribed effect to establish a violation of Sec. 2(a)." *Anheuser-Busch, Inc. v FTC* (7th Cir 1961) 289 F2d 835, 843. See also *Utah Pie Co. v Continental Baking Co., supra; Maryland Baking Co. v FTC* (4th Cir 1957) 243 F2d 716, 718 (national manufacturer of ice cream cones cut prices 25 percent in small area where competitor operated, maintaining prices elsewhere; Commission's cease-and-desist order affirmed because "there is evidence that the price cut was initiated for the purpose of driving the competitor out of business. . . ."); *Forster Mfg. Co. v FTC* (1st Cir 1964) 335 F2d 47, *cert den* (1965) 380 US 906; *Moore v Mead's Fine Bread Co., supra.*

As stated in *Antitrust Developments 1955-1968*, 128:

Both the courts and the Commission have agreed with the 1955 Report that predatory below-cost pricing "inevitably frustrates competition and may therefore be the basis for finding competitive injury," even where only a single competitor is involved.

Pretrial discovery often uncovers correspondence or memoranda documenting an over-zealous anticompetitive effort. A predatory intent may be found from the discriminator's own admissions; in *Forster Mfg. Co. v FTC, supra, aff'g in part and rev'g in part* (1963) [1961-1963 Transfer Binder] FTC Dkt 7207, Trade Reg Rep ¶16,243, the seller threatened a smaller competitor: "Don't try to follow me. If you do, we will put you out of business." Subsequent below-cost pricing that destroyed the competitor was found to be injurious to competition. Alternatively, a predatory intent may be inferred from price cuts below cost. In *Utah Pie Co. v Continental Baking Co.*, *supra*, the Supreme Court found for the plaintiff on the basis that one of the defending sellers "had engaged in predatory tactics," another of the defending sellers had sold at a "price less than its direct cost plus an allocation for overhead," and another defending seller's price was "admittedly well below its costs, and well below the other prices prevailing in the market." 386 US 685 at 697, 698, 701. See also *FTC v Anheuser-Busch, Inc.*, *supra.*

Plaintiff may also establish that defendant's discriminatory pricing caused or probably will cause injury at the seller's level by showing that the lower prices in one area were in effect subsidized by the higher prices charged in another area. As stated in *Shore Gas and Oil Co., Inc. v Humble Oil and Refining Co.* (D NJ 1963) 1964 Trade Cases ¶70,990 at 78,917–78,918:

[T]o establish the necessary causative link between the price difference and the injury to competitors and competition, it must be shown that high prices aided the injurious low prices and enabled defendant to charge them. Conversely, if no relationship is shown between prices in the low price area and prices in other areas, the injured party's case fails for lack of causation. . . . When a seller underbids a competitor, thereby injuring him, the injury is an "effect" of discrimination only if the low price is supported by other prices and their profits, wherever charged. Otherwise, the low price alone has caused the injury and the price discrimination is but incidental. Thus if it is shown that the low bid is below cost, it is fairly inferrable that profits made on other prices financed the complained-of low price. If the price is completely self-sufficient, it may be inferred that no relationship between high and low prices exists, and therefore that the discrimination had not the proscribed "effect."

In *Moore v Mead's Fine Bread Co.*, *supra*, 119, 120, in which it appeared that an interstate baker, while maintaining higher prices in other areas, had cut prices approximately 50 percent in an area where a local competitor operated, the Court held that the "Robinson-Patman Act barred the use of interstate business to destroy local business . . . [and here] [t]he profits made in interstate activities would underwrite the losses of local price-cutting campaigns." See also *Balian Ice Cream Co. v Arden Farms Co.* (9th Cir 1955) 231 F2d 356, 367, *cert den* (1956) 350 US 991.

If there is no predatory below-cost pricing, the defendant may be able to establish that no injury resulted by showing that its percentage of the market declined during the period its pricing differentials were in effect, or conversely that its competitors' sales increased during that period (*Bor-*

285

den Co. v FTC (5th Cir 1967) 381 F2d 175; *Quaker Oats Co.* (1964)
[1963-1965 Transfer Binder] FTC Dkt 8112, Trade Reg Rep ¶17,134), or
that competing sellers could and in fact did easily enter the market (*Yale
and Towne Mfg. Co.* (1956) 52 FTC 1580). For example, in the *Borden*
case, the seller sold private-brand evaporated milk at lower prices than it
sold identical milk under its own private label. The court held that this
price difference was not shown to have caused injury to competition at
the seller's level because the evidence established that competing sellers
"have bettered their position in approximately the same proportion as has
Borden."

Although far more difficult to prove, injury to competition at the primary level has also been found quite often by the Commission and occasionally by the courts when there is evidence that the discriminatory price
will probably alter the market structure materially and permanently. As
recently stated by the Commission's majority in *Dean Milk Co., and Dean
Milk Co., Inc.* (1965) [1965-1967 Transfer Binder] FTC Dkt 8032, Trade
Reg Rep ¶17,357 at 22,530-22,531, *rev'd in part and aff'd in part* (7th Cir
1968) 395 F2d 696:

It is the Commission's opinion that a finding of possible substantial competitive
injury on the seller level is warranted in the absence of predation where the
evidence shows significant diversion of business from the discriminator's competitors to the discriminator or diminishing profits to competitors resulting either
from the diversion of business or from the necessity of meeting the discriminator's
lower prices, provided that these immediate actual efforts portent either a financial crippling of those competitors, a possibility of an anticompetitive concentration of business in larger sellers, or a significant reduction in the number of sellers
in the market.

The courts too have held that substantial diversion plus a portending
monopolistic position of the discriminator will provide a sufficient basis
from which to find probable injury to competition at the primary level.
See, *e.g., Volasco Products Co. v Lloyd A. Fry Roofing Co., supra; Atlas
Building Products Co. v Diamond Block and Gravel Co.* (10th Cir 1959)
269 F2d 950, *cert den* (1960) 363 US 843; *Bergjans Farm Dairy, Inc. v
Sanitary Milk Producers* (DC Mo 1965) 241 F Supp 476, *aff'd* (8th Cir
1966) 368 F2d 679.

It has been suggested that the diversion-of-business test is on the wane.
Antitrust Developments 1955-1968, 128, 129. But practitioners will be
well advised to proceed with caution in this situation in light of the
Commission's cease-and-desist order in *National Dairy Products Corp.*
(1967) [1967-1970 Transfer Binder] Trade Reg Rep ¶18,027, *aff'd* (7th
Cir 1968) 395 F2d 517. The Commission appeared to give considerable

weight to the fact that the promotional plan in question drew business away from competitors. In that case the Kraft division of National Dairy engaged in a 26-day promotional program offering retailers in the Washington, D.C. area a free case of jams and jellies for each case purchased. The Commission found that the program constituted unlawful price discrimination. It is interesting to note that the Commission in the same proceeding dismissed charges against an identical promotional program by National of yogurt and marshmallow topping in other geographic markets. The most significant difference between the two programs was the fact that the one concerned with jellies and jam was more successful.

g. [§5.40] Proving Competitive Injury at the Buyer's Level

The Supreme Court, in *FTC v Anheuser-Busch, Inc.* (1960) 363 US 536, 543–544, pointed out that

[T]he 1936 Robinson-Patman amendments to the Clayton Act were motivated principally by congressional concern over the impact upon secondary-line competition [competition at the buyer's level] of the burgeoning of mammoth purchasers, notably chain stores.

To prove that discriminatory pricing has injured competition at the buyer's level, plaintiff must "show that the favored and unfavored competitors are in actual competition, or that they would probably be in actual competition if the discrimination were not made." Patman, *Complete Guide to the Robinson-Patman Act* (1963) 60.

Whether or not the buyers in question in fact are in competition depends on the commodities being sold, the time of the sales, and the area in which and the type of customer to whom each buyer is trying to resell. Thus, if the buyers compete in different geographic areas, as in the case of automobile distributors with exclusive sales territories, there is no competition between the distributors, and any price discrimination among them cannot adversely affect competition. *Auto Imports, Ltd. v Peugeot, Inc.* (SD NY 1964) 1964 Trade Cases ¶71,098.

Also, if the buyers' functions differ, *e.g.*, one functions strictly as a wholesaler and the other functions strictly as a retailer, the fact that the former receives a better price is irrelevant for Robinson-Patman Act purposes because they do not compete for the same class of customer, and hence there can be no injury to competition. See discussion of functional discounts at §5.23.

Similarly, a supplier may sell to an ultimate consumer at a lower price than it charged its retailer, if the consumer is not a customer of the retailer. See, *e.g.*, *Secatore's, Inc. v Esso-Standard Oil Co.* (D Mass 1959)

171 F Supp 665; *Sano Petroleum Corp. v American Oil Co.* (ED NY 1960) 187 F Supp 345.

A supplier has no duty "to sell to its distributors at a price sufficiently low to enable the distributors to compete with the supplier for the business of the retailers to whom the supplier sells directly." *Guyott Co. v Texaco, Inc.* (D Conn 1966) 261 F Supp 942 at 950.

But a supplier may not sell to its retailers at a lower price than it sells to its wholesalers whose customers compete with the favored retailer because such price discrimination injures competition at the favored retailer's level, *i.e.*, at the secondary level. See *FTC v Morton Salt Co.* (1948) 334 US 37; *Guyott Co. v Texaco, Inc., supra.*

Assuming the favored and disfavored buyers are in competition with one another, plaintiff must establish a causal connection between the price differential and the alleged injury to competition. The standard for measuring the sufficiency of proof of causation is far less strict in a secondary line case than in a primary line case. See discussion of the latter at §5.39.

The statute does not require proof that the discrimination actually did injure competition but only that the probabilities are that the discrimination may injure competition. From this statutory requirement the Supreme Court in *Morton Salt Co., supra*, at 50, fashioned a causation formula for use in secondary-line injury cases to the effect that it is "self-evident . . . that there is a 'reasonable possibility' that competition may be adversely affected by a practice under which manufacturers and producers sell goods to some customers substantially cheaper than they sell like goods to the competitors of these customers." The lower federal courts and the Commission have applied this formula on frequent occasion, despite the criticism that it is hardening the formula into a *per se* rule. See, *e.g.*, *Foremost Dairies, Inc. v FTC* (5th Cir 1965) 348 F2d 674, *cert den* (1965) 382 US 959; *United Biscuit Co. of America v FTC* (7th Cir 1965) 350 F2d 615, *cert den* (1966) 383 US 926; *Reines Distributors, Inc. v Admiral Corp.* (SD NY 1967) 1967 Trade Cases ¶72,151.

Courts have found the "self evident" causal connection in suits brought by the government at the secondary level notwithstanding testimony of the disfavored buyer to the effect that he did not believe that he was or would be adversely affected. Because the Act protects "competition" and not the individual competitor, the courts reason that "the incipient harm to competition that may be present if the challenged discrimination should continue is not to be determined solely by the opinions of the store owners. The determination must be made by the Commission through an exercise of its special competence and upon the basis of all the attendant facts and circumstances with particular reference to the type of business under investigation." *United Biscuit Co. of America v FTC, supra*, at 622; *Standard Motor Products, Inc. v FTC* (2d Cir 1959) 265 F2d 674, 676, *cert den* (1959) 361 US 826.

In *National Dairy Products Corp. v FTC* (7th Cir 1968) 395 F2d 517, *cert den* (1968) 393 US 977, the court affirmed the Commission's finding of injury at the buyer's level notwithstanding testimony of nonfavored buyers that their business was not hurt by the price discrimination, stating (at 521–522):

[I]njury may be inferred even if the favored customer did not undersell his rivals, for a substantial price advantage can enlarge the favored buyer's profit margin or enable him to offer attractice services to his customers. . . . [A]ny substantial, sustained differential between competing resellers is *prima facie* injurious. "Mini-injury" is the test.

Similarly the required causal connection has been established absent any showing of change in market structure or any showing of business diversion. In *E. Edelmann & Co. v FTC* (7th Cir 1956) 239 F2d 152, 155, *cert den* (1958) 355 US 941, the court stated:

It is not necessary that a price advantage be used to lower the resale price and thereby attract business away from the nonfavored competitors [to find probable competitive injury because] sales are not the sole indicium that reflects the health of the competitive scene.

See also *Foremost Dairies, Inc. v FTC, supra*; *Moog Industries, Inc. v FTC* (8th Cir 1956) 238 F2d 43, 50, *aff'd per curiam* (1958) 355 US 411.

Probable injury to competition has been found at the buyers' level notwithstanding the fact that the product does not represent a substantial portion of the buyer's business. "Congress intended to protect a merchant from competitive injury attributable to discriminatory prices on any or all goods sold in interstate commerce, whether the particular goods constituted a major or a minor portion of his stock. Since a grocery store consists of many comparatively small articles, there is no possible way effectively to protect a grocer from discriminatory prices except by applying the prohibitions of the Act to each individual article in the store." *FTC v Morton Salt Co., supra*, 49. See also *Mueller Co. v FTC* (7th Cir 1963) 323 F2d 44, *cert den* (1964) 377 US 923; *William H. Rorer, Inc.* (1966) [1965–1967 Transfer Binder] FTC Dkt 8599, Trade Reg Rep ¶17,535.

Antitrust Developments 1955–1968, 125 concludes that "several decisions of the courts [and Commission] have likewise shown a trend away from automatic inferences of competitive injury, in favor of inquiries to determine whether the particular discrimination does in fact impair the unfavored customers' 'ability to compete.'" But the recent date of decisions in both forums that utilize the automatic inference approach cautions the practitioner in placing too much reliance on the noted "trend." See, *e.g., United Biscuit Co. of America v FTC, supra; Foremost Dairies, Inc., supra.* See also *Beatrice Foods Co.* (1969) [1967–1970 Transfer Binder] FTC Dkt 8663, Trade Reg Rep ¶19,045, in which the Commission stated (at 21,303):

> [I]t is clear that the mere existence of substantial differentials between competing purchasers in a price sensitive atmosphere is sufficient to give rise to an inference of reasonable probability of injury to competition.

An analysis of the decisions cited in favor of the conclusion that use of the inference is decreasing shows that in most instances the inference was not rejected but rather that the facts destroyed the necessary causal link. See, *e.g., American Oil Co. v FTC* (7th Cir 1963) 325 F2d 101, *cert den* (1964) 377 US 954. The cautious practitioner would therefore be well advised to assume that the automatic inference may still be made.

The "self-evident" causal connection is destroyed if the defendant can show that identical merchandise was available to the disfavored buyer either from it or its competitors at the same price as it sold to favored customers. See, *e.g., Tri-Valley Packing Association v FTC* (9th Cir 1964) 329 F2d 694; *Ark-La-Tex Warehouse Distributors, Inc.* (1963) [1963–1965 Transfer Binder] FTC Dkt 7592, Trade Reg Rep ¶16,441.

The length of time during which the price discrimination is in effect might also destroy the necessary causal connection. Temporary price differentials have been found in some circumstances not to adversely affect competition, as "there must be something more than an essentially minimal impact on competition." *American Oil Co. v FTC, supra* (no violation found on the basis of a 17-day price war among gasoline dealers in one geographic area). Compare *National Dairy Products Corp.* (1967) [1967–1970 Transfer Binder] FTC Dkt 8548, Trade Reg Rep ¶18,027, dealing with injury at the seller's level and discussed at §5.39. National argued that the 26-day promotion was temporary and too brief to cause injury; the Commission viewed the same period as unlimited because the products could be stored for a lengthy time.

Alternatively, the size of the price differential might destroy the necessary causal connection. In industries in which the net profit in sales is small, such as in the automotive parts industry, even very small price differentials have been held to adversely affect competition. See *E. Edelmann & Co. v FTC, supra*, 154. See also *Purolator Products, Inc. v FTC* (7th Cir 1965) 352 F2d 874, *cert den* (1968) 389 US 1045; *Standard Motor*

Products, Inc. v FTC, supra; *P. Sorensen Mfg. Co. v FTC* (DC Cir 1957) 246 F2d 687; *P. & D. Mfg. Co. v FTC* (7th Cir 1957) 245 F2d 281, *cert den* (1957) 355 US 884; *Whitaker Cable Corp. v FTC* (7th Cir 1956) 239 F2d 253, *cert den* (1957) 353 US 938; *Moog Industries, Inc. v FTC, supra.*

In other industries with a more generous net profit on sales, such as the candy industry, small price differentials may be found not to affect competition adversely. Thus a charge of unlawful discrimination was dismissed in *W.F. Schrafft & Sons Corp.* (1964) [1963-1965 Transfer Binder] FTC Dkt 7743, Trade Reg Rep ¶16,882 against a candy manufacturer who sold directly to retailers at 33-1/3 percent off a preticketed consumer price and 40 percent off that price to chain and department stores. The Court explained the factors it deemed persuasive (at 21,918):

In a case such as this, where there is no proof of actual competitive injury and the non-favored retailers resell the products at a preticketed price, factors such as the net profit margins of the non-favored retailers and the extent to which they take advantage of the 2% cash discount take on an added significance in determining the probability of competitive injury. . . . The non-favored retailers are engaged in different types of retail business, and the evidence reveals the net profit margins of only two [one at 2% and the other at 15%]. In addition, although we are told that competition in the sale of packaged candy is keen, so much so that the cash discount of 2% is of extreme importance, the evidence reveals that four of the five non-favored retailers did not habitually take advantage of this discount. In these circumstances, we find that there is in this record no basis for an informed determination of the probable competitive effect of Wallace's price discriminations.

See also *Fred Bronner Corp.* (1960) 57 FTC 771.

In view of the significance attached to the size of the profit margin in determining whether there is a probability of competitive injury, a tabulation of 22 industries' medians of return on sales for 1966 and 1967 published in the June, 1968 issue of *Fortune* at 206 may be of interest:

	1967	1966		1967	1966
Mining	14.8%	12.1%	Glass, cement, gypsum,		
Pharmaceuticals	9.6	10.2	and concrete	5.3%	6.7%
Petroleum refining	8.6	9.0	Farm and industrial machinery	5.2	5.8
Tobacco	8.2	8.1	Paper and wood products	4.9	5.9
Soaps and cosmetics	7.2	6.7	Motor vehicles and parts	4.4	4.8
Measuring, scientific, and			Appliances and electronics	4.2	5.1
photographic equipment	6.6	7.6	Rubber	3.5	4.7
Publishing and printing	5.9	6.7	Shipbuilding and railroad		
Chemicals	5.9	6.8	equipment,	3.5	4.4
Metal manufacturing	5.8	6.5	Apparel	3.3	4.1
Metal products	5.3	5.4	Textiles	3.1	4.4
Office machinery			Aircraft and parts	2.8	3.3
(includes computers)	5.3	4.9	Food and beverage	2.4	3.2
			All industry	5.0	5.6

A reasonable forecast of the competitive effects of a given price differential requires a careful analysis of the market in question and a thorough understanding of the business of the concern in question, its purchasers, and its purchasers' customers. Such an analysis should include an assessment of the intensity of competition, the net profit on sales, the availability of cash discounts from suppliers, the need to give cash discounts to buyers, the need to maintain sales forces, the need to engage in promotional activities, and the need to perform special customer services.

h. [§5.41] Proving Competitive Injury at the Buyer's Customers' Level

Since the Act declares price discrimination unlawful if it tends (15 USC §13(a)) "to injure, destroy, or prevent competition with any person who either grants or knowingly receives the benefit of such discrimination, *or with customers of either of them,*" a manufacturer who favors its direct-buying wholesalers over its direct-buying retailers may cause competitive injury at the third level, i.e., the retail level, if its wholesalers sell to their retailers at a lower price than the manufacturer sells directly to competing retailers. See, *e.g., Standard Oil Co.* (1945) 41 FTC 263; *Morton Salt Co. v FTC* (1948) 334 US 37. Strictly speaking (Rowe, *Price Discrimination under the Robinson-Patman Act* (1962) 196 n. 97):

The so-called "third line" injury concept comes into play only when the supplier *favors* his distributors, whose customers compete with other purchasers from the supplier, whereby competition *with* the *customer* or the purchaser may be impaired. An ordinary "secondary-line" problem arises if the supplier *favors* his retailer purchasers over his distributors, for then competition *with* the supplier's retailer customers (rather than with customers of his customers) is affected.

The concept poses a problem in that it induces the supplier to engage in resale price maintenance contrary to the prohibitions of the Sherman Act. (See Chapter 2.) The concept is seldom used and has been frequently criticized. See Rowe, *supra*, 195–205.

However, in *Perkins v Standard Oil Co. of California* (9th Cir 1967) 396 F2d 809, 813, the Ninth Circuit ruled that an integrated wholesaler-retailer of gasoline could not recover damages from Standard, its supplier, resulting from impaired ability to compete with a customer of a customer of a favored purchaser, which the court deemed a "fourth-level" injury, not protected by the Robinson-Patman Act.

The Supreme Court reversed ((1969) 395 US 642), viewing that Standard's sales to its wholesaler (Signal) at lower prices than granted plaintiff predictably caused plaintiff injury when Signal resold to Western (a majority subsidiary), which resold to Regal (also a majority subsidiary), which was the retailer competing with plaintiff. The Court relied on *FTC v Fred Meyer, Inc.* (1968) 390 US 341 to interpret broadly the term "customer" and found plaintiffs' competition impaired with Regal, which it deemed a "customer" of Standard, stating (395 US at 648):

> We find no basis in the language or purpose of the Act for immunizing Standard's price discriminations simply because the product in question passed through an additional formal exchange before reaching the level of Perkins' actual competitor.

In view of the Court's reference to a "formal exchange," the result might well have been different had the corporate line between Standard and Regal been less close. The court might have reached the same result by regarding Regal "an indirect customer" of Standard based on the close corporate relationship and Standard's awareness of the pricing problem. See discussion of indirect purchaser at §5.12.

Absent such an analysis of the *Perkins* case, immense antitrust problems would be faced by a seller forced to police pricing policies effected by buyers far down the line of distribution over whom seller had no control.

i. [§5.42] Suits against Buyers Who Induce or Receive a Discrimination

Section 2(f) of the Clayton Act as amended by the Robinson-Patman Act (15 USC §13(f)) makes it unlawful "for any person engaged in commerce, in the course of such commerce, knowingly to induce or receive a discrimination in price which is prohibited by this section."

Patman, in *Complete Guide to the Robinson-Patman Act* (1963) 15, points out that "the basic legislative purpose of subsection 2(f) was to prevent buyers from using their economic power to force monopolistic price, service or facility concessions." Congress saw "huge buying power" as the "source of the evil" whereby the seller was "compelled usually in self defense to grant the concessions granted." 79 Cong. Rec. 9078 (1935), 80 Cong. Rec. 8111 (1936). However, §2(f) has not been used as extensively as §2(a) (15 USC §13(a)).

A suit against the buyer under §2(f) requires proof of all the jurisdictional elements required to make a case against the seller under §2(a), plus the element of knowledge, *to wit*, that the buyer *knowingly* induced discriminating prices. See discussion of jurisdictional elements at §§5.10–5.22. The buyer has the benefit of any of the defenses available to the seller. See, *e.g., Automatic Canteen Co. of America v FTC* (1953) 346 US 61. See discussion of defenses at §§5.43–5.52.

The Commission contends that an affirmative case is established against the buyer upon showing that (1) the buyer induced or received more favorable price treatment than its competitors and (2) the buyer knew or should have known that the prices it received were discriminatory. *American Motors Specialties Co. v FTC* (2d Cir 1960) 278 F2d 225, 228, *cert den* (1960) 364 US 884; *General Auto Supplies, Inc. v FTC* (7th Cir 1965) 346 F2d 311. See, *e.g.*, Consent Order entered in *Connell Rice & Sugar Co.* (1969) [1967–1970 Transfer Binder] FTC Dkt 8736, 3 Trade Reg Rep ¶18,319, prohibiting a food broker from "knowingly inducing or receiving discriminatory prices."

Several courts have interpreted the section to require proof by the plaintiff of the two elements noted above, *plus* proof that the buyer knew or should have known that the price differential could not be justified, *e.g.*, cost justified or granted to meet competition. See, *e.g.*, *Mid-South Distributors v FTC* (5th Cir 1961) 287 F2d 512, *cert den* (1961) 368 US 838. See discussion of legal elements of buyer's liability in Rowe, *Price Discrimination under the Robinson-Patman Act* (1962) 437–451. See also, Patman, *Complete Guide to the Robinson-Patman Act* (1963) 157.

Knowledge can be presumed from "trade experience." As stated by the Supreme Court in *Automatic Canteen Co. of America v FTC, supra*, 80:

A buyer who knows that he buys in the same quantities as his competitor and is served by the seller in the same manner or with the same amount of exertion as the other buyer can fairly be charged with notice that a substantial price differential cannot be justified. The Commission [or a private party] need only show, to establish its prima facie case, that the buyer knew that the methods by which he was served and the quantities in which he purchased were the same as in the case of his competitor. If the methods or quantities differ, the Commission [or a private party] must only show that such differences could not give rise to sufficient savings in the cost of manufacture, sale or delivery to justify the price differential, and that the buyer, knowing these were the only differences, should have known that they could not give rise to sufficient cost savings. The showing of knowledge, of course, will depend to some extent on the size of the discrepancy between the cost differential and the price differential, so that the two questions are not isolated. A showing that the cost differences are very small compared with the price differential and could not reasonably have been thought to justify the price differential should be sufficient.

The burden is on the Commission to show that buyer had such knowledge. As the Commission recently quoted with approval in *Beatrice Foods Co.* (1969) [1967–1970 Transfer Binder] FTC Dkt 8663, Trade Reg Rep ¶19,045 at 21,312:

[I]f complaint counsel show such facts and circumstances as would have given the buyer reason to believe, based on the knowledge available to him, including knowledge of the methods of doing business in the particular industry, that the different methods or quantities could not have resulted in cost savings sufficient to justify the differential allegedly accorded him, they would have met their initial burden.

Recently the Commission found that a buyer had violated §2(f) even though it found that the seller had not engaged in unlawful price discrimination because the discount granted was justified as a discount given in good faith to meet competition. *Beatrice Foods Co., supra*. The Commission reasoned that because the buyer "knowingly induced and received discriminatory prices . . . [it] is not entitled to any benefit of [seller's] good faith defenses." It rejected the buyer's argument that a buyer was entitled to any defense, including good faith, available to the seller. The argument was based on language from *Automatic Canteen, supra*, to the effect that "a buyer is not liable under §2(f) if the lower prices he induces are either within one of the seller's defenses such as the cost justification or not known to him not to be within one of those defenses." 346 US at 74.

The Commission refused to apply the good-faith-meeting-competition defense when the buyer initiated the price break in the first place because "to hold that a buyer can escape liability merely by inducing and accepting a second discriminatory offer which meets an offer previously induced by the buyer would make a mockery of Section 2(f)."

Commissioner Elman dissented, noting (at 21,316):

We are confronted, then, with a Commission decision holding [buyer] guilty under Section 2(f) of "knowingly" inducing or receiving "a discrimination in price which is prohibited by this section," on a record which fails to show any price discrimination illegal under Section 2.

Ironically, in view of the legislative purpose of §2(f) to curb the misuse of mammoth purchasing power by large buyers, its prohibition has been directed frequently against buying associations, mainly composed of small buyers, who, "[f]aced with the competition of large national chains and other mass buyers, . . . in an effort to reduce their costs—have formed cooperatives to engage in collective buying, warehousing, and distribution functions." Dissent of Commissioner Elman in *Southern California Jobbers, Inc.* (1965) [1965-1967 Transfer Binder] FTC Dkt 6889, Trade Reg Rep ¶17,410 at 22,629. The frequency and success with which the Commission has attacked group buying should be of particular significance to the practitioner representing small business concerns. See also discussions concerning buying associations and §2(c) at §5.30 and functional discounts at §5.23.

In *Mid-South Distributors v FTC, supra*, automobile part jobbers who purchased through a buying association to obtain volume discounts not available to them purchasing in their individual capacities were charged with knowledge that the discounts were not cost justified. The jobbers knew (1) that their orders were processed in the same way whether they sent them directly or through the association, (2) that no special cost savings were effected by interposing the association, (3) that the volume discounts were generally available, and (4) that the association was formed for the purpose of creating a larger total volume in order to obtain larger volume discounts. See also *American Motor Specialties Co. v FTC, supra.* For similar cases brought under §2(a) against the seller granting discounts to group buying associations, see *Standard Motor Products, Inc. v FTC* (2d Cir 1959) 265 F2d 674, *cert den* (1959) 361 US 826; *Moog Industries, Inc. v FTC* (8th Cir 1956) 238 F2d 43, *aff'd* (1958) 355 US 411. In each of these cases the group buying association performed few if any of the traditional wholesaler's functions; the merchandise was drop-shipped and invoiced to the member retailer. The Commission, upheld by the courts, has consistently taken the position that such group buying associations are not entitled to a volume discount and has often pro-ceeded against the association members under §2(f). For discussion of volume discounts, see §5.25.

Difficult to justify, however, is the Commission's insistence, again up-held in the courts, that such group buying associations are not entitled to a functional discount even when they perform the warehousing, selling, and invoicing functions. See, *e.g., National Parts Warehouse* (1963) [1963-1965 Transfer Binder] FTC Dkt 8039, Trade Reg Rep ¶16,700. *aff'd sub nom General Auto Supplies v FTC* (7th Cir 1965) 346 F2d 311, *cert dismissed* (1965) 382 US 923; *Purolator Products, Inc. v FTC* (7th Cir 1965) 352 F2d 874, *cert den* (1968) 389 US 1045. In *National Parts Warehouse,* the Commission justified its ruling on the ground that the group buying association was merely an agent of its jobber members, which made it irrelevant "that NPW actually performs the same ware-housing functions" that nonintegrated warehouse distributors perform ((1963) [1963-1965 Transfer Binder] Trade Reg Rep ¶16,700 at 21,615). In the *Purolator* situation, the warehouse distributors maintained a central warehouse and reshipped to branch warehouses in close proximity to customers, thereby filling orders more promptly and facilitating the sell-er's distribution process. But the Commission held: "We are not of the opinion that such price discrimination may be excused by proof that the buyer receiving the more favorable price has higher internal expenses than his competitor." *Purolator Products, Inc.* (1964) [1963-1965 Transfer Binder] Trade Reg Rep ¶16,877 at 21,884.

The Commission's position regarding discounts granted group buying associations for services performed hinges upon its view that functional discounts must be granted only on the basis of the buyer's method of resale, and not on the basis of the buyer's method of purchase. This view has been cogently criticized. See, e.g., Attorney General's Report, 1955, 207. See also discussion of functional discounts at §5.23.

Contrary to the Commission, the commentators and at least one court reason that if the association is performing valuable distributing and warehousing functions, there may be a basis for finding that the association, not its members, is the actual purchaser and that the association is in competition with and receiving the same treatment as ordinary warehousing distributors. Under this analysis, there is no price discrimination. See, e.g., Alhambra Motor Parts v FTC (9th Cir 1962) 309 F2d 213, 217 n. 5, 219, 220 n. 12. On remand of this case, however, in sub nom Southern California Jobbers, Inc. v FTC, supra, the buying association was found by the Commission to have been the agent of the members, and the members were found to have purchased with knowledge. See also National Parts Warehouse, supra.

The members of the association may be able to show a cost savings to their supplier as a result of dealing with their association. Such a defense, even if not as precise as would be required to dispel a §2(a) violation (see discussion at §§5.44–5.48), may be sufficient to dispel an inference that the members knew that the discounts could not be cost justified, or may at least shift the burden to the plaintiff to show that the obvious cost savings "could not be commensurate with the price differential." See, e.g., Alhambra Motor Parts v FTC, supra. See also Automatic Canteen Co. of America v FTC, supra, 80.

The Commission has not used §2(f) to reach buyers who induce or receive discriminatory promotional services and allowances prohibited by §2(d) and §2(e) (15 USC §13(d) and 13(e)), discussed at §§5.31–5.33. In these cases the Commission relies on §5 of the Federal Trade Commission Act, 15 USC §45(a). The Supreme Court held in FTC v Fred Meyer, Inc. (1968) 390 US 341, that a direct-buying grocery chain violated Section 5 by inducing its suppliers to grant it promotional allowances not made available to competing retailers who purchased supplier's products from a wholesaler. The Court found that the retailers who bought through wholesalers were "customers" of the supplier for purposes of §2(d) and that the supplier had not made its promotional plan available to all its customers on proportionally equal terms. See also Colonial Stores, Inc. (1968) [1967–1970 Transfer Binder] FTC Dkt 8768, Trade Reg Rep ¶18,517; Grand Union Co. (1960) FTC Dkt 6973, modified on other grounds (2d

Cir 1962) 300 F2d 92; *American News Co. v FTC* (2d Cir 1962) 300 F2d 104, *cert den* (1962) 371 US 824; *Giant Food, Inc. v FTC* (DC Cir 1962) 307 F2d 184, *cert den* (1963) 372 US 910. When there is evidence of a brokerage commission, the Commission relies on §2(c) (15 USC §13(c)) discussed at §§5.27–5.30.

2. [§5.43] Defenses

Once the Robinson-Patman plaintiff has established a prima facie case (see §5.34), the defendant must shoulder the burden of proving that (1) the price differential is cost-justified, (2) the price differential was effected in good faith to meet the equally low price of a competitor, or (3) the price differential was effected in response to changing conditions affecting the market for or the marketability of the goods concerned. *Nagler v Admiral Corporation* (2d Cir 1957) 248 F2d 319. These defenses are discussed in §§5.44–5.52.

a. [§5.44] Cost Justification

The Robinson-Patman enactment specifically exempts from its coverage price differentials "which make only due allowance for differences in the cost of manufacture, sale, or delivery resulting from the differing methods or quantities in which such commodities are to such purchasers sold or delivered" (15 USC §13(a)). In short, a seller may pass on those cost savings that originate from the manufacturing or the marketing and distributing aspects of its business, but only insofar as they can be traced either to the quantity sold and delivered or the method of sale or delivery. Cost savings coming from manufacturing include, for example, administrative overhead such as billing and bookkeeping, product development and design, tooling-up, employee training, changes in wage scale, and market changes in raw materials if goods are made to the customer's order rather than for warehouse stock. See, *e.g., United States Rubber Co.* (1950) 46 FTC 998; *Thompson Products, Inc.* (1959) 55 FTC 1252. Advisory Committee on Cost Justification, Report to FTC (FTC mimeo 1956) 21-22; and Appendix A, reprinted at §5.47.

Cost savings that result from the marketing and distributing functions include advertising, sales promotion, sales accounting, freight and delivery, catalog expenses, sales and technical services, warehousing and storage, and credit and sales. *FTC v Standard Motor Products* (2d Cir 1967) 371 F2d 613; Advisory Committee, *supra*, at 22-23; and Appendix A.

Billings costs attributable to sales or delivery are recognized, but the Commission has made it clear that in its opinion billing costs constitute "a minor expense, wholly incapable of affecting the [cost justification] issue

... to any significant extent." *Southern California Jobbers, Inc.* (1965) [1965-1967 Transfer Binder] FTC Dkt 6889, Trade Reg Rep ¶17,410 at 22,623.

Advertising costs are recognized, but the difficulty in allocating them with the precision required by the Commission makes their use problematic. It has not been decided whether advertising costs might justify a price differential between branded and nonbranded goods. *FTC v Borden* (1966) 383 US 637, *reconsidered* (5th Cir 1967) 391 F2d 175, 181.

The courts and the Commission disagree on whether brokerage or sales commissions can be treated as costs for purposes of the cost justification defense. In *Thomasville Chair Co.* (1961) [1960-1961 Transfer Binder] FTC Dkt 7273, Trade Reg Rep ¶29,510, the Commission ruled that the manufacturer could not use the savings of salesmen's commissions in selling to a given group of customers to justify the favored price afforded them. The Fifth Circuit disagreed and reversed: *Thomasville Chair Co. v FTC* (5th Cir 1962) 306 F2d 541. On remand, the Commission stated that it did not "acquiesce in the opinion of the Court of Appeals as such." *Thomasville Chair Co.* (1963) [1963-1965 Transfer Binder] Trade Reg Rep ¶16,624 at 21,515. See discussion at §5.28.

If the cost study justifies all but a small portion of the price differential, the Commission has applied a *de minimis* rule and disregarded the portion not cost justified. What will be regarded as a *de minimis* differential is not certain. However, the Commission has accepted a cost study that failed to cost justify .85 percent of the price differential (*American Metal Prod. Co.* (1962) 60 FTC 1667, 1684), and has rejected one that failed to cost justify 3.5 percent of the price differential. *Thompson Products, Inc.* (1959) 55 FTC 1252, 1273-1274.

A seller may not pass on to a large purchaser "incremental" cost savings that result from the purchaser's large order. Congress reasoned that each customer, large and small, contributes to the seller's total sales volume and is therefore entitled to his proportionate share of whatever cost savings are generated from increased sales volume. 80 Cong. Rec. 9417 (1936); *Champion Spark Plug Co.* (1953) 50 FTC 30, 43.

For example, a plant with a maximum capacity of 1,000 orders per month and a breakeven point of 500 orders can take its last 500 orders with little or no increase in basic overhead. The seller cannot give the buyer who places the final order for 500 units a discount reflecting the fact that the seller's basic overhead is not increased by reason of the order. Instead, the seller must total its basic overhead, divide it by its total orders, and assess each buyer his proportionate share of the overhead costs.

299

Congress recognized that a seller's costs, other than incremental costs, frequently decrease with a greater quantity of goods purchased and may decrease depending on the seller's methods of delivery and sale; and that such cost savings should be passed on to the consumer by way of the purchaser responsible. "Where one customer orders from hand to mouth during the rush of the season, compelling the employment of more expensive overtime labor . . . while another orders far in advance, permitting the manufacturer to use cheaper off-season labor, with elimination of overtime, or perhaps to buy his raw materials at cheaper off-season prices, such savings as between the two customers may . . . be expressed in price differentials." 80 Cong. Rec. 9417 (1936).

In actuality, "the cost defense has proved largely illusory in practice." *Attorney General's Report, 1955,* 171. The defense has been raised in only a very small percentage of the §2(a) cases (price discrimination) and has been successful in very few of those. See Rowe, *Price Discrimination under the Robinson-Patman Act* (1962) 298.

There are several reasons for its lack of use and success. One is the tremendous difficulty of proving the cost defense due in part to "the elusiveness of cost data, which apparently cannot be obtained from ordinary business records" and to the fact that "whenever costs have been an issue, the Commission has not been content with accounting estimates; a study seems to be required, involving perhaps stop-watch studies of time spent by some personnel such as salesmen and truck drivers, numerical counts of invoices or bills and in some instances of the number of items or entries on such records, or other such quantitative measurement of the operation of a business." *Automatic Canteen Co. v FTC* (1953) 346 US 61, 68. Further, although the Commission has "indicated a readiness to accept cost studies 'made in good faith and in accordance with sound accounting principles' . . . no standards for testing the requisite 'good faith' or 'sound accounting principles' have as yet been promulgated." *Attorney General's Report, 1955,* 172. Finally, the preparation of a cost defense is exceedingly expensive. The very low odds of succeeding coupled with the very high cost of preparing a cost defense explains why the defense is not used frequently.

In 1953 the Commission appointed an Advisory Committee on Cost Justification and in 1956 its report was published without approval or disapproval by the Commission. The courts have received the report with enthusiasm, and it has been cited with approval by the Supreme Court. See, *e.g., United States v Borden Co.* (1962) 370 US 460, 469. Although the report is general, it presents an excellent starting point for research in this area. Appendix A to the report, entitled *Illustrative Methods and Procedures for Allocating Manufacturing and Distribution Costs*, is quite helpful and is reprinted at §5.47.

In a case brought under §2(a) the difficulties inherent in preparing a cost study fall upon the defendant, for the seller must shoulder the burden of proving that its price differential in any given case is cost justified. *FTC v Morton Salt Co.* (1948) 334 US 37, 45; *United States v Borden Co., supra*, at 467. In a §2(f) (15 USC §13(f)) case against a buyer, on the other hand, the Commission must carry the burden of proving that the buyer knew or should have known that the price differential was not justified. See §5.42.

Although estimates are not acceptable, certain procedural shortcuts may assist the defendant in some situations in preparing a cost justification. Two of these shortcuts are product-line averaging and customer grouping, discussed in §§5.45 and 5.46. Both of these shortcuts are based on reasonable sampling which "has long been a recognized technique in price discrimination cases." *United States v Borden, supra*, at 466 n. 6. To date the Commission has strictly construed what constitutes "reasonable" sampling, requiring the sampling to represent very accurately the group from which it is taken. But from the very nature of selecting a few to represent all, absent identity within the group (which would make sampling unnecessary), complete homogenity can never be achieved. See *e.g., Admiral Corporation* (1963) [1963-1965 Transfer Binder] FTC Dkt 7094, Trade Reg Rep ¶16,570; *Mueller Co. v FTC* (7th Cir 1963), 323 F2d 44, *cert den* (1964) 377 US 923.

(1) [§5.45] Product-Line Averaging

A manufacturer of a product line composed of numerous items may use the average price paid by members of one class for the entire line rather than comparing the price for each individual item in the line. The procedure was successfully used in *Sylvania Electric Products, Inc.* (1954) 51 FTC 282, 285, in which Sylvania, which sold a line of some 600 replacement tubes to Philco at a lower price than it charged its distributors, averaged its cost savings in selling to Philco. It then compared the distributors' higher price with the price it would have charged had the sale been to Philco and offered the additional costs in selling to distributors to justify the price differentials. The defense was sustained.

In *Thompson Products, Inc.* (1959) 55 FTC 1252, 1273, although the cost defense was ultimately rejected, the Commission permitted selection of 312 parts from 22,000 listed in defendant's catalog and considered them comparable for purposes of cost and price comparisons.

(2) [§5.46] Customer Grouping

The courts have permitted "the practice of grouping customers for pricing purposes," recognizing that to renounce the practice "would be to eliminate in practical effect the cost justification proviso as to sellers having a large number of purchasers, thereby preventing such sellers from passing on economies to their customers." *United States v Borden Co.* (1962) 370 US 460, 468. However, the courts have required the customer groups to be "composed of members of such selfsameness as to make the averaging of the cost of dealing with the group a valid and reasonable indicium of the cost of dealing with any specific group member." *United States v Borden, supra,* at 469.

Borden took into account cognizable cost savings such as freight, cartons, labels, sales promotions, and advertising and clerical costs, but the cost justification defense failed because the customer groupings (comparing chain stores to independents) were not "shown to be of sufficient homogeneity"; the Court noted, *inter alia,* that several of the large "independents" had comparable volumes to the chain stores. 370 US at 469. See discussion of functional discounts at §§5.23 and 5.40.

Similarly, in *National Dairy Products Corp. v FTC* (7th Cir 1968) 395 F2d 517, *cert den* (1968) 393 US 977, the court affirmed the Commission's rejection of a dairy company's cost defense that averaged the total dollar purchases of all units of a chain to reach the cost of serving the chain buyer. As stated by the appellate court (395 F2d at 526):

The cost of selling a given volume of milk to one store is the same whether that store is part of a group or chain or is an independent. Therefore, when the group or chain receives a greater discount than the independent, the seller is bowing to the size of the buyer and not making "due allowance" for cost savings.

Similar results were reached in *Mueller Co. v FTC* (7th Cir 1963) 323 F2d 44, 47, *cert den* (1964) 377 US 923; the defense failed to establish that a "stocking" discount given to a class of customers called "stocking jobbers," as opposed to customers classified as "non-stocking jobbers," was cost justified when it was shown that some members of the class received a "stocking discount" although "no warehousing function was provided." In short, the class was not sufficiently homogenous. See also *William H. Rorer, Inc.* (1966) [1965–1967 Transfer Binder] FTC Dkt 8599, Trade Reg Rep ¶17,535.

The Commission has repeatedly tried to narrow the judicially approved customer-grouping approach and reinstate a customer-by-customer analysis of costs. In Advisory Opinion Digest 198 (1968) [1967–1970 Transfer Binder] Trade Reg Rep ¶18,237, the Commission refused to permit a manufacturer to pass on a 5 percent cost savings in freight per truckload orders based on a study showing that the manufacturer's savings in truck-load orders was in excess of 5 percent. The Commission reasoned that the manufacturer was precluded from passing on an average savings to his customers because all customers were not similarly situated; the freight savings on truckload from a nearby customer in close proximity was less than 5 percent, and the freight savings from a customer more distant was over 5 percent. In short, the Commission required a customer-by-customer dispensation of cost savings.

In *American Motors Corp.* (1964) [1965-1967 Transfer Binder] FTC Dkt 7357, Trade Reg Rep ¶17,297, *rev'd* (6th Cir 1967) 384 F2d 247, *cert den* (1968) 390 US 1012, the Commission refused to accept a cost defense that divided customers into two groups: four distributors who received a 3 percent discount, and 6,000 dealers who were not given the discount. The Commission relied on the *Borden* rule of homogeneity and held that the 6,000 dealers were not sufficiently homogeneous to be classed together for purposes of determining the cost of selling to them as a group because the cost of selling to a particular dealer within that group might be the same or even less than the cost of selling to one of the four distributors; and in a few instances the distributors were given extra sales assistance, one of the extra cost factors attributed to dealers.

The Sixth Circuit, rejecting the Commission's contention, stated (384 F2d at 254):

The needed homogenity is not dependent upon the size or style of doing business, provided American Motors' method of using [the dealers] to market its products exposed it to the "selfsameness" and uniformity in its burden of costs. The evidence disclosed that the merchandizing distributors supplied for themselves a sales staff which carried on at their own expense the functions which American Motors had to perform, at its expense, for the regular dealers.

In answer to the Commission's contention that a few of the 6,000 dealers performed for themselves functions performed by the distributors, making the cost study invalid under the *Borden* rule of homogenity, the court distinguished the *Borden* case on its facts, stating (384 F2d at 256-257):

The price differentials made by Borden were between its chain store and its independent store customers, and it relied in part for its claim of extra cost of doing business with the independent stores upon the extra personnel required to service them. It also relied in part upon the greater volume of purchasing by the chain stores. . . . In *Borden* the cost savings alleged to have been experienced with the chain stores was arrived at by lumping all of such savings together and striking an average. Of this, the Supreme Court said ". . . the favorable cost

303

comparisons between the chains and the larger independents were for the greater
part controlled by the higher *average volume* of the chain stores in comparison to
the *average volume* of the . . . independents . . . it [also] attributed to many
independents cost factors *which were not true indicia of the cost of dealing with
those particular consumers. . . .*" In contrast to the foregoing, [American Motors]
[d]id not *average* the volume of sales or the lesser cost of selling to the respective
merchandising distributors. [Its] study [was made] by separate [geographic] zones
and, in each, *separately* analyzed the cost savings experienced in doing business
with [each of the four distributors] as compared with the cost of doing business
with the regular dealers in the particular zone under examination. . . . [American
Motors] [d]id not attribute to its regular dealers "cost factors which were not true
indicia of the cost of dealing with those particular consumers [here regular deal-
ers]." . . . It is true that [American Motors] did not make a detailed report as to
the extra cost of doing business with each of the 6,000 dealers, but . . . the
Commission failed to point to one individual dealer who was not enjoying the
extra services the cost of which was part of the justification for the price differentials. The admitted minimal departures from strict uniformity did not, in our
view detract from the legitimacy of [the] conclusions. . . . In *Borden*, . . . [t]he
studies appeared to be made on estimates. . . . [E]ach independent was assigned a
portion of the total expenses involved in daily cash collections, although it was
not shown that all independents paid cash and in fact Borden admitted only "*that
'a large majority' did so.* . . ." "[Borden's] studies indicated only that a *large
majority* of independents took these services on a daily basis. . . ." "[Borden]
estimated that *about two thirds* of the independent stores received the 'optional
customer service' on a daily basis and that '*most store customers* pay the driver in
cash daily.' " . . . The [American Motors] study did not rely on *majorities, estimates, or approximations.* . . . [It] studied *all* the retail outlets in a particular zone
and *all* of the transactions in that zone over the period of the study. [They]
testified that the studies made were sufficiently extensive in area and time to be
typical of the entire United States. The Commission does not contend otherwise.
We think that, considering that perfection cannot be obtained, [the American
Motors Study] can fit into the [Borden rule governing customer grouping]. . . .

See also the cost justification study that the court exonerated in *Morton
v National Dairy Products Corp.* (ED Pa 1968) 1968 Trade Cases ¶72,612,
aff'd (3d Cir 1969) 414 F2d 403, *cert den* (1970) 396 US 1006.

The conclusions to be drawn from the decisions to date are that although the practitioner need not analyze costs on a customer-by-customer
basis, he must formulate his comparable groups with great care. As noted
above, the Commission interprets the grouping requirement more strictly
than do the courts.

The *American Motors* case, *supra*, provides a precedent for dividing
into zones the geographic area covered by the seller and for exhaustively
analyzing the costs of dealing with each customer within a given zone,

taking into account all transactions with each customer over a representative period of time such as one fiscal year. Testimony of one familiar with business costs in all zones *plus* a corroborating spot check that costs in the other zones were typical of the zone analyzed would satisfy the *American Motors* test for customer grouping. Within one zone one might reasonably class together, for example, all customers who rate a full-car delivery at the rail siding versus customers for whom the carload must be broken down. Similarly, if the cost includes sales assistance, the classification could properly consist of all customers who use the supplier's personnel versus all customers who provide their own. These classifications would satisfy the *Borden* rule of homogeneity by including in one group all customers, regardless of size, who create similar costs for the seller.

(3) [§5.47] Appendix A, Report of Advisory Committee on Cost Justification (1956): Illustrative Methods and Procedures for Allocating Manufacturing and Distribution Costs

I. Costs of manufacture

A. In general

What are commonly designated as manufacturing costs (including product development and other prerequisite costs) are likely to be segregated to show cost differences resulting from differing methods and quantities of sale only where goods are made upon customer order. Manufacturing costs applicable for cost-justification purposes are those which vary either directly or indirectly with the factor on which the price differential is based. For example, if the price differential is based on the number of units of product per order, then all those manufacturing costs which vary per unit of product with the size of the order, either directly or indirectly, are generally applicable in the cost justification process. The amount of the cost difference is equal to the amount of the variation in the per unit cost of the product.

B. Determination of manufacturing cost differences

In applying this general principle to a specific case, the first step is to divide the total expenses of manufacturing into groups, each group representing the total cost of some manufacturing activity or function; for example, product development and design, tooling, production, production control, purchasing, etc. Whether these functional expense groups will tend to vary per unit of product with the price-differentiating factor depends on the circumstances of the situation under review, and can be determined by the use of reason. Assume, for illustration, that all the expenses of the production control operation are considered as one functional group, that the price differential is based upon quantity per sales order, that all goods are manufactured for stock, that all orders are filled from this stock, and that all customers buy comparable assortments of goods. Under these circumstances, since production control affects operations prior to finished goods storage, the size of the customer's order will have no direct effect on the production control operation, and it becomes difficult to measure the effect, if any, that production control expenses may have on any cost difference. However, if materials are scheduled into production only after receipt of an order, it is likely that production control cost per unit of product will vary with the size of the order. Certain of the expenses involved will be uniform per order, regardless of its size. Others may vary, but not proportionally. The cost per unit of product will therefore decrease as the size of the order increases, and vice versa.

Examples of other manufacturing cost differences to be recognized because of varying quantities of over-all or individual production orders, traceable directly or indirectly by relative contribution to classes of customers, include: product development and design, tooling, varying manufacturing methods, set-up and make-ready, fluctuation in efficiency due to interruptions of production flow, employee training costs, methods and standards development, product costing, and others.

Costs in the manufacturing area which do not directly vary with the price-determining factor, but which can be shown to vary with costs which do so vary, are also applicable to the cost-justification procedure. In many cases the best way to give recognition to this fact is to include a proper proportion of such indirectly varying costs among the costs of the operating functions. In other cases it is more convenient to deal with them separately.

An example of such indirectly varying costs may be vacation pay. If each employee is allowed a two-week vacation for which he receives four per cent of his annual wage, this expense varies, not with the size of individual orders, but with the number of payroll dollars. Applicable to each dollar of payroll included in the functional cost grouping, therefore, is an additional four cents for vacation pay. This item may be included among the costs of each separate function in the first instance, or it may be more convenient to compute vacation pay applicable to all payroll items and to add the resultant amount of variations to the answer otherwise obtained. The precise method of computation is unimportant;: what is important is the recognition of the principle, so that complete and accurate results may be obtained.

The preceding illustrations relate to a situation in which the price-differentiating factor is the number of units of product in the sales order. This is not the only possible source of manufacturing cost differences. For example, the timing of orders may be fully as important as their size, and may affect the costs of manufacture, sale, and delivery. If it can be shown, for instance, that orders properly timed with respect to production schedules have a normal cost resulting from orderly scheduling of production factors and processes, whereas ill-timed orders cause interruptions in production flow, require overtime labor, the utilization of abnormal sources of material, and similar excessive costs, cost differences may justify the offering of price inducements for orders placed reasonably in advance or penalties for orders placed on a spot basis.

The principle here is the same as in any other instance. Those functions, the costs of which vary with the price-differentiating factor, are the applicable functions, and the amount of the cost justification is measured by the variation in unit costs.

II. Distribution costs

A. In general

The costs of sale and delivery are commonly known as distribution or marketing costs. The terms should be construed broadly. The costs of sale and delivery are, in general, the sum of the costs of obtaining sales orders and the costs which are incurred because sales orders have been received. Sometimes these costs are described as "order-getting" and "order-filling" costs. If these terms are understood broadly enough, they clearly describe the costs of sale and delivery. As noted before, the distinction between these costs and costs of manufacture is of negligible significance for Robinson-Patman Act purposes, since the same rule applies to all.

As in the case of manufacturing costs, the costs which are applicable to the problem of cost justification are those which vary, directly or indirectly, with the factor on which the price differential is based. A wide variety of such factors may give rise to variations in the costs of sale and delivery. The number of units per order, the total volume of purchases over a period of time, the timing of orders, the selection of modes of delivery or of channels of trade, and many other circumstances surrounding sales transactions may affect the unit costs of sale and delivery.

B. Functional method of distribution cost analysis

While in individual cases other approaches to the technique of cost analysis may be preferable, and should be acceptable to the Commission, the functional method has many advantages. This involves the collection of distribution costs by operations or functions. The term "function" in distribution cost accounting is comparable to "cost center" in manufacturing cost accounting. A distribution function may be defined as an operation or activity at the lowest practical level of supervision for which costs can be isolated and collected. Organization lines tend to follow functions performed. Thus the cost functions will tend to coincide with lines of authority and responsibility as established by management.

Among the considerations of importance in classifying distribution cost functions are the following:

1. Cost functions should include only similar operations. The commingling of unlike activities, with different rates of change relative to the price-differentiating factor, will be confusing, even though they may be under the same supervisor.

2. An organization division or department may perform only one function, but it frequently embraces several.

3. The size of a specialized distribution operation has no necessary relationship to whether or not it shall be considered as a function for cost justification purposes. Such a function may be the aggregate of several accounting units established for internal control purposes.

Since methods of organization and operation differ among companies and industries, distribution cost functions also differ. The examples and definitions given below, therefore, must be understood to be purely illustrative and not to be exhaustive, conclusive, or such as would fit any specific company. The illustrations are used merely to put into concrete terms the principles which the Committee has in mind.

The following might be the distribution cost functions of an integrated manufacturing company:

Transportation
Advertising
Sales Promotion
Selling and Technical Service
Warehousing
Operating Service
Sales Accounting and Credit
Sales Management

The transportation function includes the cost of transporting the goods from the place of production to the market in which they are to be sold, and then to the customer. Transportation may require one or more movements and involve several types of transportation facilities.

The advertising function is the cost of demand creation through non-personal presentation of goods or services. The usual means are newspapers, magazines, radio, television, outdoor signs, motion pictures, direct-mail, and catalogs.

The sales promotion function is similar to the advertising function in that its purpose is demand creation. This function differs from advertising only in the medium used. Mass circulation methods are not involved. Instead, the costs cover the display of the product itself, the use of point-of-sale material, the making of demonstrations, or the giving of premiums.

The selling functions involve those costs for the activities of personnel engaged in personal demand creation through direct contact with prospective buyers or their customers. They also include technical services performed for the purpose of aiding customers and prospective customers in the use of the products or service, giving technical advice and assistance in the operation of the customer's business.

Warehousing comprises the storing and handling of goods. The costs are primarily for space, stock handlers, and stock handling equipment.

The operating service function includes the cost of sales office clerical work and administration of the physical aspects of the distribution operations. Usually these activities are of greater importance when an organization is decentralized than when it is centralized.

The sales accounting and credit functions include the cost of billing, sales statistics, inventory accounting, accounts receivable and credit.

Sales management is a function which represents the responsibility for the entire marketing operation. Included in this function may be the determination of what to produce or purchase for resale, how much to make, when it should be procured or manufactured, where the products can be sold, and who will sell them.

It is to be noted that all of the functions thus described are subject to vertical subdivision for cost analysis purposes, the character and degree of such subdivision depending on the variety of tasks performed in each function, the specialization of supervision and personnel, and the purpose of the analysis. Such subdivisions are often called subfunctions, but their nature and significance are identical with the functions earlier described. The functions are also subject to horizontal subdivision in terms of geography, product lines, channels of trade, and the like. These subdivisions are apt to be very important for reduction of the scope of a cost study by elimination of costs not germane to the inquiry and by confining attention to an acceptable sample.

The costs of each distribution function consist of the familiar natural expense categories found in every classification of accounts, such as salaries, supplies, travel, communication, space costs, insurance, taxes, and so forth.

Having established satisfactory functional cost categories, it remains to determine costs by segments of the business, such as products or customers. For this purpose, costs may be roughly divided into two groups: those which are direct as respects the business segments involved, and those which are not. Direct costs are those which can be readily identified with the segment being costed. The application of these direct costs to specific segments of the business can be definitely measured, and no problems of proration or allocation exist. (It should be noted that costs which are direct as to certain segments, e.g., products, may be indirect as to other segments, e.g., customers, and vice versa.) Direct costs are usually identified with the units or segments to be costed at the time they are incurred—in other words, in the basic account classification and the original recording of expenses.

After ascertaining the direct costs, it remains to assign the indirect costs. These costs are collected as totals of functions not chargeable directly. Assignment of these indirect costs is done by measuring the activity or output of the function in terms of units of functional service which can be counted or measured, and then applying to each business segment the amount of the functional cost which is in proportion to its use of or responsibility for the units of functional service.

A simple example makes this process clear. If the function is personal selling, one possible unit of functional service in a customer analysis may be sales calls. If customers are divided into classes A, B, and C, and if 10 per cent of the calls are made on Class A, 30 per cent on Class B, and 60 per cent on Class C customers, then the three classes share the cost of personal selling in those proportions.

Procedure for other functions is similar. The steps are as follows:

1. Ascertain the total cost of the function.

2. Decide on an appropriate service unit by which the performance output of the function may be measured.

3. Measure the number of service units required by each segment to be costed—in the example above, by the three classes of customers.

4. Apply the costs of the function to the segments in proportion to the service units required.

Having measured or computed all direct and indirect functional costs, the total cost of each business segment is the total of the items so ascertained. Cost differences are then computed per unit of product, per dollar of actual or list sales, or in such other terms as may be appropriate.

C. *Principles of functional costing*

While it is not intended to list all conceivable functions with service units available for each, or otherwise to particularize, a few observations may be useful guides to functional costing.

At the outset, caution should be exercised with respect to overemphasis on the distinction between direct and indirect costs. This distinction should not be made for minor items of cost or for those where treatment of potentially direct items by a satisfactory application of the indirect procedure will produce completely reliable results. Substantial elements of direct costs are ordinarily so designated and recorded in the original bookkeeping process. Establishment and maintenance of the necessary bookkeeping routines for isolating all direct costs is burdensome and is justified only where amounts involved are appreciable and satisfactory results cannot be obtained by other and less expensive methods. In many cases the indirect functional approach, using an uncontroversial unit of functional service, will produce acceptable results.

Functions vary widely in their closeness to the business segments being costed. Some such relationships are very close and the appropriate measuring factor (the service unit) is easily identified and perhaps easily counted in total and in relation to the segments. The relationships of other functions to the costing segments are more remote, and the choice of a service unit which will adequately measure a given relationship is of greater difficulty. In many cases more than one service unit might be chosen. The precise choice will depend on two main considerations: (1) which service unit most closely approximates a satisfactory measure of benefit or activity in terms of rational analysis; (2) which service units can most readily and economically be counted both in total and in terms of the costing segments. Different service units will yield different dollars-and-cents results, and a particular service unit should not be chosen merely because it maximizes cost differences. Where the choice is otherwise a matter of indifference, however, there can be no objection to the choice of the method which produces the most desirable results.

The choice of both functions and service units must be in accordance with the circumstances of each case. To the extent that the functions listed heretofore cannot be assigned directly, the service units shown below have been found useful. Some of the units are more appropriate for commodity analysis than for customer analysis, and vice versa.

Transportation: the ton-mile, a weight unit not modified by distance, a bulk unit, a customer stop.

Advertising: square inches of advertising space, time of advertising personnel, number of pieces of advertising material furnished (direct mail and dealers' helps), number of commercials.

Sales promotion: number of promotion calls, time of sales promotion personnel, pieces of promotional literature.

310

Selling and technical service: number of calls, time spent in calls. Time spent in travel to and from territory and between customers is often handled on per-call basis, even though time with customers is used for direct selling.

Warehousing: space or volume units for storage; weight or volume units for receiving and shipping; time units, invoices, or invoice lines for order-filling costs.

Operating service: treated as overhead of selling and technical service function and allocated on same basis.

Sales accounting and credit: number of orders or invoices or invoice lines, number of transactions, number of accounts.

Sales management: treated as overhead of the functions managed, and allocated either on basis of all costs previously charged or on basis of payroll of persons supervised.

(4) [§5.48] Quantity Limits

Section 2(a) of the Clayton Act as amended (15 USC §13(a)) provides in part "that the Federal Trade Commission may . . . fix and establish quantity limits . . . where it finds that available purchasers in greater quantities are so few as to render differentials on account thereof unjustly discriminatory or promotive of monopoly in any line of commerce."

The Commission has exercised its power only once, to limit discounts in the sale of automotive replacement tires (Quantity Limit Rule 302-1, 17 Fed Reg 113), and then it was reversed. See *B.F. Goodrich Co. v FTC* (D DC 1955) 134 F Supp 39, *aff'd* (DC Cir 1957) 242 F2d 31.

The quantity limits proviso has been harshly criticized by most commentators. See *Attorney General's Report, 1955,* 177; *Antitrust Developments 1955-1968,* 136.

b. Meeting Competition

(1) [§5.49] Introduction

Section 2(b) of the Clayton Act as amended by the Robinson-Patman Act (15 USC §13(b)) provides in pertinent part that "nothing herein contained shall prevent a seller rebutting the prima facie case . . . by showing that his lower price or the furnishing of services or facilities . . . was made in good faith to meet an equally low price of a competitor, or the services or facilities furnished by a competitor."

The Supreme Court held that this proviso provides a complete defense to an alleged price discrimination charge under §2(a) that will justify price discounts even though injury to competition results. *Standard Oil Co. v FTC* (1951) 340 US 231. It also applies to a suit brought against a buyer under §2(f) (15 USC §13(f); see discussion at §5.42) and constitutes a defense to a criminal charge under §3 of the Robinson-Patman Act (15 USC §13a; see discussion at §5.7) of below-cost pricing with a predatory intent.

Recently the Second Circuit, in *Rabiner & Jontow, Inc. v FTC* (2d Cir 1967) 386 F2d 667, 671, *cert den* (1968) 390 US 1004, held that "even though petitioner is under a cease and desist order, it is free to establish its own nondiscriminatory promotional plan and, when necessary, offer certain customers the same amount as a competitor whose allowance it may have to meet [for the reason that] the 'good faith meeting of competition' defense [is] 'implicit in every order issued under authority of the Act, just as if the order set [it] out *in extenso.*'"

The meeting-competition defense also applies to the grant of promotional allowances and services. See *Guides for Advertising Allowances* (1969) 34 Fed Reg 8285; *FTC v Exquisite Form Brassiere, Inc.* (DC Cir 1961) 301 F2d 499, *cert den* (1962) 369 US 888.

To prove the defense, it is essential to have a system of recording information received about competitor's offers. See §§5.10 and 9.61. Some sellers, relying on this defense when submitting a competitive bid, state that on proof of a lower bid they will meet the lower price if it is above a given minimum.

The purpose of the §2(b) proviso was to enable a supplier to protect his competitive position. Although a seller has a "substantial right of self-defense against a price raid by a competitor" (*Standard Oil Co. v FTC, supra,* 249), that protection does not run against a price raid by competitors of the seller's customer. Thus, when a gasoline supplier granted a lower price to a retail dealer to enable the dealer to meet the price cuts granted by a competing gasoline retailer, the Supreme Court held that the §2(b) defense was not available to a supplier to meet competition to the supplier's customers. *FTC v Sun Oil Co.* (1963) 371 US 505.

There may be two caveats to this limitation, however: The §2(b) defense may be available if (a) the customer's competition is in fact partially in competition with the supplier; or (b) the customer's competition receives a reduced price from his supplier, thus calling into play competition between the two suppliers. *Statement of Commission Policy with Respect to Anticompetitive Practices in the Marketing of Gasoline* (June 30, 1967) 3 Trade Reg Rep ¶10,373.

The meeting-competition defense has had little more success than the cost-justification defense discussed in §§5.44-5.48. As with cost justification, "the burden of establishing the §2(b) defense is upon the seller." *Tri-Valley Packing Association v FTC* (9th Cir 1964) 329 F2d 694, 704. The principal impediment to its successful use, however, has been the Commission's consistent effort to limit the defense notwithstanding the Supreme Court's pronouncement two decades ago in the *Standard Oil* case, *supra,* that the defense is absolute.

It was not until December 31, 1963, in *Continental Baking Co.* (1963) [1963–1965 Transfer Binder] FTC Dkt 7630, Trade Reg Rep ¶16,720, that the Commission filed an opinion sustaining the meeting-competition defense of §2(b). The exceptional record in *Continental Baking Co.* strongly supported the defense. It showed that (1) for many years Continental had refused to grant discriminatory discounts notwithstanding the fact that its competitors had done so, (2) Continental had lost substantial business to its competitors because of its refusal to grant discounts, (3) Continental offered discounts only to customers who in fact had been offered an equal or greater price cut by a competitor, (4) Continental used its sales representative to verify the customer's claims, and (5) Continental never lowered its price below that of its competitors. See also *Ponca Wholesale Mercantile Co.* (1964) [1963–1965 Transfer Binder] FTC Dkt 7864, Trade Reg Rep ¶16,814, and *Beatrice Foods Co.* (1965) [1965–1967 Transfer Binder] FTC Dkt 7599, Trade Reg Rep ¶17,311, in which the §2(b) meeting-competition defense was sustained by the Commission. See also *B&W Gas, Inc. v General Gas Corp.* (ND Ga 1965) 247 F Supp 339, in which the §2(b) defense was sustained in a private action.

Most of the difficulty in utilizing this defense has arisen from the restrictions that the Commission placed upon the "good faith" requirement that defendant must establish. The various elements of "good faith" are discussed below.

(2) [§5.50] Establishing Good Faith

The §2(b) (15 USC §13(b)) defense applies only if a seller can show that his price cut was "a good-faith" effort to meet the "equally low price of a competitor." *Standard Oil Co. v FTC* (1951) 340 US 231.

When the Commission first sustained a §2(b) defense (in *Continental Baking Co.* (1963) [1963–1965 Transfer Binder] FTC Dkt 7630, Trade Reg Rep ¶16,720), it stated *per* Commissioner Elman (at 21,646):

[The concept of good faith] is a flexible and pragmatic, not a technical or doctrinaire, concept. The standard of good faith is simply the standard of the prudent businessman responding fairly to what he reasonably believes is a situation of the competitive necessity. . . . Such a standard, whether it be considered "subjective" or "objective," is inherently *ad hoc*. Rigid rules and inflexible absolutes are especially inappropriate in dealing with the 2(b) defense; the facts and circumstances of the particular case, not abstract theories or remote conjectures, should govern its interpretation and application. Thus, the same method of meeting competition may be consistent with an inference of good faith in some circumstances, inconsistent with such an inference in others.

In spite of the *ad hoc* nature of the good-faith concept, the Commission, frequently affirmed by the courts, has consistently sought to limit the defense through the interpretation it gives to the good-faith concept. For example:

1. *Good faith is lacking if the price reduction is used aggressively rather than defensively.* It is frequently said that a seller may meet, not beat, his competition. If the price cut exceeds that of the competitor, good faith has generally been found lacking. See, *e.g., Purolator Products, Inc. v FTC* (7th Cir 1965) 352 F2d 874, 885, *cert den* (1968) 389 US 1045 ("Purolator goes below the prices of its competitors by 4%. Insofar as it does that, Purolator's defense of meeting competition in good faith fails for Purolator has more than met competition."). See also *Atlas Building Products Co. v Diamond Block & Gravel Co.* (10th Cir 1959) 269 F2d 950, 957, *cert den* (1960) 363 US 843; *Surprise Brassiere Co., Inc.* (1966) [1965–1967 Transfer Binder] FTC Dkt 8584, Trade Reg Rep ¶17,566, *aff'd* (5th Cir 1969) 406 F2d 711.

But it is often very difficult, if not impossible, for a seller to ascertain his competitor's prices with any precision or reliability. Thus, several courts have held that to require the seller to prove knowledge of competitor's prices is unrealistic. See, *e.g., Forster Mfg. Co. v FTC* (1st Cir 1964) 335 F2d 47, *cert den* (1965) 380 US 906. See also the vigorous dissent of Commissioner Elman in *Tri-Valley Packing Association* (1966) [1965–1967 Transfer Binder] FTC Dkt 7225, 7496, Trade Reg Rep ¶17,657 at 22,946:

Presumably, a seller could satisfy the Commission that he "used reasonable diligence in verifying the existence of a lower price of a competitor" by showing that he called his competition to ascertain whether the customer was truthfully quoting the competitor's price offer. This would take care of the seller under 2(b). But where would it leave him under the Sherman Act? Proof that two sellers discussed price and that they quoted the same price to a buyer is enough to send them both to jail for illegal price-fixing.

In general the courts require only that the seller make a reasonable effort to identify the individual competitive price in a businesslike manner. The seller is not required to have the "name and quotation" of the competing seller whose price is being met. *Forster Mfg. Co. v FTC, supra.* The Commission, on the other hand, has repeatedly taken the position that if the seller undercuts the competitor's price, the meeting-competition defense is not available. *Anheuser-Busch, Inc.* (1957) 54 FTC 277, 301–302; *National Dairy Products Corp.* (1966) [1965–1967 Transfer Binder] FTC Dkt 7018, Trade Reg Rep ¶17,656, *rev'd* (7th Cir 1968) 395 F2d 517, *cert den* 393 US 977; *Callaway Mills Co.* (1964) [1963–1965 Transfer Binder] Trade Reg Rep ¶16,800, *rev'd* (5th Cir 1966) 362 F2d 435.

Recently the Commission has taken the view that while "a seller claiming the meeting competition defense is not required to prove that its prices were in fact equal to those of its competitors, it must show the existence of facts which would lead a reasonable person to believe that its lower discriminatory price would in fact meet the equally low prices of a competitor." *National Dairy Products Corporation, supra*, at 22,923. For a similar court ruling, see *Forster Mfg. Co. v FTC, supra*.

The courts have regularly taken the position that unintentional undercuts *per se* will not preclude a finding of good faith. See, *e.g., Balian Ice Cream Co. v Arden Farms Co.* (9th Cir 1955) 231 F2d 356, *cert den* (1956) 350 US 991. *Forster Mfg. Co. v FTC, supra*.

The Seventh Circuit, in contrast to the Commission and the Second Circuit, holds that the §2(b) defense is available to a seller who, in an effort to meet competitors' prices, reduces his prices to obtain new customers as well as to retain old customers. See, *e.g., Sunshine Biscuits, Inc. v FTC* (7th Cir 1962) 306 F2d 48, 51–52, *reversing* (1961) 59 FTC 674, 680. Compare *Standard Motor Products, Inc. v FTC* (2d Cir 1959) 265 F2d 674, 677, *cert den* (1959) 361 US 826.

2. *Good faith is lacking if a reasonable man would know the competitor's price was unlawful.* The §2(b) proviso does not permit a seller to escape the sanctions of the Robinson-Patman Act merely because his unlawful practices are employed by his competitors. "[I]f the seller discriminates in price to meet prices that he knows to be illegal or that are of such a nature as are inherently illegal, . . . there is a failure to prove the 'good faith' requirement in §2(b)." *Standard Oil Co. v Brown* (5th Cir 1956) 238 F2d 54, 58. See also *A.E. Staley Mfg. Co. v FTC* (1945) 324 US 746, 753–754.

It should be noted that "it [is] not incumbent upon [the seller] to establish . . . the lawfulness of the prices which it claimed to meet." *Balian Ice Cream Co. v Arden Farms Co., supra*, at 366. The judicial view is that if plaintiff does not seek to rebut defendant's §2(b) defense on the ground that the price met was unlawful, then the competitor's price is presumed lawful. See, *e.g., FTC v Standard Oil Co.* (1958) 355 US 396; *Attorney General's Report, 1955*, 182. If the meeting-competition defense is challenged, the courts require the plaintiff to introduce proof of illegality rather than require "seller [to] carry the burden of proving actual legality." *Standard Oil Co. v Brown, supra; National Dairy Products v FTC* (7th Cir 1968) 395 F2d 517, *cert den* 393 US 977, *reversing National Dairy Products Corporation* (1966) [1965–1967 Transfer Binder] FTC Dkt 7018, Trade Reg Rep ¶17,656.

The Commission, on the other hand, requires the seller to "show that he had reason to believe that the prices he was meeting were lawful or, at least, that he had no reason to believe they were unlawful." *Knoll Associates, Inc.* (1966) [1965-1967 Transfer Binder] FTC Dkt 8549, Trade Reg Rep ¶17,668 at 22,958. See also *Tri-Valley Packing Association* (1965) [1965-1967 Transfer Binder] FTC Dkts 7225, 7496, Trade Reg Rep ¶17,235; *American Oil Co.* (1962) [1961-1963 Transfer Binder] FTC Dkt 8183, Trade Reg Rep ¶15,961.

The requirement that the price met be lawful has been criticized. See, e.g., Austin, *Price Discrimination and Related Problems Under the Robinson-Patman Act* (2d ed 1959) 99; Kaapeki, *Freedom of Pricing and Competition* (1964) 26 ABA Antitrust Section 55-68; Patman, *Complete Guide to the Robinson-Patman Act* (1963) 98.

3. *Good faith is lacking if the price cut is a facet of a general pricing system rather than an ad hoc grant of a lower price to meet a specific competitive situation.* See, e.g., Advisory Opinion Digest 36 (1966) [1965-1967 Transfer Binder] Trade Reg Rep ¶17,509; *Standard Oil Co. v FTC* (1951) 340 US 231. *Standard Motor Products, Inc. v FTC* (2d Cir 1959) 265 F2d 674, 677, *cert den* (1959) 361 US 826.

What is systematic and what is *ad hoc* is sometimes difficult to distinguish. For example, the Commission has argued that area-wide price cuts are systematic and hence the §2(b) defense inapplicable. See, e.g., *Forster Mfg. Co., Inc.* (1963) [1961-1963 Transfer Binder] FTC Dkt 7207, Trade Reg Rep ¶16,243, *rev'd and remanded* (1st Cir 1964) 335 F2d 47, *cert den* (1965) 380 US 906. However, the courts have sustained the §2(b) defense when there had been an area-wide cut. See, e.g., *Balian Ice Cream Co. v Arden Farms Co, supra,* 366-367.

In *Callaway Mills Co. v FTC, supra,* the Commission held unlawful the granting of volume discounts similar to those granted by competitors on the ground that they constituted the adoption of a "formal pricing system." The Fifth Circuit reversed, ruling that "under the facts of this case, Callaway . . . could in 'good faith' attempt to meet the competition by granting similar volume discounts especially since no workable alternative is evident." The court stated that (at 441), "there is nothing wrong per se with *adopting* a 'pricing system' used by competitors. . . . To price each style of its carpeting with specific reference to all the different styles of every competitive line, as suggested by the Commission, would require the [seller] . . . to engage in *exhaustive* cost studies on the multitude of carpets *before they are actually sold and before any discounts are given.* Such a procedure would be burdensome, unreasonable and practically unfeasible."

4. *Good faith is lacking if the seller's goods are not of like grade and quality as the goods of his competitor.* In general, a seller of a superior product cannot rely on the §2(b) defense if he reduces his price to that asked by a seller of an inferior product. See, *e.g., Purolator Products, Inc. v FTC* (7th Cir 1965) 352 F2d 874, *cert den* (1968) 389 US 1045. But see *Callaway Mills Co. v FTC, supra,* at 441, reversing the Commission's holding that it "cannot be determined whether there had been a 'good faith effort' to meet the equally low price of a competing product without clear proof that the petitioner's products were of 'like grade and quality' with that of the competition." The appellate court held that "saleability" was a better standard because "the consuming public . . . cannot easily discern differences in quality between comparable carpeting." "So long as the petitioners conclusively show that their products at various price levels generate public demand (or 'saleability') substantially equivalent to that of competitors' carpeting at the same price levels, considerations of 'grade and quality' become unnecessary and indeed superfluous." Compare *Surprise Brassiere Co. v FTC* (5th Cir 1969) 406 F2d 711, 715, distinguishing the *Callaway* case and affirming the Commission's decision (1967) Trade Reg Rep ¶18,019.

(3) [§5.51] Meeting Competition Checklist

The practitioner should respond affirmatively to the following inquiries before approving a price reduction by his client on the basis of meeting competition.

☐ Has the client documented in writing the competitor's alleged lower price offer as soon as he learned of it? See §§5.10 and 9.61.

☐ Does the documentation or the facts elicited from the client indicate that the competition to be met is the client's competition rather than the client's customer's competition?

☐ Does the documentation or the facts elicited from the client indicate that the competitor's products are of like grade and quality with those of the client, or are generally regarded by the client's customers as being of comparable grade and quality?

☐ Does the documentation or the facts elicited from the client indicate that the competitor's price is probably legal? (*E.g.,* it does not involve a delivered pricing system.)

☐ Does the documentation or the facts elicited from the client indicate reliably the probable level of the competitor's price?

☐ Does the client's proposed price reduction equal but not exceed what is reasonably believed to be the competitor's price offer?

☐ Does the client intend to reduce prices only to customers documented as having received a lower offer from the competitor as contrasted with reducing its prices throughout the area serviced by the competitor?

☐ Does the client intend to offer the reduced price to retain an old customer as contrasted with obtaining new customers? (The Commission and the Second Circuit would require an affirmative answer to this question. The Seventh Circuit would permit the client to offer the reduced price to secure new customers. See §5.50.)

c. [§5.52] Changing Conditions

Section 2(a) of the Clayton Act as amended by the Robinson-Patman Act (15 USC §13(a)), contains the following proviso:

That nothing herein contained shall prevent price changes from time to time where in response to changing conditions affecting the market for or the marketability of the goods concerned, such as but not limited to actual or imminent deterioration of perishable goods, obsolescence of seasonal goods, distress sales under court process, or sales in good faith in discontinuance of business in the goods concerned.

This proviso is "intended to provide for continuance of the normal economically justifiable freedom of action that will permit a seller to dispose of goods on hand where he is threatened with immediate or imminent loss as the result of changing marketing conditions, deterioration or obsolescence of the goods themselves or any other similar circumstance that requires the sudden and immediate movement of goods on hand to avoid losses resulting from conditions beyond his control." Patman, *Complete Guide to the Robinson-Patman Act* (1963) 88-89. See discussion of changing conditions defense in Rowe, *Price Discrimination under the Robinson-Patman Act* (1962) 322-329.

The burden is on the defendant to prove the market fluctuations affecting the market for, or the marketability of, the goods concerned. See *Huber, Inc. v Pillsbury Flour Mills Co.* (D NY 1939) 30 F Supp 108.

This defense has had scant use. In a few cases it has been rejected as inapplicable to the facts presented. See, *e.g., Balian Ice Cream Co. v Arden Farms Co.* (9th Cir 1955) 231 F2d 356, 369, *cert den* (1956) 350 US 991; *Fruitvale Canning Co.* (1956) 52 FTC 1504, 1515.

In *Valley Plymouth v Studebaker-Packard Corp.* (SD Calif 1963) 219 F Supp 608, 611-613, the district court dismissed on the basis of the changing conditions proviso a private treble-damage action by a dealer who bought his cars at a higher price than a competitor who purchased similar cars six months later as the new models were coming out. For a similar holding, see *Peter Satori of California, Inc. v Studebaker-Packard Corp.* (SD Calif 1964) 1964 Trade Cases ¶71,309.

The Commission seems to have taken a harder line than the courts in interpreting the changing-conditions defense in dealing with obsolescence due to model changes. In *Joseph A. Kaplan & Sons, Inc.* (1963) [1963-1965 Transfer Binder] FTC Dkt 7813, Trade Reg Rep ¶16,666 at 21,551, *aff'd* (DC Cir 1965) 347 F2d 785, the Commission held that a markdown of shower curtains on the ground that they were a "slow-moving" item would not constitute the changing-conditions defense which, said the Commission, required "pronounced and serious deterioration or alteration in the market conditions." The circuit court expressly stated that it did not rule on the Commission's interpretation of the changing-conditions defense. See also *D & N Auto Parts Co.* (1959) 55 FTC 1279, 1301 (price reduction in effect too long to constitute a reduction in response to changing conditions).

B. [§5.53] Criminal Litigation

Criminal sanctions are attached to Section 3 of the Robinson-Patman Act (15 USC §13a), which declares:

It shall be unlawful for any person engaged in commerce, in the course of such commerce, [1] to be a party to, or assist in, any transaction of sale, or contract to sell, which discriminates to his knowledge against competitors of the purchaser, in that any discount, rebate, allowance, or advertising service charge is granted to the purchaser over and above any discount, rebate, allowance, or advertising service charge available at the time of such transaction to said competitors in respect of a sale of goods of like grade, quality, and quantity; [2] to sell, or contract to sell, goods in any part of the United States at prices lower than those exacted by said person elsewhere in the United States for the purpose of destroying competition, or eliminating a competitor in such part of the United States; or, [3] to sell, or contract to sell, goods *at unreasonably low prices* for the purpose of destroying competition or eliminating a competitor. (Emphasis added.)

The Supreme Court defined the scope of Section 3 in *Nashville Milk Co. v Carnation Co.* (1958) 355 US 373, 377:

It prohibits three kinds of trade practices, (a) general price discriminations, (b) geographical price discriminations, and (c) selling "at unreasonably low prices for the purpose of destroying competition or eliminating a competitor."

The first prohibition is directed at "secret rebates which the seller knows are not made available to competitors of the recipient on goods of the same quality and same *quantity." Antitrust Developments 1955-1968*, 155.

The second prohibition covers "territorial price discrimination for the predatory purpose of destroying competition or eliminating a competitor." Id. It is quite similar to the civil price-discrimination cases charging

319

injury to competition at the seller's level by means of geographic price cuts. See, *e.g.*, *Moore v Mead's Fine Bread Co.* (1951) 348 US 115, 118-119. See Discussion at §5.39.

The third prohibition is directed at "unreasonably low prices," *i.e.*, generally most below-cost price cuts. See, *e.g.*, *Balian Ice Cream Co. v Arden Farms Co.* (SD Calif 1951) 104 F Supp 796, 807, *aff'd* (9th Cir 1955) 231 F2d 356, *cert den* (1956) 350 US 991. In 1963 the Supreme Court held the third clause constitutional as applied to sales made below cost with a predatory intent, without deciding whether the cost reference was to direct or fully distributed costs or some other cost level. See *United States v National Dairy Products Corp.* (1963) 372 US 29, 33.

The Supreme Court has recognized a number of potential defenses under the phrases of "acceptable business exigency," "legitimate commercial objective," or "justifying business reason." See *United States v National Dairy Products Corp., supra.* That opinion made clear that the statutory defenses of cost justification, meeting competition, as well as liquidation of excess, obsolete, or perishable merchandise under changing market conditions are all recognized. Whether other defenses might be judicially cognizable under the "legitimate commercial objective" standard posed by the Court has not yet been determined.

As noted in §5.4, violations of Section 3 may result in a fine of not more than $5,000 or imprisonment of not more than one year, or both. Corporate entities, as well as individuals, are subject to its prohibitions.

Its enforcement, unlike the other sections of the Robinson-Patman Act, is vested exclusively in the government. A private party has no right to bring an action for damages or for injunctive relief under Section 3. *Nashville Milk Co. v Carnation Co., supra.*

6

The Federal Trade Commission and the Federal Trade Commission Act

Richard B. Hoegh, Richard N. Ellner and V. Shannon Clyne

Mr. Hoegh received the BAS degree from the University of California at Berkeley in 1944 and the JD degree from Harvard Law School in 1949. He is a member of the Los Angeles County Bar Association, the State Bar of California, and the Los Angeles firm of Hahn, Cazier, Thornton, Hoegh & Leff. Mr. Ellner received the AB degree from Harvard University in 1951 and the JD degree from Harvard Law School in 1954. He is a member of the Los Angeles County and American Bar Associations, the State Bar of California, and the Los Angeles firm of Hahn, Cazier, Thornton, Hoegh & Leff. Mr. Clyne received the BA degree from Stanford University in 1965 and the LLB degree from Stanford University Law School in 1968. Mr. Clyne is a member of the Los Angeles County and American Bar Associations, the State Bar of California, and with the Los Angeles firm of Hahn, Cazier, Thornton, Hoegh & Leff.

I. Introduction

II. Substantive Law Enforced by the Federal Trade Commission

I. Introduction

A. [§6.1] Brief Description of the Federal Trade Commission

The Federal Trade Commission was established by the Federal Trade Commission Act enacted by Congress in 1914. It is composed of a chairman who serves at the pleasure of the President and four commissioners, all of whom are appointed by the President and confirmed by the Senate for staggered seven-year terms. On January 13, 1970, the Senate confirmed Caspar W. Weinberger's appointment to the Commission to fill an existing vacancy and designated him as chairman, and on July 1, 1970, Mr. Weinberger resigned as chairman of the Commission to become deputy director of the newly created Office of Management and Budget. On September 15, 1970, Miles W. Kirkpatrick was sworn in to complete Mr. Weinberger's term.

In 1969 the Commission's budget was $16,900,000.00. It employed 1,154 persons—about 400 were lawyers, and about 200 were economists and other professionals. The Commission exercises enforcement or administrative responsibilities under the Federal Trade Commission Act, 15 USC §45; the Clayton Act, 15 USC §12, as amended by the Robinson-Patman Price Discrimination Act, 49 Stat 1526; the Webb-Pomerene Export Trade Act, 15 USC §§61-65; the Packers and Stockyards Act of 1921, 7 USC §181; the Wool Products Labeling Act of 1939, 15 USC §68; the Lanham Trade-Mark Act of 1946, 15 USC §1051; the Fur Products Labeling Act, 15 USC §69; the Flammable Fabrics Act, 15 USC §1191; the Textile Fiber Products Identification Act, 15 USC §70; and the Fair Packaging and Labeling Act, PL 89-755, 89th Cong., among others.

On June 8, 1970, Chairman Weinberger announced a major reorganization plan for the Federal Trade Commission. Effective July 1, 1970, its operating bureaus were cut from five to two: the Bureau of Consumer Protection and the Bureau of Competition. Four new positions were created: economic advisor, office of congressional relations, deputy executive director of operations, and deputy executive director for management. The new organizational chart appears at page 324.

The Commission has broad power to investigate business practices and to require the submission of reports concerning business practices, to issue guidelines for business conduct, to regulate industry practices through settlement and compliance procedures or cease-and-desist orders with respect to violations of the Federal Trade Commission Act and the Clayton Act, and to prepare studies and reports to the President and Congress to point out need for new legislation.

Under Section 11 of the Clayton Act (15 USC §21), the Federal Trade Commission has concurrent jurisdiction with the Department of Justice to enforce Sections 2 (15 USC §13) (price discrimination), 3 (15 USC §14) (sales on condition that competitor's products are not sold), 7 (15 USC §18) (mergers), and 8 (15 USC §19) (interlocking directorates) of the

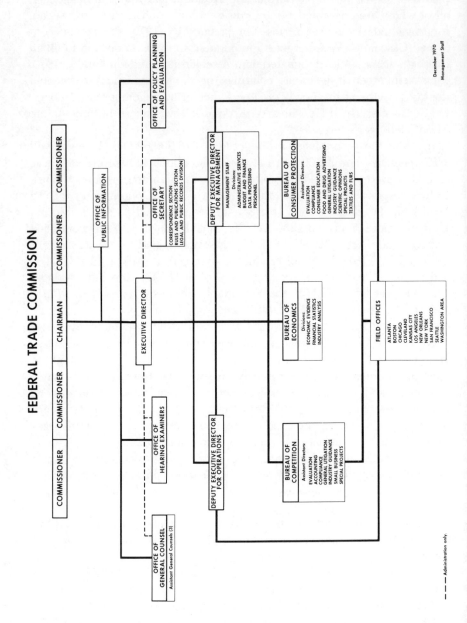

FEDERAL TRADE COMMISSION

December 1970
Management Staff

COMMISSIONER — COMMISSIONER — CHAIRMAN — COMMISSIONER — COMMISSIONER

OFFICE OF POLICY PLANNING AND EVALUATION

OFFICE OF PUBLIC INFORMATION

EXECUTIVE DIRECTOR

OFFICE OF SECRETARY
CORRESPONDENCE SECTION
RULES AND PUBLICATIONS SECTION
LEGAL AND PUBLIC RECORDS DIVISION

OFFICE OF HEARING EXAMINERS

OFFICE OF GENERAL COUNSEL
Assistant General Counsels (3)

DEPUTY EXECUTIVE DIRECTOR FOR MANAGEMENT
MANAGEMENT STAFF
Divisions:
ADMINISTRATIVE SERVICES
BUDGET AND FINANCE
DATA PROCESSING
PERSONNEL

DEPUTY EXECUTIVE DIRECTOR FOR OPERATIONS

BUREAU OF COMPETITION
Assistant Directors:
EVALUATION
ACCOUNTING
COMPLIANCE
GENERAL LITIGATION
INDUSTRY GUIDANCE
SMALL BUSINESS
SPECIAL PROJECTS

BUREAU OF ECONOMICS
Assistant Directors:
ECONOMIC EVIDENCE
FINANCIAL STATISTICS
INDUSTRY ANALYSIS

BUREAU OF CONSUMER PROTECTION
Assistant Directors:
EVALUATION
COMPLIANCE
CONSUMER EDUCATION
FOOD AND DRUG ADVERTISING
GENERAL LITIGATION
INDUSTRY GUIDANCE
SCIENTIFIC OPINIONS
SPECIAL PROJECTS
TEXTILES AND FURS

FIELD OFFICES
ATLANTA
BOSTON
CHICAGO
CLEVELAND
KANSAS CITY
LOS ANGELES
NEW ORLEANS
NEW YORK
SAN FRANCISCO
SEATTLE
WASHINGTON AREA

— — — Administration only.

Clayton Act. As a general rule, however, the Department of Justice has been active only in Section 7 (merger) cases, leaving the Commission pretty much alone in the rest of the Clayton Act area. Even with respect to mergers, the Justice Department has not been active in those areas where the Commission has traditionally operated, like the cement industry. On the other hand, the Commission has not instituted proceedings with respect to mergers in those industries, like the banking industry, on which the Department has built up an expertise.

The two agencies maintain close liaison. Prior to the institution of an investigation or litigation, the interested agency usually checks with the other to avoid wasteful overlapping of effort.

Large and small businesses alike are affected by the workings of the Federal Trade Commission. In recent years the Commission has attacked large concerns if it has found potentially detrimental use of dominant economic power. On the other hand, the Commission brings a very large proportion of its actions against smaller companies. There are a number of reasons for this seemingly disproportionately large volume of activity with respect to small companies, including a feeling that such suits are easier and less expensive to win. But perhaps more important is the fact that practically the sole source of information for the commencement of investigations is the informal complaint filed by other businesses. Small companies, far more than large companies, file informal complaints with the Commission.

A cease-and-desist order issued against a firm, regardless of its size, may result in considerable expense and inconvenience. Their restriction may last forever, and violation of their terms can result in a penalty of $5,000 per day of violation. In addition there is a growing body of case law interpreting Section 5(a) of the Clayton Act, 15 USC §16(a), which allows findings in government antitrust suits to be used by private litigants as prima facie evidence of antitrust violations in civil treble-damage suits concerning the same conduct, to allow the Commission's Decision and Order entered in cases brought under the Clayton Act to be used as prima facie evidence in private suits. See *Farmington Dowel Products Co. v Forster Mfg. Co.* (1st Cir 1969) 421 F2d 61; *Purex Corp. v The Procter & Gamble Co.* (CD Calif 1970) 308 F Supp 584; *Carpenter v Central Arkansas Milk Producers Ass'n., Inc.* (WD Ark 1966) 1966 Trade Cases ¶71,817 and discussion at §6.11. Thus a cease-and-desist order issued in Commission proceedings under the Clayton Act may expose the unsuccessful respondent to further liability under the treble-damage provision of the Clayton Act.

B. [§6.2] Brief History of the Federal Trade Commission Act

By the end of the first decade of this century, the menacing pace of American industrial and commercial concentration which had inspired passage of the Sherman Act, then more than twenty years old, again drew the attention and concern of economists and political commentators. The Sherman Act had been followed by considerable legislation on the state level (see *Laws on Trusts and Monopolies* compiled under the direction of the clerk of the House Committee on the Judiciary, Sixty-Third Congress, by Nathan B. Williams, revised January 10, 1914) and by many official investigations. (Between 1906 and 1913 the Federal Bureau of Corporations, an agency replaced by the Federal Trade Commission, turned its investigatory spotlight on the petroleum industry, the steel industry, the tobacco industry, and the farm machinery industry. See, *e.g., Report of Bureau of Corporations on the International Harvester Co.*, March 3, 1913.)

When, in 1911, Mr. Justice White, writing for the majority of the Supreme Court, announced its acceptance of the "rule of reason" in *Standard Oil Co. of New Jersey v United States* (1911) 221 US 1, congressional reaction was immediate and angry. The *Standard Oil* case in effect accepted the dissenting view of Mr. Justice White in *United States v Trans-Missouri Freight Ass'n.* (1897) 166 US 290, 354, as follows:

. . . it seems to me . . . impossible to construe the words "every restraint of trade" used in the [Sherman] act in any other sense than as excluding reasonable contracts, . . . such contracts were not considered to be . . . in restraint of trade, . . . in England [or] in this country at the time the act was adopted.

The day after the rule of reason was announced, Senator Newlands, an advocate of strong antitrust enforcement, stated on the Senate floor (47 Cong. Rec. 1225 (1911)):

The question therefore presents itself to us whether we are to permit in the future the administration regarding these great combinations to drift practically into the hands of the courts and subject the question as to the reasonableness or unreasonableness of any restraint upon trade . . . to the varying judgments of different courts upon the facts and the law, or whether we will organize, as the servant of Congress, an administrative tribunal similar to the Interstate Commerce Commission, with powers of recommendation, with powers of correction similar to those enjoyed by the Interstate Commerce Commission over interstate transportation.

Over the next three years public demand for legislation grew, and in 1914 the Clayton Act was passed to make more precise prohibitions against price discrimination, tie-in sales, stock acquisitions, and interlocking directorates feared no longer prohibited by a Sherman Act interpreted by the rule of reason. At the same time, the Federal Trade Commission Act was passed to prohibit "unfair methods of competition," a novel and general phrase that would require prospective interpretation, to plug the loopholes that inevitably appear when legislation, in this case the Clayton Act, is made quite specific. Also the Federal Trade Commission was created to implement concurrently with the Justice Department the newly enacted Clayton Act and exclusively the Federal Trade Commission Act.

II. Substantive Law Enforced by the Federal Trade Commission

A. "Unfair Methods of Competition" prohibited by Section 5 of the Federal Trade Commission Act

1. [§6.3] Early Development of "Unfair Methods of Competition"

Although the antitrust statutes have changed rather little over the years, the politico-economic setting has become more complex and the judiciary's approach more sophisticated. This is particularly true of Section 5 of the Federal Trade Commission Act (15 USC §45), which has developed into a substantive provision of great breadth. In this area it is particularly important not only to look for the cases that have been overruled but to note the fundamental change in judicial outlook. Such change renders obsolete many cases never officially overruled.

For example, in *FTC v Gratz* (1920) 253 US 421, 427, the first Section 5 case to reach the Supreme Court, the Commission was rebuffed:

The words "unfair method of competition" are not defined by the statute and their exact meaning is in dispute. It is for the courts, not the commission, ultimately to determine as matter of law what they include. They are clearly inapplicable to practices never heretofore regarded as opposed to good morals because characterized by deception, bad faith, fraud or oppression, or as against public policy because of their dangerous tendency unduly to hinder competition or create monopoly.

In short, the *Gratz* opinion held that the courts, not the Federal Trade Commission, would establish what methods of competitions are "unfair" and that practices considered lawful before the act's passage would continue to be lawful.

The *Gratz* case, although in disuse for many years, was not overruled until 1966 in *FTC v Brown Shoe Co.* (1966) 384 US 316, an opinion that

327

expressly recognized Mr. Justice Brandeis' dissenting view in the *Gratz* case as the correct interpretation of congressional intent.

Section 5(c) of the Federal Trade Commission Act expressly provides for review by a court of appeals of a Commission order to cease and desist and specifically states that the FTC's findings "as to the facts, if supported by evidence, shall be conclusive." Thus, conclusions of law are reviewable. But the question remained whether the determination that a given method of competition is unfair was a question of fact or of law. The majority in the *Gratz* case frustrated congressional design by making it strictly a matter of law within the exclusive competence of the judiciary. Subsequent cases, culminating with *Brown Shoe* have come around to the view that the Commission, not the judiciary, was intended by Congress to be the principal interpreter of "unfair methods of competition."

The Supreme Court early acknowledged that finding an "unfair method of competition" in violation of Section 5 of the Federal Trade Commission Act did not depend on finding violations of other antitrust laws. In *FTC v Beech-Nut Packing Co.* (1922) 257 US 441, the Commission attacked as an unfair method of competition a scheme for resale price fixing which the Court believed "goes far beyond" what would be held legal under the Sherman Act. 257 US at 454. Although price fixing is illegal under the Sherman Act if an agreement can be found, this scheme involved merely a "cooperative" effort of reporting and listing price-cutters, and the Commission and the respondent had stipulated that there was no contractual agreement. The Court found an implied agreement and illegality under Section 5 of the Federal Trade Commission Act, stating (at 453):

The Sherman Act is not involved here except insofar as it shows a declaration of public policy to be considered in determining what are unfair methods of competition, which the Federal Trade Commission is empowered to condemn and suppress. What shall constitute unfair methods of competition denounced by the act, is left without specific definition.

The Court recognized not only that "unfair methods of competition" encompass Sherman Act violations but also that Section 5 extends beyond the Sherman Act violations. *FTC v Cement Institute* (1948) 333 US 683, 721 n. 19.

Similarly, in *FTC v Curtis Publishing Co.* (1923) 260 US 568 and *FTC v Sinclair Refining Co.* (1923) 261 US 463, although finding no violations, the Court indicated that "unfair methods of competition" prohibited by Section 5 of the Federal Trade Commission Act encompassed Clayton

Act violations such as tie-ins, exclusive dealing arrangements, and other restrictions affecting the distribution of goods. In *Fashion Originators' Guild v FTC* (1941) 312 US 457 the Court went further and indicated that an exclusive-dealing arrangement might violate Section 5 of the Federal Trade Commission Act as an "unfair method of competition" even though it did not have the anticompetitive effects required to violate the Clayton Act.

It is now clear that the Commission may proceed under Section 5 of the Federal Trade Commission Act against methods that would violate either the Clayton Act or the Sherman Act, or it may utilize that same section to nip in the bud unfair methods of competition in their incipiency which, if not prevented, might become Clayton or Sherman Act violations when fully grown. The so-called "incipiency doctrine" was explained in *FTC v Motion Picture Advertising Service Co.* (1953) 344 US 392 at 394:

> The "unfair methods of competition," which are condemned by § 5(a) of the Act, are not confined to those that were illegal at common law or that were condemned by the Sherman Act. . . . Congress advisedly left the concept flexible to be defined with particularity by the myriad of cases from the field of business. . . . It is also clear that the Federal Trade Commission Act was designed to supplement and bolster the Sherman Act and the Clayton Act . . . to stop in their incipiency acts and practices which, when full blown, would violate those Acts . . . , as well as to condemn as "unfair methods of competition" existing violations of them.

2. [§6.4] What are Unfair Methods of Competition?

Congress enacted the "unfair methods of competition" provision in Section 5 of the Federal Trade Commission Act (15 USC § 45) as a broad and flexible standard to cope with changing conditions. New theories to support the use of that section are being employed by the Commission and, to an extent the majority in *FTC v Gratz* (1920) 253 US 421 would never have comprehended, are being supported by the judiciary.

The critical question for the attorney in this area is one of prediction: How do we know what practices, never before held to be illegal, will be attacked by the Commission under this broad provision? Although concrete standards are not built into the statute, there are several guidelines in the cases.

The broadest guideline is that an unfair method of competition in violation of Section 5 of the Federal Trade Commission Act is established by proof of conduct that "runs counter to the public policy declared in the Sherman and Clayton Acts . . ." *Fashion Originators' Guild v FTC* (1941) 312 US 457, 463. See discussion of development of this theory at

§6.3. Hence violations of the Sherman Act and the Clayton Act are also violations of Section 5 of the Federal Trade Commission Act even though the Commission is not vested with jurisdiction to enforce Sherman Act violations.

Since the conduct need only "run counter" to the "antitrust policies," the conduct need not actually violate the antitrust laws that announce that policy. Thus, aside from actual Sherman and Clayton Act violations, one can formulate three further guidelines to three additional areas of potential danger. First, there are practices that would violate the Sherman Act or the Clayton Act but for some restrictive provision in those acts; second, there are practices that are considered close analogues of Sherman or Clayton Act violations because their effects are the same as the practices specifically outlawed by those enactments; and third, there are practices that appear reasonably to be developing toward a restraint of trade: so-called "incipient violations."

Illustrative of the first category of cases, those that would be violations of some specific provision of the Clayton Act or Sherman Act but for some missing statutory prerequisite, stands *Beatrice Foods Co.* (1965) [1965-1967 Transfer Binder] FTC Dkt 6653, Trade Reg Rep ¶17,244, which held that Section 5 of the Federal Trade Commission Act required sole proprietorships and partnerships to meet the same standards governing mergers as Section 7 of the Clayton Act (15 USC §18) establishes for corporations. The Commission stated (at 22,335):

It is well established that Section 5 reaches transactions which violate the standards of the Clayton Act though for technical reasons are not subject to that Act, unless such application of Section 5 would be an attempt to "supply what Congress has studiously omitted" . . . or to "circumvent the essential criteria of illegality prescribed by the express prohibitions of the Clayton Act. . . . "[a]pplying Section 5 to noncorporate acquisitions effectuates, rather than circumvents or conflicts with, Congress' policy with respect to the prevention of anticompetitive acquisitions.

Similarly, in *Grand Union Co. v FTC* (2d Cir 1962) 300 F2d 92, in which it was charged that Grand Union induced discriminatory allowances from its supplier, defendant argued that such conduct was not prohibited by Section 2(d) of the Clayton Act as amended by the Robinson-Patman Act, 15 USC §13(d), which forbids suppliers to grant discriminatory allowances. The Commission held that Grand Union had violated the policy of the Robinson-Patman Act. The court affirmed the Commission's holding that inducing a discriminatory allowance constituted an "unfair method of competition" under Section 5 of the Federal Trade Commission Act and further that the omission of a specific provision outlawing the inducement was merely a legislative oversight. To the same effect see *Giant Food Inc. v FTC* (DC Cir 1962) 307 F2d 184, *cert den* (1963) 372 US 910.

Also, while Section 3 of the Clayton Act (15 USC §14) is limited to prohibiting exclusive dealing in "goods and commodities," Section 5 of the Federal Trade Commission Act can be used to stop exclusive dealing in services or real estate. Although the prohibition of Section 7 of the Clayton Act does not apply to mergers unless both companies are engaged in commerce, Section 5 of the Federal Trade Commission Act can be used to block a merger of two companies, one of which is not engaged in commerce. See discussion of the Federal Trade Commission Act and mergers at §§4.22 and 6.13.

In short, the Commission utilizes Section 5 of the Federal Trade Commission Act to stop practices that violate the spirit of the antitrust enactment in question. The courts have regularly permitted the Federal Trade Commission to proceed under the "unfair method of competition" provision of Section 5 when the practice is technically outside the more precise prohibition of another enactment.

Atlantic Refining Co. v FTC (1965) 381 US 357 exemplifies the second category of cases, those involving practices that are held to violate the unfair method of competition provision because they have the same or similar effects as practices expressly prohibited by the Sherman Act or the Clayton Act. Atlantic pushed the sale of Goodyear tires, batteries, and accessories (TBA) to its franchised service stations, and the dealers feared that their refusal to concentrate on that line would cause them to lose their franchises with Atlantic. This practice, not being a sale on condition that the buyer purchase an unwanted item from the seller, could not qualify as a tie-in specifically prohibited by Section 3 of the Clayton Act. See discussion of tie-in sales at §§3.9–3.18. The Court found that Atlantic utilized its dominant economic power in one market to coerce dealers in another market and concluded that, because the effect of the arrangement, to force a line of unwanted products on dealers, was the same as a tying arrangement, it constituted an unfair method of competition.

Atlantic Refining laid the groundwork for *FTC v Brown Shoe Co.* (1966) 384 US 316 the following year, which exemplifies the third and most controversial category of cases, those in which anticompetitive dangers are predicted. The Brown Shoe Company, which the Court characterized as "one of the world's largest manufacturers of shoes," offered attractive extra benefits in the form of bookkeeping aids, merchandising advice, discounts on rubber footwear, group insurance plan, and other assistance to those of its 650 retailers who would agree to "concentrate" their efforts in the sale of Brown Shoe products and further agree not to handle competitors' full lines, although the retailers could and did handle competitors' products. The agreement did not violate Section 3 of the Clayton Act as a tying arrangement because it was not a sale on condition that the buyer purchase an unwanted item from the seller. Nor did it constitute an unlawful exclusive-dealing arrangement because it was not a sale on condition that the buyer refrain from handling competitors' products. (For discussion of these practices, see §§3.2–3.8 and §§3.9–3.18.) The Commission attacked the practice and succeeded, after reversal at the circuit court level, in the Supreme Court. The Supreme Court, in a short, unanimous opinion, not only found it unnecessary to characterize the practice as a tying arrangement or exclusive dealing contract but upheld the Commission's determination without requiring a showing of anticompetitive effects, the *sine qua non* of the analogous Clayton Act violations, stating (384 US at 322):

[T]he Commission has the power under §5 to arrest trade restraints in their incipiency without proof that they amount to an outright violation of §3 of the Clayton Act or other provisions of the antitrust laws.

In *FTC v Texaco Inc.* (1968) 393 US 223 it appeared that Texaco encouraged its dealers to sell Goodrich tires, batteries, and accessories, but, unlike *Atlantic Refining, supra,* the record was totally devoid of any evidence of coercion. The Court found an unfair method of competition on the ground that "[t]he sales-commission system for marketing TBA is inherently coercive." 393 US at 229. See also *FTC v Motion Picture Advertising Service Co.* (1953) 344 US 392 at 394–395.

The analysis illustrated in *Brown Shoe Company* and *Texaco* resembles the *per se* approach in that it invalidates the challenged practice without extensive economic analysis to ascertain the effect on competition.

Sanctioning the Commission's use of a presumption of illegality with respect to conduct challenged as an "unfair method of competition" is significant for two reasons: (1) the presumption may invalidate activities merely predicted to have anticompetitive effect when full blown, thus getting close to an incipient, incipient violation, and (2) the presumption may result in an FTC finding of illegality that might be used in subsequent private litigation. See discussion at §6.11.

B. Unfair or Deceptive Acts or Practices

1. [§6.5] Early Development of Concept of Deceptive Practices

Under the act as it originally stood in 1914, only unfair methods of competition in commerce were held to be illegal. In 1931 the Supreme

Court held in *FTC v Raladam Co.* (1931) 283 US 643 that injury to present or potential competitors was essential to support jurisdiction under Section 5 of the Federal Trade Commission Act (15 USC § 45). Injury to consumers alone was held to be an insufficient basis for Commission action.

In 1937 Congress began to move in earnest on a bill to amend Section 5. HR Rep. No. 1613, 75th Cong. (1937), concerning Senate Bill 1077, stated:

> The words "unfair methods of competition" in Section 5 have been construed by the Supreme Court as leaving the Commission without jurisdiction to issue cease and desist orders where the Commission has failed to establish the existence of competition. In other words, the act is construed as if its purposes were to protect competitors only and to afford no protection to the consumer without showing injury to a competitor. . . .
>
> By the proposed amendment to Section 5, the Commission can prevent such acts or practices which injuriously affect the general public as well as those which are unfair to competitors. In other words, this amendment makes the consumer, who may be injured by an unfair trade practice, of equal concern, before the law, with the merchant or manufacturer injured by the unfair methods of a dishonest competitor.

The Wheeler-Lea Amendment, enacted into law in 1938, makes Section 5 of the Federal Trade Commission Act apply to "unfair or deceptive acts or practices" in addition to "unfair methods of competition" previously condemned under the act. By thus extending the law to cover (a) practices injurious to the public without regard to the existence of competitive injury and (b) individual or occasional acts as well as established methods or practices, Congress sought to give the consumer direct protection against unfair practices.

2. [§6.6] What are Deceptive Practices?

The phrase "acts or practices" is deliberately broad. Any business activity is included within the prohibition if it tends to create a deceptive impression on the public in general or a given customer.

Most industries come within the reach of the Federal Trade Commission Act's prohibition against deceptive acts or practices. There are a few statutory exceptions:

1. Section 5(a)(6) (15 USC § 45(a)(6)) of the act exempts banks, common carriers subject to ICC or CAB regulation, meat packers, and poultry dealers (to a qualified degree);

2. Insurance companies are covered only to the extent that they are not regulated by state law. (See Insurance Antitrust Moratorium Act of 1945, 15 USC §§1011-1015.)

333

Since persons, partnerships, and corporations are all within the Federal Trade Commission's jurisdiction under Section 5(a)(6) of the Federal Trade Commission Act, the form of business organization is irrelevant. Also, both products and services are covered.

Actual deception is not a required element of proof. It is sufficient if the act, practice, or representation has the capacity or tendency to deceive (*FTC v Algoma Lumber Co.* (1934) 291 US 67, 81; *Portwood v FTC* (10th Cir 1969) 418 F2d 419 (capacity to deceive revealed by exhibits); *Pep Boys—Manny, Moe & Jack, Inc. v FTC* (3d Cir 1941) 122 F2d 158, 161) or that there is a "fair probability" that the ultimate consumer would be deceived. (*Herzfeld v FTC* (2d Cir 1944) 140 F2d 207, 208). See also *FTC v Winsted Hosiery Co.* (1922) 258 US 483, 494. The Commission is free to construe an ambiguous statement in the most unfavorable light. Thus, in *Murray Space Shoe Corporation v FTC* (2d Cir 1962) 304 F2d 270, 272, the court held that "statements susceptible of both a misleading and a truthful interpretation will be construed against the advertiser." Further, the Commission can infer within the bounds of reason that deception once found will constitute a material factor in the purchaser's decision to buy. *FTC v Colgate-Palmolive Co.* (1965) 380 US 374.

The determination that a representation is deceptive is a question of fact that the Commission is empowered to make. It is not required to obtain consumer testimony or conduct a survey of the public before it rules that the representation is misleading. *FTC v Colgate-Palmolive Co., supra.* The fact that the respondent has complied with postal or state labeling requirements does not prevent the Commission from finding deception. By and large the Commission considers the effect on the "ordinary" purchaser, the "public" or the "average" man. The courts have pointed out that this may include the gullible, the unsophisticated, and the ignorant. In *Aronberg v FTC* (7th Cir 1942) 132 F2d 165, 167, the court stated:

The law is not made for experts but to protect the public, —that vast multitude which includes the ignorant, the unthinking and the credulous, who, in making purchases, do not stop to analyze but too often are governed by appearances and general impressions.

The Commission will consider the effect of the entire representation, advertisement, or label as well as the effect of individual words. Omissions may be as important as statements on labels. In fashioning a remedy the Commission may not only prohibit deception but is also empowered to require affirmative disclosures. It can even order the dropping of a trade or corporate name that carries a false implication. *Herzfeld v FTC, supra; Deer v FTC* (2d Cir 1945) 152 F2d 65.

It is important to bear in mind, therefore, that representations should be examined with a view to ensuring that they are true under all the circumstances unless suitable qualifications accompany the representations. Material facts must be disclosed. Placing qualifications or explanations in small print or inconspicuous locations may not be sufficient to counteract the misleading effect of other contents of the label or representation.

Labels especially should be carefully examined. In *Korber Hats, Inc. v FTC* (1st Cir 1962) 311 F2d 358, 361 the court pointed out:

While advertising and labelling are frequently considered together, there is good reason to insist upon a higher degree of veracity in the latter. It may well be argued that consumers accept labelling statements literally while perhaps viewing with a more jaundiced eye the vaunted claims of the advertising media.

FTC v Colgate-Palmolive Co., supra, at 387–390, is informative. In holding that mock-up demonstrations could not be used as proof of a product's effectiveness unless the fact of the simulation is revealed to the viewing audience, the court provided a brief resume of a number of practices held in prior cases to be deceptive. According to the court:

☐ It is "a deceptive practice to state falsely that a product ordinarily sells for an inflated price but that it is being offered at a special reduced price, even if the offered price represents the actual value of the product and the purchaser is receiving his money's worth."

☐ It is a deceptive practice "for a seller to misrepresent to the public that he is in a certain line of business, even though the misstatement in no way affects the qualities of the product. . . . 'If consumers or dealers prefer to purchase a given article because it was made by a particular manufacturer or class of manufacturers, they have a right to do so, and this right cannot be satisfied by imposing upon them an exactly similar article, or one equally as good, but having a different origin.' "

☐ It is a deceptive practice to fail to disclose that products are re-processed, even though the re-processed products are as good as new.

☐ "[I]t is a deceptive practice to misappropriate the trade name of another."

☐ It is a deceptive practice "to state falsely that a product has received a testimonial from a respected source."

☐ It is a deceptive practice to state falsely "that their product claims have been certified."

3. [§6.7] Assessment of the Commission's Prevention of Deceptive Practices

Recently the Commission has been severely criticized for failing to utilize the deceptive practice prohibition to stop deceptive schemes practiced against "the poor, uneducated and elderly, particularly in the urban ghettos." *Report of the ABA Commission to Study the Federal Trade Commission* (Sept. 15, 1969) 37 (hereafter referred to as the "ABA Commission Report"). See also Cox, Fellmeth, and Schultz, *The Consumer and the Federal Trade Commission* (1969), generally referred to as the "Nader Report."

The Commission's most substantial program in the area of consumer protections has been its efforts to prevent deception in labeling. However, this program also has been criticized on the grounds that "the FTC has tended to select relatively trivial practices for staunch enforcement measures" issuing "complaints attacking the failure to disclose on labels that 'navy shoes' were not made by the Navy, that flies were imported, that Indian trinkets were not manufactured by American Indians, and that 'Havana' cigars were not made entirely of Cuban tobacco." *ABA Commission Report*, 39.

Whether the Commission's deceptive practices enforcement program taken as a whole consists, as it has been described, of a "preponderance of trivia," the inconvenience, expense, and exasperation to one's clients who are affected is in no way lessened. Hence it is well for the practitioner to be aware of the activities that attract Commission action in this area. One might keep in mind that in 1969 the Commission issued 65 complaints against alleged deceptive practices, entered 68 cease-and-desist orders against such practices, and took 174 assurances of voluntary compliance to stop such practices. *ABA Commission Report*, 20 and 22.

C. [§6.8] The Federal Trade Commission's Power to Enforce Provisions of the Clayton Act

As already noted, the Federal Trade Commission has exclusive authority to enforce Section 5 of the Federal Trade Commission Act (15 USC §45), and the Justice Department has exclusive authority (along with private plaintiffs) to enforce the Sherman Act. However, the Commission may indirectly enforce the provisions of the Sherman Act as such violations have been held to constitute "unfair methods of competition" under Section 5 of the Federal Trade Commission Act. See §§6.3–6.4.

Section 11 of the Clayton Act (15 USC §21) gives the Commission concurrent authority with the Justice Department and private plaintiffs to enforce Sections 2, 3, 7, and 8 of the Clayton Act, 15 USC §§13, 14, 18,

19, which prohibit, respectively, price discrimination, exclusive dealing, mergers, and interlocking directorates. Price discrimination, prohibited by Section 2 of the Clayton Act as amended by the Robinson-Patman Act, is discussed in §§5.6–5.26. Exclusive dealing, prohibited by Section 3 of the Clayton Act, is discussed in §§3.2–3.8. Mergers regulated by Section 7 of the Clayton Act are discussed in Chapter 4. Interlocking directorates in banks or corporations engaged in interstate commerce are prohibited by Section 8 of the Clayton Act, discussed briefly in §4.13. Section 10 of the Clayton Act (15 USC §20) also concerns such directorates, but in connection with common carriers.

III. Commission's Formal Proceedings

A. [§6.9] Sanctions

Each violation of a final FTC order is subject to a civil penalty of up to $5,000. 15 USC §§21(l) and 45(l). Each day of a continuing failure or neglect to obey an order constitutes a separate offense. The United States may recover the penalty in a civil suit brought by the Department of Justice in a United States District Court.

The only issue present in such a suit is whether the respondent violated the Commission order. Mitigating circumstances that may reduce the amount of the penalty include good faith and lack of intent to violate the order, long observances of the order, and delay by the FTC in objecting to the deviation from the order.

B. [§6.10] Tolling of Statute of Limitations

Section 5(b) of the Clayton Act, 15 USC §16(b), provides in part:

Whenever any civil or criminal proceeding is instituted by the United States to prevent, restrain, or punish violations of any of the antitrust law, . . . the running of the statute of limitations in respect of every private right of action arising under said laws and based in whole or in part on any matter complained of in said proceeding shall be suspended during the pendency thereof and for one year thereafter. . . .

Minnesota Mining & Manufacturing Co. v New Jersey Wood Finishing Co. (1965) 381 US 311 held that the institution of a Federal Trade Commission action charging violation of Section 7 of the Clayton Act (15 USC §18) (mergers) tolled the statute of limitations governing a private action based on the same acquisition.

Lippa's, Inc. v Lenox, Inc. (D Vt 1969) 305 F Supp 182 held that resale price maintenance activities attacked by the Federal Trade Commission as an unfair method of competition under Section 5 of the Federal Trade Commission Act (15 USC §45) tolled the statute of limitations governing a private treble-damage action arising out of the same activities, notwithstanding the Federal Trade Commission Act was held by the Supreme Court in *Nashville Milk Co. v Carnation Co.* (1958) 355 US 373 not to be an "antitrust law." See holdings contrary to *Lippa* in *Rader v Balfour* (ND Ill 1968) 1969 Trade Cases ¶72,709; *Laitram Corp. v Deepsouth Packing Co.* (ED La 1968) 279 F Supp 883.

See discussion of Section 5(b) of the Clayton Act and tolling of statute of limitations pending government proceedings at §§2.39–2.43, 12.14, and 13.29.

C. [§6.11] Use of Commission's Findings in Subsequent Treble-Damage Actions

Section 5(a) of the Clayton Act, 15 USC §16(a), provides in part:

A final judgment or decree . . . rendered in any civil or criminal proceeding brought by . . . the United States under the antitrust laws to the effect that a defendant has violated said laws shall be prima facie evidence against such defendant . . . as to all matters respecting which said judgment or decree would be an estoppel as between the parties thereto: *Provided,* That this section shall not apply to consent judgments or decrees entered before any testimony has been taken. . . .

This section enables private litigants to use the findings in government suits as prima facie evidence that an antitrust violation has taken place. In short, when such findings are available, a private party plaintiff enjoys the benefit of a rebuttable presumption.

The question whether a Commission order is entitled to be given prima facie effect under the statute has engendered a good deal of controversy, principally regarding whether (1) an FTC proceeding is a "civil or criminal proceeding brought by the United States," (2) an FTC order is a "judgment or decree," and (3) an FTC order is "final." See cases and commentary cited in *Farmington Dowel Products Co. v Forster Mfg. Co.* (1st Cir 1969) 421 F2d 61, 67 n. 8, 75 n. 37.

In *Farmington Dowel,* the court ruled that an FTC order entered in a proceeding charging violation of the discriminatory pricing provisions of the Robinson-Patman Act was a final judgment or decree within the meaning of Section 5(a) of the Clayton Act. The court reasoned that the three objections voiced by prior decisions had been dispelled; the Finality

Act of 1959 (15 USC §21(g)-(l)) made Commission orders final, and the Supreme Court in *Minnesota Mining & Manufacturing Co. v New Jersey Wood Finishing Co.* (1965) 381 US 311 held that a Commission proceeding was a "civil or criminal proceeding" which is "brought by the United States."

In *Purex Corp v The Procter & Gamble Co.* (CD Calif 1970) 308 F Supp 584 the district court held that a Commission finding that Procter and Gamble's acquisition of Clorox Chemical Company violated Section 7 of the Clayton Act (15 USC §18) was entitled to prima facie effect in the subsequent private action brought by Purex against Procter and Gamble.

Although there is no Supreme Court decision on the subject, the trend is in favor of giving prima facie effect to Commission Clayton Act orders. Still unresolved is whether Commission orders arising out of violation of Section 5 of the Federal Trade Commission Act (15 USC §45) will be given prima facie effect. It should be noted that the Supreme Court in *Nashville Milk Co. v Carnation Co.* (1958) 355 US 373 ruled that Section 5 is not an "antitrust law" for purposes of Section 5(a) of the Clayton Act. However, in *Lippa's, Inc. v Lenox, Inc.* (D Vt 1969) 305 F Supp 182, the district court, in assessing the tolling provision of Section 5(b) of the Clayton Act (15 USC §16(b)), considered it significant that the conduct challenged by the Commission under Section 5 of the Federal Trade Commission Act (resale price maintenance) was in fact a Sherman and Clayton Act type of violation. For discussion of tolling provisions, see §6.10; on use of prior government decrees, see §§12.62 and 13.27.

IV. [§6.12] Commission's Informal Enforcement Program

The Federal Trade Commission is charged with regulating an infinite variety of practices of a vast number of business concerns. To avoid expensive litigation, the Commission encourages voluntary compliance with its antitrust policy. Under Sections 5(a)(6) and 6(g) of the Federal Trade Commission Act, 15 USC §45(a)(6) and 46(g), the Commission is empowered to promulgate rules and regulations relating to unlawful trade practices and to set down standards for compliance. The Commission has promulgated numerous rules and regulations in the form of FTC Guides, Trade Regulation Rules, and Advisory Opinions, each of which is discussed in §§6.13-6.16.

If there has been a violation not serious in nature, the Commission will effect enforcement in an informal fashion, discussed in §§6.16-6.19.

A. Rules and Regulations

1. [§6.13] FTC Guides, Also Known as Industry Trade Practice Conference Rules

FTC Guides are administrative interpretations of the antitrust laws concerning misuse of terms and deceptive business practices applicable to all industry or to specific industries. The Guides now include what previously had been called FTC Trade Practice Conference Rules. The rules promulgated in the past remain in effect, but as they are amended or re-released, they are called Industry Guides. Federal Trade Commission Procedures and Rules of Practice §1.6 (hereafter Commission Rules) 3 Trade Reg Rep ¶¶9801.01–9801.06.

Guides are drafted on an industry-wide basis by the Commission with the cooperation of the affected industry. Any interested person may petition for the commencement of a proceeding that will result in the issuance of a Guide. Notice of the proposed proceeding is published in the Federal Register and includes: (1) a statement of the time, place, and nature of the public proceeding; (2) reference to the statutory authority; and (3) the terms and substance of the proposed Guide. Under the Commission Rules interested persons are given the opportunity to participate in the proceeding and to make their views known in writing and, within the Commission's discretion, by oral presentation. The Guide finally adopted by the Commission must be published in the Federal Register, with a statement of its basis, purpose, and any necessary findings. The Guide becomes effective not less than 30 days after publication. A listing of the Commission's Guides can be found at 1 Trade Reg Rep ¶50.

Guides do not have the force of law. As stated in *FTC v Mary Carter Paint Co.* (1965) 382 US 46, 48:

[Guides are] not fixed rules as such, [but are] designed to inform businessmen of the factors which would guide Commission decision.

However, Guides are frequently cited by the courts in determining the propriety and the meaning of various words and phrases. See *e.g., Helbros Watch Co. v FTC* (DC Cir 1962) 310 F2d 868, 869 n. 3, in which the court, in affirming a Commission order requiring a manufacturer to cease representing certain prices as "regular retail prices," referred to the Commission's Guides against deceptive pricing.

Illustrative of the Commission's Guides are its four industry guidelines applicable to mergers:

1. Vertical mergers in the cement industry. Federal Trade Commission, *Commission Enforcement Policy with Respect to Vertical Mergers in the Cement Industry* (January, 1967) 1 Trade Reg Rep ¶4510.
2. Mergers in the food distribution industries. Federal Trade Commission, *Commission Enforcement Policy with Respect to Mergers in the Food Distribution Industries* (January, 1967) 1 Trade Reg Rep ¶4520.
3. Product extension mergers in grocery products manufacturing. Federal Trade Commission, *Enforcement Policy with Respect to Product Extension Mergers in Grocery Products Manufacturing* (May, 1968) 1 Trade Reg Rep ¶4530.
4. Mergers in the textile mill products industry. Federal Trade Commission, *Enforcement Policy with Respect to Mergers in the Textile Mill Products Industry* (November, 1968) 1 Trade Reg Rep ¶4540.

For a discussion of the overall purpose of the FTC Merger Guidelines, see Elman, *Rulemaking Procedures in the F.T.C.'s Enforcement of the Merger Law* (1964) 78 *Harv L Rev* 385. See also Friendly, *The Federal Administrative Agencies: The Need for Better Definition of Standards* (1962) 75 *Harv L Rev* 863.

The merger guidelines applicable to the cement industry and to the food distribution industries require that advance notice be given to the Federal Trade Commission prior to consummating certain mergers or acquisitions.

In 1965 the Commission set out informal guidelines for mergers in the dairy products industry in an opinion in a proceeding against one of the leading dairy firms. *Beatrice Foods Co.* (1965) [1965-1967 Transfer Binder] FTC Dkt 6653, Trade Reg Rep ¶17,244 and, in addition, the Commission's staff in 1966 proposed guidelines to apply to mergers by automotive tire producers in a report on that industry, but these guidelines have not been adopted by the Commission. Staff Report to the Federal Trade Commission, *Economic Report on the Manufacture and Distribution of Automotive Tires* (Washington, Government Printing Office, 1966). The Commission's staff has also published an economic report on the baking industry. Staff Report to the Federal Trade Commission, *Economic Report on the Baking Industry* (Washington, Government Printing Office, 1967). The Commission has also announced that it is conducting an investigation of acquisitions of independent gasoline marketers and refiner-marketers by major oil companies. (FTC Release, July 29, 1969).

The legal status and effect of the four formal statements of enforcement policy is unclear. In issuing each policy statement the Commission has emphasized that firms subject to its policy statement are not required

341

to seek Commission approval prior to the consummation of any prospective merger or acquisition but that it would continue to provide advisory opinions on the legality of particular mergers for firms that want them. See discussion of advisory opinions at §6.14.

In reaffirming its enforcement policy with respect to mergers in the textile mill products industry, the Commission has stated that the policy statements do not attempt to draw precise legal boundaries for every prospective merger but that their purpose is to identify the types of future mergers "which appear to require the Commission's attention in the discharge of its statutory responsibilities." (Federal Trade Commission, Statement reaffirming and clarifying its *Enforcement Policy with Respect to Mergers in the Textile Mill Products Industry* (FTC News Release August 18, 1969) 1 Trade Reg Rep ¶4540.10.) In a dissenting statement Commissioner Jones contended (at 6828) that "[t]he Commission's clarification statement furnishes what to me is a new interpretation of guidelines which so far as I know has never before been the basis for issuing merger guidelines in a given industry." She criticized "the ambiguity now interjected by the Commission into exactly what it intends these guidelines to mean for the industry." In her view, "[i]f guidelines were simply an indication of what industries were to be examined by the Commission and no more, then their issuance would constitute a real deception on the business community since in fact the Commission staff screens most mergers involving companies whose assets are in excess of $10 million." According to Commissioner Jones, the "publication of guidelines for a given industry was intended as a statement on the part of the Commission that mergers in these industries of the type covered by the guidelines would in all probability be *challenged* by the Commission."

At a minimum, the Commission's statements of enforcement policy tell firms in covered industries what kinds of mergers are most likely to raise concern on the part of the Commission. As a practical matter, it is unlikely that a merger failing to satisfy the guidelines will be allowed unless there are clearly mitigating circumstances.

The publication of a statement of enforcement policy regarding mergers in an industry has been held not to establish prejudgment on the part of the Commission of the issues raised in a particular case, and motions to transfer a merger proceeding to the Department of Justice and to dismiss a merger complaint on this basis have been denied. See *Lehigh Portland Cement Co. v FTC* (ED Va 1968) 291 F Supp 628, *aff'd* (4th Cir 1969) 416 F2d 971 and *Missouri Portland Cement Co.* (1969) [1967–1970 Transfer Binder] FTC Dkt 8783, Trade Reg Rep ¶18,805.

2. [§6.14] Advisory Opinions

Sections 1.1 through 1.4 of the Commission Rules (3 Trade Reg Rep ¶¶9801.01–9801.04) govern the issuance of Advisory Opinions. Any person, partnership, or corporation may request advice of the Commission "with respect to a course of action which the requesting party proposes to pursue." If practicable, the Commission will indicate its view of how it would proceed. A request for advice is ordinarily inappropriate "(a) [w]here the course of action is already being followed by the requesting party; (b) where the same or substantially the same course of action is under investigation or has been the subject of a current proceeding, order or decree . . . (c) where . . . an informed decision . . . can be made only after extensive investigation. . . .

Request for an advisory opinion should be submitted in writing to the secretary of the Commission and should fully describe the proposed course of action. The request should include an affirmative statement that the course of action is not presently engaged in or subject to investigation. If practicable, the Commission will advise, but without prejudice to its later reconsideration of its view of the practice or its power to rescind or revoke the advice if the public interest would be served; however, it will not proceed against one who has relied in good faith on its advice and who discontinues the practice on notification of rescission of the advice.

Advisory opinions have the potential of performing the desirable function of advising the business community regarding the Commission's views of concrete business problems. Unfortunately, of late, and with some justification, the Commission has been criticized for "publishing cryptic and obscure advisory opinions" and "failing to make available to the public, broad categories of information relating to its operations, particularly its determination to grant or withhold pre-merger clearances." *ABA Commission Report* 11.

Traditionally, digests of advisory opinions have been published if they are of general interest, but they do not disclose trade secrets, customer's names, or other "confidential" material. Effective October 29, 1969, the Commission advised that to conform with the letter and spirit of the Freedom of Information Act, subject to the request for confidentiality, parties requesting advisory opinions will be identified in the text of the opinions released. Commission Rules §1.4 (3 Trade Reg Rep ¶9801.04). In 1969 the FTC issued a volume containing its first 313 advisory opinion digests published between June 1, 1962, the date it commenced their publication, and December 31, 1968, together with enforcement and policy statements of special interest. The volume can be purchased for

$2.25 from the Superintendent of Documents, United States Government Printing Office, Washington, DC 20402. A listing of advisory opinions is found in 1 Trade Reg Rep ¶50.

3. [§6.15] Trade Regulation Rules

Trade regulation rules are intended to "express the experience and judgment of the Commission, based on facts of which it has knowledge derived from studies, reports, investigations, hearings, and other proceedings, or within official notice, concerning the substantive requirements of the statutes" that it administers. Commission Rules §1.12 (3 Trade Reg Rep ¶9801.12). The rules may be broad in their coverage or they may be limited to particular areas, industries, products, or geographic markets. Notice of a proposed trade regulation rule is published in the Federal Register, and interested parties may offer their views. Adopted rules are also published in the Federal Register. Commission Rules §1.6 (3 Trade Reg Rep ¶9801.06).

The Commission has initiated a trade regulation rule proceeding after commencing an adjudicatory proceeding when it appeared that the activity challenged was widespread. See, e.g., FTC Dkt 7939 (3 Trade Reg Rep at 24,624) concerning vertical integration in the cement industry.

When an adopted rule relates to an issue raised in an adjudicatory proceeding, after the respondent has had the opportunity to challenge the legality and propriety of applying that rule to his case, the Commission may rely on the rule to resolve the issue. Commission Rules §1.12 (3 Trade Reg Rep ¶9801.12). In short, the rules constitute the Commission's interpretation of substantive statutory requirements and have the force and effect of law. A listing of final trade regulation rules and proposals are found in 1 Trade Reg Rep ¶50.

The Commission is also authorized to issue quantity limit rules under Section 2(a) of the Clayton Act (15 USC §13(a)) and regulatory rules under Section 6 of the Wool Products Labeling Act (15 USC §68d), Section 8 of the Fur Products Labeling Act (15 USC §69f), Section 5 of the Flammable Fabrics Act (15 USC §1194), and Section 7 of the Textile Fiber Products Identification Act (15 USC §70e). These rules, like Trade Regulation Rules, have the force and effect of law. Commission Rules §1.13-1.14 (3 Trade Reg Rep ¶¶9801.13-9801.14).

B. Informal Enforcement Procedures

1. [§6.16] Assurance of Voluntary Compliance

In December, 1969, the Federal Trade Commission outlined its program of voluntary compliance. See 5 Trade Reg Rep ¶50,264. Its purpose was stated to be immediate cessation of questioned acts or practices with adequate safeguards against their resumption and the avoidance of expense both to the government and to the private party. If there has been no substantial violation, the Commission will enter into an agreement with a potential respondent wherein the latter gives a written assurance of voluntary compliance. In 1969 the Commission took 511 assurances of voluntary compliance. *ABA Commission Report* 22.

2. [§6.17] Informal Corrective Actions

Similar to assurances of voluntary compliance, but less formal, are "informal corrective actions," which consist of an agreement in the form of a letter or a purely verbal assurance of discontinuance of the objectional practice. The Commission accepted 5,768 informal corrective actions in 1969. *ABA Commission Report* 22-23.

3. [§6.18] Consent Decree

If the potential respondent has acted in plain disregard of the rules or guides promulgated by the Commission, and the Commission seeks to avoid the expense of adjudication, the Commission may dispose of the matter by a consent decree. In 1969, the Commission issued 220 formal complaints; 198 of those were settled by consent orders, whereas only 22 were litigated. *ABA Commission Report* 20.

4. [§6.19] Compliance Reports

The Commission requires compliance reports to be filed 60 days after the issuance of a cease-and-desist order and six months after the taking of an assurance of voluntary compliance. It has been severely criticized for not following up to see whether compliance exists in fact, not just in report. See *ABA Commission Report* 23-25.

V. [§6.20] Investigatory Powers

The FTC has very broad investigatory powers. The Commission is authorized to conduct investigations both before issuing a complaint when it believes that a violation may have occurred and after issuing an order to assure itself that compliance has been achieved.

Other statutes administered by the Commission confer authority to inspect, analyze, test, and examine wool (Wool Products Labeling Act Section 6(a), 15 USC §68d(a)), fur (Fur Products Labeling Act Section 8(c)(1), 15 USC §69f(c)(1)), textiles (Textile Fiber Products Identification

Act Section 7(d), 15 USC §70e(d)), and wearing apparel believed to be dangerously inflammable (Flammable Fabrics Act Section 5(d)(1), 15 USC §1194(d)(1)). In addition, the Commission is authorized to investigate suspected antitrust violations of export trade associations (Webb-Pomerene Export Trade Act Section 5, 15 USC §65). Also, investigation may be undertaken in order to collect facts for congressional legislative purposes or to enable the President to recommend legislation.

The Commission's investigative machinery is discussed in Chapter 10.

7

Patents and the Antitrust Law

John C. Stedman

Professor Stedman received the BA degree from the University of Wisconsin in 1928, the LLB degree from the University of Wisconsin School of Law in 1933, and the LLM degree from Columbia University in 1940. He is Professor of Law at the University of Wisconsin School of Law.

I. [§7.1] Introduction

Collision between the patent system and antitrust policies is in many
instances inevitable. The patent law authorizes the creation of individual
monopolies, although these monopolies are limited in subject matter,
geographical application, and duration. The antitrust laws are dedicated
to preventing monopoly and restraints on competition. The law man,
whether judge, practitioner, or legislator, must recognize this inherent
conflict and develop rules for avoiding or minimizing it, which requires
recognition of the purposes underlying each system, the kinds of antitrust
problems that may arise in context of the patent system, and the respective limits that each system imposes on the operation of the other.

The underlying purpose of antitrust is to preserve effective competition
in an effort to assure a satisfactory supply of goods and services at a
reasonable cost and a high level of quality and performance and to avoid
government regulation of commerce and industry. The patent system
operates on the theory that it may sometimes be necessary to substitute
the stimulus of monopoly for the spur of competition to encourage private
inventors and entrepreneurs to come up with new products and processes

and to make the results available to the public. The premise is that the risks and costs of such ventures make it unlikely that they will be undertaken without special inducement in the form of exclusive control over the source of supply and the possibility of extra profit that freedom from competition may bring. A collateral objective of the patent system is to persuade inventors to disclose their ideas to the public instead of keeping them secret, an act that may benefit the public, both short-range in terms of stimulating invention and long-range in terms of utilizing the patented ideas once the patents have expired.

Antitrust and patent objectives do not always work at cross purposes. For instance, entrepreneurs may undertake business ventures they would not be willing to risk but for patent protection. The patent system may encourage competitive research that results in new products, new processes, and a constant ferment within a given industry that contributes to, rather than impedes, economically and socially desirable competition. The patent system can also provide temporary protection to a small inventor or entrepreneur against more powerful competitors, enabling the former to get a start and gain sufficient strength to survive in the world of competition.

In spite of these occasional pro-competitive results, the antitrust laws often look in one direction and the patent system in another. The result is likely to be litigation. Many antitrust cases concerning patents have been brought, especially in the past thirty years.

Antitrust problems concerning patents can arise in a variety of ways. They may stem from efforts by the patent owner to prevent others from using the patented invention although this, without more, rarely gives rise to antitrust action. Secondly, they may arise out of the acquisition or transfer of patents by assignment. Here, also, antitrust problems are infrequent although they do arise occasionally. The third and most frequent patent-antitrust conflict arises when patents are licensed on terms that impede competition or create monopoly. See discussion at §§7.10–7.15. A fourth set of patent-antitrust problems does not, strictly speaking, entail any real conflict between patent and antitrust law. Included in this category are competitive restrictions not involving the actual assertion or waiver of patent rights, but restrictions on conduct that lie outside the patent right as such. Examples include agreements by the *patentee* not to engage in certain conduct and agreements by a licensee not to engage in activities lying entirely outside the scope of the patent, not to operate in patent areas after the patent has expired, or not to question the validity of designated patents. See discussion at §§7.16–7.20.

In resolving conflicts between patent and antitrust law, counsel must keep in mind the boundaries of the respective laws as laid down by federal statutes. The statutes are not very helpful when it comes to dealing with specific issues. They tend to speak in generalities with only minimal references to the other system. Thus, the Sherman and Clayton Acts deal broadly with monopoly and restraint of trade. Only one section, Section 3 of the Clayton Act (15 USC §14), contains any express reference to patents, prohibiting tying arrangements whether or not commodities are patented. The patent laws similarly speak in broad terms, granting an exclusive right for 17 years within the United States on the patented subject matter. Only two sections contain language that may bear on antitrust problems. Title 35 USC §261 provides that rights in a patent "to the whole or any specified part of the United States," may be assigned. Title 35 USC §271 contains a rather detailed subsection (d) which states that it shall not constitute a "misuse or illegal extension of the patent" for the patent owner to have engaged in any of the following acts:

(1) derived revenue from acts which if performed by another without his consent would constitute contributory infringement of the patent; (2) licensed or authorized another to perform acts which if performed without his consent would constitute contributory infringement of the patent; (3) sought to enforce his patent against infringement or contributory infringement.

The background and significance of this provision are discussed at §7.23.

In sum, one must look to Sections 1 (restraint of trade) and 2 (monopoly) of the Sherman Act (15 USC §§1–2) and Sections 3 (tie-ins) and 7 (mergers and acquisitions) of the Clayton Act (15 USC §§14 and 18) in determining the application of the antitrust laws. In applying these statutes, one must consider the possible qualifications imposed by Sections 261 and 271 of the patent laws.

Before turning to a detailed examination of the law, mention should be made of the "misuse" doctrine that has developed in patent law. This doctrine holds that one who has "misused" his patent shall be barred from enforcing it against others until the effects of the misuse have been dissipated. *Morton Salt Co. v G.S. Suppiger Co.* (1942) 314 US 488. Strictly speaking, the doctrine is not an antitrust doctrine since it is court-made law limited to use as a defense to patent infringement. Nevertheless, the misuse doctrine is so clearly inspired by antitrust principles and objectives and in many respects so closely follows the antitrust criteria, that any discussion of the patent-antitrust relationship must cover the misuse doctrine as well. The doctrine is discussed at §7.23.

II. [§7.2] Acquisition of Patents

The acquisition of patents can run afoul three different provisions of the antitrust laws. Acquisition agreements may be looked upon as contracts to restrain trade (*e.g.*, a company conveys to a competitor a patent on a competitive product, thereby precluding itself from selling the product in competition) and thus constitute a violation of Section 1 of the Sherman Act (15 USC §1). Acquisition of patents that enable a company to dominate a field or industry may violate Section 2 of the Sherman Act (15 USC §2), which prohibits monopolization and attempts to monopolize. See discussion of the Sherman Act in Chapter 2. Finally, X Corporation's sale of patents to Y Corporation may violate Section 7 of the Clayton Act (15 USC §18), which provides that

no corporation subject to the jurisdiction of the Federal Trade Commission shall acquire the whole or any part of the assets of one or more corporations engaged in commerce, where . . . the effect of such acquisition . . . may be substantially to lessen competition, or to tend to create a monopoly.

See discussion of Section 7 of the Clayton Act in Chapter 4.

Standing alone, the acquisition of patents is not subject to challenge under the antitrust laws. It would be a strange doctrine that set up a patent system authorizing one to obtain patents, and then imposed penalties for doing so. Indeed, the patent laws expressly provide for the assignment of patents, either at the application or issued patent stage. 35 USC §261. However, acquisitions innocent in themselves may constitute a violation of the antitrust laws if certain other facts or circumstances are present. Problems can arise in five major areas: (1) acquisition of patents by direct grant from the Patent Office; (2) purchase of patents from others; (3) acquisition pursuant to an employer-employee relationship; (4) acquisition pursuant to a grant-back arrangement; and (5) acquisition by fraud.

A. [§7.3] Acquisition by Grant from the Patent Office

There appear to be no cases in which someone who has consciously obtained patents for the express purpose of monopolizing a given field has been challenged on this basis alone. Even the more sweeping pro-antitrust decisions, such as *United States v Aluminum Co. of America* (2d Cir 1945) 148 F2d 416 and *United States v United Shoe Machinery Corp.* (D Mass 1953) 110 F Supp 295, 342, *aff'd per curiam* (1954) 347 US 521, have expressly declared that monopoly attributable to "superior products . . . economic or technological efficiency, (including scientific research), . . . or licenses . . . within the limits of law, (including patents on one's own inventions . . .)" are unobjectionable. Thus, one may safely assume that a company that embarks on a vigorous research program directed to improving its competitive position through patents will not be subjected to antitrust action even though it ultimately achieves a dominant or monopolistic position in its field. Its conduct may, however, be closely scrutinized for the presence of factors which, taken with its patent acquisitions, may add up to an antitrust violation. In several patent-antitrust cases the courts have taken critical note of the practices of defendants in amassing a huge portfolio of patents, many of them of narrow scope and doubtful validity, which defendants have used to overpower their competitors through the sheer force of numbers.

B. [§7.4] Acquisition by Purchase

Until recently, there was little disposition to look askance at acquisitions by purchase. This is no longer true. Section 7 of the Clayton Act (15 USC §18) was amended in 1950 to include asset acquisitions, with the result that a purchase of patents is now vulnerable to attack under that section. Even the Sherman Act, with its more demanding requirements, will apply to the extent that the acquisition restrains competition or strengthens one's monopoly position.

The courts draw a sharp distinction between acquisitions resulting from one's own research and acquisitions through purchase from another. *United States v United Shoe Machinery Corp.* (D Mass 1953) 110 F Supp 295, *aff'd per curiam* (1954) 347 US 521. It does not follow that all or even most outside acquisitions are objectionable. In deciding whether a given acquisition by purchase is valid, the courts will consider such factors as the nature and scope of the acquired patents, the effect of the acquisition on the purchaser's position in the industry, the extent and manner of his use of the acquired patents, whether he purchased them from a competitor or from a non-competitor, and the extent of the rights acquired, *i.e.*, whether he purchased entire patent rights or more limited rights. Courts will distinguish between the acquisition of full title or an exclusive license on the one hand, and acquisition of a non-exclusive license on the other. Courts may also consider whether the acquisition was made for the purpose of resolving a conflict or a patent dispute, since this is important in inferring the parties' intentions.

C. [§7.5] Acquisition from Employees

Acquisitions from employees have earmarks of both acquisition by direct grant and acquisition by purchase. Obviously, corporations can acquire patents directly only on the basis of work done by their employees, and even non-corporate entities undoubtedly depend largely on employed researchers. Ordinarily, no antitrust problems arise with respect to obtaining patents on the inventions made by one's employees. If an employee is subjected to a so-called "trailer clause" under which he is obligated to convey inventions made after this employment terminates, however, the situation is very different. Such agreements are permitted, subject to sharp limitations, but to the extent that they exceed the bounds of reasonableness, they are condemned. *Guth v Minnesota Mining & Mfg. Co.* (7th Cir 1934) 72 F2d 385, *cert den* (1935) 294 US 711. One who deliberately hires away the research staff of a competitor for the purpose of running the latter out of business may also be subject to antitrust action. *Perryton Wholesale, Inc. v Pioneer Distributing Co.* (10th Cir 1965) 353 F2d 618, *cert den* (1966) 383 US 945. Presumably any patents resulting from such conduct would be tainted with the wrongdoing.

D. [§7.6] Acquisition by Grant-back

Grant-back arrangements have been the target of frequent attacks under the antitrust laws. Under a typical grant-back arrangement, a patentee licenses his patent on condition that the licensee convey back to him any subsequently obtained patents or inventions in the defined area. Such an arrangement may contribute to a monopoly position or to competitive imbalance. It is also subject to the objection that the patentee is using his power to refuse a license as a means of coercing the licensee into conveying the additional technology back to him—a sort of tie-in arrangement in reverse. If permitted to operate without limitation, such a practice could quickly lead to domination of the entire field by a strong patentee. Lastly, it may frustrate the objectives of the patent system by destroying the stimulus to invent on the part of the licensee.

In times past, grant-backs were not seriously called into question and in *Transparent-Wrap Machine Corp. v Stokes & Smith Co.* (1947) 329 US 637 the Court ruled that grant-backs were not illegal *per se*. To the extent that they provide for the grant-back of *exclusive* rights (*i.e.*, either assignment or exclusive licenses), however, they have increasingly become the subject of scrutiny and criticism, and today it is the rare case in which they are upheld. Indeed, the Antitrust Division is currently taking the position that grant-back of exclusive rights is illegal *per se*. McLaren, *Patent Licenses and Antitrust Considerations* (1969) 5 Trade Reg Rep ¶50,246. The case law supporting the grant-back doctrine, in the words of one commentator, has become a "hollow reed." Austern, *Umbras and*

Penumbras: The Patent Grant and Antitrust Policy (1965) 33 *Geo Wash L Rev* 1015, 1018.

The reasons for imposing a grant-back requirement are, of course, understandable. The patentee does not relish the thought of providing a competitor with competitive ammunition in the form of a right to use his patented inventions, unless the competitor is willing to return the compliment with respect to patents that *he* acquires. The point is well taken, but only to the extent of justifying a *non*-exclusive grant-back. It can hardly justify requiring outright assignment or an exclusive license.

E. [§7.7] Acquisition by Fraud

Recently, the acquisition of patents by means of fraudulent statements or conduct has been the subject of sharp attack. The attack started in *American Cyanamid Co. v FTC* (6th Cir 1966) 363 F2d 757, an FTC proceeding involving the allegedly fraudulent procurement of the tetracycline patent. It received further impetus in *Walker Process Equipment, Inc. v Food Machinery & Chemical Corp.* (1965) 382 US 172, in which the Court held that attempts to enforce a fraudulently procured patent could give rise to a cause of action for treble damages under the antitrust law. Subsequently, charges of fraud have been asserted in a number of cases, both as a defense in infringement cases and as an affirmative cause of action under the antitrust laws. The claim of fraud has been substantiated in only a few cases. The cases make it clear that, in treble-damage suits at least, in addition to proving fraudulent conduct the plaintiff must establish that the fraud resulted in competitive injury to him. The nature of patents being what it is, the probability of success in establishing such injury seems fairly high. The related problems of fraud in procurement of patents as rendering the patent invalid and of fraudulent attempts to enforce a patent obtained in good faith as constituting "misuse" are discussed in §7.23.

III. [§7.8] Use and Suppression of Patented Inventions

No antitrust problem arises from failure of a patentee to put his invention to use. While there may be an underlying expectation in the patent law that one will put his invention to use, there is no compulsion to do so. In short, both the patent laws and the antitrust laws leave one free to engage in business or not as he sees fit. There may be good reasons for not using an invention. It may be unworkable. It may be commercially unprofitable. Its use may be prohibited by law or by the fact that it would infringe another patent. The patentee may simply by occupied with other matters.

The real issue is not whether the patentee has an obligation to make use of the invention but whether he has the right to prevent others from using it if he fails to use it. The basic proposition is that the patentee is free to exclude others from using his invention if he does not want it used. One has no general right to make use of a patented invention without the patentee's consent, even though one may be willing to pay for the privilege of doing so. The statutes give the owner of a patent the flat right to exclude others and impose no limitation or qualification on this right except with respect to use by the federal government. See 35 USC §154; 28 USC §1498(a). Limitations on this right, other than the governmental ones, are few.

If the patentee is himself making use of the invention, his right to exclude others is very broad. The law not only expressly permits him to recover damages for unauthorized use, but also grants him the right to enjoin such use. While certain conduct, discussed in §7.24, may qualify this right, the basic proposition stands. Efforts over the years to modify the law to provide for compulsory licensing have been generally unsuccessful. In this respect, United States law differs from the laws of most other countries which do typically contain compulsory working or compulsory licensing provisions. Neumeyer, *Compulsory Licensing of Patents Under Some Non-American Systems* (1958) Senate Patent Study No. 19.

The closer question is whether a patentee's obligation is different if he refuses to permit others to use his invention even though he is not using it himself. No statute requires licensing under such circumstances, and early cases held that a patentee in such a position does not, for this reason alone, have any obligation to license. *Continental Paper Bag Co. v Eastern Paper Bag Co.* (1908) 210 US 405. The courts did, however, warn that circumstances might arise in which, as a matter of equity, they might refuse to enforce the patentee's right to exclude. For instance, an *agreement* by the patentee with others that he will not grant licenses may be held illegal and, in some circumstances, a violation of the antitrust laws. *United States v Krasnov* (ED Pa 1956) 143 F Supp 184, *aff'd per curiam* (1957) 355 US 5. This doctrine would not apply to an agreement by the patentee with an exclusive licensee not to license others since, for all practical purposes, he has already given away everything he had to give. It would, however, apply to agreements not to grant licenses that he otherwise had the power to grant, as for instance, to designated groups or individuals or for given fields, or not to license without the approval of existing licensees or other parties. It may be added that agreements by persons *not* to take licenses from a patentee or not to recognize the validity of his patent, have also been held objectionable under the antitrust laws, although the basis for finding an injury to competition in such circumstances is not at all clear. See, *e.g., Jones Knitting Corp. v Morgan* (ED Pa 1965) 244 F Supp 235, *rev'd* (3d Cir 1966) 361 F2d 451.

Unilateral refusal by a non-using patentee has generally been accepted as permissible (subject to critical scrutiny), although it has been suggested that refusal may be objectionable if an actual attempt to monopolize is found to exist. *1955 Report of the Attorney General's National Committee to Study the Antitrust Laws* 231 (hereafter, *Attorney General's Report, 1955*). The rationale for this qualification is somewhat obscure, since the inherent effect of a refusal to license would seem to be an attempt to monopolize. One interesting application of this qualified approach might be a showing that the purpose behind the refusal was to protect the patentee's competitive position with respect to some product *other* than the product covered by the patent. Condemnation of such a practice might be viewed as an extension of the tie-in doctrine, discussed at §7.13, which precludes one from using a patent to protect his monopoly or competitive advantage in some product that lies outside the scope of the patent. To date, this approach to suppression apparently has not been taken.

There is one additional area in which preventing others from using the invention may violate the antitrust laws, whether the patentee is using the invention himself or not. Improper methods in asserting one's patent rights and preventing use by others may render one guilty of antitrust violation, such as the use of harassment and engagement in litigious practices including repetitious litigation, threatening of customers, or unnecessary enhancement of trial expenses, to burden an alleged infringer with unnecessary impediments, difficulties and expenses. *Kobe, Inc. v Dempsey Pump Co.* (10 Cir 1952) 198 F2d 416, *cert den* (1952) 344 US 837. Fraudulent conduct in enforcing patent rights, such as asserting the validity of a patent that one knows to be invalid, is likewise improper. See *Union Camp Corp. v Lewis* (4th Cir 1967) 385 F2d 143. Suppression of patents, extensive infringement prosecution and the like, when coupled with other practices or attitudes that clearly indicate an intent to monopolize or restrain trade beyond the legitimate enforcement of a patent, may also constitute an antitrust violation. For example, extensive infringement litigation bottomed on a large accumulation of patents might be treated as an attempt to monopolize.

IV. Restrictive Patent Licenses and Assignments

A. [§7.9] Introduction

The most difficult and frequently-arising problems involving patent-antitrust relationships concern restrictive patent licensing and assignment agreements. The patentee may find it advantageous to permit others to share in the use of the invention, or to have them assert the patent rights rather than to do so himself, and hence enter into an agreement with another party. A patentee may be unwilling to release his exclusive rights without receiving commitments in return from the other party, commitments that may have the effect of limiting competition between them or with other parties or which may tend to create some sort of monopoly control. Because of the variety and complexity of such situations, it is important to distinguish among the various types of arrangements.

A pure, simple, no-strings-attached assignment or license agreement is unlikely to give rise to antitrust problems. An assignment merely transfers from the patentee to some other person the legal right to exclude. Absent the presence of some other factors, the competition and monopoly situation remains unchanged. The grant of a license reduces the monopoly (unless the patentee agrees not to use the invention himself), since now *both* the patentee and the licensee are free to use the invention. Indeed, the antitrust laws should take a neutral attitude toward patent assignments and should welcome, not oppose, an unrestricted license grant.

Antitrust problems arise when restrictions or conditions are imposed. While the types of restrictive arrangements are so varied that it is impossible to classify them rigidly, in general the problem-creating restrictions fall into three main categories: (1) restrictions imposed on the licensee that come *within* the scope of the licensed patent in the sense that, absent a license, the prohibited conduct would constitute infringement; (2) restrictions imposed on the licensee that go beyond the scope of the licensed patent; and (3) restrictions to which the patentee himself is subjected.

While the foregoing classification provides a convenient vehicle for analyzing the existing law, the situation may be complicated by various additional factors, such as the problem of multiplicity (*i.e.*, arrangements dealing with more than one patent, more than one patentee, or more than one licensee) and problems of "remote control" (*e.g.*, situations in which the patentee attempts to extend his control beyond the immediate licensee by imposing a resale price restriction on products purchased from the licensee).

From the standpoint of legal theory, the courts have been guided at various times and in various circumstances by three main criteria:

357

(1) Under the doctrine originally enunciated in *United States v General Electric Co.* (1926) 272 US 476, the test was deemed to be one of "reasonableness," *i.e.*, whether the restriction imposed was "reasonably related" to the legitimate interests of the patentee and the protection of those interests. (2) Under the doctrine enunciated in *Motion Picture Patents Co. v Universal Film Manufacturing Co.* (1917) 243 US 502 and *Morton Salt Co. v G.S. Suppiger Co.* (1942) 314 US 488, the test was deemed to be whether the patentee, in imposing the restriction, was asserting a monopoly or restraint of competition "beyond the scope of the patent;" if so, the restriction would be tested by its effect under the antitrust laws without the benefit of any special protection that the existence of a patent might otherwise give. (3) In some instances, restrictions are expressly declared illegal by statute. See Section 3 of the Clayton Act, 15 USC §14. Obviously, these three approaches differ considerably in sweep. The last is the narrowest, whereas the first is the widest, most general—and most vague.

Penalties imposed for illegal conduct also vary. An agreement held to violate the Sherman Act may result in either criminal or civil action by the federal government or action for damages or equitable relief (usually injunction) by injured private parties. Violations of Section 3 or 7 (15 USC §18) of the Clayton Act also give rise to civil, but not criminal, action by the federal government (either the Department of Justice or the Federal Trade Commission) and to private action. Closely related to the antitrust laws is the doctrine of "patent misuse" (generally defined as attempting to assert a monopoly beyond the scope of the patent), which bars one who has misused his patent from enforcing it until the effects of the misuse have been dissipated. See discussion at §7.23. Lastly, there exists the common-law doctrine that contracts that are illegal will not be enforced by the courts.

The policy considerations in the development of the law are complicated by the fact that one starts with the fact of a legal, albeit limited, monopoly in the hands of the patentee. One may urge that any licensing arrangement, even a restrictive one, improves the antitrust situation since it reduces the monopoly that the patentee possesses to the extent that others are now free to use the invention. The argument, of course, breaks down if restrictions are imposed that go beyond the scope of the patent and prevent competitive conduct that one would be free to engage in if there were no license agreement. It does, however, have merit if the restriction is limited to the boundaries of the patent.

Several questions of basic policy arise in the context of restrictive licensing:

(1) What is the overall effect of the agreement on competition, both as between the patentee and the licensee and as between either or both of them and others?

(2) What is the possible wet-blanket effect of a strict rule concerning license and assignment restrictions on either or both the patentee and the licensee, considering the avowed objective of the patent law to stimulate and encourage invention and innovation?

(3) If one may legally assert a 100% monopoly in the invention by virtue of patent ownership, what antitrust objection is there to waiving part but not all of one's monopoly rights?

(4) What is the probable effect of restrictions on licensing practices: Will the patentee, if barred from imposing given restrictions, refuse to license, thus retaining the complete monopoly to himself, or will he grant a license on an unrestricted basis?

(5) In addition to these considerations, there remains the problem of laying down a set of workable rules that business people and the courts can live by.

These are the considerations that courts should have in mind in dealing with the issues, at least when precedents and unequivocal statutory language do not provide settled answers. Various kinds of restrictions are discussed in §§7.10-7.20.

B. Intra-patent License Restrictions

1. [§7.10] Time, Quantity, Field, and Geographical Restrictions

Certain types of intra-patent restrictions have been generally upheld on the simple theory that one is entitled to divide up his patent and dispose of—or more accurately, in the case of licenses, rent out—one part of the right, retaining the remainder to himself. The clearest examples of this are time, quantity, field of use, and geographical restrictions. A patentee may, for instance, license his patent for a period of ten years, instead of the full seventeen years, just as one may rent 40 acres of an 80-acre farm. One may license use of the invention west of the Mississippi, retaining for himself the exclusive rights east of the Mississippi. He may limit the license to the manufacture of 50,000 units of the patented product. Field of use restrictions (a license, for instance, to manufacture tires for motorcycles, but not for other vehicles) logically fall within this category, and in the past the courts have so held. *General Talking Pictures Corp. v Western Electric Co.* (1938) 304 US 175. Recently there has been some tendency to question the validity of such restrictions (McLaren, *Patent Licenses*

359

and Antitrust Considerations (1969) 5 Trade Reg Rep ¶50,246), although the logic underlying such questioning is not entirely clear to this writer.

2. [§7.11] Price, Tie-in, and Quality Restrictions

In contrast to time, quantity, field of use, and geographical restrictions, price restrictions and tie-in clauses contained in patent licenses are subject to serious question, notwithstanding that both types of restrictions may properly be viewed as operating within the confines of the patent. The difficulties that arise in these latter two areas may also arise with respect to *quality* restrictions, although there appears to have been no disposition to challenge the latter.

Price and tie-in restrictions, unlike time and quantity restrictions, cannot be viewed as reducing the monopoly by parceling out the rights in the patent. A price restriction arrangement contemplates that the patentee and the licensee will compete with each other but *not* with respect to price. A tie-in arrangement contemplates that the licensee will be free to use the invention in any way and anywhere that he pleases on condition that he buy from the patentee specified materials required in its use. Quality restrictions eliminate competition based on differences in quality, but enjoy the more favorable connotation that the patentee's objective is to compel the licensee to keep his performance up to a certain level in order not to bring the patented invention into ill repute.

Arguably, all three of these restrictions could be viewed as parceling out a share of the patent, with the licensee permitted to operate above certain levels of quality, at certain prices or with materials stemming from a certain source, and with the patentee reserving to himself the rights with respect to other prices, other raw materials, or lower quality. Realistically, this is not the patentee's objective. The courts have not attempted to deal with the problem in these refined, analytical terms. They have simply held pricing restrictions to be a "reasonable" condition for the patentee to impose (if they deem the condition valid) or an agreement between the patentee and licensee to fix prices and illegal *per se* under the antitrust law (if they deem it invalid). They view tie-in agreements as a device whereby the patentee is enabled to control, monopolize, and prevent competition in the unpatented, tied-in product, notwithstanding that the very nature of the patent monopoly is to enable the patentee to assert such control over unpatented materials to the extent that he precludes others from using the invention. The courts have shown increasing resistance to both tie-in arrangements and price restrictions.

a. [§7.12] Price Restrictions

A patentee must choose between retaining the invention exclusively to himself and reaping the financial benefits that come from being its sole user or producer and licensing others and obtaining the royalties. In the latter context arises the desire to impose price restrictions to eliminate price competition.

Until fairly recently, price restrictions based on a valid patent were deemed unobjectionable. In *United States v General Electric Co.* (1926) 272 US 476, the Supreme Court in a unanimous decision held that such a price restriction constituted a reasonable protection of the patentee's legitimate interests, reasoning that since the patentee could have prevented competition completely he should not be condemned for permitting others to use the invention subject to insulation against the ravages of price competition.

Over the years the *General Electric* doctrine has been whittled away; it has been held that the rule does not apply if

(1) The price agreement was the result of a conspiracy between the patentee and the licensee or was dictated by the licensee in *his* interests rather than by the patentee in his. *Cummer-Graham Co. v Straight Side Basket Corp.* (5th Cir 1944) 142 F2d 646, *cert den* (1944) 323 US 726.

(2) The licensee was not a manufacturing licensee, but rather a purchaser of the product for resale.

(3) The patent did not cover the entire product that was the subject of the price restriction. *United States v General Electric Co.* (D NJ 1949) 82 F Supp 753 (incandescent lamp).

(4) The price restriction was imposed on the unpatented product of the licensed invention (a process or machine). Nordhaus and Jurow (1961) *Patent-Antitrust Laws* 98-100.

Furthermore, in *Sola Electric Co. v Jefferson Electric Co.* (1942) 317 US 173, the court ruled that any patent subject to a price restriction could be challenged as to validity (thus refusing to the "estoppel" doctrine that prevailed until recently), since the agreement would be clearly invalid under the antitrust laws in the absence of a valid patent.

Also, limitations were imposed in "multiplicity" situations (*i.e.*, more than one patentee, more than one licensee, or even more than one patent). "Multiplicity" has created problems in the many areas, but they have been especially acute in the price fixing area. See discussion at §7.22. Thus, *United States v Line Material Co.* (1948) 333 US 287 held that an otherwise valid price restriction becomes invalid if two or more patentees agree to grant such restrictive licenses or authorize a single licensing agent (who may be one of them) to license for both on price-restrictive terms. The rule applies even though the inventions may be complementary, *i.e.*, both used in or essential to the product that is subject to the price restriction. Courts have also become increasingly critical of arrangements covering more than one licensee, tending to view such arrangements as a horizontal price-fix between the licensees, rather than one imposed by the patentee. *Newburgh Moire Co. v Superior Moire Co.* (D NJ 1952) 105 F Supp 372, *aff'd* (3d Cir 1956) 237 F2d 283. In addition to these modifications, the price-fixing doctrine of the *General Electric* case has come under direct frontal attack. In *United States v Line Material Co., supra,* and *United States v Huck Manufacturing Co.* (1965) 382 US 197, both subsequent to *General Electric*, the Supreme Court has divided four to four on the question whether to throw out the doctrine entirely. In view of these limitations and trends, increasing doubt has arisen whether price restrictive agreements, even in narrow form, are legal. Patent owners have shied away from this type of arrangement.

In support of price restrictions it is argued that: (1) The limitation is "reasonably adapted" to the protection of the patentee's interest (the *General Electric* reasoning); (2) the patentee is legitimately entitled to protection from price competition in view of the monopoly that he already possesses through ownership of the patent; (3) if such restrictions are prohibited, the patentee will refuse to license at all and thus a more complete monopoly will exist than would have resulted from allowing the restriction; and (4) if such arrangements are prohibited it will put a damper on the stimulus to invent and innovate that the patent system seeks to provide.

The arguments against permitting price restrictions are that: (1) they are unnecessary for the protection of the patentee's legitimate interests since he can adequately protect himself through the royalty he charges; (2) it does not follow, if such restrictions are prohibited, that the patentee will refuse to license at all since, if he cannot grant a license containing the restriction there is a good chance that he will grant one without it; (3) permitting such restrictions contributes to conspiracies and other phony arrangements in which the patent simply becomes the facade for a price-fixing arrangement; (4) price fixing does not constitute a legitimate dividing up or parceling of the patent rights; (5) the non-price-competition arrangement creates a pattern of conduct that will persist after the patent expires; (6) implicit in the arrangement is an agreement by the *patentee* that *he* will not sell at a lower price—a commitment that is *not* protectible as being within the scope of the patent (*cf.* comment in Nordhaus and Jurow (1961) *Patent-Antitrust Laws* 137); (7) the activity of the licensee to which the price restriction is addressed inevitably goes beyond the scope of the patent since it probably includes other features than the patented invention and involves the licensee's personal contributions, such as advertising and sales effort; (8) even if the result would be a refusal by the patentee to license at all, this may be the lesser of two evils because the licensee, if he cannot get a license, may find other ways of competing, for instance by inventing around the patent, by manufacturing non-infringing competitive products, or by going ahead and infringing, prepared to meet head on an attack by the patentee; and finally (9) competition that does not include price competition is of minimal value.

b. [§7.13] Tie-in Restrictions

Tie-in arrangements take a variety of forms. See discussion at §§3.9–3.18. The most common is a license to manufacture a patented product or use a patented machine or process on condition that the licensee buy the materials used in the product or process from the patentee. Closely associated is the sale by the patentee of a patented product on condition that unpatented materials used with it be purchased from him. These materials may either lie outside the patented invention but be usable in its operation (*e.g.*, the tin cans used with a canning machine), or they may be an element in the patented invention itself (*e.g.*, a chemical compound contained in a patented drug). No distinction has been made between these two types of situations in the earlier cases permitting the restrictions, in the later cases condemning them, or in the provisions of 15 USC §271 authorizing certain limitations.

Other tie-in arrangements consist, for example, of requiring a licensee to take a license under patent X as a condition of obtaining a license under patent Y (package licensing). The rendition of services may also be tied in with the license grant. More subtly, the arrangement may take the form of giving better terms to those who buy from the patentee, of requiring the licensee to *sell* products to the patentee or to give the patentee better terms in the sale of products, as a condition of receiving a license (see, *e.g.*, discussion of acquisition by grant-back at §7.6), or of granting unrestricted licenses but refusing to license persons who do not buy their raw materials from the patentee. A variation of the last arrangement consists of suing for infringement those who purchase their materials elsewhere but not those who buy from the patentee.

The patentee's usual business objective underlying a tie-in arrangement is to insulate himself from competition in the unpatented, tied goods. Faced with competition in the sale of unpatented products, the patentee seeks a competitive advantage by requiring the licensee or purchaser who wants to make or use the patented invention to purchase from the patentee the unpatented product or service he might have obtained elsewhere. Less frequently, the patentee may force the licensee to take a product he does not want at all by refusing to sell the one without the other.

More legitimate motivations may be present. The patentee may be guaranteeing the workability of the patented product and impose the tie-in condition to assure satisfactory performance. With this objective in mind, he may insist on use of the tied product or, less sweepingly, stipulate that the guarantee will not apply unless the tied product or service is used. In other instances, he may be seeking to establish the reputation of a new invention he is introducing to the market, and feel that good performance can best be assured by controlling the unpatented articles or replacement parts that are used with it. Or, he may impose the condition on the ground that materials other than his will not work satisfactorily with the invention—a questionable justification since the licensee's self-interest would then generally induce the use of the patentee's materials without his being legally required to use them. The patentee may simply be in the business of selling the unpatented product and grant purchasers of such products the right to use the patented invention. Indeed, one may suggest that, in the absence of express disclaimer by the patentee, a right of such use would be implied as a matter of law when the product is sold. In such circumstances, the patentee may have no ulterior motives. Nevertheless, the effect may be non-competitive since the purchaser may buy the non-patented material from the patentee because he gets a license under the patent that he would not otherwise have and that he presumably could not obtain in the absence of such purchase.

The most serious anti-competitive effect of a tie-in arrangement occurs when the tied product is the subject of substantial competition and especially when it requires considerable expenditure either because of high initial cost or need for frequent replenishment. If the product is unobtainable from any source except the patentee, imposition of the tie-in does not affect the competitive situation to any substantial degree (although its imposition in that case is largely superfluous). Similarly, if the tied product does not require replacement or replenishment, the clause may have much less impact than if it does.

Logically, one may regard the tie-in as merely one part of the consideration that the licensee must pay to obtain the license. So viewed, one may ask whether it is basically any different or any more harmful than simply charging a higher fee for the patented product or the patent license and letting the licensee buy the tied product where he wishes. To the licensee, it may be the same, although it may be that while he would just as soon buy the product from the patentee as from someone else, he is not willing to pay a higher price for the tying product or the patent license. But whatever the views of the licensee, from a competition standpoint the difference may be very significant. The arrangement *does* preclude sales to the licensee by an outsider and thus insulates the patentee against such competition.

So much for the variation, motivations, and competitive effects of tie-in arrangements. Such arrangements, depending on the circumstances, may run afoul of the antitrust laws in three ways. They may constitute a contract in restraint of trade under Section 1 of the Sherman Act (15 USC §1), a monopolization or attempt to monopolize under Section 2 (15 USC §2), or a violation of Section 3 of the Clayton Act (15 USC §14), which provides:

> It shall be unlawful ... to lease or make a sale or contract for sale of goods, wares, merchandise, machinery, supplies, or other commodities, whether patented or unpatented, ... on the condition, agreement, or understanding that the lessee or purchaser thereof shall not use or deal in the goods, wares, merchandise, machinery, supplies, or other commodities of a competitor or competitors of the lessor or seller, where the effect of such lease, sale, or contract for sale or such condition, agreement, or understanding may be to substantially lessen competition or tend to create a monopoly in any line of commerce.

Under the Sherman Act, tie-in arrangements have been held to be virtually illegal *per se* if (1) the tying product represents a monopoly or unique product in an economic sense so as to give the seller a leverage that can be used to induce purchase of the tied product and (2) the amount of commerce in the tied product is substantial. *International Salt Co. v United States* (1947) 332 US 392. For Clayton Act purposes, it is enough that *either* of these conditions exists. *Times-Picayune Publishing Co. v United States* (1953) 345 US 594. Possession of a patent is held to provide sufficient uniqueness or monopoly. *International Salt Co. v United States, supra; cf. Northern Pacific Railway Co. v United States* (1958) 356 US 1. Thus, any patent tie-in arrangement inevitably violates the Clayton Act, and also the Sherman Act if there is a substantial amount of commerce in the tied product. See discussion of tie-ins at §§3.9–3.18.

In deciding whether a tie-in agreement in fact exists, the courts do not require that there be an actual written or express oral understanding. They will find such an agreement on the basis of actual practices engaged in. In *Leitch Manufacturing Co. v Barber Co.* (1938) 302 US 458, the Court found such an agreement even when no express or implied understanding existed, simply on the basis of the patentee's refusal to permit use of the invention except by persons who bought the tied article from him.

Tie-in arrangements not only violate the antitrust laws, but are also viewed as a "misuse" under the patent laws, *i.e.*, a use of the patent to control the unpatented tied-in material and thus to extend the monopoly beyond the scope of the patent. Indeed, the misuse doctrine developed out of cases dealing with tie-in arrangements. *Leitch Manufacturing Co., supra; Morton Salt Co. v G.S. Suppiger Co.* (1942) 314 US 488; *Chemical Co. v Ellis* (1942) 314 US 495. The misuse doctrine, which renders patents unenforceable during such time as the effects of the misuse continue, is discussed at §7.23.

Notwithstanding the sweeping condemnation of tie-in arrangements, a few practices do appear to be permissible, at least under the law as it presently stands. In *Dehydrating Process Co. v A.O. Smith Corp.* (1st Cir 1961) 292 F2d 653, *cert den* (1961) 368 US 931, it was held that the seller of a patented silo could require the buyer to use the seller's unloading device when it was shown that other devices would not work satisfactorily and that the patentee's good will would suffer if other devices were used. *United States v Jerrold Electronics Corp.* (ED Pa 1960) 187 F Supp 545, *aff'd per curiam* (1961) 365 US 567 dealt with the requirement by the patentee of a community antenna television system that the purchaser have his servicing done by the patentee. The court held that in the initial stages, only the patentee was competent to provide adequate service and that poor servicing would have given the system a bad name. In some instances, courts have permitted tie-ins when the patentee was guaranteeing the sold product. *Electric Pipe Line, Inc. v Fluid System, Inc.* (2nd Cir 1956) 231 F2d 370. See *International Salt Co. v United States, supra.*

It should be noted that some types of tie-in arrangements do not come within the purview of Section 3 of the Clayton Act, although they may be viewed as a misuse under the patent laws or a violation of Section 1 or 2 of the Sherman Act. Since Section 3 of the Clayton Act speaks only of the sale of physical commodities and tie-in of one *sale* with another, it is inapplicable to patent arrangements in which a patent *license*, rather than the *sale* of a patented product, is the tying factor. It is also inapplicable to arrangements in which the patentee requires the licensee or purchaser to convey or sell him something in return, as would be the case, for instance, with a grant-back.

An interesting relationship exists between the tie-in doctrine and the patent law that applies to the repair or reconstruction of a patented product. Under general patent law, the owner of a patented product is free to repair the product, but not to rebuild or reconstruct it. In the recent landmark case of *Aro Manufacturing Co. v Convertible Top Replacement Co.* (1961) 365 US 336, using the tie-in doctrine as an analogy, the Supreme Court ruled that a patentee cannot prohibit, on the ground that it constitutes a reconstruction, the replacement of an unpatented part in a patented product that one owns.

The strict rules regarding tie-in arrangements pose a serious problem for the patentee to the extent that he is doing business in both the tying and the tied areas. If he is in the business of selling the tied product and at the same time has a patent license to grant, he is faced with substantial limitations on his freedom to use his patent in the traditional sense. He must either refuse to grant a license under the patent entirely, not only to the purchaser of the material, but to others as well, or handle the sale of the product and the grant of a patent license independently from each other and if he grants a license to the purchaser of his products, offer to license all others on comparable terms. Otherwise, his only choices are to sell the entire patented equipment and supplies as a single unit, dispose of his patent, or simply not enforce it at all. In spite of these obvious hardships, the courts have held to very strict rules concerning tie-ins and show no disposition to relax them—even in the face of efforts by Congress to soften the impact of the doctrine through enactment of 15 USC §271.

c. [§7.14] Quality Restrictions

Quality restrictions are similar to price and tie-in restrictions in the sense that they do not constitute a "Balkanizing" of the patent into lesser monopolies or a reservation by the patentee to himself of certain exclusive areas, but instead contemplate sharing production and use with the licensee, subject to express conditions. Unlike price and tie-in restrictions, quality restrictions are imposed for the purpose of *maintaining* a level of quality (presumably for the purpose of preserving the integrity and reputation of the invention) rather than for the purpose of imposing limits on competition. Thus, no adverse effect upon competition arises and there is no reason to challenge the restriction under either the antitrust laws or the misuse doctrine.

It is conceivable, of course, that quality limitations might be used to restrain competition—for instance, by imposing *maximum* quality restrictions, or by setting minimum restrictions (to which the patentee is not subject) so high as to insulate the patentee from price competition or from competition in the lower quality market. The writer is not aware of the existence of these types of restrictions and in their absence, one would not expect "quality" cases to arise.

3. [§7.15] Further Limitations on the Validity of the Intra-patent Restrictions

Even within the limited areas in which a restrictive license is considered valid, there are certain conditions that must be met: (1) the restriction must be held rigidly within the confines of a valid patent and the area (geographical, time, and subject matter) that the patent covers; (2) the arrangement must not involve "multiplicity," i.e., more than one patentee, more than one licensee, or more than one patent; and (3) the patentee must not assert the restriction beyond the immediate licensee by attempting to impose a servitude that will operate by remote control on successive holders or users of the patented invention. These three qualifications have been noted in the discussion of price restrictions at §7.12 and are discussed more fully at §§7.16–7.19, since the doctrines apply not only to intra-patent restrictions, but to other types of restrictions as well.

C. [§7.16] Restrictions That Go beyond the Scope of the Patent

The discussion of restrictions imposed on the licensee in §§7.10–7.15 has been directed to restrictions that fall within the scope of the patent in the sense that the patentee, possessed of a legal right to exclude others from using the invention, waives his right of exclusion with respect to part, but not all, of the monopoly area. Analytically, even such things as price restrictions and tie-ins can be brought within this classification inasmuch as in the absence of a license, the licensee could not sell the product at *any* price, or use the invention with *any* unpatented products whether purchased from the patentee or not. The patentee who grants a license containing an intra-patent restriction is comparable to the owner of a 160 acre farm who rents out the southwest 40, but keeps the remainder to himself.

Quite different are licenses that impose obligations lying *outside* the scope of the patent, either requiring the licensee to do things he would not be required to do in the absence of the license agreement or forbidding him to do things he would be free to do in the absence of the agreement.

Here, again, the variety of restrictions is almost endless. For our purposes, however, they fall into three moderately well-defined groups: (1) restrictions that lie clearly outside the patent and its scope as, for instance, an agreement not to manufacture or sell unpatented products that compete with the product covered by the license (see §7.17); (2) restrictions on conduct partly within and partly beyond the scope of the patent, as, for instance, an agreement not to export products made under the license to countries where no patent protection exists, or restrictions on the unpatented product of a patented process (see §7.18); (3) restrictions on conduct that, although not within the licensed patent, is collaterally related as, for instance, an agreement to pay royalties or an agreement not to challenge the validity of the licensed patent (see §7.19).

It does not follow that all or even most of such restrictions are illegal under the antitrust laws or objectionable as constituting a "misuse." An agreement to pay a royalty for the privilege of using the invention, for instance, may be so clearly reasonable as to be subject to no serious challenge. A requirement that the licensee avoid misrepresenting the unpatented product of a licensed process would clearly lack any anticompetitive effect and would not constitute a "misuse." Such restrictions must stand on their own feet, and meet the antitrust or "misuse" attack on the merits; unlike the intra-patent restrictions discussed at §§7.10-7.15, they cannot take refuge in the proposition that they simply represent a limited and partial waiver of the patent monopoly rather than a commitment by the licensee not to do something he would otherwise be free to do.

If this analysis of the situation is kept in mind, it will help to clarify some otherwise puzzling legal doctrine.

1. [§7.17] License Restrictions Having No Relation to the Patent

Restrictions that lie completely outside the patent are comparable to tie-in arrangements in that the patentee uses his power to withhold the license as a means of bending the licensee to his will in some completely unrelated respect. If such restrictions restrain competition or create a monopoly situation, they are doubly objectionable, since the patentee not only extends his monopoly beyond the scope of his patent, contrary to the tie-in doctrine, but also enters into an outright agreement not to compete that can find no protective umbrella in the patent.

The most common example of this type of restriction is a commitment by the licensee not to engage in the production and sale of competing unpatented products. These restrictions are uniformly held objectionable to the extent that they restrain competition, as they usually do. *McCullough v Kammerer Corp.* (9th Cir 1948) 166 F2d 759. A closer question is posed when the restriction requires a licensee to use his "best efforts" to exploit the patented invention without expressly barring activity in other areas. Such a requirement appears reasonable in terms of patentee protection, especially if the license is exclusive and the royalty is keyed to the extent of the licensee's use. Yet, broadly interpreted in favor of the patentee, such an agreement can have the effect of preventing the licensee from engaging in other commercial activity. Whether it will be held valid or invalid will depend on the circumstances and how the court interprets the agreement and evaluates its impact, effect and intent. On the whole, it has not been subject to serious question.

2. [§7.18] Restrictions Partly within and Partly beyond the Scope of the Licensed Patent

If the limitation imposed applies to activity that is partly *within* the patent (and is legal as so applied) and partly *beyond*, the question is closer. The situation can arise in a variety of ways:

(1) Suppose the owner of a carburetor patent licenses an automobile manufacturer to build not more than 100,000 automobiles containing the carburetor. He could not prevent the manufacture of additional automobiles *not* containing the carburetor, but he could limit the quantity of carburetor-using automobiles even though the carburetor is only one small element in the entire machine. See Nordhaus and Jurow (1961) *Patent-Antitrust Laws* at 152-157. To hold otherwise would cast doubt on every conceivable limitation, since it would be a rare case in which a product did not contain *something* from outside the patent—at least in terms of production activity, sales and advertising. In contrast stand price restrictions. The courts have held—possibly reflecting the basic doubt as to the validity of the restriction itself—that a patentee cannot fix the licensee's sale price of an entire product if the licensed product covers only an element in it. *United States v General Electric Co.* (D NJ 1949) 82 F Supp 753.

(2) Suppose the patentee imposes an otherwise valid restriction (quantity limit or geographical limit) for a specified number of years that extends beyond the expiration date of the patent or, by its terms, continues in effect after the patent is held invalid. Such a restriction is legitimate as long as there is a patent in force, but it becomes unsupportable once the patent expires or is held invalid. *United States v National Lead Co.* (SD NY 1945) 63 F Supp 513, 523-524, *aff'd* (1947) 332 US 319.

(3) Suppose the licensee agrees not to export the product into foreign countries. The United States patent is limited geographically to the United States. Some courts in the past have held such restrictions valid, on the ground of "reasonableness," on the theory that the patentee can bar the manufacture of the product or limit use of the process, or on the ground that he may be precluded by the existence of patents in the foreign country (which may be true, but seems irrelevant). The current trend is to hold that such limitations upon export go beyond the legitimate exercise of patent rights. See Nordhaus and Jurow (1961) *Patents and Antitrust Laws* 144-152.

(4) Suppose the owner of a patented machine or process imposes price, use, or comparable restrictions on a licensee with respect to the unpatented product of the machine or process. Although some early decisions treated such restrictions as proper, under current doctrine they are uniformly condemned, consistent with the prevailing tendency to hold the patentee strictly to the limits of his patent and the immediate operations under it.

(5) Suppose the patentee attempts to extend the limitation beyond the immediate licensee, imposing a servitude, so to speak, on the patented product enforceable against successive users or purchasers. Illustrative of such limitations are resale price limitations or limitations on the field in which a patented product can be used. Well-settled doctrine holds that such "remote control" is not permissible; the power to assert the patent does not extend beyond the immediate licensee. *Keeler v Standard Folding Bed Co.* (1895) 157 US 659. *Cf. General Talking Pictures Corp. v Western Electric Co.* (1938) 304 US 175. Without going into the reasoning that underlies the judicial conclusion (the arguments do not hold up very well, as a matter of logic), suffice it to say the doctrine appears to be firmly established and the courts show no disposition to question or change it. Any agreement that purports to bind subsequent purchasers or obligates the licensee to impose restrictions on such purchasers will, then, be clearly beyond the scope of the patent, however valid the restrictions might be with respect to the immediate licensee. Indeed, recent decisions holding that a patentee cannot restrict the licensee himself from selling drugs in bulk or from selling to certain classes of customers, indicate that the doctrine is not only as firmly established as ever, but may even be expanding. *United States v Glaxo Group Ltd.* (D DC 1969) 163 US PQ 668.

3. [§7.19] Restrictions Collateral to the License Agreement

Some conditions, although not involving the waiving of one's exclusive rights, are so closely identified with the patentee's interests as to become a necessary part of the license transaction.

The most obvious of these conditions is the obligation to pay royalties or some other consideration for the privilege of using the invention. The "consideration" one may pay for the license right can take many forms. Although most commonly it consists of money payments, it may take other forms, such as commitments not to do something one would otherwise be free to do, discussed in §§7.16–7.18, the conveyance of some other property (a sort of tie-in), or a license back under one's own patents (grant-back agreements would come within this category). The mere statement of these collateral types of consideration points up two features of the arrangement: (1) the collateral commitment may be challengeable under tie-in theories, *i.e.*, that the patentee is using his patent to extend his monopoly and (2) patent laws do not protect from antitrust attack the collateral commitment having adverse competitive consequences.

While monetary royalty payments generally are unobjectionable, they are not immune from attack and appear to be becoming more vulnerable. For example, in *Brulotte v Thys Co.* (1964) 379 US 29 the Supreme Court ruled that a royalty extending beyond the term of the patent so that a licensee continues to pay royalties on products he produces after the patent has expired, extends the patent beyond its legitimate scope and is illegal. The *Brulotte* ruling has given rise to a number of subsidiary questions. If some but not all the licensed patents expire, must the royalty be reduced? Some courts hold that it must, others that it need not, and the issue remains in a state of flux. *Rocform Corp. v Acitelli-Standard Concrete Wall, Inc.* (6th Cir 1966) 367 F2d 678 holds illegal a requirement for the continued payment of royalties after the main patent expires; *McCullough Tool Co. v Well Surveys, Inc.* (10th Cir 1965) 343 F2d 381, 409–410, *cert den* (1966) 383 US 933, holds that continuation of royalties while some of the licensed patents remain unexpired, is not illegal. If a patent covers only part of the product or indeterminate parts of a group of products, can the royalty be fixed on the basis of the entire production? This practice was held legal in *Automatic Radio Manufacturing Co. v Hazeltine Research, Inc.* (1950) 339 US 827 but subsequently in *Zenith Radio Corp. v Hazeltine Research, Inc.* (1969) 395 US 100 the Court held such a condition illegal unless required by the circumstances and voluntarily accepted by the licensee.

The Fifth Circuit ruled in *LaPeyre v FTC* (5th Cir 1966) 366 F2d 117 (violation of Federal Trade Commission Act), criticized in Baxter, *Legal Restrictions on Exploitation of the Patent Monopoly: An Economic Analysis* (1966) 76 *Yale LJ* 267, that a patentee may not discriminate among licensees in the rates he charges. Other factors were present in the *LaPeyre* case, however, and it seems unlikely that discrimination would normally be condemned.

The Seventh Ciruit in *American Photocopy Equipment Co. v Rovico, Inc.* (7th Cir 1966) 359 F2d 745 raised questions concerning excessive royalties, but the courts generally have not challenged them on this ground.

The fundamental principles applicable to royalties seem to be as follows:

(1) As long as the patent right exists the amount of royalty the patentee charges should be a matter for him to decide.

(2) Once the patent expires, a royalty arrangement cannot be used to affect the production or pricing practices of the licensee. Thus, a continuing royalty on unpatented products might be objectionable, whereas a continuing obligation to pay for a given period irrespective of the fact or amount of production might be acceptable as comparable to a lump sum royalty paid in installments.

(3) Discriminatory royalties, in the absence of some obligation to license applicants generally or some association with other objectionable practices, are probably permissible.

(4) A royalty arrangement that has the effect or purpose of influencing the licensee with respect to the production or sale of unpatented products may be treated as going beyond the legitimate scope of the patent monopoly. Royalty arrangements that are without business necessity based on production of unpatented products or that increase the rates if unpatented products are manufactured fall into this category.

(5) Finally, a royalty arrangement used to evade the prohibitions of the tie-in doctrine would be objectionable if, for instance, the patentee charges a lower royalty if the licensee purchases his raw materials from the patentee, than if he purchases them elsewhere. *Barber Asphalt Corp. v La Fera Grecco Contracting Co.* (3d Cir 1940) 116 F2d 211.

Another collateral condition frequently imposed on the licensee in the past was an agreement not to contest the validity of the patent or patents under which he was licensed. This type of agreement creates a conflict between two basic policies; a policy in favor of subjecting patents to attacks on validity to expose spurious patents and to open to public use the "inventions" covered, and a policy against permitting a licensee, who has accepted the benefits of a patent license and acquiesced in the presumed validity of the patent, from repudiating his agreement by challenging the patent's validity. For years an accommodation between these two policies existed; it was settled law that a patentee could not require a licensee to concede the validity of patents under which he was *not* licensed or on which the license was no longer in effect, but that an agreement not to challenge patents under which he did have a license was valid and enforceable. Indeed, even in the absence of such an agreement, settled common law doctrine held that the licensee was estopped from challenging the licensed patent. This is no longer the law. In *Lear, Inc. v Adkins* (1969) 395 US 653 the Supreme Court threw out the estoppel doctrine and held that a licensee may challenge the validity of the licensed patent, and any agreement prohibiting him from doing so is unenforceable as contrary to public policy. Still unanswered is the question whether the imposition or attempt to enforce an agreement prohibiting a licensee from challenging a patent gives rise to a cause of action under the antitrust laws. See, e.g., *The Bendix Corporation v Balax, Inc.* (7th Cir 1970) 421 F2d 809, *cert den* (1970) 399 US 911. It seems unlikely that it would, insofar as the conduct occurred prior to the 1969 *Lear* decision. Attempts to impose or enforce such an agreement subsequent to that decision pose a different question.

D. [§7.20] Restrictions Imposed on Patentee

Restrictions imposed on the patentee, like restrictions imposed upon the licensee, take many different forms. The general law with respect to such restrictions is relatively simple. Restrictions on the patentee are not imposed under the patent, and hence receive no protection from the patent laws or existence of the patent. To the extent that they restrain trade, lessen competition or contribute to monopoly, they are treated as if no patents were present. For example, an agreement by the patentee not to engage in the production or marketing of certain goods would have no better standing from an antitrust standpoint than if there were no patents.

Certain restrictions imposed on the patentee have not been the subject of serious antitrust attack, probably because of their integral relationship to accepted patent transactions, and their marginal adverse effect from an antitrust standpoint. For example, a patentee who imposes a price restriction on his licensee is probably committed (implicitly) not to sell below that price himself. Otherwise, the licensee would be put in an impossible position competitively. Yet, price restrictive agreements (see §7.12), condemned for other reasons, have not been criticized on this score.

Also, a patentee who assigns his patent to another party has been held estopped from challenging the validity of the patent in a subsequent suit against him for infringement. *Westinghouse Electric & Manufacturing Co. v Formica Insulation Co.* (1924) 266 US 342; *cf. Scott Paper Co. v Marcalus Mfg. Co.* (1945) 326 US 249. To the extent that this doctrine still is viable, the assignor-patentee could presumably *agree* not to challenge the validity of the patent. In the light of *Lear, Inc. v Adkins* (1969) 395 US 653, the assignor-estoppel doctrine may be rejected as was the licensee-estoppel doctrine and with it, the assignor-patentee's agreement not to challenge the validity of an assigned patent.

Finally, a patentee who grants an exclusive license in effect agrees not to license others. To the extent that the agreement is limited to the area of exclusivity, the limitation appears legitimate because the patentee has no remaining rights to grant in that area. But to the extent that he grants non-exclusive licenses or limited exclusive licenses and subjects himself to a veto power on the part of existing licensees before granting licenses to others the limitation is deemed objectionable. *United States v Krasnov* (ED Pa 1956) 143 F Supp 184, *aff'd per curiam* (1957) 355 US 5.

E. [§7.21] Assignments

The foregoing discussion of restrictive agreements has been directed to licensing arrangements. Restrictions on both patentee and assignee seem to occur less frequently and less justifiably in assignments.

There are some clear legal distinctions between licenses and assignments. A license is a *waiver* of the right to exclude. An assignment is a *transfer* of the right to exclude. Grant of a license reduces the patent monopoly; assignment does not. Licenses may vary greatly in scope. Assignments are generally of the *entire* right to exclude, although a limited assignment is sometimes permissible as, for instance, the assignment of a joint interest in the patent, or assignment of the rights for less than the entire United States (expressly provided for by 35 USC §261). Sometimes, as a practical matter, assignments and licenses are indistinguishable when, for instance, the patentee grants a license to X and, whether as a result of express agreement, mutual understanding, or course of conduct, refrains from licensing anyone else or from using the invention himself.

From an antitrust standpoint, it is hard to justify any restrictions beyond those inherent in the assignment, *i.e.*, those that exist as a matter of law making any *agreement* on the part of patentee or licensee superfluous. For example, an assignee for a limited geographical area would have no rights outside that area; an assignee of a joint interest in the patent as a tenant in common would have no right beyond what that tenancy gave him; an assignor of a patent would be estopped from challenging the validity of the patent, assuming the assignor-estoppel doctrine is still in effect.

In short, certain limitations may be imposed on the patentee or assignee by law or by the limited nature of the assignment, but any agreement to a limitation that goes beyond this, like restrictions on the patentee or extra-patent restrictions on a licensee, cannot take refuge in patent doctrine but must stand on its own feet. Illustrative of a qualification to this rule: The Assignee or co-owner of a patent might agree that he would not grant licenses under the patent without the assignor's consent even though, under the law, a co-owner has the right to grant such licenses. Conversely, a series of assignment agreements entered into between various parties and covering different areas, resulting in a "Balkanization" of the United States competitively speaking, might be attacked as a division of territories contrary to the antitrust laws, even though 35 USC §261 permits assignment of patent rights for only a part of the United States.

Limited assignments, whether in terms of assigning the right to exclude with respect to less than all of the entire patent rights or in terms of a joint ownership arrangement, are awkward things in the patent system. In addition, the lack of any legitimate need for restrictions except in rather special circumstances, plus the attendant difficulty of justifying the imposition of restrictions, results in a paucity of restrictive assignment agreements. Antitrust problems do arise in the case of assignments, but most of them arise out of the transfer as such, or out of the "multiplicity" aspect (patent pools and interchanges), discussed at §7.22.

F. [§7.22] Combinations of Patents, Patentees and Licensees ("Multiplicity")

We have heretofore been discussing restrictions imposed on licensee, assignee or patentee unilaterally, *i.e.*, a single patentee, single licensee, etc. Even as to those restrictions that may be acceptable in single situations, the existence of two or more parties or two or more patents may change the picture. Three types of situations present themselves: (1) two or more patentees get together and initiate a joint program; (2) a patentee enters into license agreements with two or more licensees who may be in actual or potential competition with each other; and (3) even though there be only one patentee and one licensee, a number of patents is involved. A patent pool in which, typically, several patentees throw their respective patents into a common pot and make licenses available to each other and sometimes to others on varying conditions, has characteristics of all three of these.

There is no basic objection to multiple patentees agreeing to license their patents. Indeed, such arrangements, without restriction, are conducive to the competition sought by the antitrust law. If, however, the parties agree upon restrictions, for example as to resale prices or territories, or agree not to license certain parties or not to grant licenses without the consent of the others, the agreements are viewed as a horizontal conspiracy among the patentees. To the extent that the agreements restrain competition, they are not protected from operation of the antitrust laws. *United States v Line Material Co.* (1948) 333 US 287.

Even if no restrictions are contained in the licenses themselves, combinations of patentees may have an adverse competitive effect, as for instance, when a selected group combines its economic and patent power to the exclusion of outsiders or when patents are combined in a single person augmenting his control or domination of an industry.

Even if there is only one patentee, difficulties may arise if restrictions are imposed on multiple licensees. Unrestricted licenses pose no problem since they further competition rather than limit it. Imposition of price restrictions, however, may have the effect of eliminating price competition among a number of competitors who, unlike the patentee, cannot justify the restraint on competition on the grounds of owning a patent. *Newburgh Moire Co. v Superior Moire Co.* (D NJ 1952) 105 F Supp 372, *aff'd* (3d Cir 1956) 237 F2d 283. Field or geographical restrictions may have the effect of dividing up territories or "Balkanizing" the market, thus restraining trade on a horizontal basis. While such arrangements are not treated as illegal *per se,* if the court finds that the arrangement actually restrains trade and that the various licensees accepted the licenses with knowledge that others are participating in the arrangement, or if it finds that the arrangement was really induced by the licensees rather than the patentee, it is likely to find a violation of the antitrust laws. Compare *United States v Sealy, Inc.* (1967) 388 US 350, holding unlawful a trademark licensing arrangement that allocated territories.

"Discrimination" may also become a problem when there are multiple licensees. It has generally been held that a patentee may discriminate between potential licensees, granting a license to one person but not to another. If a patentee grants licenses on more favorable terms to one licensee than to another and the discrimination adversely affects competition, courts have sometimes found the practice illegal, although other factors involving questionable competitive practices have also existed. *LaPeyre v FTC* (5th Cir 1966) 366 F2d 117. And see Oppenheim and Weston (3d ed 1968) *Federal Antitrust Laws* 684-686. As a practical matter, most patentees avoid such discriminatory practices by including in the agreement (probably at the insistence of the licensee) a "most favored licensee" clause providing that, if more favorable terms are granted to some other licensee, the named licensee will also be given the benefit of the better terms.

The last category is that of multiple patents or so-called "package licensing." There is no prohibition against a patentee granting a license under more than one patent in a single license agreement. The broader the license the more freedom from patent monopoly there is. The difficulty arises when the patentee attempts to tie one patent to another by requiring that one take a license under *all* the listed patents. The courts have treated such mandatory package licensing as objectionable, using the analogy of the tie-in doctrine. *Zenith Radio Corp. v Hazeltine Research,*

Inc. (1969) 395 US 100. A doubtful exception exists when it is found that the invention covered by patent X cannot be used without the invention covered by patent Y. *International Manufacturing Co. v Landon, Inc.* (9th Cir 1964) 336 F2d 723. The ban does not, of course, extend to situations in which the licensee is given a choice of taking either the package or taking a license under whatever individual patents he wishes, unless the conditions imposed make the choice an illusory one. There are many legitimate, practical business reasons for licensing patents as a package that make it advantageous in some situations not only to the patentee but to the licensee as well.

The patent pool, in which two or more patentees license each other under their respective patents on varying terms, is a common phenomenon. The overlap of patents, with the consequent blocking of each patentee from taking full advantage of the latest technology, may make pooling or, in its more limited form, cross-licensing, indispensible if the latest technology is to be utilized. A pool, for all practical purposes, dissolves the patent system vis a vis the participants insofar as the pooled technology is concerned, except as it may provide for the collection and allocation of royalties. Thus, as a general proposition, a patent pool may be viewed as contributing to competition rather than restraining it (except to the extent that elimination of patent protection may tend to discourage competitive research).

Difficulties with a patent pool arise in two situations: (1) when the pooling arrangement contains restrictive provisions concerning, for instance, price, territory, or quantity of production, and (2) when the pool is "closed," *i.e.*, limited to a selected group of participants with outsiders excluded. In the first situation, if the restrictions eliminate price competition, divide territories or fields of operation, or limit production, both the antitrust laws and the misuse doctrine come into play, since the combination of patentees bars them from the protective umbrella of the patent grant. If a pool is closed, competition may exist between the participants in the pool, but their combined advantages and economic strength may give them an unwarranted advantage over excluded competitors, and adversely affect competition or create a monopoly. While the closed pool has not been subjected to as strict scrutiny as the restrictive pool, it is still suspect. If the pool is too limited to have any serious impact, as when it is entered into for the purpose of resolving mutual impediments or when reasonable limitations (such as those relating to performance, quality, reputation, or financial reliability) exist for denying admission to the pool to certain parties, it may be found permissible. See general discussion in *Attorney General's Report, 1955*, 242–247. To avoid lengthy litigation it has been a fairly common practice for parties to include in the settlement of interference actions a provision for cross-licensing under any patent that may issue. Abuse sometimes attending this otherwise legitimate practice (see, *e.g.*, *American Cyanamid Co. v FTC* (6th Cir 1966) 363 F2d 757) caused Congress in 1962 to require that such settlement agreements be filed with the Patent Office and be available for inspection by government agencies. 35 USC §135(c).

V. [§7.23] Misuse Doctrine

The "misuse" doctrine has come into increasing use over the years. Its basic thrust is well stated in *Morton Salt Co. v G.S. Suppiger Co.* (1942) 314 US 488 at 493:

Where the patent is used as a means of restraining competition with the patentee's sale of an unpatented product, the successful prosecution of an infringement suit even against one who is not a competitor in such sale is a powerful aid to the maintenance of the attempted monopoly of the unpatented article, and is thus a contributing factor in thwarting the public policy underlying the grant of the patent. . . . Equity may rightly withhold its assistance from such a use of the patent by declining to entertain a suit for infringement, and should do so at least until it is made to appear that the improper practice has been abandoned and that the consequences of the misuse of the patent have been dissipated.

The *Morton Salt* statement taken literally seems to limit the misuse doctrine to situations in which (1) equitable relief is sought in an infringement suit; (2) enforcement of the patent against the alleged infringer would aid in the extension of the monopoly beyond the scope of the patent; (3) the misuse takes the form of impairing competition, *i.e.*, includes practices contrary to the policies of the antitrust law; and (4) the misuse causes injury to the party charged with infringement and would be furthered by prevailing in the infringement suit. Most of the cases do deal with situations in which these limitations are present; however, the courts have not held themselves strictly within these limits.

The misuse doctrine originated as a patent law doctrine; its sources can be found in cases decided soon after enactment of the Sherman Act, well before antitrust enforcement had really gotten under way. *Morgan Envelope Co. v Albany Perforated Wrapping Paper Co.* (1894) 152 US 425. Initially, it relied upon well-settled principles of estoppel, clean hands, and contract. If, for example, a patent license expressly required the licensee to use the patentee's unpatented materials the court might hold the condition to be contrary to public policy and unenforceable. Having so held, the objectionable provision would be blue-pencilled out of the license agreement and the license permitted to stand as amended. The doctrine developed into a rule that the objectionable restriction tainted the patent, irrespective of the existence of a contract and of whether it was the contracting licensee or an unrelated third party who was objecting to the practice. *Leitch Manufacturing Co. v Barber Co.* (1938) 302 US 458. Thus, the improper practice could be set up as a defense even by a party with whom the patentee had no contractual relation. As a practical matter, in most cases the parties setting up the defense (typically, defendants in suits for infringement) have been directly and adversely affected by the offensive conduct. The typical situation in which the doctrine developed was a suit brought on a contributory infringement theory against a seller of the unpatented material, or a suit for direct infringement brought against a party buying from some other source, usually with the supplier joined in the suit as a contributory infringer.

The doctrine started with a situation in which the unpatented material lay completely outside the patent but was usable with the patented invention (for instance, raw materials used with a patented machine or process). It expanded to situations in which the unpatented material was one of the elements in the patented combination (for instance, one of the unpatented chemicals in a patented drug compound). With the impetus provided by the broad language of *Morton Salt*, the doctrine has come to apply to *any* extension of the monopoly beyond the scope of the patent, as for example the inclusion of services, assertion of rights beyond the geographical or time limit of the patent, or objectionable price provisions. Nordhaus and Jurow (1961) *Patent-Antitrust Laws* 119. It is conceivable that the doctrine might be carried to the point that any misuse of the patent would come within the ban, as for example misrepresentations as to the efficacy of the patented invention, misrepresentations or concealment of pertinent evidence bearing on the validity of a patent, or harassment of infringers or possible infringers.

Historically, the misuse doctrine has been closely associated with the doctrine of contributory infringement. It became common practice, when a patentee discovered that a user of his invention was buying raw materials from someone else, regardless of whether the user was an actual licensee or an unlicensed third party, to bring suit against the supplier of the materials rather than against the direct infringer, charging the former with knowingly contributing to the infringing conduct of the latter. The tied product was usually a staple article of commerce and one that was in need of frequent and extensive replenishment—circumstances that made it worth the patentee's while to try to control sales, and the contributory infringement action proved to be one of the most effective methods of using patents to control unpatented products.

In *Mercoid Corp. v Mid-Continent Investment Co.* (1944) 320 US 661 the product tied to the patent was a highly specialized element (an unpatented electric control) in the patented combination (a furnace system) and was one that was built especially for the use and not usable for other purposes, as most staple products are, nor did it ordinarily require replacement or replenishment. The corporate holder of the patent rights was in the business of manufacturing the switches in question, not in the furnace business. It sold the switches with the understanding that any purchaser was free to use them in the patented furnace system. Defendant, Mercoid, was a competing seller of switches which it sold to customers for use in the patented combination—an act of infringement on the customer's part. The patentee sued Mercoid for contributory infringement. The Court held the patentee to be guilty of a misuse under the *Morton Salt* doctrine and in violation of the antitrust laws.

The *Mercoid* decision was strongly criticized by the business community and the patent fraternity. Efforts to limit the doctrine through Congressional action were enacted as part of the overall 1952 Patent Law Revision. Title 35 USC §271 provides in part as follows:

(c) Whoever sells a component of a patented machine, manufacture, combination or composition, or a material or apparatus for use in practicing a patented process, constituting a material part of the invention, knowing the same to be especially made or especially adapted for use in an infringement of such patent, and not a staple article or commodity of commerce suitable for substantial noninfringing use, shall be liable as a contributory infringer.

(d) No patent owner otherwise entitled to relief for infringement or contributory infringement of a patent shall be denied relief or deemed guilty of misuse or illegal extension of the patent right by reason of his having done one or more of the following: (1) derived revenue from acts which if performed by another without his consent would constitute contributory infringement of the patent; (2) licensed or authorized another to perform acts which if performed without his consent would constitute contributory infringement of the patent; (3) sought to enforce his patent rights against infringement or contributory infringement.

A careful reading of this language indicates an intent to overturn the *Mercoid* decision, although the legislative repudiation does appear to be limited to this case, and not to extend to the contributory infringement doctrine generally, as is evident from the fact that subsection (c), reestablishing application of the contributory infringement doctrine to sales of unpatented items, limits its application to the sale of items "constituting a

material part of the invention" and that are "not a staple article or
commodity of commerce suitable for substantial noninfringing use." Furthermore, the sweeping provisions of subsection (d) are limited in their
application to "contributory infringement" as defined in subsection (c).
Also, although subsection (d) expressly declares that the conduct there
specified shall not constitute a "misuse," it is silent as to whether it might
or might not still constitute a violation of the antitrust laws, unless the
"illegal extension" terminology is deemed to refer to the antitrust laws.

Enactment of the quoted provisions of Section 271 reconfirms the
existence of a legitimate area in which the contributory infringement
doctrine can operate—an existence some had suggested was brought to
an end by *Mercoid*. At the same time, the enactment keeps the operation
of the doctrine within strict and narrow limits, narrower than its application had been in times past. While preserving the general doctrine that
one who deliberately assists another in infringing will be treated as a
contributory infringer, following the analogy of the contributor to any
kind of tort, it laid down specific requirements regarding its application to
the sale of unpatented materials. For such a sale to constitute contributory infringement, the product must be a non-staple product, must have
been sold knowing that it would be used in an infringing manner, and
must be a material part of the invention. If these conditions are met, it is
immaterial whether the product is used with a patented process or is an
actual ingredient of the patented invention itself. Section 271 seems to
reject the extreme holding in the *Mercoid* case, since there the unpatented article was a non-staple specially adapted for use in the invention,
but does not condone common tie-ins of staple products like salt, cement,
and asphalt. Nor, presumably, is application of the antitrust laws affected,
barring the unlikely interpretation of the "illegal extension" reference as
constituting a repeal by implication.

Generously interpreted, the provisions of Section 271 could substantially limit the sweep of the misuse doctrine. However, it has not been
generously interpreted. There are several possible reasons for this: the
strong predisposition of the Supreme Court in favor of the antitrust laws
and their use to keep patent practices within limits; the generality of the
language employed in Section 271, especially subsection (d); the facts that
earlier attempts to enact these provisions on their merits had been unsuccessful and they came into the law only as part of an overall package
revision; and finally, because the bill was presented to and enacted by
Congress as a codification and most of the substantive changes were
glossed over. Wiviott, *Patent Law—Test of Invention* (1956) 38 *J Pat Off
Soc* 527. Although a few cases have held that the section modified the law

to some extent, in general the courts, including the Supreme Court, have been inclined to apply the tie-in doctrine in misuse cases in much the same fashion as they did prior to 1952. *Aro Manufacturing Co. v Convertible Top Replacement Co.* (1964) 377 US 476; *Calhoun v United States* (Ct Cl 1964) 339 F2d 665. In the absence of further action by the Congress, this approach seems likely to continue.

The misuse doctrine, as stated in *Morton Salt*, holds that disability to enforce the patent continues only until the effect of the misuse has been dissipated. The courts have been slow to find dissipation. Consequently, a finding of misuse may, as a practical matter, be tantamount to nullifying the patent because of the difficulty of correcting the situation to the satisfaction of the courts prior to expiration of the patent. Non-action or discontinuance of the objectionable conduct standing alone is unlikely to provide the necessary corrective. Some affirmative action, such as public repudiation of the practice by the patentee coupled with conduct to support the repudiation, is usually necessary. Kins, *Dissipation of Patent Misuse* (1968) 1968 *Wis L Rev* 918.

The antitrust law and the misuse doctrine, although similar in content and in substantial conformity as to objectives, are not completely co-extensive. Conduct may constitute a misuse of the patent without violating the antitrust laws, as for example when the adverse effect upon competition is minimal or when there is no interstate commerce. *Berlenbach v Anderson and Thompson Ski Co.* (9th Cir 1964) 329 F2d 782. Also, Section 3 of the Clayton Act (15 USC §14) does not apply to grant-backs and to tie-ins of materials with patents; yet, both of these practices would be treated as a misuse. As a practical matter, it is a rare case in which a given course of conduct constitutes a misuse but does not violate the antitrust laws, because tie-ins are treated as virtually a *per se* violation of the antitrust laws and the mere existence of a patent is generally deemed sufficient to create the control that is necessary to a finding of antitrust violation in tie-in cases. See discussion of tie-ins at §§3.9–3.18.

The impact of the misuse doctrine is less severe than the typical antitrust decree in four respects: (1) There is the possibility that the patent's enforceability may be restored; consequently, one may hesitate to invest substantial efforts or sums in a usage that ultimately may be enjoined. (2) Application of the misuse doctrine is limited to the patents that have been misused, whereas antitrust decrees often require compulsory licensing of other patents, existing and future, as well. Staff Report, *Compulsory Patent Licensing Under Antitrust Judgments* (1960) Senate Judiciary Subcommittee on Patents, Trademarks, and Copyrights. (3) The misuse doctrine has been limited to patents and probably does not extend to

related know-how, whereas antitrust decrees typically require the licensing of the know-how as well. (4) The misuse doctrine is defensive, rendering a patent unenforceable against an infringer or licensee, whereas antitrust
actions may result in injunctive action against related activities, recovery of treble damages, and imposition of criminal penalties.

The misuse doctrine, invoked most frequently in tie-in arrangements,
may pose a serious dilemma for the patentee who is not in a position to
sell the entire product covered by the patent or who is in the business of
selling products usable with a patented process on which he owns the
patent. He can stop selling the product, abandon the patent, or sell the
patent—all of them drastic solutions. The most practical approach is to
treat the material he sells and the patent as entirely separate things and
transact his business with each one separately and independently, selling
the product as if he had no patent and granting licenses on terms that
have nothing to do with whether the licensee is a customer with respect
to the product. See §7.13.

It is conceivable that the drastic impact of the misuse doctrine may
discourage one from entering into research and development activity that
one would otherwise undertake, or from granting licenses. Both of these
possibilities are probably more than offset by the fact that enforcement of
the misuse doctrine may discourage a patentee from engaging in undesirable practices, or may encourage others to engage in competitive research or to challenge the validity and enforcement of questionable patents. Even so, the misuse doctrine constitutes a severe sanction, a form of
confiscation that is not typically imposed upon one who uses his property
in an illegal manner. It sets a high standard for patentees and demonstrates
the relative importance that courts attach to the preservation of
antitrust objectives. Some of its extremes might be avoided if its invoca-
tion could be limited to infringement defendants actually damaged by the
improper conduct, to situations in which enforcement of the patent
would actually further the injury (a qualification that is found in *Morton
Salt* but tends largely to be ignored) and, in tie-in cases, to the tie-in of
replenishable and staple products.

VI. [§7.24] Remedies and Relief

Judgments in actions by private parties or the Antitrust Division under
the Sherman or Clayton Acts often contain provisions peculiarly applicable to patents. The most significant and controversial are those compelling patent licenses. Patent-antitrust decrees usually require that improp-

erly used patents and related patents become the subject of compulsory licensing. Sometimes, depending on the circumstances, even unrelated patents are included. Inasmuch as the patent law expressly gives the patentee the right to exclude others from use of the invention and imposes no obligation to grant licenses, the compulsory licensing provision represents a serious inroad upon one's patent rights. In *Hartford-Empire Co. v United States* (1945) 323 US 386 the Court justified the imposition of this relief on the ground that under the antitrust laws the court may order whatever remedy or relief it reasonably deems necessary to restore competition and the conditions of competition.

Difficult questions arise with respect to the nature and sweep of the compulsory license. Much controversy has concerned the question of royalty-free licenses or public dedication of the patents, as contrasted to reasonable royalty licenses. In the former instances, the effect is obviously to confiscate the patent as occurs with the application of the misuse doctrine. Here, however, the confiscation is permanent, not just for the period during which the adverse effects of the misconduct continue. Critics opposing royalty-free licensing, contend that it is confiscatory and unconstitutional; supporters justify the practice on the ground that in many instances effective competition cannot be restored except by withdrawing the patent and all the advantages that the patentee has, including the right to compensation from persons who use the invention. The United States Supreme Court has not conclusively and unequivocally passed on the question. *United States v National Lead Co.* (1947) 332 US 319; *but cf. Hartford-Empire Co. v United States, supra.* But the prevailing view is that royalty-free licensing or dedication is permissible where the circumstances are appropriate (*United States v General Electric Co.* (D NJ 1953) 115 F Supp 835), and the inclusion of royalty-free provisions in consent decrees is common.

Other sweeping provisions in patent decrees include the requirement for licensing related patents obtained in the future (usually limited to a five or ten year period) and the requirement for licensing know-how and engineering services. *Besser Manufacturing Co. v United States* (1952) 343 US 444; Hollabaugh and Rigler, *Scope of Relief in Government Patent and Know-How Antitrust Cases* (1966) 28 *U Pitt L Rev* 249. These provisions have been included because a decree that is limited to existing patents and does not include know-how and services often leaves the licensee in a competitively inferior position as compared to those who have access to the know-how and the accumulation of future patents.

Decrees also contain miscellaneous provisions designed to protect licensees and license applicants, as well as provisions that make it easier for

385

them to obtain such licenses and harder for the patentee to engage in obstructive and delaying tactics. Thus, patent decrees typically provide that the court may set a temporary royalty rate if the parties cannot agree on a reasonable royalty, to be followed, if necessary, by a proceeding to determine a reasonable rate. Decrees usually prohibit the patentee from imposing various listed restrictions and limitations on the licensee, preserve in the licensee the right to cancel the license, and prohibit the patentee from transferring his patents to others in order to avoid the conditions of the decree. Stedman, *Patent and Trademark Relief in Antitrust Judgments* (1949) 10 *Fed Bar J* 260.

As previously noted, the typical antitrust decree has a broader sweep than the misuse doctrine, because of its inclusion of additional sanctions and additional patents and know-how and because of its non-cancellable nature. Since the misuse doctrine bars recovery of royalties or damages for infringement during the period it is in operation, it amounts in effect to a royalty-free license. In contrast, the typical antitrust decree permits the patentee to collect a reasonable royalty. Thus, but for the inclusion of additional sanctions, the patentee could find himself in a better position after losing an antitrust action than he would be if no such action had been brought and he were subject to the misuse defense.

In addition to antitrust actions based on the Sherman and Clayton Acts brought by the Antitrust Division or private parties, the Federal Trade Commission has concurrent jurisdiction over patents when Clayton Act violations are present, although traditionally it has shown little tendency to get into the patent field. Its jurisdiction under the antitrust laws arises when there is a violation of either Section 3 (15 USC §14) (tie-ins) or Section 7 (15 USC §18) (acquisition of assets) of the Clayton Act. See discussion of FTC in Chapter 6. In *American Cyanamid Co. v FTC* (6th Cir 1966) 363 F2d 757, referred to as the *Tetracycline* case, the FTC attacked certain patent activities as unfair methods of competition in violation of Section 5 of the Federal Trade Commission Act (15 USC §45). That case dealt with a fraud on the Patent Office in obtaining the key tetracycline patent and a conspiracy to fix prices and control the marketing of tetracycline through an agreement entered into by the conspirators in settlement of an interference action concerning that patent. The FTC found the respondents in violation of the Federal Trade Commission Act and issued a cease and desist order. Although FTC cease and desist orders are generally more limited than judgments issued by the Department of Justice, they can be fairly extensive. In the *Tetracycline* case, the FTC did not declare the patent in question invalid, but it did require that it be licensed on a reasonable royalty basis. The FTC presumably could prevent the acquisition of further patents or require the divestiture of patents already acquired, as for example when there has been an illegal acquisition of a patent.

The patent provisions contained in the typical antitrust decree may be appropriate and necessary to the restoration of competition if the patents have played an active role in the antitrust violation. Some patent consent decrees have been criticized on the ground that drastic patent penalties have been imposed when the patents or patent practices were not the heart of the objectionable antitrust conduct, and when the decree leaves objectionable practices untouched, suggesting that the decree reflects a horse trade, with the defendant unwarrantedly giving up his patent rights in order to escape other more serious but legitimate sanctions. Crews, *Is It Necessary to Sacrifice Patent Property in Antitrust Consent Decrees?— The Effect Upon the Patent System* (1959) 41 *J Pat Off Soc* 801. Such decrees discredit the patent institution and fail to provide relief called for by the public interest.

Drastic patent provisions have been criticized on the ground that their inclusion will discourage research, invention, and developmental activity and thus defeat the purposes underlying the patent system. Spencer, *Threat to Our Patent System* (1956) 34 *Harv Bus Rev* 21. The argument has little credence insofar as existing patents are concerned. One can hardly contend that inventive activity should be encouraged by permitting one to engage in illegal acts with impunity. The argument carries more weight when the licensing of *future* patents is at issue, since one may be discouraged from making inventions and obtaining patents if the law is going to compel him to license or dedicate those he does obtain.

VII. [§7.25] Procedure and Jurisdiction

A few procedural and jurisdictional features that attend patent-antitrust cases can be noted briefly. Both antitrust issues and the misuse defenses may arise in connection with private patent litigation, with the following jurisdictional complexities:

(1) Patent litigation based on contract is based on the common law over which the state courts have jurisdiction, subject to removal to the federal courts if there is diversity of citizenship. In the state courts, *defenses* of misuse, unenforceability, antitrust violation or unfair competition, and counterclaims for unfair competition or violation of state statutes, will also lie. Counterclaims based on the federal antitrust laws will not lie, since they fall within the exclusive jurisdiction of the federal courts.

(2) If the common-law action is removed to federal court on diversity grounds, the enumerated defenses would lie and, in addition, the federal court would have jurisdiction over an affirmative antitrust counterclaim.

(3) In *United States v Farbenfabriken Bayer, A.G.* (D DC 1968) 1968 Trade Cases ¶72,569, *cert den* 393 US 216, 959, *final judgment* (D DC 1969) 1969 Trade Cases ¶72,918 the court held in an antitrust action that jurisdiction over a foreign patentee can be obtained pursuant to 35 USC §293 based on his use of his patents. This application of §293 clearly was not in the minds of Congress when it enacted the statute. However, its language giving the District of Columbia district court "the same jurisdiction to take any action respecting the patent or rights thereunder that it would have if the patentee were personally within the jurisdiction of the court" is broad enough to cover the court's ruling.

(4) If an action is brought for patent infringement, the action must be brought in federal courts. Title 28 USC §1338 provides:

(a) The district courts shall have original jurisdiction of any civil action arising under any Act of Congress relating to patents, copyrights and trade-marks. Such jurisdiction shall be exclusive of the courts of the states in patent and copyright cases.

(b) The district courts shall have original jurisdiction of any civil action asserting a claim of unfair competition when joined with a substantial and related claim under the copyright, patent or trade-mark laws.

Because subsection (a) vests jurisdiction of patent infringement suits in the federal courts, which also have jurisdiction of antitrust suits, jurisdictional problems are not likely to arise. Jurisdictional problems are further minimized because subsection (b) permits common-law actions for unfair competition, over which the federal courts would not otherwise have jurisdiction, to be brought in connection with a patent infringement suit provided the patent claim is related and substantial. Although subsection (b) was primarily designed to enable the patentee to join a claim for unfair competition with his claim for infringement, it is equally available for a counterclaim by the defendant provided the requirements of relatedness and substantiality are met. The federal court also has jurisdiction to entertain the defenses of misuse, antitrust violation, and unfair competition set up by the alleged infringer. Complex matters of joinder may arise if an antitrust issue is raised in an infringement suit or a declaratory judgment action. For instance *I.C.E. Corp. v Armco Steel Corp.* (SD NY 1961) 201 F Supp 411 held that an antitrust claim cannot be joined with a charge of patent invalidity in a declaratory judgment action. *Emhart Corp. v Continental Can Co.* (SD NY 1964) 144 US PQ 122 held that in an infringement suit brought by a patentee, a defendant cannot counterclaim for invalidity on antitrust grounds, if the matter is not related to the patent infringement claim and if there has been no injury to the defendant. An easing trend is indicated, however, in *Components, Inc. v Western Electric Co.* (D Me 1970) 167 US PQ 583, where the court permitted joinder of a misuse and an antitrust count in a declaration judgment action asserting that a patent was invalid and not infringed.

Following traditional doctrine with respect to antitrust defenses, courts have held that one cannot set up an antitrust defense in an infringement suit unless the patent is directly connected with the illegal conduct that forms the basis for the antitrust defense. *Dole Valve Co. v Perfection Bar Equipment, Inc.* (ND Ill 1970) 311 F Supp 459, 165 US PQ 337. In contrast, many courts permit one to assert a misuse defense even though the charged misuse has no relation to the issues in the case being tried. *The Ansul Co. v Uniroyal, Inc.* (SD NY 1969) 306 F Supp 541.

If both patent and antitrust issues arise in a case, the question is posed whether one should be tried before the other. In support of separation, it is pointed out that disposition of one of the issues may have the effect of disposing of the other. While *Attorney General's Report, 1955,* 249, suggested mandatory separation, the prevailing doctrine continues to be that both the questions whether or not to separate and, if separation is deemed desirable, which issue shall be tried first, lie in the discretion of the trial court.

Finally, the difference in sanctions between the antitrust doctrine and the misuse defense has resulted in some differences in terms of proof. The fact that the antitrust laws provide for more sweeping relief in civil judgments, mandatory treble damages, and the imposition of criminal penalties, understandably disposes the courts to be more demanding in proof, in establishing the relevance of the challenged conduct to the patent, and in procedural requirements, when the issues are cast in terms of antitrust rather than misuse.

VIII. [§7.26] Conclusions

Much of the difficulty in the patent-antitrust area is the basic conflict that exists between the patent system and antitrust policy. The patent system objective is to promote invention and innovation through the grant of limited monopolies, whereas the antitrust law objectives are to prevent monopoly, economic concentration, and restraint of trade, for the benefit of both the consumer (purchaser) and the business community. Since the patent and antitrust statutes are in many respects too general to provide the answers to specific issues, the burden falls on the courts to resolve or minimize the conflicts or decide which policy shall control. It is understandable if the decisions are sometimes pragmatic rather than logical; absent specific direction from Congress, the situation calls for pragmatism.

The problem is aggravated by our lack of information concerning the operations of each system in the areas in which they interact and the effect of applying doctrines and rules from one area on the objectives of the other institution. We need to learn more about the interaction of the two and to reevaluate existing rules in the light of what we learn.

Although the critics of the present "detente" are legion (some deeming the antitrust laws much too hard on the patent system and others deeming it much too easy), it may be that the present rapprochement is a fairly reasonable one. The complaint that the law in its present state fails to tell one what he can and cannot do with his patent is one that permeates the antitrust field. It is not limited to patents. Actually, on the whole the law is fairly predictable. The patent area has its share of *per se* rules, and whatever else may be said of the *per se* doctrine, it does tell one quite plainly what he can and cannot do and reduces the duration, complexity, and cost of litigation. Most of the uncertainty exists in the areas in which the law is still developing so that the rules have not yet crystallized.

The bias of most courts (especially the federal appellate courts) in favor of antitrust, where it and the patent system collide, is apparent. While patent holders may wish the law were otherwise, this approach serves to keep patent operations within bounds, and there is no persuasive evidence that application of broad antitrust rules has had a deleterious effect on the invention and innovation process.

Remaining trouble spots include:

(1) Tie-in arrangements, with the attending problems of dealing with specially-devised items, tie-in of nonreplenished items, treatment of "reasonable" restrictions such as those relating to guarantees, good-will and market reputation, and indirect efforts to reach tie-in objectives through discriminatory practices.

(2) Acquisition of massive portfolios of patents, posing such problems as monopoly and economic concentration (especially on the part of very large concerns), package licensing, and royalty determinations.

(3) Joint ventures, with the attendant problems of establishing proper limits of legitimacy, and possible distinctions based on whether the participants are large or small.

(4) Patent pools and interchanges, with the attending problems of restrictive licensing conditions, restrictions on participation, practices in the formulation and allocation of royalties, and the effect on both the competitive structure and inventive-innovative activity.

(5) Licensing practices involving such problems as discrimination between licensees, refusals to license, exorbitant royalties.

(6) The policies and scope of antitrust relief as presently applied in patent cases, especially the practices relating to compulsory licensing.

(7) Miscellaneous procedural problems in litigation, such as the rules concerning joinder, related claims, and counterclaims, and the appropriate areas for operation of the antitrust counterclaim and the misuse defense.

(8) International arrangements concerning patents, and the host of problems involving antitrust considerations that attend such arrangements.

(9) In addition to the foregoing are various collateral problems including (a) the prevailing lack (especially at the international level) of information and control with respect to patent practices that have a bearing on antitrust policies, (b) federal government policies with respect to patents, both in the allocation of patent rights arising out of government-sponsored research and development (as well as the practices followed in awarding research and development contracts) and in the administration of patent rights held by the government, and (c) interaction of the law and practices relating to patents with those relating to trade secrets and know-how, and their effect in antitrust terms.

Some of these problems may, on closer examination and more intensive exploration of the facts, turn out to be nonexistent. The solutions we are now applying may prove in some instances to be superior to any possible alternative. Some of the approaches one might explore are obvious; others are less so. But such exploration—and implementation in the light of the results—would clearly benefit both the antitrust and the patent structure.

8

Trade Associations

James C. McKay

Mr. McKay received the BS degree from Cornell University in 1938 and the JD degree from Georgetown University in 1947. He is a member of the District of Columbia Bar Association, the District of Columbia Bar, and the Washington, D.C. firm of Covington and Burling.

III. [§8.17]   The Role of the Company Attorney

IV.   Controversial Association Activities

A. [§8.18] Introduction
B. [§8.19] Standardization of Product
   1. *[§8.20] Checklist for Validity*
   2. *[§8.21] Adverse Effects*
   3. *[§8.22] Enforcement*
C. [§8.23] Ethical Codes and Their Enforcement
D. [§8.24] Seals of Approval
   1. *[§8.25] Checklist*
E. [§8.26] Customer Credit Information
F. Statistical Programs
   1. *[§8.27] Price Reporting*
   2. *[§8.28] Statistical Forecasting*
   3. *Procedures for Conducting Statistical Programs*
      a. [§8.29] Advisory Opinions
      b. [§8.30] Confidential Data
      c. [§8.31] Distribution

V. [§8.32]   Conclusion

I. [§8.1] Introduction

The association together of men with like interests is about as natural a phenomenon as one could imagine. Alexis de Tocqueville articulated this sentiment in 1835 in *Democracy in America:*

> Americans of all ages, all conditions, and all dispositions constantly form associations. They have not only commercial and manufacturing companies, in which all take part, but associations of a thousand other kinds, religious, moral, serious, futile, general or restricted, enormous or diminutive. The Americans make associations to give entertainments, to found seminaries, to build inns, to construct churches, to diffuse books, to send missionaries to the antipodes; in this manner they found hospitals, prisons, and schools. If it is proposed to inculcate some truth or to foster some feeling by the encouragement of a great example, they form a society. Wherever at the head of some new undertaking you see the government in France, or a man of rank in England, in the United States you will be sure to find an association.

The 1969 Directory of National Trade and Professional Associations of the United States lists in excess of 4,000 national trade and professional associations. According to the compilers, more than 160,000 sales meetings, 30,000 conventions, and 4,300 trade shows are held each year by United States associations.

Just as natural as the desire of men with common interests to associate together is the urge to discuss common problems and to seek ways to solve them. When representatives of competing businesses engage in such discussions and efforts there is a danger that they may, unless checked, slip into areas forbidden by the antitrust laws. It is the task of the trade-association attorney to prevent such a happening, and he should start by familiarizing himself with the pertinent statutes.

A. [§8.2] Pertinent Statutes

Trade-association attorneys should be familiar with a number of Federal laws, including the Robinson-Patman Act, the Federal Trade Commission Act, and the Sherman Act, and with the leading decisions under those statutes. Other statutes that affect trade associations include, for example, the Webb-Pomerene Act §§1-5, 15 USC §§61-65, exempting qualifying export trade associations; the Capper-Volstead Act §§1-2, 7 USC §§291-292, exempting certain activities of agricultural cooperative associations; and the Interstate Commerce Act §5b, 49 USC §5b, exempting certain activities of common carrier rate bureaus.

In general, the Robinson-Patman Act prohibits a supplier from favoring one or more of its customers over other competing customers, for example by giving a lower price, a larger advertising allowance, or extending more valuable merchandising services. Section 5 of the Federal Trade Commission Act (15 USC §45) is designed primarily to prevent unfair trade practices of all kinds, many of which also violate common law.

Generally of greater significance to the trade-association attorney than the Robinson-Patman Act or the Federal Trade Commission Act is the Sherman Act, Section 1 of which (15 USC §1) broadly prohibits agreements, combinations and conspiracies in restraint of trade, and Section 2 of which (15 USC §2), *inter alia*, prohibits combinations or conspiracies to monopolize. Proof of unlawful activity under these provisions does not require evidence of a formal agreement or understanding on the part of the conspirators. As a matter of fact, more often than not such proof is circumstantial. *American Tobacco Co. v United States* (1946) 328 US 781,

809–810 (involving Section 2 of the Sherman Act. "No formal agreement is necessary to constitute an unlawful conspiracy. The essential combination or conspiracy in violation of the Sherman Act may be found in a course of dealing or other circumstances as well as in an exchange of words."); *Interstate Circuit, Inc. v United States* (1939) 306 US 208, 227 (involving Section 1 of the Sherman Act. "It is elementary that an unlawful conspiracy may be and often is formed without simultaneous action or agreement on the part of the competitors. [citations] Acceptance by competitors, without previous agreement, of an invitation to participate in a plan, the necessary consequences of which, if carried out, is restraint of interstate commerce, is sufficient to establish an unlawful conspiracy under the Sherman Act.") Thus, a general rise in industry prices following a meeting of competitors at which prices were shown to have been discussed may give rise to an inference of conspiratorial activity.

Trade associations are peculiarly vulnerable to Section 1 of the Sherman Act because a trade association is a ready-made combination. (The extent to which the Supreme Court will strain to find a combination is apparent from its decision in *Albrecht v The Herald Company* (1968) 390 US 145.) Nearly every act taken by the membership constitutes an agreement among competitors. When competitors take "consciously" parallel action, the courts have inferred a conspiracy (*Interstate Circuit v United States* (1939) 306 US 208) unless the nature of the industry otherwise explains the parallel action. (*Theatre Enterprises Inc. v Paramount Film Distributing Corp.* (1954) 346 US 537.) Once the agreement is found or inferred, the sole remaining question is: Does the agreed-to activity unreasonably restrain trade?

B. [§8.3] Forbidden Activities in General

Most persons are cognizant of the fact that price fixing by competitors is illegal; antitrust cases frequently are front-page news. There is no question but that a *per se* violation of Section 1 of the Sherman Act (15 USC §1; see §2.26) occurs when a trade association takes steps to achieve price uniformity or stability within the industry. See, *e.g.*, *United States v Gasoline Retailers Ass'n. Inc.* (7th Cir 1961) 285 F2d 688, holding unlawful a continuing agreement made between a union and gasoline-station operators through their trade association. In an effort to eliminate price wars, the operators agreed to refrain from displaying signs showing the price of gasoline on station premises or giving trading stamps to customers. Yet the Antitrust Division continues to obtain indictments charging price fixing in increasing numbers each year against trade associations and their members, and plaintiffs continue to bring and win treble-damage civil actions (see Chapter 12) in ever greater numbers based on price-fixing arrangements. Heavy fines are levied, imprisonment is threatened or incurred, enormous verdicts are recovered, and costly settlements are negotiated. Many thousands of dollars that might have been used by association members to improve their industry and promote their sales are literally wasted.

Probably, the reason this effort by members of trade associations to fix prices persists is because it is natural for businessmen to seek ways to maximize profits, and agreements for an industry-wide price increase appear to be such a simple way to do so. Agreements are often detected, for industry-wide price hikes attract the attention of government agencies as well as customers.

Equally tempting as a mode of increasing profits are agreements among competitors to discontinue producing a "cheap" item that is "disrupting" the market and that is kept as a product line only because a few "mavericks" insist on selling the product (see §2.28). Such agreements constitute *per se* violations of Section 1 of the Sherman Act, and participants are subject to government prosecution (see Chapter 11) and treble-damage actions (see Chapter 12).

Other activities constituting *per se* violations of Section 1 of the Sherman Act include agreements to allocate customers (see §2.30), to divide markets (see §2.29), to restrict the volume of production or sales (see §2.28), to engage in boycotting activities (see §2.31), and to channel distribution (see §2.28).

Still other activities, while not *per se* unlawful, may be forbidden because their purpose or effect is to suppress competition. Such activities include product standardization, discussed at §§8.19-8.20; enforcement of ethical codes, discussed at §8.23; seals of approval, discussed at §§8.24-8.25; customer credit information, discussed at §8.26; and statistical programs, discussed at §§8.27-8.31.

C. [§8.4] Legitimate Activities in General

It is not possible to discuss all the numerous activities that a trade association may properly conduct. They include a multitude of subjects, such as wages and fringe benefits, public relations, labor relations, plant safety, government relations, education and training programs, health programs, product research, product publicity, and taxes.

These activities are described as legitimate because as associations normally engage in such activities, they have no antitrust repercussions. However, as with the more controversial activities discussed at §§8.18–8.31, these so-called "legitimate" activities may become unlawful if they are part of an anticompetitive scheme. For example, issuance by an association of a "product research" report, not scientifically substantiated, disparaging a technically sound product for the purpose of destroying its competition, would clearly constitute a violation of the Sherman Act (15 USC §§1–7) as well as of the Federal Trade Commission Act (15 USC §§41–58) notwithstanding the fact that issuance of such reports is generally considered a legitimate activity.

A number of the above activities involve communications with the public or some special segment of it and can often better be handled by an association than by a single company. An association representing an entire industry is particularly effective in dealing with the government. See Executive Order No. 11007 (1962) 27 Fed Reg 1875 for rules governing government–industry advisory committees. Also, an association may lobby for the benefit of the industry it serves. See *Eastern Railroad Presidents Conference v Noerr Motor Freight, Inc.* (1961) 365 US 127, 139, holding that forty-one truck operators and their trade association had no cause of action against twenty-four railroads, an association of their presidents, and a public relations firm for lobbying for laws destructive to the trucking industry, notwithstanding that the lobbying may have had an anticompetitive purpose and actually caused injury. For further discussion of the *Noerr-Pennington* doctrine, see §2.47. On lobbying, see Federal Regulation of Lobbying Act, 2 USC §§261–270.

Other activities mentioned above involve research and analysis, which may benefit all members of the industry. Doing such work through the association spreads the cost, prevents duplication, and may result in a higher quality study for large and small companies alike.

In connection with association research, it should be noted that a trade association, because it is composed of a group of competitors, does not have the same patent rights as an individual patentee. An association must offer to license all competing companies for a reasonable compensation. *Hartford Empire Co. v United States* (1945) 323 US 386, 413–418, clarified at 324 US 570 (1946). It cannot fix the licensee's sale price, limit the licensee's production, or restrict the licensee's use to a specified geographic area. *Standard Sanitary Manufacturing Co. v United States* (1912) 226 US 20. In contrast, a member company holding a patent may keep the patent for itself (*Continental Paper Bag Company v Eastern Paper Bag Company* (1908) 210 US 405, 428–429), assign all or part of it (35 USC §261), or license one or many users. (*Cutter Laboratories, Inc. v Lyophile-Cryochem Corp.* (9th Cir 1949) 179 F2d 80 at 92–93). A company may restrict its assignee to a particular geographic area (35 USC §261; *Ethyl Gasoline Corporation v United States* (1940) 309 US 436, 456), to a particular use (*General Talking Pictures Corporation v Western Electric Co.* (1938) 305 US 124, 126-127), to a particular production volume (*United States v Parker-Rust-Proof Co.* (ED Mich 1945) 61 F Supp 805, 812), and probably to a specified sales price (*United States v Huck Manufacturing Co.* (ED Mich 1964) 227 F Supp 791, 803-804, *aff'd per curiam* (1965) 382 US 197; *United States v General Electric Co.* (1926) 272 US 476). On patents and antitrust, see Chapter 7.

II. [§8.5] Role of Trade-Association Counsel: Preventive Measures

As noted above, it is not very difficult to recognize hardcore antitrust violations. Most trade-association executives, as well as the members, recognize such violations as quickly as do their attorneys. The attorney's principal goal is to discourage the members from following a seemingly easy—but frequently disastrous—path to higher profits. That goal will be reached, if ever, through careful adherence to a number of simple and relatively inexpensive procedures.

A. [§8.6] Review of Trade-Association Bylaws

Every trade association should have a set of bylaws as a basic charter of its operations. If the association is to be newly formed, the attorney should draft the bylaws; otherwise, he should carefully study them, and revise them if necessary.

1. [§8.7] Statement of Purpose

The purposes of the association should be clearly stated in the bylaws, and those purposes, of course, must be lawful. *Advertising Specialty National Ass'n v FTC* (1st Cir 1956) 238 F2d 108, 116-117. A safe and effective statement of purpose might simply recite:

The purpose of the Association shall be to promote the interests of the industry by providing for an organization through which the industry may undertake those lawful activities that can be conducted most effectively by cooperative effort.

Obviously, a self-serving statement such as this would be of little avail in a legal action brought against the association if its activities were in fact unlawful. *American Column & Lumber Co. v United States* (1921) 257 US 377, 392.

2. [§8.8] Provisions Governing Admission and Expulsion from Membership

Among the more important provisions of the bylaws are those relating to eligibility for membership, admission to membership, and expulsion from membership. In every industry there is probably at least one so-called maverick, disliked by others because he does not follow what is generally thought to be conventional business practices and frequently "disrupts" the market. The temptation is to keep him out of the association. Such an action, however, raises questions about the true purpose of the association, and whether the association is open only to companies that follow certain practices.

If the association truly reflects the interests of the entire industry, there is no legitimate reason why all members of the industry should not readily be admitted. This is not to say, for example, that wholesalers must be admitted to a trade association of manufacturers or vice versa. In fact, so-called "vertical" membership in an association should be avoided because it presents a temptation to unlawful efforts to "stabilize" the industry. *United States v Frankfort Distilleries* (1945) 324 US 293, 295-296; *Advertising Specialty National Ass'n. v FTC* (1st Cir 1956) 238 F2d 108.

But certainly every manufacturer in an industry should be eligible for membership in an association that purports to represent all the manufacturers in that industry. Moreover, each manufacturer should be admitted automatically to membership, and not be required, in order to join, to obtain the favorable vote of the majority of the members or other governing committee. *Associated Press v United States* (1945) 326 US 1, holding exclusion from membership, being of crucial competitive significance, constituted a violation of Section 1 of the Sherman Act (15 USC §1). *Cf.* Advisory Opinion Digest 152 (1967) [1967-1970 Transfer Binder] Trade Reg Rep ¶18,125.

In addition to industry restriction, some associations restrict membership to a defined geographic area. The area of competition rather than the situs of the main office should govern in such situations. See *American Federation of Tobacco Growers v Neal* (4th Cir 1950) 183 F2d 869, 873 holding it an unreasonable restraint of trade in violation of Section 1 of the Sherman Act to exclude a tobacco cooperative from membership in an association that controlled tobacco selling in the Danville market on the ground that its warehouse was outside the city limits. An acceptable bylaw requirement would be one that provided:

Any firm, partnership, or corporation actively engaged in the ____(e.g. manufacture)____ **of** ____(describe the industry's products)____**immediately prior to application for membership is eligible for membership in the association.**

No member should be subject to expulsion except for reasons unrelated to competition or commercial considerations. The bylaws might provide:

Any member more than three months in arrears in payment of dues or assessments may be expelled from the association upon an affirmative vote of a majority of the entire membership.

But eligibility for membership or continued membership should not be conditioned on, for example, in maintaining a minimum inventory. *Montague & Co. v Lowry* (1904) 193 US 38, 47. Nor should bylaws contain provisions expelling members who advertise prices. See *United States v Utah Pharmaceutical Ass'n.* (D Utah 1962) 201 F Supp 29, *aff'd per curiam* (1962) 371 US 24 and *Northern California Pharmaceutical Association v United States* (9th Cir 1962) 306 F2d 379, *cert den* (1962) 371 US 862, both holding that the adoption, dissemination, and promotion of a price schedule with the intent to produce price uniformity violates Section 1 of the Sherman Act. Similarly, members cannot be expelled for violating bid depository rules adopted by the association prohibiting discounts exceeding a specified percentage on combination bids and requiring large bid fees and bid withdrawal fees. *United States v Bakersfield Associated Plumbing Contractors, Inc.* (SD Calif 1958) 1958 Trade Cases ¶69,087, *modified* (1958) 1959 Trade Cases ¶69,266. Such restrictive provisions have a direct bearing on competition and are unlawful.

3. [§8.9] Dues

The bylaws may include a provision for the payment of dues. Dues are frequently assessed members in proportion to their production or sales, with a minimum requirement. The bylaws might provide:

The association may from time to time establish dues to be paid by each member on the basis of its _____(e.g., sales/production)_____ **of** _____(describe the industry's prod-ucts)_____ **provided that no member shall pay annual dues of less than** _____(e.g., $500)._____

The bylaws may also require an admission fee. Care should be taken not to set either the minimum dues or the admission fee so high that small companies are effectively excluded from membership. This is particularly so when high dues or high admission fees are not necessary to operate the association.

4. [§8.10] Voting

It is not unusual for members paying higher dues to believe that they should be entitled to voting rights in proportion to their financial contribution to the association. However, such a provision should be avoided to preclude any inference that the association is dominated by the larger members. The bylaws should provide:

Each member is entitled to only one vote.

Oppenheim, *Federal Antitrust Laws* (3d ed, 1968).

B. Preparing for and Attendance at Meetings

1. [§8.11] Agenda

The trade-association attorney should always review in advance of general circulation the proposed agenda of meetings in order to eliminate items that may be of questionable legality. For example, a member of the beverage bottling industry may suggest that the agenda for an association meeting include the subject "elimination of container-return allowances," and it may be placed on a proposed agenda. It will be obvious to the association attorney that because the suggested topic is directly related to prices and may not be the subject of joint discussion or action by competitors, it cannot be included on the agenda and cannot be discussed at the meeting. (On forbidden topics, see §8.12.) The improper item should be promptly removed from the proposed agenda even though those conducting the meeting agree that the subject will not be discussed, for agendas may be used as evidence of what occurred at the meeting and may be given greater credibility than a member's recollection. See *Appalachian Apple Service, Inc.* (1954) [1954–1955 Transfer Binder] Trade Reg Rep ¶25,169, page 35,319, holding that a report written shortly after the meeting in question should be given greater weight. To the same effect see *United States v Gypsum Co.* (1948) 333 US 364, 396, in which the Court held that if "testimony is in conflict with contemporaneous documents, we can give it little weight, particularly when the crucial issues involve mixed questions of law and fact."

2. [§8.12] Discussions at Meetings: Forbidden Topics

During a meeting, the association attorney frequently will be relatively inactive. His presence alone ought to assure that members will not engage in improper discussions, but he should be alert and quick to advise when a discussion is approaching "off-limits" character. He should not hesitate to remind the members of the fate of antitrust violators who get caught. It should be emphasized that company officials have served jail sentences and have been heavily fined for antitrust law violations. See, for example,

United States v American Radiator & Standard Sanitary Corp. (WD Pa 1968) [US Antitrust Cases Summaries (1961-1970) Transfer Binder] Trade Reg Rep ¶45,066 at 52,636 (jail sentences and fines up to $40,000). The members should also be told that the government often seeks dissolution of trade associations, as well as the entry of burdensome injunctive provisions against the member companies. And mention should be made of the multimillion-dollar jury verdicts that juries sometimes award. It is hoped that recitation of such grim events will remind the participants that antitrust violators are frequently caught and that the consequences can be disastrous.

Despite the presence of counsel, there sometimes is an almost overwhelming urge on the part of competitors gathered together at least to talk about prices. In theory, Section 1 of the Sherman Act (15 USC §1) cannot be violated by mere price discussions among competitors. The danger is that the discussions will lead to tacit understandings affecting prices. If it happens that a general price increase becomes effective shortly after a meeting at which prices were "discussed," neither the government nor a treble-damage plaintiff would have much difficulty in connecting the two events. See *Safeway Stores, Inc. v FTC* (9th Cir 1966) 366 F2d 795, 799, *cert den* (1967) 386 US 932. Accordingly, price discussions among representatives of member companies should be prevented, if possible, by the trade-association attorney.

Similarly, discussions among competitors concerning inventories, production, and costs of individual companies should also be avoided even though such discussions alone would not constitute a violation of Section 1 of the Sherman Act. *Maple Flooring Manufacturers Ass'n. v United States* (1925) 268 US 563; *Container Corp. of America v United States* (1969) 393 US 333. See discussion of statistical programs at §§8.27-8.31.

There is also a continuing temptation among members of an association to discuss so-called "trade abuses" and to consider joint action to eliminate them. The difficulty is that activities that certain association members regard as being abuses may be regarded by the government and the perpetrators as a form of competition. The association may not engage in any effort to eliminate a trade abuse in such a way as unreasonably to restrain competition, even though the abuse does in fact exist. In *Fashion Originators' Guild v FTC* (1941) 312 US 457, an association's program designed to stop, by group boycott, the "unethical and immoral" practice of "style piracy" was held to violate Sections 1 and 2 of the Sherman Act, Section 3 of the Clayton Act (15 USC §14), and Section 5 of the Federal Trade Commission Act (15 USC §45); in *Sugar Institute, Inc. v United States* (1936) 297 US 553, 576 and 601, an association's program to abolish a "vicious and discriminatory system of secret concessions" by requiring its members to announce in advance their prices and terms and conditions of sale and to adhere to such prices and terms until they had made another announcement was held unlawful; in *Standard Sanitary Manufacturing Co. v United States* (1912) 226 US 20, an association's effort to eliminate, by group boycott, sales of inferior products, or so-called "seconds," was held unlawful. Thus, trade-association counsel should discourage discussions or joint action relating to any trade abuse that may be thought to exist in the industry if the so-called "abuse" constitutes a form of competition, albeit undesirable.

The FTC has advised trade associations that members should not discuss and seek a guarantee from members' suppliers that a quoted price will remain firm for a definite number of days on the ground that there is

. . . too grave a danger that it would serve as advice whereby the concerted power of members of the local association, and even of the national association, might be brought to bear to coerce the producers, or their association, to conform pricing policies to the standard desired, or at the very least as an invitation to enter into agreement among themselves to do so.

Advisory Opinion Digest 137 (1967) [1967-1970 Transfer Binder] Trade Reg Rep ¶18,041.

Similarly, the Commission has advised that an association should not issue a code that describes "fair and adequate" profit levels (Advisory Opinion Digest 115 (1967) [1965-1967 Transfer Binder] Trade Reg Rep ¶17,878) or the prices members are to be paid (Advisory Opinion Digest 15 (1966) [1965-1967 Transfer Binder] Trade Reg Rep ¶17,456), and should not prepare and distribute a standard rate and service-pricing manual for use by association members (Advisory Opinion Digest 158 (1968) [1967-1970 Transfer Binder] Trade Reg Rep ¶18,148).

In this connection see also discussions of standardization at §§8.19-8.22 and ethical codes at §8.23.

3. [§8.13] Rump Meetings

Members are occasionally tempted to hold rump sessions before or after the formal meeting, perhaps on the assumption that what the attorney doesn't know won't hurt the members. If the attorney suspects that such meetings are being held—and perhaps even if he has no suspicions—as a preventive measure, he should point out to the members that the informality and relative obscurity of these meetings are no protection and may even be quite incriminating.

4. [§8.14] Meeting of Committees

Many associations are so large as to make it impracticable to hold meetings of the entire membership. Those associations conduct most of their business through committees, with the governing bodies meeting perhaps once or twice a year. Trade-association counsel should attend all meetings of the governing body and of any committee that has the power to develop policies or to make final decisions about the association's programs and activities, particularly those committees whose activities in any way involve relations with customers or suppliers. Without clear and demonstrable business reasons, the formation of such committees should be avoided if possible, since they can be fertile hatching grounds for anticompetitive activity. Some committees will not warrant substantial attention of the trade-association attorney; for example, a public relations committee, a government committee, a plant safety committee, or an education and training committee probably would not engage in activities with antitrust overtones. See discussion of legitimate activities in general at §8.4. Nevertheless, the attorney should remain generally aware of the activities of all committees to assure himself that they are within legal bounds.

C. [§8.15] Review of Minutes

Complete and accurate minutes should be prepared by the appropriate staff member after all meetings of the association or its committees. Minutes of meetings attended by the attorney should be reviewed by him before distribution to the membership. Minutes, like the agenda, can be used as circumstantial evidence of what occurred at the meeting. The attorney should make certain that the minutes accurately reflect the business transacted at the meeting and contain no ambiguous phrases that might be misinterpreted by the membership or anyone else. Possible pitfalls cannot be predicted with certainty, but an alert attorney ought to recognize them on sight. For example, careless and incorrect usage of words like "agree" or "understanding" might create ambiguity. If, for example, the members had agreed at a meeting that the standards should be changed to eliminate an obsolete design, carelessly drawn minutes might recite that the members had agreed not to manufacture the design; but while the members of an association may properly agree to eliminate an obsolete design from the standards, they may not lawfully agree to stop manufacturing it. See discussion of standardization at §§8.19–8.22. The minutes should be modified to reflect correctly the action in fact taken by the association.

D. [§8.16] Review of Association Files

Another precautionary step that ought to be taken by the trade-association attorney is a periodic—perhaps once a year—review of the files of the association, particularly the correspondence files. What are the members saying to the association executive and staff, and vice versa? Are they discussing matters that neither appeared on any agenda nor were considered at any meeting? If so, what is the nature of the discussions?

The periodic review of files is a part of the attorney's "watchdog" duties. However, its primary purpose is to remind and discourage, not to search and destroy. Thus, if the attorney discovers a damaging piece of correspondence, he may not ethically—or perhaps legally—advise the destruction of the document. See 18 USC §§1503 and 1505 declaring it a federal offense punishable by $5,000 fine and/or imprisonment of up to five years for persons who corruptly obstruct the due administration of justice; *United States v Solow* (SD NY 1956) 138 F Supp 812 concerning the destruction of four letters to prevent their production before a pending grand jury investigation. His only recourse is to investigate the circumstances, make certain that no illegal activity is in progress—and if so, stop it—and take all reasonable steps to insure against a repetition of the incident. Beyond that, the attorney and the trade-association members can only hope for the best.

III. [§8.17] The Role of the Company Attorney

The preceding discussion has been directed at the attorney who represents the trade association. What is the role of the attorney who represents a member company or a company that desires to join an association or to participate in the formation of an association? He should ascertain that there is a legitimate need for a trade association in the industry. Sometimes a trade association is born because of a specific and immediate problem of an emergency nature confronting the whole industry. Other associations are formed because of a recognition that the welfare of the industry requires cooperative action in certain areas where cooperation is permissible under the law, such as standardization, public relations, education, and government relations. If the association is to be newly formed, the company attorney should investigate the facts and circumstances surrounding the movement leading to the decision to organize the group to better understand its purposes and proposed programs.

If the association already exists, the company attorney should review the bylaws, the prior minutes, agendas, and other publications of the association. From this review the attorney should attempt to ascertain and comprehend its standing committees, the code of ethics, its purposes, and its principal programs. In either case, if the association has no substantial activities beyond the holding of meetings, the attorney would be justified in questioning the purpose and intentions of the group, and further investigation would be called for. In addition, the attorney ought to attend a few meetings, question officials of his client about their participation in association affairs, and review his client's files relating to the association.

The activities of associations normally will extend far beyond the mere holding of meetings. The great bulk of association work is accomplished by committees engaged in work designed to improve the industry as a whole. Such an association should give company counsel little concern. However, he should "touch base" with his company representative from time to time in order to keep abreast of all association activities, and he should feel no reluctance to attend association meetings occasionally, even after he is satisfied about the propriety of the association's activities. The trade-association attorney probably would welcome the opportunity to discuss association problems with company counsel and to acquire any fresh ideas that may evolve from those discussions. By the same token, the company counsel would become more knowledgeable concerning association activities and would be in a better position to advise his client.

If the company attorney concludes that the association is conducting one or more unlawful activities, he should advise an immediate resignation, not merely a withdrawal from active participation in association affairs. Continued membership alone, with knowledge of illegal activities, may be sufficient to implicate the client. *Phelps Dodge Refining Corp. v FTC* (2d Cir 1943) 139 F2d 393, 396.

IV. Controversial Association Activities

A. [§8.18] Introduction

Although trade associations run afoul of the antitrust laws from time to time, most of their activities are perfectly legitimate. A few of the more important, and controversial, ones from an antitrust standpoint are discussed below. They include standardization programs, adoption of seals of approval, collection and dissemination of customer credit information, statistical programs, and miscellaneous activities.

B. [§8.19] Standardization of Product

Standardization of product is a legitimate activity of a trade association, if it is not a facet of an effort to fix prices or to eliminate competitive products or competitors or otherwise to restrict competition.

Proposed standards can run the gamut from the very dangerous to the
very safe. At the safe extreme are proposals that clearly have no antitrust
significance and that account for the overwhelming majority of standardization programs. Generally they concern industry nomenclature describing the products' size or material content. Thus, no antitrust problems
flow from a determination that commercial standards require that all bolt
holes be of a certain diameter or that metal not be labeled "fourteen
karat gold" unless it contains a specified percentage of gold. Nor would
an investigator's eyes light up if he uncovered a requirement that all suits,
coats, and dresses bearing a given size fall within an agreed range of
measurements. The commercial need for such agreement in industry is
obvious.

At the other end of the spectrum are the standardization activities
involving serious antitrust risk because of their anticompetitive purpose or
effect. For example, in *Radiant Burners, Inc. v Peoples Gas Light & Coke
Co.* (1961) 364 US 656 a manufacturer of gas heaters successfully sued a
trade association and ten members on the ground that the association
gave seals of approval to gas burners not on the basis of objective tests
but for anticompetitive purposes, that the association refused to certify
plaintiff's technically sound gas burner, and that two member gas companies refused to provide gas for plaintiff's burner, all in violation of Section
1 of the Sherman Act (15 USC §1).

In *National Macaroni Manufacturers Ass'n. v FTC* (7th Cir 1965) 345
F2d 421, the court found anticompetitive in effect a resolution adopted
by a majority of association members (over the strong objections of some
members) seeking to induce suppliers of durham wheat to blend it with
less costly wheat, stating:

[W]here all or the dominant firms in a market combine to fix the composition of
their product with the design and result of depressing the price of an essential
raw material, they violate the rule against price-fixing agreements as it has been
laid down by the Supreme Court.

It is not the standardization of products that is unlawful; it is the use of
standardization to force uniform prices or otherwise to eliminate some
aspect of competition among the members of an industry. As stated in
Bond Crown & Cork Co. v FTC (4th Cir 1949) 176 F2d 974, 979:

The standardization of product . . . would be innocent enough by itself, but not
when taken in connection with standardization of discounts and differentials,
publication of prices with agreements not to charge less than a minimum, . . .
freight equalization . . . and such uniformity of prices throughout the industry as
to leave no price competition of any sort anywhere.

Very often it is obvious from the product that there is no business justification for more uniformity of product design, except to facilitate more uniform pricing. For example, in *C-O-Two Fire Equipment Co. v United States* (9th Cir 1952) 197 F2d 489, 493, *cert den* (1952) 344 US 892, the court noted:

[S]tandardization of a product that is not naturally standardized [fire extinguishers] facilitates the maintenance of price uniformity.

The court found a violation of the Sherman Act, stating (197 F2d 497):

Here, . . . we have in addition to price uniformity, the other so-called plus factors. . . . They include a background of illegal licensing agreements containing minimum price maintenance provisions, an artificial standardization of product, a raising of prices at a time when a surplus existed in the industry, and a policing of dealers to effectuate the maintenance of minimum price provisions. . . .

To the same effect are *Fort Howard Paper Co. v FTC* (7th Cir 1946) 156 F2d 899, *cert den* (1946) 329 US 795, invalidating standardization of sizes and weights of crepe paper; and *Milk and Ice Cream Can Institute v FTC* (7th Cir 1946) 152 F2d 478, invalidating standardization of milk cans.

If an adequate business reason exists for issuing uniform standards for a given product line, no violation will be found. For example, in *United States v National Malleable & Steel Castings Co.* (ND Ohio 1957) 1957 Trade Cases ¶68,890, *aff'd per curiam* (1958) 358 US 38, an agreement among manufacturers of railroad couplings to manufacture one standard coupling was held not to violate the antitrust laws on the ground that the agreement was necessary to remove obsolete couplings and enhance safety in the railroad industry.

Recently the Commission approved a discussion among association members of how a product should be labeled to comply with a ruling of a governmental agency. Advisory Opinion Digest 133 (1967) [1967-1970 Transfer Binder] Trade Reg Rep ¶18,022 (1967).

The United States government encourages—even insists upon—standardization in some industries and frequently cooperates with association committees in the development and modification of standards. See, for example, the motor vehicle safety standards that Congress has enacted in the National Traffic and Motor Vehicle Safety Act of 1966, 15 USC §§1381-1425, and the various product standards published by the Commerce Department that have been approved by a consensus of an industry. Such government cooperation does not necessarily insulate the resulting standard from a charge of illegality, but it helps. See *United States v Socony-Vacuum Oil Co.* (1940) 310 US 150, 226-227, in which the Court stated:

Though employees of the government may have known of those programs and winked at them or tacitly approved them, no immunity would have thereby been obtained. . . . The fact that the buying programs may have been consistent with the general objectives and ends sought to be obtained under the National Industrial Recovery Act is likewise irrelevant to the legality under the Sherman Act. . . .

In each instance the question is whether the standardization activities are designed to restrain or result in a restraint of trade.

1. [§8.20] Checklist for Validity

In passing on the validity of any suggested new standard, the attorney should get the answers to a number of questions:

1. Who is requesting the new standard? If the request comes from consumers rather than suppliers, the association members' motivation is more likely proper.

2. What is the purpose of the new standard? Most standards have legitimate purposes: to decrease costs, to correct a deficiency, to increase safety features, or to benefit consumers in other ways.

3. What is likely to be the commercial impact of the proposed standard? This question is interrelated with the second question. A new standard that is likely to raise the costs of certain suppliers and make it difficult for them to compete, or to eliminate the production of certain items (to the ire of the consumer and the principal suppliers of the item in question), must be carefully examined by the trade-association attorney before passing on its propriety.

4. To what extent is the proposed standard based on engineering or technical considerations rather than commercial considerations? This question also overlaps the question of motivation and purpose. Standards that are confined to engineering or performance characteristics or to safety measures are less likely to have antitrust implications than those that have been developed for commercial considerations.

5. Is any disinterested body such as the Bureau of Standards or the American Standards Association participating in the development of the standard? Many industry standards are developed in cooperation with disinterested agencies. In such instances, interested parties are given an opportunity to object to any proposed standard that might have adverse effects. Participation by such organizations will not protect a standard that offends the Sherman Act, but the likelihood that the standard will be illegal is lessened if it is promulgated, for example, under the auspices of the Bureau of Standards.

2. [§8.21] Adverse Effects

One of the principal problems relating to standardization programs arises when the standard or proposed standard has or will have a substantial adverse economic effect on a minority of the industry. The effect might come, for example, from eliminating from the standard a product or the size or design of a product manufactured by the minority; or it might come from requiring certain manufacturers to incur substantial costs in order to conform to the standard.

The adoption of a standard that discriminates against products or adversely affects one or more members of the industry, or both, will not necessarily constitute a violation of the Sherman Act. Unless the standard represents an effort to fix prices of otherwise to restrain competition, it is likely that its legality or illegality will be determined by application of the so-called "rule of reason." *Standard Oil Co. of New Jersey v United States* (1911) 221 US 1; *United States v American Tobacco Co.* (1911) 221 US 106. See discussion at §2.25. In applying the rule of reason, the courts generally consider the association's intent in promulgating the new standard. If the intent of the association members is found to have been to benefit the public, rather than to restrain competition, there is a reasonable possibility that no antitrust violation will be found even though some members of the industry are adversely affected by the standard. See *Structural Laminates, Inc. v Douglas Fir Plywood Ass'n.* (D Ore 1966) 261 F Supp 154, *aff'd per curiam* (9th Cir 1968) 399 F2d 155, 156, *cert den* (1969) 393 US 1024, holding unproved plaintiff's assertion that defendant's efforts to have an association change industry standards stemmed from a desire to suppress competition; and *United States v Johns-Manville Corp.* (ED Pa 1966) 259 F Supp 440, 453, upholding industry tests as "scientifically justified" notwithstanding that they tended to suppress competition. If a standard constitutes a bald effort to fix prices, intent is immaterial and Section 1 of the Sherman Act (15 USC §1) will have been violated.

3. [§8.22] Enforcement

Standards should be issued only in the form of recommendations. Adherence by members of the industry must be voluntary, and the standard should recite that the adoption and use of the standard is voluntary. Although it is appropriate for association members to agree on what should be included in the commercial standards, it is not appropriate for the members to agree that they will all adhere to the standards. Such an agreement could constitute a *per se* violation of Section 1 of the Sherman Act (15 USC §1; see §2.26).

Moreover, there should be no arrangement or understandings among the members on the policing of industry practices, or on procedures for advertising or cataloging nonstandard items, or on the basis for pricing nonstandard items. The question whether a member will or will not adhere to the standards must be made unilaterally by that member, and his adherence must not be coerced, directly or indirectly. If his refusal to conform constitutes an unfair trade practice, he will be subject to the appropriate legal sanctions. See §8.23.

C. [§8.23] Ethical Codes and Their Enforcement

Closely related to standardization and seals of approval are ethical codes. These express the consensus of the industry on what is proper in commercial uniformity, technical proficiency, or moral conduct. If a member of an industry competes in ways different from the majority's, whether with a different but competitive product line or with a different sales approach, other members may regard the product as "substandard" or the approach as "unethical." The difference between what is aggressive competition and what is unethical conduct may be in one's point of view.

But rules of conduct do have a place in industry. Generally the mere announcement of a code of ethics will have no anticompetitive effects, although there is precedent for holding that rules of conduct are anticompetitive on their face. For example, in *Union Circulation v FTC* (2d Cir 1957) 241 F2d 652, agencies selling magazine subscriptions door-to-door agreed to refuse to hire a solicitor employed by another agency in the preceding year. The object was to curtail deceptive selling practices on the theory that solicitors would observe the rules of conduct more readily if their movement was curtailed. The court found the agreements not a reasonable attempt at self-regulation by members of an industry because the "... reasonable foreseeable effect of the 'no switching' agreements will be to impair or diminish competition existing among subscription agencies, and to prevent would-be competitors from engaging in similar activity."

Similarly, in *New Orleans Chapter, Associated General Contractors of America, Inc. v United States* (1969) 396 US 115, the Court granted the government's motion for summary judgment, holding that an association bidding rule requiring members to include quantity survey costs and chapter dues in bids violated Section 1 of the Sherman Act (15 USC §1).

Also, in *Eastern States Lumber Ass'n. v United States* (1914) 234 US 600, 614, the Court found unlawful efforts by an association of retail lumber dealers to prevent (by boycotting violators) sales by wholesalers directly to consumers. The Court noted:

An act harmless when done by one [refusal to deal] may become a public wrong when done by many acting in concert, for it then takes on the form of conspiracy.

The Commission has advised an association that it could not approve a bylaw provision forbidding members from advertising that its service is faster and better in other towns than that of members who are actually in business in those towns on the ground that ". . . advertising is an element or form of competition and any agreement among competitors to refrain from legitimate and truthful advertising restricts competition." Advisory Opinion Digest 80 (1966) [1965-1967 Transfer Binder] Trade Reg Rep ¶17,637.

Frequently, rules of conduct are anticompetitive in the manner in which they are enforced. For example, in *Silver v New York Stock Exchange* (1963) 373 US 341, the Court held that refusal to give grounds or a hearing before removing direct wire connections to the Exchange offended notions of fairness and constituted a group boycott, a *per se* violation of Section 1 of the Sherman Act (15 USC §1; see §§2.3, 2.26-2.32). Such conduct is not excused under the partial exemption to the antitrust laws created by the self-regulatory scheme of the Securities Exchange Act of 1934 because the unfair manner in which defendants acted took them outside the authority vested in them by the act.

Similarly, in *Mechanical Contractors Bid Depository v Christiansen* (10th Cir 1965) 352 F2d 817, *cert den* (1966) 384 US 918, the court found that sanctions—in the form of fines, foreclosure from submitting bids through the depository, and circulation of the names of violators—that were actually used to enforce rules requiring the use of the bid depository and prohibiting submission of bids for partial work violated Sections 1 and 2 of the Sherman Act notwithstanding the purpose had been regulation and control of industry, not price fixing, because the rules restricted freedom of competition.

Even if the association has the best motives in enacting and seeking to enforce its code of ethics, efforts that have anticompetitive effects violate the Sherman Act and its good motives are no defense. As stated in *Standard Sanitary Manufacturers Co. v United States* (1912) 226 US 20, 49, dealing with a group of manufacturers who sought to prevent through boycotts the sale of inferior goods:

The law is its own measure of right and wrong, of what it permits, or forbids. . . .

See also *Fashion Originators' Guild v FTC* (1941) 312 US 457, 465, holding that manufacturers violated the Sherman Act, the Clayton Act, and the Federal Trade Commission Act by refusing to sell to retailers who dealt in copied women's clothing designs and textiles.

In the last three decades both the Commission and the courts have been wary of disciplinary procedures set up by trade associations, fearing that associations thus become

... an extra-governmental agency, which prescribes rules for the regulation and restraint of interstate commerce, and provides extra-judicial tribunals for determination and punishment of violations and thus "trenches upon the power of the national legislature and violates the statute."

Fashion Originators' Guild v FTC, supra.

Earlier the Court had praised voluntary industry self-regulation, noting that "voluntary action to end abuses and to foster fair competitive opportunities in the public interest may be more effective than legal processes," although it held that an arrangement whereby members of an association reported their prices and agreed to adhere to them for a specified time produced unlawful price uniformity and could not be justified by a desire to rid the industry of secret rebates. *Sugar Institute v United States* (1936) 297 US 553, 598.

The FTC has approved an association's requirement of adherence to the Commission's trade practice rules for the industry as a condition of membership; significantly, it expressly noted that the association did not propose to enforce the rules but only required a pledge of adherence. Advisory Opinion Digest 64 (1966) [1965-1967 Transfer Binder] Trade Reg Rep ¶17,580.

Clearly, the safe course for trade associations is to avoid sanctions for violators of industry codes of ethics because of the anticompetitive effects that usually result. This "safe course" is consistent with the view taken by the Commission of the trade association's proper role. Some associations have their ethics committees work with the Federal Trade Commission to develop trade-practice conference rules setting forth rules of conduct for the industry, which purport to "express the experience and judgment of the Commission, based on facts of which it has knowledge derived from studies, reports, investigations, hearings, and other proceedings, or within official notice, concerning the substantive requirements of the statutes which it administers." Federal Trade Commission Procedure and Rules of Practice §1.12, Trade Reg Rep ¶9801.12.

The Commission expressly prohibits trade associations from penalizing violations of trade practice rules, including a stock provision in all such rules that a trade association may form a trade practice committee to discuss trade practice rules with the Commission, but it may not

(1) Interpret the rules;

(2) Attempt to correct alleged rule violations;

(3) Make determinations or express opinions as to whether practices are violative of the rules;

(4) Receive or screen complaints of violations of the rules; or

(5) Perform any other act or acts within the authority of the Federal Trade Commission or any other governmental Agency or Department.

Federal Trade Commission Trade Practice Conference Rules §16.1 (1956) Trade Reg Rep ¶40,230, 16 CFR Chap. 1, subchap. B, Part 16.

Trade practice rules are not enforceable as such. Violations must be challenged under the usual antitrust enactments, and the Commission frequently proceeds under Section 5 of the Federal Trade Commission Act (15 USC §45), which declares unfair practices unlawful. Thus, one who concedes violating a trade practice rule might vindicate his conduct and establish that the rule in question was improperly adopted by the Commission.

D. [§8.24] Seals of Approval

Closely related to standardization programs are efforts by trade associations to develop a so-called "seal of approval" to be affixed to products that meet certain minimum specifications. Again, there is nothing improper about such a program so long as it does not have an unduly restrictive effect on competition.

A typical program was attempted by the American Gas Association, which adopted a seal of approval to be affixed to gas burners that passed tests conducted in the association's laboratories. The program ran into difficulties when the association and its members were sued by a manufacturer whose product did not pass the test. Both the district court and the Seventh Circuit ruled that the complaint failed to state a cause of action; however, the Supreme Court ruled to the contrary because the plaintiff had specifically alleged that his product had been excluded from the market by a collective refusal to deal. *Radiant Burners, Inc. v Peoples Gas Light & Coke Co.* (1961) 364 US 656.

The Commission has approved the award of a certificate of accreditation in the cement industry to upgrade the quality of building material. The awards were made objectively and there was "no requirement for any applicant as to the length of time in business, his capital, or size of operation." Advisory Opinion Digest 350 (1969) [1967-1970 Transfer Binder] Trade Reg Rep ¶18,826. See discussion at §8.19.

1. [§8.25] Checklist

An experienced trade-association attorney or executive should instinctively recognize a program or proposed program likely to have anticompetitive results. The following criteria should be observed by an association undertaking a program that includes seals of approval:

1. There should be a legitimate need for setting minimum specifications that a product must meet to qualify for the seal of approval.

2. The specifications should provide *minimum* requirements, but no producer should be prevented from adhering to specifications higher than the minimums.

3. The minimum specifications should be objective and reasonable and, if practicable, should be drafted by an impartial organization.

4. The testing organization should be impartial and should not be composed of representatives of companies that are members of the association.

5. Organizations that are not members of the association should be permitted to have their products tested and to obtain the seal of approval if their products comply with the applicable specifications. If the association is the testing organization, it would be appropriate to charge nonmembers a reasonable fee for testing services.

6. The advertising or promotion of the seal of approval should affirmatively promote the excellence of products that bear the seal of approval but should not disparage products that do not bear the seal.

7. Any manufacturer, whether or not an association member, must remain free to produce goods that fail to meet the minimum specifications without fear or coercive action or threats by the association or its members.

8. There must be no collective action by the association or its members to persuade customers not to purchase products that do not bear the seal of approval.

E. [§8.26] Customer Credit Information

The collection and distribution by trade associations of credit information concerning delinquent customers should be approached with caution. This activity can give rise to more problems than it solves in some instances because customers may become irate and resort to legal action if they are cut off from supplies because of a poor credit rating. On possible libel action see annotation at 30 ALR2d 776 (1953). Protection from antitrust exposure cannot be guaranteed. The danger, as with all reporting programs (see §§8.27-8.32), is that if the fact of delinquency is made generally known, very little more than mere refusals to sell may be deemed group decisions, notwithstanding the language in the *Cement* case quoted below.

If an association does engage in the collection and distribution of credit information, procedures should be established assuring that only facts—and correct facts—concerning the customer's credit record be disclosed, that there is no control over the extension of credit by association members, that no comment is made about the delinquent customers, and that customers are promptly removed from the delinquency list on payment of past obligations. See, for example, *Cement Manufacturers Protective Ass'n. v United States* (1925) 268 US 588, 599-600, approving the reporting without comment of delinquent accounts and the amount of the delinquency on the ground that the reporting provided information that fellow members could use in "the exercise of [their] individual judgment determining, on the basis of available information, whether to extend credit or to require cash or security from any given customer." See also *United States v The Cincinnati Fruit and Produce Credit Ass'n.* (SD Ohio 1956) 1956 Trade Cases ¶68,248, holding that the United States failed to establish a *per se* violation of Section 1 of the Sherman Act; the association's bylaw fixed the number of days' credit that should be extended by members and forbade sales on credit to delinquent customers, whose names were circulated.

An association should take care that members are not prohibited from selling to customers on a cash basis to avoid the implication that the association will blacklist delinquent customers of its members. *Swift and Company v United States* (1905) 196 US 375, 394; *United States v First National Pictures, Inc.* (1930) 282 US 44, 50, 54. Similarly, agreements by competitors to extend uniform credit terms involve unnecessary risk; decisions on credit are best made unilaterally. Note the position of the government in the *Cincinnati Fruit and Produce* case, *supra*, at 71,151 to the effect that such agreements constitute *per se* violation; and *United States v Long Island Sand & Gravel Ass'n.* (SD NY 1940) 1940-1943 Trade Cases ¶56,048 in which producers of sand and gravel were prohibited by consent decree from agreeing among themselves to adopt uniform terms for extending credit.

F. Statistical Programs

1. [§8.27] Price Reporting

Many association members, particularly sales people, consider the collection and dissemination of industry statistics to be the most important of all trade-association activities. Many trade associations conduct a statistical program of one kind or another, varying widely in scope and variety. Before *United States v Trenton Potteries Co.* (1927) 273 US 392 established that price fixing is illegal *per se*, the Supreme Court, in *American Column & Lumber Co. v United States* (1921) 257 US 377, struck down an "Open Competition Plan" that called for the daily reporting of all sales, purchases, production, and stocks and the regular reporting of price changes. The views of each association member on expected market conditions were solicited, including predictions relating to price and production. The Supreme Court found that the plan was intended to increase prices, restrict production, and curtail entry of competitors into the hardwood field and concluded that it constituted an unreasonable restraint of trade. To the same effect, see *United States v American Linseed Oil Co.* (1923) 262 US 371.

Some years later, in *Sugar Institute v United States* (1936) 297 US 553, the Supreme Court invalidated another price-reporting plan developed by a trade association. In this one, members of the association reported price changes to become effective on a given date in the future and agreed to adhere to reported prices.

The activities involved in the *Hardwood* and *Sugar Institute* cases were drastic, and there is little likelihood that an association would now adopt such a program. But the desire for information on prices remains, and the question is whether an association should engage in any kind of price-collection program, regardless of its purpose.

The mere exchange of current or past pricing information does not in itself constitute a violation of the antitrust laws, particularly if the report reflects only composite or average figures. *Maple Flooring Manufacturers Ass'n. v United States* (1925) 268 US 563, 586, holding it lawful for an association to send a statistical report that did not identify the parties to transactions, stated:

... trade associations or combinations of persons or corporations which openly and fairly gather and disseminate information as to the cost of their product, the volume of production, the actual price which the product has brought in past transactions, stocks of merchandise on hand, approximate cost of transportation from the principal point of shipment to the points of consumption, as did these defendants, and who, as they did, meet and discuss such information and statistics without however reaching or attempting to reach any agreement or any concerted action with respect to prices or production or restraining competition, do not thereby engage in unlawful restraint of commerce.

See also *Cement Manufacturers Protective Ass'n. v United States* (1925) 268 US 588, holding that although specific sales were identified and disseminated, the purpose was demonstrably to prevent fraud in the industry, and therefore there was no violation of the antitrust laws; and *Tag Mfrs. Institute v FTC* (1st Cir 1949) 174 F2d 452, holding that the regular reporting of price lists and price revisions as well as of terms of sales and off-list sales and dissemination to members, consumers, and public agencies, did not violate Section 5 of the Federal Trade Commission Act (15 USC §45).

Notwithstanding the nice distinctions drawn in the foregoing cases, many trade-association counsel traditionally have cautioned against collection and dissemination of price information. Caution was justified in *United States v Container Corp. of America* (1969) 393 US 333; the Supreme Court reversed the district court's dismissal of the government's complaint challenging as a violation of Section 1 of the Sherman Act (15 USC §1) a program providing for the furnishing of price information among competitors on specific request. The Court viewed the case as ". . . unlike any of the other price decisions we have rendered." Manufacturers of corrugated paper containers voluntarily exchanged prices on specific sales to identified customers, information very different from the statistical reports revealing averages involved in *Maple Flooring Manufacturers.* The conceded purpose for the exchange of specific prices by competing sellers was ". . . to compete effectively for the business of a purchaser," again different from the demonstrated purpose for exchanging specific prices in the *Cement Manufacturers* case, *i.e.,* to protect ". . . their legal rights from fraudulent inducements to deliver more cement than needed for a specific job."

In the *Container Corp.* case, concluding that neither the purpose nor the result of the price exchange was to impair competition, the district court emphasized four findings (among 362) to support its decision upholding the exchange:

(1) "The price trend of all corrugated containers was downward . . . [while] labor rates, machinery and equipment costs and other production costs . . . increased." (273 F Supp at 61);

(2) "Purchasers frequently shifted their business from one supplier to another." (273 F Supp at 60);

(3) "[T]he uncontested statistical data in the record demonstrates the absence of any uniformity, harmony, stability or parallelism in prices." (273 F Supp at 61);

(4) "In determining the price to be charged or quoted" defendants considered "many factors" besides competitors' prices, including current plant production load; suitability of his equipment for order; availability of any special materials needed to produce the order; convenience of

customer's plant; size of order; customer's credit rating; growth prospects of the account; experimental . . . character of the order; prices of . . . recent sales to the customer; customer loyalty; and effect of the order on costs. 273 F Supp at 26–27.

The Supreme Court acknowledged these findings but mentioned four others in reversing the district court's decision:

(1) "The [eighteen] defendants account for about 90% of the shipment of corrugated containers from plants in Southeastern United States."

(2) "While containers vary as to dimensions, weight, color, and so on, they are substantially identical, no matter who produces them, when made to particular specifications."

(3) "Suppliers . . . do not exceed a competitor's price. . . . Where a competitor was charging a particular price, a defendant would normally quote the same price or even a lower price."

(4) "Capacity . . . exceeded the demand from 1955 to 1963, the period covered by the complaint. . . . Yet . . . the industry has expanded in the Southeast from 30 manufacturers with 49 plants to 51 manufacturers with 98 plants . . . and entry into the industry [is] easy."

From these findings the Supreme Court found the "inferences are irresistible that the exchange of price information has had an anticompetitive effect in the industry, chilling the vigor of price competition."

Although the majority opinion acknowledged that "price information exchanged in some markets may have no effect on a truly competitive price," if the market is "dominated by relatively few sellers," the product is fungible, "competition for sales is price," and "demand is inelastic," it concluded that "the exchange of price data tends toward price uniformity" and is therefore unlawful.

As Justice Fortas points out in his concurring opinion, the majority opinion does not hold that the price-exchange program is illegal *per se.* However, considering the great ease of entering the market, the frequent switching of suppliers, and the other market factors cited by both the district court and the Supreme Court, it is difficult to imagine any price-exchange program identifying specific transactions that could excape the stamp of "illegal" after the *Container Corp.* case. Certainly, if the product is relatively standardized and the market is relatively concentrated, the risk of such activity can hardly be justified. If there are numerous competitors and product variations in the market, price uniformity is less likely, and the lack of price uniformity may negate the inference of price stabilization. See, *e.g., Tag Mfrs. Institute v FTC* (1st Cir 1949) 174 F2d 452.

In all cases counsel for the trade association will be well advised to have a clear business reason as exemplified in the *Cement* case, *supra*, before an exchange program is undertaken and to be aware that clearly the safest course is to avoid such programs. Since meaningful trends can generally be obtained from composite figures, there is little reason for an exchange program that identifies transactions. The risk of severe injunction provisions is very real. The final judgment in *Container Corp.* entered in accordance with the Supreme Court's ruling enjoined defendants for 10 years from exchanging price data. (MD NC 1970) 1970 Trade Cases ¶73,091.

2. [§8.28] Statistical Forecasting

A trade association may want to undertake a statistical forecasting project for the purpose of predicting future production by members of the industry. Such a program might involve the collection of monthly shipments made by members of the association for a number of years in the past. Thereafter, the figures would be consolidated to show total industry monthly shipments for the period. On the basis of past history of production, as well as seasonal and other factors, a forecast would then be made as to the future production of the industry.

The trade-association attorney should scrutinize such a proposed program with great care, particularly if the association members are relatively few and the product is relatively highly standardized. Care should be taken to assure that the figures submitted by each individual company are not revealed to other members of the association. Otherwise, it may be concluded that the individual submissions in reality constitute production quotas. An agreement among competitors to limit production would be a *per se* violation of Section 1 of the Sherman Act (15 USC §1; see §2.26). *Hartford-Empire Company v United States* (1945) 323 US 386, 406–407. *United States v United Fruit Co.* (ED La 1958) 1958 Trade Cases ¶68,941 and *United States v Standard Oil Co. of California* (SD Calif 1959) 1959 Trade Cases ¶69,399, both involving consent decrees prohibiting defendants from limiting production or selling quotas.

Statistics submitted pursuant to a forecasting program should, if feasible, be collected, compiled, and distributed by an independent organization. Furthermore, the compilations and forecasts that are disseminated to the association members preferably should not include any analysis— and certainly no recommendations—of any kind.

3. Procedures for Conducting Statistical Programs

a. [§8.29] Advisory Opinions

There are many industry statistics that can be collected and disseminated with safety. Thus, it is perfectly legal for an association to establish

421

a program under which the members periodically submit data concerning production, sales, inventories and the like. The FTC will issue advisory opinions on any "proposed course of action" relating to practices subject to the jurisdiction of the Commission. Requests should be addressed to the Secretary. Opinions will be issued "where practicable." An example of that practice is the issuance on January 27, 1968, of an advisory opinion on the question of the legality of a trade association's proposal that members of the association exchange copies of their labor contracts. The Commission ruled that it had no objection so long as the information was not used for illegal purposes. However, the Commission warned that, since labor costs are a significant element of price, the proposed program should "be used with extreme care."

If an association wishes to collect information about industry wages and fringe benefits, it would be preferable—as with other statistical programs —not to link information with specific members, and comments and recommendations should be avoided. The information should, if feasible, be collected, compiled, and disseminated by an outside organization. See §8.30.

b. [§8.30] Confidential Data

Since much statistical information is regarded by a manufacturer as highly confidential, some associations do not allow the information to be collected by the staff. Accordingly, statistics often are submitted by the members to an independent establishment, such as a certified public accounting firm. That firm collects, compiles, and distributes the statistics without revealing any information about or to individual members.

Despite all reasonable precautions, the confidentiality of statistical information submitted by individual members may be breached if the association or the accounting firm is served with a subpoena duces tecum calling for its production. It is not unusual for the Antitrust Division, the FTC, or civil litigants to attempt in this manner to obtain confidential data for use in actions brought against individual members of the association. The FTC has been successful in such efforts, as shown by the decision of the Seventh Circuit in *FTC v St. Regis Paper Company* (7th Cir 1962) 304 F2d 731, 734, in a proceeding brought against a partner in an accounting firm to enforce a subpoena duces tecum issued by the Commission. The court rejected a contention that the accountant-client privilege protected from disclosure statistical information collected by an accounting firm from members of a trade association on the ground that "the rigid rules of evidence in civil suits did not apply to the proceedings before the administrative agency."

Similar information was required to be produced by an accounting firm in *FTC v Tuttle* (2d Cir 1957) 244 F2d 605, *cert den* (1957) 354 US 925. The Second Circuit overruled the argument that the Commission did not have the power to obtain by subpoena the statistical reports of member companies other than the company under investigation. The court also ruled in effect that, even if the subpoenaed documents were properly classified as trade secrets, there was no prohibition against the Commission's obtaining such information by subpoena; there is only a prohibition against the publication of "trade secrets and names of customers" (244 F2d at 616).

It appears that the only practical way for the association to guard against such an intrusion would be to adopt procedures under which the individual company submissions are retained no longer than is necessary to carry out the association's statistical program.

If no such procedure is adopted, or if, in any event, confidential data must be produced in connection with litigation, the associaton's only recourse would be to seek a protective order from the court limiting to the fullest possible extent the persons having access to the information.

c. [§8.31] Distribution

The distribution of the compiled statistics, as a general rule, should not be confined to members of the association. The reports should be made available to the public, which includes customers as well as nonmembers eligible for membership. As stated in *Tag Mfrs. Institute v FTC* (1st Cir 1949) 174 F2d 452, 462:

There has been some tendency to look askance at reporting agreements between competitors, where the information exchanged is reserved exclusively to themselves and withheld from buyers or the public generally. Presumably this is because such secrecy more readily suggests the inference that the agreement is inspired by some unlawful purpose and precludes the argument that the information thus secretly exchanged serves a function similar to that of market information made available through the activities of commodity exchanges, trade journals, *etc.* See *American Column and Lumber Co. v United States*, 1921, 257 U.S. 377, 411, 42 S. Ct. 114 66 L. Ed. 284, 21 A.L.R. 1073; *Sugar Institute, Inc. v. United States*, 1936, 297 U.S. 553, 596-597, 56 S. Ct. 629, 80 L. Ed. 859 with which cf. *Maple Flooring Manufacturers Ass'n. v. United States*, supra, 268 U.S. at pages 573-574, 45 S. Ct. 578, 69 L. Ed. 1093.

The association may make a reasonable charge for supplying the information. "Non-members of the association may be charged a higher fee than members provided it represents no more than a reasonable differential to insure that members and non-members of the association alike pay an equal share of the costs necessary to support the program." See Advisory Opinion Digest 152 (1967) [1967-1970 Transfer Binder] Trade Reg Rep ¶18,125, page 20,562.

Making the reports available to the public insures that neither customers nor competitors will be competitively disadvantaged when dealing with association members. As mentioned in the *Tag Mfrs.* case, it also develops the argument that such reports give information no different from that available in trade journals, census reports, and the like.

Availability in this context means reasonable notice of when, where, and how the report may be obtained. It also means that the notice of availability be made at the same time as the information is provided to the association's members. *United States v Western Pine Ass'n.* (SD Calif 1941) 1940-1943 Trade Cases ¶56,107, §111(g) Consent Decree. The notice may be printed on invoices or other literature mailed by members to parties with whom they have business contacts. See *Tag Mfrs. Institute v FTC, supra.* Submission of the report to a public agency such as the Department of Justice does not suffice as adequate notice of availability. *American Column & Lumber Co. v United States* (1921) 257 US 377, 411. Although there may be some doubt about how little notice will suffice in a given situation, there is no question but that the greater the notice the less the antitrust risk. *Maple Flooring Manufacturers Ass'n. v United States* (1925) 268 US 563, 573-574. Some associations periodically submit their compiled statistics to the Bureau of the Census.

V. [§8.32] Conclusion

There is no certain way of preventing a trade association from being subjected to antitrust attack by the government or by private parties. A company attorney when informed by his client of unlawful activity by the association should advise his client to resign forthwith in writing lest, as a member, the client be charged with knowledge of a conspiracy. The most that a trade-association attorney can reasonably be expected to do is continuously and constantly watch over and guide the activities of his client and periodically remind the members of the disastrous consequences that frequently stem from antitrust violations. If the members listen to his warnings and heed his advice, the association should flourish and accomplish its legitimate goals—the overall improvement of the industry.

BIBLIOGRAPHY

1. Books

Lamb and Kittelle: *Trade Association Law and Practice* (1956);

Oppenheim: *Federal Antitrust Laws, Cases and Comments* (1968), 141–177;

Toulmin: *Antitrust Laws* (1950) §§7.3–7.61.

2. Articles

Brass: *Antitrust Division Looks at Trade Associations* (1963) 30 *DC BJ* 287;

Exclusion from Private Associations (1965) 74 *Yale LJ* 1313;

Galgay: *Antitrust Considerations in the Exchange of Price Information Among Competitors* (1963) 8 *Antitrust Bulletin* 617;

Kern: *Price Reporting by Trade Associations* (1955) 6 *ABA Antitrust Section Report* 80;

Sprunk: *Trade Associations and the General Practitioner* (1956) 29 *Ohio BJ* 791;

Symposium on Trade Associations (1965) 27 *ABA Antitrust Section Report* 127;

Timberlake: *Standardization and Simplification Under the Antitrust Laws* (1944) 29 *Corn LQ* 301;

Wilson: *Federal Trade Commission Looks at Trade Associations* (1963) 30 *DC BJ* 297;

Withrow: *Trade Associations* (1959) 4 *Antitrust Bulletin* 173.

3. Other Cases

Silver v New York Stock Exchange (1963) 373 US 341;

United States v Oregon State Medical Society (1952) 343 US 326;

United States v National Ass'n. of Real Estate Boards (1950) 399 US 485;

FTC v Cement Institute (1948) 333 US 683;

United States v Socony-Vacuum Oil Co. (1940) 310 US 150;

FTC v Pacific States Paper Trade Association (1927) 273 US 52;

United States v American Linseed Oil Co. (1923) 262 US 371;

Eastern States Lumber Ass'n. v United States (1914) 234 US 600;

C-O-Two Fire Equipment Co. v United States (9th Cir 1952) 197 F2d 489, *cert den* (1952) 344 US 892;

Montrose Lumber Co. v United States (10th Cir 1941) 124 F2d 573;

Standard Containers Mfrs. Ass'n. v FTC (5th Cir 1941) 119 F2d 262;

Council of Defense v International Magazine Co. (8th Cir 1920) 267 F 390;

United States v Food & Grocery Bureau (SD Calif 1942) 43 F Supp 966.

9

Compliance

Joseph F. Brodley

Mr. Brodley received the BA degree from the University of California at Los Angeles in 1949, the LLB degree from Yale University in 1952, and the LLM degree from Harvard University in 1953. He is Alcoa Foundation Professor of Law at Indiana University.

VII. Periodic Reviews and Checkups of Antitrust Compliance Program

A. [§9.68] Need for Periodic Review
B. [§9.69] Periodic Checkups
C. [§9.70] Spot Checks on Specific Problem Areas
D. [§9.71] Antitrust Investigation of a Company to be Acquired

I. Introduction

A. [§9.1] Scope

On the premise that preventive antitrust law can be of great benefit, this chapter deals with the development and execution of an effective antitrust compliance program. The problems discussed include the reasons for having a compliance program (§§9.2–9.4), the proper formulation of a program (§§9.6–9.7), the making of an initial antitrust inventory (§§9.8–9.49), the development of compliance procedures and guidelines, the execution and maintenance of a compliance program after it has been adopted (§§9.50–9.66), the possibility of obtaining government advice and clearance of questionable transactions (§9.67), and the education of company employees to develop an understanding of antitrust and a desire to comply with the law (§9.53).

The compliance program outlined here is a thorough one and necessarily requires adaptation to the problems and budgetary limitations of a particular company. For some smaller firms, this program will be too elaborate, and counsel will have to simplify it, after an assessment of his client's antitrust risks.

B. Reasons for Having a Compliance Program

1. [§9.2] Risks of Not Having a Compliance Program

Since any effective antitrust compliance program requires considerable effort and is bound to be expensive, the question arises whether a smaller firm should have a formal compliance program at all. The growing reach of antitrust doctrine, the constantly increasing number of private antitrust actions, and the undiminished vigor of government enforcement, both state and federal, has materially increased the risk of antitrust involvement for the smaller firm. In recent years, the majority of antitrust actions have been brought against companies not included in the *Fortune* list of the 500 largest industrial companies. The great financial burden of protracted antitrust litigation, not to mention the risk of crushing damages or almost equally onerous settlements, bears with particular weight on the smaller firm. Criminal indictment of top officers is more likely in the smaller corporation, where responsibility for a particular series of illegal actions can be more readily traced to top management.

The specific risks involved in an antitrust action include the following:

Criminal action by the United States or a state with the risk of substantial fines and even jail sentences. Each criminal violation subjects the offender, who may be an individual, to a maximum fine of $50,000. Congress is seriously considering an increase in penalties. On May 19, 1970, the Senate Antitrust Subcommittee approved S3036, which increases the maximum fine to $500,000. The House passed a companion bill, HR 14116, in February, 1970. Even if a business executive is not sentenced to jail, the requirement that he report to a probation officer for several years is not a contingency for which he is likely to be emotionally prepared. (In the *Electrical Cases (e.g., Philadelphia v Westinghouse Electric Corp.* (ED Pa 1962) 210 F Supp 486, *Commonwealth Edison Co. v Allis Chalmers Mfg. Co.* (ND Ill 1962) 211 F Supp 729) seven defendants were sent to jail while twenty-four others, having also received jail sentences, were placed on probation for five years. Subsequently, defendants in several other cases have received jail sentences and been placed on probation.)

Government civil action resulting in a sweeping decree that may place the firm at a severe competitive disadvantage. A decree of this kind may enjoin action that is perfectly legal in order to close all possible roads to the violation attacked and may in some cases require the divestiture of plants and companies. In almost every case a decree will provide for continuing jurisdiction by the court for years and will give the government continuing access to the company's records and personnel.

Private treble-damage and injunctive actions possibly resulting in substantial damages and/or injunctive relief that may void existing contracts or transactions. The potential of private litigation has been increased by the recent amendment to Federal Rule of Civil Procedure 23 drastically expanding class actions. Moreover, under the doctrine of "fraudulent concealment," applied in the *Electrical Cases* and subsequent antitrust proceedings, the usual four-year statute of limitations in antitrust actions may be tolled until the conspiracy is actually discovered. *Westinghouse Electric Corp. v Pacific Gas & Electric Co.* (9th Cir 1964) 326 F2d 575; see Costikyan, *The Statute of Limitations and Fraudulent Concealment,*

1966 NY State Bar Assoc. Antitrust Law Symposium 126 (citing numerous cases).

The expense and burden of antitrust proceedings, which can last for many years and entail extraordinary legal fees as well as costly loss of key executive time. In the smaller corporation, the top officers will likely be called as trial and deposition witnesses, requiring days or weeks for both testimony and preparation.

Following issuance of a court decree or a commission cease-and-desist order, the possibility of future contempt-of-court proceedings or heavy penalties for subsequent violations. Violations of an FTC cease-and-desist order can subject a company to a maximum penalty of $5,000 for each day of a continuing violation. 15 USC §45(l).

In assessing the antitrust risk it must be borne in mind that antitrust proceedings are most often initiated by complaints or reports to government antitrust authorities (Department of Justice, FTC, or a state attorney general). These reports may come from worried or envious competitors, disgruntled customers or suppliers, government agencies with which the company may have had some relationship, unhappy or vindictive employees, unwilling takeover-targets, or anyone else with a motive to hurt the company or block it from taking a planned course of action.

2. [§9.3] Benefits of Having a Compliance Program

There are also positive reasons for having a compliance program. To the extent that a firm can know what it can and cannot do under the antitrust laws, it is freer to compete vigorously within permissible areas. Company employees who realize clearly that they have no alternative to competing energetically for business can direct their time, energies, and resources to that end.

Most legitimate corporate objectives can be guided or reshaped by experienced counsel so that they will not violate the antitrust laws. Even though reshaped or rearranged objectives are more expensive than the originals, they will be cheaper than a protracted antitrust suit.

C. [§9.4] Caveat: Ineffective Compliance Programs

If a compliance program is adopted, care must be taken to ensure it is effective; an ineffective program is worse than none. The existence of an ineffective compliance program may lull management into thinking that the company is complying with the antitrust laws. At the same time, the existence of the compliance program can be used by adversaries to establish guilty knowledge. For example, if Jones, the sales manager of a company with a compliance program, attends a meeting with competitors at which there was a casual discussion of prices, the existence of a compliance program of which Jones is aware is evidence that Jones knew the extreme sensitivity of meeting with competitors to discuss price, and that he and his company therefore consciously and deliberately intended to join the criminal conspiracy.

D. [§9.5] Role of Legal Counsel in Formulating and Executing a Compliance Program

The burden of executing and administering a compliance program, particularly that of a smaller firm, will fall on the company's regular attorney. His knowledge of the company, its operations, the economic market in which it functions, its personnel, documents, and records, makes him the most logical person for developing and executing a successful compliance program.

If the company's regular attorney lacks antitrust experience he may find it helpful—and in the long run economical—to consult an antitrust specialist. He should understand how to make good use of a specialist. Consultation might range from one or a few meetings between the company's attorney and the antitrust specialist not attended by the client, to the retention of the specialist to review with the company's attorney particular aspects of the compliance program. Occasions that might call for consultation or retention include the initial formulation of the company's compliance program; revision of the program when market conditions or antitrust doctrine change; and the handling of any serious antitrust problems (for example, litigation or a merger) that may arise. For further discussion concerning the use of an outside consultant, see §9.64.

II. Formulation of a Compliance Program

A. [§9.6] Understanding the Basic Provisions of the Antitrust Laws and the Economics of the Industry Involved

No effective antitrust compliance program can be formulated without understanding the essential provisions of the antitrust laws. These include the Sherman Act, Clayton Act, the Robinson-Patman Act, Section 5 of the Federal Trade Commission Act, and applicable state antitrust laws.

State laws will not be discussed in this chapter. They vary considerably in their content and in the extent to which they are enforced. The firm that is complying with federal law is not apt to have major antitrust difficulty under state laws, which are for the most part not as comprehensive as the federal law. Occasionally, a state provision may be stricter than the comparable federal provision, e.g., Hawaii Rev Laws 1965 Supp §205A-4, declaring unlawful some individual refusals to deal that would be unlawful if done by agreement. There may also be a problem of federal-state conflict; see Barnett, *Problems of Compliance—Conflicts in State and Federal Antitrust Enforcement* (1965) 29 ABA Antitrust Section 285.

In addition, an applicable antitrust exemption will modify the impact of the antitrust statutes. Extreme care must be exercised in advising a firm operating within the immunity of an antitrust exemption, for outside the precise scope of the exemption the firm remains fully subject to the antitrust laws.

For a discussion of the basic provisions of the antitrust laws, see the previous chapters of this book discussing these provisions in the context of specific business transactions.

The attorney formulating an antitrust compliance program must also understand the economics and competitive realities of the industry. An attorney who has long handled the affairs of a firm will probably have such a background and understanding. Nevertheless, he should check his knowledge and make certain it is current. He can discuss informally general conditions in the industry and any special problems of the firm with officers and employees of the company.

If the attorney has no background in the industry, he must acquire a basic grasp of industry problems. This can be gained through discussions and through reading the literature, trade journals, special industry studies (particularly special reports of the FTC, Congressional investigations, or other governmental studies), reported cases and consent decrees concerning the industry, and, if available, the trial record of any antitrust proceeding in the last ten years involving the industry.

B. [§9.7] Essential Steps in Formulating a Compliance Program

The development of a successful compliance program can be broken down into the following essential steps:

1. Taking an antitrust inventory of the company. (See §§9.8–9.46.)

2. Obtaining full management backing of the compliance program. (See §§9.49–9.52.)

3. Formulating effective operating procedures and guidelines to ensure antitrust compliance. (See §§9.50–9.66.)

4. Making appropriate use of government advisory and clearance programs (See §9.67.)

5. Making provision for periodic checkups and review of compliance program. (See §§9.68–9.71.)

6. Orienting company personnel, including the development of a basic feeling and understanding for the antitrust laws. (See §§9.50–9.58.)

III. The Antitrust Inventory

A. [§9.8] Who Should Conduct the Antitrust Inventory?

The first step in an antitrust compliance program is to take a full antitrust inventory to determine the exact antitrust posture of a firm and to uncover any existing antitrust problems.

The company's regular counsel, who knows his client's operations and problems, will normally be the best qualified person to conduct the antitrust inventory. While counsel may want to consult an antitrust specialist (see §9.64), the outside specialist's role should be primarily advisory; an unknown antitrust lawyer attempting to interview executives may not be able to obtain the kind of detailed and revealing information available to the company's regular attorney.

B. [§9.9] Objectives and the Necessity for Thoroughness

The basic objectives of the antitrust inventory are these:

1. To identify any antitrust problems, actual or potential.

2. To identify executive or employee attitudes that could create antitrust problems if not corrected.

3. To understand the company's operations and problems in its various markets in order to decide how best to develop an effective compliance program that will prevent future problems.

4. To determine whether the company may be subject to antitrust restraints imposed by others. This is not ordinarily thought of as part of an antitrust compliance program, but if the company is being restrained by others' antitrust violations, it may be difficult or impossible to develop in company personnel the proper attitude toward compliance. They may, with some justice, believe that the firm cannot succeed unless it "meets fire with fire," or, worse yet, joins an existing antitrust conspiracy. Institution of an effective compliance program may not be possible unless action is taken to correct antitrust abuses by competitors.

An antitrust inventory must be thorough if it is not to generate a false and dangerous sense of complacency. The lawyer unacquainted with antitrust proceedings should realize that an antitrust case is an enormously elaborate and protracted proceeding. A grand-jury investigation, for example, can easily last months or even years, and require the production of thousands—in some cases millions—of documents, and require the calling and recalling of scores of witnesses, month after month. And this is only the investigative stage; the actual litigation can be even more extensive. In the course of these proceedings, a company's operations and records will be searched with a thoroughness seldom matched in other fields of litigation.

It follows that unless the antitrust inventory in conducted with comparable thoroughness it is likely to miss the very problems that would be uncovered in a searching antitrust investigation and litigation. See generally Hale, *Preventive Law: Experience in the Antitrust Field* (1965) 38 *So Calif L Rev* 391, 395-400.

C. Substantive Matters That Should Be Reviewed

1. [§9.10] Ascertain the Markets in Which the Firm Does Business

The first step in conducting the antitrust inventory is to ascertain the markets in which the firm competes, *i.e.*, the area or areas in which the firm is effectively involved in competition with other firms. The market for antitrust purposes is of two kinds: the product market, and the geographical market.

The *product* market refers to the particular product or products that the firm produces or sells, or the services which it renders. For example, the product market of a grocery store is normally defined as the retail distribution of food products; this market is comprised of several narrower submarkets, the retail distribution of particular kinds of food products, *e.g.*, fluid milk or bread. Similarly, the product market of a motion-picture theater would normally be defined as the exhibition of motion pictures; it could also be defined more narrowly as the exhibition of first-run motion pictures.

Each firm is also engaged in one or more *geographic* areas, or markets; the grocery store and the motion-picture theater serve a particular city or a particular section of the city.

Market definition is not always required; thus, it does not ordinarily matter in a price-fixing or boycott case what market the affected product is in. Market definition is acute, however, in any case in which there must be a measurement of market share, *e.g.*, mergers, monopoly cases, and requirements contracts, or in cases in which there is a cross-influence between two markets, *e.g.*, tie-ins. In these situations, unless counsel has some notion of the relevant product and geographic markets, it will be impossible for him to understand the competitive position of the firm and the legality or illegality of its actions. The author of this chapter has expressed the view that prevailing antitrust doctrines view many non-*per se* areas of antitrust against the background of the structural characteristics of the markets affected. This would make market definition crucial in most, if not all, cases arising outside the *per se* areas. See Brodley, *Oligopoly Power under the Sherman and Clayton Acts: From Economic Theory to Legal Policy* (1967) 19 *Stan L Rev* 85. But see Handler, *Some Novel Theories of Antitrust Liability* (1967) 37 *Antitrust LJ* 50.

In the technical language of the recent Department of Justice *Merger Guidelines* (Trade Reg Rep ¶4430):

A market is any grouping of sales (or other commercial transactions) in which each of the firms whose sales are included enjoys some advantage in competing with those firms whose sales are not included.

Although the decisions supply the legal rules (see generally *Brown Shoe Co. v United States* (1962) 370 US 294, 325; *United States v Aluminum Co. of America* (2d Cir 1945) 148 F2d 416, 424–26), the market definition inquiry is essentially an economic and business study.

The best short statement of the factors relevant to product-market definition is set forth in *Brown Shoe Co.*, in which the Court said that market boundaries might be determined by the presence of the following economic factors:

☐ [lack of] reasonable interchangeability of use . . . [between] the product itself and substitutes for it,
☐ industry or public recognition of the market as a separate economic entity,
☐ the product's peculiar characteristics and uses,
☐ unique production facilities,
☐ distinct customers,
☐ distinct prices,
☐ sensitivity to price changes, and
☐ specialized vendors.

No one factor is necessarily decisive, but the more of these criteria that a hypothesized product market fulfills, the more likely it is to be held a separate product market.

Definition of the geographic market is perhaps even less certain than that of the product market. The recent Department of Justice *Merger Guidelines*, recognizing that "data limitations or other intrinsic difficulties . . . often make precise definition of geographic markets impossible," simply defines the geographic market as "any commercially significant section of the country (even as small as a single community)" if the sellers to be included in the defined market make significant sales to purchasers in that geographic area. This makes almost any geographic area (*e.g.*, a state, a city, a metropolitan area) a possible geographic market. This becomes the geographic market under the *Merger Guidelines* unless the party seeking to overcome the market as thus defined can demonstrate that sellers outside the defined market are under no disadvantage in selling to purchasers within the defined market. (This would tend to show that the geographic market has been defined too narrowly.) Relevant evidence would include a showing of absence of any appreciable differences in significant transportation costs, distribution facilities, customer inconvenience, or established consumer preference for existing products. *Merger Guidelines*, Trade Reg Rep ¶4430 at 6683. See §§2.55-2.57.

If a firm's share of the market is small under any possible market definition, market definition may lose much of its importance. More frequently, the market share will vary dramatically depending on how the market is defined. See *United States v Aluminum Co. of America* (1964) 377 US 271.

Thus, however difficult evaluation of market data may be, it is nonetheless necessary for effective antitrust review. There is no simple way to accomplish this. The ten-part questionnaire at §9.11 may be useful in assembling relevant data. The questionnaire is complex, difficult to fill out, and when filled out, even more difficult to evaluate. Yet, it is only a starting point for analysis. The problem is compounded because, as the Supreme Court has held, it is possible in Clayton Act cases, and now apparently in Sherman Act cases, to have within a defined market "submarkets . . . which, in themselves, constitute product markets for antitrust purposes." *Brown Shoe Co., supra*, at 325; *United States v Grinnell Corp.* (1966) 384 US 563.

Counsel can obtain some assistance from the company's executives in determining the appropriate markets. Businessmen's ideas of the areas of effective competition are not conclusive, but they may be extremely helpful. The outside antitrust specialist may be able to provide crucial assistance in this difficult area. An economist familiar with the industry may also be helpful.

2. [§9.11] Market Definition Questionnaire

A. Product Market

1. Products (or product lines), their physical characteristics and uses *(e.g.)*:

Product	Major Physical Characteristics	Prime Uses
1. Cellophane (plain)	1. Heat sealability if coated Printable Highly transparent Low tear strength High bursting strength High water absorption in 24 hour immersion High moisture permeability Very low gas (flavor type) permeability Large dimension change with humidity difference Excellent resistance to grease and oils Adequate for use on wrapping machine	1. 7% of wrapping for bakery products 25% of wrapping for candy 32% of wrapping for snacks 35% of wrapping for meat and poultry 27% of wrapping for crackers and biscuits 47% of wrapping for fresh produce 34% of wrapping for frozen foods.
2. Aluminum Foil	2. No heat sealability Printable Opaque Low tear strength Low bursting strength No water absorption in 24 hour immersion Very low moisture permeability Very low permeability to gases No dimension change with humidity difference Excellent resistance to grease and oil Adequate for use on wrapping machine	2. 2% of wrapping for bakery products 32.5% of wrapping for candy .8% of wrapping for snacks .1% of wrapping for meat and poultry .2% of wrapping for crackers and biscuits .1% of wrapping for fresh produce .7% of wrapping for frozen foods
3. Waxed Paper (18 Lbs. or over)	3. Heat sealability Normally printed before waxing Commercially transparent High tear strength Good bursting strength Low water absorption in 24 hour immersion Low-Medium moisture permeability High permeability to gases Moderate dimension change with humidity difference No resistance to grease and oils Adequate for use in wrapping machines	3. (figures below include various other types of papers) 88.6% of wrapping for bakery products 21.6% of wrapping for candy 4.4% of wrapping for snacks 57.5% of wrapping for meat and poultry 63.2% of wrapping for crackers and biscuits 45.6% of wrapping for fresh produce 60.3% of wrapping for frozen foods

A. Product Market (cont'd)

1. Products (or product lines), their physical characteristics and uses *(e.g.)*: (cont'd)

Product	Major Physical Characteristics	Prime Uses
4. Sulphite (high finish wrapper and label paper)	4. No heat sealability Printable Opaque High tear strength Medium bursting strength High water absorption in 24 hr. immersion Very high moisture permeability High permeability to gases Moderate dimension change with humidity differences No resistance to grease and oils Adequate for use in wrapping machine	4. See % for all papers above
5. _____	5. _____	5. _____

2. Customers (by name or category) to whom product or product lines are sold:

Product	Customers
1._____	1._____
2._____	2._____
3._____	3._____

(NOTE: Questions 1 and 2 furnish basic data about the company's own products, which will then be compared with data about competitive and substitute products.)

3. Competitive products (products having same physical characteristics and uses to be placed tentatively in the same product market):

Company's Product	Corresponding Competitive Products	Name of Producer of Competitive Product
1._____	1._____	1._____
2._____	2._____	2._____
3._____	3._____	3._____

4. Substitute products (products having similar but not identical physical characteristics and uses, and which may or may not be included in the product market depending on other factors—see below in this form):

Company's Product	Substitute Products	Producer of Substitute
1._____	1._____	1._____
2._____	2._____	2._____
3._____	3._____	3._____

5. Physical characteristics and uses of substitute products. (Similarity of physical characteristics and uses tends to place substitute products in the same product market.):

Substitute Products	Physical Characteristics	Uses
1._____	1._____	1._____
2._____	2._____	2._____
3._____	3._____	3._____

6. Price history over last 10 years. (Similarity of price and coinciding price changes tend to place competitive or substitute products in the same product market. Graphing this information may show similarities much more vividly.):

Company's Product	Competitive Products	Substitute Products
1._____	1._____	1._____
2._____	2._____	2._____
3._____	3._____	3._____

7. Common customers. (Common customers tends to show identity of markets.):

Name of Customer	Company's Product Sold to Customer	Competitive Products Sold to Customer	Substitute Products Sold to Customer
1.	1.	1.	1.
2.	2.	2.	2.
3.	3.	3.	3.

B. Geographic Market

8. Geographic markets served by company products (*"geographic service area"*). (This information tentatively indicates the various geographic markets and the competitive products within each, but see items 9 and 10):

Company's Product	Geographic Service Area	Competitive Products Produced and Sold in Geographic Service Area
1.	1.	1.
2.	2.	2.
3.	3.	3.

9. Significant cost or other economic disadvantages, if any, of competitive products produced outside but sold within the geographic service area. (The greater the disadvantage to outside competitive products, the more likely that they fit into a separate geographic market.):

Company's Product	Competitive products produced outside geographic service area	Geographic area in which competitive product sold	Economic disadvantage (if any) of outside competitive product in sales made within company's geographic service area
1.	1.	1.	1.
2.	2.	2.	2.
3.	3.	3.	3.

10. Significant cost or other economic advantage or disadvantage of competitive products produced within subareas of company's service area. (The more it appears that products produced within some distinctive subarea of the company's service area have a significant advantage or disadvantage, the more likely it is that this subarea itself comprises a separate geographic market.):

Company's product	Geographic service area	Possible subarea within geographic service area	Competitive products sold in each such possible subarea	Products subject to any special economic advantage or disadvantage in subarea	Nature of economic advantage or disadvantage
1.	1.	1.	1.	1.	1.
2.	2.	2.	2.	2.	2.
3.	3.	3.	3.	3.	3.

COMMENT: This illustration is taken from the facts given in *United States v E.I. duPont de Nemours & Co.* (1956) 351 US 377.

3. [§9.12] Ascertain the Market Structure and Relative Position of the Firm in Its Market

Having defined the relevant product and geographic markets, it is necessary to ascertain the relative position of the firm in that market. This determination has growing relevance for antitrust not only in mergers but in other antitrust areas as courts direct increasing attention to whether a questioned trade practice will strengthen the position of a dominant or important firm in a concentrated market (a market in which a very few firms produce the bulk of the goods). Following economic usage, the cases frequently refer to such a market as a concentrated or tight oligopoly market. It is thought that this kind of market structure is conducive to undesirable economic behavior. "... a concentrated market structure ... tends to discourage vigorous price competition and to encourage ... inefficient methods of production. ...." Department of Justice *Merger Guidelines*, Trade Reg Rep ¶4430 at 6682. See *United States v Aluminum Co. of America* (1964) 377 US 271, 280; *United States v Philadelphia Nat'l. Bank* (1963) 374 US 321. See generally, Brodley, *Oligopoly Power under the Sherman and Clayton Acts* (1967) 17 *Stan L Rev* 285.

Five factors help determine the relative position of a firm in its market:

1. Market share, clearly the most important factor. See §9.13.
2. Trend toward competition. See §9.14.
3. Total number of firms in the market. See §9.15.
4. Ease of entry of new firms. See §9.16.
5. Product differentiation, *i.e.*, the degree to which the company's products are distinguished and differentiated by buyers from the products of the company's competitors.

a. [§9.13] Market Share

As stated, market share, the percentage of the total market occupied by the firm, is the most important bench mark of the firm's market position. It can be measured in several ways, *e.g.*, in terms of gross sales, assets, net worth, or productive capacity. Gross sales is the most common yardstick used, but other factors may serve as a better measure of a firm's relative importance in particular industries, *e.g.*, in banking, total assets and deposits. In order to judge the degree of concentration in the market counsel should get fairly specific information on the relative size of his client and other firms in the market.

For example, if firm A has 5% of a market shared with seventy-five other firms, no one of which has more than a 10% share, the market is unconcentrated. A merger by firm A with a competitor that has no more than a 5% share would be permitted under the Department of Justice's *Merger Guidelines* (Trade Reg ¶4430 at 6684).

On the other hand, if firm A has 10% of its market, ranking fifth in a market in which the four leading firms have 75% of the market, the market is highly concentrated (a concentrated oligopoly market) and under the *Merger Guidelines* firm A could not merge with any firm with a market share of 2% or more (Trade Reg Rep ¶4430 at 6684). Further, vertical mergers and other types of market conduct will also be scrutinized more critically, since the market is apt to be viewed as not fully competitive. (See *Merger Guidelines*, Trade Reg Rep ¶4430 at 6682.)

If firm A is a struggling new entrant with 3% in a market shared with ten other firms, the four largest of which have 80% of the market—a highly concentrated market—mergers and other market conduct tending to increase the power or share of the market leaders will raise severe antitrust problems. But the successful entry of firm A will increase the number of competitors and, potentially, the competitiveness of the market. Firm A might be given greater competitive freedom *e.g.*, permission to merge with another small company, but counsel may want to seek advance clearance under the Department of Justice or FTC advisory and clearance program. See §§9.67 and 4.75-4.76.

b. [§9.14] Trend toward Concentration

Market structure also has a time dimension. It is important to know whether there is a tendency toward concentration, a tendency that the decisions view as highly adverse to competition. See *e.g.*, *Brown Shoe Co. v United States* (1962) 370 US 294, 332-33.

In its *Merger Guidelines*, the Department of Justice defined a trend toward concentration as existing if the aggregate market share of the largest firms in the market (from the two largest to the eight largest) had increased by 7% or more of the market over any base year from five to ten years prior to the merger. (Trade Reg Rep ¶4430 at 6684.)

c. [§9.15] Number of Firms in Market

In *United States v Von's Grocery* (1966) 384 US 270, the Supreme Court treated as significant a decrease in the sheer number of firms in the market.

d. [§9.16] New Entry

New entry into the market, and even the mere threat of new entry, adds to the competitiveness of the market and is becoming a factor of some importance in decisions. See *United States v Penn-Olin Chem. Co.* (1964) 378 US 158; *FTC v Procter & Gamble Co.* (1967) 386 US 568.

The form in §9.17 may be useful in assembling market concentration data.

4. [§9.17] Form for Measuring Market Share

1. Product_____
2. Geographic Market_____
3. Basis on which market share is to be measured_____
4. Market-share data   (gross sales, total assets, etc.)

	Company's mkt share	Mkt share of 4 largest firms	Mkt share of 8 largest firms	No. of firms in market	No. of firms leaving mkt by merger in last year	No. of firms entering mkt in last year
Current Year	____%	____%	____%	____	_____	_____
1 year ago	____%	____%	____%	____	_____	_____
2 years ago	____%	____%	____%	____	_____	_____
3 years ago	____%	____%	____%	____	_____	_____
5 years ago	____%	____%	____%	____	_____	_____
10 years ago	____%	____%	____%	____	_____	_____

5. List any special economic factors explaining above figures (*e.g.,* new patents or patent expirations, innovations, heavy advertising, new entrants into market, obsolescence, declining profitability):

_____
_____
_____
_____

6. List any potential market entrants:

Name of firm	Nearest product market in which presently engaged	Nearest geographic market in which presently engaged	Asset size of firm	Source of belief that firm may enter market
1._____	1._____	1._____	1._____	1._____
	_____	_____	_____	_____
2._____	2._____	2._____	2._____	2._____
	_____	_____	_____	_____

5. [§9.18] Understand the Firm's Internal Structure and Relationships

Counsel should understand the internal structure of the firm and the relationships among its various parts. For example, does it have separate subsidiaries? Do these subsidiaries compete with each other? Is the firm vertically integrated? Is the firm both seller and buyer to the same outside companies?

a. [§9.19] Competition within the Firm: Intraenterprise Conspiracy

It is important to know if separate units of the firm compete indirectly and, if so, whether they are separate corporate entities or simply divisions or departments of a single corporate entity. It is also significant whether their affiliation is public knowledge or whether they are held out as separate competitors.

Despite viable precedents holding that affiliated corporations are capable of conspiring with each other in violation of the antitrust laws (*Kiefer-Stewart Co. v Joseph E. Seagram & Sons* (1951) 340 US 211, 215; *Timken Roller Bearing Co. v United States* (1951) 341 US 593, 598), the doctrine of "intraenterprise conspiracy" is seldom applied. One situation, however, is sensitive; if a company has separate corporate subsidiaries engaged in competition and holds them out to the public in some way as unaffiliated competitors (*e.g.*, by failing to disclose the affiliation), the doctrine may be invoked. If counsel discovers such a situation, he should explore the possibility of changing the practice or the corporate form, for example, by using corporate divisions instead of separate subsidiaries. See discussion at §2.11. See generally Willis & Pitofsky, *Antitrust Consequences of Using Corporate Subsidiaries* (1968) 43 *NYU L Rev* 20.

b. [§9.20] Vertical Integration

Vertical integration exists when a firm is its own supplier or customer for some economically distinct product. Vertical integration of either the company or its market competitors is relevant to many antitrust issues, *e.g.*, mergers, requirements contracts, franchise arrangements, exclusive distributorship arrangements, and fair trade. In particular, if a firm supplies or sells to firms with which it also competes, it is engaged in "dual distribution." This should be an area for antitrust scrutiny, since abuses can (or at any rate many think they can) easily occur. For example, the existence of dual distribution was held to bar a company from engaging in fair trade under the McGuire Act (15 USC §45). *United States v McKesson & Robbins, Inc.* (1956) 351 US 305.

Some illustrations may be apposite: If, from its own iron-ore mine, a steel company supplies its own ore and also sells iron ore to its competitors, it is integrated backward to the raw-material source and is engaged in dual distribution. If drug wholesaler B owns retail stores in competition with other retailers who are customers of B's wholesale division, B is integrated forward into retailing and is likewise engaged in dual distribution.

To determine the significance of vertical integration and dual distribution it is frequently necessary to ascertain the degree of concentration and vertical integration in the market. For example, in the steel company example, if a firm that does *not* own a source of iron ore can buy ore from among several sources of ore that are not vertically integrated, the market structure clearly raises less potential for antitrust problems than if the iron-ore market is highly concentrated and vertically integrated.

If vertical integration links two markets, either one of which may be concentrated, it is frequently necessary to determine the degree of concentration existing in both markets and the extent to which the two markets are vertically integrated. To measure concentration in the markets, fill out the form at §9.17 for each market. To determine the degree of vertical integration in market X, list each firm in the market known to be vertically integrated into a related market and total their market shares in X. This gives the degree of vertical integration in market X. For example, steel makers A, B, C, and D are integrated backward into iron ore. Their combined market shares of steel sales in the United States is 50%. Therefore, the United States steel-making market is 50% vertically integrated with iron ore. Conversely, if the combined market share of iron-ore production held by the same steel companies is 75%, the iron-ore market is 75% integrated with steel making.

c. [§9.21] Joint Ventures

A joint venture is a partial combination of assets between two firms to engage in a particular business. It may take the form of joint ownership of stock of a third firm. It is distinguished from a merger in that the latter is a total pooling of the assets of two firms.

Counsel should determine whether the company is engaged in any joint ventures. Antitrust difficulties come from the joint venture's reduction of competition between the parents or between one or more of the parents and the joint venture itself. Difficulties may appear in many forms; if, for example, firms A and B, competitors, form a joint venture C in their own market, the effect is that through their control of the joint venture, they will be fixing a competitor's price, a clear antitrust problem.

If firms A and B, competitors, form a joint venture C that will not compete with them but will be a customer for their output, firms A and B must operate carefully not to compromise their own competitive relationship. In addition, the joint venture might be challenged as an undesirable vertical integration foreclosing a substantial part of the end market from A and B's competitors. There may be problems even if firms A and B are not competitors. If, for example, A and B form a joint venture C to enter a new market, but A is a potential entrant into market X, and X is concentrated, the loss of a potential competitor may be held to injure competition. See *United States v Penn-Olin Chemical Co.* (1964) 378 US 158.

Joint ventures may raise other kinds of antitrust problems, *e.g.*, reciprocity relationships between parent and joint venture. See §9.22. The field is relatively uncharted and counsel must remain alert to developing trends. See Brodley, *Oligopoly Power under the Sherman and Clayton Acts: From Economic Theory to Legal Policy* (1967) 19 *Stan L Rev* at 329–337; Pitofsky, *Joint Ventures Under the Antitrust Laws: Some Reflections on the Significance of Penn-Olin* (1969) 82 *Harv L Rev* 1007.

d. [§9.22] Reciprocity

If the firm is both customer and supplier to the same company, and if it attempts in any way to utilize its patronage from suppliers to increase sales to the suppliers, or companies related to them, there may be problems under Section 1 of the Sherman Act (15 USC §1). As companies continue to grow and diversify, the opportunities for direct and indirect reciprocal buying multiply. Counsel must be alert to spot the possibilities, which may change frequently as a growing firm adds new product lines, or which may develop in connection with a merger or joint venture. See further discussion at §9.32.

Examples of reciprocal relationships are easy to imagine; eraser manufacturer A purchases substantial quantities of office supplies from B. Any attempt by A to condition its continued purchase of office supplies on B's purchases of erasers from A will involve A in a reciprocity agreement violating Section 1 of the Sherman Act (15 USC §1). See §2.35.

6. [§9.23] Learn the Firm's Antitrust History

Counsel must thoroughly understand the antitrust history of the firm. As part of his antitrust inventory he should analyze the following items:

a. All antitrust litigation and antitrust investigations affecting the firm.

b. All consent decrees that have been entered against the firm. Decrees ordinarily contain no expiration date.

c. All FTC cease-and-desist orders that have been entered against the firm.

d. The antitrust history of the industry. Have there been any industry-wide investigations by the FTC or antitrust cases or proceedings against other firms in the industry? At a minimum, counsel should consult the table of cases and FTC proceedings in the CCH Trade Regulation Reporter. It would also be desirable to ask company executives and trade-association officials about prior antitrust proceedings in the industry.

7. [§9.24] Review All Acquisitions of Stock or Assets

Recent Supreme Court decisions have made acquisitions of stock or assets particularly sensitive antitrust acts. The government rarely attacks long-standing acquisitions although it clearly has the power to do so. *United States v E.I. du Pont de Nemours & Co.* (1957) 353 US 586. But the company's history of acquisitions may be important in determining the legality of a new acquisition or, for that matter, of some other antitrust-significant act. This is particularly true if an acquisition is one of a series that tends to concentrate the market or preclude market entry. More recent acquisitions raise the possibility of direct attack by the Department of Justice, the FTC, or even a private litigant. On acquisitions and mergers generally, see Chapter 4.

Counsel will want to ask these questions, among others, about past acquisitions:

☐ When was the acquisition made?

☐ What was acquired? If it was a going company, what was its relevant market share? See §§9.10–9.17.

☐ Is there a vertical relationship between the markets of the client and the acquired firm? If so, how concentrated are the vertically related markets, and has the acquisition resulted in dual distribution? See §9.20.

☐ If there is no horizontal or vertical relationship between the client and the acquired firm, was the client prior to the merger a potential entrant into the acquired firm's market? There would be potential for entry, for example, if the two firms were in closely related product markets, or if the two firms were in the same product market in distinct geographical areas. If the client was a potential entrant into the acquired firm's market, was that a concentrated market? Was the client recognized by other firms as a potential market entrant? Do internal memoranda or other documents identify the market as one of potential entry?

☐ Was any government clearance obtained prior to the acquisition? See §9.67.

☐ Were any distributors or suppliers terminated after the acquisition? If so, were they injured? If they were, they are likely sources of antitrust litigation against the client.

8. Understand the Firm's Operations

a. Relationships with Competitors; Trade-Association Activities

(1) [§9.25] Importance

Counsel should probe thoroughly all relationships between the firm and its competitors. Violations in this most sensitive area often raise Sherman Act problems and frequently result in criminal indictment. Trade-association activities, since they provide a place for direct meetings between competitors, must be reviewed with special care. For discussion, see Chapter 8.

(2) [§9.26] Relationship with Competitors

If any agreements or understandings exist between the company and one or more of its competitors covering prices, allocation of customers or markets, or otherwise directly affecting the competitive relationship between the firms, the situation is most serious and the matter should be investigated fully. Some subjects are permissible for agreement among competitors, *e.g.*, patent licensing (if there are no anticompetitive restrictions) (see Chapter 7), and ethical advertising codes like the tobacco industry's (see §8.23). Obviously, any improper agreements should be terminated immediately in writing or by a memo in the file.

If there have been meetings or contacts apart from normal trade-association activity between any executive or employee of the company and any representatives of competitors, a full and detailed investigation should be made and unless the matter was wholly innocuous, top management should be informed at once.

Businessmen may understand that they are not permitted to enter into agreements with their competitors, but not realize that a court may infer agreement or conspiracy from the mere fact of a conversation followed by joint action. See §§2.9-2.11.

For example, Smith, sales manager of B, suggests to Jones, sales manager of A, "We sure are knocking ourselves out trying to bid every job. Why don't you bid the jobs within 50 miles of your plant, I'll bid those within 50 miles of my plant, and we'll fight over the rest?" Jones, not sure that Smith is serious, shakes his head and says, "Nothing doing." When he gets back to his plant Jones decides to follow such a bidding policy, and Smith makes a similar decision. These facts create a clear risk that a conspiracy will be inferred.

A conspiracy could also be inferred from a simple letter from a sales-man to his sales manager stating, "I have reason to believe our competitor will be increasing his bid price by 10% on his next bid." The letter may be a purely innocent attempt to diagnose competitive action, but it is open to a more sinister interpretation. The salesman would be well ad-vised not to speculate on paper about what he thinks a competitor will do in the future.

In general, counsel should determine the attitude of the company's executives toward competitors. Do they look upon their competitors as if they belonged to the same club, or do they manifest an attitude of vigor-ous competition? The former view may suggest that there are serious antitrust problems below the surface.

(3) [§9.27] Trade-Association Activities

If the company belongs to any trade associations, counsel should find out what takes place at trade-association meetings. Trade-association activi-ties are not inherently unlawful, but meetings bring competitors togeth-er and thus provide opportunity for improper discussions. Questions to ask about the company's trade-association activities are:

☐ To what trade associations does the company belong?
☐ What is the purpose of each?
☐ Does the company have a copy of the trade association's bylaws and does it receive the minutes and agenda of association meetings? If not, it should!
☐ Does a study of the bylaws, minutes, agenda, and other trade-association documents raise questions? If so, counsel should ask them.
☐ What company personnel go to the trade-association meetings?
☐ Does the trade association have a lawyer and does he attend all meet-ings? He should.
☐ What committees or groups within the trade association do company personnel belong to?
☐ At trade-association meetings or conventions does the conversation ever drift into sensitive areas, either at the meetings or at social affairs outside the meetings? Company personnel attending meetings should be interviewed.

For further discussion, see Chapter 8.

b. [§9.28] Relationships with Suppliers and Customers

The firm's relationships with its suppliers and customers present antitrust problems in the forms of resale price maintenance, price discrimination, tie-in sales, requirements and exclusive dealing contracts, customer and territorial restrictions, reciprocity, and dual distribution.

Pricing problems are briefly discussed in §§9.36–9.39. The other supplier/customer problems are discussed at §§9.29–9.35. The trend of recent decisions has been to narrow the range of restrictions that a firm can impose on its customers or extract from its buyers.

(1) [§9.29] Tie-In Sales

If the company uses a desired product or product line to force customers to take also a less desired product or product line, and if competition is held to be restrained, both Section 1 of the Sherman Act (15 USC §1) and Section 3 of the Clayton Act (15 USC §14) may have been violated.

For example, if a liquor wholesaler insists that a liquor retailer buy a case of Dry Gulch Blended Gin with every case of Golden Lift Scotch, the tie-in arrangement tends to restrict competition in the gin market. Actual practices may be much more subtle, for example, offering customers a single package of related products that cannot be purchased separately. Sometimes it is not easy to determine whether two distinguishable but functionally related goods are a single product, so that no tie-in exists, or several products, resulting in a tie-in. Recent decisions have tended to separate functionally related goods, making possible a finding of an illegal tie-in, and generally to expand the scope of tying as a *per se* offense. See *Fortner Enterprises, Inc. v United States Steel Corp.* (1969) 394 US 495, and *Associated Press v Taft-Ingalls Corp.* (6th Cir 1965) 340 F2d 753, *cert den* (1965) 382 US 820.

Specific questions to uncover tie-ins include:

☐ Does the company sell two or more distinguishable products or services together?

☐ If it does, are customers permitted to buy each separately?

☐ If customers are permitted to buy them separately, are the separate products priced in a way that makes separate purchasing more expensive or more difficult or inconvenient?

☐ Do any customers in fact purchase less than the total package of products? If not, a serious question is raised as to whether, either by pricing or other means, there is in fact a tie-in situation.

☐ Are any unusual credit arrangements offered? If so, they must be analyzed in the light of *Fortner, supra.*

If the company insists that the various products are actually a single product, counsel must probe whether this is so. Practices of other firms and customer attitudes are relevant.

For further discussion of tie-in sales see §§3.9–3.18.

(2) [§9.30] Requirements and Exclusive-Dealing Contracts

If the company sells goods under contracts or arrangements that limit the purchaser in buying the goods of the company's competitors, and if there is an appreciable effect on competition, there is a serious antitrust question under Section 3 of the Clayton Act (15 USC §14) and possibly under Section 1 of the Sherman Act (15 USC §1). The courts may hold that the seller's competitors are "foreclosed" or shut out of the market by the agreement. An exclusive dealing contract usually prohibits the buyer from handling products that compete with those of the seller. One form of exclusive dealing is the requirements contract, which obligates the buyer to purchase all or part of his requirements of a given product from the seller. These arrangements, obviously, foreclose the seller's competitors from this portion of the market.

To uncover requirements and exclusive-dealing contracts, counsel should probe all written and oral agreements, and all sales practices. A good question to ask is whether any of the company's customers in fact buy from the company's competitors. If not, the exact reason should be determined, for there is a strong possibility of exclusive dealing.

Exclusive dealing is not always illegal. The quantity of the product sold or the share of the market foreclosed may be too small possibly to injure competition. In addition, exclusive dealing otherwise illegal may be held permissible if it is conducted by a new market entrant or a failing company or if it is compelled for technological reasons. See *United States v Jerrold Electronics Corp.* (ED Pa 1960) 187 F Supp 545, *aff'd per curiam* (1961) 365 US 567.

For further discussion of requirements and exclusive-dealing contracts see §§3.2–3.8.

(3) [§9.31] Customer and Territorial Restrictions

Restriction by a company of the customers to whom or the territory in which its own customers may resell the company's product was declared illegal *per se* by the Supreme Court in *United States v Arnold, Schwinn & Co.* (1967) 388 US 365. See further discussion at §§3.19–3.24. Examples of arrangements:

☐ Company A appoints one wholesale distributor in each state under a contract prohibiting sales activities and sales outlets outside the state. This is a territorial restriction, illegal *per se* except in an agency or consignment situation, discussed below.

☐ Company A, an automobile manufacturer, prohibits dealers from making sales to fleet buyers. This is a customer restriction, illegal *per se* if imposed on an independent customer.

☐ Company A appoints one wholesale distributor in each state and provides in the distributorship agreement that the distributor's "primary zone of operations" is his home state. This is probably not illegal *per se* since the distributor is not prohibited from selling outside the primary zone, but it is easy to see how the contract might be administered to make it impossible or virtually impossible to sell outside the zone. If it is, the agreement would become illegal.

The Supreme Court in *Schwinn* was careful to distinguish independent distributors and agents or consignees. In arrangements with the latter, the manufacturer retains ownership of the goods and a customer or territorial restriction is not illegal *per se* if the agency or consignment is bona fide. Such arrangements may be illegal, but they will be judged by the rule of reason. See §§2.25, 2.26. See also *National Institute on Sales & Distribution of Goods* (1968) 37 *Antitrust LJ* 1; Bock, *Antitrust Issues in Restricting Sales Territories and Outlets* (1967) National Industrial Conference Board Study no. 98.

Specific questions to uncover customer and territorial restrictions include:

☐ What are the relevant provisions in the company's written distributorship agreements?

☐ What oral agreements or understandings are entered into with customers?

☐ Does the company maintain records of the territory or customers to which its distributors resell? If so, for what purpose?

☐ If the company sells through agents, consignees, or franchisees, are the relationships more than paper designations? *E.g.*, who bears the risk of loss; who supplies financing or insurance?

☐ Has the company terminated any distributors? If so, were any of them selling in territories or to customers in a manner different from other distributors? Actions often speak louder than words. If a company terminates dealers who sell more widely than its other dealers, the burden will be on the company to show that it is not carrying out territorial or customer restrictions.

(4) [§9.32] Reciprocity

Reciprocity is the use of buying power to induce sales of a company's products. It has been identified by the Supreme Court as an anticompetitive practice (*FTC v Consolidated Foods Corp.* (1965) 380 US 592, 594) because it tends to reduce competition on the merits for the products involved. See generally, Hausman, *Reciprocal Dealing and the Antitrust Laws* (1964) 77 *Harv L Rev* 873. Outright reciprocity agreements ("I'll buy from you if you buy from me.") or reciprocity by coercion ("You had better buy from me if you want me to buy from you.") are illegal *per se* under Section 1 of the Sherman Act (15 USC §1). *United States v General Dynamics Corp.* (SD NY 1966) 258 F Supp 36. Less overt reciprocity may also raise antitrust questions.

For example, steel company A follows a definite policy, known to suppliers, of buying all its chemical requirements from firms that buy steel from the company and polices the policy by keeping detailed records. From such systematic reciprocal buying practices, there is a clear risk that a court would infer a reciprocity agreement, since company A's suppliers were aware of the practice. The Department of Justice has taken the position that such practices are illegal even without agreement. See Flinn, *Reciprocity and Related Topics under the Sherman Act* (1968) 37 *Antitrust LJ* 156.

Questions to elicit information about reciprocity arrangements include:

☐ Does the company maintain any records by which purchases and sales to particular firms are compared or matched?

☐ Does it distribute purchasing figures to sales personnel or sales figures to purchasing officials?

☐ Do purchasing officials accompany sales personnel when calling on customers?

☐ Does the company have a "Trade Relations Department?"

☐ Does it belong to any trade-relations associations (a trade association composed of purchasing officials from various companies)?

☐ Is there any practice or procedure by which buying is concentrated on customers or potential customers? This can probably occur only if purchasing officials are informed about, or have access to, sales figures.

Affirmative answers to *any* of these questions raise serious question whether reciprocity is company policy.

For further discussion of reciprocity see §§2.35, 4.31.

(5) [§9.33] Other Supplier and Customer Problems

Terminations of suppliers or customers often lead to lawsuits or complaints to antitrust enforcement agencies. If there have been or are likely to be such terminations, counsel should:

☐ Review all agreements and written correspondence and memoranda relating to the termination.

☐ Interview the company personnel who handled the transaction. It is probably desirable to prepare memoranda of the interviews, but counsel should take care not to lose the attorney-client privilege. See §9.65.

(6) [§9.34] Relations with Some Trade Associations

Relationships between the company and any trade associations or similar groups to which its suppliers or customers belong are potentially troublesome. For example, if a trade association persuaded an appliance manufacturer to adopt a fair-trade program, both would be guilty of illegal price fixing, although the manufacturer's unilateral establishment of a fair-trade program in states permitting it would ordinarily be perfectly legal. See generally §§3.25–3.40. On trade associations, see Chapter 8.

(7) [§9.35] Dual Distribution

"Dual distribution" exists when a firm simultaneously supplies (or is supplied by) and competes with another firm.

Dual distribution raises the possibility of discrimination against or unfair treatment of the supplier or customer who is dependent for his supplies or sales on his competitor. The legal rules are by no means settled, but counsel should examine for possible abuses. These can take the form of a "price squeeze," in which the company raises prices to its competitor-customer while lowering its own prices to their mutual end-product customers; or a "supply squeeze," in which the company cuts down on supply to its competitor-customer in a time of scarcity while offering ample goods to their mutual end-product customers. See *United States v McKesson & Robbins, Inc.* (1956) 351 US 305; and Jones, *Marketing Strategy and Government Regulation in Dual Distribution Practices* (1966) 34 *Geo Wash L Rev* 456. Various problems may also arise under the price-discrimination sections of the Robinson-Patman Act. See §5.23 and *Dual Distribution*, Nat'l Institute on Sale and Distribution of Goods (1968) 37 *Antitrust LJ* 168.

c. [§9.36] Pricing Practices

Pricing is possibly the most sensitive area in antitrust. Frequent and persistent questions arise under Section 1 of the Sherman Act (15 USC §1) and under the Robinson-Patman Act. They can be divided into problems of price identity, resale-price maintenance, and price discrimination.

(1) [§9.37] Price Identity

Counsel should determine whether the company's prices are identical with those of its competitors and if so, why and for how long. If there is a formal agreement or "informal understanding" with competitors on prices or if the pricing mechanism is such that price identity is unlikely in the absence of agreement, there is potential trouble that counsel should deal with immediately.

Price fixing may be obvious—for example, two contractors frequently submit identical bids—or it may be covert, with bidders following formulas in pricing or allocating work. For example, it may appear consistently that when firms A, B, and C bid on jobs, the bid of one of the three is considerably below the other two. Such a bidding pattern may suggest allocation of jobs and "collusive bidding," which is just as illegal as outright price fixing.

Counsel should learn whether price information is exchanged with competitors, perhaps through trade associations. Such reporting could be held conspiratorial, and should be stopped. Indeed, almost any industry-wide system of price reporting, even without action between competitors, is a potential problem and should be reviewed carefully. See *United States v Container Corp. of America* (1969) 393 US 333.

(2) [§9.38] Resale Price Maintenance

Although resale price maintenance through fair trade is perfectly legal in many states, proper administration of a fair-trade program can be a delicate matter. See *United States v McKesson & Robbins, Inc.* (1956) 351 US 305, 316, reciting that fair-trade laws should be narrowly construed since "resale price maintenance is a privilege restrictive of a free economy." For more extended discussion of fair-trade programs, see §§3.28–3.36.

Among the questions counsel should ask about a company's fair-trade practices:

In fair-trade states—

☐ Does the company operate within the precise limits of fair-trade laws in the states that permit fair trade?

☐ Does the company avoid making any use of fair-trade contracts in non-fair-trade states?

☐ What methods does the company use to maintain fair-trade prices?

☐ Does the company enforce its fair-trade program diligently and uniformly in fair-trade states?

☐ Does the company solicit the support of its distributors or retailers in enforcing its fair-trade program? Does it ask its distributors or retailers to police their competitors' adherence to fair-trade prices? These practices could lead to an inference of conspiracy between the company and its distributors or retailers.

In non-fair-trade states—

☐ Does the company suggest resale prices and refuse to deal with buyers who do not adhere to the suggested prices? If the answer is yes, the company is operating in one of the most hazardous of all antitrust areas, for while the company may suggest prices and refuse to deal with price cutters, it is strictly forbidden to enter into any agreement or understanding with its distributors about their resale prices. See

United States v Parke, Davis & Co. (1960) 362 US 29 and *Albrecht v Herald Co.* (1968) 390 US 145. For discussion, see §§3.25–3.29, 3.37–3.39.

☐ Does the company refuse to deal with price cutters? If so, learn the exact mechanism by which it stops selling to them. See discussion above.

☐ Does the company ever reinstate price cutters? If so, how does the company satisfy itself that they will in the future adhere to suggested prices? Any discussion of price prior to reinstatement could lead to inference of agreement in non-fair-trade states.

☐ Does the company take any other steps against those not maintaining suggested prices?

(3) [§9.39] Price Discrimination

To avoid Robinson-Patman problems, the company should charge the same price to all its customers who are in direct or indirect competition with each other. In exploring price discriminations, counsel can question along these lines:

☐ Have there been sales in interstate commerce? Ordinarily, at least one of the two or more sales constituting the discrimination must cross a state line to invoke Robinson-Patman jurisdiction. See §5.17.

☐ Have there been secret rebates? These are automatically suspect; the secrecy suggests unlawful discrimination.

☐ Were the prices lower to meet equally low prices of competitors on specific sales? This constitutes a statutory defense to price discrimination, provided the company meets, but does not "beat," the competitor's price on specific sales. The defense is hedged with technical requirements. See §§5.49–5.51.

☐ If quantity discounts are given, can they be cost-justified? That is, are the discounts no greater than the cost saving in selling that quantity to that customer? Cost justification is an exceedingly complicated and difficult undertaking, only rarely successful. See §§5.44–5.48.

☐ Are functional discounts valid? Discounts to buyers based on differences in their business functions are generally permitted. Thus, a manufacturer may sell at a lower price to wholesalers than he does to retailers. But classifications must reflect actual differences in functions performed, and not be merely paper classifications. See §5.23.

☐ Are prices geographically uniform? If the company charges different prices to customers in different geographic areas and hence not in competition with each other, there may nevertheless be an injury to the company's competitors. This is known as primary-line discrimination. See §§5.24–5.39.

☐ Are merchandising and promotional allowances and services fairly given? The firm's payments, allowances, or furnished services or facilities for promotional efforts by customers—*e.g.*, display racks, posters, sales training, and advertising allowances—must be available to all competing customers "on proportionally equal terms." 15 USC §13(e). The inquiry can be highly technical. Various defenses to straight price discrimination are not available. See §§5.31–5.33.

☐ Does the company sell its products under a delivered-pricing system? If so, counsel should learn how the system works. This can be a complex undertaking, probably requiring expert accounting assistance. A delivered-pricing system can raise highly involved problems under the Sherman, Robinson-Patman, and Federal Trade Commission Acts concerning price fixing among the firms adhering to the system of price discrimination among customers. See §5.24 and *FTC v Cement Institute* (1948) 333 US 683; *FTC v A.E. Staley Mfg. Co.* (1945) 324 US 746; *Corn Products Co. v FTC* (1945) 324 US 726.

☐ Does the company as a *buyer* obtain from its suppliers price concessions that are not available to its competitors? This is especially important if the company is a large buyer relative to competitors purchasing from the same supplier. Inducing an unlawful price discrimination is a violation of the Robinson-Patman Act. See §5.42.

For further discussion of price discrimination, see Chapter 5.

d. [§9.40] Interlocking Relationships with Other Firms

Counsel should determine whether there are any interlocking relationships between the company and other firms, particularly if they are competitors. Joint occupancy of directorships of competitors violates Section 8 of the Clayton Act (15 USC §19) but beyond that, the existence of an interlocked board or interlocking stock ownership with a competitor, or with a customer or supplier, is a clear warning signal to counsel to inquire into the relationship between the interlocking firms. A common director or officer may funnel price or other information from a competitor; an interlocking relationship with a supplier or customer may lead to favoritism. Any such interlocks should be terminated. See Travers, *Interlocks in Corporate Management and the Antitrust Laws* (1968) 46 *Tex L Rev* 819. Development in the securities law field of the doctrine of "deputization"—that a director or officer sitting on the board of a related company is the company's deputy—creates an additional hazard. See *Feder v Martin Marietta Corp.* (2d Cir 1969) 406 F2d 260, *cert den* (1970) 396 US 1036. See §4.13.

e. [§9.41] Patent, Licensing, and Trademark Agreements

Counsel should review all patent, licensing and trademark agreements. (On patent problems generally see Chapter 7.) Antitrust problems come both in cross-licensing situations and in attempts by the patentee to extend his patent monopoly. As an example of the first, if company A, located in Atlanta, grants company B an exclusive license to use its patented machine in ten northern states and company B, located in Boston, grants A an exclusive license to use its competing patented machine in ten southern states, the result is to give A exclusive rights to use both machines in the South and B exclusive rights to use both machines in the North. Either license might be unobjectionable in itself, but the two together could be held an unlawful division of the market between competitors.

Among the questions counsel should ask, probably in conjunction with the company's patent counsel, are:

☐ Has the company entered into cross-licensing agreements with competitors or otherwise pooled its patent holdings with a competitor? These arrangements may be sensitive; see §7.22.

☐ Are any of the company's patents known to be invalid? If so, has the company made any efforts to enforce them? Enforcement of clearly invalid patents could be held to violate the Sherman Act. See §7.8.

☐ Are patent licensees restricted concerning territory, competing products, resale prices, or customers? Each of these restrictions could raise antitrust questions. See Chapter 7.

☐ Do patent licenses provide for quotas, patent grant-backs, purchases of unpatented supplies, or royalties payable after some or all patents have expired?

☐ Are royalty rates uniform, or do they discriminate in favor of one or more licensees? On pricing in general, see Chapter 5.

☐ Does the company insist on package licensing of patents whether or not the licensee wants the full package? On tying arrangements, see §§3.9–3.18.

f. [§9.42] Firms in Industries Subject to Antitrust Exemptions

A number of industries, *e.g.*, ocean shipping, labor unions, agricultural cooperatives, and insurance, are in varying degrees exempt from the antitrust laws. But all antitrust exemptions have limits. If his client does business in a field where an exemption exists, counsel should:

☐ Review the statutes and cases to determine, as far as possible, the exact scope of the exemption.

☐ Review the company's operations to determine whether it has in any way exceeded the scope of its exemptions or used the leverage of its exemption to obtain an advantage in some nonexempt market operation. If, for example, a labor union, which enjoys an antitrust exemption to bargain collectively with employers, agrees with existing firms that it will not permit union members to work for any firms seeking to enter the market, the union has exceeded the scope of its exemption and, along with the employers, has violated the Sherman Act. See generally §§2.14–2.22. *Antitrust Exemptions* (1967) 33 *Antitrust LJ* 1.

D. Conducting the Antitrust Inventory

1. [§9.43] Study of Corporate Records

Generally, counsel should begin his antitrust inventory by studying the pertinent corporate records. Counsel should approach the job with the attitude that potentially every piece of paper in the possession or control of the corporation may some day turn up before a federal grand jury or government prosecutor or in the hands of adverse counsel in antitrust litigation. This may happen years after everyone in the company has all but forgotten that the paper ever existed. Indeed, as former Assistant Attorney General Donald Turner has commented, ". . . documentary evidence is usually more important than testimony in our investigations and litigations." (Quoted in Beckstrom, *Destruction of Documents with Federal Antitrust Significance* (1966) 61 *Nw UL Rev* 687, 716.)

A study of the corporate documents will also give counsel the background to conduct thorough interviews with corporate personnel and will suggest particular areas to explore.

Among the records that should be reviewed are:

☐ All antitrust files (if there are any).
☐ Minutes of board of directors meetings and meetings of important committees within the corporation, particularly in the areas of price policies, sales, purchasing, and patents.
☐ The files of policy-making executives, particularly in sales, whether they are kept in a central file area or as "personal" files.
☐ Any file or file folder bearing the name of a competitor.
☐ Sales-department files, including reports from the field.
☐ Trade-association files, including reports from those attending trade-association meetings.
☐ In general, files of departments that deal with customers, suppliers, or competitors; any "trade relations" or similarly designated file.

☐ Other correspondence, interoffice memoranda, and documents relating to activities and dealings with competitors, customers, and suppliers.

Review of files can be very time-consuming and therefore expensive for the client. Counsel will have to judge how far to go and how much time to spend. Frequently, he may develop leads that will enable him to go directly to sensitive documents. If counsel finds himself bogged down in documents, he may find it helpful to stop looking at files temporarily and conduct some interviews with corporate personnel to guide his further examination of documents.

2. [§9.44] Interviews

The study of the company's documents is the prelude to interviews with key company officials. Counsel should be sure to interview policy-making executives who deal with competitors, customers, or suppliers. They should be asked to supply full information about any questionable document. In addition, counsel should ask questions about each sensitive area of operations, even though he sees nothing in the documents to suggest that there may be a problem.

At least a few interviews should be conducted with sales and purchasing personnel at lower levels—e.g., branch managers, purchasing agents; and salesmen or sales managers. They should be asked generally about their operations and also for hearsay about particularly sensitive antitrust areas, e.g., meetings with competitors.

In interviewing company personnel, every effort should be made to encourage full and free disclosure of information. An effective antitrust inventory cannot be made unless there is full disclosure. One method of encouraging disclosure is to assure employees that the firm itself will impose no sanctions against them for any antitrust violations committed before a compliance program is established.

3. [§9.45] Study of Branch Operations

If the firm has branches active in sales, purchasing, or other activities important for antitrust purposes, a special study should be made of them; geographically separate branches frequently operate with a high degree of autonomy and are a source of frequent antitrust trouble. If possible, counsel should visit some or all of the branch offices, talk to the branch managers and other branch officials, and examine the files kept there.

4. [§9.46] Analysis and Recommendations

After the necessary information has been collected, counsel should prepare a report identifying the antitrust problem areas and recommending changes in the firm's operations, and, importantly, suggest legal alternatives to accomplish objectives that counsel finds are being pursued by questionable activities.

In preparing his analysis and recommendations, counsel should look not only at particular phases of a firm's operations, but at the firm's operations as a whole. If there are antitrust problems, counsel should seek the reason and the importance of the area in the firm's total operations. He will thus be better able to propose steps to prevent problems from arising and to formulate legal alternatives to questionable activities.

But beware: The widening scope of civil discovery makes it unclear how far counsel's report, which may contain a virtual index of antitrust offenses, is privileged from discovery or grand jury subpoena. Counsel's report may be based on disclosures by corporate personnel, some of whom could be held not to have been in an attorney-client relationship with counsel (See §9.65.) The report will also be based, in part at least, on corporate documents to which the privilege does not apply. Even if the report is held privileged, the privilege could be lost by too wide a dissemination within the corporation. In the event of antitrust litigation, counsel can expect that the report will be sought by adverse counsel, and he cannot be certain that production will not be required.

Faced with these difficulties, counsel may want to report past antitrust violations and derelictions orally to the company's top management. Written recommendations should be made for future corporate action. This is necessary so that management will have a clear and permanent guide for its compliance program.

IV. An Effective Compliance Program

A. [§9.47] Background of Knowledge

An effective compliance program must be developed against a background of knowledge of the firm and its operations. Once this is achieved through the antitrust inventory (see §§9.8-9.46), the existing antitrust problems of the firm identified, and necessary corrective action taken, counsel can take a longer view and proceed to formulate an effective antitrust compliance program.

B. [§9.48] Developing Sensitivity for the Antitrust Laws and the Will to Comply

The most important objective of an antitrust compliance program is to develop among responsible corporate personnel a basic feeling or sensitivity for the antitrust laws and the will to comply with them. Unless such attitudes are developed, policy statements, procedures, and guidelines will be futile. Evidence of a widespread failure to develop the proper attitudes runs through the congressional hearings on the *Electrical Cases* conspiracies. These cases resulted in jail sentences for high corporate executives and the payment of hundreds of millions of dollars to treble-damage plaintiffs. See *Hearings on Administered Prices before Antitrust and Monopoly Subcommittee of Senate Judiciary Committee* (Pts 26 and 27 (1961)) 86th Cong., 2d Sess. and 87th Cong., 1st Sess. (cited below as *Hearings*).

It appears from the hearings and from various analyses that the motivations to antitrust violations include:

☐ A desire to avoid meeting competition and instead to reach an accord with competitors to "live and let live."

☐ A possibly groundless lack of confidence that the company or an executive can succeed in a confrontation with competitors.

☐ A lack of understanding of the seriousness of violations of the antitrust laws or a feeling that they constitute only a "technical" violation of law.

☐ A belief that certain conduct is not really wrong; for example, price fixing when prices have been fixed at "fair" levels.

☐ A belief that the violation will not be detected.

☐ A feeling that top management is either unconcerned or tacitly expects its employees to engage in activities that are in fact antitrust violations.

☐ The development of a prohibited practice in the industry, with a resulting dulling of the sense of wrongdoing.

See *Hearings, passim*; Whiting, *Antitrust and the Corporate Executive II* (1962) 48 *Va L Rev* 1, 15-18; Withrow, *Making Compliance Programs Work* (1962) 7 *Antitrust Bulletin* 607.

To fight these motivations and to develop feeling for the antitrust laws requires more than rote learning of what the laws forbid; it requires a positive appreciation of the basic objectives of the antitrust laws. Teaching this may require vigorous orientation of company personnel by management with the assistance of counsel. On orientation of company personnel, see §9.53.

C. [§9.49] Importance of Attitude of Top Management

No compliance program can be effective unless company personnel come to believe that the program is wholeheartedly supported by top management. The congressional investigation of the *Electrical Cases* conspiracies revealed that in some companies, although top management was on record as being in favor of antitrust compliance, middle management did not really believe top management meant what it said. See Whiting, *Antitrust and the Corporate Executive II* (1962) 1, 16, notes 48–50 (citing *Hearings, supra*).

V. [§9.50] Antitrust Compliance Procedures and Guidelines for Operations

Sections 9.51–9.66 describe the detailed procedures and suggest guidelines for day-to-day administration of the firm's compliance program. Some of these procedures, guidelines, and forms will be more pertinent to some clients than others, and budgetary limitations may compel counsel to make a comparative evaluation.

The major elements of a compliance program are:

1. A statement of management policy directing employees to adhere strictly to the antitrust laws. See §§9.51–9.52.

2. An effective antitrust orientation program that will instill a basic feeling for and understanding of the antitrust laws. See §9.53.

3. A limited number of specific guidelines on prohibited activities to keep employees out of important danger areas. See §9.54.

4. A checklist of activities that are to be engaged in only with the specific clearance of legal counsel. Lack of consultation between attorneys and operating personnel was another major lesson of the *Electrical Cases*. See §9.55.

5. A requirement that employees engaging in sensitive activities execute certificates concerning their activities. See §§9.56–9.58.

6. An effective documentation and records-retention program to ensure that any questionable areas of operation are fully documented and the documents retained for a substantial time. Destruction of records should be in accordance with an established company record-retention policy. See §§9.59–9.62.

A. [§9.51] Statement of Management Policy on Antitrust Compliance

It is desirable to have a short and definite statement of the basic management policy of complying with the antitrust laws. Unlike some of the more detailed rules and guidelines, which may have to be changed or amended as antitrust doctrine develops, the statement of management policy can reflect a continued and unchanging attitude of antitrust compliance. Most important, such a statement serves to make it clear that employees are not being asked merely to comply with specific company directives, but are expected to comply with the spirit as well as the letter of the antitrust laws. The form suggested goes one step further and combines antitrust compliance with ethical business conduct.

A general statement will not be meaningful unless management convinces its employees that it means business. The president of Westinghouse Corporation made his point this way (*Hearings*, p 17606):

Gentlemen, let me make it unmistakably clear that my position is not being taken just "for the record." Let me repeat: I mean business. We must abide by the laws.

B. [§9.52] Form for Statement on Antitrust Compliance

Policy

It is the policy of _____(Name of company)_____ to comply fully with all laws governing its operations and to conduct its affairs in keeping with the highest moral, legal, and ethical standards.

Compliance with the law, including antitrust and trade regulations, means not only following the law, but so conducting our business that the Company will deserve and receive recognition as a good and law-abiding citizen, alert to its responsibilities in all areas of good citizenship. Even when the law is not applicable, standards of ethics and morality relate to our activities and require the same diligence and attention to good conduct and citizenship.

Any clear infraction of the applicable laws or of recognized ethical business standards will subject an employee to disciplinary action, which may include reprimand, probation, suspension, reduction in salary, demotion, or dismissal, depending on the seriousness of the offense. By way of example, clear-cut price-fixing or bid-rigging acts or illegal activities with competitors to divide or allocate markets or customers will result in dismissal.

Responsibility

There is both a company obligation and an individual obligation to fulfill the intent of the above policy. It is not expected that every employee, or every member of management, will be fully versed in the law affecting his responsibilities. However, it is expected that every employee with significant responsibilities will have a working knowledge of the law relevant to his activities and will seek guidance from a superior or the company's attorney concerning any matter on which he has any question.

Furthermore, it is the responsibility of every individual in the Company who in any way may affect the Company's compliance with the antitrust laws and with standards of ethical and moral conduct to carry out the corporate policy.

The Company's attorney is responsible for constant review and interpretation of the laws and should be called upon for guidance and consultation if questions arise regarding the policy. It is the responsibility of each employee, if he is in any doubt whether a particular act or course of action is legal, to seek guidance and advice from the Company's attorney.

————(Signature of president of company)————

COMMENT: This form is adapted from the form used by Westinghouse Corporation, set out in the congressional hearings on the *Electrical Cases.* See *Hearings,* 17130. There are several points to note in this statement: Responsibility for compliance is placed on every employee; legal advice should be available to every employee without risk; and antitrust compliance is put in the context of business ethics and economics. See Kerr, *The Westinghouse Experience: One Company Reviews Its Antitrust Program.*

C. [§9.53] Understanding of the Antitrust Laws

No attorney should undertake to establish and administer an antitrust compliance program unless he can communicate a fundamental belief in and understanding for what our antitrust laws seek to do. For example, if an attorney says, "This is a lot of nonsense, but here is what you have to do technically," he may undermine the company's entire compliance program.

In the development and administration of the compliance program, the attorney should attempt to communicate to company personnel a feeling, perhaps through a number of concrete examples, for what the antitrust laws are trying to do and for the value of that objective. Among the points that counsel might make are the following:

☐ Compliance with the antitrust laws is much like following the rules of the game in competitive sports. The boxer who takes a "dive" is an object of derision and contempt. The businessman who rigs bids is doing the same thing.

☐ The businessman in the United States enjoys great freedom to manage his business and to establish prices and other conditions of sale. This freedom is based on the belief that freely competing businesses will be more efficient and will produce more innovations and industrial progress than centralized government planning.

☐ Preservation of freedom of business initiative is possible only so long as the antitrust laws are complied with. For if the fundamental premise of business freedom—independent and competitive business decision—is absent, then the reason for preserving business freedom disappears. Clearly, if a choice is presented between businessmen acting to rig and control markets, and business direction by government authorities subject to public scrutiny, it is not difficult to foresee which will be preferred.

☐ The businessman who competes takes many risks by that fact alone. He may find his investments and large amounts of time and effort washed away by competition. He is asked to accept this as part of the workings of competition, a necessary price that must be paid for a free competitive system. When this independent businessman is injured or destroyed and forced from the market—not by losing in fair competition, but by collusive action or abuse of market power—there is a perversion of the competitive system. Such events tend to undermine our free economic system.

Through arguments such as these counsel must communicate to others a feeling for the objectives of antitrust laws. He must somehow get across the two basic tenets, sometimes at odds, that are present in our antitrust laws: the mandate to compete vigorously, as required particularly by the Sherman and Clayton Acts; and the prohibition against using unfair and discriminatory trade practices in competing, as stated in the Federal Trade Commission and Robinson-Patman Acts.

A confession of unsuccessful communication of proper understanding for the antitrust laws was expressed in the congressional hearings (17705) on the *Electrical Cases* by one high corporate executive, as follows:

Senator Kefauver: Your enforcement broke down admittedly, as you said. Where did it break down?

Mr. Cordiner: I think it broke down in that in our teaching we were not able to get through the message that this is a personal individual situation, that you have to have a deeply seated conviction, that this is a moral issue with an individual, and a legal issue, and that it is just good business to have all-out competition without any understanding with your competitor.

For an entire opening talk on compliance, see Withrow, *The Antitrust Laws and Corporate Personnel: What Type of Educational Program is Needed* (1962) 4 *Corporate Practice Commentator* 1, Appendix.

D. [§9.54] Specific Guidelines for Activities

Counsel should not try to make businessmen antitrust experts. It is possible, however, to establish a limited number of guidelines on clearly prohibited activities. Examples of guidelines:

Guideline One:
All company personnel are prohibited from having discussions with competitors or attending meetings with competitors at which anyone discusses or mentions prices, terms or conditions of sale, allocations of customers or territories, or any other subject affecting competition.
Guideline Two:
All company personnel are prohibited from having discussions with outsiders or attending meetings with outsiders at which anyone discusses or mentions boycott or refusal to deal with any supplier or customer.

Companies have, as a general principle, the right to choose the firms with which they will do business, but they frequently run into antitrust difficulties in making the selection. Attending meetings, conferences, or discussions with persons outside the company allows the inference that there was an agreement, which would make the subsequent refusal to deal an illegal boycott.

Often employees do not understand that their mere presence at a meeting at which improper subjects are discussed will be sufficient to compromise them. For example, the following excerpt from the congressional hearings on the *Electrical Cases* conspiracies (*Hearings*, 17890–17891) illustrates the dangers in attending a meeting where the wrong subjects are discussed. The witness was the sales manager of a minor company in the electrical industry:

Mr. Turner [committee counsel]: I would like to get into the very heart and center of these meetings.
You say that you did not come away from the meeting with the knowledge in your mind that there was an agreement to increase the price?
Mr. Scarola: That is correct, Mr. Turner.
Mr. Turner: You are stating that under oath.
Mr. Scarola: Yes sir.
Mr. Turner: You say I misunderstood you when I talked to you before?
Mr. Scarola: Oh, yes, sir.
Mr. Turner: All right. What did you come away with, specifically, an impression that someone was going to raise the price?

Mr. Scarola: Mr. Turner, I just came away with a hope that someone would raise the price, and that the market would stabilize due to my own picture.
Mr. Turner: Did you ever say at a meeting that you would go along with a raise in price?
Mr. Scarola: No, sir.
Mr. Turner: You never told anybody at any of these meetings --
Mr. Scarola: No, sir.
Mr. Turner: That you attended that you would go along with a raise in price if the price was raised?
Mr. Scarola: No, sir.
Mr. Turner: Did you ever tell anyone at these meetings that you would not go along with the raise in price?
Mr. Scarola: No, sir.
Mr. Turner: Did you ever give any indication in these meetings as to what your company would do in the event of a raise in price?
Mr. Scarola: No, sir.
Mr. Scarola: . . . I sat in these meetings more as an observer. . . .

What the witness apparently did not fully appreciate is that despite his testimony that he agreed to nothing, and that he attended these meetings as an "observer," his mere presence at the meeting was sufficient to permit a court or jury finding that he was part of the conspiracy, particularly if his company followed the same course of action as others who attended the meeting.

Guideline Three:
 All company personnel are prohibited, except with express approval of legal counsel, from discussing with any customers or suppliers of the company any action, including action on prices, that the company might take with respect to other suppliers or customers.

Such discussions can lead to inferences and possible allegations of improper agreement. However, there may be occasions when such discussions would be permissible competitive action to sell a customer or to negotiate buying terms with a supplier. Hence, this guideline is not an absolute prohibition, but an admonition to consult a lawyer.

E. [§9.55] Checklist of Acts That Require Clearance of Legal Counsel

The legality of many actions with antitrust implications depends on the surrounding circumstances. Improper pursuit of legitimate objectives violates the antitrust laws; the impropriety can sometimes be cured or, if not, the acts forbidden. To encourage that counsel is consulted before rather than after the fact, company officials can be given a checklist of actions that they are not permitted to undertake until after counsel has been consulted. A checklist should include the following items:

☐ Termination or refusal to deal with any customer or supplier.
☐ Submission of a bid or price known to be identical with that of a competitor.
☐ Correspondence with competitors.
☐ Meetings with competitors, including trade-association activities.
☐ Major changes in prices or price schedules.
☐ Offering any customer prices or conditions of sale more favorable than those offered to other customers.
☐ Purchase from any supplier at prices or terms more favorable than those the supplier is known to offer to other customers.
☐ Acquisition of patents or issuance of patent licenses.
☐ Action or response to any complaint from a supplier, competitor, or customer claiming injury or discrimination by the company.
☐ Making or revising a distributorship contract.
☐ Acquisition or merger, whether accomplished by stock purchase or asset acquisition.
☐ Allocation of scarce products between customers.
☐ Entry into a joint venture.
☐ Marketing of a new product.
☐ Offering unusual sales promotional arrangements.

F. Certificates of Employees

1. [§9.56] Certificate That Employee Has Read the Company's Statement on Antitrust Compliance

Certificate

I have read the statement of antitrust compliance and ethical conduct of _____(Name of company)_____. I understand it and agree that I will not engage in any activities opposed to the statement.

_____(Signature of Employee)_____

Dated:_____

COMMENT: This certificate is adapted from the Westinghouse certificate, which is set forth in the Hearings on Administered Prices. See *Hearings*, 17128.

2. [§9.57] Certificate of Independent Pricing

Certificate

I have caused an investigation to be made of all prices currently being quoted, bid, or charged by ____(Name of company or department)____ and I have satisfied myself that all prices quoted, bid, or charged since ____(Date)____ on the sale of products for which I have responsibility have been set in accordance with the company's policies on antitrust compliance and ethical conduct and in conformity with the law, including antitrust and trade regulation laws.

____(Signature of Employee)____

____(Title)____

Dated:_____

COMMENT: This certificate, which calls the antitrust compliance policy forcefully to the attention of pricing officials, is adapted from the Westinghouse certificate, which is set forth in the Hearings on Administered Prices. See *Hearings,* 17128. Westinghouse reported that it required such certificates to be executed quarterly, and that periodic audits insured that the certificates were being executed. *Ibid.* A smaller company might wish to have such certificates executed semiannually or perhaps only annually.

3. [§9.58] Certificate by Employee Attending Meeting with Competitors

Certificate

On ____(date)____ I attended a meeting or gathering at ____(Address)____ for the purpose of _____ or to discuss _____ at which representatives of competing companies were present. The gathering was ____casual/coincidental [or] called/sponsored by (Name)____. Representatives of competing companies with whom I had personal contact were: ____(Names and titles)____.

I certify that while I was in attendance, there was no discussion relating to terms or conditions of sale, or to prices to be quoted, bid, or charged any third party, or relating to choice of customers, allocation of business, or market shares for any product or products, or relating to any other matter inconsistent with the complete independence of ____(Name of company)____ in its commercial activities.

I further certify that I did not participate in any incidental, collateral, or other discussions of any of these matters in any informal gathering, "side-bar discussion," "rump session," social or unofficial meeting, conference, or conversation.

Dated:_____

_____(Signature of Employee)_____

_____(Title)_____

COMMENT: This form is taken from the forms used by Westinghouse Corporation, set out in the Hearings on Administered Prices, *Hearings*, 17127, contained also in Whiting, *Antitrust and the Corporate Executive II* (1962) 48 *Va L Rev* 1, 9, n 26.

No activity is more sensitive than meetings with competitors. The requirement that employees who do meet with competitors—for whatever reason—execute such a certificate documents the innocent nature of the meeting and reminds the employees of the care that they must take in their discussions with competitors, even during proper meetings.

G. Documentation and Record Retention

1. Documentation

a. [§9.59] Importance

Innocent acts may be incriminating absent adequate contemporary documentation. An overly colorful and perhaps clearly erroneous document in the company's files, or indeed in the files of a competitor or customer, can turn up years later to convict a firm of antitrust violation. Contrary oral testimony years after the event may be disregarded as self-serving. See, *e.g., United States v United States Gypsum Co.* (1948) 333 US 364, 369. Yet, had adequate contemporary documentation been made and preserved, perhaps no problem would have arisen.

b. [§9.60] Types of Activities That Should be Documented

In general, any activity that is likely to raise an antitrust problem should be documented. Therefore, no list can be complete, and counsel will have to use judgment in determining what additional matters should be included. The following types of action should ordinarily be documented:

☐ Any meeting with competitors other than trade-association meetings the proceedings of which are regularly reported.

☐ Significant changes in price, including the reason for the change, particularly if competitors make similar changes.

☐ Competitive price information, *e.g.*, prices being charged by competitors, and particularly any similar bids. Information should be obtained from customers or general sources—*never from competitors.*

☐ Acquisitions and mergers; the reasons for undertaking the acquisition and merger and the steps followed.

☐ Terminations of or refusals to deal with customers or suppliers.

☐ Discriminations in price between customers; the basis or justification for the discrimination and data supporting it, *e.g.*, if the discrimination was to meet the equally low price of a competitor or was cost-justified, supporting facts should be gathered. See §9.61.

☐ Purchasing advantages obtained from suppliers over competing purchasers; the justification for the advantage and all supporting data.

☐ Any questionable approach or offer by an outsider, even though nothing came of it, *e.g.*, a request for a price discrimination.

☐ Any over-colorful document. For example, a salesman's legitimate report of competitors' prices might carry the notation "Destroy after reading," or "For your eyes alone." The notation is so suggestive of illegal activities that an otherwise innocent report, unless explained by a further statement from the salesman, could be used years later as evidence of a price-fixing conspiracy among competitors. For a vivid catalog of such documents, see Loughlin, *The Naughty Words of Antitrust* (1968) 54 *ABAJ* 246.

Sensitive documents (which seem particularly likely to turn up in sales departments, perhaps because of the natural enthusiasm of sales personnel) should be explained, not destroyed. The selective destruction of questionable antitrust material leads to a strong inference that illegal acts have taken place. Too, it is remarkable how often previously unknown copies of destroyed documents turn up. When counsel finds suspicious material, he should obtain a full explanation and collect all documentation necessary to explain the transaction.

c. [§9.61] Form for Reporting Activities of Competitors

Competitive Activity Report

Customer's name:_____
  Address:_____
  Products affected:_____
  Present suppliers:_____
Name of competitor:_____

Competitive activity (describe prices, discounts, rebates, allowances, loans, promotions, advertising, special deals, new products, etc.):_____
If activity affects competitor's prices:
    When offered:_____
    By whom offered:_____
    To whom offered:_____
    Regular or private label:_____
    Type of service:_____
    Was offer written _____ or oral _____?
    If written, was copy obtained (attach) _____ or refused _____?
    If not obtained, was it shown to you? _____
    Source of information:_____
    Customer signature:_____
Is this report submitted for information only _____ or as a request for approval to meet activity described _____?
In your opinion, will it be necessary to meet this activity in order to (retain/gain) this business:_____
Submitted by:_____
Branch:_____ Date:_____
Branch Manager or Sales Manager:
    Noted _____ Recommended approval _____ Initials _____
    Date _____
Appropriate higher executive:
    Noted _____ Approved _____ Initials _____ Date _____

(Adapted from the form appearing in Whiting, *Compliance With the Federal Price Discrimination Laws* (July, 1966) Law Notes: ABA Sections of General Practice and Young Lawyers.)

COMMENT: Use of this form is particularly important in documenting price discriminations to meet equally low prices of competitors. It is important that the form be filled out in as much detail as possible. Use of the form would be encouraged by a policy of not permitting any discount or favored treatment of any sort to a customer unless the form is first prepared and approved. Sales personnel should be told to attempt actually to look at the written quotation or other document containing the competitor's offer or, even better, to obtain a copy and attach it to this form. *In no event should the information be obtained directly from competitors.*

2. [§9.62] Record Retention and Destruction

There is no general rule prescribing how long a company should retain records before destroying them. Practices vary widely, and some records may be needed longer than others. A period as short as four years for retention of general records appears not unreasonable provided this meets the company's business needs. See American Society of Corporate Secretaries, *Survey on Records Retention Practices* (1961), referred to in Beckstrom, *Destruction of Documents with Federal Antitrust Significance* (1966) 61 *Nw UL Rev* 687, 712-713. The following guidelines are suggested:

☐ Record retention and destruction should not be at the whim of department heads or other officials; there should be a settled company policy, in writing, on record retention and destruction.

☐ Records and files should not be "scrubbed" by removing sensitive or incriminating documents. Besides appearing to admit guilt (see §9.60), record destruction by a company under investigation by the Department of Justice or a federal agency is a criminal offense punishable by up to five years imprisonment. See, *e.g.*, 18 USC §1001 (willful concealing or covering up of a material fact), 18 USC §1503 (obstruction of due administration of justice), and 18 USC §1505 (willful destruction of documents in connection with civil investigative demand or administrative agency proceeding). It is not altogether clear that intentional destruction of sensitive documents *prior* to investigation could not also be held to be an "obstruction of justice." See Beckstrom, *Destruction of Documents with Federal Antitrust Significance* (1968) 61 *Nw UL Rev* 687, 702-704.

☐ Record destruction should be administered on a nondiscriminatory basis. All records falling within a category should be destroyed routinely at the end of the retention period.

☐ Records generated to document sensitive antitrust areas (see §§9.60-9.61) should probably not be destroyed at all, but after a time can be shipped to a warehouse for dead storage. Because extremely long time periods can become relevant in antitrust proceedings, it is almost impossible to determine when these records are no longer useful.

☐ Apart from legal records and documents collected as part of the corporation's antitrust compliance program, the length of record retention should be determined by business requirements and convenience.

H. Role of Legal Counsel in the Firm's Compliance Program

1. [§9.63] The Company's Regular Counsel

As stated above (§9.5), the company's regular counsel is normally the one to formulate and administer the firm's compliance program, although he may want to obtain specialized assistance. His role should be a continuing one in the program, with regular liaison and consultation with executives of the corporation, particularly those working in sensitive areas. At regular intervals, counsel should conduct a checkup or additional audit of the company's antitrust health. See §§9.68–9.70. These checkups will normally not have to be as thorough as the initial antitrust inventory.

2. [§9.64] The Proper Use of Specialized Antitrust Counsel

Unless the company's regular counsel is an experienced antitrust lawyer, he should establish contact and consult with specialized antitrust counsel. Appropriate occasions include these:

☐ When establishing a compliance program.
☐ When advising a firm about a questionable transaction. Counsel may want to get a written opinion from antitrust counsel; if the transaction should be challenged by a government enforcement agency, the corporate officials will be able to point out that they proceeded on the advice not only of the firm's regular counsel, but on that of an antitrust specialist specifically retained to render an impartial legal opinion.
☐ When a serious problem erupts, such as being subpoenaed in connection with a grand jury investigation, or being sued in a major antitrust damage action. It is important that experienced antitrust counsel be brought in at the earliest moment, because the initial handling of the matter can often be determinative. Bringing in antitrust counsel does not necessarily mean that the whole matter must be turned over to him. Indeed, regular counsel's intimate knowledge of the company will be vital, and a team approach should be the objective.
☐ When periodically revising the company's antitrust compliance program. In recent years, antitrust has become more complex as new concepts have been evolved. Periodic consultations with outside counsel will help keep the company's attorney abreast of developments.

3. [§9.65] Attorney-Client Privilege

The question arises whether interviews with employees during the inventory and generally in connection with the compliance program are protected by the attorney-client privilege. Corporations are entitled to the attorney-client privilege. *Radiant Burners, Inc. v American Gas Ass'n.* (7th Cir 1963) 320 F2d 314. The more difficult question is whether the interviews conducted by the company's attorney with corporate personnel are in fact communications *by the corporation* and therefore privileged.

It has been held that communications by corporate employees are *not* protected by the attorney-client privilege unless the person talking with the attorney is in a position to take at least some substantial part in a decision about advice the attorney might give to the company. *Philadelphia v Westinghouse Electric Corp.* (ED Pa 1962) 210 F Supp 483, 484; *Natta v Hogan* (10th Cir 1968) 392 F2d 686.

Clearly, lower-level company employees the attorney interviews will not be able to take any substantial part in a decision about actions of the company. Therefore, under *Philadelphia* the interviews would not be privileged. On the other hand, the decision has been criticized, and a contrary result has been reached by the Seventh Circuit, which held communications by lower-level corporate employees privileged when the communication was made at the direction of the employee's superiors, concerned a subject on which the attorney's advice was sought by the company, and which was within the scope of the employee's duties. *Harper & Row Publishers, Inc. v Decker* (7th Cir 1970) 423 F2d 487, *petition for cert granted* (1970) 399 US 903. See also *Continental Oil Co. v United States* (9th Cir 1964) 330 F2d 347. In the face of this uncertainty, counsel should not tell lower-level employees that their conversation will be privileged and should himself plan accordingly. See Willis, *The Inroads of Pretrial Discovery on Attorney-Client Privilege*, 1966 NY State Bar Ass'n. Antitrust Law Symposium 109.

Compare discussion at §10.22.

4. [§9.66] Bypassing Ordinary Channels of Intracompany Communication in Antitrust Compliance Programs

One of the lessons of the *Electrical Cases* was the apparent failure of any knowledgeable person to communicate directly with the company's attorneys or with high-level management concerning the widespread conspiratorial activities. To avoid such a problem it would be desirable to announce to company employees that anyone gaining knowledge of acts in violation of the antitrust laws is at liberty, and indeed would be expected, to communicate directly with legal counsel or directly with top management, including the president of the company. It would also be desirable to state that the disclosures will be treated confidentially. This would permit an employee to report on the activities of a superior without risking retaliatory action.

VI. Making Use of Government Advisory and Clearance Programs

A. [§9.67] Obtaining Department of Justice or FTC Clearance before Doing Questionable Acts

Two types of government clearances of a proposed transaction can be obtained. Both require submission of all data relating to a proposed transaction.

The first is the review procedure, which results in a written expression of intention by the Department of Justice not to institute criminal proceedings or to bring a civil antimerger case. For many years, the Justice Department has been willing to review proposed business transactions and issue a statement (*vel non*) of intention (the so-called "railroad release") not to institute criminal proceedings. A separate procedure (the "merger clearance") was available for mergers, which could result in either a formal or informal expression of Department of Justice views. These procedures have now been consolidated into the business review procedure, which, like its predecessors, is normally available only to check on criminal prosecution and to clear mergers.

In brief, the procedure is to write a letter to the Assistant Attorney General in charge of the Antitrust Division outlining a contemplated business transaction and requesting a business review letter. Each request must be supported by a full statement of all relevant facts. Based on the request and supporting data and, sometimes, on requested additional information and documents, the Antitrust Division will reply by letter, signed by the Attorney General, a Deputy Attorney General, or the Assistant Attorney General in charge of the Antitrust Division. The Antitrust Division may (1) state its present intention about enforcement, (2) decline to pass on the request, or (3) take other "appropriate" action. No clearance or binding statement may be given orally. The procedure is now codified at 28 CFR 50.6; 2 Trade Reg Rep ¶8559. See Turner, *An Interview* (1966) 30 ABA Antitrust Proceedings 100, 120-21.

The second type of procedure is an FTC advisory opinion, which gives the applicant the Commission's view of the legality of any "proposed course of action" subject to the Commission's jurisdiction (mergers, price discrimination, and a broad category of trade restraints under Section 5 of the Federal Trade Commission Act (15 USC §45). The FTC issues brief digests of its advisory opinions, but keeps the identity of the firm confidential. See 3 Trade Reg Rep ¶9732.

A disadvantage of seeking government clearance or an advisory opinion is that if approval is denied and the company goes ahead anyhow, the government ordinarily feels impelled to prosecute or issue a complaint. Since the government (understandably) tends to be conservative in giving approvals, the applicant, ironically, may suffer from a government action that would not have been brought if he had not applied.

If government clearance is sought, it is essential that counsel be thoroughly prepared, and that a persuasive written memorandum and, if necessary, oral presentation be made explaining the proposed action and showing why it should be allowed. Counsel may want to get help from an antitrust specialist. See discussion of clearance procedures at §§4.75–4.76, 6.14, and 11.14.

VII. Periodic Reviews and Checkups of Antitrust Compliance Program

A. [§9.68] Need for Periodic Review

Periodic review of the compliance program is necessary for at least three reasons:

☐ The facts surrounding a company's operations may change: Its relative position in its market may alter; the shape of the market itself may change; and economic conditions may change. Any of these changes can have a vital impact on the legality of various practices under the antitrust laws. For example, a firm, while small, may be perfectly free to make acquisitions of suppliers or customers that would raise the most serious problems if the firm gains a substantial market share.

☐ Antitrust law may change. Changes have been occurring with increasing frequency in recent years.

☐ Failure to conduct periodic checkups and to review compliance procedures may dull antitrust alertness among corporate personnel, who may slide back into old practices or begin dangerous new practices.

B. [§9.69] Periodic Checkups

Counsel should regularly conduct an antitrust checkup of the firm, perhaps annually in a smaller firm. The checkup should include these steps.

☐ Confer with key employees concerning the firm's activities since the last checkup to gain a general understanding of the firm's recent operations and identify any activities of particular antitrust significance.

☐ Review all investigations and litigation that have developed during the past year. From time to time investigations or litigation in nonantitrust areas will have antitrust significance.

☐ Read the minutes of the board of directors and key committees.

☐ Check all antitrust compliance certificates that have been executed during the year. See especially §§9.57–9.58.

☐ Read the documentation developed during the year to check on otherwise questionable practices. See §§9.59–9.61.

☐ Review the files of one or two key executives. A different person's files can be reviewed each year so that over a period of four or five years counsel will have reviewed the files of each executive.

☐ Look into the operations of any newly acquired company or facility. There may be antitrust problems inherited or a-borning. See §9.71.

☐ Check into anything that counsel has previously identified as sensitive or potentially troublesome.

Following the checkup, counsel should prepare a short report with any recommendations for changes in procedures and practices or in the compliance program.

C. [§9.70] Spot Checks on Specific Problem Areas

In addition to the periodic checkup, counsel may find it desirable, or even essential, to conduct spot checks, unannounced to lower management, of troublesome areas. For example, if counsel suspected an inclination toward price collusion in the sales department, he may wish to visit the department irregularly and unannounced, review selected files, and talk with various people in the department.

In addition to possibly discovering important information, irregular spot checks serve as a substantial deterrent to employees who might otherwise be tempted to violate the antitrust laws. It is also a vivid demonstration of the seriousness and importance management places on antitrust compliance.

D. [§9.71] Antitrust Investigation of a Company to be Acquired

However careful the firm's own compliance program, an acquired firm may bring with it a whole assortment of antitrust problems. Thus, before advising a firm on an acquisition of stock or of assets with assumption of liabilities, it is desirable to conduct a full antitrust inventory of the to-be-acquired firm. If the problems uncovered are sufficiently serious, counsel should assess the antitrust exposure for management so that it can decide whether to abandon the merger or to proceed, protecting itself through indemnity agreements or otherwise.

10

Meeting Government Investigations

John J. Hanson and Irwin F. Woodland

Mr. Hanson received the BA degree from University of Denver in 1948 and the JD degree from Harvard Law School in 1951. He is a member of the Los Angeles County and American Bar Associations, the State Bar of California, and the Los Angeles firm of Gibson, Dunn and Crutcher. Mr. Woodland received the BA degree from Columbia University in 1948 and the JD degree from Ohio State University College of Law in 1959. He is a member of the American Bar Association, the State Bar of California, and the Los Angeles firm of Gibson, Dunn and Crutcher.

I. [§10.1] Introduction

Antitrust laws are enforced by the United States Department of Justice and the FTC. Within the Department of Justice there is an Antitrust Division, which investigates and prosecutes violations of the antitrust laws. The division also represents the federal government in civil antitrust suits for damages.

This chapter will discuss the various means by which the Justice Department and the FTC investigate alleged violations of the law, and the role of the private attorney in meeting those investigations.

II. Investigations Conducted under the Auspices of the Antitrust Division of the Department of Justice

A. Informal Investigations

1. [§10.2] FBI Investigations

Within the FBI there is a special section available to assist the Antitrust Division of the Department of Justice in its investigations into alleged violations of the antitrust laws. The FBI may be used in an investigation at almost any point. To understand this it is probably best to examine the manner in which a Department of Justice investigation begins.

The attention of the Antitrust Division may focus on a given course of conduct for a variety of reasons. A merger, for example, may be reported in the newspapers or in trade papers. An investigation by a grand jury of a particular industry and geographic area may produce evidence of wrongdoing in another industry or area. A competitor who feels he is suffering unduly because of what he believes to be illegal activities of his competitors may complain to the Justice Department. The filing of a private antitrust suit may bring an industry to the attention of the Justice Department. In Central District of California, for example, the Los Angeles field office of the Antitrust Division is informed of every private antitrust action filed in the court. At the incipient stage of an investigation, the Antitrust Division may turn to the FBI for assistance. Interviews with persons who have knowledge of the facts can be conducted by FBI agents. The FBI can locate witnesses in different areas of the country and conduct preliminary interviews for the Antitrust Division attorneys.

FBI agents are known for their courtesy in dealing with the public, and this characteristic is perhaps best reflected in their antitrust investigations. It should be emphasized, however, that compliance with the requests of an FBI agent is voluntary. Under these conditions, the FBI is not armed with process to permit search or arrest. Rather, the agents seek to obtain information through the voluntary cooperation of the interviewees.

The procedure adopted by FBI agents will naturally vary from case to case. In some instances, they may make a tape recording of the interview. In others, they may merely take notes. In some cases, they may ask that certain documents be made available to them for copying. Usually, they will not agree to provide the interviewee with a transcript or memorandum of the interview.

It has been suggested by some writers on antitrust investigations that an interview with the FBI should be permitted only on the condition that counsel be present. As a matter of practice, the FBI does not like to conduct interviews in the presence of counsel. The reason usually given is that the government's counsel is not present and thus it would be unfair for the person being interviewed to have his counsel present and further, that such procedure would render the interview somewhat less than meaningful.

As a general rule, there is probably no advantage to a prospective defendant in granting an interview to an FBI agent, whether or not counsel is present. There are situations of course, in which the person being interviewed has no reason to believe that he or his company is a target of the investigation. He may be asked, for example, about former employment. Under these conditions, it is just as well to cooperate with the FBI. If notes are taken in the course of the interview, the interviewee should request a copy. If a recording is made of the interview, he should request a copy of the transcription, even though the request is likely to be refused.

After an interview has been conducted, the attorney for the witness or for the witness's employer should help the witness prepare a memorandum of the interview. The attorney should then make a memorandum of his own. Considerable time may elapse before the investigation is concluded, and these memoranda can aid a witness in remembering what he said.

It is a difficult task for the attorney to guide a client who is faced with an FBI investigation. If the company is one that will ultimately become a target of an investigation, it may have no knowledge that an investigation is being conducted. On the other hand, it may be discovered through a friendly exemployee who will report to his former superiors the fact that he has been approached by the FBI and questioned about activities while he was in the employ of the client. At this point, the attorney should begin to put together a dossier with respect to the investigation. The attorney should, as early as possible, attempt to learn the identities of other interviewees and what was said in each of the interviews, so he will be in a position to make preliminary evaluation of the investigation for the benefit of his client.

When an attorney learns that his client is under investigation, he must become alert to all the government's efforts to obtain information, and he must try to learn as much as he can of the progress of that investigation. Prudence dictates that he decline the invitation of the FBI to interview his client or employees of his client. The immunity of witnesses who testify before the grand jury is discussed at §10.18; it is sufficient to note at this point that a witness who talks to the FBI may thereby lose an opportunity he might have had to appear before the grand jury and thereby to obtain some degree of immunity.

Once a grand jury has returned an indictment, the Antitrust Division no longer has the power to subpoena witnesses and obtain information by compulsion. The FBI may be asked to interview witnesses or even obtain documents. The FBI may want to conduct interviews with customers or competitors of your indicted client to obtain evidence for use at the trial. The attorney must try to see to it that this information is reported to him promptly so that he can prepare a summary of what was said to the FBI agent, and also to obtain copies of any documents submitted to the FBI.

In summary, it may be stated that when the attorney believes his client is a target of an antitrust investigation by the FBI, there is ordinarily little benefit to be gained by permitting the interviews to take place. In an unusual case, if for some reason it is possible to turn over facts which, as a practical matter, would clear the client of any possible wrongdoing, it would be sensible for the interview to take place, even if counsel could not be present.

2. [§10.3] Informal Investigations by the Antitrust Division

What has been said previously about FBI investigations applies, in large measure, to investigations undertaken by attorneys of the Antitrust Division of the Department of Justice. There is, however, this difference: The Antitrust Division personnel are attorneys and are accustomed to observing the usual professional courtesies between attorneys. If a Division attorney wants to interview a client, and if it appears that there is more to be gained by permitting it than by refusing it, the Antitrust Division attorneys will generally agree to have counsel present, and if a transcript is made of the interview, they will undoubtedly make a copy available.

The question arises, of course, whether this kind of interview should be permitted. If the grand jury is in session, the client has received subpoenas, and employees have received subpoenas to appear before the grand jury, then counsel's thought must be to try to preserve the immunity from prosecution afforded to witnesses who appear before the grand jury. Thus, it is advisable to decline interviews if the interviewee is likely, absent the interview, to be called before the grand jury.

A client sometimes reports that he has had a request for an interview by the Antitrust Division in connection with an investigation it is making. The situation must be assessed, and if it appears that the client is not a target of the investigation, or if it is likely that the client, though within the target area, will not be prosecuted if the facts are known, then cooperation with the Antitrust Division may spare further expense to him.

Counsel may be able to determine whether or not the client is a target on the basis of the industry being investigated. In some cases, it can be determined from conversations with representatives of the Antitrust Division that the client is not a target, but the Antitrust Division often will be reluctant to assure counsel that the client is not a target. In view of recent Supreme Court rulings dealing with the rights to counsel and similar matters, the Antitrust Division may well advise a client that he is free to decline to participate in the interview, that he is entitled to have an attorney present, and that anything he says might be held against him. In some cases, the client may be asked to sign a written statement to the effect that such advice has been given.

3. Legal Problems Encountered in Withholding Accurate Information

a. [§10.4] Supplying False Information

When a decision has been made to cooperate in the informal investigation by either the FBI or Antitrust Division attorneys, counsel must caution his client about the compelling necessity to supply only truthful information to the investigators. While the FBI will not take a statement under oath, the Antitrust Division often, after transcribing a statement, will ask that it be signed under oath. A deliberate false written statement is, of course, perjury. Perjury, being a felony, is a more serious offense than a violation of the antitrust laws. There are, in addition, other statutory penalties for false statements and obstructing justice. See 18 USC §1001, which prescribes a fine up to $10,000, or imprisonment up to five years, or both, for knowingly making or using a false writing. It is incumbent upon the attorney, therefore, to see to it that any information that is provided by his client to the investigating authorities is truthful.

b. [§10.5] Destroying Documents

Destruction of documents once an investigation is underway is extremely ill-advised. It may be illegal, under certain circumstances, under the federal statute prohibiting acts to obstruct or impede justice. 18 USC §1503, which declares it a federal offense punishable by $5,000 fine and for imprisonment of up to 5 years for persons who corruptly obstruct the administration of justice; *United States v Solow* (SD NY 1956) 138 F Supp 812, convicting a defendant who destroyed four letters to prevent their production before a federal grand jury. The attorney must caution his client against the understandable inclination to rid himself of apparently incriminating documents. Most of these attempts are abortive in any event, since modern methods of duplicating documents almost guarantee that copies of the destroyed documents exist in other files and will ultimately be found.

B. Formal Investigations by the Grand Jury

1. The Grand Jury Generally

a. [§10.6] Introduction

The most serious form of government inquiry into violations of the antitrust laws is the federal grand jury investigation. This is so not merely because of the very broad investigative powers of the grand jury but also because the end result of the proceedings can be the return of an indictment. Conviction under an indictment carries with it fines up to $50,000 for each violation, and individuals are, in addition, subject to imprisonment for up to one year. 15 USC §1. Of course, treble-damage cases may well follow the criminal proceeding. Accordingly, the attorney who undertakes the representation of a client under investigation should have a good working knowledge of the operation of a federal grand jury.

b. [§10.7] History and Use of Grand Jury

The right of an individual to be indicted by a grand jury before he can be tried is an ancient one. It has been embodied in the Federal Constitution. US Const Amend V. The Fifth Amendment requirement of a grand jury indictment, however, refers only to "capital or otherwise infamous crime." A violation of the antitrust laws is neither capital nor infamous; in fact, it is by definition a misdemeanor, since it is not an offense "punishable by death or imprisonment for a term exceeding one year." (18 USC §1.) Traditionally, however, the Antitrust Division has used the device of the grand jury indictment in bringing criminal prosecutions under the antitrust laws. This approach is probably used in order to gain the advantage of the broad powers of the grand jury to gather evidence that can be used for a successful prosecution.

Since a violation of the antitrust laws does not fall within the grand jury provisions of the Fifth Amendment, the Antitrust Division could obviously proceed on the basis of an information rather than an indictment. This is rarely done, but it should be kept in mind that if an indictment were to be quashed for technical reasons, the government could reinstitute the proceedings by filing an information rather than obtaining a new indictment.

c. [§10.8] Grand Jury's Method of Operation

A federal grand jury must consist of not less than sixteen nor more than twenty-three members. Fed R Crim P 6(a). There are no special provisions in the law concerning the eligibility of a grand juror. The rule merely provides that "they must be legally qualified." See 28 USC §1861. The indictment may be returned only upon the concurrence of 12 or more jurors. Rule 6(f). The grand jury may not serve longer than 18 months. Rule 6(g). Local district court rules may limit the life of a grand jury, but they cannot extend it beyond the 18 month limit.

In the most populous districts of the United States it is not uncommon to find more than one federal grand jury sitting concurrently. One grand jury may be used almost exclusively for a particular antitrust investigation, although it can be used by the United States Attorney for the purpose of returning routine indictments as well. In less populated districts, however, there is generally only one grand jury which handles both the regular business of the United States Attorney as well as the antitrust business.

Access to grand jury proceedings is extremely limited. No one may be present while the grand jury is in session except the government's attorneys, the witness under examination, and the court reporter. While the grand jury is deliberating or voting, no one but members of the grand jury may be present. Rule 6(d). The limitation on access to the grand jury is significant, since it means that a witness must go before the grand jury unaccompanied by counsel, while in contrast, the government attorneys are always present, with the exceptions noted above, and in practice usually select and examine the witnesses who testify.

Even though the witness's attorney cannot be present in the grand jury room, most government attorneys will permit the witness to leave the grand jury room and consult with counsel about specific matters that arise during his grand jury appearance. We know of nothing that gives a witness an absolute right to leave the grand jury room and consult with counsel. We suggest that the witness be advised to decline to answer further questions if he is refused the right to consult with his counsel.

If a witness refuses to answer questions for whatever reason, the government attorney may bring the matter before a United States district court judge immediately, even the same day. The procedure is as follows. The government attorney gets in touch with the appropriate United States district court judge having jurisdiction over the grand jury and establishes a time for a hearing in open court. The witness is advised to appear before the court at the specified time and the government attorney appears there with the members of the grand jury. At this point, counsel for the witness can be present. The government attorney asks for an order permitting disclosure of the grand jury proceedings pursuant to Rule 6(e) and then calls the reporter to the stand and asks him to read the portion of the testimony that raises the question. The government attorney then is in a position to ask for a court order requiring the witness to answer or to be subject to contempt of court. The attorney for the witness then has an opportunity to present whatever argument is appropriate under the circumstances.

The power of the grand jury is essentially the power of the federal district court. There is no specific statutory grant of authority to a grand jury. In practice, it summons witnesses and evidence before it in its capacity as an arm of the court and it is the court's subpoena that requires attendance before it.

Grand jury subpoenas may be served at any place within the United States. It is the custom of the Antitrust Division to use the office of the United States marshal to serve a grand jury subpoena. The marshal, after effecting service, will make a return of service to the attorney of the Antitrust Division. At some point during the course of the grand jury investigation, the Antitrust Division attorney will file the subpoenas with the clerk of the court in which the grand jury is sitting. Ordinarily, the file does not contain the subpoenas of witnesses who have been served but have not appeared. However, once an indictment has been returned, the file should be complete and can be an important source of information to an attorney in determining the extent of the grand jury investigation, as well as the names of potential witnesses. Practice varies among the federal districts concerning the accessibility of this file. In the Central District of California, for example, the file may be examined only by making an application to the chief judge and obtaining his order permitting the examination. In some other districts, however, the file is maintained by the clerk and will be shown to anyone upon request.

d. [§10.9] Secrecy of Grand Jury Proceedings

While defendants in criminal trials are entitled to have their day in open court and have the right to be confronted by their accusers, the grand jury traditionally operates under a veil of secrecy. The proceedings of the grand jury are closed and, except by order of the court, remain secret. The federal practice is materially different in this regard from the practice in numerous states in which the accused has the opportunity to review all the testimony that induced the grand jury to return the indictment. (See Cal Penal Code §938.1; Iowa Code Ann §772.4; Ky Rules Crim P 5.16; Minn Stat Ann §628.04; Mont Laws 95-1406 (e); Okla Stat Ann Title 22, §340.)

While Rule 16(a)(3) of the Federal Rules of Criminal Procedure now provides for limited access to grand jury records as part of the defendant's discovery in a criminal trial (see §10.23), Rule 6 was left relatively unchanged and the secrecy of grand jury proceedings is thereby maintained.

The prohibitions against disclosure of proceedings before the grand jury, however, extend only to a juror, attorney, interpreter, stenographer, recorder, or typist. Fed R Crim P 6(e). Witnesses are not among the persons so named, and Rule 6(e) specifically provides that:

> No obligation of secrecy may be imposed upon any person except in accordance with this rule.

A witness is not obliged to keep secret either his testimony or anything he may have observed while testifying before the grand jury. If the witness is told that he may not disclose anything that happened before the grand jury or an attempt is made to swear him to secrecy, the witness should know that he can resist such suggestions.

In summary, then, the federal grand jury is a powerful investigative agency that can compel the production of documents and the testimony of witnesses to be considered in secret proceedings. At the conclusion of its deliberations, the grand jury may or may not return an indictment. If an indictment (usually called a "true bill") is returned, Rule 6(f) requires that it be returned to the district court judge in open court.

2. The Grand Jury Subpoena Duces Tecum

a. [§10.10] Subpoena Duces Tecum Addressed to Corporation

The grand jury subpoena duces tecum served on a corporation is usually the first concrete sign that the corporation is under investigation by a grand jury. Service is made by a United States marshal on an officer or duly authorized agent of the corporation. The company is directed to produce before the grand jury on a certain date documents that are usually described on a list attached as an annex to the subpoena. The annex contains certain definitions, such as an explanation of what is meant by "documents," a definition of the product under investigation, and other definitions needed to prevent ambiguity. There then follows a description of the actual documents sought. The subpoena usually provides the name, address, and telephone number of the attorney for the Antitrust Division in charge of the case.

In form, the subpoena does not differ materially from subpoenas used in civil cases. The subpoena is addressed to the company, and typically reads as follows:

You are hereby commanded to appear in the United States District Court for the ＿＿ District of ＿＿ at ＿＿ in the city of ＿＿ on the ＿＿ day of ＿＿＿＿,19＿, at ＿ o'clock ＿.M., to testify before the Grand Jury and bring with you [the documents, materials and other data set forth in the Annex attached].

This subpoena is issued on the application of the United States of America.

Dated ＿＿＿＿.

_____
Clerk

The first subpoena is usually the one that calls for the greatest volume of documents and will cover documents spanning a period of years. As the government investigator proceeds, and more information comes to hand, more particularized subpoenas duces tecum may issue.

The usual practice is to request "all documents" in each category. A typical paragraph in which the government is seeking documents reflecting the interstate commerce of the business under investigation might read as follows:

All books, records and documents that contain the following information for each of the years from January 1, 1962 to the date of this subpoena;

(a) a description of the materials and components used in the manufacture of ＿＿(your products)＿＿ in the State of:

(b) the names and addresses of the suppliers of each of the different kinds of materials and the components used in the manufacture of ＿＿(your products)＿＿ in the State of:

(c) the address of the plants, factories or warehouses of the suppliers of components and other materials.

(d) the total dollar amount of purchases of all materials and components from each of the plants listed in response to subparagraph (c) above.

Note that in this illustration the government is seeking the documents relating to presumed interstate shipment of materials and components. This request, however, is for "all books, records and documents." Similar paragraphs will be found in the subpoena relating to the personnel in charge of the operations under investigation; with respect to any significant contacts between the company and its competitors; and with respect to a whole host of other subjects. In order to satisfy the government's demand, a major effort may well be required in searching the files of the corporation for documents responsive to the call of the subpoena. The search may not be limited to a single location. In multiplant operations, the use of the word "all" generally means that searches have to be made in many plants and many offices within those plants.

In addition to the request for documents to establish interstate commerce, there will likely be requests for documents that reflect financial information, such as the dollar volume of sales or perhaps unit sales. In the case of an investigation of an alleged conspiracy involving more than a single state, the subpoena may well request documents that show economic information on a state-by-state basis.

Broad as the subpoena powers may be, no subpoena requires production of a company's entire records. In addition, the subpoena is limited usually to a single product or product line and there will be many company documents that need not be searched. When faced with a demand for a large mass of documents, it is not wise to invite the government's agent to conduct his own file search.

b. [§10.11] Subpoena Duces Tecum Addressed to Individual

In many cases, a grand jury subpoena addressed to an individual will also require the individual to bring to the grand jury any personal (as distinguished from company) documents in his possession relating to the matters under investigation. Such a subpoena duces tecum ordinarily does not present substantial file search problems but it means what it says; that the individual must bring personal papers if they are relevant.

c. Compliance with the Grand Jury Subpoena Duces Tecum

(1) [§10.12] Time and Scope   The first task of the attorney is to negotiate with the government concerning compliance with the subpoena duces tecum. The initial subpoenas to produce documents are usually issued about the same time to several companies in the industry and have return dates on about the same day. The government attorney will generally be cooperative in arranging a realistic schedule for the production of

documents. Long before the return date of the subpoena, arrangements should be made with the government to modify the return date if there are difficulties of compliance.

Once an understanding has been reached with respect to the date, other understandings can be reached with respect to the documents themselves. The government throws a very wide net and is not usually interested in everything the net is capable of bringing up. For example, if all documents relating to sales are sought, one can quite often work out an arrangement with the government whereby only sales in excess of certain dollar amounts need be included. Similarly, the government will accept summaries of certain information. Usually, a footnote to the subpoena will contain a statement similar to the following:

In lieu of producing or returning the actual documents called for in Paragraphs 1, 2, 6, 8 and 9, you may furnish an affidavit by an official of ____(your company)____ setting forth the information called for and describing the books, records and documents from which the information in the described statement was obtained, and relating the said information in each instance to the respective paragraphs and subparagraphs of this subpoena to which it pertains.

On occasion, compliance with certain paragraphs of the subpoena will be waived by the government, without prejudice, or at least total compliance will be waived with an understanding that the government will be given certain information upon request.

(2) [§10.13] The Search   Once having cleared the hurdle of negotiating the return date of the subpoena and the modification of its scope, counsel must then decide on the physical efforts that will be made to locate the documents called for.

Practice in these matters will vary depending upon the size of the client. If the company is very large with numerous files, the file search may be conducted by employees of the client company under the supervision of an attorney. To organize such a search, the attorney should make an analysis of the documents sought and should conduct a limited inspection of the files himself in order to become familiar with the type of records kept. He can then prepare directions to be used by lay personnel in searching the files for the appropriate documents. Since the determination of whether or not a document is responsive to the subpoena must ultimately be made by the attorney, the lay personnel who do the actual physical searching will turn over the documents to the attorney for a determination of responsiveness.

Whether the search is conducted by an attorney or not, it is important that a rational system for identifying the documents be adopted at the very beginning. One should know, for example, out of which file a particular document came because, while a particular document may be the only one responsive to the subpoena, other documents in the same file may be helpful in the preparation of witnesses or in explaining what appears to be damaging information in the responsive document. In addition it may be important in the day-to-day operations of the company to have a record in its files of the documents that have been removed. Before the search begins, a simple form can be designed to be inserted in the file in place of each document taken out, briefly describing the document, naming the present custodian, and giving the date of removal.

The subpoena contemplates the production of original documents. While it is sometimes possible upon agreement to offer copies in place of originals, one must be prepared to surrender the original documents. No document should be turned over to the grand jury unless a copy of it has first been made for retention. The attorney should have at his disposal throughout the investigation copies of all the documents produced.

It is desirable also to adopt some form of numbering system for the documents. If the documents are numbered when selected, the numbers will provide a continuing register of all documents submitted. Sometimes, in large investigations, the government will suggest as part of the subpoena that the documents be marked with certain initials and in a certain number series. If the numbering system suggested by the government is not feasible because of some internal system of the client's, then it is best to continue with the client's own system. The government can apparently not compel a person to number the documents, and there is no penalty for failure to follow the government's suggestion.

Although the subpoena duces tecum requires the witness to produce the documents before the grand jury, in many districts an arrangement can be made with the Antitrust Division for delivery of the documents to the attorney handling the investigation, rather than to the grand jury itself. A letter agreement is usually worked out with the Antitrust Division to provide that the corporation will have the same protection as if the documents were delivered to the grand jury. Sometimes the corporation is required to furnish a certificate that all appropriate files have been searched and all documents called for by the subpoena have been produced.

A typical letter will read as follows:

_____(Date)_____

Department of Justice
Antitrust Division
Washington, D.C. 20530

Gentlemen:

On behalf of the ABC Corporation and pursuant to the grand jury subpoena dated November 7, 1970, I hereby submit to the grand jury the enclosed documents, all of which have been numbered in accordance with the procedures outlined in your previous letter, that is, each document bears the letter "A" and the documents are numbered consecutively from 1 through 11,476.

The above enumerated documents constitute a complete response to the grand jury subpoena. As we have agreed, the ABC Corporation by delivering these documents to you for the grand jury has, in fact, submitted them to the grand jury.

Very truly yours,

_____(Signature)_____

Great care is taken by the government in the drafting of its subpoenas. On limitations, see §10.14. Similarly, great care should be exercised by an attorney in deciding whether a document falls within the call of the subpoena. Every document within the call must be produced, but documents not within the call need not, and ordinarily should not, be produced.

In the course of the file search, very damaging documents may sometimes be found that are clearly within the call of the subpoena. There is a natural tendency on the part of some companies under investigation to suppress this sort of document. In order to convince your client that the subpoenaed documents must be produced, his attention should be drawn to 18 USC §1001, which provides a $10,000 fine, or imprisonment for not more than five years, or both, for anyone who knowingly conceals a material fact. See discussion of legal problems encountered in withholding accurate information at §§10.4-10.5.

d. [§10.14] Limitations on Grand Jury Subpoenas Duces Tecum

While the subpoena duces tecum can be extremely broad, there are some limitations in the law. Grand jury subpoenas duces tecum must be issued in accordance with Rule 17(c) of the Federal Rules of Criminal Procedure. Discussions of the permissible scope of a subpoena duces tecum appear in many texts; see particularly 11 *Cyclopedia of Federal Procedure* (3d ed) §41.57. It is fair to conclude that if the documents sought can be described with specificity and if the period of time covered by the documents is not too long, a subpoena duces tecum will usually be upheld against a motion to quash, even though compliance is burdensome.

3. The Grand Jury Subpoena Ad Testificandum

a. [§10.15] Introduction

One of the more difficult problems encountered in connection with grand jury investigations occurs when an individual is subpoenaed to appear before the grand jury to testify about matters being investigated. In many cases the individuals involved will be present or former employees of the companies in the industry under investigation for antitrust violation.

By the time witnesses are subpoenaed to testify, an attorney who represents a company under investigation for antitrust violations realizes that, as a practical matter, his client may be involved in serious legal proceedings. Although no complaint has been filed and no indictment returned, the Antitrust Division or the FBI has probably interviewed informally a number of witnesses. Substantial masses of documents undoubtedly have been subpoenaed and turned over to the grand jury or to the Antitrust Division by the other companies involved, and other witnesses may well have appeared before the grand jury and given testimony. In short, a very substantial amount of activity has taken place, some of which is not apparent on the surface. It is in this context that the typical witness gives testimony before a grand jury.

b. [§10.16] Practical Operation of Grand Jury Proceedings

The subpoena ad testificandum ordinarily requires the witness to appear at the local federal courthouse. Grand juries ordinarily meet in one of the court rooms or hearing rooms in the federal courthouse building. Present while the witness testifies are a majority of the 23 grand jurors, one or more attorneys from the Antitrust Division office, a court reporter, and a bailiff. All these persons are sworn not to divulge anything that takes place before the grand jury. However, the witness himself is not barred from disclosing to others the testimony he has given. See §10.9. No other persons are permitted to be present, and, in particular, the witness is not entitled to be accompanied by his lawyer.

c. [§10.17] Preparation of Witness to Testify before Grand Jury

It is unnecessary, and beyond the scope of this chapter, to set forth what is ordinarily required in connection with the preparation of a witness for a deposition or for trial. It is sufficient to note that the same general steps must be taken in connection with preparation of a witness who is to testify before a grand jury. In addition, special problems are presented because the witness cannot be represented by counsel, and there is no one in the grand jury room to help and protect the witness, object to questions, and so forth. Time must be spent with the witness to teach him to listen carefully to questions, not to answer a question if he does not understand it, and to answer in terms of facts rather than sweeping conclusions and opinions. In the usual case, the company has already turned over masses of documents to the grand jury, and the witness may well be asked questions concerning some of these documents. He should be prepared to answer such questions.

Typically, if officers and employees of a corporate client are subpoenaed to testify, they will also want the attorney to represent him as individuals in connections with the investigation. It is desirable, however, to discuss this question at the outset with each employee or officer and advise him that he may want to consider retaining separate counsel. In any event, it should be clearly established whether or not the attorney for the company is representing the individual witness. For the implications of client status on discovery of witnesses, summaries, see §10.22.

d. [§10.18] The Privilege against Self-incrimination

The Fifth Amendment of the United States Constitution provides that no person may be compelled to testify against himself. The amendment is applicable to individuals but not to corporations. *Maricopa Tallow Works, Inc. v United States* (9th Cir 1967) 1968 Trade Cases ¶72,346, *cert den* (1968) 392 US 926 indicates the possibility that a small, closely held corporation may assert the privilege on the ground that compliance with the grand jury subpoena may tend to incriminate the stockholders.

Before December, 1970, the Immunity Act (former 15 USC §§32-33) conferred automatic immunity from prosecution on any witness testifying in response to a subpoena. The Organized Crime Control Act of 1970 repealed these sections (PL 91-452, 84 Stat 922, Sec. 209) and narrows the immunity considerably. If a witness has refused or "is likely to refuse to testify or provide other information on the basis of his privilege against self-incrimination" (18 USC §6003(b)(2)), the United States Attorney, with the approval of the Attorney General, may request an order from the district court requiring the witness to testify. The law appears to require the court to issue the order automatically.

The witness who complies with the order is granted immunity, not from prosecution for any matter concerning which he has testified, but only from use against him of "testimony or other information compelled under the order (or any information directly or indirectly derived from such testimony or other information). . . ." 18 USC §6002(3).

At least one court has held the new immunity provisions unconstitutional. *In re Joanne Kinoy* (SD NY 1971) 499 ATRR D-1, citing *Counselman v Hitchcock* (1891) 142 US 547.

e. [§10.19] Selection of Witnesses by the Government to Testify before Grand Jury

At this point it may be worthwhile to note briefly the Antitrust Division's problems and strategy concerning grand jury witnesses. By the time an investigation gets to the grand jury stage, Antitrust Division attorneys usually suspect that there has been a violation of the antitrust laws. In the usual case, proof of such a violation must be obtained either from documents in the files of the potential defendants or from testimony of the present or former employees of the company. Generally speaking, if serious antitrust violations have occurred, the Antitrust Division attorneys want to indict the highest officials in the company who are involved in the violation. The lowest level employees are usually first subpoenaed, and then the Antitrust Division gradually works up the corporate ladder. Each witness called, of course, obtains whatever immunity the law allows. Until the 1970 immunity statute (18 USC §§6001-6005), discussed in §10.18, the government had to make difficult choices about when to stop calling witnesses; if it called the top official who participated in the arrangement, it had no one left to be indicted. The government's problem is ameliorated by the new law if it is ultimately held constitutional; the government can now prosecute someone even though he testified before the grand jury, although his testimony and its fruits cannot be used against him. In a sense, the government's problem under the 1970 immunity provisions is not what witnesses to call, but when to stop asking questions.

It should be emphasized that the witness is not immune from prosecution for perjury if he gives false testimony before the grand jury. In many cases, the Antitrust Division Attorney advises the witness on behalf of the grand jury that he does have immunity but that he can be prosecuted for perjury if he lies.

f. [§10.20] Preparing a Record of Witness's Testimony

A witness who testifies before the grand jury is not entitled to receive a transcript of his testimony. However, the Antitrust Division always has a copy and may use it in the preparation of criminal and civil cases. The witness should recognize that he must live with his testimony, and if he subsequently testifies differently, the grand jury transcript may be used for impeachment.

After the witness has testified before the grand jury, he and his attorney should immediately confer and the attorney should prepare a memorandum summarizing the testimony. If this is not done immediately, it will be difficult, if not impossible, to get an accurate summary of the testimony. To protect against a waiver of the attorney-client privilege and subsequent discovery of information concerning his testimony before the grand jury, the witness should not discuss his testimony with anyone but his attorney, and he should be so instructed. See further discussion of discovery of summaries of witnesses' testimony at §10.22.

4. Subsequent Disclosure of Grand Jury Proceedings

a. [§10.21] Introduction

The secrecy of grand jury proceedings is one of those verities that is accepted by everyone. The reason and the statutory support for grand jury secrecy are discussed at §10.9. In a day when change proceeds at an ever-accelerated rate, it is not too surprising that "secret" isn't secret any more. Various inroads have been made into grand jury secrecy, and every attorney should be aware that at some point the testimony of witnesses and the documents submitted to the grand jury may be spread on an open record. Some of the areas of subsequent grand jury disclosure will be discussed in §§10.22–10.23.

b. [§10.22] Discovery of Summaries of Witnesses' Testimony

As discussed at §10.20 the lawyer should obtain from his client a summary of his testimony before the grand jury as promptly as possible after the grand jury appearance. Given a broad investigation, an attorney will accumulate a number of these summaries. These documents should be safe from any discovery on the grounds that they embody a confidential communication from a client and that summaries in their final form are an attorney work product entitled to that protection as set forth in *Hickman v Taylor* (1947) 329 US 495.

A difficulty arises when an attorney wants to know what some witness other than his own client may have said in testifying. Many attorneys will let attorneys for other witnesses read the summaries of his witnesses. Immediately apparent is the question whether this exchange of summaries between counsel vitiates either the attorney-client privilege or the protection afforded attorney work product.

The issue was presented squarely in *Continental Oil Co. v United States* (9th Cir 1964) 330 F2d 347, which held that an exchange of such memos or summaries between counsel did not waive the attorney-client privilege. The work-product rule was not discussed. The rationale for the court's decision is found in the cases cited in the opinion permitting attorneys engaged in a common defense to exchange information without losing the privilege.

It would seem therefore under present law that the summaries of client's testimony are protected by the attorney-client privilege. But the witness must be a "client." *Continental* is clear that the attorneys were counsel for the corporation *and* the witnesses. If counsel cannot represent the witness and other counsel is not representing the witness, only the protection of the work-product rule remains. If the summary is entirely the work of the witness, and the witness is not a "client," then the work-product protection should not be available and the document should be considered discoverable. Even if the summary is the "work product" of the attorney, there is recent authority that the work-product doctrine would not protect it from discovery. See *Illinois v Harper & Row Publishers, Inc.* (ND Ill 1969) 1969 Trade Cases ¶72,965, *rev'd in part, Harper & Row Publishers, Inc. v Decker* (7th Cir 1970) 423 F2d 487, *aff'd by equally divided court* 1/12/71; 39 *US Law Week* 4100; 1971 Trade Cases ¶73,430, in which the district court ruled that debriefing memoranda prepared by counsel after interviewing the witnesses who were in fact not clients but employees of the corporate client following the witnesses' testimony before the grand jury were not protected from discovery in a private treble-damage action either by the work-product doctrine or the privilege shielding communications between client and lawyer.

c. [§10.23] Disclosure of Grand Jury Testimony in Subseqent Trial

In the trial of indictments, grand jury testimony of witnesses can be used for impeachment. The Supreme Court has held that a court may also order the disclosure of grand jury minutes when there is a showing of "special and compelling circumstances sufficient to overcome the policy against disclosure." See *Atlantic City Electric Co. v A.B. Chance Company* (2d Cir 1963) 313 F2d 431, 434, citing *Pittsburgh Plate Glass Co. v United States* (1959) 360 US 395 and *United States v Procter & Gamble Co.* (1958) 356 US 677, and (1963) 10 LE2d 122, refusing to stay lower court's order making testimony available pending decision on certiorari.

As pointed out in the *Atlantic City* case, these exceptions previously had applied only to criminal cases. *Atlantic City* was the first case to permit the disclosure of grand jury testimony in a civil case, *i.e.*, a treble-damage action growing out of the prior electrical industry criminal cases.

As in the criminal cases, disclosure was ordered in *Atlantic City* after there had been review of grand jury testimony by the judge in chambers. Disclosure was ordered because of apparent inconsistencies between the witness's deposition testimony and his testimony before the grand jury. This technique of obtaining grand jury testimony is now fairly standard in antitrust cases. Usually a motion is made requesting the court to make an inspection of the transcript in chambers. If a showing of inconsistency has been made, the court will order disclosure. *Illinois v Harper & Row Publishers, Inc.* (ND Ill 1969) 1969 Trade Cases ¶72,965, *rev'd in part, Harper & Row Publishers, Inc. v Decker* (7th Cir 1970) 423 F2d 487, *aff'd by equally divided court* 1/12/71; 39 *US Law Week* 4100; 1971 Trade Cases ¶73,430.

Yet another way suggests itself because of the 1966 amendments to the Federal Rules of Criminal Procedure. Rule 16(a)(3) provides that the defendant may obtain "recorded testimony of the defendant before a grand jury."

In an antitrust case in which the defendant is a corporation, there is authority to the effect that every officer or employee of a corporation who testifies about his activities as an officer or employee in effect is giving the testimony of the corporate defendant. In *United States v Hughes* (5th Cir 1969) 413 F2d 1244, 1253, *cert granted sub nom United States v Gifford-Hill-American, Inc.* (1969) 396 US 984; *judgment vacated and mandamus dismissed as moot*, (1970) 397 US 93, the court held

under Rule 16(a)(3) the defendant corporations may discover the testimony of all present and former officers and employees concerning activities carried on, or knowledge acquired, within the scope of or reasonably relating to their employment. In so holding, we reiterate that if circumstances exist justifying the denial, restriction, or deferral of discovery in the particular case, the government may seek appropriate orders under Rule 16(e).

Documents submitted to the grand jury and grand jury transcripts are governed by Rule 16(b) and can be discovered if there is "a showing of materiality to the preparation of the defense and of reasonableness" (at 86,960). If testimony and documents are turned over to the corporate defendant under Rule 16(b), there is always the possibility that these items may then be discoverable from the corporate defendant by private plaintiffs in subsequent treble-damage actions on a general "fairness" theory. While no case has yet been presented on this theory, certain other cases, by analogy, give good indication of the direction of the wind. For example, in *Olympic Refining v Carter* (9th Cir 1964) 332 F2d 260 answers to interrogatories that had been sealed by the court in a government antitrust suit were ordered disclosed to a subsequent treble-damage plaintiff despite the fact that the interrogatories, to which objections could have been interposed, were answered only on the express understanding that they would be sealed and could never be revealed.

In a somewhat similar situation, the government had prepared a memorandum for the probation department to assist it in the preparation of a presentence report for the court, drawing on information it had developed in the grand jury investigation. Counsel for the defendants saw the government memorandum as part of the court's regular presentence procedure. In a subsequent treble-damage action, the plaintiff moved to discover the government memorandum. Defendants objected on the grounds that the information contained in it was secret grand jury testimony. The Court of Appeals made it available after some editing, on the ground that the defendants had seen it and therefore the plaintiff should. *U.S. Industries, Inc. v United States District Court* (9th Cir 1965) 345 F2d 18, *cert den* (1965) 382 US 814.

In summary, the attorney should be aware that grand jury testimony may be disclosed (1) at a subsequent criminal trial as impeachment evidence, thereby becoming discoverable in subsequent civil actions; (2) upon a showing of compelling need in a civil case even though there may have been no prior criminal trial, and (3) by discovery of government memoranda previously made available to defendants.

C. Civil Investigative Demand

1. [§10.24] History and Scope

In 1962 the Justice Department was provided with a new investigatory tool, the civil investigative demand (CID), created by the passage of the Antitrust Civil Process Act, 15 USC §§1311-1314. Prior to this legislation, the Justice Department lacked compulsory methods for obtaining information relevant to a *civil* antitrust suit prior to its filing and was required to rely on the cooperation of potential antitrust defendants and others in its efforts to secure evidence.

The Supreme Court had held that grand jury criminal procedures utilized by the department to obtain evidence for criminal antitrust actions could not be used solely to elicit evidence for a civil action. *United States v Procter & Gamble Co.* (1958) 356 US 677. Furthermore, while the Attorney General could request the help of the FTC, which has civil investigatory powers, this procedure was found to be unworkable because of the additional burden this placed on the FTC.

The basic purpose of the act is to enable the Justice Department to determine before filing a complaint whether there is sufficient evidence to warrant a civil action and, if there is, to obtain the evidence in advance. The act authorizes only the production of documents; oral testimony cannot be compelled by a CID. The act authorizes the demand to be made upon business entities; it may not be used to obtain evidence from natural persons. The act by no means precludes criminal action; a savings clause makes it clear that *any* evidence concerning *any* antitrust violation can be laid before *any* grand jury. PL 87-664 §7, 76 Stat 548-552.

Under the act, the Justice Department is authorized to serve a civil investigative demand to examine a company's books or records whenever the Attorney General has reason to believe that a company may be in possession of documentary material relevant to a civil antitrust investigation. Service of the demand may be made anywhere within the territorial jurisdiction of a United States court on any partnership, corporation, association, or other legal entity by delivering an executed copy to an authorized agent, to the company's principal place of business, or by sending it by certified or registered mail.

The contents of the demand (see form on page 508) must indicate the nature of the antitrust violation being investigated and the relevant provisions of law, describe with particularity the documentary material to be produced, prescribe a return date that allows a reasonable period of time to produce the documents, and identify the person to whom the material shall be made available. The test used to determine whether the demand complies with this provision is whether it is sufficient to inform the investigated company of the nature of the investigation and to permit a determination of the relevance of the documents demanded. *Petition of Gold Bond Stamp Co.* (D Minn 1963) 221 F Supp 391, 396, *aff'd per curiam* (8th Cir 1964) 325 F2d 1018; *Petition of Columbia Broadcasting System, Inc.* (SD NY 1964) 235 F Supp 684, 687. A demand is sufficiently specific if it states that its purpose is to determine whether there has been a conspiracy to fix prices, to refuse to deal, or to monopolize in violation of Sections 1 and 2 of the Sherman Act (15 USC §§ 1, 2). It is not necessary to specify the nature of the alleged conduct. *Petition of Gold Bond Stamp Co., supra* at 397 ("Necessarily, therefore, the nature of the conduct must be stated in general terms."); *Lightning Rod Manufacturers Ass'n v Staal* (7th Cir 1964) 339 F2d 346.

United States Department of Justice
ANTITRUST DIVISION
WASHINGTON, D.C.   20530

TO ....

....

....

....

CIVIL INVESTIGATIVE

DEMAND NO.

    This civil investigative demand is issued pursuant to the provisions of the Antitrust Civil Process Act, 76 Stat. 548–552, Title 15 United States Code Secs. 1311–1314, in the course of an inquiry for the purpose of ascertaining whether there is or has been a violation of the provisions of Title 15 United States Code Secs. .... by conduct of the following nature : ....

....

....

    You are a person under investigation and are hereby required to produce, to make available for inspection and copying or reproduction, and to deliver to a custodian named herein, at your principal place of business, designated above, the documentary material in your possession, custody or control described on the attached schedule, on the .... day of ...., 19........ at
               A.M.
.... P.M.

    For the purposes of this investigation, the following are designated as custodians or deputy custodians to whom said documentary material shall be made available and delivered : ....

....

....

    Inquiries concerning compliance should be directed to ....

....

    Your attention is directed to the provisions of Title 18 United States Code Sec. 1505 as amended which makes obstruction of this investigation a criminal offense and which is printed in full on the reverse side hereof.

    Issued at Washington, D.C. this .... day of ...., 19........

508

Assistant Attorney General

"§ 1505. Obstruction of proceedings before departments, agencies, and committees

"Whoever corruptly, or by threats or force, or by any threatening letter or communication, endeavors to influence, intimidate, or impede any witness in any proceeding pending before any department or agency of the United States, or in connection with any inquiry or investigation being had by either House, or any committee of either House, or any joint committee of the Congress; or

"Whoever injures any party or witness in his person or property on account of his attending or having attended such proceeding, inquiry, or investigation, or on account of his testifying or having testified to any matter pending therein; or

"Whoever, with intent to avoid, evade, prevent, or obstruct compliance in whole or in part with any civil investigative demand duly and properly made under the Antitrust Civil Process Act willfully removes from any place, conceals, destroys, mutilates, alters, or by other means falsifies any documentary material which is the subject of such demand; or

"Whoever corruptly, or by threats or force, or by any threatening letter or communication influences, obstructs, or impedes or endeavors to influence, obstruct, or impede the due and proper administration of the law under which such proceeding is being had before such department or agency of the United States, or the due and proper exercise of the power of inquiry under which such inquiry or investigation is being had by either House, or any committee of either House or any joint committee of the Congress—

"Shall be fined not more than $5,000 or imprisoned not more than five years, or both."

Certificate of Compliance with Civil Investigative Demand

All of the documentary material described on the attached schedule which is in the possession, custody or control of the person to which this civil investigative demand is directed has been produced and made available to a custodian named therein.

Date ....

Signature ....

Title ....

However, there are limitations imposed by the act on the use of the civil investigative demand. Section 3(a) of the Act (15 USC §1312(a)) allows the demand to be served only on a company "under investigation." But is not necessary to state in the demand that the company served is under investigation, for it is presumed that the Attorney General will act within the ambit of the act. (*Lightning Rod Manufacturers Ass'n. v Staal, supra.*) It is enough if the demand states that it is issued pursuant to provisions of the Antitrust Civil Process Act. *Hyster Co. v United States* (9th Cir 1964) 338 F2d 183.

Besides requiring that the demand be made only on a company under investigation, and call only for the company's documents, Section 3(a) also requires that the material demanded be relevant to the asserted investigation. The Ninth Circuit has held that the demand may call for material relevant to ascertaining whether one has already engaged in an antitrust violation, but not whether there has been activity that may result in a violation in the future. See *United States v Union Oil Co. of California* (9th Cir 1965) 343 F2d 29, holding improper a demand for documents relating to proposed acquisitions.

A demand has been held proper even though a similar investigation is being conducted by the FTC. *Petition of Gold Bond Stamp Co., supra.* Moreover, a stay of a civil investigative demand pending disposition of FTC proceedings has been denied since findings of fact by the FTC would not be binding on the Justice Department (*Petition of Columbia Broadcasting System, Inc., supra*).

The scope of the demand, despite the above limitations, is exceedingly broad. Section 3(a) makes the civil investigative demand available in the investigation of any "antitrust violation." Section 2(d) (15 USC §1311(d)) defines "antitrust violation" as any violation of an antitrust law or antitrust order. Section 2(b) (15 USC §1311(b)) defines "antitrust order" to include any final order, decree, or judgment of any United States court in a case arising under the antitrust laws. Therefore, the demand would be available to the Department of Justice not only in contemplated civil suits for injunctive relief or damages, but also to check on the company's compliance with an antitrust judgment. The power to serve a demand to check compliance exists as an enforcement method in addition to the usual visitation provisions contained in most antitrust judgments and the compliance investigations referred to the FTC under Section 6(c) of the Federal Trade Commission Act (15 USC §46(c)). See Trade Reg Rep ¶8591.

While the civil investigative demand is available to aid in the investigation of a violation of any antitrust law, Section 4(c) (15 USC §1313(c) limits the use of the documents to duly authorized agents of the Justice Department. Under Section 7 (Pub L 87-664 §7, 76 Stat 548-552), however, the documents may be used in a court or grand jury proceeding concerning an alleged antitrust violation conducted by a United States Attorney.

Procedurally, the civil investigative demand is limited by the rules applicable to a subpoena duces tecum served in grand jury investigations of alleged antitrust violations. See §10.14. Antitrust Civil Process Act of 1962, §3(c) (15 USC §1312(c)); *Petition of Columbia Broadcasting System, Inc., supra.* Thus, Section 3(c)(1) of the act, 15 USC §1312 (c)(1), provides that the demand cannot contain a request that would be unreasonable if contained in a subpoena duces tecum. In addition, Section 3(c)(2) of the act, 15 USC §1312(c)(2), provides that a demand may not require the production of documents that would be privileged from disclosure if demanded by subpoena duces tecum. Finally, a petition for a demand must comply with the requirements of the Federal Rules of Civil Procedure unless the rules are inconsistent with the act. Section 5(e), 15 USC §1314(e).

A proper demand requires the company to produce the requested documents and turn them over for safekeeping to a custodian designated by the Department of Justice. The custodian may make necessary copies for official use, but must upon completion of the investigation return all documents received from the company that have not passed to the control of a court or grand jury. The company can examine its documents while they are in custody of the Justice Department and can request the return of documents if no case is instituted within a reasonable time after the investigation is completed.

2. [§10.25] Constitutionality of Civil Investigative Demand

Defense attorneys mounted early attacks on the constitutionality of the CID, none of which have been successful. The demand has been upheld against charges that it constituted an unreasonable search and seizure in violation of the Fourth Amendment. *Petition of Gold Bond Stamp Co.* (D Minn 1963) 221 F Supp 391, *aff'd per curiam,* (8th Cir 1964) 325 F2d 1018, *Hyster Co. v United States* (9th Cir 1964) 338 F2d 183.

The assertion that the act permits the Attorney General to embark on a fishing expedition has been rejected on the analogy that a grand jury subpoena can be issued with no assurance that antitrust laws have actually been violated. *Petition of Gold Bond Stamp Co., supra.* Moreover, safeguards against unreasonableness are afforded by application of the Federal Rules of Civil Procedure to the demand process and by procedures that allow the demand to be enforced only in a judicial proceeding. *Hyster Co. v United States, supra.*

In *Hyster* the act also withstood attack on the ground that it constitutes a violation of the Fifth Amendment safeguard against self-incrimination. In *Hyster*, the company upon whom the demand was served argued that the demand violates the privilege against self-incrimination in that it requires implicit testimony by company employees in the process of selecting the demanded material without the opportunity of gaining immunity against self-incrimination. The court held that a corporation has no privilege against self-incrimination and cannot assert it on behalf of someone else.

3. [§10.26] Enforcement or Challenge of Civil Investigative Demand

Whenever a company served with a demand refuses to produce the documentary material, the Attorney General is empowered to bring an enforcement suit in the United States District Court in the district where the company resides, is found, or transacts business. (Antitrust Civil Process Act of 1962, §5(a), 15 USC §1314(a).) Section 5(d) of the act, 15 USC §1314(d), authorizes contempt proceedings against a company that refuses to produce when ordered to do so by the court.

Section 6 of the act amends 18 USC §1505 to impose a fine of not more than $5,000, or imprisonment for not more than five years, or both, for removal, concealment, destruction, or falsification of any documentary material requested in the demand.

The company upon whom the demand has been served may sue in the United States District Court in the district where the company resides, is found, or transacts business, to modify or set aside the demand. (Antitrust Civil Process Act of 1962, §5(b), 15 USC §1314(b).) The petition must be filed within 20 days after the demand has been served or before the demand's return date, whichever is sooner, and must be served upon the custodian named in the demand.

In most cases a company can, without fighting, negotiate the scope of the demand down to a reasonable level. The government attorneys will insist on obtaining the information they regard as important, but they will often cooperate in reducing the burden of compliance.

4. [§10.27] Compliance with Terms of Civil Investigative Demand

Compliance with the terms of a CID is precisely the same as compliance with a grand jury subpoena duces tecum, bearing in mind the limitations previously discussed. See §§10.12–10.13.

III. Investigations Conducted under the Auspices of the FTC

A. [§10.28] Introduction

Many of the problems associated with investigations by the FBI and the Antitrust Division are also present in connection with investigations by the FTC. If an investigating agency can compel a client to do an act, the client may be well advised to cooperate and avoid compulsion. If the agency cannot compel the witness to do a particular thing, cooperation is then voluntary in a true sense.

The FTC's primary powers to investigate are as follows.

1. The power to obtain by notice documents of any corporation being investigated for examination and copying. 15 USC §49. See §10.29.

2. The power to subpoena the attendance of witnesses and the production of documentary evidence. 15 USC §49. See §10.30.

3. The power to direct a corporation to file annual or special reports and to answer specific questions in writing. 15 USC §46. See §10.33.

The FTC's Procedures and Rules of Practice, hereafter called Commission Rules, are set out at 16 CFR §§1.1-4.11, 15 USCA following §45, and 3 Trade Reg Rep ¶¶9801.01-9821.11. Investigations are governed by §§2.1-2.14, FTC investigations may be commenced on the request of practically anyone, including members of the public, or by the Commission on its own initiative. Commission Rules §§2.1-2.2. Requests are made in writing, without formal procedures, and the FTC does not divulge the name of the complaining party. Commission Rules §2.2.

Commission Rules §§2.1-2.14 should be studied in their entirety by counsel facing an FTC investigation. The rules are discussed along with the powers in §§10.29-10.35.

1. [§10.29] The Power to Obtain Documentary Evidence from a Corporation by Notice

Section 9 of the Federal Trade Commission Act (15 USC §49) provides in pertinent part as follows:

For the purposes of [this act] the commission, or its duly authorized agent or agents, shall at all reasonable times have access to, for the purpose of examination, and the right to copy any documentary evidence of any corporation being investigated or proceeded against; . . .

FTC investigators have claimed in several cases that Section 9 gives them the right to review *in toto* the files of any corporation the FTC is investigating. Such an investigator probably would state that the FTC desires only documents relevant to the practices being investigated, but he may contend that he has a right to review all the corporation's documents in order to select those relevant. For an assertion of this claim, see Mueller, *Access to Corporate Papers Under the FTC Act* (1962) 11 Kan L Rev 77.

Early decisions of the Supreme Court reject the idea that an FTC investigator may come into a corporation's plant or offices and review all documents of the corporation. *FTC v American Tobacco Co.* (1924) 264 US 298. The FTC has not subsequently made a clear-cut attempt to establish that it has unlimited rights to review all documents of a corporation. One recent case that arose in a slightly different context *(United States v International Nickel Co. of Canada, Ltd.* (SD NY 1962) 203 F Supp 739) indicates that the Commission's power of access entitles it to inspect and copy only those documents relevant to its inquiry, and that the company or its attorney can select the documents called for. Notwithstanding the Supreme Court's expansion of the FTC's investigatory powers in recent years (see *e.g., United States v Morton Salt Co.* (1950) 338 US 632), it is the authors' belief that the FTC's right of access under Section 9 is no broader than its right to subpoena documents, as discussed at §10.30.

It should be noted that Commission Rules §2.11, 16 CFR §2.11, 15 USCA following §45, 3 Trade Reg Rep ¶9807.11, not only authorizes the Commission to issue an order requiring a corporation being investigated to grant access to files, but also requires any motion to limit or quash such order to be filed with the secretary of the Commission within 10 days after service or in a shorter allowed time if the date for compliance is less than 10 days. Counsel must act quickly if he intends to limit the Commission's "access to" his client's files.

2. [§10.30] The Power to Subpoena the Attendance of Witnesses and the Production of Documentary Evidence

Section 9 of the Federal Trade Commission Act, 15 USC §49, provides in part as follows:

> ... the commission shall have power to require by subpoena the attendance and testimony of witnesses and the production of all such documentary evidence relating to any matter under investigation.

Section 9 also provides that the attendance of witnesses and the production of documents "may be required from any place in the United States, at any designated place of hearing."

Under the Commission Rules, the Commission or any member of it may issue a subpoena directing the person named to appear before an FTC representative to testify and produce the documentary evidence referred to in the subpoena. Commission Rules §2.7, 16 CFR §2.7, 15 USCA following §45, 3 Trade Reg Rep ¶9807.07. It should be noted that §2.7 requires any motion to limit or quash the subpoena to be filed with the secretary of the Commission within 10 days after service, or a shorter allowed time if the return date is less than 10 days. The Commission rules on such motions, but the director or assistant director who issues the subpoena may negotiate and approve "terms of satisfactory compliance." §2.7, as amended August 12, 1969.

Testimony will be heard and documents received by the Commission, one or more members, or a representative, which means a Commission attorney. See Commission Rules §2.8(b).

Witnesses required to testify pursuant to a subpoena are entitled to be accompanied by counsel (there is nothing to indicate that the FTC has an obligation to provide counsel for a witness); Section 6(a) of the Administrative Procedure Act, 5 USC §1005(a), provides quite broadly that "any person compelled to appear . . . before any agency . . . shall be accorded the right to be accompanied, represented, and advised by counsel. . . ."

Commission Rules §2.9 state that a witness compelled to appear may be accompanied, represented, and advised by counsel as follows: Counsel may advise his client on any question and state the grounds if he has advised the client not to answer the question; counsel may object to questions on the grounds of irrelevance or privilege, and may state the grounds for the record; motions may be made to the FTC in advance of the hearing, and counsel is not permitted to interrupt the examination of the witness by making objections or statements except those listed above; and the witness, at counsel's request, in the discretion of the hearing officer, may be permitted to clarify his answers after the completion of the examination. An attorney guilty of obstructive conduct in violation of the rules may disbarred from practice before the FTC.

Although there is little law on the subject, there is some question whether the limitations placed on the right to counsel by the FTC rules comply with the Administrative Procedure Act.

a. [§10.31] Immunity under the Federal Trade Commission Act

The immunity provision of the Federal Trade Commission Act, the seventh paragraph of 15 USC §49, was repealed by the Organized Crime Control Act of 1970, PL 91-452, 84 Stat 922, Sec. 211. That Act included the General Immunity statute, 18 USC §§6001-6005, which narrows considerably the immunity derived from testifying. The immunity formerly was against any prosecution growing out of the subject matter, whereas the immunity is now only against use of the testimony of information growing out of the testimony. See 18 USC §6002. There is some question about the constitutionality of the new statute. See *Counselman v Hitchcock* (1891) 142 US 547. At least one court has held immunity provisions unconstitutional. *In re Joanne Kinoy* (SD NY 1971) 499 ATRR D-1.

An FTC subpoena requiring the production of documents is undoubtedly limited or restricted in several ways:

A subpoena requiring a corporation to produce *all* its documents may be unconstitutional because it is a constructive unlawful search and seizure in violation of the Fourth Amendment. The Fourth Amendment guards against abuse in the form of too much indefiniteness or breadth in the description of the documents to be produced. *Oklahoma Press Publishing Co. v Walling* (1946) 327 US 186. An FTC subpoena duces tecum that is reasonably specific and properly limited in its scope does not violate the Fourth Amendment.

A corporation cannot avoid producing documents on the ground that it may incriminate itself because the self-incrimination provisions of the Constitution are inapplicable to corporations.

Although a person may decline to produce personal documents in his possession on the ground of self-incrimination (absent an immunity statute), a company officer cannot refuse to produce records he holds as a representative because the self-incrimination provisions are not applicable under these circumstances.

Partnership records pose special problems. The decisions provide no clear answers about when the partnership records are so constituted that any partner or all partners might invoke the Fourth and Fifth Amendments. Several cases have held that a partner holding records to which a subpoena is directed may claim privilege: *United States v Linen Service Council* (D NJ 1956) 141 F Supp 511; *United States v Lawn* (SD NY 1953) 115 F Supp 674; *In re Subpoena Duces Tecum* (ND Calif 1948) 81 F Supp 418; *United States v Brasley* (WD Pa 1920) 268 F 59. In another group of cases, the privilege was not thought to invalidate the subpoena. *United States v Wernes* (7th Cir 1946) 157 F2d 797; *United States v Onassis* (SD NY 1955) 133 F Supp 327; *United States v Onassis* (D DC 1954) 125 F Supp 190. In a carefully reasoned opinion, after considering the two groups of cases just cited, the Second Circuit denied the privilege to a man who was a general partner in five limited partnerships. *United States v Silverstein* (1963) 314 F2d 789.

While there is authority both ways, it would seem that the privilege against self-incrimination could be asserted successfully against a subpoena for partnership records by any partner when the partnership is an intimate one. Members of a large partnership that approaches the image of a corporation could probably not assert successfully the privilege against a subpoena directed to the partnership records. The records in question would be treated as they were in *Silverstein, supra.*

The Supreme Court in recent years has handed down a number of decisions protecting the rights of persons charged with "common crimes," including crimes of violence. There has been a hue and cry in many quarters that the Supreme Court has gone too far in protecting the rights of "criminals" and has failed to protect the general public. These decisions have not yet been applied specifically in the antitrust field, but it is quite possible that the businessman will receive the same protection that others charged with crime have received. Accordingly, much that is true today about the permissible scope and nature of antitrust investigations may change in the future. The attorney should save and assert every right the client may have.

b. [§10.32] Power to Enforce Subpoenas

Although Commission Rules §2.13, 16 CFR §2.13, 15 USCA following §45, 3 Trade Reg Rep ¶9807.13 generically provides that the Commission or the Attorney General may take "appropriate action . . . including actions for enforcement, forfeiture, or penalties or criminal actions" "in cases of failure to comply with Commission investigational processes," the Federal Trade Commission Act sets forth specific and strong means by which the Commission may enforce its subpoena powers.

Section 9 of that act, 15 USC §49, authorizes the Commission to "invoke the aid of any court of the United States in requiring the attendance and testimony of witnesses and the production of documentary evidence." That section also authorizes the United States district courts to order compliance and expressly provides that failure to obey a court order to appear before the Commission to produce documentary evidence or to testify may be punishable as contempt of court. Section 9 also authorizes the Commission to request the Attorney General to apply to the United States district court for a writ of mandamus commanding compliance with the Commission's order. In addition, Section 10 of the act, 15 USC §50, provides that any person who neglects or refuses "to attend and testify, or to answer any lawful inquiry or to produce documentary evidence . . . in obedience to the subpoena or lawful require-

ment of the commission," shall be punished by a fine of from $1,000 to
$5,000 and/or by imprisonment up to one year.

3. [§10.33] Power to Direct a Corporation to File Annual or Special Reports

Section 6(b) of the Federal Trade Commission Act, 15 USC §46(b),
empowers the Commission

> To require, by general or special orders, corporations engaged in commerce,
> excepting banks and common carriers subject to the Act to regulate commerce,
> or any class of them, or any of them, respectively, to file with the commission in
> such form as the commission may prescribe annual or special, or both annual and
> special, reports or answers in writing to specific questions, furnishing to the
> commission such information as it may require as to the organization, business,
> conduct, practices, management, and relation to other corporations, partnerships,
> and individuals of the respective corporations filing such reports or answers in
> writing. Such reports and answers shall be made under oath, or otherwise, as the
> commission may prescribe, and shall be filed with the commission within such
> reasonable period as the commission may prescribe, unless additional time be
> granted in any case by the commission.

It was believed for many years that Section 6(b) was intended to give
the FTC the power to gather and compile business statistics and make
economic studies, and not to assist in the enforcement of the law. But in
United States v Morton Salt Co. (1950) 338 US 632, the Supreme Court
held that the FTC had the power under Section 6(b) to require a corporation to file reports showing how it had complied with a court decree
enforcing a cease-and-desist order under Section 5 of the Federal Trade
Commission Act 15 USC §45); and in *St. Regis Paper Co. v United States*
(1961) 368 US 208, the Supreme Court held that the FTC had the right to
compel an acquiring company to furnish a special report relating to the
acquisition, which the FTC claimed was in violation of Section 7 of the
Clayton Act (15 USC §18). See also *FTC v Washington Fish & Oyster Co.*
(9th Cir 1959) 271 F2d 39, in which the court upheld the Commission's
right to investigate compliance with an order issued under the Clayton
Act.

4. [§10.34] Premerger Notification

For several years various bills have been introduced in Congress, the
effect of which would give the FTC the power to require certain corporations planning to merge to give the FTC advance notice of the proposed merger or acquisition. None of these bills have been enacted into
law.

The FTC has achieved the same end by adopting on April 8, 1969, under existing legislation, a "Resolution Requiring Notification of and Submission of Special Reports Relating to Large Corporate Mergers." The FTC adopted this resolution at a time when it stated that "all previous levels of merger activity were eclipsed in 1968" (FTC News Release, April 13, 1969). The notification and reporting requirements imposed by the resolution are set out at §4.72.

The Commission subsequently adopted FTC Form 6-21 (4-69), reproduced at pages 212–213, requiring a great deal of detailed information, including the consummation date, the manner in which the transaction is to be carried out, and a description of the stock or assets to be acquired and the consideration to be paid. The food and cement industries are required to fill out special forms.

As noted above, the resolution requires that notice be given "no less than 60 days prior to the consummation of the merger or acquisition." On the face of it, this would appear to prevent a company from merging for at least a period of 60 days. However the FTC has no power to issue a temporary restraining order or a preliminary injunction in merger cases. The Commission, in June of 1969, clarified the resolution by stating that it was not intended to prevent mergers and acquisitions from being consummated within the 60-day period. If the acquisition or merger is to be consummated in less than 60 days, the reporting company is required only to give notice as soon as practicable.

Apparently the only penalty the Commission might seek to impose for failure to file a special report is that imposed by Section 10 of the Federal Trade Commission Act (15 USC §50), which provides that if failure to file a report "shall continue for thirty days after notice of such default, the corporation shall forfeit to the United States the sum of $100 for each and every day of the continuance of such failure. . . ."

After the notification and the filing of the Special Report, it seems clear that the Commission staff makes a preliminary determination whether the proposed acquisition might violate Section 7 of the Clayton Act (15 USC §18). If it does not appear to raise problems, that is the end of the matter. If the information on the Special Report indicates the possibility of an antitrust violation, the next step is usually a letter from the Commission to the reporting company requesting additional detail. Although the Special Report form can usually be completed within a couple of weeks, the information requested by the follow-up letter often requires several weeks to collect and furnish to the Commission. The Commission obviously is examining the acquisition and may well decide to challenge it. At this stage of the proceeding, counsel can perform a most valuable

519

service for his client. In addition to furnishing the information requested, we believe counsel and the reporting company should collect and furnish to the Commission all information indicating that the proposed acquisition does not violate Section 7 or any other provision of the antitrust laws. As a practical matter, the battle may well be won or lost at this stage, since the Commission has lost very few acquisition cases.

For further discussion see §§4.71–4.73.

B. [§10.35] Informal Investigations

Some of the investigatory powers of the FTC are summarized in §§10.24–10.34. Although these powers are broad, they are not unlimited; there are some things the lawyer can do.

The first step in an FTC investigation is often the appearance at the company's offices of the FTC investigator with a request that he be permitted to talk with a person of authority. The investigator is usually an attorney on the FTC's staff and often will desire first to talk informally with a responsible official and then to review the records of the company.

The first step that such a company official should take is to advise the FTC investigator to see the company's attorney to discuss the matter. Granting unlimited access to the company's files and an unlimited right to discuss any matters with any and all company officials is probably an unwise procedure to follow. The FTC investigator may state that any company that has nothing to hide should permit the investigator unlimited access and interviews. The difficulty with doing so is that it may result in a disruptive, time-consuming investigation and possibly an FTC proceeding that would not otherwise have been filed. A company's records may contain isolated statements or references that indicate some possible violation of the law. If the investigator seizes on them, it may take the company months or years and many thousands of dollars to present a true and accurate picture.

The company's attorney should meet with the FTC investigator and inquire about the nature and purpose of the investigation. Commission Rules §2.6, 16 CFR §2.6, 15 USCA following §45, 3 Trade Reg Rep ¶9807.06, provides:

> Any person under investigation compelled or requested to furnish information or documentary evidence shall be advised with respect to the purpose and scope of the investigation.

The director of the former FTC Bureau of Field Operations has stated that an investigating attorney, if asked to do so, will reduce his request for information to writing and that he should be able to "prepare one immediately in the office of a potential witness." (Williams, *Investigations by the Federal Trade Commission* (1965) 27 ABA Antitrust Section 71, 72.) Mr. Williams further stated:

Whether a request for information is made orally or in writing, it is always prefaced by a full explanation of the business conduct under investigation, the statutory provision involved in the investigation, and an outline of the categories of documents to be examined. Our field attorneys are instructed to make every effort to aid and assist potential witnesses or the party under investigation to understand exactly the nature and scope of the investigation. . . .

An appropriate way to handle the FTC's request for documents is to suggest that the investigator prepare a letter addressed to the company listing the documents requested. The company's attorney can review the letter with the FTC attorney and work out some reasonable accommodation about the categories of the documents to be produced for inspection and the time schedule for production. A practical approach is to produce promptly those documents readily available and produce later those that require a search of the company's files.

The FTC investigator may want to interview the representatives of the company. It is difficult to give general advice on this; in many cases it will be desirable to permit such an interview but in others, it will not.

Little is to be gained by misleading the investigator about the nature and scope of your compliance with his request. If you and your client do not intend to cooperate, more may be lost by indicating a willingness to cooperate and then failing to do so than if you had merely stated your intention not to cooperate in the first instance.

11

Government Enforcement: Criminal and Civil

Edwin M. Zimmerman

Mr. Zimmerman received the AB degree from Columbia University in 1944 and the LLB degree from Columbia University School of Law in 1949. He was a Professor at the Stanford Law School from 1959 to 1969 and served as Assistant Attorney General of the Antitrust Division from 1968 to 1969. He is a member of the American Bar Association, the District of Columbia Bar, and the Washington, DC firm of Covington & Burling.

III.   Complaints of Alleged Violations

IV. [§11.14]   Business Review Procedure

V.   Consent Decree Procedure

I. Organization of the Antitrust Division

A. Duties and Functions

1. [§11.1] Antitrust Laws

The Department of Justice has exclusive jurisdiction to enforce the Sherman Act and shares with the Federal Trade Commission the authority to enforce the Clayton Act. Within the Department of Justice the assistant attorney general in charge of the Antitrust Division is assigned responsibility for enforcement of the federal antitrust laws. The division's enforcement activities include the investigation of possible antitrust violations through a variety of methods including the civil investigative demand (see §§10.24-10.27) and the grand jury (see §§10.6-10.23), the preparation and trial of antitrust cases, the taking of appeals where necessary, and the policing and enforcement of final decrees. When appropriate, the Sherman Act is enforced by criminal actions; otherwise, civil suits are brought that seek relief designed to restore competitive conditions and to ensure that those conditions are maintained; frequently, criminal actions are accompanied by civil suits that seek injunctive relief. The criteria for choosing between criminal and civil enforcement are discussed in §11.7.

2. [§11.2] Other Laws

In addition to its responsibilities to enforce the Sherman and Clayton Acts, the division participates from time to time in regulatory agency proceedings involving competitive issues. For example, the division, representing the Department of Justice, may intervene in proceedings before the Interstate Commerce Commission or the Federal Maritime Commission considering the merger of regulated carriers. The division is also allotted a portion of the Department of Justice's responsibility for the supervision of government litigation in the courts. In particular, the division represents the United States as a statutory defendant or respondent in suits to review orders of the Interstate Commerce Commission, the Federal Communications Commission, the Federal Maritime Commission, and the Atomic Energy Commission. The division also represents the Civil Aeronautics Board in suits seeking review of the board's orders and supervises litigation in the Supreme Court concerning the Federal Trade Commission. It also has special responsibilities in connection with the enforcement of a number of other acts of Congress and Presidential Orders, such as the Defense Production Act, the Federal Aviation Act, the Federal Trade Commission Act, the Interstate Commerce Act, and Executive Order 10936 on identical bids. The Antitrust Division is assigned certain special duties such as reporting and advising on the competitive effects of certain governmental and industrial activities connected with national defense programs, the Small Business Administration, the Interstate Oil Compact, and the disposal of government-owned rubber-producing facilities and surplus property. Finally, representatives of the Antitrust Division sit on *ad hoc* interagency committees that deal with ongoing major policy questions in which issues of economic regulation are important.

B. [§11.3] Structure of the Antitrust Division

The precise organization of the division varies from time to time. The division is headed by an assistant attorney general, a presidential appointee. He is assisted by a deputy assistant attorney general (formerly called the first assistant) who helps exercise general supervision over the entire division and serves as the assistant attorney general in the latter's absence.

Under the present organization the assistant attorney general and the deputy are assisted by a director of operations, a deputy director of operations, and the director of policy planning and his deputy. The director of operations and the deputy director of operations supervise the

525

division personnel principally concerned with investigatory and litigation activities—the four Washington litigation sections and the seven field offices. See §11.4. The director of policy planning and his deputy supervise the activities of personnel whose principal functions are other than those of investigation and litigation—*i.e.*, the nonlitigating activities of the appellate, economic, evaluation, foreign commerce, judgments, and public counsel and legislative sections. See §11.5.

1. [§11.4] The Litigating Sections and Field Offices

The Antitrust Division is organized into twelve sections in Washington and seven field offices. Four of the sections in Washington are principally concerned with investigation and litigation. These are the general litigation section, the special litigation section, the trial section, and the special trial section. The titles of these litigating sections have lost their original significance, and the assignment of investigations and cases among these four is on the basis of familiarity of each section with particular industries. The ongoing enforcement activity against patent licensing restrictions has recently given rise to a special patent unit which investigates and litigates problems in the patent licensing field and which is also supervised by the office of the director of operations.

The seven field offices are principally concerned with investigation and litigation. They are presently in Atlanta, Chicago, Cleveland, Los Angeles, New York, Philadelphia, and San Francisco. Investigations and litigation are assigned either to Washington litigating sections or to the field offices on the basis of geographic convenience. The field offices handle investigations and litigation in areas conveniently reached from those offices, particularly if the problems are local. Each section and field office is headed by a chief and an assistant chief.

These litigating sections and field offices investigate complaints, conduct preliminary inquiries and grand jury investigations, request FBI investigations, prepare civil investigative demands, and try both civil and criminal cases.

2. [§11.5] The Specialized Sections

The specialized sections are all in Washington. They consist of the appellate section, the economic section, the evaluation section, the foreign commerce section, the judgments section, and the public counsel and legislative section. There is also an administrative section. While several of these sections do, from time to time, engage in litigation within their own specialized areas, investigation and litigation are not their principal functions. A consumer affairs section has recently been established

10

to enforce existing consumer-protection legislation, to handle FTC civil penalty cases, and to represent consumer interests in regulatory proceedings.

The appellate section handles the division's appellate work under the federal antitrust laws and under various statutes for the regulation of different types of businesses by federal administrative agencies. Hence the appellate section is concerned with the review of orders of the Civil Aeronautics Board, the Federal Communications Commission, the Federal Maritime Commission, the Interstate Commerce Commission, the Federal Aviation Agency, and the Atomic Energy Commission as well as Supreme Court matters involving the Federal Trade Commission.

The economic section provides technical assistance to the litigating sections and field offices in the conduct of investigations and trials. It is also responsible for the planning and conduct of economic research and the analysis of economic data relating to all phases of antitrust enforcement. It is assigned responsibility for implementation of Executive Order 10936, which requires periodic reports to the President and Congress on the status of the Identical Bid Program—which surveys identical bids in excess of $10,000 to public agencies.

The evaluation section is a floating resource that is used from time to time in the preparation of cases of special complexity or for the preparation of policy positions on intragovernmental matters and otherwise makes recommendations on specific actions that should be taken to implement the basic policy objectives of the division.

The foreign commerce section provides a liaison between the division, the State Department, and other governmental agencies in connection with all division cases, investigations, and other matters relating to foreign commerce, nationals, or governments. From time to time, the section also investigates and litigates cases in which foreign commerce is peculiarly important. It also works with the State Department in handling exchanges of views between the Department of Justice and foreign government agencies.

The judgments section prepares consent decrees and formulates and negotiates litigated judgments in civil antitrust cases in conjunction with the trial staffs. A newly established judgment enforcement unit reviews antitrust decrees, investigates to determine compliance, and initiates necessary enforcement litigation.

The public counsel and legislative section is responsible for preparation of the reports required by Congress; liaison with government regulatory agencies on matters pending before them; congressional mail; comments

on proposed legislation; surplus property disposal; small-business questions; and litigation in court or before regulatory agencies concerning
transportation, public utilities, and other regulated industries.

II. Enforcement Problems and Procedures

A. [§11.6] Jurisdictional Questions: Trade or Commerce among the Several States

An underlying Sherman Act question is that of the meaning and scope
of the statutory phrase "trade or commerce among the several States, or
with foreign nations" (15 USC §1). The phrase corresponds closely to the
language used in Article 1, Section 8, of the Constitution. It has been
construed, at least with respect to domestic commerce, to be as inclusive
as the constitutional limits of Congress' power to regulate commerce. In
United States v South-Eastern Underwriters Ass'n. (1944) 322 US 533,
558, the Supreme Court said that Congress, in passing the Sherman Act,
meant "to go to the utmost extent of its Constitutional power in restraining trust and monopoly agreements."

The words "trade or commerce" are not restricted to the production
and physical movement of goods but have been construed to include all
manner of economic activities so long as the requisite interstate effect is
found. Thus, for example, banking, insurance, finance, and the business of
conducting hospitals and making organized provision for medical care all
may come within its scope. For further discussion, see §§2.12–2.13.

The interstate requirement is fairly easy to satisfy; *Mandeville Island
Farms, Inc. v American Crystal Sugar Co.* (1948) 334 US 219, *United
States v Employing Lathers Ass'n. of Chicago* (1954) 347 US 198, and
other decisions permit the application of the federal antitrust laws to local
restraints of importance to the people and economy of particular areas if
such restraints directly or indirectly have interstate effects.

B. [§11.7] The Choice between Civil and Criminal Enforcement for Violations of Antitrust Laws

The Sherman Act provides for both civil and criminal enforcement.
The purpose of a civil suit is to bring unlawful activities to a halt and to
restore competitive conditions. The criminal action seeks the imposition
of fines and punishment on those responsible for violations of the Sherman Act. In some circumstances only a civil suit will be filed. If both
injunctive relief and criminal punishment appear appropriate, companion

civil and criminal actions will be filed. Finally, situations arise in which injunctive relief would not be effective or needed but criminal sanctions are warranted; then, only a criminal case will be filed.

If the division decides to use the criminal process, the case is ordinarily commenced through a grand jury indictment. From time to time, usually when technical reasons prevent use of a grand jury, the division will proceed by information rather than indictment. But this is relatively rare. For discussion of grand juries, see §§10.6–10.23.

The decision whether or not to indict is determined by whether the activities in question are "hard-core" offenses. In addition, the available evidence is evaluated to determine whether it would be adequate to satisfy the proof requirements for a criminal conviction.

If the activities in question constitute *per se* violations of the antitrust laws, such as price fixing, division of territories, allocation of customers, limitation of production, or group boycotts, it is highly probable that the activities will be deemed to warrant criminal prosecution. The same is true if there is evidence of a specific intent to restrain trade or to monopolize, or of a deliberate, knowing, or willful violation of the law. The evidence may consist of direct statements or predatory practices.

Criminal sanctions are also probable if there is evidence of the use of violence, threats, intimidation, or other types of "racketeering" practices to accomplish the goals of the combination or conspiracy or to monopolize or attempt to monopolize. Moreover, if a defendant has previously been found to violate the antitrust laws for similar activities, a subsequent violation may indicate a sufficient disregard for the antitrust laws and their purposes to warrant criminal prosecution.

Finally, as the law develops and civil cases demonstrate that activities are clearly and inevitably in violation of the Sherman Act, use of the criminal sanction for future violations may be expected.

If criminal proceedings are utilized, indictments against individuals will be seriously considered if there is evidence showing actual participation by the individual in the illegal conduct, agreements, or meetings at which the agreements were made or implemented; evidence showing authorization or ratification by the individual of illegal activity by subordinates; or evidence showing knowledge by the individual of the illegal activity by a subordinate in his chain of command and failure to prevent such activity.

Although the Antitrust Division typically attempts to charge those senior officials ultimately responsible for antitrust violations, corporate officers and other corporate representatives of a lesser rank, such as managers or salesmen, are also subject to the proscriptions of the antitrust laws and to criminal prosecution for violations.

The individual's culpability for participation in a hard-core violation will not ordinarily be deemed to be lessened by the fact of the existence of corporate pressure to meet sales goals or the alleged necessity to engage in illegal activities to enable a small corporation to compete with larger ones. Nor will the fact that grand jury testimony has resulted in immunity for equally culpable individual defendants (see §10.18) prevent the indictment of those individuals whose testimony was not required.

Similarly, factors such as age, ill health, lack of money, previous sanction by the corporation, etc., will not ordinarily prevent the indictment of a culpable individual but will instead be regarded as relevant to sentencing recommendations. The same is true of the fact of cooperation with the investigation and truthfulness. Exceptions may be made, however, if there is strong reason to believe that indictment would endanger the life of a prospective defendant in ill health.

If the conduct in question is a *per se* violation, and if there is persuasive evidence tying an individual to that conduct, the division would ordinarily seek to indict the individual regardless of the absence of evidence showing that the individual knew the conduct was illegal. If the offense is not of a *per se* variety, however, but is of the type made criminal because of the presence of threats or racketeering or the like, an indictment of an individual will probably not ordinarily be sought unless the evidence indicates that the individual was aware of the threats and racketeering.

C. [§11.8] Factors in Recommendations of Jail Sentences and Fines

Decisions on jail sentences and fines are ultimately made by the trial courts, and the extent to which they will be influenced by division recommendations varies greatly from judge to judge. By and large, the division's recommendations for jail sentences have been largely ignored, with a few historic exceptions. Its recommendations on fines, however, are apt to have a greater impact on the court, particularly in determining the relative magnitude of the fines to be assessed on different defendants.

While there is no ready formula from which to compute the division's probable recommendations in a particular case, it is apparent that the division considers both the nature of the offense and the character of the offender in proposing its recommendations of jail sentences and fines.

The severity of the recommended sentences or the decision not to recommend a jail sentence would be influenced by an evaluation of the following factors concerning the offense: the degree to which the unlawful activity was willfully entered into and whether disrespect for the law was apparent; the duration and the effects of the violation; and whether the offense was committed as a result of unusual circumstances or was a part of an established pattern. The division further considers the following factors concerning the offender: whether the defendant was a moving force or just another participant in the activities constituting the violation; the extent to which the defendant was acting pursuant to directions of supervisors or under other corporate pressure; the age, health, financial resources, and family responsibilities of the offender; and whether the defendant has previously been found to be in violation of the antitrust laws for similar activities.

The extent of the affirmative, truthful, and voluntary cooperation with the division during the trial may have a bearing on the recommendation, although it is division policy not to bargain with defendants concerning the recommendation of sentences that would be made in the event defendants plead *nolo* or guilty. The division seeks to avoid any suggestion that it would modify the sentence recommendation in order to induce a plea.

The question of the amount of individual or corporate fines will reflect, among other factors, the degree of involvement, the degree of leadership, the impact of the offense, the financial impact of the fine, and the defendants' attitude toward the law. In assessing corporate fines, the division gives substantial weight to the financial size of the defendants, although degrees of relative culpability and involvement are also considered.

D. [§11.9] Consenting to Nolo Contendere Pleas

Defendants in criminal actions are impelled to enter a plea of *nolo contendere* for a variety of reasons. A primary motivation is to avoid the impact of Section 5(a) of the Clayton Act (15 USC §16(a)), under which a plea or verdict of guilty may be used as prima facie evidence of an antitrust violation for purposes of a treble-damage action. A plea of *nolo contendere* has no such effect. Unless legislation is enacted to provide that *nolo contendere* pleas have the same prima facie effect as guilty pleas, the interest of defendants in *nolo* pleas will be great. If legislation, which has been proposed on several occasions, is enacted, the distinction between the *nolo contendere* plea and the guilty plea will be pursued only because of the widespread public impression that the *nolo* plea implies something less than outright guilt or because of the expectation that it may influence a judge to impose a lighter sentence than would have been imposed under a plea of guilty.

The Antitrust Division takes the position that it regards a *nolo contendere* plea as the equivalent of guilty for the purpose of the case. In either event, a defendant is subject to imposition of the same punishment, and a judgment of conviction is entered. Accordingly, the division makes it a precondition of its acquiescence to *nolo* pleas that defendants acknowledge in court that the *nolo* plea is an admission of guilt for purposes of the criminal case and that the same penalties can be imposed as upon a guilty plea. Moreover, the defendants must provide assurance that they will not, after having pled *nolo*, make public statements inconsistent with these admissions of guilt.

The division now pursues a somewhat more flexible policy than it did a decade ago in deciding whether or not to oppose a plea of *nolo*. The earlier policy of general opposition has been modified in favor of a case-by-case approach.

To begin with, the division will ordinarily oppose *nolo* pleas if one or more defendants are pleading not guilty. Since the case must go to trial, the division sees no significant savings in its resources or the court's time in consenting to disposition by way of *nolo*. Occasionally, however, the division deems it appropriate not to oppose *nolo* pleas by individual defendants even though trial against corporate defendants might be required because of pleas of not guilty. Since individual defendants are rarely named as defendants in private treble-damage actions, it is of somewhat less significance that *nolo* pleas by individuals are acquiesced in by the division. In making its determination, the division considers, among other things, whether retention of the individuals in the trial would be advantageous to prosecution of the government's case and whether health problems militate against trial of an individual.

A second major consideration that affects the government position on pleas of *nolo contendere* is whether a conviction or a plea of guilty would be of meaningful aid to private parties who may have suffered substantial damages as a result of the offense. The division, however, does make this factor automatically determinative; it now takes into account the relative capability of the private plaintiffs to pursue their suits through use of liberalized discovery and class action rules and with the help of a skilled private plaintiffs' bar. See Chapter 12. Moreover, if substantial treble-damage recoveries might have the effect of bankrupting smaller defendants, the division might acquiesce in a *nolo* plea. If there is a companion civil case that is going to trial in any event, the importance to private claimants of government opposition to a *nolo* plea is diminished. Finally, the division will be more willing to acquiesce in *nolo* pleas despite the presence of treble-damage claimants if it concludes that events since the indictment make it less likely that a conviction could be obtained after a trial.

Even without the presence of treble-damage claimants the division will oppose *nolo* pleas in cases that involve blatant violations, taking into account the duration and economic effect of the violation, the extent to which predatory or secretive activities were involved, and the presence of any coercive activities. Apparently, the larger the company the higher the standard of corporate citizenship to which it will be held and the more likely it is that the division would oppose a *nolo* plea.

In sum, therefore, the division will ordinarily, but not inevitably, oppose *nolo* pleas if substantial treble-damage claims are present, or if the violation is blatant, or if, because of not guilty pleas by some defendants, a trial is inevitable.

If the division has opposed *nolo* pleas in order to assist private claimants but the court nonetheless accepted those pleas, the division might regard consistency as requiring it to refuse to settle a companion civil suit through a consent decree. Or, in the alternative, the division might insist on the insertion of a so-called "asphalt clause" in such a decree, the effect of which is to prevent defendants from denying that the consent judgment is prima facie evidence of an antitrust violation in private treble-damage actions. In fact, however, the asphalt clause has been used rarely, and the division has not in fact insisted on a trial of the companion civil cases if an adequate consent decree was offered despite its prior opposition to a *nolo* plea that was accepted. There is some possibility, however, that on occasion, at least when the division's civil case is quite strong, an asphalt clause or litigation will be insisted on for the civil cases as to which *nolo* pleas were accepted over the government's opposition in the companion criminal case.

For further discussion, see §§13.74-13.75.

III. Complaints of Alleged Violations

A. [§11.10] Sources for Investigations

Possible violations of the antitrust laws are brought to the attention of the division in a variety of ways. These include complaints by persons, including businessmen and the consuming public, who believe that they have been victimized by unlawful conduct of suppliers, customers, or competitors; complaints made to members of Congress or other agencies of the government and forwarded to the division for appropriate action; suspected violations noted by other government agencies that are referred to the division; and articles appearing in daily newspapers and trade and other publications. Disaffected employees are a source of occasional complaints. Possible violations of the antitrust laws are also detected as a result of division staff observation and study of industry conditions. This is particularly true in the case of possibly unlawful mergers and acquisitions.

B. [§11.11] How to Complain to the Division

There is no set form required to bring a possible violation of law to the attention of the Antitrust Division. A letter addressed to the division's Washington office (Antitrust Division, Department of Justice, Washington, D.C. 20530) or to the local field office will be considered and answered. The division, however, has neither the authority nor the resources to render legal advice to the public. Hence, letters of complaint are reviewed to ascertain the need for division action to enforce the law, but the division does not advise citizens of their private rights or the merits of a claim. A letter of complaint is most effective if it supplies available detailed information pertinent to the complaint and indicates clearly in what respect the activities are thought to be violative of the antitrust laws.

The letters containing complaints are assigned to the section or field office most familiar with the industry involved. The complaint is evaluated. The evaluation may indicate the further information is needed from the complainant before an assessment of the grievance may be made. Or the letter may reveal that the complainant is protesting some personally adverse economic consequence without suggesting any evidence of illegal behavior. Or the letter may suggest a possible violation, in which case the division embarks upon its investigatory process. If the letter of complaint so requests, the name of the complainant will be kept confidential in making a further investigation.

C. [§11.12] Investigations

The initial phase of an investigation is the preliminary inquiry, the purpose of which is to ascertain whether any substantial commitment of enforcement resources is warranted. The inquiry may be conducted by letters or interviews by the staff attorney with the complainant and others having knowledge of the matter or of pertinent industry conditions. This preliminary inquiry may satisfy the division that no violation of law has occurred, in which case the matter is closed. Several hundred preliminary inquiries are conducted each year, only a fraction of which result in enforcement action. For discussion of meeting government investigations, see Chapter 10.

If the preliminary inquiry indicates the need for a fuller investigation, the division may proceed by conducting more intensive interviews by staff attorneys, by using the resources of the FBI for extensive interviews and fact gathering (see §10.2), or, if necessary and appropriate, by use of the civil investigative demand (see §§10.24-10.27) or, if authorized by the Attorney General, by a grand jury (see §§10.6-10.23).

The civil investigative demand is authorized by the Antitrust Civil Process Act and calls for the production by corporations or other legal entities of documents that may be relevant to a suspected violation of the antitrust laws. It may be enforced by compulsory court process.

If the suspected violation is of the kind that may be prosecuted criminally, a grand jury investigation may be initiated. Grand juries have power to compel the production of documents and the appearance and testimony of witnesses.

Again, the results of full investigations may indicate that a complaint is not warranted. Recommendations that a suit be brought or that an indictment be sought are made by the assistant Attorney General. The recommendations are usually initially reviewed by the director of operations, the director of policy planning, and the deputy assistant attorney general. Authority to seek the return of an indictment or to file an information or a complaint requires the approval of the assistant attorney general and the Attorney General.

D. [§11.13] Small Business Procedure

The Antitrust Division also undertakes to assist small businessmen in certain situations that may not warrant the expenditure of enforcement resources. In these situations, with the permission of the complainant, the division may bring the grievance to the attention of the company alleged to be infringing the rights of the complainant in the hope that the parties may reach a satisfactory solution voluntarily.

IV. [§11.14] Business Review Procedure

The Business Review Procedure is a device by which a description of proposed conduct may be submitted to the division for the purpose of eliciting a statement of the division's present enforcement intention concerning that conduct. The current official division description of the function, limitations, and prerequisites for this procedure follows (33 Fed Reg 2442 (1968), 2 Trade Reg Rep ¶8559 §50.6):

Antitrust Division Business Review Procedure

Although the Department of Justice is not authorized to give advisory opinions to private parties, for several decades the Antitrust Division has been willing in certain circumstances to review proposed business conduct and state its enforcement intentions. This originated with a "railroad release" procedure under which the Division would forego the initiation of criminal antitrust proceedings. The procedure was subsequently expanded to encompass a "merger clearance" procedure under which the Division would state its present enforcement intention with respect to a merger or acquisition; and the Department issued a written statement entitled "Business Review Procedure." This is a revision of that statement:

1. A request for a business review letter must be submitted *in writing* to the Assistant Attorney General, Antitrust Division, Department of Justice, Washington, D.C. 20530.

2. The Division will consider only requests with respect to proposed business conduct, which may involve either domestic or foreign commerce.

3. A business review letter shall have no application to any party which does not join in the request therefor.

4. The requesting parties are under an affirmative obligation to make full and true disclosure with respect to the business conduct for which review is requested. Each request must be accompanied by all relevant data including background information, complete copies of all operative documents and detailed statements of all collateral oral understandings, if any. All parties requesting the review letter must provide the Division with whatever additional information or documents the Division may thereafter request in order to review the matter. In connection with any request for review the Division will also conduct whatever independent investigation it believes is appropriate.

5. No oral clearance, release or other statement purporting to bind the enforcement discretion of the Division may be given. The requesting party may rely upon only a written business review letter signed by the Attorney General, Deputy Attorney General, or Assistant Attorney General in charge of the Antitrust Division.

6. If the business conduct for which review is requested is subject to approval by a regulatory agency, a review request will be considered before agency approval has been obtained (except in the case of bank mergers or acquisitions) where it appears that exceptional and unnecessary burdens might otherwise be imposed on the party or parties requesting review. However, any business review letter issued in these as in any other circumstances will state only the Department's present enforcement intentions under the antitrust laws. It shall in no way be taken to indicate the Department's views on the legal or factual issues that may be raised before the regulatory agency, or in an appeal from the regulatory agency's decision. In particular, the issuance of such a letter is not to be represented to mean that the Division believes that there are no anticompetitive consequences warranting agency consideration.

7. After review of a request submitted hereunder the Division may: state its present enforcement intention with respect to the proposed business conduct;

decline to pass on the request; or take such other position or action as it considers appropriate. Ordinarily, however, the Division will state a present intention not to bring a *civil* action only with respect to mergers, acquisitions or similar arrangements.

8. A business review letter states only the enforcement intention of the Division as of the date of the letter, and the Division remains completely free to bring whatever action or proceeding it subsequently comes to believe is required by the public interest. As to a stated present intention not to bring an action, however, the Division has never exercised its right to bring a criminal action where there has been full and true disclosure at the time of presenting the request.

9. Any requesting party may withdraw a request for review at any time. The Division remains free, however, to submit such comments to such requesting party as it deems appropriate. Failure to take action after receipt of documents or information, whether submitted pursuant to this procedure or otherwise, does not in any way limit or estop the Division from taking such action at such time thereafter as it deems appropriate. The Division reserves the right to retain documents submitted to it under this procedure or otherwise and to use them for all purposes of antitrust enforcement.

V. Consent Decree Procedure

A. [§11.15] The Division's Consent Decree Policy

By far the greater part of the division's civil antitrust cases—80 percent or more, perhaps—have been terminated by consent judgments. The chief advantage of a consent decree disposition to the division is that it enables it to secure prompt relief and use its enforcement resources on a far broader scale than would be the case if it were committed to substantial litigation of each suit filed. The division does not itself initiate settlement negotiations but is ready to discuss settlement when proposed by defense counsel. Where companion civil and criminal cases are pending, the disposition of one case cannot be in any way tied to the disposition of the other.

The usual position of the division in consent decree negotiations is to insist on relief that is much the same as the relief to which it would be entitled after successful litigation. The division may compromise on relief in settling cases when the theory under which a complaint was brought, while still tenable, is no longer as convincing as it was at the time of filing or when, after extensive discovery, it appears that the problems of proof of critical facts are far harder than anticipated. Except for such situations the division treats the consent decree process as one by which it should obtain the relief to which it would be entitled after trial. However, the process of working out the details of appropriate relief in a non-litigating context may lead to a greater flexibility and appreciation of industry problems than would otherwise be the case.

The reasons for the defendant's consenting to a decree include the avoidance of the costs of litigation and the avoidance of the prima facie evidence effect that Section 5(a) of the Clayton Act (15 USC §16(a)) accords to a judgment decided adversely to defendants in a litigated case. As noted in §11.9, if a companion criminal case exists and *nolo* pleas were unsuccessfully opposed by the division, there may be some reluctance on the part of the division to enter a consent decree, or it may require an "asphalt clause," particularly if it regards its evidence as peculiarly strong. This is still the very rare exception, however.

B. [§11.16] Negotiation of Decrees

The consent decree negotiations usually take place in the first instance with the staff in charge of the lawsuit. At that point, assuming agreement on the substantive terms between defense counsel and the trial staff, the drafting of the judgment in the form of a detailed and complete decree will be undertaken by specialists in the judgments section. This draft decree must be submitted through other reviewing officials within the division and to the assistant attorney general for approval, and until such approval is forthcoming it is made clear to defendants that no action by the staff can be regarded as division acquiescence or approval of a proposed consent judgment in whole or in part.

C. [§11.17] Prefiling and Informal Commitments

From time to time a complaint and a consent decree have been simultaneously filed. The Department of Justice does not make this procedure a matter of course because of the possibility that the filing of a complaint may be delayed for an extensive period of time while negotiations, which ultimately prove fruitless, may be carried on with continuation of the complaint of injurious practices. However, if the Antitrust Division is satisfied that effective relief can be quickly arrived at because the defendants demonstrate a genuine interest in negotiating relief promptly, it will consider prefiling negotiations, and prefiling has been used more frequently recently.

Only occasionally is the Department willing to forgo bringing suit against an allegedly unlawful practice or relationship upon receiving a commitment that the practices or relationships would be discontinued. Such cases usually include special circumstances such as the fact that the impact of the law may have been unclear, that recurrence was unlikely, and that mere cessation was adequate relief. But in the vast majority of cases the division regards a decree as necessary in order to provide an adequate assurance against recurrence and a disincentive against violation in the first place.

D. [§11.18] The Role of Third Parties

In order to provide opportunity for information, comment, or criticism from persons or firms not parties to an action in which a consent judgment is negotiated, the Department of Justice ordinarily makes the proposed consent judgment public at least 30 days before it is to be entered in court. During the 30-day period, during which the proposed judgment is on file in court, the Department will receive and evaluate any written comments, views, or allegations relating to the proposed judgment. During this 30-day period interested parties have often filed briefs as *amici* before the court entering the decree. The Department reserves the right to withdraw or withhold its consent to the entry of the decree in the event the views presented convince it that the judgment is inappropriate, improper, or inadequate. If the Department does not withdraw its consent, the judgment can be entered at the end of the 30-day period on the motion of either party or on the court's own motion without any further hearings.

A problem that has been arising with increasing frequency in recent years, coincident with the rise of a well-organized treble-damage claimant's bar, is that of attempted intervention by prospective claimants into the lawsuit for the purpose of protesting the terms of a consent judgment, to insist on the requirement of an "asphalt clause" (see §11.9), to affect the subsequent interpretation and enforcement of the decree, or to insist on a full trial rather than a negotiated settlement.

The Antitrust Division has consistently taken the position that these applicants have no right to intervene under Federal Rule of Civil Procedure 24(a) because an interest in obtaining damages is not an interest within the meaning of the rule, because the damage claimants are not impaired in their ability to protect whatever "interest" they claim to have in the government's suit, and because the division is adequately representing the interests of the damaged applicants.

Similarly, the division has opposed discretionary intervention under FRCP 24(b) on the grounds that the proposed judgment adequately protects the public interest in the maintenance of competition and that the orderly administration of justice would be disrupted by the intervention. The division typically agrees to the appearance of the applicants as *amici*

539

for purposes of making their views known to the court and to some degree extends its cooperation to prospective private treble-damage plaintiffs short of permitting them to interfere with the division's discretion to settle its cases. Thus, in resisting intervention by treble-damage claimants who object to the decision to enter a consent judgment without an "asphalt clause," the division points out that antitrust indictments and complaints are frequently detailed in setting forth alleged violations, thereby providing the private plaintiff's lawyer with a basis for structuring his discovery efforts. Also, in appropriate cases the division does not object to the entry of orders impounding grand jury testimony and documents produced in response to grand jury subpoenas, thereby ensuring that if a litigant shows particular need for portions of the grand jury testimony or for grand jury documents, the material will remain available to him. On availability of grand jury proceedings, see §§10.21-10.23. The Department, however, takes the position that documents received from potential defendants during the course of a non-grand jury investigation and documents that constitute internal Department memoranda summarizing the investigation are protected from disclosure under the Freedom of Information Act (5 USC §552) by the exceptions in that statute for intra-agency memoranda and investigatory files compiled for law enforcement purposes.

At this point the Department has been generally successful in its opposition to intervention. See, *e.g., United States v Blue Chip Stamp Company* (CD Calif 1967) 272 F Supp 432, *aff'd sub nom Thrifty Shoppers Scrip Co. v United States* (1968) 389 US 580; *United States v Harper & Row Publishers, Inc.* (ND Ill November 27, 1967) *unreported opinion, aff'd sub nom City of New York v United States* (1968) 390 US 715.

The division distinguishes the one Supreme Court case in which intervention was allowed to challenge a decree, *Cascade Natural Gas Corp. v El Paso Natural Gas Co.* (1967) 386 US 129, arguing that it is limited to the situation in which intervention is permitted to help ensure that the parties carry out the Court's prior mandate for complete divestiture. The intervention issue will no doubt be the subject of further litigation.

12

Plaintiff's Prosecution of Federal Treble-Damage and Injunction Cases

Matthew P. Mitchell

Mr. Mitchell received the BA degree from Amherst College in 1954 and the MA degree from the University of California at Berkeley in 1957; he received the LLB degree from the University of California at Berkeley in 1960 and the Dr. Jur. degree from the University of Koeln, Germany in 1961. He is a member of the California State Bar and the San Francisco firm of Feldman, Waldman and Kline.

I. [§12.1] Scope

This Chapter discusses the special problems of private treble-damage actions under the federal antitrust laws. It presupposes that the antitrust laws have been violated. Whether there has been a violation is treated in the other chapters of the book.

The chapter deals only with the private right of action under federal law; private actions may be available under state statutes as well. Since federal subject-matter jurisdiction is tied to interstate commerce, actions under state statutes may be useful in obtaining compensation for injuries arising out of purely local anticompetitive conduct.

Many procedural problems come up in the course of a plaintiff's antitrust case. Effective use of federal discovery procedures is vital. The vigorous defense of a private antitrust action ordinarily entails lavish use of motions, both procedural and substantive. See §12.71. A full-dress discussion of federal procedural matters is beyond the scope of this chapter. See Lavine & Horning, *Manual of Federal Practice* (McGraw-Hill, 1967, and *Supplement*, 1970).

II. [§12.2] Perspective

Successful private antitrust actions are a relatively new phenomenon. There have probably been more private antitrust actions filed in the last dozen years than in all the prior 69 years in which such actions were possible. Now, for the first time, private antitrust actions are causing substantial sums of money to change hands. The possibility that large corporations will have to pay large private antitrust judgments against them is being mentioned for the first time in the reports of financial analysts. Conversely, the businessman who has suffered injury as a result of antitrust violations is now able for the first time to seek compensation with a reasonable probability of success.

The change has been wrought in part by the massive electrical-equipment conspiracy cases, which have educated a generation of federal judges and the American public in the ways of the gentlemen-conspirators. In part, the change has been due to the private antitrust bar, which has learned its trade through a generation of chronic litigation in the motion-picture industry. In part, the trend results from a long series of decisions of the United States Supreme Court, which has repeatedly held that the antitrust laws must be liberally construed in favor of plaintiffs. These decisions recognize the critical importance of the antitrust laws to the American free-enterprise system and the pivotal role of the private plaintiff in antitrust enforcement. (Private filings are now many times more numerous than suits by the Justice Department.)

Private antitrust litigation is rapidly becoming a major legal speciality in metropolitan centers. The possibility of private antitrust actions is also increasingly important throughout the country, particularly from the potential plaintiff's point of view. Businessmen in remote areas or smaller cities are more likely than those in large cities to fall victim to anticompetitive practices if only because the monopolist's "divide and conquer" tactics are more effective in a small and isolated market than they are in a major metropolitan marketing area.

Trial of private antitrust cases is not an arcane art; private actions are commonly tried to juries, and the issues are within the comprehension of any competent trial lawyer. But the recognition of antitrust implications of commercial facts, and the discovery and marshalling of evidence for use in antitrust trials are large-to-massive undertakings for the neophyte.

III. The Federal Cause of Action

A. [§12.3] The Statutory Bases for Recovery

The federal statute creating a private right of action for treble damages under the antitrust laws is Section 4 of the Clayton Act, 15 USC §15:

Any person who shall be injured in his business or property by reason of anything forbidden in the antitrust laws may sue therefor in any district court of the United States in the district in which the defendant resides or is found or has an agent, without respect to the amount in controversy, and shall recover three-fold the damages by him sustained, and the cost of suit, including a reasonable attorney's fee.

The Sherman Act and the Clayton Act as amended are "antitrust laws," as are Sections 73–76 of the Wilson Tariff Act (15 USC §§8–11). Insofar as it amends Section 2 of the Clayton Act (15 USC §2), the Robinson-Patman Act is an antitrust law. But Section 3 of the Robinson-Patman Act (15 USC §13(a)) is not an amendment to the Clayton Act and violation of Section 3 of the Robinson-Patman Act will not support a private action. *Nashville Milk Co. v Carnation Co.* (1958) 355 US 373. See also 15 USC §12.

The code sections most commonly relied on to support private actions under the antitrust laws are Section 1 of the Sherman Act (15 USC §1), dealing with combinations, contracts and conspiracies in restraint of trade (see Chapter 2); Section 2 of the Sherman Act (15 USC §2), dealing with monopolization and attempts to monopolize (see Chapter 2); Section 2 of the Clayton Act as amended by the Robinson-Patman Act (15 USC §13), dealing with discrimination in prices or other price-related practices (see Chapter 5); and Section 3 of the Clayton Act (15 USC §14), dealing with tying and exclusive dealing contracts (see Chapter 3). Of course, other sections of the antitrust laws may give rise to private actions if the violations are such as to cause private injury. Thus private actions are possible under Section 7 of the Clayton Act (15 USC §18), dealing with mergers (see Chapter 4) and Section 10 of the Clayton Act (15 USC §20), dealing with purchases by common carriers with interlocking directorates. See,*e.g., Klinger v Rose* (SD NY 1968) 291 F Supp 456.

1. [§12.4] Jurisdiction over Federal Private Antitrust Actions

Jurisdiction over private treble-damage cases is exclusively in the federal district courts. 15 USC §15. The remedy for violation of the federal antitrust laws may not be pursued in state courts. *Engelhardt v Bell & Howell Co.* (8th Cir 1964) 327 F2d 30, 35; *L.S. Good & Co. v H. Daroff & Sons, Inc.* (ND W Va 1967) 263 F Supp 635, 643. A New York court has held that an antitrust violation by the plaintiff in a state-court action cannot be raised as a defense in that action. *Chicken Delight, Inc. v DeTomasso* (NY Sup Ct 1970) 1970 Trade Cases ¶73,047.

Moreover, a contractual agreement to submit future antitrust disputes to arbitration is void and unenforceable. *Associated Milk Dealers, Inc. v*

Milk Drivers Union Local 753 (7th Cir 1970) 422 F2d 546; *Power Replacements, Inc. v Air Preheater Co.* (9th Cir 1970) 426 F2d 980. But once the antitrust dispute exists, it may be settled and the parties may be able to agree enforceably on a settlement via arbitration. *Power Replacements, Inc., supra.*

Federal subject-matter jurisdiction exists only if the complained-of activities affect interstate commerce. See *Food Basket, Inc. v Albertson's, Inc.* (10th Cir 1967) 383 F2d 785. Jurisdiction over the person of the defendant, at least when it is a corporation, is easily obtained insofar as service of process is concerned. See §12.52. Venue, on the other hand, can be a problem. See §12.51.

In most types of cases, the "commerce" requirements are easily met. See, *e.g. Perryton Wholesale, Inc. v Pioneer Distributing Co.* (10th Cir 1965) 353 F2d 618, *cert den* (1966) 383 US 945. But see *Page v Work* (9th Cir 1961) 290 F2d 323, *cert den* (1961) 368 US 875. A more stringent "commerce" requirement comes into play in actions based on the Robinson-Patman Act. See *Food Basket, Inc. v Albertson's, Inc., supra.*

If interstate commerce is lacking, suit under a state antitrust law may provide a satisfactory alternative to a federal treble-damage action. Ordinarily, such a case would be brought in the state court. If the plaintiff and the defendant are of diverse citizenship and the existence of the interstate commerce required for federal antitrust jurisdiction is doubtful, it may be possible to plead the same facts in two counts in federal court; a count under the federal antitrust laws, and a count under the state antitrust statute, with diversity of citizenship as the basis of federal jurisdiction under 28 USC §1332. Of course, diversity jurisdiction does not exist unless the amount in controversy is at least $10,000, exclusive of interest and costs.

There is authority for the proposition that a claim under a state antitrust law may not be properly included under the doctrine of "pendent jurisdiction" in a case brought under the federal antitrust laws, absent diversity. See *McKeon Construction v McClatchy Newspapers* (ND Calif 1969) 1970 Trade Cases ¶73,212.

FRCP 23 permits a plaintiff to bring his private antitrust suit as a class action if (a) the class is so numerous that joinder of all members of the class is impracticable, (b) there are questions of law or fact common to the class, (c) the claims or defenses of the representative parties are typical of the claims and defenses of the class, (d) the representatives will fairly and adequately protect the interest of the class, (e) the questions of law or fact common to the members of the class predominate over questions affecting only individual members, and (f) a class action is superior to other available methods for fair and efficient adjudication of the controversy.

The availability of a class action may make possible the prosecution of private actions that would otherwise not be worth bringing because of the relatively small recovery likely to be obtained by a single plaintiff. See, e.g., *Eisen v Carlisle & Jacquelin* (2d Cir 1968) 391 F2d 555; *Siegel v Chicken Delight, Inc.* (ND Calif 1967) 271 F Supp 722. On the other hand, courts have not always been quick to approve class antitrust actions if the circumstances of the various class plaintiffs were expected to differ substantially. See, e.g., *Lah v Shell Oil Co.* (SD Ohio 1970) 50 FRD 198; *William Goldman Theatres, Inc. v Paramount Film Distributing Corp.* (ED Pa 1969) 1970 Trade Cases ¶73,211.

Increasingly, defendants in major price-fixing cases have been using the class suit as a means of lining up all potential plaintiffs and negotiating a mass settlement. See, e.g., *West Virginia v Chas. Pfizer & Co.*(SD NY 1970) 314 F Supp 711.

Under FRCP 23, a member of the class must be given notice and unless he elects not to be bound, he will be deemed a member of the class and bound by any judgment entered in the lawsuit. A member of the class will be bound by a settlement, and unless he intervenes or objects, he will not be entitled to appeal the decision. See *Research Corp. v Asgrow Seed Co.* (7th Cir 1970) 425 F2d 1059.

But care must be taken by a potential plaintiff; if he does not file suit, relying on his being a member of a class on whose behalf a class action has been commenced, he may find his claims barred if the statute runs and the court subsequently concludes that the suit may not be maintained as a class suit. See *Utah v American Pipe and Construction Co.*(CD Calif 1970) 1970 Trade Cases ¶73,143.

2. [§12.5] "Business" or "Property" Defined

The statute requires plaintiff to show injury to his "business or property." A purchaser who pays too much for a commodity because the sellers have conspired to fix high prices is injured in his property to the extent of the overcharge. *Chattanooga Foundry and Pipe Works v Atlanta* (1906) 203 US 390, 399.

Similarly, a contract is property. If defendants conspire to prevent plaintiff from deriving the benefits of the contract, he may recover although he does not yet have a "business." *Waldron v British Petroleum Co.* (SD NY 1964) 231 F Supp 72, 86. See also *North Texas Producers Association v Young* (5th Cir 1962) 308 F2d 235, 243, *cert den* (1963) 372 US 929.

A man who has been gainfully employed and is subsequently black-listed has suffered injury to his business although he has been an employee rather than an employer. *Radovich v National Football League* (1957) 352 US 445; *Nichols v Spencer International Press, Inc.* (7th Cir 1967) 371 F2d 332. But see *Centanni v T. Smith & Son, Inc.* (ED La 1963) 216 F Supp 330, 338, *aff'd per curiam* (5th Cir 1963) 323 F2d 363.

Where the plaintiff has no firm contract, and has not yet gone into business, he has been injured neither in his business nor in his property and may not recover. *Martin v Phillips Petroleum Co.* (5th Cir 1966) 365 F2d 629, *cert den* (1966) 385 US 991; *Duff v Kansas City Star Co.* (8th Cir 1962) 299 F2d 320; *Cohen v Curtis Publishing Co.* (D Minn 1963) 229 F Supp 354, 364, *app disms'd* (8th Cir 1964) 333 F2d 974, *cert den* (1965) 380 US 921.

3. [§12.6] The Elements of the Private Cause of Action for Treble Damages

Even though injury may be caused by a contract, the private antitrust case sounds in tort. In order to prevail, the private treble-damage plaintiff must prove violation, impact, and damages.

The "violation" must be a violation of the "antitrust laws." (15 USC §15.) For discussion of the statutory bases for action, see §12.3. Because the same conduct may violate several sections of the antitrust laws, private cases are commonly brought under more than one section. See §§12.18-12.23.

It has been generally accepted among lower federal courts that the plaintiff must show *proximate* cause, not merely causation in fact. The "standing" rules discussed in §12.27 are best understood as arbitrary rules attempting to define outer limits of proximate cause. "Impact" is shorthand for "injury to the plaintiff proximately caused by the defendant's antitrust violation."

"Damages" is shorthand for "proof sufficient to permit the trier of fact to make a reasonable estimate of the amount of monetary damage the plaintiff has suffered." Proving damages with mathematical precision is rarely if ever possible. Once impact has been shown, the plaintiff may prove the amount of damage by any facts upon which the trier of fact can reasonably base an estimate. See §§12.35-12.36.

B. Practical Factors in Assessing a Plaintiff's Case

1. [§12.7] Evaluating a Plaintiff's Case

Cautious practitioners do not take a plaintiff's treble-damage antitrust case unless a violation of the antitrust laws has apparently occurred and the plaintiff has suffered substantial injury as a result, but they do not turn down a plaintiff's case merely because the prospective plaintiff cannot deliver direct evidence of the violation. Circumstantial proof of violation is likely to be the only available proof, particularly in conspiracy cases. See *Girardi v Gates Rubber Company Sales Division, Inc.* (9th Cir 1963) 325 F2d 196.

In most plaintiff's cases, discovery is everything. The importance of discovery is generally recognized by federal courts, but it helps greatly to be able to make a strong showing of "probable cause" for believing that plaintiff will ultimately recover, especially when the equities for and against discovery are closely balanced. If, after a reasonable amount of discovery, plaintiff is unable to come up with evidence tending to support a cause of action, he runs the risk of suffering an adverse summary judgment. If the facts are extreme enough, the summary judgment will be upheld on appeal. See *First Nat'l. Bank v Cities Service Co.* (1968) 391 US 253, *reh den* (1968) 393 US 901.

2. [§12.8] Checklist for Interview with Plaintiff

No single list of questions can adequately prepare the attorney for his first interview with a prospective antitrust plaintiff. As the nature of the case unfolds, further avenues of inquiry will suggest themselves. But certain basic facts that will be significant in almost every instance should be obtained as soon as possible:

Client's name, address, phone.

Client's conception of injury:
☐ Overcharge or underpayment
☐ Exclusion or foreclosure
☐ Predatory practices
☐ Amount of injury

Client's conception of violation:
☐ Conspiracy
☐ Monopoly
☐ Unlawful vertical restriction
☐ Attempt to monopolize

Business organization of plaintiff:
☐ Proprietorship
☐ Partnership
☐ Corporation

Business organization of any affiliated persons and organizations:
☐ Common ownership or management with other businesses
☐ Subsidiary corporations
☐ Any changes in form of business entity?

Nature of business.

General factors of scale:
☐ Size of client's business
☐ Size of prospective defendants' businesses

Jurisdictional and venue factors:
☐ Location of plaintiff
☐ Location of defendants
☐ Main situs of violation and injury

Discovery against defendants:
☐ How much evidence does client now have to prove violation?
☐ What kind of discovery will be necessary to get the essential facts from defendants?
☐ How much does client know about defendants' organization, operations and record-keeping procedures?

Plaintiff's ability to respond to discovery:
☐ How extensive are client's business records?
☐ Will client submit to searching discovery by defendants?
☐ Trade secret problems
☐ Income tax problems
☐ Other possible sources of embarrassment

Damage information:
☐ How long has client been in business?
☐ What is client's history of success?
☐ What is evidence that violation caused deterioration in business position?

Logistical position of client:
☐ Can client afford time and expense of trail preparation?
☐ Can client afford to pay a reasonable fee?

3. [§12.9] Estimating Potential Net Recovery

In evaluating the plaintiff's probable monetary recovery, the attorney should consider:

1. apparent actual damage (see §§12.18–12.23, 12.35–12.37);
2. the trebling feature of the statute;

3. the probable "reasonable attorneys' fees" based on the amount of the recovery (see §12.38);

4. probable delay in obtaining and collecting a judgment.

The estimate of the potential recovery must be discounted for the possibility of an adverse judgment. At the evaluation stage, however, a great many factual questions probably will remain unanswered pending discovery. Unless the client has access to the inner workings of the defendant's business, the client's initial evidence may be a pale reflection of evidence later uncovered.

Apparent damage figures should be checked against the net worth of the plaintiff, its prior history of profits, its previous rate of growth, and any other factors that will indicate whether the scale of the preliminary damage estimate is within reasonable limits.

In an "overcharge" case (see §12.18) damages cannot exceed purchase price, and will ordinarily not exceed 25%–35% of purchase price. If damage is in the destruction of a new and promising business, however, it is often difficult to find guidelines for possible recovery. *Farmington Dowel Products Co. v Forster Mfg. Co.* (1st Cir 1969) 421 F2d 61; *Volasco Products Co. v Lloyd A. Fry Roofing Co.* (6th Cir 1965) 346 F2d 661, *cert den* (1965) 382 US 904. *Cf. Kobe, Inc. v Dempsey Pump Co.* (10th Cir 1952) 198 F2d 416, *cert den* (1952) 344 US 837.

4. [§12.10] Logistics of a Plaintiff's Case

The main logistical problem in evaluating a plaintiff's case is whether lawyer or client can afford to bring it. Even if the prospective defendants have clearly violated the antitrust laws, counsel should not take the case without considering these factors:

1. What is the proper forum for the case? See §12.51.

2. What is the probable actual damage? How much is a jury likely to return? What is the probable attorney's fee award?

3. What will it cost to prepare the case? How much to prove liability? How much to prove damages? See §§12.35–12.37.

    a. How much travel and other non-recoverable expense will there be? See §§12.11, 12.39.

    b. Will expensive (non-recoverable) accounting testimony be needed to prove liability? Damages? See §§12.11, 12.39.

    c. How many witnesses will have to be deposed? How many documents copied? See §§12.53–12.60.

    d. How much will the plaintiff be able to help in doing discovery work? In responding to discovery?

e. How much effort will be involved in plaintiff's response to discovery? How much will it cost the plaintiff to devote his own time to litigation?

4. Can the plaintiff pay the expenses as they accrue? See §12.11.

5. Can the plaintiff put out a substantial retainer at the beginning of the case? See §12.11.

5. [§12.11] Costs and Fee Arrangements

Most attorneys are not in a position to advance costs on the scale required for antitrust litigation, and most would prefer not to await the outcome of protracted litigation without being paid something for their effort. It is bad practice to agree to advance costs. It is probably bad practice to take a case without a substantial retainer; the prospective plaintiff is more likely to make a full and candid disclosure of the facts if he is not gambling exclusively with the attorney's time.

Otherwise, fee arrangements are limited only by the ingenuity of attorney and client, and their respective bargaining positions. An antitrust plaintiff's best asset may be a cause of action for treble damages; contingent fees are both common and proper. See *Farmington Dowel Products Co. v Forster Mfg. Co.* (1st Cir 1969) 421 F2d 61. Generally speaking, smaller and more difficult cases would seem to call for a larger contingent fee, on a percentage basis, than larger clear-cut cases. All of the factors that a court considers in fixing the "reasonable attorney's fee" may properly be considered in agreeing on a fee with the client. See §12.38.

However, the amount of the usual "reasonable attorney's fee" is *not* adequate for contingent fee work; the court does not determine the "reasonable" fee as if it were a contingency. See §12.38. Attorney and client may agree between themselves upon a different amount—one-third of the total recovery including the court-awarded attorney's fee, for example. Professional ethics set an upper limit on the fee regardless of the agreement. *Farmington Dowel Products Co. v Forster Mfg. Co., supra.*

If the client is thoroughly solvent, a modest minimum fee on an hourly basis, together with a small contingency, may be a good compromise. Net costs to the client may be substantially less than under a straight contingent-fee arrangement and the attorney has the benefit of assured income during the progress of the litigation as well as a reward for success.

A graduated contingency (*e.g.*, 25% of the settlement before pre-trial, 30% of settlement before verdict, 35% of settlement before briefs on appeal, 40% thereafter) permits early settlement without penalizing the plaintiff. It also protects the attorney if the litigation drags on.

Difficult contingent fee problems arise when a case is settled for a patent license or some other non-monetary consideration. The possibility of such a settlement should be anticipated to the extent possible. Then agreement on the valuation of such a non-monetary settlement as between attorney and client should be reached, or a formula for arriving at a valuation agreed upon. Arbitration may be a simple, speedy solution if valuation is likely to prove difficult and the ability of attorney and client to agree is doubtful.

The final agreement should always be reduced to writing.

C. [§12.12] Statute of Limitations

The Sherman Act (1890) provided for treble damages, but prescribed no period of limitation for bringing suit; the most appropriate statute of limitations of the state in which the federal court sat applied. *Chattanooga Foundry and Pipe Works v Atlanta* (1906) 203 US 390.

The Clayton Act (1914) did not prescribe a period of limitation, but it did provide (38 Stat 731):

... Whenever any suit or proceeding in equity or criminal prosecution is instituted by the United States to prevent, restrain or punish violations of any of the antitrust laws, the running of the statute of limitations in respect of each and every private right of action arising under said laws and based in whole or in part on any matter complained of in said suit or proceeding shall be suspended during the pendency thereof.

Finally, in 1955, Congress amended the Clayton Act to provide a four-year limitation period (15 USC §15b). It also amended the tolling provisions of Section 5 of the Clayton Act by adding a proviso (15 USC §16(b)):

Provided, however, That whenever the running of the statute of limitations in respect of a cause of action arising under section 15 of this title is suspended hereunder, any action to enforce such cause of action shall be forever barred unless commenced either within the period of suspension or within four years after the cause of action accrued.

Although pre-1955 cases antedate the present statute of limitations for federal actions, they continue to be valuable precedent for at least three purposes:

1. Establishing when the cause of action accrued for statute of limitations purposes (see §12.13);

2. Applying the doctrine of "fraudulent concealment" to toll the running of the statute of limitations (see §12.15); and

3. Construing the statutory tolling provision based on the pendency of a related government case (see §12.14).

1. [§12.13] Accrual of the Cause of Action

When did the plaintiff's cause of action accrue? The answer determines whether a suit has been brought too late, too soon, or on time. If the cause of action is more than four years old when suit is brought, it is likely to be barred by the statute of limitations. If the cause of action has not yet arisen when suit is brought, then damages may not be recovered at all. Unfortunately, there is no simple rule for determining when antitrust causes of action arise.

Some antitrust injuries take place at a reasonably definite time (*e.g.,* cancellation of a dealership; a particular sale at a conspiratorially fixed price). Other kinds of injuries arise out of a more or less continuous course of dealing, such as predatory or monopolistic pricing (see, *e.g., Atlas Building Products Co. v Diamond Block & Gravel Co.* (10th Cir 1959) 269 F2d 950, *cert den* (1960) 363 US 843; *Hanover Shoe, Inc. v United Shoe Machinery Corp.* (MD Pa 1965) 245 F Supp 258, *vacated* (3d Cir 1967) 377 F2d 776). Still other injuries arise out of conduct that might be described as "episodic." See *Braun v Berenson* (5th Cir 1970) 432 F2d 538; *Hoopes v Union Oil Co.* (9th Cir 1967) 374 F2d 480.

The basic rule on limitations is that the statute begins to run (unless tolled for some reason) at the time of the defendants' last act causing the injury. In *Steiner v 20th Century-Fox Film Corp.* (9th Cir 1956) 232 F2d 190, the injury occurred, and the statute began to run, when defendants forced plaintiff to accept a long-term lease at an inadequate rental, although the injury would actually be suffered on the installment plan into the future. The corollary, of course, is that an action could have been brought immediately for the whole injury, although the lease might have many years to run. See *Twentieth Century-Fox Film Corp. v Brookside Theatre Corp.* (8th Cir 1952) 194 F2d 846, *cert den* (1952) 343 US 942.

The last word on the subject is the Supreme Court's decision in *Zenith Radio Corp. v Hazeltine Research, Inc.* (1971) 39 *Law Week* 4250, finally upholding a treble-damage judgment in favor of Zenith in the face of a belatedly-raised statute of limitations defense. Zenith's damage claim was based upon its exclusion from Canadian markets by an illegal patent pool. Zenith attempted to prove damages for only four years, although the illegality of the patent pool and its adverse effect upon Zenith's business had been apparent for many prior years.

The Supreme Court's *Zenith* decision is flawed, since the district court may have decided that the statute of limitations defense had been waived. The Supreme Court holds that a decision on that ground would have been proper, if that was what the district court had had in mind.

But *Zenith* does set out a method for determining when the statute of limitations begins to run as to future damages (39 *Law Week* at 4256):

In antitrust and treble damage actions, refusal to award future profits as too speculative is equivalent to holding that no cause of action has yet accrued for any but those damages already suffered. In these instances, the cause of action for future damages, if they ever occur, will accrue only on the date they are suffered; thereafter the plaintiff may sue to recover them at any time within four years from the date they were inflicted.

The Supreme Court's *Zenith* solution thus brings the statute of limitations cases into focus with cases on post-complaint damage recovery. Although the law in this area is still in flux, the Ninth Circuit's discussion of *Twentieth Century-Fox Film Corp. v Brookside Theatre Corp.*, *supra*, in *Flintkote Co. v Lysfjord* (9th Cir 1957) 246 F2d 368 may prove prophetic.

2. [§12.14] Statute of Limitations Tolled by the Pendency of a Related Government Case

Civil or criminal proceedings instituted by the United States to prevent, restrain, or punish violations of the antitrust laws toll the statute of limitations on private claims "based in whole or in part on any matter complained of " in the government case. Clayton Act Section 5, 15 USC §16(b). And see *Twentieth Century-Fox Film Corp. v Goldwyn* (9th Cir 1964) 328 F2d 190, 214, *cert den* (1964) 379 US 880.

FTC proceedings *to enforce the antitrust laws*, as well as Justice Department cases, will toll the statute of limitations under 15 USC §16. *Minnesota Mining & Manufacturing Co. v New Jersey Wood Finishing Co.* (1965) 381 US 311. However, the FTC can enforce only the *Clayton* Act, not the Sherman Act, directly. The FTC sometimes attacks Sherman Act violations indirectly as "unfair trade practices" under Section 5 of the Federal Trade Commission Act, 15 USC §45. It is safer to assume that an FTC proceeding under the Federal Trade Commission Act does *not* toll the statute, even if the challenged "unfair trade practice" seems to be a Sherman Act offense. But *cf. Farmington Dowel Products Co. v Forster Mfg. Co.* (1st Cir 1969) 421 F2d 61.

A suit brought by the United States as a damage claimant under 15 USC §15a does *not* toll the statute of limitations. 15 USC §16(a), as amended (1955) 69 Stat 283.

The plaintiff's problem is whether the case he proposes to bring is sufficiently similar to a "government" case to permit him to safely withhold suit until the government finishes its case.

The Supreme Court's decision in *Zenith Radio Corp. v Hazeltine Research, Inc.* (1971) 39 *Law Week* 4250 has confirmed the most sweeping decisions of the lower courts. If a private plaintiff can prove, in his lawsuit, that a particular defendant was a participant in an antitrust violation which was the subject of an earlier government case, then the statute of limitations is tolled as to that defendant notwithstanding the fact that the defendant in the private case was not a defendant in the earlier government case and was not even shown to have been a co-conspirator by the government's proof. A broader reading of the tolling statute as it concerns parties would be hard to imagine. For further discussion, see §2.41.

3. [§12.15] Fraudulent Concealment

Fraudulent concealment of a cause of action under the antitrust laws tolls the running of the statute of limitations. See *Westinghouse Electric Corp. v Pacific Gas and Electric Co.* (9th Cir 1964) 326 F2d 575 and cases there cited. If there has been concealment, the statute of limitations begins to run when the plaintiff discovers that he can bring suit. *Moviecolor Ltd. v Eastman Kodak Co.* (2d Cir 1961) 288 F2d 80, 83, *cert den* (1961) 368 US 821; *Public Service Co. v. General Electric Co.* (10th Cir 1963) 315 F2d 306, *cert den* (1963) 374 US 809.

It has been said that mere ignorance of the basis of a claim is not sufficient—there must be some diligence on the part of the plaintiff and fraudulent concealment, mistake, or misrepresentation that frustrated the plaintiff's efforts to find out the truth. See *Laundry Equipment Sales Corp. v Borg-Warner Corp.* (7th Cir 1964) 334 F2d 788.

If it is appropriate, plaintiff should plead fraudulent concealment (see §12.50), alleging justifiable ignorance up to a point less than 4 years before the date on which he filed his complaint and alleging circumstances (such as the filing of an indictment, testimony of a witness before a congressional committee, etc.) that revealed the previously-concealed cause of action.

The defendant raises a prima facie defense to all injuries incurred more than 4 years prior to the filing date of complaint by pleading the statute of limitations contained in 15 USC §15b. The plaintiff has the burden of showing defendant's fraudulent concealment of the facts that would give the plaintiff knowledge of his cause of action, and of showing the plaintiff's ignorance in fact. Unless there is "no genuine issue as to any material fact" bearing on the fraudulent concealment issue, it is a fact question for the jury. Compare *Pan American Petroleum Corp. v Orr* (5th Cir 1963) 319 F2d 612 with *Moviecolor Ltd. v Eastman Kodak Co., supra.*

If a corporation has a cause of action but is controlled by the wrong-doers and cannot bring suit, a belated shareholder's suit might still be timely although officers and directors of the corporation have long known of the violation and participated in it if the plaintiff can show no "possibility that an informed stockholder or director could have induced the corporation to sue." See *International Railways v United Fruit Co.* (2d Cir 1967) 373 F2d 408, *cert den* (1967) 387 US 921.

4. [§12.16] "Tacking" of Tolling Provisions

When there are several different successive bases for tolling a statute of limitations, they may be "tacked" to toll the statute of limitations for extended periods of time. See *Union Carbide and Carbon Corp. v Nisley* (10th Cir 1961) 300 F2d 561, 567–572.

An ordinary "tacking" situation is one in which the government has brought a criminal action and followed it with a civil suit that continues to "pend" after the criminal action has been disposed of. Since the government criminal suit tolls the statute of limitations until it is concluded and for one year thereafter, it is sufficient if the government's civil suit is filed within that extra year. See *Maricopa County v American Pipe and Construction Co.* (9th Cir 1970) 431 F2d 1145, *pet for cert filed* 11-27-70. Another common situation is a conspiracy that is fraudulently concealed for a period of time but becomes known as the result of a government proceeding against the conspirators. The statute of limitations is tolled until disclosure of the conspiracy by the doctrine of fraudulent concealment (see §12.15); it is tolled thereafter by the pendency of the government litigation. See §12.14.

Although there is an informal division of labor between the Antitrust Division and the FTC that generally precludes simultaneous prosecution of the same offenses, it might sometimes happen that an FTC proceeding gives rise to a subsequent Antitrust Division prosecution based on facts divulged during the FTC investigation. The tolling period created by the pendency of FTC proceedings might then be extended by the subsequent Antitrust Division prosecution.

During the Second World War a special statute tolled the statute of limitations as to all acts, offenses, or transactions not already barred, from October 10, 1942 through June 30, 1946. PL 740, 77th Cong., 2d Sess., 56 Stat 781, as amended, PL 107, 79th Cong., 1st Sess., 59 Stat 306. Although the statute is now of largely historical interest, it is conceivable that other types of tolling might take a case back to 1946 and make the statute meaningful. It is likely that a similar statute would be passed in a future national emergency to preserve claims until the nation returned to something resembling a normal state.

D. [§12.17] Injury and Causation

Although there are no theoretical limits to the types of trade practices actionable by private plaintiffs under the federal antitrust laws, most plaintiffs' cases run to fairly standard patterns. Problems of causation are best understood in the context of these typical antitrust violations and the resulting injuries. See §§12.18–12.23.

The effects of an antitrust violation tend to reverberate throughout the economy. Those effects are usually felt most keenly by those closest to the violation. To prevail, the private plaintiff must prove that his injury was not only caused by the violation but proximately caused by it. See §§12.26, 12.27.

1. Types of Plaintiffs' Antitrust Cases

a. [§12.18] Monopoly Pricing Cases

These cases are generally brought under Sections 1 and 2 of the Sherman Act (15 USC §§1 and 2). The plaintiff has bought (or leased or licensed) from a member of the price-fixing conspiracy and paid too much because the conspiracy has had monopoly pricing power. See *Chattanooga Foundry and Pipe Works v Atlanta* (1906) 203 US 390. Alternatively, the plaintiff has sold (or leased or licensed) to a member of a price-fixing conspiracy and has received too little. See *Twentieth Century-Fox Film Corp. v Goldwyn* (9th Cir 1964) 328 F2d 190, *cert den* (1964) 379 US 880; *American Crystal Sugar Co. v Mandeville Island Farms, Inc.* (9th Cir 1952) 195 F2d 622. It is conceptually immaterial whether the plaintiff faces monopoly pricing as a buyer or as a seller. *Mandeville Island Farms, Inc. v American Crystal Sugar Co.* (1948) 334 US 219, 236.

Usually, the monopolistic price is the result of a conspiracy, but "single-firm" monopoly is also possible. See *Hanover Shoe, Inc. v United Shoe Machinery Corp.* (1968) 392 US 481.

b. [§12.19] Coercion or Vertical Restriction Cases

These cases resemble the monopoly pricing cases in that the plaintiff is injured by someone with whom he does business, and not by his competitor. Commonly, the plaintiff is a dealer or distributor in some merchandise or service that he purchases from the defendant. The dealership or distributorship franchise contains vertical restrictions on the plaintiff's pricing, territory, or type of customer who may be served. (See Chapter

3.) The restrictions interfere with the plaintiff's business freedom and reduce his profits. The fact that the plaintiff has himself participated in the unlawful agreement by adhering to it does not of itself preclude recovery. See §12.69.

Examples of this type of case: Plaintiff's freedom to set his own resale prices may have been wrongfully abridged by the defendant. See *Albrecht v Herald Co.* (1968) 390 US 145; *Simpson v Union Oil Co.* (1964) 377 US 13. For further discussion, see §§3.25–3.36. Or, in order to get the lease to defendant's service station, the plaintiff is obliged to take all of his tires, batteries and accessories from the defendant as well. The arrangement is likely to be unlawful. If so, the plaintiff has an action against the supplier under Section 3 of the Clayton Act, 15 USC §14, and perhaps under Section 1 of the Sherman Act, 15 USC §1. *Lessig v Tidewater Oil Co.* (9th Cir 1964) 327 F2d 459, *cert den* (1964) 377 US 993; *cf. Associated Press v Taft-Ingalls Corp.* (6th Cir 1965) 340 F2d 753, *cert den* (1965) 382 US 820. But *cf. Amplex of Maryland, Inc. v Outboard Marine Corp.* (4th Cir 1967) 380 F2d 112, *cert den* (1968) 389 US 1036; *Scanlan v Anheuser-Busch, Inc.* (9th Cir 1968) 388 F2d 918.

A recent and much-criticized case is *Fortner Enterprises, Inc. v United States Steel Corp.* (1969) 394 US 495. In that case, U.S. Steel had provided a developer with 100% financing (covering land as well as buildings) on condition that the builder purchase steel houses from U.S. Steel. The builder liked the financing, but shortly concluded that he would prefer building wooden houses to purchasing steel houses. U.S. Steel stood on its contract and Fortner sued, alleging an illegal tie-in between credit and houses.

Although the number of houses involved in Fortner's development represented a tiny portion of the total construction in the area, and although there were other financial institutions presumably willing to lend to Fortner on some terms, the Supreme Court found it possible that the financing terms offered by U.S. Steel were unique and therefore could constitute a tying product. The Supreme Court accordingly reversed the summary judgment which had been granted to U.S. Steel. Four Justices dissented. They pointed out that U.S. Steel was simply granting a concealed price reduction in the price of its houses; the money that U.S. Steel lent to Fortner was obtained by it in the financial market and was in no way unique. U.S. Steel might have escaped the Fortner problem if it had limited its advances of credit to the goods it was selling—*i.e.*, the houses.

In *Siegel v Chicken Delight, Inc.* (ND Calif 1970) 311 F Supp 847, it appeared that plaintiffs had been granted franchises on the condition that they would purchase certain items from the franchisor for use in their businesses. There was no separate license fee for the franchise, and the franchisor expected to make its profit by selling to its franchisees.

In defense of the scheme, Chicken Delight, the franchisor, argued that the two methods of extracting a franchise fee from the franchisee were equivalent in effect and that legality should not depend on the franchisor's method of exploiting his franchisees. The court disagreed, noting that the form chosen was a classic tie-in arrangement, coercively binding the franchisees to a sole source of supply. The franchisor might have achieved a similar result by lawful means, but had in fact opted in favor of an unlawful method of exploiting its trade name and know-how.

See also *Advance Business Systems and Supply Co. v SCM Corp.* (4th Cir 1969) 415 F2d 55, *cert den* (1970) 397 US 920.

For further discussion of tie-ins, see §§3.9–3.18.

c. [§12.20] Foreclosure Cases

The foreclosure cases are the mirror image of the coercion cases. They are the cases in which a plaintiff has been excluded from an advantageous business arrangement by an unlawful combination or agreement that makes potential business contacts (customers or suppliers) unavailable to him. The nature of the injury is a loss of business, the resulting loss of profits, and possibly a diminution in the good will of the plaintiff's business.

For example, if plaintiff is unable to sell his products to all of the Richfield Oil Company dealers, he may have a cause of action under Section 1 of the Sherman Act, 15 USC §1, or under Section 3 of the Clayton Act, 15 USC §14, or both. See *Karseal Corp. v Richfield Oil Corp.* (9th Cir 1955) 221 F2d 358. *Cf. Northern Pacific Railway Co. v United States* (1958) 356 US 1.

Advance Business Systems and Supply Co. v SCM Corp. (4th Cir 1969) 415 F2d 55, *cert den* (1970) 397 US 920 is typical of a successful foreclosure case. It was brought by a competitor foreclosed from selling in a market controlled by tie-in arrangements and other anticompetitive practices employed by a seller of office machinery. The plaintiff was unlawfully hampered in its efforts to sell supplies to the users of office equipment.

In theory, both parties to the respective agreement might be proper defendants. In fact, plaintiff may not want to sue his potential business partners; he can confine his suit to the competitor who has tied up his customers with restrictive agreements.

The plaintiff may similarly have been deprived of a customer or of a source of supply by a merger. However, private actions under Section 7 of the Clayton Act (15 USC §18) are relatively rare, and the availability of a private action under that section has only recently been generally recognized. See §12.33.

A form of foreclosure used competitively in the home construction industry has produced several decisions. Typically, in an effort to increase its business, an electric (or gas) utility offers a reduced charge for installing its line from curb-side to building-site if the builder will install exclusively or primarily electric (or gas) appliances in the house. In *Washington Gas Light Co. v Virginia Electric and Power Co.* (ED Va 1970) 309 F Supp 1119, the practice was held to violate Section 3 of the Clayton Act and Section 1 of the Sherman Act. A contrary result was reached in *Gas Light Co. v Georgia Power Co.* (MD Ga 1970) 313 F Supp 860.

d. [§12.21] Discrimination Cases

There are two kinds of discrimination cases. Primary line cases involve predatory discriminations used as weapons by a seller to injure or destroy his competitors. They can be thought of as "dirty tricks" or "competitor" cases, and are brought primarily under Section 2 of the Clayton Act as amended by the Robinson-Patman Act, 15 USC §13. See, *e.g., Utah Pie Co. v Continental Baking Co.* (1967) 386 US 685. The same conduct may constitute both an illegal discrimination and an attempt to monopolize in violation of Section 2 of the Sherman Act, 15 USC §2. *Food Basket, Inc. v Albertson's, Inc.* (10th Cir 1967) 383 F2d 785. See §12.22.

The other kind of price discrimination case is the secondary line case, in which a seller discriminates between purchasers who compete among themselves. The plaintiff is the disadvantaged competitor who does not receive the benefit of the discrimination. The plaintiff sues under Section 2 of the Clayton Act as amended by the Robinson-Patman Act for failure to receive the benefit accorded to his competitor.

Price discrimination is only one of several kinds of Robinson-Patman violations for which plaintiff may sue. He may also sue for the adverse impact of discriminatory promotional or advertising allowances, or for injuries resulting from unlawful discounts in lieu of brokerage. 15 USC §2(c), 2(d), and 2(e).

Apart from the problems of proving violation of the Robinson-Patman Act (see Chapter 5), proof of injury and damages in discrimination cases can be tricky and frustrating. See §12.31.

e. [§12.22] "Dirty Tricks" or "Competitor" Cases

Sometimes a single firm, or conspiracy of firms in the same business, will attempt to monopolize the business by running its competitors out of the business. The attempt violates Section 2 of the Sherman Act, 15 USC §2. If two or more persons jointly attempt to monopolize, their conduct is almost inevitably a violation of Section 1 of the Sherman Act, 15 USC §1, as well.

The means used by monopoly-minded defendants may include tying contracts, probably unlawful under Section 3 of the Clayton Act, 15 USC §15 (see §§3.9–3.18), and discriminatory regional price-cutting, violating Section 2 of the Clayton Act as amended by the Robinson-Patman Act, 15 USC §13. See §12.21 and §5.39. Other weapons include boycotts induced by the defendants' market power and consequent leverage over plaintiff's suppliers or customers, probably constituting violations of Section 1 of the Sherman Act. See *Klor's, Inc. v Broadway-Hale Stores, Inc.* (1959) 359 US 207.

Other acts of defendants, for example espionage of trade secrets, sabotage, fomenting labor trouble, trade libel, and palming off, may be damaging, and may even be independent torts. Acts of this character may be highly probative of predatory intent even if they do not constitute independent antitrust violations.

But this kind of act is not necessary to a cause of action; in *American Tobacco Co. v United States* (1946) 328 US 781, the Court said (at 809):

It is not of importance whether the means used to accomplish the unlawful objective are in themselves lawful or unlawful. Acts done to give effect to the conspiracy may be in themselves wholly innocent acts. Yet, if they are part of the sum of the acts which are relied upon to effectuate the conspiracy which the statute forbids, they come within its prohibition.

When this sort of "commercial mayhem" is used, the wounds are as various as the weapons. They may include, in a predatory pricing case, lost sales, reduced prices on sales actually made, and injury to the good will of the business. *Atlas Building Products Co. v Diamond Block & Gravel Co.* (10th Cir 1959) 269 F2d 950, 958, *cert den* (1960) 363 US 843.

f. [§12.23] Retaliation or Revenge Cases

In some cases, plaintiffs have been permitted to recover when the direct cause of their injury was not so much the defendant's antitrust violation as defendant's retaliation against plaintiff's refusal to go along with the violation.

For example, in *Simpson v Union Oil Co.* (1964) 377 US 13, defendant attempted unlawfully to control the plaintiff's retail gasoline prices. In fact, the plaintiff set his own prices; defendant retaliated by cancelling plaintiff's service station lease. The Supreme Court said that the plaintiff could recover damages for the cancellation.

In *Alles Corp. v Senco Products, Inc.* (6th Cir 1964) 329 F2d 567, the plaintiff refused to compel an affiliated corporation to enter into an exclusive-dealing contract with the defendant. Defendant thereupon cancelled the plaintiff's dealership. The complaint was held to state a cause of action under Section 3 of the Clayton Act (15 USC §14), although no tying contract had in fact been entered into.

The *Alles* case seems to conflict directly with *Leo J. Meyberg Co. v Eureka Williams Corp.* (9th Cir 1954) 215 F2d 100, *cert den* (1954) 348 US 875, which holds that a *refusal* to sell except with the unlawful condition is not enough to create a cause of action under Section 3 of the Clayton Act; a completed sale subject to the challenged condition must be proven. *Meyberg* was distinguished in *Lessig v Tidewater Oil Co.* (9th Cir 1964) 327 F2d 459, *cert den* (1964) 377 US 993. Its present strength is uncertain.

The Tenth Circuit recently held that there is no valid distinction between a plaintiff injured for refusal to participate in an antitrust violation and a plaintiff who participated against his will and to his damage. See *Sahm v V-1 Oil Co.* (10th Cir 1968) 402 F2d 69. On the other hand, in *Quinn v Mobil Oil Co.* (1st Cir 1967) 375 F2d 273, *pet disms'd* (1967) 389 US 801, the First Circuit refused to permit recovery to a plaintiff who had refused to participate in an antitrust violation and had been injured as a consequence.

Absent direct evidence that a dealer has been terminated for refusal to participate in an antitrust violation, it still may be possible to obtain sufficient circumstantial evidence to permit a plaintiff to recover. However, in the absence of some anticompetitive motive that would support an inference that defendant supplier has terminated plaintiff distributor in order to further some scheme that violates the antitrust laws, the plaintiff may have grave difficulty in making that showing. See *Joseph E. Seagram and Sons, Inc. v Hawaiian Oke and Liquors, Ltd.* (9th Cir 1969) 416 F2d 71, *cert den* (1970) 396 US 1062, *reh den* (1970) 397 US 1003; *Daily Press, Inc. v United Press International* (6th Cir 1969) 412 F2d 126, *cert den* (1969) 396 US 990.

2. [§12.24] Causation in Fact

In theory, plaintiff should prove that he would have been better off "but for" the defendant's violation of the antitrust laws. In practice, the net overall impact of a violation on a plaintiff's economic position is often ignored and the court concentrates on the immediate and direct effects. See, for example, §12.25.

Nevertheless, plaintiff must prove that his injury was "proximately" caused by the defendant's violation (see §12.26), and that presumes some preliminary showing of causation in fact. For example, if the alleged violation is a conspiracy to fix prices, plaintiff must show that the price he paid was raised by the conspiracy.

a. [§12.25] The Passing-On Defense

Suppose the plaintiff buys widgets from the defendant at $1.50 each, and subsequently discovers that defendant has been secretly conspiring with other widget manufacturers to raise the price of widgets. Suppose further that plaintiff proves that he could have bought widgets for $1.00 each in the absence of the conspiracy. Has the defendant's conspiracy actually injured plaintiff?

There is no single answer to this question. The plaintiff may have absorbed the overcharge and suffered reduced profits as a consequence. On the other hand, if the plaintiff is a "middleman" he may have suffered no damage because he may have "passed on" the overcharge to his own customers. Indeed, if the plaintiff is a middleman and figures his selling price on the basis of his costs plus a percentage of markup, he makes more money on an item that he purchases for a high price than he would have made by purchasing the same item at a lower price, unless the high price reduces his volume so substantially as to offset increased unit profit.

A workable body of law on "passing on" was developing in the lower courts when the Supreme Court decided *Hanover Shoe, Inc. v United Shoe Machinery Corp.* (1968) 392 US 481.

The Supreme Court's decision in *Hanover Shoe* is obviously based on policy considerations rather than economic analysis and adopts a highly simplistic view (at 494): "Our conclusion is that Hanover proved injury and the amount of its damages for the purposes of its treble-damage suit when it proved that United had overcharged it during the damage period and showed the amount of the overcharge . . . ." In reaching that conclusion, the Supreme Court relied on earlier cases (not all of them under the antitrust laws) in which the "possibility that plaintiffs had recouped the overcharges from their customers was held irrelevant in assessing damages." (392 US at 490.)

In *Hanover Shoe*, the Supreme Court recognized two possible exceptions to its general rule (392 US at 494):

[1.] We recognize that there might be situations—for instance, when an overcharged buyer has a pre-existing "cost-plus" contract, thus making it easy to prove that he has not been damaged—where the considerations requiring that the passing-on defense not be permitted in this case would not be present.

[2.] We also recognize that where no differential can be proved between the price unlawfully charged and some price that the seller was required by law to charge, establishing damages might require a showing of loss of profits to the buyer.

The real problem with *Hanover Shoe* is with assessing the extent to which it overrules prior decisions of lower courts which had attempted to draw lines between cases in which the "first purchaser" was the proper plaintiff and those in which the "first purchaser" effectively passed on the overcharge, thereby avoiding any damage to himself and putting the next purchaser in line as a potential plaintiff injured by the original overcharge.

The leading cases allowing the passing-on defense as against a plaintiff who was the first purchaser from the overcharging defendant were the "middleman" cases. Typically, the plaintiff purchased from the defendant, tacked on a percentage markup based on the purchase price, and resold to his own customers. There was respectable authority that the middleman who first purchased from the overcharging seller was not injured by the overcharge and therefore could not recover against the seller. See *Freedman v Philadelphia Terminals Auction Co.* (3d Cir 1962) 301 F2d 820 and the "oil jobber" cases cited at 833 n 7. It is not clear whether those cases are overruled by *Hanover Shoe* (See 392 US at 490, n 8), or fall within the exceptions mentioned by the Supreme Court (392 US at 494): ". . . for instance, when an overcharged buyer has a pre-existing 'cost-plus' contract, thus making it easy to prove that he has not been damaged . . . ."

The best explanation for the Supreme Court's result in *Hanover Shoe* is pure public policy—if the injury is deemed to be passed on there is no logical way to stop the chain short of the ultimate consumers, who are too diffuse and uninterested to bring a lawsuit, even with the aid of the new federal class suit rules.

Rather than permit the defendant to escape liability, the Supreme Court opted to give a cause of action to the "first purchaser" with very little regard to whether the first purchaser was in fact injured.

The second problem that the Supreme Court's simplistic rule solves neatly, if not satisfactorily, is the problem of proof surrounding a passing-on defense. It seems to say that if there is any doubt about the fact of passing on (*i.e.* anything other than a pre-existing cost-plus contract), the first purchaser is the proper plaintiff. Only when the fact of passing on is so clear as to be substantially beyond argument could it be raised as a defense.

The effect of *Hanover Shoe* on the passing-on doctrine has now been felt in several large conspiracy cases. In each case defendants were alleged to have engaged in a massive price-fixing conspiracy. In each case the distribution system included middlemen. In each case numerous purchasers of the product in question sued and the court was required to decide who in the chain of purchase and resale was a permissible plaintiff.

In *Philadelphia Housing Authority v American Radiator & Standard Sanitary Corp.* (ED Pa 1970) 50 FRD 13 plaintiff homeowners alleged that the prices of the plumbing fixtures in their homes had been unlawfully inflated by a price-fixing conspiracy. The court concluded that homeowners were too remote from the defendant plumbing-fixture manufacturers to recover damages for the overcharges. The decision strongly suggests that contractors who purchased plumbing fixtures and incorporated them into the finished house were the proper plaintiffs to recoup overcharges on the fixtures.

In contrast, in approving a settlement in the broad-spectrum-antibiotic cases, Judge Wyatt of the Southern District of New York observed that the settlement offer made to drug wholesalers and retailers was generous. Judge Wyatt felt that these middlemen would be unlikely to prove damages since any overcharges in sales made to them had probably been passed on. See *West Virginia v Chas. Pfizer & Co.* (SD NY 1970) 314 F Supp 711.

The rule of *Hanover Shoe* will undoubtedly be salutary if the first purchaser is a public agency that will pass on any recovery in the lawsuit to the taxpayer. See *Public Utility District No. 1 v General Electric Co.* (WD Wash 1964) 230 F Supp 744, based on this policy consideration. On the other hand, if a contractor constructs a major project for a public agency on a negotiated contract in which the contract price is predicated on artificial price levels for materials, the contractor will recover from the overcharging suppliers although his bid has protected him against any loss and it is in fact the public agency that suffers. If the public agency preserves its right to sue suppliers for overcharges by entering into a cost-plus contract, it is likely to suffer from the inefficiencies that attend cost-plus contracts. Perhaps the solution is for the ultimate purchaser to issue a fixed-price contract which assigns to it any claims the contractor may have against the original supplier for overcharges. See further discussion of the passing-on doctrine at §2.49.

3. [§12.26] Proximate Cause

The statute says that "*any* person who shall be injured in his business or property by reason of anything forbidden in the anti-trust laws may sue . . ." (15 USC §15; emphasis added). The Supreme Court has said that ". . . to state a claim upon which relief can be granted under [Section 1 of the Sherman Act], allegations adequate to show a violation and, in a private treble damage action, that plaintiff was damaged thereby are all the law requires." *Radiant Burners, Inc. v Peoples Gas Light & Coke Co.* (1961) 364 US 656, 660. *Cf. Mandeville Island Farms, Inc. v American Crystal Sugar Co.* (1948) 334 US 219, 236. The Supreme Court has also observed, generally, that it should ". . . not add requirements to burden the private litigant beyond what is specifically set forth . . .[in the antitrust] laws." *Radovich v National Football League* (1957) 352 US 445, 454.

Nevertheless, the lower federal courts have required that the antitrust plaintiff prove that he was *proximately* injured by the defendant's violation. See *Highland Supply Corp. v Reynolds Metals Co.* (8th Cir 1964) 327 F2d 725, 732.

One expression of the requirement is the Ninth Circuit's "target area" test, enunciated in *Karseal Corp. v Richfield Oil Corp.* (9th Cir 1955) 221 F2d 358. The common tort law concept of "foreseeability" has been suggested as a test of proximate cause. See *Hoopes v Union Oil Co.* (9th Cir 1967) 374 F2d 480, 485; *Twentieth Century Fox Film Corp. v Goldwyn* (9th Cir 1964) 328 F2d 190, 220, *cert den* (1964) 379 US 880.

Proximate cause is not synonymous with sole cause; "substantial" cause has been held sufficient. See *Continental Ore Co. v Union Carbide & Carbon Corp.* (1962) 370 US 690, 702; *Haverhill Gazette Co. v Union Leader Corp.* (1st Cir 1964) 333 F2d 798, 805–806. In *Standard Oil Co. of Calif. v Perkins* (9th Cir 1967) 396 F2d 809, the Ninth Circuit seemed to hold that plaintiff was required to segregate his damages and that the defendant would not be responsible for damages from other causes. The Supreme Court subsequently reversed, finding in substance that the defendant could be found responsible for most of the possible sources of plaintiff's damages and that there was no showing that the jury had improperly included a damage award for any non-recoverable items. *Perkins v Standard Oil Co. of Calif.* (1969) 395 US 642.

More recently, the Ninth Circuit has said that "legal cause exists between the antitrust wrong and the injury if that wrong is a substantial factor in bringing about the injury. It need not be the sole or the 'controlling' cause of the injury." *Mulvey v Samuel Goldwyn Productions* (9th Cir 1970) 433 F2d 1073, *pet for cert filed* 2-22-71.

Much of the law of proximate cause has been crystalized in the "standing to sue" cases, which define categories of plaintiffs who may and may not seek redress for their injuries under the antitrust laws. See §12.27.

a. [§12.27] Standing to Sue

The lower federal courts limit recovery to plaintiffs with standing to sue. "Standing" cases establish arbitrary categories of plaintiffs who may sue under the antitrust laws and other categories of plaintiffs (*e.g.*, creditors, shareholders, landlords) who may not. Analytically, the standing rules are rules of proximate cause.

The main justification for the "standing" concept is that it permits an early identification of cases in which the plaintiff will never be able to recover because, as demonstrated by undisputed facts or by his own complaint, he will never, as a matter of law, be able to prove injury proximately caused by the defendant.

The objection to the standing rules, aside from the fact that the statute does not mention them and the Supreme Court has never approved them, is that they invade the province of the jury by arbitrarily settling the factual issue of proximate cause. Recent Ninth Circuit cases have questioned the whole concept of arbitrary standing rules. See *Hoopes v Union Oil Co.* (9th Cir 1967) 374 F2d 480; *Harman v Valley Nat'l. Bank* (9th Cir 1964) 339 F2d 564.

Some of the categories of plaintiffs who have been held not to have standing:

1. Shareholders, officers and employees of corporations. See *Kauffman v The Dreyfus Fund, Inc.* (3d Cir 1970) 434 F2d 727; *Ash v International Business Machines, Inc.* (3d Cir 1965) 353 F2d 491, *cert den* (1966) 384 US 927; *Walker Distributing Co. v Lucky Lager Brewing Co.* (9th Cir 1963) 323 F2d 1, 10. *But cf. Dailey v Quality School Plan, Inc.* (5th Cir 1967) 380 F2d 484, permitting the sales supervisor for a corporation to sue a conspiracy in which his employer participated.

2. Creditors of injured parties. *Martens v Barrett* (5th Cir 1957) 245 F2d 844, 846.

3. Landlords, when the injury is to the lessee. *Harrison v Paramount Pictures, Inc.* (ED Pa 1953) 115 F Supp 312, *aff'd per curiam* (3d Cir 1954) 211 F2d 405, *cert den* (1954) 348 US 828. *But cf. Steiner v 20th Century-Fox Film Corp.* (9th Cir 1956) 232 F2d 190 (lessee alleged to be a participant in the unlawful conspiracy).

4. A patentee who has given an exclusive license for the term of a patent. *Productive Inventions, Inc. v Trico Products Corp.* (2d Cir 1955) 224 F2d 678, *cert den* (1956) 350 US 936.

5. Suppliers to customers directly injured by the violation. *Volasco Products Co. v Lloyd A. Fry Roofing Co.* (6th Cir 1962) 308 F2d 383, 393–395, *cert den* (1963) 372 US 907. The *Volasco* case is not the law in the Ninth Circuit, at least when the supplier's product undergoes no change in form but is simply resold through distributors. See *Karseal Corp. v Richfield Oil Corp.* (9th Cir 1955) 221 F2d 358.

6. Franchisors of appraisers excluded from appraisal work by insurers who agree upon other appraisers to the exclusion of franchisee. *Nationwide Auto Appraiser Service, Inc. v Association of Casualty and Surety Companies* (10th Cir 1967) 382 F2d 925.

Purchasers of goods the prices of which have been artificially inflated by an antitrust violation such as price fixing may or may not have standing to sue, depending on their privity or lack of privity with the seller, and the nature of their relationship with the seller. The first purchaser will ordinarily have standing. See *Hanover Shoe, Inc. v United Shoe Machinery Corp.* (1968) 392 US 481. Although *Hanover Shoe* did not say so in terms, it would appear that purchasers from the first purchaser would not have standing to sue the antitrust defendant. Whether they would have standing to sue the first purchaser on a quasi-contract theory in order to share in his recovery is a matter not related to the standing question. In at least one instance, the United States took the position that it is entitled, by reason of grant to a state agency for a project, to share in a recovery that the state obtained for overcharges on material that went into the project. (GAO; B-162652, 11/27/67, 36 *USL Week* 2348.)

If the first purchaser has a cost-plus contract with the ultimate purchaser so that it can be demonstrated beyond any real doubt that the first purchaser has no injury, then it would appear that the first purchaser has no standing to sue. See *Hanover Shoe, supra.*

For further discussion see §2.48.

4. Special Problems under Particular Code Sections

a. [§12.28] Special Problems in Rule of Reason Cases; the Public Injury Doctrine

In *Klor's, Inc. v Broadway-Hale Stores, Inc.* (9th Cir 1958) 255 F2d 214, involving the Sherman Act, the Ninth Circuit held that proof of "public injury" was an essential part of the plaintiff's case in a private action. The Supreme Court's resounding reversal of that decision should have laid the public injury requirement to rest. See *Klor's, Inc. v Broadway-Hale Stores, Inc.* (1959) 359 US 207. But Timberlake, *Federal Treble*

Damage Antitrust Actions (1965) Chapter 15 seems to suggest that the requirement lives on, although possibly assimilated into another of the "elements" of a private cause of action.

If proof of public injury means proof that the defendant has violated the antitrust laws, then it remains a necessary element of a plaintiff's case. If the public injury doctrine would permit a proven violator of the antitrust laws to escape liability because *only the plaintiff* has apparently been injured, then it was laid to rest in *Klor's*.

Injury to the plaintiff does not in and of itself prove an antitrust violation; there are doubtless commercial torts of various kinds that inflict serious injury without amounting to antitrust violations. Violation of a public law, on the other hand, would seem to cause "public injury" as a matter of definition.

b. [§12.29] Special Problems under Section 1 of the Sherman Act

Price-fixing, bid-rigging, market-allocation and group-boycott cases present no question of the existence of a violation. A conspiracy for any of those purposes is *per se* unreasonable and therefore illegal unless expressly exempted by statute from the operation of the Sherman Act.

Off-beat situations that must be tested by the rule of reason (see §§2.25-2.26) can present serious "violation" problems under Section 1 of the Sherman Act. "Reasonableness" ought to be treated as a jury question in almost every case. Lower federal courts, however, have sometimes disposed of such cases on motion. See *Packard Motor Car Co. v Webster Motor Car Co.* (DC Cir 1957) 243 F2d 418, *cert den* (1957) 355 US 822 (dealer cut off at instigation of single competing retailer on a "one-of-us-has-got-to-go" ultimatum); *Ace Beer Distributors, Inc. v Kohn, Inc.* (6th Cir 1963) 318 F2d 283, *cert den* (1963) 375 US 922 (competitor talked supplier into shifting business from plaintiff to him); *Savon Gas Stations Number Six, Inc. v Shell Oil Co.* (4th Cir 1962) 309 F2d 306, *cert den* (1963) 372 US 911 (fence erected by defendant on his own property limited access to plaintiff's station).

Reasonableness can be a formidable defense; the Ninth Circuit has held it not unlawful for several sellers to replace a common distributor even if the result is to put the distributor out of business and they know it. See *Joseph E. Seagram and Sons, Inc. v Hawaiian Oke and Liquors, Ltd.* (9th Cir 1969) 416 F2d 71, *cert den* (1970) 396 US 1062, *reh den* (1970) 397 US 1003, in which the court recognized, however, that an anticompetitive motive on the part of the defendants would have converted reasonable conduct on the part of the defendants into unreasonable conduct and produced an entirely different result. See also *Bridge Corp. of America v The American Contract Bridge League, Inc.* (9th Cir 1970) 428 F2d 1365, *cert den* (1971) 91 SC 940.

Even when a refusal to deal with a distributor is based on objections to his choice of customers, there is authority for the proposition that the refusal to deal can be reasonable, at least in special circumstances. In *Tripoli Co. v Wella Corp.* (3d Cir 1970) 425 F2d 932, *cert den* (1970) 400 US 831, it appeared that the distributor was selling professional hair styling products at retail. The manufacturer refused to deal further with the distributor on that ground, pointing out that the products were potentially dangerous and they should therefore be sold only through professional hair stylists. The Third Circuit found the limitation on resale to professionals not unreasonable and denied the plaintiff recovery. In fact, the manufacturer could presumably have protected itself by enclosing more adequate instructions with the product, by placing warning labels on the packages, or by compelling the distributor to obtain product liability insurance covering the supplier.

The District of Columbia Circuit Court has also held that an accrediting agency that reviews non-profit institutions may reasonably refuse accreditation to a commercial junior college on the grounds that the profit motive might adversely influence the quality of education in the commercial junior college. See *Marjorie Webster Junior College, Inc. v Middle States Association of Colleges and Secondary Schools, Inc.* (DC Cir 1970) 432 F2d 650, *cert den* (1970) 400 US 965.

In *United States v Container Corp. of America* (1969) 393 US 333, the Supreme Court held that a regular exchange of price information among competitors had the likely effect of eliminating or at least reducing price competition, and, therefore, violated Section 1 of the Sherman Act. The Court did not find that there had been, in fact, any agreement among competitors to fix prices as such, but the majority was convinced that the exchange of price information "chilled the vigor" of price competition. So far, private plaintiffs have had little success in founding private actions on exchanges of price information between competitors. Se *Di-Wal, Inc. v Fibreboard Corp.* (ND Calif 1970) 1970 Trade Cases ¶73,155.

If the plaintiff himself participated in an unlawful restraint of trade he may still bring suit, at least if his participation in the particular restraint was grudging. See discussion of the in pari delicto defense at §§ 12.69 and 2.46. Moreover, it appears that the unlawful agreement ("contract, combination, or conspiracy") that must be shown in a Section 1 Sherman Act case can be an agreement between the plaintiff and the defendant. See *Perma Life Mufflers, Inc. v International Parts Corp.* (1968) 392 US 134 at

142, relying on *Albrecht v Herald Co.* (1968) 390 US 145, 150 n. 6 and *Simpson v Union Oil Co.* (1964) 377 US 13.

All three of these cases dealt with vertical restrictions placed by large companies on their franchisees. *Simpson* and *Albrecht* dealt specifically with vertical price fixing. *Albrecht* squarely holds that the franchisee (operator of a newspaper-delivery route) must be free to set his own prices, whether his pricing decisions are advantageous to the supplier (or the ultimate consumer) or not. In *Albrecht*, the newspaper-route operator charged more for home delivery than the recommended price, and lost his distributorship as a result. The Eighth Circuit felt that the supplier had a right to protect the consumers from overcharges, but the Supreme Court disagreed, placing primary importance on unfettered market conditions: "The assertion that illegal price fixing is justified because it blunts the pernicious consequences of another distribution practice is unpersuasive. If, as the Court of Appeals said, the economic impact of territorial exclusivity was such that the public could be protected only by otherwise illegal price fixing itself injurious to the public, the entire scheme must fall under Section 1 of the Sherman Act." (390 US at 154).

c. [§12.30] Special Problems under Section 2 of the Sherman Act

Section 2 of the Sherman Act (15 USC §2) gives rise to private actions for damages arising out of monopolization, conspiracy to monopolize, and attempt to monopolize.

The most difficult question in monopolization cases is, "monopolize what?" The plaintiff must prove intentional monopolization of a "relevant market". Having the only theatre in town does not necessarily give its owner "monopoly" power. *United States v Griffith* (1948) 334 US 100, 106. A patent may be so narrow in scope as to convey less than a "monopoly" in Sherman Act terms. *Walker Process Equipment, Inc. v Food Machinery & Chemical Corp.* (1956) 382 US 172, 177–178.

The burden of proving "relevant market" facts is formidable, in spite of recent cases construing the concept with some flexibility. See, *e.g.*, *United States v Grinnell Corp.* (1966) 384 US 563; *United States v Pabst Brewing Co.* (1966) 384 US 546. See discussion of relevant market at §§4.24–4.26.

It may be easier to prove an attempt to monopolize. In *Lessig v Tidewater Oil Co.* (9th Cir 1964) 327 F2d 459, *cert den* (1964) 377 US 993 the Ninth Circuit held that "when the charge is attempt (or conspiracy) to monopolize, rather than monopolization, the relevant market is 'not in issue.'" (327 F2d at 474.) Neither is the probability of success in monopolizing an issue: "... specific intent itself is the only evidence of dangerous probability the statute requires—perhaps on the not unreasonable assumption that the actor is better able than others to judge the practical possibility of achieving his illegal objective." (327 F2d at 474.)

On this point, *Lessig* has not been followed in other circuits, but the Ninth Circuit has subsequently reaffirmed its position in *Industrial Building Materials, Inc. v Interchemical Corp.* (9th Cir 1970) 1971 Trade Cases ¶73,399.

d. [§12.31] Special Problems under Section 2 of the Clayton Act

The coverage of Section 2 of the Clayton Act as amended by the Robinson-Patman Act (15 USC §13) is limited to tangible personal property, described as "commodities," "goods, wares, or merchandise," and "products or commodities." Generally, see Chapter 5.

The plaintiff planning to plead discrimination should bring it under the appropriate subsection. Section 2(a) (15 USC §13(a)) is the basic price discrimination subsection. It is subject to a cost justification defense not available under other subsections. It also requires the plaintiff to prove incipient threat to competition or a tendency to monopoly, or show that the effect of the discrimination may be to injure, destroy, or prevent competition with any person who either grants or knowingly receives the benefit of the discrimination or with customers of either of them.

By contrast, other subsections of Section 2 of the Clayton Act are essentially *per se* in their approach. They outlaw discriminations in the form of dummy brokerage (15 USC §13(c)); advertising allowances (15 USC §13(d)); and services or facilities (15 USC §13(e)).

Understandably, plaintiffs prefer the relatively simple proof required under 15 USC §13(c), (d), and (e). The law on what constitutes a violation of which subsection is still in a state of flux. In *Empire Rayon Yarn Co. v American Viscose Corp.* (2d Cir 1966) 364 F2d 491, *cert den* (1967) 385 US 1002 the plaintiff abandoned its Section 2(a) price discrimination claim in favor of a more easily proven Section 2(c) dummy brokerage claim with fatal results; the Second Circuit held that the complaint did not state a claim on which relief could be granted under Section 2(c), and the Section 2(a) claim had been abandoned. See discussion of these essentially *per se* sections at §§5.10–5.17, 5.29.

Of course, discrimination between two purchasers implies two comparable sales. Absent facts tending to show predatory purpose, or other special circumstances, an isolated sale at a special price is an insufficient basis on which to predicate a case. See, *e.g.*, *International Film Center, Inc. v Graflex, Inc.* (3d Cir 1970) 427 F2d 334. For further discussion of comparable sales see §§5.13–5.19.

FTC v Fred Meyer, Inc. (1968) 390 US 341 added a new wrinkle to the rules on discriminatory allowances in the "dual distribution" situation (see §5.31). A direct-buying retailer induced a promotional allowance not available to several of its retailer-competitors who bought the same manufacturers' merchandise through distributors. The Supreme Court stated (at 357):

We conclude that the most reasonable construction of §2(d) is one which places on the supplier the responsibility for making promotional allowances available to those resellers who compete directly with the favored buyer.

As *Fred Meyer* makes clear, both the knowing recipient of favored treatment and the discriminating seller are responsible for violations of the Robinson-Patman Act.

Under 15 USC §13(b) a seller may meet in good faith the equally low price of a competitor without liability. The "meeting competition" defense is also available to a defendant charged with granting discriminatory advertising or promotional allowances or with providing discriminatory promotional services under 15 USC §13(d) and 13(e). *Exquisite Form Brassiere, Inc. v FTC* (DC Cir 1961) 301 F2d 499, *cert den* (1962) 369 US 888. On what constitutes meeting competition, compare *Callaway Mills Co. v FTC* (5th Cir 1966) 362 F2d 435 with *Surprise Brassiere Co. v FTC* (5th Cir 1969) 406 F2d 711. For further discussion, see §§5.49-5.51.

e. [§12.32] Special Problems of Section 3 of the Clayton Act

Section 3 of the Clayton Act (15 USC §14) deals with exclusive dealing and tie-in contracts. These contracts require a purchaser not to deal with others as a condition of dealing with the seller (or lessor, etc.). There are two potential classes of plaintiffs, the purchaser who is precluded from looking elsewhere for a more competitive source of supply, and the defendant's competitors who are excluded from the purchasers' business.

Karseal Corp. v Richfield Oil Corp. (9th Cir 1955) 221 F2d 358 is typical of cases brought by the defendant's excluded competitor. Defendant Richfield compelled its dealers to purchase their requirements of tires, batteries and accessories from Richfield-approved sources. Plaintiff attempted unsuccessfully to sell his non-approved Karseal wax to the Richfield dealers and ultimately recovered damages. *Richfield Oil Corp. v Karseal Corp.* (9th Cir 1959) 271 F2d 709.

Lessig v Tidewater Oil Co. (9th Cir 1963) 327 F2d 459, *cert den* (1964) 377 US 993 is typical of cases brought by the purchaser, in this case one who was precluded from obtaining tires, batteries, and accessories from sources other than his gasoline supplier.

Section 3 of the Clayton Act reaches only transactions in "goods, wares, merchandise, machinery, supplies or other commodities . . . ." Section 1 of the Sherman Act (15 USC §1), however, reaches transactions in land or services. See *Fortner Enterprises, Inc. v United States Steel Corp.* (1969) 394 US 495; *Northern Pacific Railway Co. v United States* (1958) 356 US 1.

In *Washington Gas Light Co. v Virginia Electric and Power Co.* (ED Va 1970) 309 F Supp 1119, defendant electrical power utility charged an installation fee for electrical power lines that was inversely proportional to the number of electrical appliances which the builder put into his new homes. The court held this a violation of Section 3 of the Clayton Act. The decision is probably wrong in apparently treating power as a commodity, but the error is moot inasmuch as the court also found a violation of Section 1 of the Sherman Act. See also *Advance Business Systems and Supply Co. v SCM Corp.* (4th Cir 1969) 415 F2d 55, *cert den* (1970) 397 US 920.

The circuits are split in their treatment of cases in which the seller terminates a dealership because the dealer refuses to enter into an exclusive dealing or tie-in contract. The Ninth Circuit, reading the statute literally, has held that in order to prevail the plaintiff must show that a sale has actually been made. *Leo J. Meyberg Co. v Eureka Williams Corp.* (9th Cir 1954) 215 F2d 100, *cert den* (1954) 348 US 875. Compare *Alles Corp. v Senco Products, Inc.* (6th Cir 1964) 329 F2d 567 sustaining a claim by a plaintiff terminated for refusal to compel an affiliated corporation to agree to a contract that *would have been* unlawful under Section 3. The *Alles* opinion does not mention *Leo J. Meyberg. Cf. Amplex of Maryland, Inc. v Outboard Marine Corp.* (4th Cir 1967) 380 F2d 112, *cert den* (1968) 389 US 1036.

Of course, the whole concept of a "tie-in" is that one product or service is sold on condition that the buyer take some other product or service in the bargain. Absent the coercive condition there is no violation. See *Glen Mfg. Inc. v Perfect Fit Industries, Inc.* (2d Cir 1970) 420 F2d 319, *cert den* (1970) 397 US 1042. For further discussion of tie-ins, see §2.32 and §§3.9–3.18.

f. [§12.33] Special Problems under Section 7 of the Clayton Act

Section 7 of the Clayton Act (15 USC §18) outlaws mergers if the effect "may be substantially to lessen competition, or to tend to create a monopoly" *now or in the future*. Mergers of all kinds quite commonly cause realignments of trade relationships and management shakeups. Almost inevitably, mergers work to the disadvantage of the merged companies' trading partners, competitors, and/or employees.

It now seems generally accepted that Section 7 of the Clayton Act gives rise to a private action for treble damages. See *Gottesman v General Motors Corp.* (2d Cir 1969) 414 F2d 956; *Dailey v Quality School Plan, Inc.* (5th Cir 1967) 380 F2d 484; *Kirihara v The Bendix Corp.* (D Haw 1969) 306 F Supp 72; *Isidor Weinstein Investment Co. v Hearst Corp.* (ND Calif 1970) 310 F Supp 390. *But cf. Dailey v The Quality School Plan, Inc.* (5th Cir 1970) 427 F2d 1080.

There is no real doubt that a private plaintiff may enjoin threatened violations of Section 7 of the Clayton Act under Section 16 of the Clayton Act (15 USC §26). *Allis-Chalmers Manufacturing Co. v White Consolidated Industries, Inc.* (3d Cir 1969) 414 F2d 506, *cert den* (1970) 396 US 1009; *American Crystal Sugar Co. v The Cuban-American Sugar Co.* (2d Cir 1958) 259 F2d 524. A district court has recently held, in denying a motion to dismiss, that it is not prepared to conclude summarily that divestiture may never be an appropriate remedy in a private action. *J.D. Burkhead v Phillips Petroleum Co.* (ND Calif 1970) 308 F Supp 120. See §12.40 on injunctions. For discussion of mergers generally, see Chapter 4.

5. [§12.34] Assignment and Survival of Actions

A private right of action under the antitrust laws is assignable, and survives the death of either the plaintiff or the defendant. *Isidor Weinstein Investment Co. v Hearst Corp.* (ND Calif 1969) 303 F Supp 646. See *Hicks v Bekins Moving & Storage Co.* (9th Cir 1937) 87 F2d 583, 585; *Cinnamon v Abner A. Wolf, Inc.* (ED Mich 1963) 215 F Supp 833.

No case has been found in which an *inter vivos* assignment of the treble damage cause of action was held to convey less than a right to treble damages. In *Gerr v Schering Corp.* (SD NY 1966) 256 F Supp 572, the court says (at 574) that there is "... little doubt but that treble damage claims are assignable ...." See also *Standard Oil Co. of Calif. v Perkins* (9th Cir 1967) 396 F2d 809. Mr. Perkins ultimately prevailed. See *Perkins v Standard Oil Co. of Calif.* (1969) 395 US 642. An assignment for collection is valid, if clearly alleged. *California League of Independent Insurance Producers v Aetna Casualty & Surety Co.* (ND Calif 1959) 175 F Supp 857. The assignee must plead facts showing that his assignor would be entitled to recover. *Northern California Monument Dealers Ass'n. v Interment Ass'n.* (SD Calif 1954) 120 F Supp 93.

But the question remains whether the right to *treble* damages and attorney's fees survives. In *Rogers v Douglas Tobacco Board of Trade, Inc.* (5th Cir 1957) 244 F2d 471, 483, the Fifth Circuit said that only actual damages could be recovered from the estate of a deceased defendant. In

Haskell v Perkins (D NJ 1928) 28 F2d 222, *rev'd on other grounds* (3d Cir 1929) 31 F2d 53, *cert den* (1929) 279 US 872, the trial judge refused to treble the jury's verdict in favor of plaintiff, on motion of plaintiff's executor. The *Haskell* case has been criticized in subsequent decisions. See *Barnes Coal Corp. v Retail Coal Merchants Ass'n.* (4th Cir 1942) 128 F2d 645, 649.

The plaintiff's right to recovery probably ought to be treated as "unitary" for all purposes. Nothing in the statute suggests that the plaintiff has one cause of action for his actual damage and another for an additional two times his actual damage, plus attorney's fees. Cases attempting to characterize the private right of action are not unanimous, but there is substantial authority for treating the whole bundle of plaintiff's rights as a unit in the context of the statute of limitations (*Sun Theatre Corp. v RKO Radio Pictures, Inc.* (7th Cir 1954) 213 F2d 284). *Cf. Leh v General Petroleum Corp.* (9th Cir 1964) 330 F2d 288, 299 *rev'd* (1965) 382 US 54.

E. Impact and Damage Rules

1. [§12.35] Proving Damages

The standard of proof for the *amount* of damage is much looser than for the *fact* of damage. Once the fact of damage has been established, the amount may be proven by any evidence permitting a jury to make ". . . a just and reasonable estimate of the damage based on relevant data . . . ." *Bigelow v RKO Radio Pictures, Inc.* (1946) 327 US 251, 264.

It may be possible to prove damages by several different methods. See *Twentieth Century-Fox Film Corp. v Goldwyn* (9th Cir 1964) 328 F2d 190, 213, *cert den* (1964) 379 US 880. The limitation, for practical purposes, is cost; the *Goldwyn* record shows $117,781.58 in non-recoverable accounting expenses (328 F2d at 221-223).

A realistic estimate of damages made by the plaintiff himself may be more satisfactory than a "top dollar" computation made by a qualified expert, but based on false or questionable premises. Compare *Joseph E. Seagram and Sons, Inc. v Hawaiian Oke and Liquors, Ltd.* (9th Cir 1969) 416 F2d 71, *cert den* (1970) 396 US 1062, *reh den* (1970) 397 US 1003 and *Herman Schwabe, Inc. v United Shoe Machinery Corp.* (2d Cir 1962) 297 F2d 906, with *Story Parchment Co. v Paterson Parchment Paper Co.* (1931) 282 US 555 and *Rangen, Inc. v Sterling Nelson & Sons, Inc.* (9th Cir 1965) 351 F2d 851, 856, *cert den* (1966) 383 US 936.

The reason for the liberal rule on proof of the amount of damage is that the defendant's violation almost inevitably makes it impossible to know with precision what "might have been" in the absence of a violation.

Plaintiff ordinarily has no trouble showing from his own books and records what actually happened to him. He has invoices to show prices actually paid or received; books of account to show his actual profit or loss; his own salesman's testimony of unsuccessful attempts to sell, and his production manager's testimony on the plaintiff's capacity to deliver.

The problem is, what would have happened to the plaintiff in the absence of a violation? To establish a "competitive norm", the plaintiff must ordinarily look to some other point in time or space for a comparable business situation not tainted by antitrust violations. For example, he may look to his profit-and-loss picture at a time prior to the restraint. *American Crystal Sugar Co. v Mandeville Island Farms, Inc.* (9th Cir 1952) 195 F2d 622, 625–626. Or he may look to the market situation after the restraint, as when a government decree has dissipated, or at least reduced, the impact of the violation. *Herman Schwabe, Inc. v United Shoe Machinery Corp., supra.* He may look to contemporaneous results in a different but comparable geographic area where the impact of the restraint does not reach. *Elyria-Lorain Broadcasting Co. v Lorain Journal Co.* (6th Cir 1966) 358 F2d 790. If the damage is loss of future profits in a brand-new business, market surveys may be probative. *Kobe, Inc. v Dempsey Pump Co.* (10th Cir 1952) 198 F2d 416, 427, *cert den* (1952 344 US 837.

Should the plaintiff insist on a jury determination of damages? Or is it better to try the case to the court? There is no single answer. At one end of the spectrum, damage evidence too unreliable even to submit to a jury might sustain some damages if submitted to the court. *Herman Schwabe, supra*, at 912. Also, it may be possible to overturn a demonstrably inadequate award on appeal in a judge-tried case. *Elyria-Lorain, supra.* But for the run-of-the-mill case in which a solid damage picture can be presented, most plaintiffs' attorneys strongly favor the jury and its inscrutable verdict.

A perplexing problem is whether future damages are sufficiently clear to be recoverable in the present. The Supreme Court, in a rare departure from its liberal view of antitrust damage proof, has suggested that future lost profits that may result from continuing unlawful activity of competitors are too speculative to be recovered until they have actually occurred. See *Zenith Radio Corp. v Hazeltine Research, Inc.* (1971) 39 *Law Week* 4250.

However, there is no suggestion in *Zenith* that future damages resulting from the loss of a business or from the execution of a disadvantageous contract would not remain immediately recoverable. See discussion in *Flintkote Co. v Lysfjord* (9th Cir 1957) 246 F2d 368; §12.13, *supra.*

a. [§12.36] The Measure of Damages in Antitrust Cases

Some of the rules governing the measurement of damages in antitrust cases are common to all cases; other rules depend on the type of violation and injury alleged. General rules include the rule that the plaintiff is entitled to treble damages even though the defendant may have acted without malice. *Locklin v Day-Glo Color Corp.* (7th Cir 1970) 425 F2d 873. *Locklin* also establishes that antitrust damages shall not be increased to compensate for inflation between the injury and the date of judgment, and that the plaintiff is not entitled to interest until judgment is entered, notwithstanding the fact that the damages may have been determined much earlier by a master. See also *Trans World Airlines, Inc. v Hughes* (SD NY 1969) 308 F Supp 679.

Under the Tax Reform Act of 1969, PL 91-172 (1969), private antitrust recoveries remain generally taxable. See §12.85. Taxes are disregarded in computing plaintiff's damages. If the defendant's violation has given a plaintiff certain tax benefits, he is not required to take those benefits into account in computing his damages. Thus, in *Hanover Shoe, Inc. v United Shoe Machinery Corp.* (1968) 392 US 481, Hanover Shoe claimed damages arising out of United Shoe Machinery's practice of leasing shoe machinery rather than selling it. Hanover "expensed" its rental payments, thereby obtaining tax deductions larger than those it would have obtained if it had purchased shoe machinery and depreciated it. Hanover was not required to take its tax savings into account in computing damages. The Supreme Court said (392 US at 503): ". . . the rough result of not taking account of taxes for the year of injury but then taxing recovery when received seems the most satisfactory outcome."

In addition to the principles applicable to all types of private antitrust cases, there are special rules that depend on the type of case involved and the nature of the injury.

In an "overcharge" case, the damages are the amount of the overcharge. See *Chattanooga Foundry and Pipe Works v Atlanta* (1906) 203 US 390, 396; *Thomsen v Cayser* (1917) 243 US 66, 88.

In *American Crystal Sugar Co. v Mandeville Island Farms, Inc.* (9th Cir 1952) 195 F2d 622, 625, dealing with un underpayment (the mirror image of an overcharge), the Ninth Circuit said:

The measure is concededly the difference, trebled, between the amounts actually realized by appellees during the critical crop years from the sale of their beets to Crystal, and what they would have realized during the period had the unlawful price fixing combination not been in existence.

In "exclusion" cases, the measure of damages is loss of net profit on the lost business. *Rangen, Inc. v Sterling Nelson & Sons, Inc.* (9th Cir 1965) 351 F2d 851, *cert den* (1966) 383 US 936; *Richfield Oil Corp. v Karseal Corp.* (9th Cir 1959) 271 F2d 709. Loss of profit may be shown to result from an increase in costs due to the violation. *Atlas Building Products Co. v Diamond Block & Gravel Co.* (10th Cir 1959) 269 F2d 950, 958–959, *cert den* (1960) 363 US 843.

Plaintiff may recover "loss of profit" damages although its business remained profitable on an overall basis. *Mechanical Contractors Bid Depository v Christiansen* (10th Cir 1965) 352 F2d 817, 821, *cert den* (1966) 384 US 918; *Herman Schwabe, Inc. v United Shoe Machinery Corp.* (2d Cir 1962) 297 F2d 906, 910.

If the general level of market prices has been reduced to the plaintiff's detriment, he recovers the difference between prices obtained and prices that would have been obtained in the absence of the violation. *Story Parchment Co. v Paterson Parchment Paper Co.* (1931) 282 US 555, 561–562.

In "destruction of business" cases, damages for loss of going concern are recoverable. *Story Parchment, supra; Farmington Dowel Products Co. v Forster Mfg. Co.* (1st Cir 1969) 421 F2d 61. Damages for injury to good will may be recovered even if the plaintiff's business has not been totally destroyed. *Atlas Building Products Co. v Diamond Block & Gravel Co., supra; Bruce's Juices, Inc. v American Can Co.* (SD Fla 1949) 87 F Supp 985, *aff'd* (5th Cir 1951) 187 F2d 919.

If there is enough "commerce" to support proof of an antitrust violation, damages for *all* injury may be recovered, including injury resulting from intrastate transactions. *Perryton Wholesale, Inc. v Pioneer Distributing Co.* (10th Cir 1965) 353 F2d 618, 623, *cert den* (1966) 383 US 945.

It seems to have been generally assumed that in "primary line" discrimination cases (see §§5.39 12.21); the measure of damages is the same as in other "competitor" cases—plaintiff must prove loss of profits or loss of goodwill or both. *Atlas Building Products Co. v Diamond Block & Gravel Co., supra.*

In "secondary line" discrimination cases (see §§5.40, 12.21), the rule is much less certain. For simplicity of proof, it would be desirable for plaintiff to prove damages by the difference between the price it paid (or the services or allowances it received) and the prices (or services or allowances) which it would have received if it had been given the same beneficial treatment as its more fortunate competitors. In fact, however, this rule has not prevailed and the cases on measure of damages are in serious conflict. In *Enterprise Industries, Inc. v Texas Co.* (2d Cir 1957) 240 F2d 457, 458–460, *cert den* (1957) 353 US 965, plaintiff's case was dismissed for failure to show "consequential" damages in the form of lost profits resulting from a price discrimination in favor of the plaintiff's competitors. The Second Circuit reversed a judgment for the plaintiff based on the difference between the price plaintiff was required to pay for gasoline and the price given its favored competitors. The case has been followed in the Second Circuit. See *Guyott Co. v Texaco, Inc.* (D Conn 1966) 261 F Supp 942. It is discussed and followed in *Sano Petroleum Corp. v American Oil Co.* (ED NY 1960) 187 F Supp 345 at 357.

The Ninth Circuit has held to the contrary in *Fowler Manufacturing Co. v Gorlick* (9th Cir 1969) 415 F2d 1248, *cert den* (1966) 396 US 1012. See also *State Wholesale Grocers v Great Atlantic and Pacific Tea Co.* (ND Ill 1961) 202 F Supp 768.

Insofar as the rule of *Enterprise Industries, Inc., supra,* requiring proof of "consequential damages" is based on the proposition that a discriminatory price is an overcharge that may have been "passed on," it would not seem to survive the Supreme Court's decision in *Hanover Shoe, Inc. v United Shoe Machinery Corp.* (1968) 392 US 481.

The picture becomes even more complicated if the amount of the discrimination and the consequential damages of the discrimination are treated as alternative remedies. The question then becomes whether the amount of the discrimination becomes a "ceiling" or a "floor" for the plaintiff's possible recovery. In *Bruce's Juices, Inc. v American Can Co.* (1947) 330 US 743, 757, the Supreme Court said "if the prices are illegally discriminatory, petitioner has been damaged, in the absence of extraordinary circumstances, at least in the amount of that discrimination." See also *Reid v Doubleday and Co.* (ND Ohio 1955) 136 F Supp 337, a price discrimination case holding that the disadvantaged purchaser is not necessarily limited to damages based on the amount of the discrimination, but may be able to collect consequential damages on sales lost due to his inability to compete. Setting a ceiling rather than a floor was *Sun Cosmetic Shoppe, Inc. v Elizabeth Arden Sales Corp.* (2d Cir 1949) 178 F2d 150, dealing with promotional allowances. Judge Hand suggested that the discrimination set the maximum amount of damages, since plaintiff would be required to advertise or hire a demonstrator if the defendant discriminatorily refused to assist him, and the measure of the plaintiff's damages would be his cost in obtaining the advertising or promotional services the defendant had wrongfully failed to provide.

b. [§12.37] Measure of Damage; Unincorporated Plaintiffs

If plaintiff is a natural person and the damages consist of loss of the business, proof of the amount of damages is somewhat more complex. The plaintiff is entitled to "reasonably anticipated future profits." *Lessig v Tidewater Oil Co.* (9th Cir 1964) 327 F2d 459, 464, *cert den* (1964) 377 US 993.

Put another way, plaintiff is entitled to the value of his business as a going concern measured by the profit the business has made after deducting an amount fairly attributable to the return on capital and the labor of the owner, and the reasonable prospect that this profit would have continued into the future, judged by the circumstances existing and known as of the date of the injury. See *Simpson v Union Oil* (9th Cir 1969) 411 F2d 897, 909, *rev'd on other grounds* (1969) 396 US 13.

Following the *Simpson* approach, net profits would be computed as if the owner had been paying himself a salary out of the revenue of his business. The business would be valued on the basis of its past and prospective profit picture after deduction of the owner's imputed wage. This approach requires that the owner wear two hats—employee and entrepreneur—in making the damage calculation.

The Ninth Circuit's opinion in *Simpson* leaves one important ambiguity: Is the deduction for the value of the plaintiff's own labor based on what he might have made in the same line of work as a laborer? Or is it based on what someone else would have been paid to do the owner's job? Or could it be based on what plaintiff might have earned in some other line of work? A valuation based on what plaintiff would have had to pay someone else to do the same work without taking any entrepreneurial risk seems most appropriate.

2. [§12.38] A Reasonable Attorney's Fee

Section 4 of the Clayton Act, 15 USC §15, entitles the successful plaintiff to a reasonable attorney's fee. The amount of the fee is established by the trial court, not the jury. Recovery is for the benefit of the plaintiff, not his counsel; the award neither controls nor is it controlled by the arrangement the attorney had made with his client. See *Milwaukee Towne Corp. v Loew's, Inc.* (7th Cir 1951) 190 F2d 561, 570, *cert den* (1952) 342 US 909. Factors to be considered by the trial judge in establishing a reasonable attorney's fee are said to include:

(1) Whether plaintiff's counsel had the benefit of a prior judgment or decree in a case brought by the government;

(2) The standing of counsel at the bar—both counsel receiving the award and opposing counsel;

(3) Time and labor spent;

(4) Magnitude and complexity of the litigation;

(5) Responsibility undertaken;

(6) The amount recovered;

(7) The knowledge that the court has of the conferences, arguments that were presented, and work done by the attorney for plaintiff prior to trial;

(8) What it would be reasonable for counsel to charge a victorious plaintiff.

See *Bal Theatre Corp. v Paramount Film Distributing Corp.* (ND Calif 1962) 206 F Supp 708, 716. Reasonableness is not to be decided as though the fee were a contingency. *Twentieth Century-Fox Film Corp. v Brookside Theatre Corp.* (8th Cir 1952) 194 F2d 846, *cert den* (1952) 343 US 942.

Awards have varied considerably in amount. A table of fee awards in a number of cases appears in *Hanover Shoe, Inc. v United Shoe Machinery Corp.* (MD Pa 1965) 245 F Supp 258, at 304. Generally speaking, the ratio of attorney's fee to trebled damages has been substantially greater in small-recovery cases than in very large cases. For example, in *Darden v Besser* (6th Cir 1958) 257 F2d 285, an award of $10,000 for attorney's fees was reversed as inadequate and $30,000 allowed on a recovery (after trebling) of $45,000. In *Twentieth Century Fox Film Corp. v Goldwyn* (9th Cir 1964) 328 F2d 190, *cert den* (1964) 379 US 880, a marathon case, the fee award was $100,000 as against $300,000 in treble damages (328 F2d at 221-222). In *Union Carbide and Carbon Corp. v Nisley* (10th Cir 1961) 300 F2d 561, a multi-million dollar case, 15% of the trebled amount was suggested as a reasonable attorney's fee (300 F2d at 587).

In *Courtesy Chevrolet, Inc. v Tennessee Walking Horse Breeders' & Exhibitors' Association* (9th Cir 1968) 393 F2d 75, *cert den* (1968) 393 US 938, the plaintiff had appealed from an award of damages and attorney fees on the grounds that both were inadequate ($10,200 in damages, after trebling; $5,000 in attorney fees). The Ninth Circuit reluctantly affirmed the damage award as "not clearly erroneous" but doubled the attorney fee award to $10,000. (The record contained testimony in which "a highly respected and competent member of the Los Angeles Bar estimated reasonable attorneys' fees for plaintiff in this case at $140,000 to $150,000." (393 F2d at 77.) The plaintiff has since filed a petition for certiorari.

For work done on appeal, the Court of Appeals may make an additional award. See *Twentieth Century-Fox Film Corp. v Goldwyn, supra,* at 222, 226; *Sanitary Milk Producers v Bergjans Farm Dairy, Inc.* (8th Cir 1966) 368 F2d 679, 692, and cases cited. *But cf. Washington State Bowling Proprietors Association v Pacific Lanes, Inc.* (9th Cir 1966) 356 F2d 371, 381, *cert den* (1966) 384 US 963.

Attorney's fees are probably not recoverable in an injunction suit under 15 USC §26. See *Ring v Spina* (SD NY 1949) 84 F Supp 403, 408, *modified* (2d Cir 1951) 186 F2d 637, *cert den* (1951) 341 US 935; *cf. Courtesy Chevrolet, supra.*

No attorney fees are allowable for the successful defense of a private antitrust action. *Byram Concretanks, Inc. v Warren Concrete Products Co.* (3d Cir 1967) 374 F2d 649.

3. [§12.39] Recovery of Taxable Costs

The costs recoverable under 15 USC §15 are those recoverable by the prevailing party in any sort of litigation. See 28 USC §§1920, 1923. In addition to filing and docket fees, taxable costs may include such expensive items as depositions and trial transcripts. See *Independent Iron Works, Inc. v United States Steel Corp.* (9th Cir 1963) 322 F2d 656, 678, *cert den* (1963) 375 US 922.

On the other hand, the Supreme Court recently upheld a district court (and reversed an *en banc* decision of the Second Circuit), holding that the cost of a *daily* transcript in a reasonably uncomplicated personal injury trial could not be recovered. *Farmer v Arabian American Oil Company* (1964) 379 US 227. In the same decision, the Supreme Court approved the trial court's decision not to allow travel expenses of witnesses beyond 100 miles from the location of the trial, although intimating that there might be circumstances under which the trial court would have discretion to award travel costs for longer journeys.

The expenses of accounting studies made by the plaintiff in order to prove liability and damages may not be recovered. See *Twentieth Century-Fox Film Corp. v Goldwyn* (9th Cir 1964) 328 F2d 190, 223–224, *cert den* (1964) 379 US 880. A big case can also result in substantial non-recoverable expenses for attorney's travel. See *Hanover Shoe, Inc. v United Shoe Machinery Corp.* (MD Pa 1965) 245 F Supp 258, 305, *vacated* (3d Cir 1967) 377 F2d 776, *remanded* (1968) 392 US 481.

The trial court retains substantial discretion, however, to tax or not tax various costs. See, *e.g., Advance Business Systems & Supply Co. v SCM Corp.* (D Md 1968) 287 F Supp 143, *modified and remanded* (4th Cir 1969) 415 F2d 55, *cert den* (1970) 379 US 920. In a large case, costs can be substantial, notwithstanding the limitations on recoverable items. In

Trans World Airlines, Inc. v Hughes (SD NY 1970) 312 F Supp 478, amounts recovered were apparently as follows: Damages, $137,611,435.95; attorneys' fees, $7,500,000; costs, $336,705.12. (Inferred from 312 F Supp 478, 485 and 314 F Supp 94.) At that, the costs awarded were well short of the $2,230,602 claimed by TWA. See 312 F Supp at 479.

F. [§12.40] Injunctions

A successful plaintiff may have injunctive relief against threatened future loss or damage under the antitrust laws pursuant to Section 16 of the Clayton Act, 15 USC §26. If plaintiff can show immediate danger of irreparable loss or damage, and posts a bond, he may obtain a preliminary injunction. If the plaintiff is solvent, the bond may be dispensed with. *Continental Oil Co. v Frontier Refining Co.* (10th Cir 1964) 338 F2d 780.

Plaintiffs have had considerable success in enjoining takeovers by other companies under circumstances in which the acquisitions might violate Section 7 of the Clayton Act (15 USC §18). See §12.33.

As a practical matter, the plaintiff's biggest problem is showing immediate danger of irreparable loss. Treble damages are a highly satisfactory remedy, as legal remedies go. Moreover, the filing of a treble damage suit challenging a continuing practice forces the prudent defendant to look closely at the practice, since he may be piling up additional damages that could be avoided by stopping or modifying the practice. Consequently, the filing of a treble damage action, even without a prayer for injunctive relief, may well produce much the same result as an injunction would. For these reasons, and because many antitrust plaintiffs are unable to afford the legal expense (which cannot be recovered) of obtaining an injunction, injunctions are not commonly sought and are even less often granted.

The basic papers in support of a motion for an injunction should include:

1. The motion itself, in very brief form, stating generally the substance of the injunction sought, and referring to an attached proposed form of order providing the relief sought.

2. Affidavits of competent witnesses setting out, in as much detail as is practical and reasonable, the facts that would justify the granting of the motion. The affidavits should incorporate any attached documents, excerpts from depositions, or other evidentiary matter that is available and should affirmatively show the competence of the affiants.

3. A memorandum of points and authorities, organizing and marshalling those facts that would justify the court in granting the injunction, and that are best calculated to sell the idea that the injunction not only may but should be granted.

Within limits, the District Court has considerable discretion to grant or deny a preliminary injunction pendente lite. The main factors considered in granting or denying preliminary injunctions are:

1. The probability that plaintiff will ultimately succeed.
2. Whether the injunction is to maintain the status quo or to change it.
3. Whether plaintiff's injury is really irreparable.
4. Degree of hardship to the defendant during the course of the litigation.

Plaintiffs have sought preliminary injunctions, with varying success, in a variety of situations. In *Continental Oil, supra,* a price-discrimination case, the Tenth Circuit upheld a preliminary injunction designed to maintain the spread between major and minor brand gasoline prices at a pre-price-war level. But a plaintiff attempting to prevent predatory pricing has failed for lack of proof that the pricing was more than merely competitive. See *General Gas Corp. v National Utilities of Gainesville, Inc.* (5th Cir 1959) 271 F2d 820.

In "refusal to deal" cases, there is a split on whether a defendant may stop dealing with the plaintiff because he has been sued. In *House of Materials, Inc. v Simplicity Pattern Co.* (2d Cir 1962) 298 F2d 867, the Second Circuit reversed an order granting a plaintiff a preliminary injunction against defendant's termination of contract. In *Bergen Drug Co. v Parke, Davis & Co.* (3d Cir 1962) 307 F2d 725, the Third Circuit reversed the lower court's *denial* of a preliminary injunction. The *Bergen* case would seem to embody the more persuasive reasoning. See Farber, *The Antitrust Treble Damage Defendant's Duty to Continue Business Dealings with the Plaintiff Pendente Lite—A Two Case Study* (1963) 8 *Antitrust Bulletin* 883. See also §13.51.

In *Semmes Motors, Inc. v Ford Motor Co.* (2d Cir 1970) 429 F2d 1197, a Ford dealer obtained an injunction against termination of his dealership pendente lite, notwithstanding evidence that he had defrauded his customers and Ford with phony repair and warranty claims. In affirming the grant of a preliminary injunction against cancellation of Semmes' dealership, the Second Circuit relied on the "imbalance of hardship" as between Semmes and Ford, noting that "affirmance of the temporary injunction does not depend on a holding that Semmes had demonstrated a likelihood of success. . . ."

Policy considerations in cases in which a franchisee seeks an injunction against his franchisor are different from those in cases in which a competitor seeks an injunction against another competitor. In the franchisor-franchisee situation, it may be possible for a franchisee to continue to operate notwithstanding the fact that he is at swords' points with his franchisor; regardless of the animosity, franchisor and franchisee have a common interest in the success of the franchisee's operation. There is no such "common interest" between competitors. Thus, in *H.B. Fletcher Co. v Rock of Ages Corp.* (2d Cir 1963) 326 F2d 13, the court denied an injunction compelling a defendant to supply his competitor.

It has been held not an abuse of discretion to deny an injunction on the ground that treble damages are an adequate remedy at law. *Graham v Triangle Publications, Inc.* (3d Cir 1965) 344 F2d 775. But when the effect of a refusal to deal is to create wide and hard-to-measure repercussions for the plaintiff's business, the injunction has been granted. *McKesson and Robbins, Inc. v Charles Pfizer & Co.* (ED Pa 1964) 235 F Supp 743.

The injury to the defendant arising from *granting* the injunction is also a factor that is considered. If there is no real harm to the defendant in granting the injunction, it is more likely to be granted. See *e.g., Crane Co. v Briggs Manufacturing Co.* (6th Cir 1960) 280 F2d 747.

If the plaintiff has prevailed in a private treble-damage suit, a permanent injunction may be appropriate. *Volasco Products Co. v Lloyd A. Fry Roofing Co.* (6th Cir 1965) 346 F2d 661, 667, *cert den* (1965) 382 US 904. Any problems subsequently arising under the injunction can be handled by application to the trial court for modification, even if the district court has not expressly reserved power to modify. See *Volasco, supra; Continental Oil Co. v Frontier Refining Co., supra; cf. Adelman v Paramount Pictures, Inc.* (5th Cir 1961) 296 F2d 308, *cert den* (1962) 369 US 851.

Attorney's fees are not awarded for the successful prosecution of an injunction suit under 15 USC §26, but are of course awarded for successful prosecution of a treble-damage case in which an injunction is also obtained. *Volasco Products Co., supra.*

G. Pleading and Procedure

1. [§12.41] The Complaint

The antitrust complaint, like other complaints in federal court, should be short and to the point. FRCP 8(a). See *Walker Distributing Co. v*

Lucky Lager Brewing Co. (9th Cir 1963) 323 F2d 1; Lavine and Horning, *Manual of Federal Practice* (1967) Chapter 3. The essential elements are statements of:

(1) The basis of federal jurisdiction;
(2) The basis of venue;
(3) The basis of the claim; and
(4) The relief sought.

For a sample complaint, see §§12.42–12.50.

a. [§12.42] Title and Demand for Jury

IN THE UNITED STATES DISTRICT COURT FOR THE
_____DISTRICT OF_____

ASTOUNDINGLY BETTER COMMODITIES CORPORATION,

	Plaintiff,	**No._____**

v.   **COMPLAINT**

SUPERCOLOSSAL TITANIC UNDERTAKINGS, INC. and   **JURY DEMANDED**
VULCAN WORKS CORPORATION,

Defendants.

COMMENT: For safety's sake, the demand for a jury should be endorsed on the face of the complaint as permitted by FRCP 38(b). Jury trial is a constitutional right, but may be waived by failure to demand a jury within ten days after filing the complaint. FRCP 38(d).

b. [§12.43] Pleading Jurisdiction and Venue

I
JURISDICTION AND VENUE

1. This complaint is filed pursuant to, and this Court has jurisdiction of the matters complained of under, Sections 4 and 16 of the Clayton Act, 38 Stat §§ 731 and 737, 15 USC §§15 and 26.

2. The alleged unlawful acts and violations hereinafter described have been and are in part conceived, carried out, and made effective within the _____ District of ____(name of state)____, _____Division and many of the unlawful acts

pursuant thereto have been performed by defendants in this district _____and divi-
sion_____. **The interstate trade and commerce described hereinafter is carried out
in part within this district** _____and division_____. **Each defendant transacts business in
this district** _____and division_____.

COMMENT: The statutes referred to in Paragraph 1 are the basis of
federal jurisdiction of private claims under the antitrust laws for damages
(Section 4 of the Clayton Act, 15 USC §15) and for injunctions (Section
16 of the Clayton Act, 15 USC §26).

Roman numeral headings and general topic headings (*i.e.*, JURISDIC-
TION AND VENUE) are helpful in reading a complaint and should be
used. Note, however, that the rules require that the *paragraphs* of a
complaint be numbered and that each be limited to a single subject
matter, as far as possible. FRCP 10(b). Even if several counts are used,
paragraphs should be numbered serially throughout the complaint; it is
confusing to have two paragraphs bearing the same number in the same
complaint.

Interstate commerce, here alleged generally, is the "handle" for federal
jurisdiction. Further reference to facts showing interstate commerce
should be made where appropriate in later parts of the complaint if it
appears that "commerce" will be a real issue in the case.

c. [§12.44] Pleading the Parties

II
DESCRIPTION OF THE PARTIES

**3. Plaintiff Astoundingly Better Commodities Corporation (hereinafter
"ABC") is a California corporation with its principal place of business in Los
Angeles.**

**4. Defendant Supercolossal Titanic Undertakings, Inc. (hereinafter "STU") is
a Delaware corporation with its principal place of business in Kansas City,
Missouri.**

**5. Defendant Vulcan Works Corporation (hereinafter "VW") is a Delaware
corporation with its principal place of business in Bakersfield, California.**

**6. XYZ Corporation (hereinafter "XYZ") is an Ohio corporation with its
principal place of business in Ohio. XYZ is named herein as a co-conspirator
of defendants STU and VW but not as a defendant.**

COMMENT: The draftsman should resist the temptation to launch into a
discussion of the facts of the case in connection with a description of the
parties. If co-conspirators are to be referred to in the rest of the com-

plaint, it should be made clear which parties are defendants and which are non-defendant co-conspirators. A plaintiff is not required to make all the conspirators defendants. *Walker Distributing Co. v Lucky Lager Brewing Co.* (9th Cir 1963) 323 F2d 1, 8. Counsel should have correctly identified the defendants. Large corporations commonly have numerous subsidiaries and a complicated corporate structure that makes it difficult to decide who should be sued.

d. [§12.45] Pleading Trade and Commerce

III
THE NATURE OF TRADE AND COMMERCE

7. STU is the world's largest manufacturer of whiffling machines. Its sales in the United States account for approximately 90% of all such machines sold. VW and XYZ are major users of whiffling machines and are major buyers of such machines from STU. STU sells, and VW and XYZ as well as numerous other purchasers, buy STU's whiffling machines, which are shipped from STU's plant in Kansas City to customers, including VW and XYZ, in other states.

8. The average life of STU's machinery is approximately twenty years. Over the course of their service, STU's whiffling machines require numerous spare and replacement parts. Most of such parts are supplied by STU. ABC makes parts that can be used on STU's machines and sells them in competition with STU throughout the United States. VW and XYZ are potential purchasers from defendant STU and plaintiff ABC.

COMMENT: Counsel should continue to resist the temptation to talk about the violations. At this stage, it is sufficient to explain the relationships between the parties, the general nature of the business structure and transactions, and the element of interstate commerce.

e. [§12.46] Pleading the Offenses

IV
OFFENSES CHARGED

9. In December, 1969, plaintiff ABC invented and developed a new and improved ratchet for use on whiffling machines manufactured by STU. Plaintiff ABC thereupon began to sell its new and improved ratchets to users of STU machinery, including defendant VW and co-conspirator XYZ. ABC's sales efforts were successful, and its customers expressed thorough satisfaction with the improved ABC ratchets. Approximately one year after ABC began sales of its improved ratchets, defendant VW and co-conspirator XYZ informed ABC

that they would no longer purchase ratchets from ABC. ABC is informed and believes that the refusal of VW and of XYZ to purchase ratchets from it after December, 1969 is a result of the unlawful acts of defendants STU, VW and XYZ, as hereinafter alleged.

10. ABC is informed and believes that STU has sold, leased, or discounted, or contracted to sell, lease or discount, its whiffling machines to VW, to XYZ, and to others on condition that they refrain from dealing with other sellers, including ABC. These arrangements constitute contracts, combinations, and conspiracies in restraint of trade and commerce in violation of Section 1 of the Sherman Act, 15 USC §1. They are reasonably likely to substantially lessen competition or tend to create a monopoly in spare and replacement ratchets for whiffling machines manufactured by STU, in violation of Section 3 of the Clayton Act, 15 USC §14.

11. By various means, not all of which are known to plaintiff, but which ABC is informed and believes include, without limitation, price-cutting on replacement ratchets of its own manufacture; disparagement of ABC's products; and threats of refusals to continue to deal with VW, XYZ, and others, STU has attempted to monopolize the business of supplying replacement ratchets to users of whiffling machines manufactured by STU, all in violation of Section 2 of the Sherman Act, 15 USC §2.

12. By the various means hereinbefore alleged, STU has prevented all of its competitors from selling in, and has in fact monopolized throughout the United States, the market for replacement ratchets for whiffling machines manufactured by STU in violation of Section 2 of the Sherman Act, 15 USC §2.

COMMENT: The facts that show the nature of the restraint and its impact on plaintiff should be pleaded in general terms. Here, plaintiff got started in a business and was then shut out. This is, in other words, an "exclusion" case.

In many plaintiff's cases, the nature of the violation may not be entirely clear and it is perfectly possible that the defendants' conduct violates several different sections of the antitrust laws. Although several different statutes are alleged to be violated, it is cumbersome and unnecessary to plead in separate counts; it is sufficient that the complaint separately states the violations and clearly indicates which defendant is accused of each of the violations alleged.

Pleading in the language of the statutes is cumbersome at times, but may prove to be a complaint-saver on a motion to dismiss. *Cf. Walker Distributing Co. v Lucky Lager Brewing Co.* (9th Cir 1963) 323 F2d 1, 9.

Examples of allegations of other offenses include:

(a) Basic cartel allegations:

Defendants have combined, contracted, and conspired with each other and with other non-defendant co-conspirators to eliminate competition between themselves and to suppress or eliminate the competition of others by, without limitation, the following means and methods:___(Set out all types of cartel activity known, such as price fixing, predatory price cutting, false representations, bribery, commercial espionage, intentional below-cost selling, tie-ins, exclusive dealing, inducing boycotts, inducing reciprocal dealings, fomenting labor unrest, sabotage, threats, coercion, arson, and anything else that fits the facts.)___**This agreement between defendants violates Sections 1 and 2 of the Sherman Act, 15 USC §§1 and 2.**

(b) Horizontal price-fixing:

Defendants have combined, contracted, and conspired with each other and with other non-defendant co-conspirators to fix, raise, and stabilize the prices at which they would sell ___(name of products)___ **.**

(c) Vertical price-fixing:

Defendant has compelled its franchisees, including plaintiff, as a condition of obtaining and retaining their franchises, to resell ___(name of products)___ **purchased from defendant only at prices established by defendant in violation of Section 1 of the Sherman Act, 15 USC §1.**

(d) Vertical restrictions typically contained in resale franchise:

As a condition of selling to plaintiff, defendant has, over plaintiff's objection and solely for its own benefit, insisted that plaintiff resell its products ___at prices/on terms/only to certain limited geographical areas___ **dictated by defendant. These restraints are restrictions on plaintiff's freedom to compete** ___at prices/in a manner___ **of its own choosing, and unreasonably restrain trade in violation of Section 1 of the Sherman Act, 15 USC §1.**

COMMENT: The fact that a plaintiff may have participated with its supplier in a contract that contains restrictions in violation of the antitrust laws does not necessarily prevent the purchaser from suing the supplier, even though both purchaser and supplier might be subject to prosecution by the government or liable in treble damages to any third parties who could show injury as a result. See §12.69. However, it may be important to show that although the plaintiff is a participant in the restrictive agreement, the restrictions on which he is basing his suit are restrictions of which he is the victim, not the proponent.

593

(e) Catch-all allegations:

All of the foregoing offenses charged against defendant were in furtherance of an attempt by defendant to monopolize, and defendant's actual monopolization, of the market for ____(name of product)___ in ____(geographical area)___ in violation of Section 2 of the Sherman Act, 15 USC §2.

COMMENT: Since violations of the antitrust laws commonly overlap and interlock, it may be advisable to include a general allegation tying together all of the specific types of offenses separately alleged (*i.e.*, discriminatory pricing, tying contracts, vertical price-fixing, customer and territorial restraints, etc.) as part of an overall anti-competitive plan.

f. [§12.47] Pleading Injury to the Plaintiff

V
INJURY TO THE PLAINTIFF
13. By reason of and as a direct and proximate result of the unlawful conduct alleged in paragraphs 10, 11, and 12, ABC has been injured in that:
(a) It has lost profits by reason of lost sales that it would have made in the absence of those violations;
(b) To the extent that it has been able to make sales, ABC has been obliged to sell at prices lower than it would have been able to charge under freely competitive conditions; and
(c) It has suffered a substantial injury to its good will as a result of defendants' violations.

COMMENT: In a case of this sort, the injury to the plaintiff arises out of what the defendants did, and not out of any particular statutes they violated. A general allegation of the nature of the injury should be sufficient.

Plaintiff is not required to treat each of the defendant's objectionable acts or practices as a separate violation of the antitrust laws if they are in fact parts of an overall scheme that violates the antitrust laws. Plaintiff should not attempt to subdivide its damage claim, either. Compare *Continental Ore Co. v Union Carbide & Carbon Corp.* (1962) 370 US 690.

Examples of allegations of other kinds of injury include:

(a) Refusal-to-deal cases:

As a direct and proximate result of the foregoing violations, plaintiff has been injured in its business and property in that it has been unable to obtain defendant's products, has lost the profit that would otherwise have obtained in reselling those products, and has suffered greatly in its goodwill and going concern value by reason of its inability to offer defendant's products to its customers.

(b) If the plaintiff's business is destroyed:

As a direct and proximate result of the foregoing violations, plaintiff's business has been irrevocably and completely destroyed and its value reduced from a value that plaintiff conservatively estimates at _____ to approximately _____, representing its salvage value.

(c) Price-fixing cases—plaintiff as purchaser:

As a direct and proximate result of the foregoing violations, plaintiff has been injured in its business and property in that it has been forced to pay prices for products of defendants and their co-conspirators substantially higher than the prices it would have paid in the absence of those violations.

(d) Price fixing cases—plaintiff as seller:

As a direct and proximate result of the foregoing violations, plaintiff has been injured in its business and property in that it has received for its products prices substantially lower than the prices it would have received in the absence of those violations.

(e) Vertical restraints; restrictions on resale price, territory, or customers:

As a direct and proximate result of the foregoing violations, plaintiff has been injured in its business and property in that it has lost the profits it would have obtained had it been free to offer defendant's goods for resale at prices _____to customers/to customers located in places_____ of its own choosing.

595

(f) Requirements contracts and tying contracts:

As a direct and proximate result of the foregoing violations, plaintiff has been injured in its business and property in that it has been forced to pay substantially more for the _____(name tied products)____than it would have been required to pay had it been free to purchase the _____(name tied products)____at competitive prices on the open market.

g. [§12.48] Pleading the Amount of Damages

VI
DAMAGES

Plaintiff does not now know the full extent of its damages, but believes that its total damages from all causes alleged above exceed $1,000,000. At such time as plaintiff has ascertained more clearly the extent of its damages, it will seek leave to amend to allege them.

COMMENT: It is not necessary to plead a monetary amount of damages if damages are unascertained or for practical purposes unascertainable at the pleading stage. Neither is it necessary to allocate damages to particular violations or to particular types of injury; discovery will crystalize the damage facts and theories in due course. See Timberlake, *Federal Treble Damage Antitrust Actions* (1965) 67. *But cf. California League of Independent Insurance Producers v Aetna Casualty & Surety Co.* (ND Calif 1959) 175 F Supp 857.

If a damage figure is mentioned, it should be a reasonable estimate of the probable actual damage recovery. There is no need to plead absurd figures; amendment of damage allegations upwards is freely allowed if the damage allegation turns out to be conservative.

h. [§12.49] Prayer for Relief

VII
PRAYER FOR RELIEF

WHEREFORE plaintiff prays:

1. That defendants be adjudged to have violated the antitrust laws as hereinbefore alleged;

2. That the actual damages to plaintiff's business and property proximately resulting from those violations be determined;

3. That plaintiff have judgment for three times the amount of its actual damages, together with costs and a reasonable attorney's fee, as required by law;

4. That defendants be enjoined from further violation of the antitrust laws;

5. That plaintiff have such other and further relief as the court may deem proper.

Dated:_____

_____Attorney for Plaintiff_____

COMMENT: The prayer is a necessary part of the complaint. FRCP 8(a). It may be quite general. In this example, it asks for a determination of *actual* damage by the trier of fact, but *judgment* for three times that amount. The trier of fact should not be encouraged to have anything to do with trebling. See §12.73. The prayer for injunctive relief is general; it may be the basis of whatever injunctive relief seems appropriate when all of the facts are in.

i. [§12.50] Pleading Special Matters

(a) Pleading a related government action:

Plaintiff's right of action is based in part on matters complained of in a civil proceeding instituted on _____ **by the United States in the** _____Federal Trade Commission/ United States District Court for the _____ District of _____ entitled _____(name of case)_____ . **That proceeding was instituted by the United States to prevent, restrain, and punish violations of the antitrust laws, and** _____is still pending/was dismissed on _____/resulted in a judgment which became final on _____ . **The statute of limitations on plaintiffs' right of action was tolled by the pendency of that proceeding from** _____(the date the government action was commenced)_____ **to the date of the filing of this complaint.**

COMMENT: In addition to pleading the government action, it may be desirable to incorporate into the plaintiff's complaint any relevant charging allegations of the government's indictment or complaint in the words used by the government, even if they would not otherwise have been the words chosen by the private plaintiff's attorney, so as to clearly demonstrate the close relationship between the private action and a prior government action for purposes of tolling the statute of limitations and of using a government victory as prima facie evidence in the private case under Section 5 of the Clayton Act, 15 USC §16.

(b) Pleading fraudulent concealment:

Plaintiff had no knowledge of the violations of the antitrust laws hereinbefore alleged, or of any facts that might have led to their discovery and it first became aware of the unlawful conduct alleged by _____ e.g., the institution of government proceedings against defendants in _____ /a conversation between _____ and _____ on _____ . **Plaintiffs could not have uncovered the violations at an earlier date by the exercise of due diligence inasmuch as the violations have been fraudulently concealed by defendants through various means and methods designed to avoid detection.**

H. [§12.51] Venue and Change of Venue

The "general" venue provisions for private actions under the antitrust laws are contained in Section 4 of the Clayton Act, 15 USC §15, which provides that suit may be brought ". . . in the district in which the defendant resides or is found or has an agent . . .."

There is an even broader provision governing venue over corporations contained in Section 12 of the Clayton Act, 15 USC § 22, which provides that a private action ". . . may be brought not only in the judicial district whereof [the corporation] is an inhabitant, but also in any district wherein it may be found or transacts business . . .." The "transacts business" language ordinarily permits the plaintiff to bring suit against a corporation in the district where the plaintiff was injured and presumably resides. See Annotation (1970) 3 ALR Fed 120.

It is not clear whether it is sufficient that the defendant corporation was transacting business in the district where suit is brought at the time of the injury. *Eastland Construction Co. v Keasbey and Mattison Co.* (9th Cir 1966) 358 F2d 777 so holds. *Stern Fish Co. v Century Seafoods, Inc.* (ED Pa 1966) 254 F Supp 151 on the other hand, holds that 15 USC §22 is couched in the present tense and that the defendant must be doing business in the district at the time of suit in order to sustain venue. *Hawkins v National Basketball Association* (WD Pa 1968) 288 F Supp 614 goes one step further, and states that defendant must be transacting business both at the time the complaint is filed and at the time the cause of action arose.

The "transacting business" test has been broadly construed to permit suit in a district where the defendant has minimal business contacts. See *B.J. Semel Associates, Inc. v United Fireworks Manufacturing Co.* (DC Cir 1965) 355 F2d 827; *Courtesy Chevrolet, Inc. v Tennessee Walking Horse Breeders' & Exhibitors' Association* (9th Cir 1965) 344 F2d 860.

On the other hand, not every contact of any kind has been held sufficient to support venue. See, *e.g.*, *Philadelphia Housing Authority v American Radiator & Standard Sanitary Corp.* (ED Pa 1968) 291 F Supp 252; 309 F Supp 1053; *Stern Fish Co. v Century Seafoods, Inc.* (ED Pa 1966) 254 F Supp 151; *Rhode Island Fittings Co. v Grinnell Corp.* (D RI 1963) 215 F Supp 198.

Some ingenious ideas have been developed for obtaining venue by indirection. For example, in *Giusti v Pyrotechnic Industries, Inc.* (9th Cir 1946) 156 F2d 351, *cert den* (1946) 329 US 787, the Ninth Circuit seems to have held that since all conspirators are agents for each other, one defendant in a district can subject his co-conspirators to suit in that district as their agent. Although *Giusti* has been followed reluctantly by some district courts in the Ninth Circuit, it has been rejected out of hand by other courts. See, *e.g.*, *Bertha Building Corp. v National Theatres Corp.* (2d Cir 1957) 248 F2d 833, *cert den* (1958) 356 US 936.

A defendant unincorporated joint venture has been held amenable to suit in any district where any of its joint ventures may be sued. *Hawkins v National Basketball Association, supra.*

The general venue provisions of 28 USC §§1391 and 1392 may also be considered. *Hawkins v National Basketball Association, supra*, held that a corporation is a resident of all districts of its state of incorporation and that any district in which it is transacting business is its "residence" for venue purposes. That case also held that if defendants reside for venue purposes in different districts in the same state, suit may be brought under 28 USC §1392 in any of those districts although all defendants do not transact business in all districts.

The parties apparently also have the power to agree on venue in advance. In *A.C. Miller Concrete Products Corp. v Quikset Vault Sales Corp.* (ED Pa 1970) 309 F Supp 1094, a franchise agreement had provided for jurisdiction and venue of lawsuits arising under the contract in the federal district court in Los Angeles. The agreement was enforced by the Pennsylvania court, which transferred the case to Los Angeles pursuant to 28 USC §1406(a). Note, however, that the court indicated that transfer would have been appropriate under 28 USC §1404(a) (forum non conveniens) even absent the contract provision.

The purpose of Section 12 of the Clayton Act was to permit the injured person to sue in his own district rather than a distant district in which a foreign corporation resided or could be found. See *Eastman Kodak Co. v Southern Photo Materials Co.* (1927) 273 US 359, 372–374; *United States v Scophony Corp.* (1948) 333 US 795. *Cf. United States v National City Lines, Inc.* (1948) 334 US 573. Change of venue under 28 USC §1404 is nevertheless possible in antitrust cases. *United States v National City Lines, Inc.* (1949) 337 US 78.

Choice of venue can be of great practical importance to a plaintiff; a suit that can practicably be brought in the plaintiff's home district may be hopelessly expensive and unwieldy if the case must be prosecuted elsewhere. "Unless the balance is strongly in favor of the defendant, the plaintiff's choice of forum should rarely be disturbed." *Crawford Transport Co. v Chrysler Corp.* (ED Ky 1961) 191 F Supp 223, 228, *aff'd* (6th Cir 1964) 338 F2d 934, *cert den* (1965) 380 US 954.

The rules on change of venue are subject to a large caveat if numerous cases have been brought against the same defendant in a number of districts arising out of one antitrust violation, or a connected series of violations. The enormous logistical problems created when over 1,900 separate antitrust suits were brought against the electrical equipment manufacturers has given rise to important changes in the law applicable to "multiple litigation".

The first reaction to the *Electrical Cases* was a series of ad hoc procedures developed by the Coordinating Committee for Multiple Litigation appointed by Chief Justice Warren in 1962 as a special subcommittee of the Pretrial Procedures and Practices Committee of the Judicial Conference of the United States. The coordinating committee managed to organize discovery procedures to permit expeditious preparation of the *Electrical Cases* (consisting of over 25,000 separate claims in suits in 35 districts) by ordering defendants to deposit documents in central locations accessible to all plaintiffs, by arranging for depositions to be taken only once for use in all related cases (depositions were set in type, printed and bound as paperback books in editions of hundreds of copies) and by other procedures designed to bring some order into the pretrial proceedings.

Nevertheless, until near the end of the *Electrical Cases*, the cases remained in the courts where they were filed and orders of the local district courts were required to effectuate the "national orders" recommended by the coordinating committee. After many of the electrical cases had been disposed of, motions were made in certain districts to transfer cases to other districts in which cases dealing with the same product line of electrical equipment were pending. Many of the motions were granted. See, *e.g.*, *Atlantic City Electric Co. v I-T-E Circuit Breaker Co.* (SD NY 1965) 247 F Supp 950.

Subsequently, at the instigation of the coordinating committee, Congress enacted a new transfer statute specifically directed to "multidistrict litigation". PL 90-296, 82 Stat 109; 28 USC §1407. Under 28 USC §1407(a), "when civil actions involving one or more common questions of fact are pending in different districts, such actions may be transferred to any district for coordinated or consolidated pretrial proceedings." The statute goes on to provide for a determination by a "judicial panel on multidistrict litigation" that the transfers would be "for the convenience of parties and witnesses and will promote the just and efficient conduct of such actions." The proceedings to transfer an action under the section may be initiated by the panel itself or by a motion filed by a party with the panel and also filed in the district where the action by or against the moving party is pending. The statute provides for notice and hearing, findings of fact, and conclusions of law by the judicial panel on multidistrict litigation, and for review by extraordinary writ of an order granting transfer.

The flexibility of the mandate granted to the panel on multi-district litigation is expressly stated in 15 USC §1407(f): "The panel may prescribe rules for the conduct of its business not inconsistent with Acts of Congress and the Federal Rules of Civil Procedure." The panel has subsequently issued its rules of procedure, filed October 7, 1969, effective November 25, 1969. They are set out following 28 USCA §1407.

It is impossible to say categorically whether transfer is good or bad from the plaintiff's point of view. If the plaintiff is small and his case is unique, transfer may prove disastrous. If, however, the plaintiff is adequately financed and there are numerous cases on file in the same industry, consolidation of the plaintiff's case in an inconvenient district may nevertheless be beneficial in terms of speedier and more expeditious discovery and an enhanced opportunity to divide the labors of the plaintiff's pretrial preparation with attorneys for other plaintiffs. Although many ruggedly individualistic plaintiff's attorneys chafed under the national discovery program in the *Electrical Cases*, most now agree that coordinated discovery was a tremendous boon to their pretrial preparation.

I. [§12.52] Service of Process

Section 12 of the Clayton Act, 15 USC §22, permits service of process on a corporation ". . . in the district of which it is an inhabitant, or wherever it may be found." In other words, nationwide service of process is possible. Service is made in the manner provided in FRCP 4.

Service upon natural persons is as in ordinary civil actions in Federal Court. See FRCP 4. It is thus ordinarily necessary to have the marshal catch the individual somewhere in the state with process unless out-of-state service under an appropriate "long arm" statute of the state can be effectuated. See *Chicago Football Associates v American Football League*

(ND Ill 1967) BNA ATTR No. 343(Feb 6, 1968) A-19. An appointment of someone other than the marshal to serve process may be obtained from the court. FRCP 4(c).

For discussion of service, see Lavine and Horning, *Manual of Federal Practice* (1967) and *Supplement* (1970) Chapter 3.

IV. [§12.53] Discovery and Pretrial Procedures

Skillful use of discovery tools is essential in prosecuting private antitrust cases. In the ordinary case, so much information is in the possession of the defendants and so little in the possession of the plaintiff that the plaintiff will have serious difficulty proving his case unless he can force the defendants to disclose the evidence.

For a general discussion of federal discovery, see Lavine and Horning, *Manual of Federal Practice* (1967) and *Supplement* (1970) Chapter 5.

Defendants commonly urge elaborate and complicated pretrial and discovery procedures such as those recommended in *Handbook of Recommended Procedures for the Trial of Protracted Cases* (1960) 25 FRD 351, and the *Manual for Complex and Multidistrict Litigation* prepared by a subcommittee of the Coordinating Committee for Multiple Litigation Judicial Conference of the United States, 1 PT 2 Moore's *Federal Practice* (2d ed 1970), which has succeeded the *Handbook of Recommended Procedures*.

The usual reaction of the plaintiff's attorney is to resist procedures that proliferate conferences, motions, hearings, and other preliminary matters that are thought to waste time and sap the plaintiff's energy. The plaintiff should resist bitterly any discovery procedure calculated to waste time in unproductive effort, to delay disposition of the litigation, or to run up the costs of preparing a case for trial. But that does not mean that all special procedures should be rejected out of hand. The massive electrical equipment litigation (over 2,000 cases) has demonstrated that special procedures can be of enormous benefit to plaintiffs.

Some special procedures likely to help plaintiffs in the long run include stipulations or orders:

1. That depositions taken in one case may be used in other, related litigation;
2. That documents relevant to several suits shall be deposited by defendants in a central location for common use by plaintiffs;
3. That documents to be used in a number of depositions in the same case may be marked in one single, serially-numbered series and deemed

exhibits to the deposition of any witness who testifies with respect to them;

4. That if defendants propose to use machine-tabulated statistical material in the course of their defense, they shall make the punched cards, punched tape, or magnetic tape available to plaintiffs, together with machine time and an opportunity to program the machine to "print out" statistical compilations that plaintiffs may wish to use.

Some of the procedures used in the heavy electrical cases are described in *Atlantic City Electric Co. v I-T-E Circuit Breaker Co.* (SD NY 1965) 247 F Supp 950.

The tendency of some courts to think of antitrust litigation as necessarily "big" litigation may have serious adverse effects upon the plaintiff. The appointment of a special master can be a crushing burden of expense for a plaintiff, and may amount to an abuse of discretion. *Cf. La Buy v Howes Leather Co.* (1957) 352 US 249.

However, a special master can be used to good effect in analyzing damage proof. See, *e.g.*, *Locklin v Day-Glo Color Corp.* (7th Cir 1970) 429 F2d 873. In *Trans World Airlines, Inc. v Hughes* (SD NY 1969) 308 F Supp 679, the special master was required to hear and consider an enormous mass of evidence in assessing damages after liability had been established by the defendant's default.

Nevertheless, in the ordinary case a requirement that plaintiff retain economists or accountants in order to answer interrogatories or even to try the case would seem to conflict with the plaintiff's right to try its damage case with whatever evidence it can present with its own witnesses. *Cf. Rangen, Inc. v Sterling Nelson & Sons, Inc.* (9th Cir 1965) 351 F2d 851, 856, *cert den* (1966) 383 US 936.

A. [§12.54] Ascertaining the Defendant's Internal Organization and Recordkeeping Procedures

A clear understanding of the defendant's internal organization and recordkeeping procedures should be obtained early. Antitrust defendants tend to be large corporations with elaborate organizational structure. Information passes up and down through the corporate structure, laterally from department to department, and in and out with respect to the rest of the business world. Much of that information is on paper.

The two main things that the plaintiff must learn in almost every case are who are the people in the defendant's organization who can testify meaningfully to the issues, and what documents must necessarily have been created within the defendant's organization in the course of the transactions in issue. With this information, the right people can be deposed and the existence and location of relevant documents identified preliminary to a request for production of documents.

Information on organization and document-flow can be quickly and easily obtained by interrogatories asking the defendants to describe their organizational structure, to identify the persons who occupied the relevant positions in that structure, and to identify all documents (or regularly maintained series of documents) bearing upon the issues in the case. Under FRCP 26(b) and 33, defendants may be required to answer as to anything which " . . . appears reasonably calculated to lead to the discovery of admissible evidence."

For forms of interrogatories that may be helpful, see §§12.55–12.57.

B. Forms of Interrogatories

1. [§12.55] Definitional Interrogatories

Interrogatories can be uniquely useful in an antitrust case as a means of identifying documents and witnesses. Commonly, the defendants are large corporations with complicated internal structures and enormous collections of documentary material. There is no such thing as a set of "universal interrogatories" but there are some approaches that have proven effective in cases of this kind. The interrogatories that follow can be a starting point.

Definitions at the beginning of a set of interrogatories may tend to make them tighter and harder to evade. A set of antitrust interrogatories might begin like this:

(Title of Court)

(Title of Cause)

PLAINTIFFS' _____(e.g., FIRST)_____
SET OF INTERROGATORIES PROPOUNDED TO DEFENDANT _____(name of defendant)_____

TO DEFENDANT _____(name of defendant)_____ **and to** _____, **its attorneys:**
Pursuant to Rule 33, Federal Rules of Civil Procedure, plaintiffs direct the following interrogatories to defendant _____(name of defendant)_____ **and require that the answers thereto, under oath, be served upon them within thirty days.**

DEFINITIONS

1. "You", or "_____" means defendant _____(name of defendant)_____, its subsidiaries and its merged or acquired predecessors, its present and former officers, agents, employees and all other persons acting on its behalf or on behalf of such subsidiaries or predecessors, including all past and present employees exercising discretion, making policy, and making decisions or participating in any of the foregoing functions with respect to development, evaluation, production, sale, pricing, or shipping of products.

2. "Communication" means any contact, oral or written, formal or informal, at any time or place, and under any circumstances whatsoever, whereby information of any nature was transmitted or transferred.

3. "Costs" means the price, plus any shipping and handling charges, which you pay for _____ purchased from others, or, when applied to goods manufactured by you, the computation of cost that you ordinarily use in determining the cost of their manufacture. When you are asked to state "costs" of _____ you shall state the basis on which your answer is predicated including whether the _____ is manufactured by you or purchased from others; and if manufactured by you, a description of all indirect expenses (*i.e.*, expenses other than direct labor and material costs) included in your computation. In either event, you shall state costs in your warehouse, ready for shipment to customers.

4. "Document" means any written, recorded or graphic matter, however produced or reproduced. It includes all matter that relates or refers in whole or in part to the subjects referred to in an interrogatory. If a document has been prepared in several copies, or additional copies have been made, and the copies are not identical (or which, by reason of subsequent modification of a copy by the addition of notations, or other modifications, are no longer identical) each non-identical copy is a separate "document". "Form document" means a document prepared as a matter of repetitive routine under a procedure (such as the use of printed blank forms) which eliminates the necessity for repeated production or reproduction of information that remains the same in the whole series of form documents.

5. "Identify" means:

a. Wherever in these interrogatories you are asked to "identify" a document, you shall specifically designate the type of document (*i.e.*, letter, interoffice memorandum, report, etc.), and shall state:

1. Information sufficient to enable plaintiffs to identify the document, such as its date, the name of the addressee or addressees, the name of the signer or signers, the title or heading of the document, and its approximate number of pages. Form documents may be identified by title of the form, a description of the method of preparation, and disposition of all copies;

2. The identity and address or addresses of the person or persons to whom copies were sent;

3. The present or last known location of possessor of the original of the document (or, if that is unavailable, the most legible copy).

b. Wherever in these interrogatories you are asked to "identify" a person, you shall furnish information sufficient to enable plaintiffs to identify the person, such as his name, his present whereabouts, his present position, prior relevant positions he has held and similar identifying information.

c. Wherever in these interrogatories you are asked to "identify" a communication or contact, you shall indicate whether the communication or contact was oral or written, identify the document if the communication or contact was written (or if the oral communication or contact was recorded in any manner in a document), and identify the person or persons who sent, received, or had knowledge of the communication or contact, if it was oral.

6. _____(Define collective names for groups of parties, short names for parties with long names, etc.)_____

7. _____(Define any words of art in the industry involved, including products, processes, selling plans, etc.)_____

8. "Relevant period" means from _____ to _____. Unless otherwise indicated, answers shall cover that period.

COMMENT: The title to a set of interrogatories can be very helpful. Many antitrust cases give rise to several sets, and it is wise to anticipate that each party may have to answer more than one set.

In defining terms, it is important not to broaden the scope of the interrogatories beyond all reason or to confuse the issue by transferring large parts of a question to the "definition" section by over-defining terms. Interrogatories should still be intelligible on their face, with the definitions serving to limit the possibilities for evasion through an unreasonably narrow reading of the language used in the interrogatories.

2. [§12.56] Interrogatories to Identify Defendants

1. Is there a _____(name of state—e.g., California)_____ corporation known as _____?

2. If there is a corporation known as _____ chartered in California or qualified to do business in California, then state its relationship to _____.

3. Has a California corporation known as _____, stock of which is listed on the _____ Stock Exchange, appeared to defend this action?

4. State whether you operated a _____(e.g., factory)_____ at _____ in _____, _____(e.g. California)_____ from _____ to _____, 19_____.

5. If the person operating such _____(e.g., factory)_____ from _____ to _____, 19_____, was a person or corporation other than defendant _____, identify such person or corporation.

6. Do you presently operate a _____(e.g., factory)_____ **in** _____, **California?**
7. Where is your present _____(e.g., factory)_____ **in California located?**
8. Do you operate any other _____(e.g., factories)_____ **in California?**
9. If so, where are they located?

COMMENT: It is embarrassing to find that one has sued and served a corporation or other business entity that has a name like the intended defendant but lacks such essential attributes as liability to the plaintiff or the financial responsibility to respond in damages.

To avoid the possibility that one has sued a subsidiary or related corporation and failed to bring the intended defendant into the net, interrogatories designed to identify an answering defendant are helpful. Counsel should establish not only that the defendant he has sued and served is the defendant he intended to sue and serve but also that the defendant he intended to sue and serve is the defendant in fact engaged in the type of business that gives rise to the plaintiff's claim. The above interrogatories are designed for this purpose. See §12.55 for format.

3. [§12.57] Machine Records Interrogatories

1. Do you maintain any of your business records by machine-records (computer) procedures?

2. If so, what brand, model, and configuration of machine-records machinery do you use?

3. What is the form of information input to your machine-records bookkeeping system (punched cards, punched tape, magnetic tape, other)?

4. What kinds of information do you include in the input for your machine-records bookkeeping system?

5. What kinds of information is regularly printed out by your machine-records bookkeeping system?

6. How often do you obtain each type of printout that you regularly obtain from your machine-records bookkeeping system?

7. Are any data on the operation of your _____ **facility fed into your machine-records bookkeeping system?**

8. If so, describe such data.

9. Do you obtain any printouts from your machine-records bookkeeping system with respect to the operation of your _____ **facility?**

10. If so, describe each such printout that you regularly obtain and state how often such a printout is obtained.

11. Are any data on the operation of a geographical division embracing your _____ **facility fed into your machine-records bookkeeping system?**

12. If so, describe such data.

13. Do you obtain any printouts from your machine-records bookkeeping system with respect to the operation of a geographical division embracing your _____ facility?

14. If so, describe each such printout that you regularly obtain and state how often such a printout is obtained.

15. Have you obtained any printouts, regular or otherwise, relating to _____?

16. If the answer to any part of the foregoing interrogatory is affirmative, identify each such printout.

17. Identify each of the following people:
    a. The man in charge of your machine-records bookkeeping system;
    b. The man in charge of programming the machines used in your machine-records bookkeeping system.

COMMENT: Most modern companies handle a large part of their routine business records with machine records (computer) procedures. Discovery may be directed not only to the identification of the end result of such bookkeeping procedures (the printouts) but also the input and the method in which it is handled. The input itself may be valuable. By programming a computer to manipulate inputs in different ways, it may be possible to obtain information of a type not ordinarily prepared for business purposes but highly probative of sales, pricing, cost, profit, and similar issues.

The above interrogatories are designed to obtain this information. For format, see §12.55

C. [§12.58] Obtaining the Defendant's Documents

Adequate production of the defendant's documents can make the difference between a case built on inference and a case solidly grounded on the defendant's own recorded statements and admissions. The plaintiff's problem is to get the critical documents without drowning in a sea of meaningless paper.

Changes to FRCP 34 effective July 1, 1970 have substantially repealed the whole body of law that grew up around the motion to produce documents and the necessity of showing good cause for their production. As modified, Rule 34 permits any party to request documents of another party. The request must be honored unless objection is made. If a production request is opposed, the party seeking production may pursue his request by motion under amended FRCP 37 to compel production, and to recover expenses, including reasonable attorney's fees, in making the motion.

The principal area of controversy under amended Rule 34 will probably center on the requirement that a request for documents "set forth the items to be inspected either by individual item or by category, and describe each item and category with reasonable particularity." To meet that requirement, the discovering party should have the best possible idea of what he is after. A plaintiff's designation of a "category" that includes a warehouse full of paper may be a serious tactical error. If the defendant agrees to produce, the plaintiff faces the problem of how he is going to find time and manpower to run an inspection.

Accordingly, preliminary discovery designed to pinpoint useful documents remains advisable. It can limit the adverse party's production to a manageable volume of documents without excluding important and relevant material inadvertently.

D. [§12.59] Limitation on Discovery; Time and Space

How wide should plaintiff's discovery range in time and space? In order to show the formation of a conspiracy, or a "base" for damages, plaintiff may wish to prove facts that occurred prior to the earliest time for which he can claim damage. To show the actual effects of a challenged trade practice, a plaintiff may wish to show facts that have occurred since his complaint was filed.

Similarly, to show the full scope of a conspiracy, a plaintiff may wish to show acts in furtherance of the conspiracy that occurred far away from the plaintiff's own small sphere of activity.

The usual defense tactic, both in discovery and at trial, is to try to limit the plaintiff to the narrowest possible time period and the smallest possible geographical spread.

Some limitation on scope of discovery can be accepted as a matter of self-preservation; unreasonably broad discovery is likely to inundate the plaintiff with paper, and may hurt more than it helps. But the usual problem is not too much discovery, but too little. Several Supreme Court decisions have considered the relevance of matters occurring both before and after alleged antitrust violations. *Continental Ore Co. v Union Carbide & Carbon Corp.* (1962) 370 US 690, 709-710 held it error to exclude evidence of events that occurred years before the corporate plaintiff even came into existence. In *FTC v Consolidated Foods Corp.* (1965) 380 US 592, 598, the Supreme Court held that post-complaint evidence was properly admitted in a Clayton Act case.

Standard Oil Co. of New Jersey v United States (1911) 221 US 1 is the classic case demonstrating the potential geographic scope of a major antitrust conspiracy. It is hard to imagine what that case would have come to if the government had been limited to discovery and proof of a small segment of the overall operations of the oil trust. *Cf. Banana Service Co. v United Fruit Co.* (D Mass 1953) 15 FRD 106.

E. [§12.60] Governmental Aids to Discovery and Proof

The FTC and the Antitrust Division of the Department of Justice have enormous resources for gathering antitrust evidence. The Antitrust Division may proceed by way of a grand jury, obtaining both testimony and documents. It may proceed with a civil investigative demand to obtain documents. It has the resources of the FBI at its disposal, as well as a small army of lawyers. See Chapters 10 and 11. The FTC also has broad investigative powers, which it may exercise by subpoena, questionnaire, and in various other ways. See Chapter 6.

A private antitrust plaintiff may benefit from the efforts of the government in two ways. First, he may be able to obtain some or all of the evidence that the government has collected for his own use. See §12.61. Second, if the government wins its case, the private plaintiff may be able to use the government's victory as prima facie evidence of the defendant's violation in his own private antitrust action under Section 5 of the Clayton Act, 15 USC §16(a). See §12.62.

1. [§12.61] Discovery of Evidence Collected by the Government

There is a strong public policy, embodied in statute, in favor of public disclosure of information the government obtains in civil antitrust cases. *Olympic Refining Co. v Carter* (9th Cir 1964) 332 F2d 260, *cert den* (1964) 379 US 900. On the other hand, there is a policy of secrecy, embodied in Fed R Crim P 6(e), covering grand jury proceedings in criminal cases. *U.S. Industries, Inc. v United States District Court* (9th Cir 1965) 345 F2d 18, *cert den* (1965) 382 US 814.

In both *Olympic Refining* and *U.S. Industries*, a private plaintiff was attempting to obtain access to papers filed by the government under "sealing orders" that would prevent the plaintiff from simply looking at the clerk's file in the district court. In each case a private plaintiff was granted access to at least some of the material, under protective provisions. In each case, the defendants had already capitulated, so that no trial (and no resulting public disclosure of evidence) would be had. For further discussion, see §§10.21–10.23.

Ideally, from the private plaintiff's point of view, a government case is tried. Then, even if the government loses, the private plaintiff may be able to pick up invaluable evidence with a minimum of effort.

But there is nothing to prevent a private plaintiff from outrunning the government. Private plaintiffs have been permitted to forge ahead with civil discovery at the same time the government is preparing to try related criminal cases. The Fifth Amendment constitutional privilege against self-incrimination does not bar the civil discovery proceedings, although the privilege is available and may be asserted by any natural persons who are civil defendants. *United States v American Radiator & Standard Sanitary Corp.* (3d Cir 1967) 388 F2d 201.

There has been recent controversy over the extent to which a plaintiff can discover grand jury proceedings by obtaining de-briefing memoranda prepared by defendants' lawyers after talking with witnesses emerging from the grand jury room. It seems clear that if the de-briefing memoranda are prepared within the context of a personal attorney-client relationship, they are privileged. The privilege also applies if the witness is a member of the "control group" of a corporation and he is de-briefed by the corporation's attorneys. But what about the middle-management grand jury witness who is de-briefed by the corporation's attorneys? In *Harper & Row Publishers, Inc. v Decker* (7th Cir 1970) 423 F2d 487, *aff'd by an equally divided court* (1971) 400 US 348, mandamus was granted to restrain a district judge from disclosing the de-briefing memoranda of corporate witnesses not within the control group. For further discussion see §10.22.

2. [§12.62] A Government Victory as Prima Facie Evidence

Title 15 USC § 16(a) provides that

a final judgment or decree . . . in any civil or criminal proceeding brought by or on behalf of the United States under the antitrust laws to the effect that a defendant has violated said laws shall be prima facie evidence . . . in any action . . . brought by any other party . . . as to all matters respecting which said judgment or decree would be an estoppel . . ..

as between that defendant and the United States. The section does not apply to ". . . consent judgments or decrees entered before any testimony has been taken . . .." Neither does it apply to cases in which the United States is suing as a damage claimant.

For many years it was assumed that the "United States" was the Justice Department, suing in federal court, and usually represented by Antitrust Division lawyers. In *Minnesota Mining & Manufacturing Co. v New Jersey Wood Finishing Co.* (1965) 381 US 311, the Supreme Court held that FTC proceedings would toll the statute of limitations under 15 USC §16(b) on a private right of action, at least insofar as the practices the FTC was challenging constituted violations of the antitrust laws. The

Court was not called on to consider whether the result in such an FTC proceeding would be admissible in a private lawsuit as evidence under 15 USC §16(a). However, in *Farmington Dowel Products Co. v Forster Mfg. Co.* (1st Cir 1969) 421 F2d 61, the First Circuit reviewed the authorities and concluded that the prima facie evidence provisions of 15 USC §16(a) applied equally to final determinations in favor of the United States acting through the FTC. *Farmington Dowel* was followed in *Purex Corp., Ltd. v Procter & Gamble Co.* (CD Calif 1970) 308 F Supp 584, with leave to the defendant to seek an interlocutory appeal under 28 USC §1292(b).

It is not always easy to determine whether the FTC has treated particular conduct as violative of the antitrust laws, or only violative of some broader policy set forth in Section 5 of the Federal Trade Commission Act. See, *e.g.*, *Lee National Corp. v Atlantic Richfield Co.* (ED Pa 1970) 308 F Supp 1041. The breadth of any such distinction is now in doubt as a result of *Sperry and Hutchinson Co. v FTC* (5th Cir 1970) 432 F2d 146, in which a majority of the panel held that the FTC may not enjoin conduct that does not violate at least the spirit of the antitrust laws.

A judgment by consent, before any testimony has been taken, cannot be used as prima facie evidence against the consenting defendant in a subsequent private action. A defendant's plea of *nolo contendere* in a criminal case gives rise to a consent judgment and may not be used, but a plea of guilty is usable. *Burbank v General Electric Co.* (9th Cir 1964) 329 F2d 825.

Private plaintiffs may use government victories in civil cases as prima facie proof unless the defendant capitulated and entered into a consent judgment *before any testimony was taken*. If the defendant resists until testimony has been taken and then consents to judgment, the judgment may be used against him in private actions. *De Luxe Theatre Corp. v Balaban & Katz Corp.* (ND Ill 1951) 95 F Supp 983.

But what does a government victory prove for a private plaintiff? In *Emich Motors Corp. v General Motors Corp.* (1951) 340 US 558, 568, the Supreme Court said, "we think that Congress intended to confer, subject only to a defendant's enjoyment of its day in court against a new party, as large an advantage as the estoppel doctrine would afford had the Government brought suit." The Court went on to hold (at 340 US at 569) that there is an estoppel as to all matters "'distinctly put in issue and directly determined' . . .." The difficulty is in determining what a jury's general verdict (or a simple guilty plea) has necessarily decided. Counsel must analyze the elements of the offense and the ultimate facts that would have to have been found to sustain the conviction.

A prior judgment against a defendant is nice evidence in a private case; it is in the same league with a "hot" document. But a government victory should rarely be relied on as the sole proof of any material part of a plaintiff's case. Even if the government case has been tried to the court sitting without a jury and the court has entered extensive findings of fact and conclusions of law, plaintiffs have sometimes found to their chagrin that the decision in the government case did not adequately relate to the precise facts on which their cases were based, and did not provide the necessary proof to win their cases. See *Theatre Enterprises, Inc. v Paramount Film Distributing Corp.* (1954) 346 US 537; *Eagle Lion Studios, Inc. v Loew's, Inc.* (2d Cir 1957) 248 F2d 438, *aff'd* (1958) 358 US 100.

F. [§12.63] Protective Orders

Antitrust cases commonly revolve around trade information (customers, prices, terms of sale, etc.) that may be sensitive competitive information. This may be as true of the plaintiff's business as the defendant's.

Protective orders limiting disclosure of documents, depositions, or interrogatory answers to particular individuals, to attorneys, or to attorneys and accountants for the parties are commonly granted and should be freely stipulated with the understanding that it may be necessary to lift protective orders to present evidence at trial. See *Covey Oil Co. v Continental Oil Co.* (10th Cir 1965) 340 F2d 993, 999, *cert den* (1965) 380 US 964; *Hartley Pen Co. v United States District Court* (9th Cir 1961) 287 F2d 324, 331; *Chemical and Industrial Corp. v Druffel* (6th Cir 1962) 301 F2d 126, 129.

V. Defenses

A. [§12.64] Defenses and Non-Defenses in Private Antitrust Cases

No plaintiff's case can be intelligently evaluated without considering possible defenses. Several defenses commonly used in other kinds of actions (*e.g.*, unclean hands) have little efficacy in antitrust. See §12.69. On the other hand, specific statutes confer antitrust immunity on particularly classes or conduct (*e.g.*, labor organizations). See §§12.65-12.67 and §§2.14-2.22. Baseball is a unique exempt enterprise. The exemption is without any real justification except history but enjoys continuing vitality. See *Toolson v New York Yankees, Inc.* (1953) 346 US 356; *Flood v Kuhn* (SD NY 1970) 312 F Supp 404, and §2.15.

Somewhere in between is the no-man's-land of "primary jurisdiction" in which a regulatory agency may be able to influence, if not actually determine, the outcome of a private plaintiff's antitrust case. See §12.68. For discussion of the statute of limitations, see §§12.12–12.16.

B. [§12.65] Labor Organizations

Section 6 of the Clayton Act, 15 USC § 17 contains the labor exemption to the antitrust laws. See Chapter 14. The exemption does not protect restraints of trade masquerading as labor unions. *Los Angeles Meat & Provision Drivers Union v United States* (1962) 371 US 94; *United States v Gasoline Retailers Association* (7th Cir 1961) 285 F2d 638.

An anticompetitive conspiracy between a labor union and one or more employers falls outside the exemption, but legitimate union activities, even when they have adverse competitive effects, remain exempt. Compare *American Federation of Musicians v Carroll* (1968) 391 US 99 and *Local 189, AMC & BW v Jewel Tea Co.* (1965) 381 US 676 with *United Mine Workers v Pennington* (1965) 381 US 657 and *Allen Bradley Co. v Local 3, IBEW* (1945) 325 US 797.

Subsequent history of the mine workers' litigation of which *Pennington, supra,* was a part, raises a question about the standard of proof in antitrust actions against unions. In *Ramsey v United Mine Workers* (6th Cir 1969) 416 F2d 655, *cert granted* (1970) 397 US 1006, the Sixth Circuit, *en banc,* split evenly on the standard of proof required, and accordingly affirmed the judgment of the district court. The district court had required the plaintiff to show by "clear proof," and not just by the preponderance of the evidence, that the union had conspired with employers to violate the Sherman Act. The Supreme Court reversed, holding that the "clear proof" standard does not apply to a determination of whether unlawful acts have been committed, but rather to the question whether unlawful acts were authorized or ratified by a particular defendant.

C. [§12.66] Privileged Activity of Agricultural Cooperatives

The Clayton and Capper-Volstead Acts exempt agricultural cooperatives from the operation of the antitrust laws. See §2.18. That is, the combination that creates a cooperative is not in and of itself a violation of the antitrust laws, nor does the interaction of affiliated cooperatives violate the antitrust laws. See *Sunkist Growers, Inc. v Winckler & Smith Citrus Products Co.* (1962) 370 US 19. But inclusion of non-growers in the cooperative strips the cooperative of its immunity under the antitrust laws. See *Case-Swayne Co. v Sunkist Growers, Inc.* (1967) 389 US 384.

Furthermore, an agricultural cooperative may quickly find itself in trouble when it engages in predatory activity designed to monopolize (*Maryland and Virginia Milk Producers Association, Inc. v United States* (1960) 362 US 458) or when it engages in a conspiracy with outside groups (*United States v Borden Co.* (1939) 308 US 188).

D. [§12.67] Inducing Government Action; Scope of the Privilege

A private plaintiff may wish to complain of injuries inflicted as a result of the defendant's appeal to governmental action. The extent to which his complaint will be heeded seems to depend on which branch of government the defendant goes to.

An appeal to legislative action is privileged as an exercise of free speech and of the constitutional right to petition the government, even when engaged in for anticompetitive motives. See *Eastern Railroad Presidents Conference v Noerr Motor Freight, Inc.* (1961) 365 US 127.

The immunity seems less absolute for appeals to the executive branch. Even if the government action itself may not be the basis for a damage claim, it may be evidence that can be used to support the claim of violation and as evidence of purpose and intent. See *United Mine Workers v Pennington* (1965) 381 US 657, 670, n 3. Certainly, if there is bribery of the public official, there is no immunity; the action induced is not the action of the government but rather the action of the individual in violation of his trust. See *Rangen, Inc. v Sterling Nelson & Sons, Inc.* (9th Cir 1965) 351 F2d 851, *cert den* (1966) 383 US 936.

The cases dealing with appeals to the judicial branch are in conflict. While it might seem that an appeal to the judicial branch, at least if successful, should be treated the same as an appeal to the other two branches of government, there is lower-court authority to the contrary. In *Trucking Unlimited v California Motor Transport Co.* (9th Cir 1970) 432 F2d 755, the court said (at 759), inter alia, ". . . the Sherman Act is violated by a conspiracy to unreasonably restrain or monopolize trade through the use of judicial and administrative adjudicative proceedings."

On the other hand, in *Sperry and Hutchinson Co. v FTC* (5th Cir 1970) 432 F2d 146, *pet for cert filed* 1-27-71, the majority reversed an FTC order that had enjoined S & H from suing traffickers in S & H Green Stamps. S & H had brought 43 consecutive, successful actions over about 60 years, in 8 federal districts and 19 states, to enjoin unauthorized use of S & H trading stamps. A majority of the Fifth Circuit panel said, "this court must hold that the efforts of S & H to prevent that which time and time again has been declared unlawful do not constitute practices of the type that transgresses the spirit of the antitrust laws. . . ."

Of course, if the government agency is a purchaser of goods and services and the defendant has deprived that agency of the best available prices or quality in furtherance of an antitrust violation, there is no privilege. See *George R. Whitten, Jr., Inc. v Paddock Pool Builders, Inc.* (1st Cir 1970) 424 F2d 25, *cert den* (1970) 400 US 850.

For further discussion see §§2.47, 13.31.

E. [§12.68] Regulated Industries; Primary Jurisdiction

Large portions of American industry are regulated in some way by federal or state agencies. The question arises whether regulation carries with it exemption from antitrust liability and, if not, whether it entitles the defendants to preliminary determination of legal and factual questions by the regulating agency before a private antitrust case may proceed. In answering these questions, it helps to know:

1. Is the industry or activity specifically mentioned in the federal antitrust laws? See §§12.65, 12.66. See also 15 USC §§ 13b, 13c, 17, 20, 21.

2. Are the antitrust laws specifically referred to in the statutes covering the regulated industry or activity?

3. Is the conduct complained of the subject of express regulatory power of the regulating agency?

4. Has the agency in fact regulated the conduct complained of?

5. Would the enforcement of the private antitrust remedy conflict directly with the policy of the regulatory scheme created by the regulatory statute?

In general, repeal of the antitrust laws by implication is not favored, and even approval by a regulatory body does not necessarily immunize conduct unless a statute expressly says so. On the other hand, an agency may have "primary jurisdiction" that can be the basis for a stay of court proceedings to decide legal and factual questions that can significantly affect the outcome of litigation. See *Carnation Co. v Pacific Westbound Conference* (1966) 383 US 213; *Carter v American Telephone & Telegraph Co.* (5th Cir 1966) 365 F2d 486, *cert den* (1967) 385 US 1008.

Reference is inappropriate, however, if the administrative agency has no particular expertise, could not decide the crucial issue within the scope of its jurisdiction, or would not itself have jurisdiction. See *Local 189, AMC & BW v Jewel Tea Co.* (1965) 381 US 676, 684–688.

Since federal law is paramount to state law, states have limited power to create antitrust immunity in the absence of statute. *Cf. Parker v Brown* (1943) 317 US 341.

The intricacies of immunity and primary jurisdiction are discussed at length in *Marnell v United Parcel Service* (ND Calif 1966) 260 F Supp 391.

Industries in which primary jurisdiction and related problems have been litigated include:

1. Transportation: *Carnation Co. v Pacific Westbound Conference*, supra; *Pan American World Airways, Inc. v United States* (1963) 371 US 296; *Georgia v Pennsylvania Railroad Co.* (1945) 324 US 439.

2. Finance: *United States v Philadelphia Nat'l. Bank* (1963) 374 US 321, 350-351; *Silver v New York Stock Exchange* (1963) 373 US 341.

3. Natural gas: *California v FPC* (1962) 369 US 482.

4. Communications: *United States v Radio Corp. of America* (1959) 358 US 334; *Carter v American Telephone & Telegraph Co.*, supra.

5. Agriculture: *Maryland and Virginia Milk Producers Association, Inc. v United States* (1960) 362 US 458, 463.

Even if "primary jurisdiction" is not relevant, a regulatory body may appear as amicus curiae with devastating consequences. See *Empire Rayon Yarn Co. v American Viscose Corp.* (2d Cir 1965) 364 F2d 491, 492.

F. [§12.69] The In Pari Delicto and Unclean Hands Defenses

Not all antitrust plaintiffs have led blameless lives; even the underdog has fleas. Before filing a suit alleging lost profits, advise the plaintiff that practically every fact of his business life is probably relevant to some phase of his case and is probably discoverable. A plaintiff unwilling to submit to substantially unlimited discovery probably should not bring a suit seeking loss-of-profits damages.

But wrongdoing by an antitrust plaintiff—even in the antitrust area—is not itself grounds for refusing to take a case. Unclean hands of the plaintiff, even if those hands were dirtied in a related antitrust violation, is no defense to the plaintiff's action. *Kiefer-Stewart Co. v Joseph E. Seagram & Sons, Inc.* (1951) 340 US 211; *United States v Schenley Industries, Inc.* (SD NY 1966) 1966 Trade Cases ¶71,897.

In *Perma Life Mufflers, Inc. v International Parts Corp.* (1968) 392 US 134, the Supreme Court came to grips with the in pari delicto defense. The plaintiffs were franchisees operating Midas Muffler Shops under franchise agreements with defendant that contained numerous objectionable clauses including resale price maintenance, exclusive dealing, and exclusive territorial restrictions. Of course, all of the franchisees had accepted contracts containing the restrictive provisions on which they based their suit. In *Perma Life Mufflers, Inc. v International Parts Corp.* (7th Cir 1967) 376 F2d 692, the Seventh Circuit concluded (at 699) "it would be difficult to visualize a case more appropriate for the application of the *pari delicto* doctrine." The Supreme Court reversed by a clear majority. However, there were four opinions in addition to the opinion of the Court, expressing a whole panorama of viewpoints.

Mr. Justice Black, for the majority, indicated that the application of the in pari delicto doctrine to antitrust cases was inappropriate and that public policy encouraged the plaintiff's suit even if he might be (at 139) "no less morally reprehensible than the defendant". However, the majority rejected a suggestion that the plaintiffs had actively supported the entire restrictive program and participated in its formulation and encouraged its continuation. It viewed the situation as one in which the plaintiffs had eagerly sought franchises but (at 139) "did not actively seek each and every clause of the agreement." Mr. Justice Black observed that many of the restrictions were clearly to the detriment of the plaintiffs, and that they would not have been instigated by the plaintiffs.

Mr. Justice White, in a concurring opinion, raised serious doubts about a general rule permitting co-conspirators to sue each other in all circumstances for injuries resulting from the conspiracy, and concluded (at 146) that he would deny recovery when plaintiff and defendant bear substantially equal responsibility, but permit recovery in favor of the one less responsible if one is more responsible than the other.

Mr. Justice Fortas suggested (at 148) that a conspirator might be barred as to the portion of an agreement in which he actively collaborated but not as to the portions of an agreement that he did not originate as a substantially equal bargaining partner.

Mr. Justice Marshall concurred in the result, but suggested (at 149-150) that if Perma Life could have shown that it had traded certain restrictions favorable to it for restrictions favorable to the franchisees, the franchisees should then be barred from seeking damages as to the agreement as a whole.

Justices Harlan and Stewart concurred in part, and dissented in part: They concluded (at 154-155) that the in pari delicto defense, properly defined, should be an available defense but that "coercion" of the plaintiffs to enter into an unlawful agreement would create an exception to the in pari delicto rule.

Although the case is clouded by facts tending to indicate that the plaintiffs were not willing participants in the challenged portion of their franchise agreements, *Perma Life* clearly stands for the proposition that, absent a conspiracy between substantially equal bargaining partners, one conspirator can sue another for resulting damage under the antitrust laws. This is true even though, as between the plaintiffs and the defendant, there is a conspiracy that would subject both plaintiff and defendant to prosecution by the government or to private suit by third parties injured by the conspiracy.

The defense of in pari delicto, then, would seem to be limited to the situation in which a willing member of a conspiracy turns on his co-conspirators and seeks damages resulting from the conspiracy in which he participated as a full and equal partner. See *Pennsylvania Water & Power Co. v Consolidated Gas Electric Light & Power Co.* (4th Cir 1953) 209 F2d 131.

For further discussion, see §2.46.

G. [§12.70] Coercion of the Defendant as a Defense

Members of a conspiracy not uncommonly join as a result of pressure put upon them by the other conspirators. For example, a motion picture distributor may agree to distribute its pictures in accordance with the wishes of some of its more powerful customers to the detriment of other potential customers. The distributor's freedom of choice is controlled by coercive means. Or, in a price-fixing conspiracy, one or more of the conspirators may have joined as a result of policing activity on the part of the other members. See *United States v General Motors Corp.* (1966) 384 US 127; *FTC v Cement Institute* (1948) 333 US 683. Vis a vis third parties, a participant in a conspiracy is still a conspirator, regardless of his reason for joining the conspiracy. But an unwilling participant in an antitrust violation may be able to sue the principal perpetrator of the violation and recover, notwithstanding his own involvement, except in rather limited circumstances. See the discussion of in pari delicto and unclean hands at §12.69.

H. [§12.71] Motions

Filing and service of the complaint in a private action under antitrust laws often signals the beginning of a "war of the motions". The principal motions (excluding motions in support of or resisting discovery) are set out in FRCP 12 and 56. Rule 12 provides for defenses and objections that may be raised by motion and Rule 56 deals with summary judgment. Rule 12 ties in with Rule 56, providing that motions to dismiss for failure to state a claim upon which relief can be granted and motions for judgment on the pleadings are to be treated as motions for summary judgment if matters outside of the pleadings are considered in connection with the motions.

Often, the purpose of motions directed to the pleadings and raising substantive issues is not so much to throw out the plaintiff's case in its entirety as it is to cut it down, chop it up, or disfigure it so as to greatly reduce the damages or impair the chances of success at trial. Typically, the motions are for partial summary judgment to establish that some or all of plaintiff's claims are barred by the statute of limitations, or otherwise barred in whole or in part. See §§12.64–12.69.

Other motions may be directed to the misjoinder or non-joinder of parties under FRCP 21. Again, the purpose is to structure the law suit in a manner different from that chosen by the plaintiff. Generally, the broad provision for joinder of claims and parties contained in Rules 18 and 20 should permit the plaintiff to keep all of the parties whom he has named as defendants in the case, although Rule 20(b) gives a court discretion to order separate trials or make other orders to prevent delay or prejudice.

VI. [§12.72] Antitrust Violation as an Affirmative Defense in Contract and Infringement Actions

A private plaintiff may want to use the fact of an antitrust violation to avoid performance of a contract instead of (or in addition to) using his treble-damage and injunctive remedies under 15 USC §§15 and 26. His ability to do so depends on the circumstances.

An early case held that a purchaser could defend a suit for the price of goods purchased by showing that the seller had monopolized those goods and was attempting, by suit, to extract a monopoly price. *Continental Wall Paper Co. v Louis Voight and Sons Co.* (1909) 212 US 227. It has been held that an illegal tying contract cannot be enforced by suit. *Associated Press v Taft-Ingalls Corp.* (6th Cir 1965) 340 F2d 753, 768–769, *cert den* (1965) 382 US 820. One member of a cartel arrangement may not have an accounting to use ". . . the aid of the court to compel the other wrongdoer to disgorge its share of the spoils." *Farbenfabriken Bayer A.G. v Sterling Drug, Inc.* (3d Cir 1962) 307 F2d 207, 210, *cert den* (1963) 372 US 929.

Yet, a contract of purchase and sale made *in connection with* an unlawful agreement is enforceable. *Kelly v Kosuga* (1959) 358 US 516. Nor is it a defense to a note to show that the note was given in lieu of payment of accounts receivable and that the accounts receivable arose out of sales at discriminatory prices adverse to the purchaser. *Bruce's Juices, Inc. v American Can Co.* (1947) 330 US 743.

The Sixth Circuit suggested a reconciliation of the cases in *Kentucky Rural Electric Cooperative Corp. v Moloney Electric Co.* (6th Cir 1960) 282 F2d 481, *cert den* (1961) 365 US 812. There, the plaintiff sought damages for the defendant's refusal to pay it commissions on resales of equipment. The Sixth Circuit held that since payment of commissions would have, in and of itself, violated the Robinson-Patman Act, plaintiff could not prevail. It distinguished cases in which the plaintiff had engaged in collateral antitrust violations from cases in which, if the defendant had done what plaintiff had asked him to do, *that transaction itself* would have violated the law.

The cases in the patent area are simpler. Patent misuse is both a defense to an infringement action and the basis for a treble damage recovery. *Mercoid Corp. v Mid-Continent Investment Co.* (1944) 320 US 661; *Kobe, Inc. v Dempsey Pump Co.* (10th Cir 1952) 198 F2d 416, *cert den* (1952) 344 US 837. Cf. *Walker Process Equipment, Inc. v Food Machinery & Chemical Corp.* (1965) 382 US 172; *Brulotte v Thys Co.* (1964) 379 US 29. See Chapter 7.

VII. [§12.73] Jury Instructions in Private Cases

Any antitrust case worth trying to a jury is worth a hand-tailored set of jury instructions. They can and should be couched in terms of the contentions of the parties and the factual context of the case, so long as they are fair. See *Lessig v Tidewater Oil Co.* (9th Cir 1964) 327 F2d 459, 466, *cert den* (1964) 377 US 993.

Judge William C. Mathes prepared a set of general instructions for use in antitrust cases. See 28 FRD 457. These form instructions, sometimes modified, are collected in Mathes & Devitt, *Federal Jury Practice and Instructions* (1965). The Northern District of Illinois has adopted form instructions in criminal cases that appear to be substantially stricter than instructions to which a private plaintiff is entitled, at least in the Ninth Circuit. See 36 FRD 457, 471.

Lengthy approved instructions on damages are set out in *Richfield Oil Corp. v Karseal Corp.* (9th Cir 1959) 271 F2d 709, 715 n. 4.

One of the continuing battles in jury trials of antitrust cases is whether treble damages should be mentioned to the jury. Timberlake (*Federal Treble Damage Antitrust Actions* (1965) 280) urges that the overwhelming weight of authority and the better view holds that the jury should be advised of the fact of trebling. He says (at 283) that this may be done both by counsel and in the charge and that both methods have been approved. Judge Mathes suggests (28 FRD at 467) a full reading of 15 USC §15, followed by an instruction to disregard the part about trebling, costs, and attorney fees.

Plaintiff's attitude toward mention of trebling in front of the jury is analogous to defense counsel's attitude about the mention of liability insurance in negligence cases. Mention of trebling will probably influence the jury to the plaintiff's detriment. The jury is not required or permitted to do the trebling, and should not be permitted to take it into consideration. There is substantial authority for the proposition that trebling should not be mentioned to the jury; a simple instruction to return actual damage "no more and no less" should be sufficient to protect the defendants against any greater verdict than that to which plaintiff is entitled.

Cases holding that trebling may be mentioned to the jury include *Bordonaro Bros. Theatres, Inc. v Paramount Pictures, Inc.* (2d Cir 1953) 203 F2d 676, 679. Cases holding that trebling should not be mentioned to the jury include *Sablosky v Paramount Film Distributing Corp.* (ED Pa 1955) 137 F Supp 929, 941–942.

The damage instruction approved in *Richfield Oil Corp. v Karseal Corp., supra,* does not mention trebling.

VIII. Settlement

A. [§12.74] Joint Tortfeasors

Most of the problems in settling private antitrust actions revolve around the joint tortfeasor rule. In a conspiracy case, the antitrust plaintiff may sue any or all of the co-conspirators, and may collect all or a portion of the damages against any conspirator against whom he obtains judgment. Problems arise from settlements with less than all of the defendants or proposed defendants.

The plaintiff must consider these questions:

1. Will a release of the settling defendant operate as a release of the other defendants? See §12.81.

2. Should plaintiff give a release, a covenant not to sue, or both? See §12.81.

3. Assuming that plaintiff can preserve his case against the remaining defendants while settling with one, must he account for money received from the settling defendant? See §12.82.

4. Should plaintiff give a covenant not to claim against the remaining defendants damages inflicted by the settling defendant? See §12.82.

5. Should the plaintiff's attorney agree as part of the consideration for a settlement not to represent any future plaintiffs against the same defendants? See §12.83.

6. What are the probable tax consequences of settlement? See §12.85.

B. [§12.75] Formalities of a Settlement

Ordinarily, a settlement with less than all defendants should be accomplished with the following formal documents:

1. A letter to opposing counsel carefully setting forth the agreement of the parties, and describing papers without agreement on which there will be no settlement. See §12.76.

2. A covenant not to sue in a form that guarantees the survival of the plaintiff's claim against remaining defendants. See §12.78.

3. A dismissal without prejudice. See §12.79.

4. A release and covenant not to sue running from the defendant to the plaintiff and its officers, directors, heirs, assigns, etc. See §12.77.

5. A check payable to plaintiff's attorney as trustee, or payable jointly to the plaintiff and to his attorney.

A settlement is a contract and is presumably governed by the law of the state in which it is made or to be performed, under conflicts rules. It may be subject to state law governing such matters as the statute of frauds. *Winchester Drive-In Theatre, Inc. v Warner Bros. Pictures Distributing Corp.* (9th Cir 1966) 358 F2d 432.

1. [§12.76] Form of Settlement Letter

Dear _____(name of defendant's attorney)_____:

This will confirm our conversation looking toward settlement of this case by a net payment of _____ by your clients to my clients, which I understand your clients are prepared to pay. My clients are prepared to accept that sum in settlement of this litigation provided that we can agree on the terms of settlement papers. I anticipate no difficulty in arriving at such an agreement, but I want you to understand clearly that until such papers have been drafted, approved, executed, and delivered, we will not have a settlement.

I enclose a form of release and covenant not to sue, which my clients will require of your clients. Please review it, and if it is satisfactory, have your clients execute it.

623

I enclose a copy of a dismissal without prejudice that we are prepared to give you in connection with the settlement.

Would you please supply me, at your earliest convenience, with the form of covenant not to sue that you would like to have my clients execute in connection with this settlement. Please keep in mind our express understanding that this settlement must not prejudice my clients' claims against other defendants remaining in this litigation. That should be spelled out clearly.

When you prepare a check, please make it payable _____jointly to the plaintiffs and to me/to me as trustee for plaintiffs_____ .

Very truly yours,

_____(attorney for plaintiffs)_____

COMMENT: The reason for leaving the job of drafting the covenant to be signed by plaintiffs to the attorney for the defendants is two-fold. First, it is a matter of allocation of labor—if possible the plaintiff's attorney should let the defendants' attorney do the work. Second, and perhaps more important, the defendants must be satisfied with the form of release, and the quickest way to arrive at a satisfactory solution is to let the defendants produce the first draft. For comparison purposes, a form of covenant appears at §12.78.

2. [§12.77] Form of Release (Running to Plaintiff)

RELEASE

Whereas there is presently pending in the United States District Court for the _____ District of _____ an action entitled _____ v _____ , Civil Action No. _____ ; and

Whereas _____(name of plaintiffs)_____ and _____(name of defendants)_____ desire to settle and terminate all disputes among themselves including, but not by way of limitation, the above mentioned Action No. _____ ; and

Whereas _____(defendants)_____ desire to assure _____(name of plaintiffs)_____ no action will be brought by _____(defendants)_____ against _____(plaintiffs)_____ by reason of any matter, cause or thing, occurring from the beginning of the world to the effective date of this covenant not to sue:

Now, therefore, in consideration of settlement of the aforementioned

action as between ___(name of plaintiffs)___ **and** ___(name of defendants)___ , ___(name of defendants)___ **hereby release** ___(name of plaintiffs)___ **from all claims, demands, causes of action, obligations, damages and liabilities of every kind including, without restricting the generality of the foregoing, all costs, expenses, attorney fees and all other claims of whatever kind arising out of Civil Action No.** ___.

In addition, ___(name of defendants)___ **covenant as follows:**

1. ___(name of defendants)___ **will not bring, commence, institute, maintain or prosecute any action at law or proceeding in equity, or any legal proceedings whatsoever or other claim for damages or relief whatsoever against** ___(name of plaintiffs)___ **based in whole or in part upon any act or omission of** ___(name of plaintiffs)___ **up to and including the date of this covenant not to sue, including, without restricting the generality of the foregoing, any claim, demand, cause of action, obligation, damage or liability based upon, arising out of, or connected in any way whatsoever with any act, cause, or matter which is in whole or in part the subject of Civil Action No.** ___.

2. This covenant not to sue may be pleaded as a full and complete defense to, and may be used as a basis for an injunction against, any action, suit or any other proceeding that may be instituted, prosecuted or attempted by ___(name of defendants)___ **in breach of this covenant not to sue.**

3. This covenant not to sue is and shall be binding on ___(name of defendants)___ **and their successors or assigns and shall inure to the benefit of** ___(name of plaintiffs)___ **and their successors and assigns with respect to any and all claims, known or unknown, that** ___(name of defendants)___ **may have against** ___(name of plaintiffs)___ **on the effective date of this covenant not to sue.**

4. ___(Name of defendants)___ **represent and warrant that** ___(name defendants' attorneys)___ **are the attorneys employed to represent them with respect to this covenant not to sue and all matters covered by it; that** ___(name of defendants)___ **have been fully advised by their attorneys of their rights and duties concerning the execution of this covenant not to sue.**

___(name of defendants)___

COMMENT: Any settlement should protect the plaintiff from claims for costs, expenses, and suits for abuse of process or malicious prosecution as well as any possible counterclaims or cross-complaints that might arise out of the relationships between the parties. For discussion of releases and covenants, see §12.81.

3. [§12.78] Form of Covenant Not to Sue (Running to Defendant)

COVENANT NOT TO SUE

Whereas there is presently pending in the United States District Court for the _____ District of _____ an action entitled _____ v _____, Civil Action No. _____; and

Whereas ____(name plaintiffs)____ desire to settle and terminate their disputes with defendant _____ including, but not by way of limitation, the above mentioned action No. _____; and

Whereas plaintiffs desire to assure defendant _____ that action No. _____ will not be further prosecuted against that defendant and that no other action will be brought by plaintiffs by reason of any matter, cause or thing, occurring from the beginning of the world to the effective date of this covenant not to sue:

Now, therefore, in consideration of (a) the payment by defendant _____ to plaintiff of the sum of _____, the receipt and sufficiency of which are hereby acknowledged; and (b) the execution by defendant _____ of a covenant not to sue in a form satisfactory to plaintiffs, and the promises and acts hereinafter stated, plaintiffs covenant as follows:

1. Plaintiffs will immediately cause Civil Action No. _____ now pending in the United States District Court for the _____ District of _____, to be dismissed without prejudice as to defendant _____ only.

2. Plaintiffs will not bring, commence, institute, maintain, or prosecute any action at law or proceeding in equity against defendant _____ or any legal proceeding whatsoever or other claim for damages or relief whatsoever against defendant _____ based in whole or in part on any act or omission of defendant _____ up to and including the date of this covenant not to sue, including, without restricting the generality of the foregoing, any claim, demand, cause of action, obligation, damage, or liability based upon, arising out of, or connected in any way whatsoever with any acts, cause, or matter which is in whole or in part the subject of Civil Action No. _____.

3. This covenant not to sue may be pleaded as a full and complete defense to, and may be used as a basis for an injunction against, any action, suit, or any other proceeding that may be instituted, prosecuted, or attempted by plaintiffs in breach of this covenant not to sue.

4. This covenant not to sue is and shall be binding on plaintiffs' successors or assigns and shall inure to the benefit of defendant _____ and its successors and assigns with respect to any and all claims, known or unknown, that plaintiffs may have against defendant _____ on the effective date of

this covenant not to sue. This covenant not to sue shall not inure to the benefit of anyone with respect to claims that plaintiff may have against persons other than defendant _____, including without limiting the generality of the foregoing, ____(list all other defendants in the case)____, on the effective date of this covenant not to sue.

5. Plaintiffs represent and warrant that ____(plaintiffs' attorneys)____ are the attorneys employed to represent them with respect to this covenant not to sue and all matters covered by it; that plaintiffs have been fully advised by the attorneys concerning their rights with respect to the execution of this covenant not to sue; that the named attorneys are authorized and directed to receive on behalf of plaintiffs the consideration provided for by this covenant not to sue; and that the named attorneys are authorized and directed to execute stipulations and take all necessary action to dismiss without prejudice Civil Action No. _____ as against defendant _____ only, as provided in paragraph 4 of this covenant not to sue.

6. It is understood and agreed that in the execution of this covenant not to sue, plaintiffs in Civil Action No. _____ do not accept the consideration provided for in this covenant not to sue as full compensation to plaintiffs for the damages alleged to have been suffered by plaintiffs in their complaint in Civil Action No. _____, or for allowable costs and attorneys' fees in Civil Action No. _____, or otherwise, and that plaintiffs accept the consideration as only partial compensation therefor; and that plaintiffs in Civil Action No. _____ do not in any manner or respect waive, relinquish, release, or discharge any claim or claims against any person, firm, or corporation other than defendant _____, including, but not by way of limitation, its claims against defendants ____(list all other defendants in the case)____; and that plaintiffs in Civil Action No. _____ specifically retain their claims and causes of action against the remaining defendants in Civil Action No. _____ and otherwise.

COMMENT: For discussion, see §12.81.

4. [§12.79] Form of Stipulation and Order for Dismissal Without Prejudice

(Title of Court)

(Title of Cause)   No. _____

DISMISSAL WITHOUT PREJUDICE

It is hereby stipulated by and between plaintiffs _____ and defendant _____, by and through their respective attorneys, that the above action may be dismissed without prejudice as to defendant _____ only. Defendant _____ shall bear its own costs.

This dismissal is not intended to and does not dismiss this action, or any part of it, as to any other defendants.
Dated: _____

_____
Attorney for Plaintiffs

_____
Attorney for Defendant

IT IS SO ORDERED:

_____
United States District Judge

5. [§12.80] Letter of Authorization to Accept Fee

It is nice to have happy, solvent clients who never quibble about a bill for attorney's fees. It is better still to have the money. In some jurisdictions, it may be proper for the defendant to write a check to plaintiff's attorney as trustee. Such a check should be deposited in the attorney's trustee account and separate checks written to the plaintiff and to the attorney himself when the defendant's check clears the bank. Alternatively, if the settlement check is payable jointly to the plaintiff and its attorney, it may be desirable to obtain permission from the plaintiff to endorse the check on its behalf and deposit it in the attorney's trustee account for disbursement. A suitable form of letter, to be written by the client to the attorney, follows:

Re: _____(Give name and number of case and the court in which it is pending)_____

Dear _____(name of plaintiff's attorney)_____:

This will authorize you to deposit the settlement check for $_____ to be received from defendant _____ in your trustee account and to disburse $_____ of that amount to yourself as the balance due on your fees.

Please remit the remaining $_____, less any outstanding charges for expenses, and provide us with an accounting for the expenses.

Very truly yours,

_____(name of plaintiff)_____

C. [§12.81] Releases and Covenants Not to Sue

Releases in tort cases (such as antitrust cases) have been a traditional trap for the unwary, since at common law the release of one joint tortfeasor was a release of all. The rule has been gradually eroded. The Supreme Court's decision in *Zenith Radio Corp. v Hazeltine Research, Inc.* (1971) 39 *Law Week* 4250 has apparently completed the revolution with the holding that "a party releases only those others whom he intends to release." Still, to be sure that the intention is clear, it remains desirable to identify remaining defendants *not* intended to be released in a release given to other defendants.

A covenant not to sue gives rise to damages for continued prosecution of the case against the party to whom the covenant has been given. Damages include defendant's attorneys' fees for defending the merits of the case, but of course do not include anything on account of efforts expended to establish the existence of the covenant in the first instance. *Winchester Drive-In Theatre, Inc. v Warner Bros. Pictures Distributing Corp.* (9th Cir 1966) 358 F2d 432, 436.

Counsel should beware of the broad boilerplate that defendants like to put into their releases. Unless the plaintiff is willing to release all the world of all responsibility for everything, counsel should be sure he knows who all the "officers, directors, employees, heirs, assigns, parents, subsidiaries, affiliates, etc." are, and knows what possible claims exist between the broad class of people who are being released and the plaintiff giving the release.

Sometimes releases are obtained under conditions of oppression and plaintiffs have subsequently attempted to avoid their effect on that ground. Attempts in this direction have not been notably successful. See, e.g., *S.E. Rondon Co. v Atlantic Richfield Co.* (CD Calif 1968) 288 F Supp 879.

D. [§12.82] Offset for Settlements

When a plaintiff has settled with one defendant prior to trial, the amount received must be deducted from the *trebled* amount awarded by the court at the trial of the remaining defendants. *Flintkote Co. v Lysfjord* (9th Cir 1957) 246 F2d 368, 398, *cert den* (1957) 355 US 835.

Except for this offset requirement there is no contribution among antitrust defendants. Indeed, the law on contribution as such is extremely sparse. There does not seem to be any case definitely establishing whether state law or federal law applies.

In *Webster Motor Car Co. v Zell Motor Car Co.* (4th Cir 1956) 234 F2d 616, 619, the court suggested that Maryland law would apply to an antitrust recovery and that contribution might be had. However, in the subsequent case of *Goldlawr, Inc. v Shubert* (3rd Cir 1960) 276 F2d 614, 616, the court suggested that federal common law applies and that there is no federal right of contribution among joint tortfeasors.

In the face of these rules, co-defendants sometimes contract among themselves to divide their responsibility to the plaintiff. For example, in an overcharge case, the defendants may agree that each will be responsible for damages arising out of the sales that it has made to the plaintiff, and will require as a condition of any settlement with the plaintiff that the plaintiff agree to withdraw its claims on account of purchases from the settling defendant.

Suppose that a plaintiff agrees to such a settlement, and then proceeds to trial against the remaining defendants on the basis of purchases from those remaining defendants only. Are the remaining defendants entitled to the offset prescribed in *Flintkote*? Any rational interpretation of the defendants' damage-sharing contract would seem to preclude a claim of offset if the consideration for settlement was a reduction in the portion of the plaintiff's claim that went to trial against the remaining defendants. Nevertheless, the careful practitioner may wish to assure himself in advance that the remaining defendants will not claim offset if he removes the settling defendant's transactions from his claims presented at trial.

E. [§12.83] Attorney's Covenant Not to Represent Other Plaintiffs

Defendants have sometimes requested as a condition of settlement that a plaintiff's attorney promise never to represent any other plaintiff in an antitrust suit against them. Such a covenant is unwarranted and unfair, and against public policy. See ABA Disciplinary Rule 2-108B (1970). It precludes other potential plaintiffs from obtaining the best available counsel. It requires the plaintiff's attorney to provide a portion of the consideration for settlement; it makes the plaintiff's attorney, and not merely the plaintiff, a party to the settlement agreement.

An attorney's covenant that he does not presently know of any other potential or contemplated litigation against the same defendant arising out of the same facts may be given. But an attorney should not covenant to refuse the next case that walks in his door, and if further litigation is contemplated on behalf of other clients, his disclosure of that contemplated litigation must be exclusively within the discretion of those other clients.

F. [§12.84] Settlement by Sale of the Plaintiff's Business

It is sometimes possible to effect settlement of an antitrust case by selling the plaintiff's business to the defendant. Of course, if such a sale is likely to lessen competition or tend to create a monopoly, settlement may in itself violate Section 7 of the Clayton Act, 15 USC §18.

One advantage of settlement by sale of the business may be the opportunity to obtain capital gain tax treatment on the portion of the consideration properly allocable to the value of the business as such.

G. [§12.85] Tax Treatment of Antitrust Recoveries and Settlements

The Tax Reform Act of 1969, PL 91-172 (1969) completely altered the tax treatment of antitrust judgments and settlements, both for the defendant who pays and for the plaintiff who receives. Section 902 of the Tax Reform Act of 1969 amended IRC §162 and §904 of the Tax Reform Act added a new IRC section—§186.

IRC §162 as amended affects the deductibility of payments made by antitrust defendants to antitrust plaintiffs. Section 162 prohibits any deduction for two-thirds of the amount paid by an antitrust defendant to an antitrust plaintiff (whether by way of judgment or settlement) when the defendant has previously been convicted or has pleaded guilty or *nolo contendere* in a related criminal action. The two-thirds nondeductibility rule applies to payments to private litigants on account of violations that occurred before final judgment of conviction. Section 162 does not apply, however, to any conviction or plea before January 1, 1970, nor to any plea or judgment on or after that date in a new trial following appeal of a conviction obtained before that date.

When defendant has not been criminally charged with an antitrust violation, payment made by him to a private plaintiff apparently remains fully deductible. See Rev Rul 66-330, 1966-2 Cum Bull 44 (attorney's fees); Rev Rul 64-224, 1964-2 Cum Bull 52 (treble damage claims).

New IRC §186 is important to the plaintiff. The idea behind the section is that if a plaintiff has suffered losses in the damage years but has never had the tax benefit of offsetting those losses against profits (because there have never been profits or because the tax-loss carry-forward expired before profits were obtained) it would not be fair to tax the plaintiff on his ultimate recovery. Section 186 requires that the net recovery (after costs and attorneys' fees) be included in gross income. The net recovery is called the "compensatory amount". A deduction is then allowed, consisting of the smaller of the compensatory amount or the amount of the "unrecovered losses sustained as a result of" the antitrust violation. The actual mechanics of applying §186 to a particular situation are considerably more complicated than the foregoing would indicate, as they entail carefully defined accounting requirements and appropriate application of the tax-loss carry-back and carry-forward provisions of the code. At this writing, no regulations have been issued under the section.

It is important to note that, from the plaintiff's point of view, it is immaterial whether the defendant has ever been convicted or sued civilly or criminally by the government.

From the defendant's point of view, the critical question in determining the deductibility or nondeductibility of payments to a plaintiff will be whether or not the private action is "related" to the violation of which the defendant has been criminally convicted. Cases under 15 USC § 16(b), which tolls the statute of limitations during the pendency of a government case when the private suit is based "in whole or in part on any matter complained of" in the government case may be helpful in resolving this question. See §12.14. There is a distinction, of course, between the tax problem and the rule on tolling of the statute of limitations. The two-thirds nondeductibility rule is based on a judgment by trial or by plea, in a criminal case. Tolling of the statute of limitations is based on the pendency of *any* enforcement action by the government, civil or criminal, including enforcement actions by the FTC, and excluding only government suits to collect damages.

BIBLIOGRAPHY

ABA Section of Antitrust: *Antitrust Developments—1955-1968: A Supplement to the Report of the Attorney General's National Committee to Study the Antitrust Laws (1955)*;

Antitrust Laws with Amendments 1890-1966 (1966) (Udell, compiler) USGPO;

Areeda: *Antitrust Analysis: Problems, Text, Cases* (1967) Little, Brown;

Austin: *Price Discrimination and Related Problems Under the Robinson-Patman Act* (2d rev ed) (1959) ALI-ABA;

Barnett: *Joint Action by Competitors to Influence Public Officials: Antitrust Exemption or Trap?* (1969) 24 *Bus Law* 1097;

Clark: *The Treble Damage Bonanza: New Doctrines of Damage in Private Antitrust Suits* (1954) 52 *Mich L Rev* 363;

Comanor: *Vertical Territorial and Customer Restrictions: White Motor and Its Aftermath* (1968) 81 *Harv L Rev* 1419;

Congress and the Monopoly Problem, History of Congressional Action in the Antitrust Field 1890-1966 (1966) H. R. Select Comm. on Small Business, 89th Cong., 2d Sess.;

Dession: *The Trial of Economic and Technological Issues of Fact* (1949) 58 *Yale LJ* 1019;

Farber: *The Antitrust Treble Damage Defendant's Duty to Continue Business Dealings with the Plaintiff Pendente Lite—A Two Case Study* (1963) 8 *Antitrust Bulletin* 883;

FTC Bureau of Economics: *Economic Report on Corporate Mergers* (1969);

Guilfoil: *Damage Determination in Private Antitrust Suits* (1967) 42 *Notre Dame Lawyer* 647;

Hale and Hale: *Competition or Control VI: Application of Antitrust Laws to Regulated Industries* (1962) 111 *U Pa L Rev* 46;

Heyman: *Patent Licensing and the Antitrust Laws—A Reappraisal at the Close of the Decade* (1969) 14 *Antitrust Bulletin* 537;

Keck: *The Schwinn Case* (1968) 23 *Bus Law* 669;

Mathes: *Jury Instructions and Forms for Federal Civil Cases* (1961) 28 FRD 401;

Mathes and Devitt: *Federal Jury Practice and Instructions, Civil and Criminal* (1965) West;

McAllister: *The Big Case: Procedural Problems in Antitrust Litigation* (1950) 64 *Harv L Rev* 27;

National Institute on Preparation and Trial of an Antitrust Treble Damage Suit (1968) 38 ABA Antitrust LJ 1;

Neale: *Antitrust Laws of the United States of America; a Study of Competition Enforced by Law* (1960) Cambridge University Press;

Note: *Application of the Sherman Act to Attempts to Influence Government Action* (1968) 81 *Harv L Rev* 847;

Note: *Clayton Act §4—Standing—Antitrust Violator May Be Liable for Damages Resulting from Overcharges in Sales by Non-Conspiring Competitors* (1969) 82 *Harv L Rev* 1374;

Note: *Private Treble Damage Antitrust Suits: Measure of Damages for Destruction of All or Part of a Business* (1967) 80 *Harv L Rev* 1566;

Note: *The Super Bowl and the Sherman Act: Professional Team Sports and the Antitrust Laws* (1967) 81 *Harv L Rev* 418;

Pitofsky: *Joint Ventures Under the Antitrust Laws: Some Reflections on the Significance of Penn-Olin* (1969) 82 *Harv L Rev* 1007;

Pollock: *Automatic Treble Damages and the Passing-On Defense: The Hanover Shoe Decision* (1968) 13 *Antitrust Bulletin* 1183;

Pollock: *Standing to Sue, Remoteness of Injury, and the Passing-On Doctrine* (1966) 32 ABA Antitrust LJ 5;

Private Antitrust Enforcement (1966) 32 ABA Antitrust LJ 1;

Rowe: *Price Discrimination Under the Robinson-Patman Act* (1964 Supplement) Little, Brown;

Scott: *Significant Developments in Private Antitrust Suits* (1968) 37 ABA Antitrust LJ 790;

Scott and Rockefeller: *Antitrust & Trade Regulation Today: 1967* (1967) Bureau of National Affairs;

The Supreme Court, 1968 Term (1969) 83 *Harv L Rev* 60;

Timberlake: *Federal Treble Damage Antitrust Actions* (1965) Callaghan & Co.;

Turner: *Definition of Agreement under the Sherman Act: Conscious Parallelism and Refusals to Deal* (1962) 75 *Harv L Rev* 655;

Turner: *The Scope of Antitrust and Other Economic Regulatory Policies* (1969) 82 *Harv L Rev* 1207;

Wiprud: *Antitrust Treble Damage Suits Against Electrical Manufacturers: The Statute of Limitations and Other Hurdles* (1962) 57 *Nw UL Rev* 29;

Wright: *Legal Cause in Treble Damage Actions Under the Clayton Act* (1967) 27 *Md L Rev* 275.

13

Defense of Civil and Criminal and Treble-Damage Cases

Andrew C. Hartzell, Jr. and Joseph Barbash

Mr. Hartzell received the BA degree from Yale University in 1950 and the LLB degree from Yale Law School in 1953. He is a member of the Association of the Bar of the City of New York, the Cleveland, New York State, and American Bar Associations, and the New York City firm of Debevoise, Plimpton, Lyons and Gates. Mr. Barbash received the AB degree from Rutgers University in 1941 and the JD degree from Harvard Law School in 1948. He is a member of the Association of the Bar of the City of New York, the New York State and American Bar Associations, and the New York City firm of Debevoise, Plimpton, Lyons and Gates.

I. [§13.1] Defending a Federal Trade Commission Proceeding

Investigations by the Federal Trade Commission often proceed desultorily for months or even years. A client who dispatchfully handles his own affairs may become complacent when he hears nothing from the Commission for a year or more after providing information to one of its investigating attorneys. Just as all seems to be forgotten, the complaint arrives in the mail.

A. [§13.2] Consent Orders

The Commission may send with the complaint a proposed form of cease-and-desist order and invite the respondent to negotiate a settlement on the terms indicated in the order. FTC Procedures and Rules of Practice ("Commission Rules") §2.31, 3 Trade Reg Rep ¶9807.31. In that event the lawyer's first task is to find out whether his client can live with the proposed order, particularly if the same order is likely to be entered anyhow after costly litigation.

Promptness is necessary in deciding on consent negotiations because the Rules require that the Commission be notified within 10 days whether a respondent is interested in a consent order. Commission Rules §2.32, 3 Trade Reg Rep ¶9807.32. The 10-day period commences with the date of "service"—*i.e.*, the date on which the complaint and proposed consent order are delivered to the respondent. Commission Rules §4.4(c)(1), 3 Trade Reg Rep ¶9821.04.

The word *negotiate* is something of a euphemism; the order sent with the complaint is usually close to the only order that the Commission will accept, and absent special circumstances, respondent should not expect to achieve substantial revisions by negotiations. Nonetheless, under Commission Rules §2.32, 3 Trade Reg Rep ¶9807.32, the respondent is afforded the opportunity to negotiate *pro se* or through counsel with respect to the contents and the terms of the proposed consent order and should take advantage of the opportunity to present his position and marshal the facts and law in his favor. Respondent must realize that a consent order may be very serious in its effects upon him, for it may last forever unless limited in time, and a violation of its terms can result in a penalty of up to $5,000 per violation or per day of violation, which the United States can recover in a civil suit filed in a United States District Court. Section 5(l) of the Federal Trade Commission Act, 15 USC §45(l) and Section 11(l) of the Clayton Act, 15 USC §21(l). The sole issue in such a case is whether the respondent violated the order, although mitigating circumstances such as good faith or delay by the FTC in objecting to the conduct may be introduced in an effort to reduce the amount of the penalty.

If a respondent is willing to negotiate a consent order, a letter to that effect must be sent to the Secretary of the Commission within 10 days. The trial attorney who is handling the matter for the Commission ("complaint counsel") will then arrange a meeting to discuss the terms. Complaint counsel is connected with the operating *bureau* that handles the type of trade practice challenged in the complaint, such as the Bureau of Competition. (The various units of the Commission are listed in 3 Trade Reg Rep ¶9799.)

Consent negotiation meetings are arranged informally, are usually held in Washington, D.C., and should generally be attended by the attorneys only. Some clients want to appear and explain their cases in the hope of obtaining a more lenient consent order. This is usually the wrong approach since that which makes business sense to a client may not always be consistent with the refinements of the law. A lawyer negotiating alone and then reporting back can usually accomplish more.

At consent negotiation meetings the Commission is usually represented by complaint counsel and by one or two members of the Consent Order Section. Complaint counsel often has a more flexible approach to the terms of the order than his colleagues. The consent order staff tends to strive for boiler plate provisions taken from orders in similar cases. Since all consent orders must be approved by the Commission, the staff naturally feels more comfortable with language that has already passed Commission review. Innovative phraseology is therefore an uphill struggle in negotiations. On the other hand, the *addition* of new paragraphs in otherwise standard form orders is sometimes acceptable even though these paragraphs may actually qualify the impact of boiler plate language. Of course it is necessary that the facts provide a valid basis for the additional specially constructed paragraphs.

Respondent's counsel should not commence negotiations before reviewing both consent and litigated orders in similar cases. The substance of such orders is available in 3 Trade Reg Rep ¶15,000 under the heading "New FTC Complaints, Orders, Stipulations," but it is usually necessary to consult the FTC official reports for the full texts. If these reports are unavailable, the text of particular orders can be obtained, at 30 cents per page, by writing or telephoning Legal and Public Records Division, Federal Trade Commission, Pennsylvania Avenue and Sixth Street, N.W., Washington, D.C. 20580. Many proposed consent orders, in addition to barring the unlawful conduct charged in the complaint, prohibit related lawful conduct and to that extent are like a penalty rather than an injunction. Some proposed orders require affirmative action not strictly necessary to correct illegal conduct. An attorney who examines orders in cases similar to his own will quickly see that some respondents have accepted these prohibitions perhaps too quickly, while others have obtained deletion of the "extra" provisions. Illustrative is the Commission's tendency to insert prohibitions on fair-trade contracts for one or two years and a requirement that terminated dealers be reinstated in proposed consent orders concerning complaints that manufacturers have unlawfully fixed dealer resale prices and terminated pricecutters. Neither provision would seem appropriate in a cease-and-desist order whose function, like an injunction, is to prevent *future* violations and not to punish past transgressions. *FTC v Ruberoid Co.* (1952) 343 US 470, 473. Yet some respondents have acquiesced in such provisions while others have succeeded in removing them. Obviously counsel should be armed with the latter orders when he seeks to temper the proposal made to his own client.

Theoretically a respondent can appeal to the full Commission if an impasse is reached in negotiations with the staff. But rarely will the Commission overrule or even modify the staff's recommendation to relieve a respondent. For practical purposes, the negotiation stands or falls on the staff's recommendation. On the other hand, the Commission with some frequency goes further than the staff and rejects an order the staff has approved on the ground that it is too lenient.

The product of successful consent negotiations is a document entitled "Agreement Containing Consent Order to Cease and Desist" of which the order itself is only a part. On rare occasions the staff, to reduce the risk of unwanted precedents, will agree to a provision in the "agreement" portion of the document which it would not include in the "order" itself. This may take care of a respondent's particular requirements, such as the timing for the effective date of the order or some similar type of provision that can be placed outside the order itself. Commission Rules §2.33, 3 Trade Reg Rep ¶9807.33 expressly provides that "the agreement may contain a statement that the signing . . . is for settlement purposes only and does not constitute an admission by any party that the law has been violated as alleged in the complaint."

Basic boiler plate in the agreement includes an admission of all jurisdictional facts; agreement that the complaint may be used to construe the order; that the order shall have the same force and effect as other orders; that the Commission may withdraw its acceptance of the agreement for 30 days; and waivers of further procedural steps, of the requirement that the Commission's decision contain findings, and of rights to appeal or to challenge the order. Commission Rules §2.33, 3 Trade Reg Rep ¶9807.33.

Section 2.34(a) of the Rules, 3 Trade Reg Rep ¶9807.34, provides that a consent agreement may be submitted to the Commission within 30 days of respondent's acceptance of the invitation to negotiate. If the initial discussions appear fruitful, the staff can always obtain at least one 30-day extension of this timetable from the Commission. Being anxious to resolve negotiations, the staff is understandably reluctant to publicize that such extensions are routinely available. In complex cases, such as merger proceedings, in which divestiture of assets and similar complicated relief are required, many additional months may be granted.

If negotiations are successful, the staff sends a final form of agreement containing a consent order to respondent for signature. After this agreement is executed and returned to the Commission, there may be another long lag before the Commission reviews it. Sooner or later the respondent is notified of its decision. Usually, the agreement and the order are accepted. In that event, they are publicly announced, and in accordance with Commission Rules §2.34(b), 3 Trade Reg Rep ¶9807.34, placed on the public record at the Commission's Washington, D.C., offices for 30 days. Barring objections from third parties which the Commission feels require changes, the consent agreement and order are entered.

Occasionally, the Commisssion will reject the proposed agreement and order, sending back a different form of order with directions that respondent accept it without further discussion or proceed to litigation.

Even then a respondent is not finished. He will quickly be notified that within 60 days he must file a detailed compliance report explaining to the Commission precisely what changes he has undertaken in his business to comply with the order. Commission Rules §3.61(a), 3 Trade Reg Rep ¶9815.61. Although the Compliance Report is not due for 60 days from the date that the consent order becomes final, the Commission requires that the necessary business changes be in effect from the first day the order becomes effective.

It should be noted that under Commission Rules §2.34(d), 3 Trade Reg Rep ¶9807.34, after a complaint has issued, it will be very difficult absent special circumstances for a respondent to secure a second chance at the consent order procedure, although the Commission can withdraw a matter from adjudication for the purpose of negotiating a settlement.

B. Adjudicative Proceedings

1. [§13.3] Prehearing Matters

If the complaint is served without an invitation to negotiate a consent order, or if negotiations fail, respondent must prepare for the hearing. The Commission sends with the complaint a notice naming the hearing examiner to whom the proceedings have been referred. The notice will also state that the hearing will commence, usually in Washington, D.C., 30 days after service of the complaint. Commission Rules §3.11(b), 3 Trade Reg Rep ¶9815.11. This comes as a shock to lawyers schooled in the delays of regular court proceedings. Respondent's counsel must now quickly focus on the issues raised by the complaint; the processes of the Commission are commendably rapid in moving the matter to trial. Counsel's immediate tasks are to read with care the Commission's Rules of Practice for Adjudicative Proceedings, §§3.1–3.72, 3 Trade Reg Rep ¶9815.01–9815.72, and then to work out procedural timetables for responsive pleadings, discovery, and trial.

a. [§13.4] Responsive Pleadings

In accordance with Commission Rules §3.11(b), 3 Trade Reg Rep ¶9815.11, the complaint will apprise respondent of the statutory provisions allegedly violated and provide a reasonably definite summary of the activities constituting the alleged violation.

Respondent's answer is required to be filed within 30 days after service of the complaint, except that a slightly different timetable governs if he files a motion for more definite statement on a showing that "he cannot frame a responsive answer," which is rarely the case. Commission Rules §§3.11(c), 3.12(a), 3 Trade Reg Rep ¶9815.11, 9815.12.

If allegations of the complaint are contested, the answer must admit, deny, or explain (e.g., respondent has no knowledge sufficient to enable it to admit or deny) each fact alleged in the complaint. Failure to do so causes the unanswered allegation to be deemed admitted. An answer admitting all the material allegations of the complaint waives a hearing as to the facts, but the respondent is entitled to reserve the right to submit proposed findings and conclusions to the hearing examiner and to appeal the initial decision to the Commission. Commission Rules §3.12, 3 Trade Reg Rep ¶9815.12.

b. [§13.5] Timetable for Hearings

Although the hearing will not actually be held in 30 days as stated in the notice, respondent's counsel should promptly get in touch with complaint counsel whose name is provided with the complaint. If the hearing is expected to last 5 days or more, he should suggest to complaint counsel alternative dates for a prehearing conference to be held before the hearing examiner, and one or both attorneys should then get in touch with the hearing examiner and set the time and place for such a conference. This can be done informally by telephone. The hearing examiner will then issue an order (form below) which schedules the prehearing conference and sets forth certain procedural matters that opposing counsel should discuss and, if possible, agree upon in advance of the conference. Commission Rules §3.21(a), 3 Trade Reg Rep ¶9815.21.

ORDER CANCELLING INITIAL HEARING
AND SETTING PREHEARING CONFERENCE

IT IS HEREBY ORDERED that the initial hearing set in the complaint to commence on _____ in Washington, D. C., is hereby cancelled.

IT IS FURTHER ORDERED that a prehearing conference is set herein to begin at _____, local time, on _____, in Room _____, The 1101 Building, 11th Street and Pennsylvania Avenue, N.W., Washington, D.C.°

Each party shall be represented at this conference by the attorney who is expected to conduct the trial for such party. This prehearing conference will be stenographically reported, but shall not be made public unless all parties so agree.

This conference is set to consider:

1. Simplification and clarification of the issues;
2. Stipulations, admissions of fact and of the contents and authenticity of documents;
3. Expedition in the presentation of evidence, including, but not limited to, restriction of the number of expert, economic or technical witnesses, the organization and marking of documentary evidence, the period of time to be covered by the evidence, the place of hearings and the trial schedule;
4. Such other matters as may aid in the orderly disposition of the proceeding, including disclosure of the names of witnesses or furnishing for inspection or copying of non-privileged documents, papers, books or other physical exhibits, which constitute or contain evidence relevant to the subject matter involved and which are in the possession, custody or control of any party to the proceeding.

Counsel for all parties are directed to confer by correspondence or otherwise at least several days in advance of such conference, with respect to all subjects referred to herein, as well as other things which any counsel desires to be considered at the conference.

Counsel for all parties are directed to be prepared to make oral or written statements of their position as created by the pleadings. These statements will be considered to be tentative and will be received without prejudice to later modification or amendment.

°The hearing examiners, and hearing rooms, are currently located in this building near the main Commission building.

c. [§13.6] Prehearing Conference and Discovery Timetable

At the prehearing conference, respondent's counsel should ask for a list of the documents that complaint counsel intends to offer in evidence and for the names and addresses of his expected witnesses. Complaint counsel will have assembled his documentary evidence and his list of expected witnesses during the investigation preceding service of the complaint and will be able to supply the lists at the prehearing conference or shortly thereafter. Although some complaint counsel are reluctant to identify their witnesses for fear that respondent's counsel will interview them, the Commission's practice is to require complaint counsel to provide the information. Respondent's counsel therefore should take a firm position in requesting it. Reciprocally, he will be required to supply complaint counsel—although usually at a later date—document and witness lists, to the extent known in advance, to be used in defense. At the prehearing conference respondent's counsel should try to work out a schedule that gives him time to obtain and examine the proposed Commission evidence before he is required to supply his own documents and witness lists. Obviously his defensive evidence will depend in large measure on the nature of complaint counsel's evidence. The importance of establishing clear and firm procedural timetables at the prehearing conference is demonstrated by *Pacific Molasses Co. v FTC* (5th Cir 1966) 356 F2d 386, overturning a Commission order because complaint counsel failed to supply documentary evidence and a list of witnesses 15 days before the hearing as specified at the prehearing conference and incorporated in a prehearing order.

The examiner may propose that the hearing commence 30 to 90 days after the prehearing conference. Respondent's counsel and, to a lesser extent, complaint counsel usually want a longer period for preparation, but it is to be anticipated that in most cases the hearing examiner will insist on trial within two or three months.

d. [§13.7] Discovery

After respondent obtains a list of the Commission's documentary evidence, complaint counsel may ask for an admission of certain facts and of the genuineness of specific documents. Either side can do this under Commission Rules §3.31(a), 3 Trade Reg Rep ¶9815.31. Such admissions are deemed made unless within 10 days the party served with the request either denies the requested matter or states in detail why he can neither admit nor deny it, or files written objections on the ground that some of or all the matters are privileged or irrelevant or otherwise improper, simultaneously requesting a hearing. If objections are filed, the hearing examiner will set a hearing on the objections. Commission Rules §3.31(b), 3 Trade Reg Rep ¶9815.31(b).

In most cases the documents that the Commission intends to use have been obtained during the investigatory stage from respondent's own files by means of the Commission's extensive subpoena powers and "access to" corporate files. See discussion of investigations at §§10.28–10.35.

The Commission treats an admission of genuineness of documents such as letters or memoranda as an admission not only that the document is what it appears to be but also that it was in fact sent to the named addressee. *Frito-Lay, Inc.* (1964) [1963-1965 Transfer Binder] Trade Reg Rep ¶16,969. A respondent is free to produce witnesses to explain away or contradict the interpretations that the Commission intends to place on a document. However, this may require seeking out witnesses from many parts of the country, often a difficult and expensive task. Respondent's counsel must recognize before the hearing the problems of rebuttal that arise once complaint counsel obtains an admission of genuineness.

Respondent's counsel will want to interview the witnesses whose names appear on complaint counsel's list. If the witnesses are unwilling to be interviewed, a real problem is presented. Although Commission Rule §3.33, 3 Trade Reg Rep ¶9815.33, provides that a party can apply to the hearing examiner for a deposition order, an order normally will not be issued "to obtain evidence from a person relating to matters with regard to which he is expected to testify at the hearing. . . ." Unlike judicial proceedings in which depositions are regularly employed for discovery purposes, in Commission proceedings depositions are intended only to obtain testimony from witnesses who may not be available at the hearing or from a person who has helpful information for a respondent but who is not expected to be a Commission witness. Although the hearing examiner has broad discretion to permit or refuse depositions, the Rules of the Commission apparently do not contemplate depositions of Commission's witnesses purely for the purpose of discovering in advance what their testimony will be. This unsettled aspect of Commission procedure is discussed in Harris, *FTC Pretrial Discovery Procedures* (April 1966) 30 ABA Antitrust Section Reports 136; Stewart and Ward, *FTC Discovery: Deposition, The Freedom of Information Act and Confidential Informants* (April 1968) 37 ABA Antitrust LJ 248; and Dixon, *Administrative Delay Revisited, id* 281.

2. [§13.8] Hearing and Connected Matters

The place of the hearing will be determined at the prehearing conference. It is usually held in the city nearest to most of the expected

Commission witnesses. When necessary, an application can be made to the hearing examiner to have the hearing conducted in two or more cities, but the Commission tries to avoid this unless clusters of witnesses at different points make it advisable.

Respondent may apply to the hearing examiner for compulsory process to require testimony or the production of documents at the hearing. Generally there is no problem. The hearing examiner makes his rulings ex parte; denials can be appealed to the Commission within five days "upon a showing that the ruling involves substantial rights and will materially affect the final decision and that a determination of its correctness before conclusion of the hearing is essential to serve the interests of justice." Commission Rules §3.35(b), 3 Trade Reg Rep ¶9815.35. Problems may develop if respondent seeks to obtain documents from the Commission's "confidential records." The Commission's Rules require that the application for such disclosure be specific, state the "nature of the information to be disclosed," its relevance, the reasonableness of the application, and the fact that the information is not otherwise available. Commission Rules §3.36(b), 3 Trade Reg Rep ¶9815.36.

A hearing is like a non-jury trial, but with important variations. Usually there are no opening statements or pretrial briefs, although there is no rule against them. If a respondent believes it will help him, he can suggest such procedures in advance to the hearing examiner after advising complaint counsel.

The main difference between a Commission hearing and a non-jury trial is the informality of the hearing and the readiness of examiners to admit all kinds of evidence. Hearing examiners are frequently well-acquainted with similar cases—although this cannot be automatically assumed—and they tend to admit documentary evidence with little regard to formal proof of its authenticity or relevance. Strict rules of evidence are ignored on the theory that the hearing examiner has the expertise to separate the pertinent and reliable facts from the bulk of the evidence presented.

The importance of this administrative approach to fact finding cannot be overstated. Too often counsel familiar with judicial rules of evidence are astonished that the hearing examiner will admit almost everything into evidence and sort it out later. Many elaborate defense stratagems are undermined because they are built on the false premise that normal rules of evidence prevail. Not only do hearing examiners accept bulk documentary exhibits with little if any authentication, but they permit any type of questions and answers full of hearsay, opinion evidence, and speculation. See, *e.g.*, *Phelps Dodge Refining Corp. v FTC* (2d Cir 1943) 139 F2d 393 (refusal to reverse for Commission's *use* of hearsay). Counsel accustomed more to the courtroom than to administrative agencies will be surprised to find how quickly a hearing examiner will make factual findings based on a single or casual statement by a witness. The words "burden of proof" do not, in practice, have the same meaning as in a court of law. Even slight evidence is often sufficient to prove a point. This attitude may be of as much benefit to respondent as to complaint counsel, but the fact that it prevails must be taken into account.

These casual standards of proof have far-reaching consequences. Once the hearing examiner reaches his determination of the facts, his findings will very likely be adopted on appeal to the full Commission. And factual determinations by the Commission are almost unassailable if respondent takes the case to a court of appeals. The Commission is presumed to have a special expertise on the statutes it administers, as indeed it has, and this presumption cloaks its factual findings with a special authority that has all but foreclosed federal appellate courts from overturning them. *FTC v Universal-Rundle Corp.* (1967) 387 US 244, 250; *Moog Industries, Inc. v FTC* (1958) 355 US 411, 413. This substantial immunity from judicial review seems to have encouraged a liberal attitude on admissibility and a readiness to reach conclusions although proof may be minimal.

a. [§13.9] Submission of Proposed Findings, Order and Memorandum of Law

After the hearing is concluded, the examiner is required to submit his written opinion and recommended order within 90 days. Commission Rules §3.51(a), 3 Trade Reg Rep ¶9815.51(a). The examiner generally sets up a schedule providing that both sides submit proposed findings of fact and supporting briefs within 30 days and counter-proposed findings and reply briefs within 15 additional days. Commission Rules §3.46, 3 Trade Reg Rep ¶9815.46. This leaves the hearing examiner another 45 days to prepare his opinion and recommended order. No special format is required for proposed findings or briefs. Complaint counsel usually submits a single document containing proposed findings, a recommended order, and a memorandum of law. Most Commission cases do not deal in the peripheral or cloudy areas of legal controversy, and the issues are generally more factual than legal. This is usually reflected in complaint counsel's proposed findings by major emphasis on the facts and on the reasons for a recommended order without extensive argumentation on the law. Respondent's counsel may be inclined to emphasize the law more than the facts, but this is usually a mistake before the hearing examiner. The better approach in most cases is to present painstakingly clear proposed factual findings in numbered paragraphs, well-documented with specific page references to the record. The legal points can then be argued in a separate brief. Legal arguments, of course, must not be neglected, particularly if they are to be argued again before the Commission or in the appellate courts, but the best way to win the case before the hearing examiner is on the facts rather than on the law.

Respondent's proposed findings and brief to the hearing examiner will recommend that the complaint be dismissed. Complaint counsel's proposed findings, however, will set forth a proposed order against respondent. This usually contains all the provisions of the order proposed at the time the complaint was served and may also have additional provisions added as a result of evidence offered at the hearing. The new provisions may appear for the first time in complaint counsel's proposed findings; if so, respondent's only opportunity to oppose these provisions will be in his counter-proposed findings and reply brief. Thus, when at the conclusion of the hearing the examiner sets the time schedule for proposed findings, respondent should be careful to preserve his right to file counter-proposed findings and a reply brief.

b. [§13.10] Final Argument

The examiner will offer both parties an opportunity for oral argument immediately after the reply papers are served. The invitation should be accepted and if not made, solicited. The oral argument is respondent's only opportunity to debate the entire case before the hearing examiner after all the facts are in and the legal issues drawn, and when all parties know the terms of the order that complaint counsel seeks. These arguments are generally held in Washington, D.C. Frequently the hearing examiner sets no time limit on either party's presentation. The hearing examiner's decision, and particularly the scope of the order which he recommends to the Commission, can often be substantially influenced by the oral argument. It is far more important than oral arguments on appeal since the hearing examiner will at that time be fully versed in the case and prepared to devote all his attention to it on the day the argument is presented.

3. [§13.11] Initial Decision

After the hearing examiner prepares his opinion and recommended order, he sends the text to the Commission's reproduction department. This is usually done on the ninetieth day after the conclusion of the hearing. The reproduction department often takes one or two weeks to process the material, and respondent will hear nothing for that additional period after the announced deadline. When the decision is ready, it is mailed to both parties, and a copy is sent to the Commission's Office of Information, which prepares a press release. The release is distributed a day or two after the decision is mailed to the respondent. This means in significant cases that respondent may be called by newspaper reporters for comments only a few hours after he receives the decision in the mail.

If neither side appeals, the hearing examiner's opinion and recommended order automatically become the decision of the Commission 30 days after service on the parties. Commission Rules §3.51(a), 3 Trade Reg Rep ¶9815.51(a). The Commission has the right on its own initiative to review a hearing examiner's decision and recommended order, even if neither party appeals, but this is not often done.

4. [§13.12] Appeal to the Commission

On receipt of the hearing examiner's opinion and recommended order, both sides have only 10 days within which to file a notice of intention to appeal. Commission Rules §3.52(a), 3 Trade Reg Rep ¶9815.52(a). Frequently there are cross-appeals on different sections of the hearing examiner's proposed order.

On appeal to the Commission, the initial brief is required to be filed only 30 days after receipt of the initial decision. Commission Rules §3.52(b), 3 Trade Reg Rep ¶9815.52(b). Extension of time for filing briefs can be obtained for good cause on application to the Commission. Generally, however, the Commission expects the proceeding to go forward rapidly.

The answering brief is due 30 days after the service of the initial brief, and the reply brief is due 7 days after receipt of the answering brief or on the day preceding oral argument before the Commission, whichever comes first. Commission Rules §3.52(c), (d), 3 Trade Reg Rep ¶9815.52(c), (d).

Briefs are limited to 60 pages including appendices unless leave is obtained from the Commission. Commission Rules §3.52(b), 3 Trade Reg Rep ¶9815.52(b), provides for the form of briefs to be filed with the Commission, and that section should be studied carefully. In summary, the appeal brief is required to contain, in the order indicated:

1. A subject index with page references, and an alphabetical table of cases, textbooks, statutes, and other material cited, with page references;
2. A concise statement of the case;
3. Questions urged;

4. Argument presenting points of fact and law relied on with references to the record, and the law relied upon;
5. A proposed form of order for the Commission's consideration in lieu of the order contained in the initial decision.

These briefs are similar to appellate court briefs, subject to the important exception that the Commission reviews the record as at a trial *de novo* and is fully authorized to make its own factual determinations and to accept or reject the facts found by the hearing examiner. Commission Rules §3.54, 3 Trade Reg Rep ¶9815.54.

Oral arguments are scheduled before the five members of the Commission promptly after receipt of reply briefs. This means that most cases are argued before the full Commission in Washington within two or three months after the initial decision. Each side is allowed 45 minutes. At the commencement of the argument, complaint counsel customarily introduces respondent's counsel to the Commission. Since respondent is usually the party who has appealed, or is treated as the appealing party if there are cross-appeals, respondent's counsel speaks first and may reserve a portion of his time for rebuttal. Surprisingly, there are comparatively few oral arguments presented to the Commission. Nonetheless the members of the Commission have numerous functions in addition to hearing oral arguments, and it cannot be assumed that they are all fully familiar with the case even though they will almost surely have read the briefs before the argument. The members of the Commission invariably question counsel extensively during the entire period of oral presentation, and counsel should not expect to have more than a few minutes for uninterrupted presentation.

C. [§13.13] Appeal to the Courts

After oral argument, the Commission will render its opinion and final order. This may be issued at any time from three months to a year after oral argument. Once the opinion and final order are issued, complaint counsel has no further opportunity to appeal. The commission's decision is for him truly final. Respondent, however, is now presented with his first chance for review in the courts since he is entitled to have his case heard in a United States court of appeals.

A respondent who decides to seek review can do so in the court of appeals in any district where he resides or does business or where any alleged act or practice which was the subject of the proceeding took place. Section 5(c) of the Federal Trade Commission Act, 15 USC §45(c), for proceedings brought under that act and Section 11(c) of the Clayton

Act, 15 USC §21(c), for proceedings brought under that act. Thus, in many Commission proceedings, and clearly in those involving nationwide conduct, the respondent has a choice of any one of the eleven federal circuits.

It is always difficult to select the circuit that will be most receptive to respondent's point of view. The question of law at issue and how particular courts of appeal have dealt with appeals from Commission decisions in similar cases certainly should be considered. Seeking the best circuit from the client's point of view may result in an East-Coast company's appealing to the Seventh Circuit in Chicago or to the Ninth Circuit in California. There is no rule of thumb; respondent's counsel must make his own choice based on his knowledge of the issues and of the attitudes of the courts. No decision is perfect, for it is impossible to predict what panel of three judges in a given circuit may ultimately hear the appeal. This adds a further element of chance to such forum shopping.

The petition for review must be filed in the selected appellate court within 60 days of service of the Commission's final order and at the same time served on the secretary of the Commission in Washington, D.C. The form of the petition and of other papers and briefs on appeal are prescribed for all courts of appeals by the Federal Rules of Appellate Procedure, which became effective July 1, 1968. In addition, some courts of appeals have local rules that supplement the new uniform appellate rules. For a complete survey, see Lavine and Horning, *Manual of Federal Practice Supplement* (McGraw-Hill, 1970). In the appellate court, the Commission is represented by attorneys from the Office of the General Counsel rather than by the attorneys who handled the case before the hearing examiner and the Commission.

The filing of a petition for review automatically suspends the effect of a Commission order, which otherwise becomes "final" 60 days after service, *i.e.*, receipt by respondent. Section 5(b), (c), (d), 15 USC §45(b), (c), (d), for proceedings under the Federal Trade Commission Act; Section 11(c) of the Clayton Act, 15 USC §21(c), for proceedings under the Clayton Act. Thus by taking the case to the court of appeals, a respondent may delay the effective date of the order by a year or more even if the appeal is unsuccessful.

Three basic questions are presented in deciding whether an appeal is worthwhile. First, is there a reasonable chance of upsetting the Commission's finding of fact? Second, even if the factual findings cannot be disturbed, is the final order so broad and vague, or so severe, that it may be modified or set aside on appeal? Third, will the time purchased by the appeal, assuming it is not frivolous, better enable the respondent to implement the changes required by the order?

1. [§13.14] Attacking the Commission's Findings of Fact

There is rarely much chance of upsetting the Commission's findings of fact. Congress has designated the Commission to be the fact finder, and whether its findings are said to require supporting "evidence" or "substantial evidence" or "evidence in the record as a whole," in practice its factual determinations will stand unless the supporting evidence is *de minimis*. See Jaffe, *Judicial Control of Administrative Action* (1965), Chapter 15. The following cases, in which successful assaults were made on Commission findings, are exceptions to the rule: *Marcus v FTC* (2d Cir 1965) 354 F2d 85, 87 (single invoice not "substantial evidence of misrepresentation"); *Brown Shoe Co. v FTC* (8th Cir 1964) 339 F2d 45, 56, *rev'd on other grounds* (1966) 384 US 316 (two dealer incidents not sufficient to support Commission finding of unlawful price maintenance); *Rayex Corp. v FTC* (2d Cir 1963) 317 F2d 290, 294–295 (two incidents of preticketing at artificially high prices insufficient to justify order); *Timken Roller Bearing Co. v FTC* (6th Cir 1962) 299 F2d 839, 842, *cert den* (1962) 371 US 861 (one dealer incident not sufficient to support Commission finding that manufacturer cancelled dealers who carried competitive lines).

2. [§13.15] Attacking the Terms of the Commission's Order

Respondents have fared better in attacking the terms of the order issued by the Commission, although here, too, the Commission has broad discretion. The Supreme Court has repeatedly stated that the Commission has authority to frame orders to cope with the unlawful practices found to exist. *Jacob Siegel Co. v FTC* (1946) 327 US 608, 611. It may in some circumstances prohibit "related unlawful acts" if that is required to prevent easy skirting of the order by minor variations on the unlawful theme. *NLRB v Express Publishing Co.* (1941) 312 US 426, 436. In other cases courts have upheld orders prohibiting lawful conduct if such prohibitions were essential "to prevent a continuance of the unfair competitive practices found to exist." *FTC v National Lead Co.* (1957) 352 US 419, 430.

On the other hand, when the Commission has exceeded what courts consider proper remedial objectives, its orders have been modified or set aside. In *William H. Rorer, Inc. v FTC* (2d Cir 1967) 374 F2d 622, 626, and in *Country Tweeds, Inc. v FTC* (2d Cir 1964) 326 F2d 144, 148–149, the court struck provisions prohibiting unlawful conduct different from what was proved to have taken place. The court stated in *Rorer* (at 627) that "it is incumbent upon the Commission to shape all provisions of its order realistically to the violation it has found. . . ." An even stricter standard applies when an order prohibits conduct that is concededly lawful. Thus, in *Federated Nationwide Wholesalers Service v FTC* (2d Cir 1968) 398 F2d 253, the court set aside a prohibition against respondents' truthfully representing that they were "wholesalers," stating (at 260) that the Commission's discretion "does not immunize from review an order such as this one which sweeps across lawful and unlawful behavior without distinction." In *Lenox, Inc. v FTC* (2d Cir 1969) 417 F2d 126, a vertical price-fixing case, the court eliminated from an order a prohibition against fair trade contracts on the ground that the provision was "punitive."

Similarly, orders are sometimes objectionable because they are too broad and ambiguous. See, *e.g., Country Tweeds, Inc. v FTC, supra,* (striking from Commission order a paragraph prohibiting "misrepresenting in any manner" fabric quality at 148); *Libbey-Owens-Ford Glass Co. v FTC* (6th Cir 1965) 352 F2d 415, 418 (striking from Commission order a provision against "otherwise misrepresenting the grade or quality of glass used in any window"); *Korber Hats, Inc. v FTC* (1st Cir 1962) 311 F2d 358, 363–364 (criticizing provision in Commission order directed to "any words or phrases which, directly or indirectly," misrepresent country of origin). A respondent can sometimes gain help from the Supreme Court's statement in *FTC v Henry Broch & Co.* (1962) 368 US 360, 367–368 that

[t]he severity of possible penalties prescribed . . . for violations of order . . . underlines the necessity for fashioning orders which are, at the outset, sufficiently clear and precise to avoid raising serious questions as to their meaning and application.

3. [§13.16] Time Element in Effecting Required Changes

Absent an appeal the Commission requires the changes in business practices commanded by its order to be put into effect on the date the order is received. In some circumstances abrupt changes of old practices may be very difficult. The difficulties may be increased if competitors are still utilizing old practices to respondent's competitive disadvantage.

In such cases of hardship respondent may petition the Commission to stay its order until the Commission has obtained industry compliance or at least restricted respondent's closest competitors. In *Moog Industries, Inc. v FTC* (1958) 355 US 411 the Supreme Court ruled (at 413–414) that such a petition fell within the "discretionary determination by the administrative agency" which the Court would not reverse "in the absence of a patent abuse of discretion" and would not even entertain unless it had first been clearly presented to the Commission.

In *FTC v Universal-Rundle Corp.* (1967) 387 US 244, the Commission ordered discontinuance of truckload discounts that were generally granted in the industry. Respondent sought a stay of the order on the ground that its competition utilized the discount, that it was smaller than most of its competition, and that it would suffer great and irreparable harm if its competition were permitted to grant the discount while respondent was restrained from so doing. The Commission denied respondent's petition, and the court of appeals found that the denial constituted an abuse of discretion. The Supreme Court reversed the appellate court on the ground that respondent failed to put sufficient facts before the Commission to document its assertion of widespread use of the discount and resulting hardship to respondent. Perhaps respondent's proof could have been stronger, but the tone of the court's opinion raises doubts as to whether any respondent might obtain a stay if the Commission has refused it.

An appeal, although costly, will secure some period of delay in which to battle with these problems.

D. [§13.17] Certiorari

If a respondent loses in the court of appeals, his final option is to apply for certiorari in the Supreme Court of the United States. If a respondent wins in the court of appeals, the Commission itself may similarly apply to the Supreme Court. As with all petitions for certiorari, the Supreme Court is unlikely to review the case unless the decision raises a significant question of antitrust law and policy that the Supreme Court feels should be determined for guidance in future cases. The strategy, tactics, and procedures followed in the Supreme Court Federal Trade Commission cases do not differ materially from those employed in other trade regulation cases taken to the Supreme Court.

II. Defending a Private Treble-Damage Action

A. [§13.18] Guides to Handling the Big Case

Numerous trial techniques have been developed for handling the Big Case. The Prettyman Report in 1951 (13 FRD 62) pointed the way and was followed by a series of later attempts to expand upon and improve that pioneering effort. These include:

☐ Seminar on Protracted Cases for Federal Judges (1958) 23 FRD 319.

☐ *Streamlining the Big Case*—Report of Special Committee of the Section of Antitrust Law, ABA, September 1958. (Not officially published.)

☐ *Handbook of Recommended Procedures for the Trial of Protracted Cases Adopted by the Judicial Conference of the United States* (March 1960) 25 FRD 351.

☐ *Manual for Complex and Multidistrict Litigation*, Board of Editors of the Federal Judicial Center (1970) (which supersedes the 1960 *Handbook*, amends the 1969 *Manual*, and is referred to hereafter as the "1970 Manual").

Counsel defending a treble-damage action should be familiar with at least the most recent of these guides, although they are by no means handbooks for defense strategy. Indeed, they were designed primarily to solve the court's problems, or perhaps even the plaintiff's problems, in expediting preparation and trial. The guides are useful to defense counsel because they alert him to the authority and techniques that have been organized against delay and obfuscation of issues and make clear to him that he faces not only a formidable body of substantive law favorable to plaintiffs' cases but an equal body of procedural law fashioned by experienced judges and practitioners to move a case rapidly and effectively to and through trial. In addition, the 1970 Manual is helpful in its forms, its appendix *Decisions on Important Issues of Law*, i.e., procedural issues, and its extensive discussion of how expert opinion, computer data, samples, polls, and survey evidence may be used (pp. 320–359).

B. [§13.19] Immediate Action upon Receipt of a Complaint

As the federal district courts have exclusive jurisdiction of treble-damage actions under the federal antitrust laws, counsel must observe and use the Federal Rules of Civil Procedure. When a complaint is served, counsel should first answer these questions:

1. *What date was the complaint filed*, regardless of the date of service? FRCP 3 provides that an action is commenced upon *filing the complaint* in court; for purposes of both the all-important statute of limitations and certain discovery procedures, this date controls.

2. *What date was the complaint served?* FRCP 12 provides that the answer and most motions must be served within 20 days after service of the complaint.

3. *Was service valid?* FRCP 4 provides the usual methods of service. There are significant differences, however, in the territorial limits of ser-

vice on individuals and on corporations in treble-damage suits. An individual can be served (a) within the state in which the district court sits (FRCP 4(f)) or (b) outside the state if the forum state has a "long arm" statute permitting extraterritorial service on those who commit torts or make contracts within the forum state *and* if the treble-damage claim is based on such a tort or contract (FRCP 4(e)). Personal jurisdiction obtained by valid service does not, however, ensure proper venue. The treble-damage venue statute, 15 USC §15, provides that a defendant may be sued in any district where he "resides or is found or has an agent." This slightly expends the normal venue provisions of 28 USC §1391(b), which specifies the district where all defendants reside, or in which the claims arose, but usually an individual defendant cannot be reached except where he resides unless he is "caught" and served while visiting the forum state. *International Business Coordinators, Inc. v Aamco Automatic Transmissions, Inc.* (SD NY 1969) 305 F Supp 361.

A corporate defendant is treated differently. In addition to the rules discussed above, a special venue and service provision found in 15 USC §22 provides that a corporation may be sued in any judicial district "whereof it is an inhabitant," and "also in any district wherein it may be found or transacts business. . . ." If suit is brought in any such district, the corporation may be served in any *other* district "of which it is an inhabitant, or wherever it may be found." Under this broad provision, a corporation can be sued anywhere it "transacts"—in the ordinary businessman's sense—any regular or significant amount of business. It cannot escape by arguing that this business is exclusively interstate in character, amounts to only a minute percentage of its overall business, or is insufficient to require qualification under state law. *Eastman Kodak Co. v Southern Photo Materials Co.* (1927) 273 US 359; *Levin v Joint Commission on Accreditation of Hosps.* (DC Cir 1965) 354 F2d 515, 517. In most cases counsel for corporate antitrust defendants will face an uphill battle to defeat venue or jurisdiction. Only on rare occasions have they succeeded. See *Public Service Co. v Federal Pacific Elec. Co.* (D NM 1962) 210 F Supp 1; *Ohio-Midland Light & Power Co. v Ohio Brass Co.* (SD Ohio 1962) 221 F Supp 405.

4. *Are there jurisdictional and venue defenses?* If a defendant has valid jurisdictional or venue defenses, they must be asserted promptly, or they may be waived. Decision on whether to raise such defenses must be weighed with other initial discovery strategy discussed below.

5. *What is defendant's initial discovery strategy?* In the past, the FRCP barred a plaintiff from beginning discovery for 20 days after commencing suit. Defendants often served interrogatories or deposition no-

tices promptly and thus obtained "priority" of discovery, which some districts allowed. FRCP 26(d), effective July 1, 1970, has undermined this strategy by providing that unless the court orders otherwise, the fact that one party is conducting discovery shall not operate to delay any other party's discovery.

Defense counsel should nevertheless normally consider interrogatories as the first step in discovery. A defendant can serve interrogatories under FRCP 33 as soon as an action is commenced—*i.e.*, filed. These interrogatories should probe in depth the allegations of the complaint and require plaintiff to set forth the basis for each of his allegations, the identity of his prospective witnesses, and a list of all the documents on which he relies for each allegation and the location of the documents. The interrogatories may impose a heavy burden on plaintiff, but they are often justified by the sweeping allegations found in many antitrust complaints. FRCP 33 requires the plaintiff to object to interrogatories within 10 days and to answer those not objected to within 15 days. As a practical matter it may be difficult either to object or to answer in that time; furthermore, due to the broad scope of federal court discovery, the chances of successfully objecting to interrogatories are limited. Thus, plaintiff's counsel is often forced to request an extension of time, and defendant's counsel has the opportunity to ask reciprocally for additional time to respond to the complaint and to bargain for a working agreement that he will be allowed to proceed with depositions *after* the plaintiff answers the interrogatories and after defendant has had the opportunity to examine plaintiff's documents. Thus the use of interrogatories may help in arranging a stipulation governing several successive stages in the discovery process.

Defendant's counsel may serve deposition notices instead of interrogatories. This is usually unwise at the outset because most treble-damage actions involve considerable documentation, and it is well for defendant to learn what the plaintiff's documents show far in advance of taking depositions. Defense counsel needs time to analyze, from an examination of plaintiff's files, the business facts underlying the claim. Most treble-damage plaintiffs are either customers or competitors of the defendant, and thus defendant usually has in its employ experts in the same business who can provide counsel with assistance in examining plaintiff's files, as well as other available materials, to determine the strengths and weaknesses of plaintiff's case. This is particularly true on issues of competitive injury and damages. Indeed, defense counsel should use this expertise from the outset in all aspects of the litigation and not try to go it alone without business guidance.

C. Preliminary Motions

1. Transfer of Venue

a. [§13.20] Complete Transfer

Normally, the plaintiff's choice of forum will govern if it meets the statutory venue requirements. However, under 28 USC §1404(a), which Congress enacted in 1948 to permit transfer rather than outright dismissal under the earlier and harsher doctrine of *forum non conveniens*, a defendant may move to have the action transferred for "the convenience of the parties and witnesses" and in the "interest of justice." *Norwood v Kirkpatrick* (1955) 349 US 29, 32; *Van Dusen v Barrack* (1964) 376 US 612, 616. Transfer is possible only to another district or division where the action might have been brought. If the action has been brought by a relatively small plaintiff in his own district against a relatively large out-of-state corporation, the chances of transfer are minimal. The purpose of the antitrust venue statute was to permit a plaintiff to seek damages on his home ground. On the other hand, when a large corporate plaintiff is locked in battle with another large corporate defendant, the courts are naturally more ready to transfer an action if it has been brought in a plainly inconvenient forum, even if that happens to be the principal location of the corporate plaintiff. For example, in a large treble-damage suit raising issues that relate to an entire industry—such as a monopolization case—the most convenient forum for trial of the action may be a forum at the source of the industry's activities. Thus, a case involving the mining industry might best be tried in the geographic area where the sources of proof are most available, even though the headquarters of both parties may be in another jurisdiction.

In determining the most convenient forum, courts generally look to such factors as the relative ease of access to sources of proof, both documentary and otherwise; the availability of compulsory process for obtaining live witnesses at the trial rather than having the trial on depositions; the cost of obtaining willing witnesses; the desirability in "cases which touch the affairs of many persons . . . for holding the trial in their view and reach rather than . . . where they can learn of it by report only"; and other practical problems that make "trial of a case easy, expeditious and inexpensive." *Gulf Oil Corp. v Gilbert* (1947) 330 US 501, 508–509. For a transfer of a treble-damage suit, see *Kansas City Power & Light Co. v I-T-E Circuit Breaker Co.* (WD Mo 1965) 240 F Supp 121, *mandamus den* (8th Cir 1965) 343 F2d 361.

b. [§13.21] Discovery Transfer

Transfer of actions for discovery purposes only are in a different category as a result of 28 USC §1407, which Congress enacted in 1968. That section provides for the appointment of a judicial panel with power to order the temporary transfer of civil actions to a single district for the purpose of coordinating pretrial proceedings. After the discovery proceedings are completed, the action is returned to its original district for trial. This section has great advantages to a corporate defendant who is being sued by different plaintiffs in different districts.

Such transfers are made only when a number of different damage actions against the same defendant have common questions of fact. This is often the case when treble-damage suits are based on prior government proceedings. A defendant of course will always know when he is facing similar suits in other districts, but counsel should specifically inquire.

The panel of judges appointed to handle applications for transfer for discovery purposes have adopted provisional rules of procedure which appear in 44 FRD 391–393 (1968). These rules deal with the place and manner of filing papers for consideration of the panel, the submission of proof of facts, and other related matters. In addition, counsel should consult the *1970 Manual.*

2. [§13.22] Plaintiff's Statutory Basis for Suit

An antitrust treble-damage action can be brought only for violation of one of the "antitrust laws" as defined in Section 1 of the Clayton Act, 15 USC §12. Those laws are the Sherman Act, the Wilson Tariff Act and an amendment to it, and the Clayton Act, including the Robinson-Patman amendments. If the suit is brought under some other statute, it is not a treble-damage antitrust suit.

Nashville Milk Co. v Carnation Co. (1958) 355 US 373 held that Section 3 of the Robinson-Patman Act, 15 USC §13(a), was not one of the "antitrust laws" for violation of which a private treble-damage action would lie. Similarly, *Schnabel v Volkswagen of America Inc.* (ND Iowa 1960) 185 F Supp 122 held that the Automobile Dealers Franchise Act, 15 USC §§1221–1225, was not one of the defined "antitrust laws," and therefore extraterritorial service of process under the Clayton Act was not available to plaintiff. Further, private actions may not be brought for violation of the Federal Trade Commission Act, 15 USC §45 et seq., which prohibits "[u]nfair methods of competition" and "unfair or deceptive acts or practices," and hence it is not itself one of the "antitrust laws" for purposes of a treble-damage action. A practice that violates the Federal Trade Commission Act may also violate a defined antitrust law, in which event a private suit would lie for the violation. Other practices, however, could violate the former statute and hence give rise to Federal Trade Commission proceedings, without providing a basis for private suits. For example, an incipient tying arrangement held illegal under the Federal Trade Commission Act in *FTC v Brown Shoe Co.* (1966) 384 US 316 may have fallen short of having sufficient potential anticompetitive effects required to constitute a violation of Section 1 of the Sherman Act (15 USC §1) or Section 3 of the Clayton Act (15 USC §14). A buyer's inducement of discriminatory promotional allowances for itself, although held to violate the Federal Trade Commission Act in *Grand Union Co. v FTC* (2d Cir 1962) 300 F2d 92, would not give rise to a private suit since the Robinson-Patman Act, which prohibits supplying such services, fails to make it unlawful for a buyer to induce or receive them. Thus only the supplier of the service, and not the buyer who may have forced it, is subject to a treble-damage suit. Compare also *Atlantic Refining Co. v FTC* (1965) 381 US 357 and *Lee National Corp. v Atlantic Richfield* (ED Pa 1970) 308 F Supp 1041. See discussion of the Federal Trade Commission Act at §§6.3–6.4.

3. [§13.23] Standing to Sue

There are certain categories of plaintiffs that may lack standing to sue for treble damages even if a defendant has violated the "antitrust laws." Judicial theory basically has been that these categories of plaintiff are not entitled to the windfall of treble-damages because they were not within the "target area" of the violation, even though they may have suffered incidental injury. The categories are discussed at §§2.48, 12.27.

Since these categories have been developed by judicial decision, defense counsel should always consider whether the plaintiff in his case may be in still another category equally too remote from injury to be permitted to sue.

4. [§13.24] Survival and Assignment

Similar to standing is the argument that the right to *treble* damages does not survive against the personal representative of a decedent defendant. *Rogers v Douglas Tobacco Board of Trade, Inc.* (5th Cir 1957) 244 F2d 471. Unless the tort is one that was actionable at common law, no claim may survive at all. On the other hand, with respect to the plaintiff's capacity, the prevailing view is that a treble-damage claim is assignable (*Isidor Weinstein Investment Co. v Hearst Corp.* (ND Calif 1969) 303 F Supp 646), although a contrary argument would seem available based on the theory that "penalty suits" ought not to be marketable. For further discussion see §12.34.

5. [§13.25] Effect of Arbitration Clause

If an action is based on an alleged unlawful written contract, defendant's counsel should inquire whether the contract contains an arbitration clause and if so whether an argument can be made that certain underlying factual issues should first go to arbitration before any ruling on antitrust issues. Compare *A&E Plastik Pak Co. v Monsanto Co.* (9th Cir 1968) 396 F2d 710, in which the antitrust suit was stayed pending arbitration of certain issues, with *American Safety Equipment Corp. v J.P. Maguire & Co.* (2d Cir 1968) 391 F2d 821, holding that validity of an agreement under the antitrust laws was not itself an arbitrable issue.

6. [§13.26] Business or Property?

The statute requires that the type of injury plaintiff claims be injury to his "business or property." Thus if the plaintiff is not in business, but merely claims that an intention to enter into business was frustrated by defendant's act, plaintiff must prove that he was ready and prepared to embark—indeed, that he was virtually embarked—on his new enterprise. The courts will not permit a plaintiff to discover an antitrust violation and then construct a case for damages on the theory that he would have gone into the business adversely affected but for the violation. Compare *Deterjet Corp. v United Aircraft Corp.* (D Del 1962) 211 F Supp 348 with *Broadcasters, Inc. v Morristown Broadcasting Corp.* (D NJ 1960) 185 F Supp 641 and with *Duff v Kansas City Star Co.* (8th Cir 1962) 299 F2d 320.

Of course a person may suffer injury to "property" even if he is not in business. Compare *Washington Professional Basketball Corp. v National Basketball Association* (SD NY 1956) 147 F Supp 154 with *Volasco Products Co. v Lloyd A. Fry Roofing Co.* (6th Cir 1962) 308 F2d 383, *cert den* (1963) 372 US 907. See also *Waldron v British Petroleum Ltd.* (SD NY 1964) 231 F Supp 72 for a discussion of the distinction between "business" and "property."

7. [§13.27] Prior Government Decree

If the government has obtained a decree under the antitrust laws against a defendant, private plaintiffs invariably allege that decree in the complaint. Because of their adverse emotional impact, defendant should attempt to strike such references. Although litigated final decrees entered in government suits brought under the "antitrust laws" can be admitted in evidence against the defendant as prima facie evidence by virtue of Section 5(a) of the Clayton Act, 15 USC §16(a), subject to limitations as to time and subject matter which the Court must explain to the jury, allegations regarding the decrees should not be permitted in the pleading itself any more than other selected evidence. The pleadings are before the judge and available to the jury at all times, and there is no reason to risk the prejudice that would arise from the unexplained allegations of a prior government judgment.

Some government decrees are not admissible in evidence against a defendant; those should be stricken from the complaint. They include "nonfinal" decrees. *International Shoe Machine Corp. v United Shoe Machinery Corp.* (1st Cir 1963) 315 F2d 449, 457; Federal Trade Commission decrees issued in cases brought under the Federal Trade Commission Act which is not one of the "antitrust laws" (see discussion at §6.10); *nolo contendere* pleas in a government suit (*Philadelphia v Westinghouse Electric Corp.* (ED Pa 1961) 1961 Trade Cases ¶70,143 and *Atlantic City Electric Co. v General Electric Co.* (SD NY 1962) 207 F Supp 620. Under the express proviso of Section 5(a) of the Clayton Act, "consent judgments or decrees entered before any testimony has been taken" are not given prima facie effect. Also inadmissible are decrees with respect to a time period, or with reference to a party, not directly involved in the private suit. *Dart Drug Corp. v Parke, Davis & Co.* (D DC 1963) 221 F Supp 948 at 950, *aff'd* (DC Cir 1965) 344 F2d 173 and *Paramount Film Distributing Corp. v Village Theatre, Inc.* (10th Cir 1955) 228 F2d 721, 726-727. In *Control Data Corp. v International Business Machines Corp.* (D Minn 1969) 306 F Supp 839, *interlocutory appeal denied* (8th Cir 1970) 421 F2d 323, references to government decrees against the defendant rendered beyond the statute of limitations period were stricken, the court also holding that no reference to them could be made at the trial. The court recognized the importance of its decisions, however, and authorized an intermediate appeal under 28 USC §1292(4).

8. Statute of Limitations

a. [§13.28] General Rule

Section 4(b) of the Clayton Act, 15 USC §15(b), provides a four-year statute of limitations for private anti-trust suits. The statute begins to run from the time the cause of action "accrues." This accrual date varies for different types of violations. *Momand v Universal Film Exchange, Inc.* (D Mass 1942) 43 F Supp 996, 1006, *aff'd* (1st Cir 1948) 172 F2d 37, *cert den* (1949) 336 US 967.

In cases of continuing illegal acts, damages sustained more than four years prior to suit are not recoverable. For example, if because of a conspiracy a plaintiff purchases at artificially high prices over a period of years, he cannot recover for purchases made more than four years before he files suit. The same limitation applies to a purchaser discriminated against under the Robinson-Patman Act.

If the plaintiff sues for defendant's unlawful refusal to deal, he probably cannot recover if the refusal occurred more than four years prior to suit, even though it continued up to the date of filing the complaint. *Ansul Co. v Uniroyal Inc.* (SD NY 1969) 306 F Supp 541. *Contra: Flintkote Co. v Lysfjord* (9th Cir 1957) 246 F2d 368, 394, *cert den* (1957) 355 US 835. For discussion of refusals to deal, see §§3.37–3.40. Similarly, claims based on other types of completed wrongs that could have been sued on more than four years before the action was filed are barred, even though additional damages may be sustained within the four-year period. *Twentieth Century-Fox Film Corp. v Brookside Theatre Corp.* (8th Cir 1952) 194 F2d 846, *cert den* (1952) 343 US 942.

In *Metropolitan Liquor Co. v Heublein, Inc.* (ED Wis 1969) 305 F Supp 946 plaintiff claimed that a merger, which occurred more than four years before suit, violated Section 7 of the Clayton Act, 15 USC §18, since it resulted in plaintiff losing its position as sole distributor of the acquired firm's wine. The court ruled the cause accrued at the time of the change in plaintiff's distributorship status rather than at the time of the alleged Section 7 violation. See discussion at §§2.38, 12.12.

b. [§13.29] Exceptions

There are two important exceptions to the four-year statute. First, the pendency of a government action, civil or criminal, tolls the statute for the period of the government action and for one year thereafter. Section 5(b) of the Clayton Act, 15 USC §16(b). The tolling applies to a private action "based in whole or in part on any matter complained of" in the government proceeding. The period of the government action includes any period within which any appeal or petition for certiorari might be taken from a final judgment. *Russ Togs, Inc. v Grinnell Corp.* (SD NY 1969) 304 F Supp 279, *aff'd* (2d Cir 1970) 426 F2d 850, *cert den* (1970) 400 US 878. Plaintiff, however, must sue within one year of the termination of the government suit. He cannot take advantage of any part of his four-year litigation period that existed at the time the government suit was commenced. The government suit suspension period may in effect give a private plaintiff the right to collect damages for a period longer than the normal four-year period.

Although Justice Department suits under the antitrust laws clearly toll the statute for private suits, the law is unsettled as to whether all types of FTC proceedings do so. In *Minnesota Mining and Manufacturing Co. v*

New Jersey Wood Finishing Co. (1965) 381 US 311, the court held that an FTC action brought under Section 7 of the Clayton Act (15 USC §18) tolled the statute. Section 7 of the Clayton Act is, of course, one of the defined "antitrust laws." Most FTC proceedings, however, are brought under Section 5 of the Federal Trade Commission Act, 15 USC §45, which is not one of the defined "antitrust laws." It has nevertheless been held in *Lippa's, Inc. v Lenox, Inc.* (D Vt 1969) 305 F Supp 182 that if the FTC proceeding was to prevent or restrain conduct that was a violation of one of the defined "antitrust laws"—such as price fixing prohibited by the Sherman Act—then the FTC action tolls the statute even though it was not brought "under" the antitrust laws. Decisions in three other districts, however, have reached an opposite result. *Rader v Balfour* (ND Ill 1968) 1969 Trade Cases ¶72,709; *Laitram Corp. v Deepsouth Packing Co.* (ED La 1968) 279 F Supp 883; *Y & Y Popcorn Supply Co. v ABC Vending Corp.* (ED Pa 1967) 263 F Supp 709. See discussion of tolling at §§2.39–2.43, 6.10, 12.14, 12.16.

Second, even if there is no government suit, a plaintiff may allege that fraudulent concealment of the antitrust violation tolled the statute of limitations. See *Kansas City v Federal Pacific Electric Co.* (8th Cir 1962) 310 F2d 271, *cert den* (1962) 371 US 912. See discussion at §§2.44, 12.15.

If the unlawful conduct is by its nature self-concealing, it is unlikely that a court will require the plaintiff to show that there were affirmative acts of concealment in addition to the fraud itself. *Kansas City v Federal Pacific Electric Co., supra,* footnote 9. When concealment is pleaded, defense counsel should keep in mind the need to develop documentary and other evidence during discovery to show that plaintiff was aware of defendant's conduct and that either there was no concealment or that the statute should not be tolled beyond the time plaintiff's awareness began. Often defendant's own files will contain evidence of plaintiff's knowledge of the unlawful action.

9. [§13.30] Regulated Industries: Exemptions and Primary Jurisdiction

Various industries are regulated in one form or another so as to exempt certain conduct of their members from the antitrust laws. See discussion at §§2.14–2.22. Defense counsel should be quick to seize upon such a defense if it applies to his own client.

In addition to specific statutory exemption of certain conduct and practices, it can be argued that there are certain implied exemptions resulting from the fact that particular industry practices may be subject to administrative regulation even if the agency has not yet specifically regulated the practice. The criteria for developing such an argument are discussed in

Silver v New York Stock Exchange (1963) 373 US 341. But see the limitations expressed in *Thill Securities Corp. v New York Stock Exchange* (7th
Cir 1970) 433 F2d 264.

Even if a defendant cannot convince the court that the conduct under
attack is exempt from the antitrust laws, the additional argument can be
made that the federal regulatory authority concerned with the industry
involved should decide in the first instance certain questions of fact and
law before a federal court determines how the antitrust laws apply. This
is the doctrine of "primary jurisdiction." If that doctrine can be successfully invoked, a treble-damage action may be stayed for years while the
regulatory agency wrestles with the facts and the law involved. For discussion see §12.68.

10. [§13.31] Efforts to Influence Governmental Action

If the plaintiff's treble-damage suit is essentially grounded on defendant's efforts to obtain legislative or executive action, the claim may be
dismissed even if the defendant was motivated by anticompetitive reasons
and acted jointly with others to damage the plaintiff. In *Eastern Railroad
Presidents Conference v Noerr Motor Freight, Inc.* (1961) 365 US 127 and
again in *United Mine Workers v Pennington* (1965) 381 US 657 the Supreme
Court held that joint efforts to influence public officials do not
violate the antitrust laws even when intended to eliminate competition.
381 US at 658. In *Sun Valley Disposal Co. v Silver State Disposal Co.* (9th
Cir 1969) 420 F2d 341 summary judgment for defendant was affirmed on
this basis. For limitations on the *Noerr* rule see *Trucking Unlimited v
California Motor Transport Co.* (9th Cir 1970) 432 F2d 755; *Woods Exploration & Producing Co. v Aluminum Co. of America* (SD Tex 1971) 5
Trade Reg Rep ¶73,422.

See further discussion at §§2.47, 12.67.

D. [§13.32] Appraising the Substantive Allegations of the Complaint

In examining the substantive allegations of the complaint, defense
counsel should keep in mind certain considerations beyond the immediate
legal issues. First, virtually all treble-damage actions come under the
strong control of the court, sometimes at the outset, but in virtually every
case many months before actual trial. The issues in the case will be
carefully framed and set forth in pretrial orders, and the court will undoubtedly control discovery to the point of practically eliminating surprise. This is usually to the advantage of defense counsel. Second, defense
counsel should work out his own view of the issues as promptly as possible and use this work as a guide in conducting discovery, in developing

defenses, and ultimately in preparing the pretrial statements for the court. In analyzing the complaint, therefore, defense counsel should be simultaneously outlining for himself the issues to be explored on discovery and keeping an eye on the types of proof that will be most pertinent to those issues.

A treble-damage complaint must allege two elements. First, it must allege a violation of one of the antitrust laws. Second, it must allege damages to the plaintiff proximately caused by the violation. Both points merit critical examination.

1. Violation

a. [§13.33] Per Se Type Violations

Whether a complaint adequately charges an antitrust violation depends in part on the type of violation. Some practices are considered so intrinsically anticompetitive and lacking in any redeeming virtue that the Supreme Court has classified them as *per se* illegal. *Northern Pac. Ry. Co. v United States* (1958) 356 US 1, 6. See discussion at §2.26. They include:

1. Price fixing, whether horizontally among competitors or vertically between a supplier and his customers. *United States v McKesson & Robbins, Inc.* (1956) 351 US 305. See discussion at §§2.27–2.28.

2. Group boycotts—that is, joint refusals to sell or to buy. *Klor's, Inc. v Broadway-Hale Stores, Inc.* (1959) 359 US 207. See discussion at §2.31.

3. Territorial or customer restrictions imposed by a supplier on his customers purchasing for resale. *United States v Arnold, Schwinn & Co.* (1967) 388 US 365. See discussion at §§3.19–3.24.

4. Most tie-in arrangements, in which the availability of one product is conditioned on the recipient also taking another product. *Fortner Enterprises, Inc. v United States Steel Corp.* (1969) 394 US 495. See discussion at §2.32 and §§3.9–3.18.

5. Section (c) of the Robinson-Patman Act (15 USC § 13(c)) deals with brokerage payments. See discussion at §§5.27–5.30. Sections (d) and (e) (15 USC §13(d) and (e)) deal respectively with payments for promotional services and facilities and with providing such services and facilities. See discussion at §§5.31–5.33. These sections of the act are in effect *per se* provisions; plaintiff must come specifically within their terms in alleging a violation, but if he does so it is not necessary for him to show that any of the acts or practices charged had an adverse effect on competition. Such an effect is conclusively presumed.

Except with respect to some tie-in allegations, a treble-damage complaint alleging one or more of the described practices is sufficient to charge a violation of the antitrust laws regardless of whether the circumstances of the situation appear to defendant as reasonable or unreasonable, regardless of how much commerce is affected by the alleged violation, and regardless of whether there appears to be any "public injury" resulting from the violation. This is so well settled that defense counsel is wasting his time if he challenges the legal sufficiency of the complaint on the ground that the *per se* type of practice might be reasonable in the circumstances, or on the ground that not enough "public injury" is alleged.

There is one critical consideration, however, that applies to virtually all the *per se* offenses: there must be two distinct parties involved. That is, because Section 1 of the Sherman Act (15 USC §1) and Section 3 of the Clayton Act (15 USC §14), under which most *per se* violations fall, require contracts, combination or conspiracy. If the opposite can be shown, the charge will fail. Thus a corporation and its officers were not considered to be two different entities for the purposes of a joint refusal to deal (*Nelson Radio and Supply Co. v Motorola, Inc.* (5th Cir 1952) 200 F2d 911, 914, *cert den* (1953) 345 US 925); a corporation and its sales representative were not considered two entities so as to make it unlawful for the corporation to fix the prices at which its goods were sold by the agent (*Fagan v Sunbeam Lighting Co.* (SD Ill 1969) 303 F Supp 356); and when a dealer in a manufacturer's goods acted as an agent with respect to some sales, the imposition by the manufacturer of territorial and customer controls on those sales was not treated as though imposed on a separate party (*United States v Arnold, Schwinn & Co., supra*). Similarly, the unincorporated divisions of a corporation were held incapable of conspiring with each other in a group boycott. *Joseph E. Seagram and Sons, Inc. v Hawaiian Oke and Liquors, Ltd.* (9th Cir 1969) 416 F2d 71, *cert den* (1970) 396 US 1062, *reh den* (1970) 397 US 1003; see also *Cliff Food Stores, Inc. v Kroger, Inc.* (5th Cir 1969) 417 F2d 203.

For further discussion, see §2.11.

b. [§13.34] Non Per Se Type Violations

If the complaint alleges a non-*per se* type of violation, the opportunity for challenging its legal sufficiency is not entirely foreclosed, although even if a motion were successful, the plaintiff would undoubtedly be allowed to amend. Typical non-*per se* charges include:

1. Exclusive selling allegations, which charge that a supplier agreed to deal with only one outlet in a particular area and refused to sell to the plaintiff who desired to be an additional outlet in the same area. It is fairly well settled that this type of allegation does not state a violation of

the antitrust laws unless it is claimed that the arrangement was for the purpose of giving the single outlet a market monopoly in violation of Section 2 of the Sherman Act. *Schwing Motor Co. v Hudson Sales Corp.* (D Md 1956) 138 F Supp 899, *aff'd* (4th Cir 1956) 239 F2d 176, *cert den* (1957) 355 US 823 is the leading case. A terminated automobile dealer's complaint was dismissed, the court holding that Hudson's agreement with another dealer to terminate sales to the plaintiff was not illegal but was within Hudson's right of customer selection, that the relevant market for determining if there was a monopoly was the market for automobiles generally rather than simply Hudson automobiles, and that the elimination of the plaintiff would not leave the remaining dealer with a monopoly in the automobile market since many other dealers sold other makes of cars competing with him. See also *Ace Beer Distributors, Inc. v Kohn, Inc.* (6th Cir 1963) 318 F2d 283, *cert den* (1963) 375 US 922; *Joseph E. Seagram and Sons, Inc. v Hawaiian Oke and Liquors, Ltd.* (9th Cir 1969) 416 F2d 71, *cert den* (1970) 396 US 1062, *reh den* (1970) 397 US 1003.

2. Exclusive dealing allegations based on Section 1 of the Sherman Act (15 USC §1) or the more specific provisions of Section 3 of the Clayton Act (15 USC §14), which charge that plaintiff's supplier prohibited him from selling competing products. On occasion the same charge may be made by one of the supplier's competitors who will claim that he was foreclosed from one or more outlets which were prohibited from dealing with him. Exclusive dealing restrictions are illegal if they threaten to bring about a substantial lessening of competition or tend to create a monopoly. See discussion at §§3.2–3.8. Thus a complaint fails to show the necessary competitive consequences if it claims only that defendant restricted plaintiff's outlet and does not allege that he imposed similar restrictions on other outlets or affected a substantial volume of commerce. Similarly, if the defendant supplier was breaking into a new market or was a new company competing with much larger rivals, the exclusive dealing requirements imposed on even a large number of outlets may not have threatened competitive injuries sufficient to render them illegal. See discussion at §§3.6–3.8. Even in a few situations involving tie-ins, it has been suggested that the reasonableness of requiring one type of product to be used with another from the same manufacturer saved the arrangement from illegality. See discussion at §§3.17–3.18. In any of these cases the scope of the possible business justification should be analyzed and explored before discovery and should be developed on discovery, if possible, from statements and information carefully extracted from plaintiff's own witnesses and documents.

3. Price discrimination claims based on the Robinson-Patman Act, in which potential injury to competition is a required element in showing illegality. Defense analysis requires that such charges be broken down further, depending on the level at which the price discrimination is said to have occurred.

a. Primary line discrimination: When the seller complains that his competitor has discriminated in price in selling to one or more customers and has thereby taken the favored customer from the plaintiff, the discrimination is said to be at the "primary line"—that is, competition between sellers. Since in many cases rival sellers are able to counter the price reduction with their own reduced prices, it may be difficult for a plaintiff in a primary line case to demonstrate that the discrimination actually threatened to reduce competition generally even though it may have resulted in plaintiff's losing a few customers. See discussion at §5.39.

b. Secondary line discrimination: When the discrimination is alleged to be in favor of one customer and to the detriment of the plaintiff who is also a customer, and plaintiff and the favored customer are reselling the product in competition, the discrimination is referred to as "secondary line discrimination." Here the courts are ready to infer, rather automatically, that if there is a price discrimination, there is also injury to competition, even if only one reseller is affected. This may not be logically consistent with the competitive injury requirement as applied in primary line cases, but it is a reality the defendant must face. See discussion at §5.40.

c. [§13.35] Appraising the Alleged Violation

Surprisingly, Federal Trade Commission decisions can be a source of assistance to defendants. As discussed in Chapter 6, the FTC is an expert body which, among other things, enforces the Robinson-Patman Act and Section 3 of the Clayton Act (15 USC §14). It does not bring actions under the Sherman Act as such but uses the more general provisions of Section 5 of the Federal Trade Commission Act (15 USC §45) when it charges conduct that may also violate the Sherman Act. FTC decisions often deal in depth with requirements for competitive injury relevant to charges in complaints based on the Robinson-Patman Act and on Section 3 of the Clayton Act. Sometimes the Commission dismisses a charge because a particular practice was not shown to have had a sufficient adverse competitive effect to be unlawful, or because a particular practice did not meet some esoteric requirement of a Robinson-Patman Act provision. Rulings on such points carry considerable weight in the federal courts and can sometimes be used, particularly on motions for summary judgment, to convince trial courts to make refined rulings, rather than to apply the statutes bluntly against a defendant and leave the amount of damages the only debatable area.

Defense counsel's task in appraising the violation allegations is to identify the main elements of the offense which must be alleged and ultimately proved. The chances of successfully moving on the ground that a violation has not been pleaded are remote, but if the essential elements of the offense are grasped at the outset discovery may be geared to pinning the plaintiff down on facts which could ultimately lead to a successful motion for summary judgment. In this task, defense counsel might use as his handbook *Antitrust Developments 1955-1968*, published by the Antitrust Section of the American Bar Association which, with its annual pocket supplement, is an excellent working guide. In Robinson-Patman Act cases, Rowe, *The Robinson-Patman Act* (1964) is an exhaustive analysis of the thickets of that statute.

2. [§13.36] Private Injury

The complaint must also assert a logical connection between the claimed violation and the injury suffered by the plaintiff. This connection is usually clear from the pleading—but it too must be carefully reviewed, as the following examples demonstrate.

a. In horizontal price-fixing suits, when the plaintiff purchased at a conspiratorially high price, there is an obvious connection between the illegal act and the resulting injury. Defense counsel must be sure, however, that he recognizes the full sweep of possible injury claims. In *Washington v American Pipe & Construction Co.* (SD Calif 1968) 280 F Supp 802 the court recognized that plaintiffs might be entitled to recover from one defendant conspirator damages resulting from overcharges to plaintiff on purchases from (1) defendant, (2) nondefendant co-conspirators, and (3) nondefendants who were not conspirators but whose prices were higher as a consequence of generally increased market prices resulting from the conspiracy.

Furthermore, it may not be clear even to the plaintiff at the outset of the action whether he was damaged only by the amount of the overcharge or whether he also suffered damage because by paying a higher price he was retarded from expanding his operations or, if a reseller, from fully exploiting his market potential by keeping his resale price low. Both the amount of the overcharge and the loss of additional business can be recovered on adequate proof. Defense counsel's task is to pin the plaintiff down on discovery and try to eliminate or at least reduce the claims based on the second classification of damages.

b. In vertical price-fixing suits, the injury may be unclear or nonexistent. A supplier who unlawfully fixes dealer resale prices may have caused the dealer no harm at all. Indeed, the dealer's profits may have been increased since even an illegal price fixer does not normally require dealers to sell at a price so high as to reduce their overall profit. On the other hand, a dealer who sues because he was terminated for failing to adhere to his supplier's unlawful price-fixing requirements may claim damages for lost profits as a result of having lost the manufacturer's line. The issue in such a case is not whether he was damaged, but whether he was damaged *by the violation*. The "violation" was the termination for failing to adhere to the seller's price, not the price fixing. Thus the issue is whether the termination was a unilateral act of the manufacturer, in which case it was probably legal, or whether it was a termination pursuant to a "contract, combination or conspiracy"—*i.e.*, a "joint" act—in which case it was illegal. The courts have never adequately dealt with the problem. A defendant still has a chance of defeating a termination suit by showing that damages resulted from a unilateral termination and not from some prior antitrust violation. *Carbon Steel Products Corp. v Alan Wood Steel Co.* (SD NY 1968) 289 F Supp 584; *Quinn v Mobil Oil Co.* (1st Cir 1967) 375 F2d 273, *pet disms'd* (1967) 389 US 801.

Discovery in this type of action should be directed to developing a record showing that the termination was indeed a unilateral business decision, regardless of the supplier's good or evil motivation. Such a showing is difficult in view of Supreme Court decisions that find "joint" conduct on the basis of very slight proof (*Albrecht v Herald Co.* (1968) 390 US 145), but the *Carbon Steel* decision and others discussed in that opinion show that it is by no means an impossible task. See also *Dart Drug Corp. v Parke, Davis & Co.* (DC Cir 1965) 344 F2d 173.

c. In exclusive-dealing cases plaintiff may also have difficulty demonstrating damages caused by the alleged violation. Usually no damage is sustained as a result of the exclusive dealing requirements, and the plaintiff sues only when the supplier terminates dealing. The issue again is whether the termination is a unilateral legal termination or a termination illegal because it is part of a "contract, combination or conspiracy." *McElhenney Co. v Western Auto Supply Co.* (4th Cir 1960) 287 F2d 524.

d. In most cases dealing with alleged conspiracies to prevent plaintiff from obtaining a raw material needed in manufacturing, the damages sought are open to question because in such cases the plaintiff may be claiming he was put out of business or his production seriously disrupted. *Wolfe v National Lead Co.* (9th Cir 1955) 225 F2d 427, *cert den* (1955) 350 US 915, and *Continental Ore Co. v Union Carbide & Carbon Corp.*

(1962) 370 US 690 are leading examples of this type of claim, in which the full range of plaintiff's business operations are open to investigation, and defendant's objective will be to determine what *other* causes may have been responsible for the claimed damages.

e. In Robinson-Patman Act cases, the connection between the violation and the injury varies considerably, depending on the type of violation alleged. Here too, in discovery, defense counsel must try to pinpoint the proof that the plaintiff will offer to show the connection between the alleged discrimination and the claimed damages and then construct a defense that traces the damages to factors *other* than the discrimination. For a discouraging but realistic comment on what is required to show a causal connection between a price discrimination and claimed damages, see *Perkins v Standard Oil Co. of California* (1969) 395 US 642.

E. [§13.37] Answering the Complaint

The answer in a treble-damage case should follow the same format as in other actions. Defendant need not rise to the bait of framing a verbose or argumentative answer even if the complaint sets forth a long recitation of business grievances. No benefit is likely to result from arguing one's case in a pleading; a more summary answer is not only contemplated by the Federal Rules of Civil Procedure but is normally the better defense strategy. To respond to factual allegations that are partially accurate but that are burdened with such loaded introductory phrases as, "To carry out the unlawful combination and conspiracy, defendant in the course of its business did . . . ," one might state that "defendant denies the allegations of paragraph _____ of the complaint and avers that. . . ." setting forth a brief nonargumentative statement of the essential facts.

1. [§13.38] Affirmative Defenses

Defense counsel should consider possible affirmative defenses but must recognize that the federal policy of permitting private enforcement of the antitrust laws by treble-damage suits has resulted in Supreme Court decisions severely limiting the use of certain types of affirmative defenses. Typical affirmative Sherman Act defenses include (1) statute of limitations, discussed at §§13.28–13.29 and §§2.38–2.44; (2) in pari delicto and unclean hands, discussed at §§2.46, 12.69; (3) releases, discussed at §2.45.

In Robinson-Patman Act suits the "cost justification" and "changing conditions" defenses found in Section 2(a) and the meeting-competition defense found in Section 2(b) are affirmative defenses that must be pleaded and proved. 15 USC §13. In addition, Section 4 of the Robinson-

Patman Act (15 USC § 13b) grants a limited exemption to certain cooperative associations. These defenses are discussed in more detail in
Chapter 5.

2. [§13.39] Counterclaims and Cross-claims

Counterclaims and cross-claims must be considered just as in any other
federal court action. *Magna Pictures Corp. v Paramount Pictures Corp.*
(CD Calif 1967) 265 F Supp 144, 153) held that if the defendant has an
antitrust counterclaim against the plaintiff arising out of the transactions
or occurrences that are the subject matter of the original suit, it must be
asserted under FRCP 13(a) or it will be lost. Similarly, *Old Homestead
Bread Co. v Continental Baking Co.* (D Colo 1969) 1969 Trade Cases
¶73,002 permitted a defendant charged with conspiracy to monopolize
the market for bakery products in a western regional area to file a cross-
claim against certain co-defendants asserting that the latter sold at unreasonably low prices and thereby forced the cross-claimant to meet the
prices.

F. [§13.40] Appraising the Damage Allegations of the Complaint

In analyzing the complaint it is crucial to determine whether a logical
connection exists between the claimed violation and the claimed damages. It is in the area of disproving damages that defense counsel may
find his greatest opportunities for success. He should keep in mind that he
can lose the battle as to violation but still win the war of damages.

At the same time defense counsel must recognize that the fact finder,
particularly if it is a jury, has great latitude in treble-damage actions to
determine the amount of damages proximately caused by the violation.
Defense counsel therefore cannot simply oppose the plaintiff's showing of
damages. He must assume the more affirmative role of demonstrating, as
if he were plaintiff's counsel in a case against some other defendant, that
the damages that plaintiff claims either did not occur at all or were
caused by factors other than the antitrust violations. Unless he prepares
for such an affirmative showing he may end up with a large verdict
against the defendant which, although based on relatively thin evidence,
cannot be upset on appeal.

1. [§13.41] Fact of Damage

Under general legal principles a plaintiff is required to prove the damage portion of his case by a fair preponderance of the evidence just as
he is required to prove any other essential ingredient for recovery. In

antitrust suits, however, there has developed a more refined rule to the effect that while the "fact" of damage must be proved under normal standards, plaintiff's burden in establishing the amount or quantum of damages is reduced once some damage has been demonstrated.

The distinction between the degree of proof necessary to prove the fact of damage and the lesser proof necessary to prove the quantum of damages derives from *Story Parchment Co. v Paterson Parchment Paper Co.* (1931) 282 US 555. The rule has been often restated and is now well settled. *Bigelow v RKO Radio Pictures, Inc.* (1946) 327 US 251 (refusal to provide first-run films except after delay period); *Continental Ore Co. v Union Carbide & Carbon Corp.* (1962) 370 US 690, 700-701 (refusal to supply raw material); *Perkins v Standard Oil Co. of California* (1969) 395 US 642 (price discrimination suit).

As a consequence of this rule there have been relatively few reported cases in which defendants have succeeded in demonstrating that no damages were proximately sustained as a result of the alleged violation. Stated differently, unless a defendant can succeed in showing that plaintiff was outside the target area of injury and hence lacked standing to sue, the odds are against demonstrating that there was in fact no damage as a consequence of the violation.

One of the few cases in which the defendant succeeded in disproving the fact of damage was *Wolfe v National Lead Co.* (9th Cir 1955) 225 F2d 427, *cert den* (1955) 350 US 915. Plaintiff there claimed a conspiracy to restrict the supply of titanium, an ingredient used in manufacturing paint, during 1947 and 1948 when titanium generally was in short supply. The shortage eased in 1949, and plaintiff secured as much as it desired that year. Although plaintiff's net profits were much greater in 1947 and 1948 than in 1949, plaintiff contended that they were attributable to alternative products it sold when it was unable to manufacture items using titanium. It claimed that when titanium became available in 1949, its profits on sales of titanium pigments were larger and were a larger portion of all sales than in 1947 and 1948. Plaintiff's method of calculating its claimed differences was exposed as fallacious since it used a gross rather than a net profit theory, failed to consider all relevant factors of comparative costs, and also failed to show that the titanium portion of its business was not provided in 1949 at the expense of other phases of its business. The trial court dismissed the action for failure to prove the fact of injury, and the appellate court affirmed, holding that plaintiff's gross profit theory had no probative value and that it was wholly speculative if plaintiff suffered any damage even assuming, defendants were guilty of the violation charged.

Continental Ore Corp. v Union Carbide & Carbon Corp., supra, raised
a similar issue. Plaintiffs claimed that defendants conspired to monopolize
the supply of vanadium, an ore used in hardening steel. A jury verdict was
rendered for defendants and affirmed on appeal, the Ninth Circuit holding that there was insufficient evidence to justify a finding that defendants' alleged illegal acts caused plaintiffs' business failure. The Supreme
Court reversed, ruling that there was sufficient evidence for the jury to
find that the defendants were guilty of the alleged illegal practices and
that shortage of vanadium was the type of consequence that would "reasonably be expected to follow" from the illegal conduct. The causation
issue arose in the context of whether plaintiffs had sought out alternative
supply sources. The Supreme Court said it was for the jury to decide
whether the plaintiffs had done all that could be reasonably expected to
obtain alternative sources. Thus the question of the plaintiffs' duty to
mitigate damages was implicitly recognized, although stated in the language of proximate cause.

2. [§13.42] Amount of Damages

Although the fact finder is entitled to make reasonable estimates of the
amount of damages, the estimates must be based on what might be called
hard source data. Defense counsel must be prepared to attack estimates
that are based on assumptions or on unproved source data. Acceptable
source data varies from case to case, but examples would be (1) past
profits of a business compared with profits during the period of an illegal
restraint, (2) comparative profits of a similar enterprise if there are any,
and (3) in some price discrimination cases, differences equal to the
amount of the alleged discrimination. Defense counsel should seek to
discover whether plaintiff has source data of this type, supported by
appropriate documents, or whether the damage claims are estimated on
the basis of assumptions for which there is no concrete support.

Defense counsel must also be ready to challenge the validity of plaintiff's theories of damage. For example, an owner-operator of a gasoline
station who is put out of the retail gasoline business by an oil company's
unlawful refusal to deal has not been deprived of the physical assets
owned, and it may be presumed, unless he can demonstrate otherwise,
that he will continue to enjoy a return on his investment in the property
by putting it to the best alternative use through lease, sale, or his own
entry into another business. Similarly, if plaintiff as an individual has
certain inherent earning power, that earning power has not been taken
from him and can still be used. Both return on capital and the value of
labor must therefore be eliminated from plaintiff's damage claim in an

action charging unlawful dealer termination because plaintiff has lost neither by the termination. As stated in *Standard Oil Co. of California v Moore* (9th Cir 1957) 251 F2d 188, 219, *cert den* (1958) 356 US 975: "It follows that the only value which his business had before it was closed that it did not have afterwards was its 'going concern' or 'good will' value."

In measuring "going concern" or "good will" value, the test should be what a prospective purchaser would pay for the business over and above a fair return on the capital and the value of the owner's labor. The fair market value should be limited to the profit potential of the business, for that is all that could be transferred to a purchaser. The special value of the business to plaintiff does not affect its market value. In measuring the recoverable market value, the best test is to consider the business's net profits before termination. In projecting those profits into the future, however, a potential purchaser of the business would take into account the contingencies inherent in the type of business under consideration, such as changing neighborhoods, new product developments, the likelihood that the supplier for entirely different and wholly legitimate reasons might cease doing business, and similar factors.

Further illustration of these rules is found in *Simpson v Union Oil Co. of California* (9th Cir 1969) 411 F2d 897, *rev'd on other grounds* (1969) 396 US 13. A gas station dealer was terminated for refusing to adhere to an unlawful price-fixing requirement. Plaintiff's accountant witness testified that the plaintiff had lost $160,000 as a result of the termination. This conclusion was based on the dealer's life expectancy of 24 years and what the accountant estimated to be the annual earnings potential of the business, $10,500. The jury rendered a verdict for that amount. The district court granted a motion for a new trial on the ground that the damage award was too high. An accountant and an economist, both of whom testified for defendant, stated that the business had no net profits once the owner's wages were deducted and therefore had no "going concern" value. The court of appeals particularly noted that the plaintiff's earning power was undiminished and that the jury should not have measured damages by a standard applicable to personal injury cases in which a plaintiff has been permanently disabled. After the termination plaintiff had gone to work for another service station where he earned more than when he had had his own business. Although the court did not speak in terms of a plaintiff's duty to minimize damages by pursuing alternative work, it was recognized that lost earnings could not be recovered if plaintiff earned more in his subsequent employment.

Although the Supreme Court denied certiorari on the damage issue in *Simpson*, Justice Black in a separate opinion disagreed with the damage standards applied by the lower courts, preferring the standards applicable to personal injury cases. He believed that the jury had a right to award damages of $160,000, based on the assumption that plaintiff had a life expectancy of about 25 years and "no one can say with any absolute assurance that the jury verdict was in excess of the immediate and long-term returns he might have realized from his business during that period." 396 US at 15. Justice Black's view would result in much larger verdicts in the case of a younger man with a longer life expectancy and smaller damages for an older plaintiff. The appellate court's damage standard based on "going concern" value would result in the same award regardless of the plaintiff's life expectancy since it depends on the market value—*i.e.*, the value to a hypothetical willing purchaser. Defense counsel may choose to emphasize one theory or the other, depending on the age and circumstances of the particular plaintiff.

3. [§13.43] Use of Experts in Appraising Plaintiff's Alleged Damage

The use of accountants, economists, and other experts is always a problem for defense counsel. The plaintiff has an advantage in that he knows his business, what is behind the profit and loss figures and the figures on his balance sheet, and what hidden economic or business factors peculiar to his own operation may have affected his "business and property" more than any antitrust violation by the defendant. In most cases defense counsel will need one or more experts to assist him in evaluating the type and amount of injuries plaintiff claims. The best way to decide what expert is needed is to discuss the matter in depth with defendant's own marketing and accounting personnel and solicit their recommendations as to outside experts in the type of business. In most treble-damage cases other than those involving the economics of an entire industry, theories are less important than business facts. Defense counsel first and foremost needs an accountant experienced in the type of business and industry involved. This expert's function should be to analyze each segment of plaintiff's business and each portion of plaintiff's damage proof. The results can then be reviewed if necessary by a general economist to appraise the validity of the economic theories that plaintiff's experts construct on the basis of such records. Defense counsel must comprehend all phases of each expert's analysis. It serves no purpose for the experts to know the answers if the bases for their conclusions are obscure to defense counsel. In the last analysis it is his task to organize the presentation of this material in court as well as to derive from it the leads necessary for effective cross-examination of plaintiff's experts in order to undermine their conclusions.

G. Use of Discovery by Defendant

1. [§13.44] Ascertaining and Review of Documentary Evidence through Use of Interrogatories and Motions to Produce

Defense counsel should gear his discovery to the principal issues of liability and damage that emerge from his analysis of the claims and the available defenses.

Generally the defendant will first want answers to interrogatories, including identification of the documents on which plaintiff relies. Next, defendant will seek production of the documents either by an FRCP 34 motion to produce or by a formal stipulation with plaintiff's counsel in lieu of a motion. After review of the answers to interrogatories and examination of the plaintiff's documents, defense counsel should be ready to depose plaintiff's personnel and other witnesses.

Usually documents rather than the testimony of witnesses are at the heart of discovery in treble-damage actions. Most cases are based not on a single instance of wrongdoing in the life of a business but rather on its policy and practices over an extended period of time. Since virtually every business keeps records, the factual story is usually found in those records. Oral testimony is usually necessary to explain, clarify, and supplement the record, but it does not often alter the essential facts that emerge from a systematic study of the documents. This principle of course applies both to plaintiff's and defendant's documents, and defense counsel must launch a thorough, systematic review of his own client's documents at the same time he is taking steps to obtain review of the plaintiff's documents.

Each type of business has its own vocabulary, and counsel must quickly learn the vocabulary and idiom of the industry with which the case deals. Abbreviations, slang, and cryptic comments will be commonplace in the working records of both parties, particularly in such fruitful sources of information as salesmen's call reports, standard intracompany memo forms with respect to individual transactions, and similar working papers found in virtually every enterprise. The uninitiated lawyer can miss vital points if he fails to understand fully the words, symbols, and forms of the particular business.

All businesses try to minimize operating costs. This universal objective leads to the establishment of as much routine as possible, which is reflect-

ed in (a) organization charts that describe both the chain of command
and job functions, (b) standard forms to permit recurring tasks to be done
in the same way with a minimum of human thought and effort, and
(c) standard routing procedures for the forms. Counsel should determine
both the organization and the "routine systems" of plaintiff and of his
own client; he can then judge where the controlling facts of the case are
likely to be found. He can also cut through objections that both his client
and his opponent will raise as to the volume and complexity of his documentary demands.

The above emphasis on routine files does not mean that the files of
executive personnel, or records kept under more general classifications,
should be overlooked. On the contrary, most policy decisions relevant to
antitrust violations, or to the injuries giving rise to the suit, are made by
higher ranking officials of the respective companies. But such officials
may be too alert to antitrust considerations to leave a record of what
motivated them on important actions; furthermore, they often have the
largest stake in the outcome of the case, and this affects even an honest
person's view of events. Defense counsel needs to know the underlying
facts revealed by the more routine documents in order to test and challenge the information obtained from higher officials.

Discovered documents, whether obtained from the plaintiff or the defendant, are only as useful as their indexing. The indexing method must
be worked out in each case, but defense counsel should always have (1) a
chronological file of all documents, each document in that file indicating
its source; (2) a witness file, in which the documents relating to particular
witnesses are included, and (3) a subject or issues file in which the documents are organized according to the subject or issues with which the
case deals. Tables of contents should be prepared for categories (2) and
(3), to be revised as discovery proceeds and as new categories and subcategories become necessary. In some cases separate drawers of bulk documents must be maintained, with appropriate cross-references in one or
more of the categories indicated above. Efforts spent at the outset in
organizing the cataloging of documents will pay for itself 100-fold as the
case proceeds.

2. [§13.45] Use of Depositions

Depositions of the plaintiff or of third-party witnesses usually have four
general objectives. First, defendant will want to determine what direct
evidence the plaintiff has about the alleged antitrust violation and what
parts of the claim are based on suspicion, surmise, and hearsay. This
approach will usually eliminate some issues of fact the defendant might

have thought important but which are not actually being disputed, will disclose other factual issues previously unknown or overlooked, and will often lead to the identity of witnesses of which the defendant had no prior knowledge. Second, defendant should pin the plaintiff down to the particular grievances asserted and attempt to obtain concessions eliminating others. The Federal Rules of Civil Procedure permit questions requiring plaintiff to explain his case and his theories, and defendant should not retreat before objections that legal conclusions are being sought from lay witnesses. Third, pertinent documents from the plaintiff's files should be identified, and those that are unclear to defense counsel should be explained. Plaintiff's witnesses will sometimes concede that all or part of the claim may be based on specific documents only and on assumptions derived from such documents. If so, defendant will gain a better understanding of the exact evidence that must be met in defeating the claim. Fourth, depositions should explore in detail the basis for plaintiff's alleged damages.

3. Special Aspects of Discovery in Antitrust Cases

a. [§13.46] Grand Jury Proceedings

Grand jury testimony normally is secret, but trial judges have discretion to lift the secrecy, discreetly and within limitations, when particularized need is shown. *United States v Procter & Gamble Co.* (1958) 356 US 677, 683; *Dennis v United States* (1966) 384 US 855, 873-874. This rule can sometimes work to the advantage of a defendant in a treble-damage action, although it is usually more of a disadvantage if there has been earlier grand jury testimony on the subject matter of the action.

In taking the deposition of plaintiff's officials, or of other witnesses, defendant may find their memory is faulty about particular business facts. This may be due to lapse of time, recalcitrance, or otherwise. Documents may have been discovered that qualify or contradict the current testimony of a witness. Any of these circumstances may be sufficient to warrant a trial court's releasing to defense counsel all or part of the witness's earlier grand jury testimony on the same subject. See, *e.g., Illinois v Harper & Row Publishers, Inc.* (ND Ill 1969) 1969 Trade Cases ¶72,965, *rev'd in part, Harper & Row Publishers, Inc. v Decker* (7th Cir 1970) 423 F2d 487, *aff'd by equally divided court* 1/12/71; 39 *Law Week* 4100; 1971 Trade Cases ¶73,430. For discussion, see §§10.21-10.23.

But the rule is even more useful to plaintiffs, to whom it of course also applies. If defense witnesses exhibit their own memory failures during depositions, plaintiff's counsel can use that fact as a basis for requesting previous grand jury testimony of those witnesses. To the extent possible, defense counsel should prepare his own witnesses both for depositions and for trial testimony with this problem in mind. The problem can be acute when a subordinate employee, who was granted immunity as to his testimony before the grand jury, is now faced with the prospect of having the former testimony given to plaintiff's counsel in the treble-damage suit. On immunity and grand jury proceedings, see §§10.18–10.20.

b. [§13.47] Attorney-Client Privilege

A related aspect of discovery has to do with the attorney-client privilege, which is also discussed in *Illinois v Harper & Row Publishers, Inc.* (ND Ill 1969) 1969 Trade Cases ¶72,965, *rev'd in part, Harper & Row Publishers, Inc. v Decker* (7th Cir 1970) 423 F2d 487, *aff'd by equally divided court* 1/12/71; 39 *Law Week* 4100; 1971 Trade Cases ¶73,430. With respect to corporations, the rule now prevailing in some districts is that the privilege applies only to communications between counsel for the corporation and members of the corporate "control group," defined as corporate officials who seek and use the attorney's advice in deciding corporation action and policy in the litigation. The proposed Federal Rules of Evidence would adopt this "control group" concept, although they would extend its applicability to employees "having authority to obtain legal services" as well as to those able to act on legal advice. In *Harper & Row v Decker, supra,* the court of appeals for the Seventh Circuit, reversing the district court by granting the unusual remedy of mandamus, held that the privilege would apply if the employee, even if not a member of the "control group," makes the communication at the direction of his superiors and

the subject matter upon which the attorney's advice is sought by the corporation and dealt with in the communication is the performance by the employee of the duties of his employment.

Thus there is now a conflict in the circuits which the Supreme Court failed to resolve in *Harper & Row, supra.*

In any event, defense counsel must recognize the possibility that his discussions with subordinate corporate officials may not be privileged. On the other hand, disclosure between the employee and his personal counsel would be privileged. Thus in the *Harper & Row* case, even the trial court recognized the privilege as to communications between a witness and a lawyer who had previously prepared wills for the witness's family, thus establishing a personal attorney-client relationship, while refusing to recognize the privilege as to communications between the defendant corporation's attorneys and other subordinate employees.

Similar considerations apply to de-briefing memoranda which attorneys for corporate defendants may have prepared after an employee testified before the grand jury. See §13.48. These were at issue in *Harper & Row, supra*. Although grand jury proceedings are themselves secret, no rule of secrecy can be imposed on a witness himself. Thus any witness is free to disclose what he testified to before the grand jury, and corporate counsel's memoranda as to such grand jury testimony may or may not be protected by the attorney-client privilege in many instances depending on the resolution of the questions indicated above.

For further discussion of these matters, see Chapter 10.

c. [§13.48] Work Product

Counsel must also take into account the work product rule. For example, in *Illinois v Harper & Row Publishers, Inc.* (ND Ill 1969) 1969 Trade Cases ¶72,965, *rev'd in part, Harper & Row Publishers, Inc. v Decker* (7th Cir 1970) 423 F2d 487, *aff'd by equally divided court* 1/12/71; 39 *Law Week* 4100; 1971 Trade Cases ¶73,430, the court of appeals found that the de-briefing memoranda, even if not protected by the attorney-client privilege, qualified as work product despite the finding by the district court that the lawyers who had prepared them had "functioned primarily as investigators." The court pointed out (at 492), however, that the

. . . less the lawyer's "mental processes" are involved, the less will be the burden to show good cause. *United States v Swift & Co.* (ND Ill 1959), 24 F.R.D. 280, 284.

The appellate court also indicated that a finding of good cause required for the production of work product should not rest on merely a conclusion that a six-year lapse of time would "inevitably cause memories to dull" and an examination that showed that this was the case in some instances. Counsel should be aware, however, that the *Harper & Row* court is somewhat more sympathetic to the confidentiality of communications and work product than have been other courts and that the law in this area is very much in flux. Compare *Kagan v Langer Transport Corp.* (SD NY 1967) 43 FRD 404, 405 with *Richards-Wilcox Manuf. Co. v Young Spring & Wire Corp.* (ND Ill 1964) 34 FRD 212.

Before making a de-briefing memorandum, therefore, defense counsel should check very carefully the current situation in the circuits that are or may be relevant to his treble-damage suit. He also should check whether the applicable rules can be used to the defendant's advantage. While copies of de-briefing memoranda are often sought by plaintiff's counsel, defense counsel may in some cases find it of use to obtain such de-briefing memoranda during discovery from third parties who testified before a grand jury and whose testimony may be of use to the defense in a later private suit.

For further discussion, see §10.22.

H. [§13.49] Trials

The key difference between most treble-damage trials and other trials is that most federal judges seize control at the outset or, in any event, long before trial begins. If the judge does not do so, defense counsel has ample authority to request and to obtain such judicial control.

Defense counsel should seek to eliminate as much surprise as possible from the plaintiff's case by thorough discovery and by motions many months before the commencement of the trial for one or more detailed and binding pretrial orders. Defense counsel, more than plaintiff's counsel, will need that time to rebut the evidence, and particularly the damage evidence, on which the plaintiff relies. Special emphasis should be placed on limiting the plaintiff's proposed exhibits at trial to those marked and given to defense counsel in pretrial discovery.

Most plaintiffs' counsel demand a jury trial, although nonjury trials are easier to handle and less expensive for both parties. Jury trials are usually more of a risk and burden to defense counsel than to plaintiff's counsel. The latter is intent on making out the defendant to be a wrongdoer and then providing the jury with an opportunity to render a large verdict that may be virtually impossible to upset on appeal. Defense counsel's task is to clarify, simplify, and abstract the critical violation evidence and the critical damage elements for clear and simple jury presentation. To counteract the atmosphere of dirty dealing that the plaintiff will attempt to create, he must strive to show the jury the reasonableness of defendant's conduct regardless of how much that conduct may technically violate the antitrust laws. He must seek to rebut plaintiff's damage evidence and to convince the jury that the plaintiff's business situation is not attributable to any illegal conduct by defendant but was caused by other factors. Defense counsel may undermine the plaintiff's position in the jury's eyes, both by raising evidential objections to damage testimony on the grounds that it is speculative or lacks factual support, and by affirmatively explaining what defendant contends was the *real* cause of any actual injury.

Simplicity and clarity of presentation are essential in jury trials. Whatever the merits of the jury system in evaluating damages in personal and other "human experience" cases, it is undeniable that even the most sophisticated juror will have great difficulty in evaluating complex business facts and needs the most careful explanation from defense counsel to evaluate business conduct and its consequences. The judge's charge to the jury may meet all legal requirements, but it is difficult to believe that in most antitrust cases the jury comes away with anything more than a general impression of how the law applies. Unless defense counsel persistently proceeds along a clear and well-defined outline of his basic position throughout the trial, he will not obtain from the jury the type of analysis that is most likely to avoid an emotional verdict.

No attempt is made here to deal with the many questions of trial procedure that occur in antitrust cases as well as in other federal court litigation. It may be briefly stated that in nonjury cases, it is essential to prepare a comprehensive brief which should be submitted to the trial judge at least a week in advance of trial so that he will have at hand throughout the proceedings a ready reference statement of defendant's position. At the same time it is probably unnecessary to spend much time, if any, on an opening statement. Similarly, at the conclusion of a nonjury trial, a posttrial brief and findings of fact and conclusions of law will undoubtedly be required.

In jury trials the situation is completely different, and the greatest care must be taken in preparing an opening statement that will give the jury a framework for understanding the evidence that is to be presented. In a jury case, also, great care must be taken in preparing requested charges on the critical issues of fact and law. Defense counsel should prepare the charges well in advance of trial and supplement them as necessary while the trial proceeds.

It is not advisable for defense counsel to try most antitrust cases alone. He should have at least one, and preferably two, assistants with him in the courtroom. The first assistant should be an experienced attorney fully equipped to interrogate some of the witnesses and to comment and advise the principal counsel. The second assistant should be in charge of maintaining orderly files so that counsel can obtain in a moment any document he desires. The greatest single trial difficulty in an antitrust case is keeping the vast number of documents in organized and serviceable form throughout the trial.

I. [§13.50] Settlements

Most treble-damage actions are settled before trial. Decision on settlement requires a balance of the litigative risk against the fact that treble damages may be awarded against defendant and that he may have to pay the plaintiff a reasonable attorney's fee. 15 USC §15.

Often the defendant will resist settlement because it will set a precedent that will stimulate other suits against him on the same charges. But a judgment against him, particularly in a nonjury decision that finds its way into reports, is even more likely to stimulate other claims. Opinions rendered on pretrial motions in the case may have the same effect. If a defendant faces substantial risk in litigation, early settlement reduces the risk of adverse publicity.

It is usually possible to obtain as a facet of settlement an agreement from the plaintiff and his counsel that no publicity will be given by them to the settlement. Plaintiff's interest is generally limited to his situation. Plaintiff's lawyers are generally willing not to publicize matters since by tradition lawyer-generated publicity is unethical. Thus in any settlement, the release itself, or a separate agreement, should specifically provide that neither plaintiff nor his counsel will publicize the action or the settlement, and their response to any unsolicited inquiries will be limited to the statement that the action was settled and dismissed with prejudice. Defendant's counsel should also include in such agreement, when possible, a commitment by plaintiff that if the agreement is violated, and if the violation causes another suit, plaintiff will be responsible for defendant's costs in defending the suit. If resumption of business with a terminated dealer is the consideration for settlement, defense counsel will want to retain the right to terminate dealings again, with a waiver of liability by plaintiff, if the plaintiff violates the silence covenant and thus stimulates a lawsuit by another party. Although there may be public policy objection to agreements that impose too high a price for breaking the silence covenant, defense counsel's principal concern should be to obtain the practical protection achieved by such agreements, which are not often broken.

J. [§13.51] Cutting Off the Plaintiff

The immediate reaction of a defendant named in a private antitrust suit brought by a customer or supplier is to stop doing business with his adversary. It is impossible to give a definite answer as to whether he may lawfully do so. In the Third Circuit it has been held that defendant cannot do so if the termination stifles the main action and perhaps furthers the alleged monopoly plaintiff charges. *Bergen Drug Co. v Parke, Davis & Co.* (3rd Cir 1962) 307 F2d 725. The Second Circuit, while reversing a district court's holding that a defendant's refusal to deal with a plaintiff was as a matter of law an antitrust violation, held that in an appropriate "case a court might restrain a defendant from attempting to coerce a plaintiff into discontinuing a lawsuit." *House of Materials, Inc. v Simplicity Pattern Co.* (2d Cir 1962) 298 F2d 867, 871.

It would appear, therefore, that an injunction might be allowed if a cutoff is being used as a means of furthering an illegal restraint or series of restraints on other dealers or customers. Despite the *Simplicity Pattern* decision, most courts under present law would probably find that such a cutoff was invalid for that reason. Furthermore, unless there is an express agreement to the contrary, there is some room for a dealer to argue under common-law principles that he cannot be arbitrarily terminated if he has made an investment on the assumption that the dealership will be continued for a reasonable time.

Automobile dealers are specifically protected by 15 USC §§1221–1225 against badfaith terminations, and in automobile dealer suits the dealer has a much better chance of obtaining a preliminary injunction. *Semmes Motors, Inc. v Ford Motor Co.* (SD NY 1969) 1969 Trade Cases ¶72,964, *modified* (2d Cir 1970) 429 F2d 1197.

III. Defending a Government Civil Suit

A. [§13.52] Introduction

A government civil antitrust suit, because it is governed by the Federal Rules of Civil Procedure, is similar in many ways to any federal question nonjury litigation in the federal courts. In complexity and the nature of the issues, it is like a private treble-damage suit. But when the government, through the Antitrust Division of the Department of Justice, moves against a client, counsel must face special problems, some imagined and others real. They stem largely from the peculiar position of the government, its resources, the deference paid it by the Supreme Court in antitrust cases in recent years, its pre-complaint procedures, and the use to which a government judgment can be put in subsequent private treble-damage litigation.

It is impossible to deal here with the various aspects of federal litigation. In the previous sections a number of aspects of private antitrust suits have been discussed that are equally applicable to a government civil suit. The purpose of the succeeding sections is to point out what is distinctive about the government civil antitrust suits, particularly Clayton Act Section 7 (15 USC §18) suits and Sherman Act Sections 1 and 2 (15 USC §§1 and 2) "economic" suits.

B. [§13.53] The Government's Pre-Complaint Discovery

A client served with an Antitrust Division civil complaint is rarely surprised, for usually there has been considerable pre-complaint discovery.

If the complaint charges that a merger violated Section 7 of the Clayton Act (15 USC §18), the client probably received, shortly after the merger was announced, a letter from the head of the Antitrust Division or of one of its local offices, countersigned by a subordinate, asking, among other things, for facts concerning its production and sales in various markets, estimates of its position in those markets, and its previous acquisitions and mergers. Similar facts were probably automatically reported to the Federal Trade Commission if the merger was between a corporation with at least $240,000,000 in assets and a corporation with at least $10,000,000 in assets. (Federal Trade Commission Order Requiring Filing of Special Report, May 6, 1969) See discussion in §§4.71–4.73. This information is usually made available to the division. If the complaint charges some other violation, the defendants were probably previously served with a civil investigative demand that asked for documents and statistics. Conceivably there was a grand jury investigation, although this is less likely since the enactment of the statute authorizing the civil investigative demand. See discussion in Chapter 10.

Counsel's first step after reading the complaint, therefore, should be to review and discuss with the client all materials furnished to the government and start considering what other materials should be prepared before answer.

C. [§13.54] Cooperation among Multiple Defendants

In a merger case brought pursuant to Section 7 of the Clayton Act (15 USC §18) the defendant is usually alone; in other civil cases brought by the Antitrust Division conspiracies are charged, and this means at least one co-defendant, sometimes several.

It is important to realize that counsel for co-defendants are expected to cooperate with each other in antitrust cases, as in other cases, and this applies to a government suit. To do so is not evidence of a conspiracy, and neither the division nor the courts will consider that it is.

Yet it is desirable that the communication be between *counsel* —and not the defendants themselves. While the exchange of information with other counsel for other defendants is not likely to destroy the attorney-client privilege or the work-product protections, a document may well become unprotected if it is distributed through the executive suite of a co-defendant. In addition, information counsel may want to share with counsel for the other defendants may be the kind that the client, for business reasons, will not want to reveal to competitors, and it is entirely possible to work out arrangements with other counsel under which that information is not revealed to their clients unless it becomes necessary to present the material at the trial.

Co-defendants' counsel not only can share information, but they can and should share the expense of preparation. Ordinarily counsel for one of the defendants—usually the largest—takes the lead, but it is expected that others will assume some of the responsibilities. Frequently counsel act by the committee system with its advantages and disadvantages. Each counsel, after consulting his client, must work out a satisfactory balance that will ensure that the client's interests, which are not necessarily identical with those of the leader or the other defendants, will receive adequate protection and, at the same time, will minimize the expenses of duplication and unnecessary conferences.

The problem extends throughout the case—during pleading, preparation, discovery, settlement conferences, the pretrial conference, the trial itself, determining whether to appeal, the appeals, and the settlement of the decree if the ultimate holding is that the defendants have violated the law.

D. [§13.55] Objections to Jurisdiction or Venue

Counsel should immediately examine the complaint, of course, for jurisdictional and venue objections, although there are not likely to be any to a government civil antitrust action. Jurisdiction is almost inevitable unless the client is an individual or a corporation that does not do business in the United States. Venue is proper if the defendant is doing business in the district in which the suit is brought.

E. [§13.56] Transfer of Venue Based on Inconvenient Forum

Immediate consideration should be given, however, to whether the district chosen by the government is an inconvenient forum and whether a motion should be made to transfer it to another district. For example, if in a merger case all the principal offices and records of the merged companies are in the Northern District of Illinois, but the action is brought in the Southern District of New York where one company has a sales office, it is very possible that the action can be transferred to Illinois. The primary issue for the court is the convenience of the court and the parties in trying the lawsuit. See discussion at §§13.20–13.21. In deciding whether to press the issue, however, counsel will want to consider the attitudes in the alternative judicial districts toward similar cases and, if time matters, the calendar situation in the alternative districts.

F. [§13.57] Preparing the Answer

Preparing an answer in an Antitrust Division case calls for the same care and conservatism required in any lawsuit. The possibility of a counterclaim against the government, of course, is practically nonexistent, and affirmative defenses are rare. No statute of limitations is applicable in injunctive actions brought by the government, and the laches defense, although it should be considered, has become practically worthless. Section 4b of the Clayton Act (15 USC §15) provides for four-year statute of limitations on government civil actions seeking damages. If the defendant is in a regulated industry, the doctrine of primary jurisdiction—that the regulating agency, such as the CAB or the ICC, either approved the defendant's conduct or should have an opportunity to pass on it—may be available. See discussion at §13.30.

Yet preparing an answer is difficult. Most Antitrust Division complaints, including Section 7 (15 USC §18) complaints, contain a number of allegations about industry structure and the business of the client that seem both true and innocuous but are slanted toward showing illegality. It is important to take care, for example, to avoid acquiescing to a limited market definition that may haunt defendant later. Since many of the government's allegations cannot readily be answered without time-consuming investigation, defendants often ask for an extension of time in which to answer, and ordinarily the government will grant one, except when it is asking for immediate injunctive relief.

G. [§13.58] Obtaining Expert Assistance

In a merger case brought pursuant to Section 7 of the Clayton Act (15 USC §18) or another kind of case requiring market analysis, counsel should get expert nonlegal help and get it early. Minimally this requires that the client assign to the case an officer who knows the company's marketing situation and its products plus subordinates who have worked with the preparation of annual reports and submissions to the Bureau of Census. Counsel and the client should also consider whether they want to employ an economist, either a man who has studied the industry or an expert in the analysis and presentation of economic data in antitrust cases or, in the unusual situation, both. If an economist is to assist in preparation, counsel should get him early to mark out his areas of responsibility— to prepare well, but at the same time to keep costs down and avoid duplication and wild goose chases. It is preferable that counsel, not the client, employ the economists and other experts, in order to improve the possibilities of protecting the expert's communications from discovery.

Compare Friedenthal, *Discovery and Use of an Adverse Party's Expert Information* (1962) 14 *Stan L Rev* 455, 472–473 with *Carpenter-Trant Drilling Co. v Magnolia Petroleum Corp.* (D Neb 1969) 23 FRD 257, 262 and *United States v 38 Cases, More or Less* (WD Pa 1964) 35 FRD 357, 361. The proposed Federal Rules of Evidence, if enacted, will protect the expert's communications even if he is employed directly by the client, if he is employed "to assist in the planning and management of litigation."

H. [§13.59] Considerations

Most antitrust cases, including cases brought by the government, are settled before trial. Most Antitrust Division civil cases, particularly Section 7 (15 USC §18) cases, are costly and drawn out. The client will not only incur substantial attorneys' fees that cannot be recovered but also will lose in large gulps the time of executives and employees at various levels. In addition, it will have to produce countless documents and subject itself to scrutiny of entire operations. These costs will be incurred whether or not the division wins, but if it wins, and in recent years the division has won most economic cases that have gone to the Supreme Court, serious consequences will follow.

Section 5 of the Clayton Act (15 USC §16) enables a judgment in an Antitrust Division suit to be used as prima facie evidence of violation in a private antitrust suit. *Gottesman v General Motors Corp.* (2d Cir 1969) 414 F2d 956; *Kirihara v Bendix Corp.* (D Haw 1969) 306 F Supp 72; *Metropolitan Liquor Co. v Heublein, Inc.* (ED Wis 1969) 305 F Supp 946. A consent decree, "before any testimony has been taken," by the express terms of the statute is not prima facie evidence of violation, although certain parts of the government record could be admissible against the defendant. Thus, the defendant who permits a determination to be made against it in an Antitrust Division suit tempts a prospective plaintiff that otherwise may not want to incur the considerable expense of showing a violation, particularly in an economic case. In recent years, the growth of the class suit, with its potential for enormous recoveries, makes this consideration somewhat less important, but still antitrust lawyers representing plaintiffs prefer a case in which a government judgment can be used as prima facie evidence of violation.

In addition, in a Section 7 case the usual remedy after an adverse judgment is divestiture of the assets or stock acquired, and similar extreme remedies are possible in other kinds of economic cases. *E.g., United States v Grinnell Corp.* (1966) 384 US 563. Thus, there are great incentives for a defendant to settle unless it is confident it can win or it concludes that protracted litigation is less costly than the terms the division may require.

The division, on the other hand, has less incentive to settle, since it considers that it has chosen its cases with care. Nonetheless it will usually discuss settlement, albeit at a high price. The trial of an antitrust case, particularly an economic case, is a commitment of important resources. Although the government is not under the same kind of economic pressure that squeezes a private litigant, the division is beset by budgetary difficulties and is not oblivious to the fact that in the long run it may be in the public interest to settle a matter short of divestiture or some other onerous remedy than to pursue a complicated case to its conclusion. Ordinarily a defendant's chances of obtaining a favorable settlement diminish as the department's investment in the case increases, for the risk of loss is small, and the consequence of loss is not as onerous as it is for the defendant. Many cases are settled at the time the complaint is brought as a result of discussions initiated by the defendant when the division makes its first inquiry or indicates that it will sue.

Moreover, the earlier the settlement the less information is available to private plaintiffs, for although a settlement deprives a private plaintiff of a prima facie determination of violation, as a practical matter he still has access to much of the case the division has built up, at least when it becomes part of the record. See *Olympic Refining Company v Carter* (9th Cir 1964) 332 F2d 260, *cert den* (1964) 379 US 900.

In advising the client whether, when, and on what terms to settle, counsel must ask and try to approach answers to these questions, among others:

1. What are the chances for success?
2. If the government wins, what relief is it likely to ask for and what relief is it likely to get?
3. What will be the cost of litigation in terms of counsel fees and executives' time?
4. Are there skeletons in the closet that may be exposed in intensive discovery?
5. What are the possibilities of a treble-damage suit?
6. What can be gained from time?

One thing *not* gained from time is the running of the statute of limitations in treble-damage suits. 15 USC §16(b). See discussion at §13.29.

I. [§13.60] Negotiating Consent Decrees

In working out the terms of the consent decree, precedent is always persuasive, although the department insists it is not bound by consent decrees entered into in other cases. Thus, before discussing terms with the division, counsel should study carefully consent decrees entered in similar cases, particularly recent cases. The full text of Section 7 (15 USC §18) consent decrees may be found in the Trade Regulation Reporter. In addition, the ABA has prepared a highly useful analytical collection of provisions from consent decrees entered since 1955. *Antitrust Consent Decree Manual* (1969) ABA Section of Antitrust Law. Also useful is a compendium of abstracts from consent decrees, indexed by industry and by issues, prepared by the American Enterprise Institute. *Antitrust Consent Decrees 1906-66* (1968) American Enterprise Institute for Public Policy Research.

Most consent decrees contain a provision that the defendant does not admit a violation of the law and that there has been no adjudication of violation. In some instances, the division has not consented to such a term and indeed has insisted on a provision in which the defendant agrees not to contest the allegation of violation in damage suits by states and other governmental agencies. If the division insists on this, there is nothing counsel can do about it—except perhaps limit its impact or litigate to a judicial decision on the merits. The division, according to *Antitrust Developments 1955-1968* at 227, has not followed this practice in recent decrees but has indicated that it may instead refuse to enter into a consent decree and litigate in situations of this kind.

In negotiating the decree, particularly at an early stage, counsel should keep in mind that the client almost certainly knows more about the industry than the government. This confers an advantage, but only if counsel is in a position to make use of the information. Frequently this requires the closest coordination not only with the client's officers but also with house counsel.

Negotiations are multidimensional. Ultimately, the result must satisfy the lawyers handling the case, the chief of their section, and the judgments section, which occasionally regards its boiler plate provisions as something akin to the Holy Writ. It is vital, therefore, not to build up antagonisms at any level—which means, as a rule, that counsel must appreciate that representatives of the division are able, dedicated men whose points of view necessarily differ somewhat from theirs. And counsel must realize that although the division has new leadership every few years, much of "the staff" remains, and their experience gives them authority and influence in decision making.

The job is not completed even after agreement is reached at all levels. In recent years the division, as a matter of policy, has published the terms of the consent decree as a proposed decree that does not become final for thirty days, during which time anyone can raise objections to it. While objections are seldom made and infrequently successful, the objections must be met before the decree can be entered. Indeed, intervention by third parties can under some circumstances prevent the entry of the decree. See *Cascade Natural Gas Co. v El Paso Natural Gas Co.* (1967) 386 US 129.

If no one objects before the end of the thirty-day period, or if any objections are either found groundless or resolved, the decree is submitted to a judge who enters a consent judgment. Usually he retains jurisdiction to punish violations of the decree or to receive requests for modification.

J. [§13.61] Analyzing Market Structure: "the Numbers Game"

Most civil economic cases brought by the division, including all Section 7 (15 USC §18) cases, involve one or more variations of what has been invidiously described as the "numbers game" and more euphemistically as "market structure." If there was ever any doubt about the importance of the numbers game, it was removed by the long-promised publication by the Antitrust Division in 1968 of its *Merger Guidelines,* which emphasized "market structure," and which is still the rule book of the game as played by the Antitrust Division and may be useful in the courts. See *Allis-Chalmers Mfg. Co. v White Consolidated Industries, Inc.* (3d Cir 1969) 414 F2d 506, *cert den* (1970) 396 US 1009. To play this game, counsel must find out, for the client company and others in the relevant industries, what is the "market share," *i.e.*, percentage of total production or sales, of a distinctive product. See discussion at §§4.21–4.37.

A good first move is a conference with those responsible for market research in the client's organization. Whether they are in a distinct department or just part of the sales force, they will have a good idea of how the company stands vis-a-vis other companies in production of the product, the extent to which the product competes with other products, and the geographic boundaries of the market. In any event, counsel should get copies of all reports prepared by them relating in any way to the marketing of the relevant products. If nothing else, they will give counsel a lead into how the products are reported to the Bureau of the Census and to the client's trade associations, the two principal sources of industry statistics. Indeed, counsel should get copies of all relevant reports in all the client's files, whether or not prepared by a company employee, as the division will probably ask for all these reports in its first discovery motion (even if it has asked and received them before in the precomplaint inquiry or civil investigative demand), and counsel should know what they contain.

It is relatively easy to determine approximately the total production of a product from published Census figures. But counsel can stop here only if they are willing to accept the Census classification as a line of commerce and if they are content with knowing only their client's share of that line of commerce. In order to explore market position on other bases, counsel must go to the trade associations. But again they will provide total figures—not individual figures. They may give counsel the client's rank, but not how other companies rank or what their percentages may be. Of course, counsel can ask the individual companies, but this is one kind of information that a competitor is most reluctant to disclose to another competitor—even respected counsel for that competitor—and it may be necessary to use formal discovery, including subpoenas addressed to the trade associations or to other collectors of information on an individual and, it is hoped, confidential basis—such as Dun & Bradstreet. This means, moreover, that the information will automatically be made available also to the division.

Informal preliminary explorations should be made thoroughly and early on the basis of regional markets as well as a national market. Regional delineation is hard to make, and regional information is hard to come by. Indeed, there is some evidence that the question of whether a regional market exists may depend on whether information is collected and available on the basis of that region.

The information regarding market structure should be collected early because in an economic case whether the client can and should settle often depends on its market share and the market structure. If the case is tried, its presentation may well depend on these considerations. For example, it may not be worth arguing that X is the relevant product market, and Y is not, if both X and Y could give the client approximately the same percentage of a market, and other factors (including concentration, its position, new entrants, etc.) are approximately similar.

K. Discovery by the Government

1. [§13.62] Limiting Government Discovery Demands

Soon after the answer is served, the division usually initiates discovery—starting sometimes with interrogatories, sometimes with a motion to produce documents, sometimes by taking depositions of officers of the defendants or of other companies in the industry. Almost invariably one device is followed by another as the division counsel assigned to the case take full advantage of all the tools available under the Federal Rules of Civil Procedure.

As in its civil investigative demands, the division's interrogatories and motions to produce are often excessively broad and far-ranging, and frequently they cover time periods that seem irrelevant. Counsel should not assume that this is done to harass the defendants; it stems from a number of factors in varying combinations. First, in merger cases particularly, the division counsel usually know far less about the business of the defendants than their counsel—even after reading the defendants' responses to the precomplaint inquiries. Second, division counsel frequently are uncertain about the direction they want to take in the case. Third, they want to make sure that nothing conceivably relevant escapes the net. Finally, they really do not know the state of the defendants' files and how difficult it is to assemble the documents and information demanded.

It is important to keep these facts in mind, because it is possible to negotiate the scope of the discovery—as to subject matter, time, and the files to be searched—and all these factors play a part in the negotiations.

Unlike an opponent in a private suit, the division is not constrained in its initial demands or in negotiating the scope by the fact that the defendants have their turn. It is very much aware, on the other hand, that a defendant can obtain relief from the district judge, who usually prides himself on his independence and neutrality vis-a-vis the Justice Department and is often annoyed about being required to step into discovery controversies, particularly if there are complicated economic questions. The division, like private litigants, is subject to the rule in many districts that requires counsel to try to settle discovery problems. It is very important for counsel to make clear to the division from the outset that they are not afraid to litigate discovery questions—not because they want to hide something dreadful, but because their client is entitled to some privacy and to minimal inconvenience and expense.

Unless there are special reasons for doing otherwise, defendant's counsel should try to limit discovery. Little is to be gained from opening up the files to the division at any time, and it is doubtful that the division will drop the suit simply if it finds that in general the defendant is well behaved by the division's standards. Nor is the division usually deterred from examining documents because of their sheer volume—although the production of several truckloads of paper in one case is said to have resulted in the reduction of the scope of a demand, and doubtless the probability of unmanageable volume may persuade the division to cut down its demand.

On the other hand, failure to limit discovery to the extent possible can have serious consequences for a defendant: (1) it may incur completely unnecessary substantial expenses; (2) it may produce documents that would lead the division to bring a suit in another area; (3) it may unnecessarily put into the record ammunition for private plaintiffs.

2. [§13.63] Producing Documents for the Government

A file search in a division civil suit is much like that in any other lawsuit—except that the sheer volume of documents may require special attention to organization and special efforts to minimize expense. As in answering a civil investigative demand, it is ordinarily more economic, efficient, and expedient for the initial combing to be done by a reasonably intelligent nonlawyer company employee who can understand what a document says but does not understand all the nuances of the case. The documents should then be read again by counsel to determine that they are clearly called for. A record should be kept—but not on the document—showing the file from which each document originated, and, of course, copies of all documents should be made before they are turned over to the division. It is often preferable to keep the originals, as the division will usually accept copies, at least until division counsel decide whether they want to use the documents at the trial.

As the defendant is not required to incur the cost of making copies, it may be desirable simply to make the documents available for inspection—and this often is done when extensive volume is involved. Many antitrust defendants prefer, however, to incur the expense of making copies and shipping them to the division rather than have the division representatives around the company offices. This problem can be avoided, of course, by making the documents available at the offices of counsel.

On the government's motion to produce, the defendant usually produces those documents then in its files. This does not close out production, for the division may and sometimes does ask that production be updated. Thus every defendant should realize that what its executives do and write, including intracorporate memoranda, may ultimately have to be shown to the division and may be used as evidence against it in the action or some other action. This applies to speeches, prospectuses, and reports to stockholders—all of which should be reviewed by counsel for their implications for the litigation. In some instances, defendants' counsel may want the division to update what it has produced. Between the defendants' discovery motions and the beginning of the trial the division may have added greatly to its store of information and may have changed its theories.

3. [§13.64] Depositions by the Government

The division may examine the defendants—through depositions of its executives at various echelons, or it may take the depositions of witnesses—often executives of other companies in the defendants' industry.

When the government notices a deposition in an antitrust case the considerations are generally the same as in other actions governed by the Federal Rules, with a few exceptions in economic cases.

First, the areas of possible inquiry are so extensive that often it is hard to prepare for the deposition unless counsel can find out what the division has in mind before the deposition. Defendants' counsel can usually obtain more information prior to the deposition of a nonparty witness than an officer of a defendant. A division representative usually interviews the nonparty witness before the deposition is taken, and he or his counsel will usually tell defendants' counsel about the interview. There is nothing confidential about the predeposition interview, and there is nothing collusive about defendant's competitor telling defendant's counsel about it. Counsel should make every effort, of course, to interview the witness to ascertain what kind of cross-examination may be worthwhile.

The deposition of a defendant is another matter. Here the division has not conducted an interview, and here counsel must be prepared for anything that may be permissible under the rules. It is not likely that a sales manager will be examined on production, but counsel cannot count on it. If the client's chief executive officer is to be examined, a special caveat must be observed. He must be warned against succumbing to the temptation to explain it all to the division lawyer in the hope that this will convince the division to go away. He must realize that he is in a litigation situation against an ardent, intelligent opponent prepared to go to the end.

This does not mean, of course, that either counsel or the client should forget that settlement is always possible and that the showing made by the client's executives may bear on how favorable a settlement can be achieved.

Counsel should also consider that it may be possible to provide the government with a substitute for the depositions of the client's executives. Sometimes this can be done by submitting data and information in the form of a stipulation. Aside from other obvious advantages, this can save the time and nerves of important executives.

L. Discovery by the Defendant

1. [§13.65] Interrogatories and Motions to Produce

In government civil cases, the defendant's discovery usually begins by serving the government with interrogatories. Drawn carefully, these can serve several important functions: (1) they force the division to narrow the issues; (2) they can ferret out what the division has accumulated to date from other sources, and (3) they will give some indication of what the division plans to use at the trial.

The division may be reluctant to cooperate, particularly at an early stage, and may object to the interrogatories or may try to give evasive answers. But if the interrogatories are framed in terms of the complaint, the judge will usually require answers and responsive ones. *United States v Continental Can Company* (SD NY 1958) 22 FRD 241; *United States v West Virginia Pulp and Paper Company* (SD NY 1964) 36 FRD 250.

At an appropriate time, which, because of the government's steps to update what has been produced earlier, may be on the eve of trial, defendant may make a motion to produce to ascertain what documents the government will actually use. The division usually will provide copies of the documents it plans to use without any motion, but a motion may be necessary to obtain documents the government has obtained from others. Again, counsel must indicate that they are ready to litigate if they cannot have what they think should be made available.

2. [§13.66] Depositions by Defendant

Examination of the government as a party is all but impossible. Defendant's deposition taking is limited to third-party witnesses. Most corporations do not want their executives to be witnesses in other people's antitrust cases—particularly against the government. There is a reluctance to risk exposure of the corporation's own business skeletons, a fear of reprisal by the division, and a realization that it is going to take a good deal of the executives' time. Also, a deposition risks building up a record that, although not later admissible in a private action except for impeachment, may give leads to a private plaintiff in the event the case is settled by a consent decree.

Frequently defendant gains little by taking a witness' deposition, unless he may not be available for the trial. When counsel's objective is simply statistical data, it may be less expensive and less disturbing to the non-party competitor to take a deposition upon written interrogatories.

M. [§13.67] Assigning a Judge

In some districts, for example, the Central District of California, a single judge is assigned automatically to a case as soon as it is commenced and all motions are heard by that judge, who will also sit at the trial. In other districts, for example, the Southern District of New York, either party may request the chief judge to assign a judge for all purposes, and in an economic case he will ordinarily do so. Usually the division makes this request because the division is interested in expediting the proceedings, and the appointment of a single judge will expedite the disposition of all motions.

N. [§13.68] The Trial

Government civil antitrust suits are equity actions and are tried without a jury. In recent years, almost all have been tried before a single judge. Under the Expediting Act (49 USC §44), the division can obtain a three-judge court, as it did in *United States v Paramount Pictures, Inc.* (SD NY 1946) 70 F Supp 53 *aff'd in part, rev'd in part, remanded* (1948) 334 US 131, but the complaints of an overworked federal judiciary have effectively discouraged the exercise of this option, and it is likely that Congress will make it unavailable by an amendment of the act.

The conduct of the trial and the rules of evidence are similar to other nonjury civil cases in the federal courts. Special problems arise, in most economic cases, however, because of the extraordinary range of evidence that may be pertinent. Just keeping track of the documents and the testimony requires sharp focus on proper organization. During the pretrial conference or at the trial the division and, frequently, the judge will press for stipulations that will shorten the trial, and counsel must be prepared to make relatively speedy appraisals of the effect of these on his client's case as well as his client's purse. See 1969 *Manual for Complex and Multi-district Litigation* 30-54, Federal Judicial Center.

Counsel must be prepared for judicial impatience toward certain types of evidentiary objections. Counsel need not eschew making the objections, of course, and should protect the client's position for the record. Practically, however, counsel should realize that the division will be permitted to introduce just about every document from a defendant's files that is arguably relevant—with the judge indicating that he will take the document subject to connection, that he will consider the objections in weighing the value of the document, and that authenticity will be assumed unless the defendant has some basis for putting it into issue.

O. [§13.69] The Decree

As violation and damages pervade a private antitrust suit, violation and relief pervade a government suit.

While in a treble-damage suit, separation of the two issues is usually difficult if not impossible (see 1969 *Manual* 71-72), in a government suit the two basic issues are not so entwined and can often be tried separately. Frequently, therefore, the trial is completed, and the parties submit proposed findings of fact and conclusions of law and briefs before there is any reference to the terms of the decree. If the decision is against the government, there is no need to go into the decree. If the judge finds a violation, the decree is all important.

The usual procedure is for the division to propose a decree. Sometimes this is followed by negotiations. If not, or if the negotiations are unsuccessful, the court will hear argument on the decree, and if either party requests, will hear witnesses. But to wait until this point may be tactically dangerous. By this time it may be too late to persuade the court to do anything but award what the division requests. Thus it is important, in presenting the case, to set the stage for a sympathetic approach to the decree.

P. [§13.70] The Appeal

Under the Expediting Act, 49 USC §45, as of February 1970, the appeal from a final decree in an Antitrust Division civil proceeding—whether under Section 7 (15 USC §18) or another antitrust law—must go directly to the Supreme Court, and interlocutory appeals are not available. See Stern and Gressman, *Supreme Court Practice* (4th ed 1969) 44–48.

While technically the appeal to the Supreme Court is of right, this has not meant that a losing defendant gets a full opportunity to argue the appeal in the Supreme Court. It has to file a Statement of Probable Jurisdiction, and frequently the division or the solicitor-general, who at this point may be in charge of the case, counters by asking that the Supreme Court affirm without further proceedings. Occasionally this maneuver has been successful, *e.g.*, in *United States v Loew's, Inc.* (1950) 339 US 974. Thus it has been dangerous to be content with showing jurisdiction. Counsel must undertake the more difficult burden of showing that the decision below probably should be reversed, which can be done in papers opposing the government's motion, but the stage should be set in the Statement of Probable Jurisdiction.

The government, however, is almost invariably successful in obtaining a full-dress appeal if it loses in the district court and wants to appeal under the Expediting Act. The record of the Division in the Supreme Court, particularly in Section 7 cases, surpasses that of any champion. Thus it has been important to concentrate—if the defendant has won below—on persuading the division that it should not file an appeal. This is done informally, of course, and sometimes requires concessions by the defendant.

IV. Defending a Criminal Suit*

A. [§13.71] Introduction

Criminal antitrust suits are prosecuted by the Antitrust Division of the Department of Justice. The government trial attorneys are usually the same lawyers who handled the grand jury proceedings prior to the indictment and are thus familiar with the evidence in support of the charges. At the outset they may well be better prepared than counsel for the defendant. Most criminal antitrust suits involve alleged price fixing among several defendants, and counsel for one defendant may not be fully informed of all the evidence presented to the grand jury. Hence, it is essential that all defense counsel meet promptly to exchange information about grand jury documents and witnesses; they will also want to work out procedures for defense, including division of work on certain factual or legal issues. The extent to which counsel participates in such joint defense efforts naturally depends on the position of his client in the group of defendants.

Many of the substantive issues in criminal suits are the same as in private treble damage actions. The procedure, however, is governed by the Federal Rules of Criminal Procedure, and reference in this section to a Rule will be to the Criminal Rules. Most lawyers called upon to defend antitrust suits are not regular practitioners at the criminal bar. Since criminal pretrial procedures differ materially from those in civil cases, special emphasis is placed on them in the following discussion.

B. Arraignment and Pleas

1. [§13.72] Procedure

Normally arraignment is the first event after an indictment or information is issued. It consists of reading the indictment or information to the defendant in open court or informing him of the substance of the charge. He must be given a copy of the indictment or information and is then called upon to plead. Rule 10.

Under Rule 43, a corporation may appear by counsel, while a natural defendant must be present at the arraignment and at every stage of the trial unless the court otherwise permits, which it may do, since the offense is punishable by fine, or imprisonment for not more than one year, or both.

*We are indebted to John G. Koeltl, Harvard Law School, 1971, for his assistance in preparing this section.

2. [§13.73] Motions that Must Be Made at or before Arraignment

Rule 22 provides that a motion to transfer may be made at or before arraignment or at such time as the court or the Rules prescribe. See §13.82. A motion to dismiss under Rule 12 because of defects in the institution of the prosecution or in the indictment itself, "shall be made before the plea is entered, but the court may permit it to be made within a reasonable time thereafter." See §§13.77–13.78. Before the plea is entered, the defendant should routinely move for an extension of time within which to make motions that counsel may deem desirable. Federal Defenders Program (1967) *Handbook on Criminal Procedure* §4.19.

Because of the discretion available to the court in timing these motions, it is customary at arraignment for the court to fix a time within which the defendants may file motions—both Rule 12 motions and other types such as a motion for a bill of particulars. See Cox, *The Criminal Antitrust Case—Indictment Through Trial* 1963 NYS Bar Assn Antitrust Law Symp 96, 98 (hereafter sometimes cited as Cox); and 1 Wright (1969) *Federal Practice and Procedure* §192 (hereafter sometimes cited as Wright).

3. Pleas at Arraignment

a. [§13.74] Availability

The defendant may plead guilty, or, with the consent of the court, *nolo contendere*. Rule 11. Before accepting either a plea of guilty or *nolo contendere* the court must address the defendant personally, determine that the plea is made voluntarily with understanding of the nature of the charge, and that the defendant understands the consequences of the plea. Most antitrust defendants are well advised in advance and are able to respond affirmatively.

b. [§13.75] Considerations Affecting the Choice of Plea

It may be to the antitrust defendant's advantage to enter a plea of *nolo contendere* and to convince the judge to accept it. Although a *nolo* plea subjects a defendant to the same criminal liability as a guilty plea or a conviction, a *nolo* plea, unlike a guilty plea or a conviction, "does not constitute prima facie evidence in a private suit under Section 5(a) of the Clayton Act" if entered before any evidence is taken. Clabault and Burton (1966) *Sherman Act Indictments, 1955–1965* at 21. Thus it offers the same advantage against exposure to private suits as settlement of a government civil action. See §13.59. For a corporate defendant this advantage is usually decisive.

While a *nolo* plea cannot be introduced at a subsequent civil trial as prima facie evidence, the cases are not wholly consistent on whether references may be made to such pleas in a later private suit. See §13.27. In *Minnesota v United States Steel Corp.* (D Minn 1968) 44 FRD 559, the court struck all allegations in the original and amended complaints to the various government indictments that had resulted in *nolo* pleas, reasoning that such allegations were so prejudicial that no reference should be made to them. But in *Polychrome Corp. v Minnesota Mining and Manufacturing Co.* (SD NY 1966) 263 F Supp 101 the plaintiff was allowed to amend his complaint to state the beginning and termination dates of the criminal proceeding, even though it was resolved by a plea of *nolo contendere*; the court thought this essential to allow the plaintiff to take advantage of Section 5(b) of the Clayton Act (15 USC §16(b)), which tolls the statute of limitations for private plaintiffs during the pendency of a government suit. See §13.29. In *Pfotzer v Aqua Systems, Inc.* (2d Cir 1947) 162 F2d 779, Judge Learned Hand held that a *nolo* plea could be used in a private treble damage action to impeach a witness. See Note, *Nolo Pleas in Antitrust Cases* (1966) 79 *Harv L Rev* 1475, 1477.

If the consequences of a *nolo* plea are to be excluded from a later private suit, so must certain other materials connected with it. In *Polychrome Corp. v Minnesota Mining and Manufacturing Co., supra,* the court, while permitting plaintiff to refer to the prior criminal action in his pleadings, refused to admit remarks of the court and pre-sentence memoranda relating to a *nolo* plea to support the charge in a civil case that defendant " 'admitted the allegations of the indictment and was convicted and fined for its violation . . . .' " Such materials, however, are not always immune from discovery; production of pre-sentence memoranda has been ordered in some circumstances. *U.S. Industries, Inc. v United States District Court* (9th Cir 1965) 345 F2d 18, *cert den* (1965) 382 US 814; *Philadelphia Electric Co. v Anaconda American Brass Co.* (ED Pa 1967) 275 F Supp 146. *But cf. Hancock Brothers, Inc. v Jones* (ND Calif 1968) 293 F Supp 1229 (trial judge did not abuse his discretion in denying production of pre-sentence memoranda).

The Antitrust Division has weighed a number of factors in determining whether to oppose a *nolo* plea, including the importance of facilitating private litigation, the nature of the violation, its duration and economic effect, the degree of predatory activity involved, the previous antitrust record of the defendants, and the reason for the violation. Clabault and Burton (Supp 1968) *Sherman Act Indictments, 1955-1965* at 22-24. See Note, *Section 5 of the Clayton Act and the Nolo Contendere Plea* (1966) 75 *Yale LJ* 845. As a condition for not opposing such pleas, the Antitrust Division has required that the defendants understand that a *nolo* plea is the equivalent of a guilty plea for purposes of the criminal action and that the penalties are the same, including the possibility of a jail sentence for individual defendants. The defendants may have to agree that they will not make any public statements inconsistent with their admission of guilt in the criminal case. Clabault and Burton, *supra*, at 22-23. See further discussion at §11.9.

In spite of frequent government opposition to a *nolo* plea, the overwhelming majority of courts have allowed such pleas. See Clabault and Burton (Supp 1968), *supra*, at 1-16 (lists of all antitrust cases between 1955-1968 in which *nolo contendere* pleas were denied or accepted over government opposition); Note, *Section 5 of the Clayton Act and the Nolo Contendere Plea, supra,* at 859-860. ("Between 1954 and 1964 the courts allowed nolo pleas over the objection of the Government in 99 of the 124 contested motions.") *Cf. United States v American Bakeries Co.* (WD Mich 1968) 284 F Supp 864 and *United States v American Bakeries Co.* (WD Mich 1968) 284 F Supp 871 (consideration of some factors which a court may consider in determining whether to accept a *nolo* plea).

C. [§13.76] The Bill of Particulars: Clarifying the Indictment

A motion for a bill of particulars seeks to have the government explain more fully the charges made in the indictment. A bill of particulars can be a vital defensive weapon in restricting the government's proof, as the decision in *United States v Chas. Pfizer & Co.* (2d Cir 1970) 426 F2d 32 demonstrates. There, a guilty verdict in a price-fixing case was reversed because the government departed in its proof from the theory set forth in its bill of particulars. A motion for a bill of particulars may be made before arraignment, within ten days after arraignment, or later as the court permits. Rule 7(f). It is customary for the court at arraignment to specify when such a motion must be made. Extensions of time may be sought under Rule 45(b).

Since the purpose of a bill of particulars is far from clear, courts have hedged on the permissible scope of this device. For example, it has been said that bills of particulars are not intended to "give defendants a preview of the government's case" but "to aid the accused in preparation of his defense, to prevent surprise at trial and to permit the accused, 'after judgment, . . . to plead the record and judgment in bar of a further prosecution for the same offense.'" *United States v McCarthy* (SD NY 1968) 292 F Supp 937, 940. This lack of clarity has produced inconsistent rulings on what particulars may be required. Cox, *The Criminal Antitrust Case—Indictment Through Trial,* 1963 NYS Bar Ass'n Antitrust Law Symp 102-103. Even under a narrow view, a defendant in a conspiracy case should be able to obtain the names of his co-conspirators since he should be allowed to know with whom he allegedly conspired. *United States v Fuel Oil Dealers' Division* (ED Pa 1968) 1968 Trade Cases ¶72,619 (indictment under Section 1 of the Sherman Act). Similarly, he should be able to discover the dates and details of the alleged conspiracy so that he understands exactly the nature of the indictment. *United States v Fuel Oil Dealers' Division, supra; United States v U.S. Steel Corp.* (SD NY 1964) 233 F Supp 148, 152 (dictum) (Weinfeld, J.) (price-fixing conspiracy). For antitrust decisions allowing more extensive bills of particulars, including requiring the government to submit or identify any documents constituting express agreements, and to identify all individuals named in grand jury testimony who attended any meetings alleged in the indictment, as well as the approximate times and places of such meetings, see *United States v American Oil Co.* (D NJ 1966) 259 F Supp 851; *United States v U.S. Steel Corp.* (SD NY 1964) 1964 Trade Cases ¶71,276; and *United States v Taylor Forge & Pipe Works* (SD NY 1964) 1964 Trade Cases ¶71,277. Note, *Discovery in Criminal Antitrust Cases* (1964) 64 *Col L Rev* 735, 749.

D. Pretrial Motions: Defense and Objections

1. [§13.77] Framework of Rule 12: Raising Defenses and Objections

Rule 12(a) limits defense pleas to not guilty, guilty, and *nolo contendere*. Other defensive pleas such as pleas to the jurisdiction may be raised only by motion.

Rule 12 motions fall into three classes, depending on when they must be made. Motions to dismiss for lack of jurisdiction or for failure to charge an offense may be made at any time during the proceedings. Rule 12(b)(2).

Defenses and objections based on defects in the indictment or information itself, or in the institution of the prosecution, may be raised only by motion before trial, and are otherwise waived. Rule 12(b)(2). The Rule requires that such a motion "shall be made before the plea is entered, but the court may permit it to be made within a reasonable time thereafter." Rule 12(b)(3). It is customary for the court at arraignment to set a time limit. These defenses and objections include "illegal selection or organization of the grand jury, disqualification of individual grand jurors, presence of unauthorized persons in the grand jury room, [and] other irregularities in grand jury proceedings...." Advisory Committee Notes, 18 USCA Rules 12(b)(1) and 12(b)(2).

Defenses capable of determination before the main trial but generally requiring a factual presentation constitute the third group of defenses that Rule 12 governs. Such defenses may be raised by pretrial motion, but failure to do so does not constitute a waiver. Although no time limit is specified, "the sensible resolution is that the matters . . . are waived if not raised at the trial." 1 Wright (1969) *Federal Practice and Procedure* §193. The defenses include former jeopardy, former conviction, former acquittal, statute of limitations, and immunity.

Rule 12 applies only to the types of defenses and objections discussed above, which could formerly have been raised by pleas, demurrers, and motions to quash. Rule 12(a); 1 Wright, *supra*, §191. Other rules govern motions concerning such matters as discovery, including disclosure of grand jury minutes; subpoenas; depositions for the defense; bills of particulars; transfer to another place for trial; suppression of illegally seized evidence; and dismissal for want of a speedy trial. *Id.*

2. Rule 12 Motions

a. [§13.78] Procedural Irregularities in the Grand Jury Proceedings and Technical Defects in the Indictment

Defenses and objections based on technical irregularities are probably of little use in a criminal antitrust case. Motions to dismiss based on procedural irregularities in the impanelling or conduct of the grand jury are difficult to win "because the courts tend to overrule the motions unless the defendants can make a particularized showing of prejudice, which is difficult to do." Cox, *The Criminal Antitrust Case—Indictment Through Trial,* 1963 NYS Bar Ass'n Antitrust Law Symp 98. Objections to the form of the indictment, as for example failure to meet the technical requirements of Rule 7(c), are similarly unsuccessful because the indictment will usually be in a conventional form traditionally approved by the courts. Courts have demonstrated an impatience with arguments that an indictment is too vague or indefinite or omits essential elements of the crime. *United States v A.P. Woodson Co.* (D DC 1961) 198 F Supp 579.

If an indictment is too indefinite, the proper remedy is a motion for a bill of particulars. If it contains immaterial, irrelevant, and prejudicial material, then a motion to strike is appropriate. Rule 7(d). But even prejudicial allegations may not be struck if evidence of the allegations is admissible and relevant. *United States v Chas. Pfizer & Co.* (SD NY 1963) 217 F Supp 199, 201.

Finally, it seems futile to have the indictment dismissed on these technical grounds, since the government, without leave of court, may file an information. Under Rule 7(a) an information can be used to prosecute a Sherman Act charge since the offense is punishable by a term not exceeding one year. Even if the statute of limitations has run, this course apparently is open to the government. See 18 USC §§3288–3289.

b. [§13.79] Improper Joinder

Offenses may be joined in the same indictment though they must be charged in a separate count for each offense, if they "are of the same or similar character or are based on the same act or transaction or on two or more acts or transactions connected together or constituting parts of a common scheme or plan." Rule 8(a). Defendants may be jointly indicted if they "have participated in the same act or transaction or in the same series of acts or transactions constituting an offense or offenses." Rule 8(b). A motion will lie objecting to "misjoinder," *i.e.,* joining offenses or defendants other than those whom Rule 8 permits to be joined; "duplicity," *i.e.,* charging two or more separate offenses in the same count; and "multiplicity," *i.e.,* charging the same offense in more than one count. See 1 Wright (1969) *Federal Practice and Procedure* §142. Such a motion, raising a non-jurisdictional defect, unless prejudice can be demonstrated, should be made before trial on pain of waiver. Relief from prejudicial joinder is discussed in §13.81.

Misjoinder does not often occur in an antitrust context, since the allegations of a conspiracy automatically justify joinder of many defendants, and since the crimes charged are usually of the same character and constitute part of a common scheme.

c. [§13.80] Improper Venue

Rule 18 provides that "except as otherwise permitted by statute or by these rules, the prosecution shall be had in a district in which the offense was committed." The 1966 amendment to the Rule abolished the significance of divisions within a district by allowing the court to fix the place of trial within the district "with due regard to the convenience of the defendant and the witnesses."

Because the overt acts of an antitrust conspiracy are often alleged to have occurred in many districts, there is usually a wide choice of venue open to the government. See 18 USC §3237(a); 1 Wright, *Federal Practice and Procedure* §303. It is more probable that the venue, though technically correct, may be inconvenient and that a motion to transfer would be proper. See §13.82.

3. Other Pretrial Defenses and Objections

a. [§13.81] Relief from Prejudicial Joinder

Under Rule 14 the court may order an election or separate trials of counts, grant severance of defendants or provide "whatever other relief justice requires", if it appears that a defendant or the government is prejudiced by a joinder of offenses or of defendants. Under the 1966 amendment, "in ruling on a motion by a defendant for severance the court may order the attorney for the government to deliver to the court for inspection *in camera* any statements or confessions made by the defendants which the government intends to introduce in evidence at the trial." Recent cases have found sufficient prejudice involved in the admission in evidence against a defendant of a statement or confession made by a co-defendant to require reversal of a decision to deny severance. Advisory Committee Notes, 18 USCA Rule 14. "The purpose of the amendment is to provide a procedure whereby the issue of possible prejudice can be resolved on the motion for severance." 1 Wright, *Federal Practice and Procedure* §223.

Severance in an antitrust conspiracy case is very difficult to obtain: "There is a great reluctance to put the government and the courts to the burden of separate trials in which the proof would be almost identical, and there is a great faith in the ability of the court by suitable instructions to cure any prejudice and to guide the jury through the complex proof in a long and complicated case." 1 Wright, *supra*, §226. *See United States v American Oil Co.* (D NJ 1968) 291 F Supp 968 and *United States v Greater Blouse, Skirt & Neckwear Contractors' Ass'n, Inc.* (SD NY 1959) 177 F Supp 213, 221-222.

b. [§13.82] Motions to Transfer

Transfer motions under Rule 21 should be made promptly at or before arraignment although Rule 22 indicates it may be possible to make such motions later. Delay may result in denial of the motion. See 1 Wright, *Federal Practice and Procedure* §361.

The second part of Rule 21 allows the court upon motion of the defendant to transfer the proceedings to another district "for the convenience of parties and witnesses, and in the interest of justice . . .." Rule 21(b). The 1966 amendments permit transfer to districts even though the offense was not committed there. Explicit reference to "the convenience of parties and witnesses, and in the interest of justice" makes it clear that the rule is intended, like its civil counterpart, to provide for a convenient forum for trial. See Advisory Committee Notes, 18 USCA Rule 21; 1 Wright, *supra*, §344; *cf.* Cox, *The Criminal Antitrust Case—Indictment*

Through Trial, 1963 NYS Bar Ass'n Antitrust Law Symp 99-100. The Supreme Court seems to have approved a definition of "in the interest of justice" that would include such factors as: "(1) location of corporate defendant; (2) location of possible witnesses; (3) location of events likely to be in issue; (4) location of documents and records likely to be involved; (5) disruption of defendant's business unless the case is transferred; (6) expense to the parties; (7) location of counsel; (8) relative accessibility of place of trial; (9) docket condition of each district or division involved; and (10) any other special elements which might affect the transfer." *Platt v Minnesota Mining & Manufacturing Co.* (1964) 376 US 240, 243-244. For an application of these factors under the amended rule, see *Jones v Gasch* (DC Cir 1967) 404 F2d 1231, *cert den* (1968) 390 US 1029. See also §13.20.

c. [§13.83] Motions to Suppress Illegally Seized Evidence

A person aggrieved by an unlawful search and seizure may move under Rule 41(e) for the return of the property and its suppression as evidence. The motion must be made before trial or any hearing in which the evidence is to be used unless the opportunity did not exist or the defendant was unaware of the grounds for the motion; the court in its discretion may entertain the motion at the trial or hearing.

d. [§13.84] Motion to Dismiss for Want of a Speedy Trial

If there is unnecessary delay in bringing a defendant to trial, the court may dismiss the indictment under Rule 48(b). This discretionary power to dismiss is independent of Rule 12, so that the procedural requirements of that rule are irrelevant to this motion. See *United States v Apex Distributing Co.* (9th Cir 1959) 270 F2d 747, 754 n. 17, 755-756.

E. [§13.85] Discovery

Traditionally, discovery has been much more limited in criminal than in civil litigation; secrecy until trial has prevailed in criminal cases. See generally Traynor, *Ground Lost and Found in Criminal Discovery* (1964) 39 *NYU L Rev* 228.

Recently, however, the Supreme Court has acknowledged the "growing realization that disclosure, rather than suppression, of relevant materials ordinarily promotes the proper administration of criminal justice." *Dennis v United States* (1966) 384 US 855, 870. The 1966 amendments and recent cases have implemented this more liberal attitude. See generally Rezneck, *Pretrial Discovery in Federal Courts,* in *Criminal Defense Techniques* (1969) Chap. 10 (R. Cipes ed.).

The most extensive discovery devices should be available in a criminal antitrust case. The standard arguments against criminal discovery—that it would promote perjury when the defendants realized how to tailor their stories to circumvent government evidence, that it would encourage the elimination or intimidation of vital witnesses—have less force in such a case, especially if the proof is mainly documentary. Extensive pretrial disclosure facilitates the management and speed of otherwise cumbersome and protracted trials. The *Manual for Complex and Multidistrict Litigation* (1970) (hereafter referred to as the *1970 Manual*) recommends at §6.2:

In complex criminal cases, the judge should encourage the use of discovery to the extent authorized under Rule 16 and the last sentence of Rule 17(c), F.R. Cr. P., to give each side access, well in advance of its use, to documentary evidence and other material made available by the rules.

1. [§13.86] Rule 16: Discovery and Inspection

Rule 16, amended in 1966, now provides the most important method of defense discovery in criminal cases. On defendant's motion, under Rule 16(a), the court may order inspection and copying of relevant (1) statements by the defendant; (2) results or reports of physical or mental examinations, and of scientific tests or experiments made in connection with the particular case; and (3) defendant's grand jury testimony.

Rule 16(b), while allowing discovery of more extensive materials, conditions disclosure on a showing of materiality and reasonableness, and opens the defense to reciprocal discovery by the government. More specifically, it provides that the court may order that defendant be allowed to inspect and copy documentary and physical material in the government's possession or control if defendant demonstrates its materiality to the preparation of his defense and the reasonableness of his request. Under Rule 16(c), if the court grants a motion under Rule 16(b) or 16(a)(2), it may, upon motion by the government, condition its order by requiring that defendant permit the government, upon showing of reasonableness and materiality to the preparation of the government's case, to inspect and copy similar material that the defendant intends to produce at the trial and that is within his possession or control. Disclosure by the government under Rule 16(b) specifically excludes a broad work product classification and statements made by government witnesses or prospective government witnesses (other than the defendant) who are covered by the Jencks Act. See §13.94. Similarly, defense disclosure under Rule 16(c) need not include a broad work product classification and statements

made by the defendant or by witnesses or prospective witnesses for either
side, to the defendant, his agents or attorneys.

a. [§13.87] What Showing Must Defendant Make to Obtain Broad Discovery?

Unlike Rule 16(b), which requires a showing of materiality and reasonableness as a specific prerequisite to discovery, Rule 16(a) contains no
such express requirements. Because the items listed in Rule 16(a) should
always be important to the defense, it is reasonable that the defendant
should not have to make any particular showing of need in the specific
case; rather, the defendant should have "virtually an absolute right to
their discovery." Rezneck, *The New Federal Rules of Criminal Procedure*
(1966) 54 *Geo LJ* 1276, 1277; 1 Wright (1969) *Federal Practice and Procedure* §253.

Some courts, however, relying on the fact that the rule states only that
a court "may" order discovery, without requiring disclosure, have required a showing of various degrees of "need". Most of these decisions
requiring a showing of need have occurred in the Southern District of
New York. See 1 Wright, *supra*, §253 n. 35.

On the other hand, Judge Frankel of that court, after reviewing the
history and rationale of the rule, has concluded that "defendants should
routinely be given documents [under 16(a)] without any special showing
of any kind, unless the Government can demonstrate some particularized
and substantial reasons why this should not be allowed in a particular
case." *United States v Projansky* (SD NY 1968) 44 FRD 550, 552. The
Seventh Circuit has followed Judge Frankel's rationale in *United States v
Isa* (7th Cir 1969) 413 F2d 244, in which it reversed a conviction because
the lower court denied defendant's motion to produce recordings of conversations between him and an Internal Revenue agent. The court reasoned that the burden should be on the government to demonstrate
under Rule 16(e), which covers motions for protective orders, that discovery
or inspection should be denied, rather than on defendant to show
sufficient reasons for such discovery. *But cf. United States v American Oil
Co.* (D NJ 1968) 286 F Supp 742 (discovery under Rule 16(a)(3) is still a
question of judicial discretion dependent on balancing competing
interests).

In contrast to Rule 16(a), Rule 16(b) requires a showing of reasonableness and materiality for the materials it names. An antitrust defendant
usually can meet these standards for a broad range of documents. See
Rezneck, *supra*, 1279. The Advisory Committee Notes, 18 USCA Rule 16,
explain that specific designation of the items sought is not required of

defendant. The requirement of reasonableness permits the court "to define and limit the scope of the government's obligation to search its files while meeting the legitimate needs of the defendant." Similarly, a defendant should not have to lay a foundation of materiality for each item sought since he cannot be expected to know "the exact nature of what he has not seen"; "delineation of the subject matter sought" should be sufficient. *United States v Hughes* (5th Cir 1969) 413 F2d 1244, 1254, *cert granted sub nom United States v Gifford-Hill-American, Inc.* (1969) 396 US 984; *judgment vacated and mandamus dismissed as moot,* (1970) 397 US 93. As a practical matter, it would be difficult for the government to object if defense counsel copied the same subject matter categories used in the grand jury subpoenas for the documents the defendant seeks. In most cases the grand jury will have sent the same form of subpoena to most defendants and other witnesses and defense counsel will either have a copy or can easily get one.

b. [§13.88] Timing of Discovery Motions under Rule 16

Rule 16(f) provides that motions under Rule 16 must be made within 10 days after arraignment or "at such reasonable later time as the court may permit." Making such motions early will enable the judge, at pretrial hearings, to encourage the parties to engage in mutual disclosure that would facilitate the trial. This will help defendant to obtain pretrial discovery somewhat similar to that available in a civil case. This is also consistent with the spirit of the amendments to the Criminal Rules, which contemplate voluntary compliance by the parties rather than judicial resolution of discovery issues. See 1 Wright (1969) *Federal Practice and Procedure* §257. See also sample pretrial order No. 11, *1970 Manual* 197.

c. [§13.89] Who is a Defendant under Rule 16(a)

Rule 16(a) gives a "defendant" the right to obtain *his* testimony before a grand jury and *his* statements in the hands of the government. Counsel for a defendant corporation should attempt to construe the rule as broadly as possible in order to obtain testimony and statements by its present and former employees, officers, and directors.

The Antitrust Division has argued that a corporation may obtain grand jury testimony of only those witnesses who responded to a subpoena duces tecum addressed to the corporation itself. See *Antitrust Developments 1955-1968,* 232. While the issue has arisen under Rule 16(a)(3), relating to grand jury testimony, the government presumably takes the same position under Rule 16(a)(1) since neither section defines "defendant".

The courts have in general been more liberal in granting discovery. In *United States v Aeroquip Corp.* (ED Mich 1966) 41 FRD 441, the court permitted as a matter of right under Rule 16(a)(3) pretrial disclosure to a corporate defendant of the grand jury testimony of corporate officers who were officers at the time they testified and of other individuals who testified in response to subpoenas duces tecum directed to the corporation. *United States v American Oil Co.* (D NJ 1968) 286 F Supp 742 refused to distinguish discovery under Rule 16(a)(3) from discovery of grand jury testimony under Rule 6(e) (see § 13.91), but did require disclosure of grand jury testimony of all persons who, when they testified, were officers or employees of any of the moving corporations. In *United States v United Concrete Pipe Corp.* (ND Tex 1966) 41 FRD 538, the court was more liberal, granting discovery to the corporate defendant of the grand jury testimony of its present and former officers. This decision was broadened on a writ of mandamus in *United States v Hughes* (5th Cir 1969) 413 F2d 1244, *cert granted sub nom United States v Gifford-Hill-American, Inc.* (1969) 396 US 984; *judgment vacated and mandamus dismissed as moot,* (1970) 397 US 93.

It would seem that the *Hughes* rationale would apply equally well under Rule 16(a)(1) to statements by officers, directors and employees, both past and present, concerning activities carried on or knowledge acquired, within the scope of or reasonably related to their employment. These statements should also be discoverable by the corporation as a matter of right before trial. It would be unreasonable to define "defendant" one way when an officer or employee testifies before the grand jury, and another way when his statement is otherwise in the possession of the government. See discussion of grand jury testimony in subsequent trial at § 10.23, and secrecy of grand jury proceedings at § 10.9.

2. [§ 13.90] Other Modes of Discovery of Grand Jury Testimony

Because of its importance in a criminal antitrust case (see Archer, *Discovery for Defendant's Counsel in Criminal Antitrust Cases* (1965) 20 *Bus Law* 911, 915), a defendant should utilize all possible methods of obtaining grand jury testimony. If the person who testified before the grand jury is not a defendant, even in the broad sense discussed in § 13.89, his testimony might still be obtained on a different basis, at least after he has testified on direct examination at trial.

a. [§ 13.91] Grand Jury Transcripts: Rule 6(e) and the Dennis Case

Rule 6(e) provides that grand jury transcripts may be disclosed if "directed by the court preliminarily to or in connection with a judicial proceeding or when permitted by the court at the request of the defendant upon a showing that grounds may exist for a motion to dismiss the indictment because of matters occurring before the grand jury." The traditional learning under this rule has been that the defendant is required to establish a "particularized need" before obtaining access to a grand jury transcript. See *Pittsburgh Plate Glass Co. v United States* (1959) 360 US 395. In *Dennis v United States* (1966) 384 US 855, however, the Court reversed a conviction because of the government's failure to disclose the grand jury transcript of the witnesses it called. Placing new stress on the value of disclosure, the Court explained (at 873) that in "our adversary system for determining guilt or innocence, it is rarely justifiable for the prosecution to have exclusive access to a storehouse of relevant fact. Exceptions to this are justifiable only by the clearest and most compelling considerations." The Court found that disclosure was required for a number of particular reasons in *Dennis*. Since those reasons underlay the extensive language respecting the liberalization of discovery, it was unclear whether *Dennis* was maintaining the particularized need standard and demonstrating how it was met in that case, or whether it was urging that the standard be relaxed.

Professor Wright has stated that under a "fair reading" of *Dennis* a defendant is entitled to at least the relevant portions of a trial witness's grand jury testimony. 1 Wright (1969) *Federal Practice and Procedure* §108. The Second Circuit in *United States v Youngblood* (2d Cir 1967) 379 F2d 365, 370 has laid down a strong rule granting defendants such a right of access to grand jury testimony after the testimony of a government witness:

> . . . the district courts of this circuit at the request of the defendant should order that the defendant be allowed to examine the grand jury testimony of those witnesses who testify at his trial without requiring him to show any particularized need for this material; we are holding that a defendant should be entitled to see all the grand jury testimony of each witness on the subjects about which that witness testified at the defendant's trial.

See also *Melton v United States* (10th Cir 1968) 398 F2d 321. Other courts have read *Dennis* more restrictively, and still require some showing of need. See, *e.g.*, *White v United States* (5th Cir 1969) 415 F2d 292 (per curiam), *cert den* (1970) 397 US 993; *National Dairy Products Corp. v United States* (8th Cir 1967) 384 F2d 457, *cert den* (1968) 390 US 957 ("particularized need" must still be shown, but is sufficiently shown when prosecution introduces grand jury testimony); *United States v American Oil Co.* (D NJ 1968) 286 F Supp 742 (discovery under Rules 6(e) or

16(a)(3) requires the court to use its discretion in balancing competing interests).

Even if the liberal interpretation of *Dennis* followed by the Second Circuit is employed, grand jury testimony is available for impeachment only after the government witness has testified. Unlike Rule 16(a)(3), *Dennis* dealt with disclosure after direct examination, not pretrial discovery. "The traditional attitude has been one of great reluctance to make grand jury minutes available if they are sought merely for purposes of discovery. That attitude is likely to continue." 1 Wright, *supra*, §108. See, e.g., *United States v Burgio* (SD NY 1968) 279 F Supp 843, 846–847; *United States v Birrell* (SD NY 1967) 276 F Supp 798, 825.

There is some authority, however, for the position that the court may require such disclosure before trial on a clear showing of need. In *United States v Hughes* (5th Cir 1968) 388 F2d 236, the court held that it had not been an abuse of discretion for the district judge in *United States v Venn* (SD Fla 1966) 41 FRD 540 to allow the defendant corporation pretrial access to grand jury testimony of its officers, directors, agents and employees, though not its former employees, on the bases of a court's inherent power to manage the trial, Rules 6(e), 16(a)(3), and *Dennis*. However, when grand jury testimony is sought for pretrial discovery purposes, particularized need will still have to be demonstrated. See *United States v Hughes* (5th Cir 1969) 413 F2d 1244, 1247, *cert granted sub nom United States v Gifford-Hill-American, Inc.* (1969) 396 US 984; *judgment vacated and mandamus dismissed as moot*, (1970) 397 US 93; *cf. United States v Cullen* (ED Wis 1969) 305 F Supp 695 ("pretrial discovery [of grand jury testimony] is still not permitted absent a showing of particularized need").

This use of the court's discretion to require pretrial disclosure of grand jury transcripts in antitrust cases may become more popular since it has been specifically approved in the *1970 Manual* §6.1, at 96–97 and n. 146.

Further, even if pretrial discovery is not allowed, the court in its discretion might allow the defendant to see the grand jury testimony of government witnesses before the witness actually testifies. This would avoid lengthy delays while defense counsel examined the transcripts before cross-examination. *United States v Cullen, supra; United States v Venn, supra; 1970 Manual, supra.*

b. [§13.92] Alternate Argument under Rule 16(b) to Obtain Grand Jury Transcripts

If no particularized need can be shown, then the defense might attempt to obtain pretrial discovery of grand jury testimony under Rule

16(b). It can be argued that grand jury transcripts are documents, and consequently subject to defense discovery upon a showing of reasonableness and materiality to preparation of the defense. In *United States v Hughes* (5th Cir 1969) 413 F2d 1244, *cert granted sub nom United States v Gifford-Hill-American, Inc.* (1969) 396 US 984; *judgment vacated and mandamus dismissed as moot*, (1970) 397 US 93, it was asserted on a writ of mandamus that to deny defendants access to grand jury testimony they sought in order to prove a charge of double jeopardy was reversible error. The court agreed. It found that such transcripts were discoverable under Rule 16(b) if reasonableness and materiality could be proved.

The Fifth Circuit, however, no longer seems committed to that position. In *James v United States* (5th Cir 1969) 416 F2d 467, 476, *cert den* (1970) 397 US 907, it stated in a footnote that such testimony should be discoverable under Rule 6(e) rather than Rule 16(b) since the specific should control the more general rule. See 1 Wright (1969) *Federal Practice and Procedure* §108. The decision is unclear since the court did not overrule *Hughes*, which had approved the use of Rule 16(b), but distinguished it on the basis that in that case materiality had been shown.

3. [§13.93] Subpoenas for the Production of Documentary Evidence and Objects: Rule 17(c)

Rule 17(c) is a general grant of power to the court to issue subpoenas for the production of books, papers, documents, etc. The court may direct production before trial or before the time when the objects are to be offered in evidence. Thus on its face Rule 17(c) could be used as a discovery device. Defendant's counsel should be aware that the Supreme Court has held that "rule 17(c) was not intended to provide an additional means of discovery. Its chief innovation was to expedite the trial by providing a time and place *before* trial for the inspection of the subpoenaed materials." *Bowman Dairy Co. v United States* (1951) 341 US 214, 220. Lower courts have held, moreover, that Rule 17(c) is merely a method for the production of objects that may be used in evidence, and pretrial inspection is only a provision for convenience. *United States v Murray* (2d Cir 1962) 297 F2d 812, 821, *cert den* (1962) 369 US 828; *In Re Magnus, Mabee & Reynard, Inc.* (2d Cir 1962) 311 F2d 12, 15, *cert den* (1963) 373 US 902. *United States v Fassler* (SD NY 1968) 46 FRD 43, 45. So applied, the rule is of less help to antitrust defendants than to those accused of simpler offenses. Prosecution documents in an antitrust case, because of their size and complexity, usually require time and study before defendant is prepared to explain or rebut them. Defendants accused of less complicated, albeit more serious, offenses may need only a few minutes before trial to prepare against a few prosecution documents. Defense counsel should be ready to argue that the more numerous and complicated the government's documents, the earlier they should be disclosed under Rule 17(c).

4. [§13.94] Discovery under the Jencks Act

Jencks v United States (1957) 353 US 657 held that a criminal action had to be dismissed when the government refused to comply with an order to produce relevant statements or reports in its possession given by government witnesses touching the subject matter of their testimony at the trial. Fearing that this would lead either to a wholesale dismissal of government cases or to unreasonable disclosure of government evidence, Congress enacted the Jencks Act, 18 USC §3500. This statute now provides that statements or reports in the possession of the United States that were made by government witnesses or prospective government witnesses to an agent of the government will not be subject to subpoena, discovery, or inspection until after the witness has testified on direct examination at trial. The statute provides for *in camera* review by which the court may excise portions that do not relate to the subject matter of the testimony of the witness.

Motions for the disclosure of such statements should be made during trial. It may be possible, when a large volume of material is involved, to obtain discovery in advance of testimony. See *United States v Cobb* (SD NY 1967) 271 F Supp 159, 164; 8 *Moore's Federal Practice* (1969) §16.01. Such procedures might be worked out at a pretrial hearing. See *1970 Manual* §6.1. Such an arrangement saves trial time, since defense counsel would not have to halt proceedings to read the documents after direct testimony.

The Jencks Act has been held to be an exclusive means of discovery for the subjects with which it deals. *Palermo v United States* (1959) 360 US 343. Hence, if the government witness never testifies, his statement to the government would not be discoverable. Further, if the government does not agree to disclose before trial a statement from one of its witnesses who will testify, it cannot be required to do so until after direct examination. See generally, 2 Wright (1969) *Federal Practice and Procedure* §417.

The most disputed question of application under the Jencks Act is whether information in the hands of the government is really a statement or report covered by the Act and, if it is covered, whether it fits into the narrower definition of statement that would make it discoverable by the defense. See *Palermo v United States, supra.* See generally 2 Wright, *supra,* §417.

5. [§13.95] Defense Motions for Disclosure

In *Brady v Maryland* (1963) 373 US 83, the Supreme Court held (at 87) that "the suppression by the prosecution of evidence favorable to an accused upon request violates due process where the evidence is material either to guilt or to punishment, irrespective of the good faith or bad faith of the prosecution." Thus, the prosecution is under an obligation to turn over to the defense favorable evidence, should the defense so request.

While the *Brady* opinion dealt with admissible evidence, it is unclear that mandatory disclosure should be so limited. See, *e.g.*, *Giles v Maryland* (1967) 386 US 66, 96 (Fortas, J., concurring) (prosecution's duty to disclose material facts to defense should be extended, in certain circumstances, even to inadmissible evidence).

It is not clear how a *Brady* type motion for disclosure should be phrased. It would be difficult for a defendant to describe specifically evidence that the government might be suppressing and about which he knows nothing. But dragnet requests to disclose evidence " 'favorable to or tending to exculpate or establish any defenses to prosecution of defendant' " are not well received by the courts. See *United States v Birrell* (SD NY 1967) 276 F Supp 798, 826. But see *Antitrust Developments, 1955-1968*, 235.

It is unsettled when the prosecution should have to disclose favorable evidence. If it disclosed all such evidence before trial, it would exceed the standards set down in the Jencks Act since some favorable evidence would surely consist of statements by government witnesses to government agents, otherwise undiscoverable until after direct examination. See *United States v Leighton* (SD NY 1967) 265 F Supp 27, 35; *United States v Manhattan Brush Co.* (SD NY 1965) 38 FRD 4, 7. It would also be difficult for the government to tell, before presentation of the defendant's case, what evidence is actually relevant or helpful to possible defenses.

Nevertheless, some courts have recognized that there are situations in which an adequate defense depends upon viewing favorable government evidence before trial. Realizing this, Judge Mansfield in *United States v Cobb* (SD NY 1967) 271 F Supp 159, 164, left up to the good conscience of the government what evidence to produce prior to trial, subject "to the sanction that if it delays disclosure until trial, it may risk the granting of a motion for a mistrial." In *United States v Gleason* (SD NY 1967) 265 F Supp 880, Judge Frankel called on the prosecution to inform the court before trial of any evidence it had that might be exculpatory on the theory that the court could order pretrial disclosure if it found the information important to the defense. Judge Frankel (at 887) specifically rejected the notion that the Jencks Act might restrict disclosure until after direct testimony by a government witness. The *Gleason* approach was disapproved, however, by Judge Tyler in *United States v Kaminsky* (SD NY 1967) 275 F Supp 365, 368.

At a minimum it seems that the government has a responsibility to disclose evidence favorable to the defense at a time when it might still be useful; if it withholds all such evidence until after direct examination it risks a mistrial. "Without [guidelines from the appellate courts], however, it is at least clear that exculpatory information having a material bearing on defense preparation—*e.g.*, suggestive of affirmative defense theories such as insanity or self-defense—should be disclosed well in advance of trial." 8 *Moore's Federal Practice* §16.06[2] (1969). Otherwise, *Brady* would be emasculated when evidence was critical to the preparation of the defense but the government withheld it till after direct examination.

Defendant should raise the question of when favorable evidence must be disclosed at a pretrial conference so as to enlist the aid of the judge in bringing about an agreement to resolve the matter. See *1970 Manual* §6.1.

6. [§13.96] Pretrial Conferences

Rule 17.1 as amended in 1966 establishes the basis for the pretrial conference in criminal cases by authorizing the court upon motion of any party or upon its own motion to hold one or more conferences to consider such matters "as will promote a fair and expeditious trial." The Rule, according to the Advisory Committee Notes, 18 USCA Rule 17.1, was cast in broad language in order to accommodate all types of pretrial conferences. See generally West, *Criminal Pre-trials—Useful Techniques* (1961) 29 FRD 436.

The pretrial conference is particularly useful in a large criminal antitrust case. *1970 Manual* §6.1. Such a conference should so streamline the case that trial time is substantially reduced. It should bring about agreement on mutual discovery and defense discovery by right under Rule 16 (see §§13.85–13.88); discovery of grand jury transcripts under the *Dennis* case, Rule 6(e), the inherent power of the court, or Rule 16(b) (see §§13.89–13.92); disclosure of statements covered by the Jencks Act before trial (see §13.94); *Brady* motions for pretrial disclosure of evidence favorable to the defense in the possession of the government (see §13.95); and other procedural problems such as severance. Sample pretrial orders are recommended in the *1970 Manual*.

7. [§13.97] Effect of a Related Civil Case on a Criminal Prosecution

Since broader discovery is allowed in a civil than in a criminal case, a simultaneous civil suit may greatly increase disclosure. This can help the prosecution because of its increased access to defense information and witnesses; it can also help the defense since it may result in pretrial access to Jencks Act materials and grand jury testimony. See §§13.89–13.94. In *United States v Kordel* (1970) 397 US 1, the Supreme Court dealt with convictions of two defendants for violating the Federal Food, Drug, and Cosmetic Act. The convictions occurred while the Food and Drug Administration was pursuing a nearly contemporaneous civil condemnation proceeding based on the same violation. The corporation, which had received government interrogatories in the civil case, moved to stay the civil proceedings or in the alternative to extend the time to answer the interrogatories until after disposition of the criminal proceedings. After those motions were denied, the corporation, through one of the defendants, answered the interrogatories. The Court rejected the contention that the answers to the interrogatories were involuntarily given and represented violations of defendants' Fifth Amendment rights, reasoning that the defendant who answered could have asserted his privilege against self-incrimination. Since the other defendant never answered the interrogatories his privilege against self-incrimination was not abridged. "The respondents press upon us the situation where no one can answer the interrogatories addressed to the corporation without subjecting himself to a 'real and appreciable' risk of self-incrimination. For present purposes we may assume that in such a case the appropriate remedy would be a protective order under Rule 30(b), postponing civil discovery until termination of the criminal action. But we need not decide this troublesome question." 397 US at 8–9.

In response to the contention that a simultaneous civil action should invalidate the conviction on grounds of due process or under the court's supervisory power over federal courts, the court noted that the public interest might demand swift civil enforcement by an agency, yet there may be insufficient evidence at that time to begin a criminal prosecution. "It would stultify enforcement of federal law to require a governmental agency such as the FDA invariably to choose either to forgo recommendation of a criminal prosecution once it seeks civil relief, or to defer civil proceedings pending the ultimate outcome of a criminal trial." 397 US at 11. The court laid down a general standard of "special circumstances" that might indicate that the criminal prosecution would have to be overturned.

Since the Court rejected any blanket rule delaying civil proceedings, until the conclusion of a criminal trial, the best course for defense counsel would be to move in the civil case, on the basis of specified special circumstances, to delay proceeding on such matters as answering extensive interrogatories, or to adopt appropriate protective orders, while the criminal proceeding is still being prosecuted. See *United States v American Radiator & Standard Sanitary Corp.* (3d Cir 1967) 388 F2d 201, *cert den* (1968) 390 US 922; *Kaeppler v Jas. H. Matthews & Co.* (ED Pa 1961) 200 F Supp 229; *Perry v McGuire* (SD NY 1964) 36 FRD 272; *cf. Campbell v Eastland* (5th Cir 1962) 307 F2d 478, *cert den* (1963) 371 US 955; *United States v Maine Lobstermen's Ass'n.* (D Me 1958) 22 FRD 199.

8. [§13.98] Depositions: Rule 15

Depositions, like subpoenas under Rule 17(c), are included among discovery devices more to warn against their misuse than to recommend them as affirmative discovery tools. Unlike depositions in the Federal Rules of Civil Procedure, they are not used for discovery purposes, nor are they available to the government. (Title 18 USC §3503, which is part of the Organized Crime Control Act of 1970, provides for depositions even for the government in exceptional circumstances if the Attorney General or his designee certifies that the legal proceeding in which the deposition is sought is against a person who is believed to have participated in an "organized criminal activity." Hopefully this will never be construed to mean antitrust cases.) The defendant under Rule 15 has a limited right to take depositions if it appears that a witness may be unavailable for trial. The Advisory Committee explained that "it was contemplated that in criminal cases depositions would be used only in exceptional situations, as has been the practice heretofore." Advisory Committee Notes, 18 USCA Rule 15(a). The rule specifies that a deposition should be taken in the manner provided in civil actions, and dictates the circumstances under which it may be used at trial.

F. [§13.99] Trials

Criminal antitrust suits are tried before a judge and jury. The strategy and tactics useful in civil antitrust jury trials are also helpful here. See §13.49. Certain additional considerations merit brief comment.

The government begins with a psychological advantage with the jury since the attorneys prosecuting the case have no personal stake in the outcome. The jury may be inclined to give more weight to the prosecution's view of the evidence than to defendant's. In addition, the government, unlike a private treble damage plaintiff, does not have to prove damages. It need only prove commission of the offense charged.

Defense counsel, however, does not lack compensating advantages. In most criminal cases such as theft, assault or murder, a crime has indisputably been committed, and the issue is whether the defendant is the guilty person. In criminal antitrust cases, the charge is usually conspiracy to fix prices or to monopolize, and the issue is not identification of the wrongdoer, but whether there has been a wrong committed. This distinction should be pointed out to the jury. Defense counsel should also emphasize that in order to decide the case the jury must look into the minds of the defendants to determine whether there was or was not an unlawful conspiracy. Obviously this is a more difficult task than to decide whether a particular defendant was the person who committed an undisputed crime; and not only is the antitrust jury required to probe the defendant's mental processes—a task fraught with possibilities for error—but it must do so as to business matters, in which the line between unilateral lawful conduct and that degree of consensus that equals unlawful joint conduct is itself shadowy and elusive. In short, only with the clearest evidence could a fact-finder confidently decide that an illegal conspiracy or agreement existed. Thus, when charges in a criminal antitrust case are placed in their proper setting it might be said—and defense counsel should say it both briefly in his opening statement and more explicitly in his closing statement—that such charges are the hardest possible ones to prove, the margin for error is great, the presumption of innocence is applicable, and the jury's obligation to demand proof beyond any reasonable doubt is essential for the proper administration of justice.

Defense counsel's opening statement, reflecting the considerations stated above, should be reasonably short and simple, focused only on the main issues the jury must decide. The jury may well be able to understand numerous points in an extended opening statement but it is foolhardy to expect the jury to *remember* these points during the trial. A few propositions that the jury can retain as a guide in appraising the evidence is the better approach.

Defense counsel, by appropriate objections, should keep the government restricted to the charges made in the indictment as more specifically identified in the bill of particulars (see §13.76). The weaker the government's case, or the more it depends on circumstantial evidence, the more tempting it will be for the government attorneys to try to prove the same point repeatedly by different means. In doing so, they may wander from the main charges of conspiracy and mislead the jury to the defendant's detriment. A classic example occurred in *United States v*

Chas. Pfizer & Co. (2d Cir 1970) 426 F2d 32, in which the government's proof and the court's subsequent charge to the jury were found to have obscured the basic theory of the government's case. The court reversed the criminal conviction and remanded the case for a new trial. The record of the case shows that the Pfizer defendants repeatedly objected to the government's tactics and thereby preserved their rights on appeal.

Defense counsel must prepare in advance of trial explanations for certain types of business conduct that will negate an inference of unlawful agreement. This requires special preparation in antitrust cases because most business decisions by their very nature can be justified on several different logical grounds. Whether counsel actually uses such affirmative explanations at trial or simply stands pat on the contention that the government has not proved a violation requires a delicate legal judgment that can only be made as the trial progresses, and as defense counsel assesses the impact of the government's evidence and the jury's awareness of the standard of proof to which the government should be held.

Guilt by association is a special hazard in criminal antitrust cases involving multiple defendants. Counsel for a leading defendant will refute directly the government's claim that any conspiracy existed at all. Counsel for a lesser defendant may take a different tack. He may find it more useful to leave direct refutation to the lead defendants, and devote his efforts to separating his own client, in the jury's mind, from the other defendants so that whether or not they are found guilty his client will be found innocent. Many opportunities for this strategy will occur in the course of the trial. For example, if there has been testimony about a particular meeting attended by several defendants, counsel might cross-examine by asking the single question whether his client was present when he is certain that the answer will be "no". Repeated use of this tactic even in the most obvious ways will help to differentiate his client from the others.

Defense counsel should not overlook the judge as a fact-finder. Not only does a judge's attitude influence the jury if the case goes to the jury, but the judge might himself dismiss the case at the end of the government's evidence if it appears that the government has not made out a prima facie case. This is by no means rare in criminal antitrust suits, in which judges feel a special responsibility because of the complex business issues involved. See, *e.g., United States v Aeroquip Corp.* (ED Mich 1968) 284 F Supp 114. Unlike civil cases so dismissed, the government cannot appeal from the dismissal of a criminal suit and the trial judge's decision is therefore final.

Great care must of course be taken in preparing instructions to the jury. All judges are well versed in the "necessary generalities" relating to burden of proof, etc. Defense counsel must frame his requests to focus fairly but with impact on the critical substantive issues developed by the evidence. Some helpful examples may be found in *Jury Instructions in Criminal Antitrust Cases* (1965) Antitrust Section of the American Bar Association; Devitt and Blackmar, *Federal Jury Practice and Instructions* (2d ed 1970).

14

Labor and Antitrust

Stefan M. Mason and Roderick M. Hills

Mr. Mason received the AB degree from Dartmouth College in 1962 and the JD degree from the University of California at Los Angeles Law School in 1967. Mr. Hills received the AB degree from Stanford University in 1952 and the LLB degree from Stanford Law School in 1955. They are members of the Los Angeles County and American Bar Associations, the State Bar of California, and the Los Angeles firm of Munger, Tolles, Hills and Rickershauser.

I. [§14.1] Introduction and Scope

Labor unions are afforded substantial immunity from prosecution under federal antitrust laws by reason of specific exemptions in the Clayton Act (15 USC §17, 29 USC §52) and the Norris-LaGuardia Act (29 USC §§101-115). Nevertheless, violations of state and federal antitrust laws may occur when union activities tend to restrain competition among employers. For example, federal Sherman Act antitrust violations have been found when (1) a union picketed independent gas station operators for the purpose of forcing them to comply with a price-fixing agreement previously made between the union and an association of operators (*United States v Gasoline Retailers Ass'n.* (ND Ind 1960) 1960 Trade Cases ¶69,596, *aff'd* (7th Cir 1961) 285 F2d 688; (2) a union and an association of plastering contractors conspired to control who could operate as plastering contractors and purchase plastering materials in the Chicago area (*United States v Employing Plasterers Ass'n.* (1954) 347 US 186); and (3) a "union" representing independent frankfurter distributors conspired with frankfurter manufacturers to fix retail prices in order to compensate the manufacturers for an increase in discounts negotiated by the "union" for its distributor-members (*United States v Olympia Provision & Baking Co.* (SD NY 1968) 282 F Supp 819, *aff'd per curiam sub nom Provision Salesmen & Distributors v United States* (1969) 393 US 480).

Since the 1890 enactment of the Sherman Act, federal and state judiciaries have attempted to balance the legitimate efforts of workers to increase their benefits by combining in exclusive bargaining unions against the somewhat contradictory government efforts to eliminate combinations that restrain competition. The contradiction is highlighted when a large union or combination of unions enter into an agreement with an association of employers.

The uncertainty flowing from these contradictory policies is heightened by a paucity of appellate decisions, by Congressional inattention, and most recently by the Supreme Court's divided decisions in *United Mine Workers v Pennington* (1965) 381 US 657 and *Local 189, AMC & BW v Jewel Tea Co.* (1965) 381 US 676.

To appreciate the conflict between the two policies, one must keep in mind organized labor's long struggle against the judicial injunction and its efforts to secure governmental protection for organizing efforts. This chapter does not attempt an analysis of that struggle, which involves far more regulation than the antitrust laws. Nor does it treat those aspects of the federal and state labor laws that regulate union conduct similar to the types of conduct regulated by the antitrust laws, *e.g.*, laws governing "hot cargo" clauses and secondary boycotts. Broadly defined, "hot cargo" refers to goods that are produced, handled or shipped by "unfair" employers; "hot cargo" clauses are agreements between labor and management whereby management agrees not to deal with other employers who are considered unfair by labor. These laws are more appropriately discussed in context with the broad and general subject of labor-management relations.

The purpose of this chapter is to alert the practitioner to the circumstances when federal and state antitrust laws may apply to labor union activities.

II. History of Labor's Antitrust Exemption

A. [§14.2] The Sherman Act

Enacted in 1890, Section 1 of the Sherman Act (15 USC §1) declares illegal "every contract, combination . . . or conspiracy, in restraint of trade or commerce among the several States." Remedies for violations include injunctive relief, contempt proceedings, treble damages, and criminal prosecution. See discussion of the Sherman Act in Chapter 2.

Until 1940, federal courts frequently held that union activities such as strikes and boycotts violated the Sherman Act because they had the effect or intended effect of substantially restraining the flow of goods in interstate commerce. See, *e.g., Coronado Coal Co. v United Mine Workers* (1925) 268 US 295 (strike), *Bedford Cut Stone Co. v Journeymen Stone Cutters' Ass'n.* (1927) 274 US 37 (boycott).

B. [§14.3] The Clayton Act

Two purposes of the 1914 Clayton Act were to exempt labor organizations from the operation of the Sherman Act and to limit the use of labor injunctions in federal courts. 15 USC §17, 29 USC §52. Restrictive judicial interpretations of the Clayton Act aborted the intended exemptions. See, *e.g., Duplex Printing Press Co. v Deering* (1921) 254 US 443; *Labor's Antitrust Exemption After Pennington and Jewel Tea* (1966) 66 *Col L Rev* 742, 743; Winter, *Labor Injunctions and Judge-Made Labor Law: The Contemporary Role of Norris-LaGuardia* (1960) 70 *Yale LJ* 70, 88.

C. [§14.4] The Norris-LaGuardia Act

Judicial enforcement of the Sherman Act against labor organizations and judicial refusal to implement the purposes of the Clayton Act caused Congress to enact the Norris-LaGuardia Act in 1932, which explicitly overturned the narrow interpretations of the Clayton Act and prohibited the issuance of injunctions in all cases involving a "labor dispute." 29 USC §§101–115. The Act defines a labor dispute as any controversy concerning a labor union's efforts to negotiate, fix, maintain or change the terms or conditions of employment. 29 USC §113(c). However, whether a court will find that a labor dispute exists seems to depend on a balancing of the contradictory policies; *e.g.*, a court will not find that a labor dispute exists unless it concludes that the suspect activity should remain immune from antitrust liability.

D. [§14.5] The Judicial Change of Heart

Evidencing a change of heart, in 1940 the Court commenced to give broader effect to the immunity legislation granted labor organizations by the Norris-LaGuardia Act. In *Apex Hosiery Co. v Leader* (1940) 310 US 469, the Court held (at 501) that the Sherman Act prohibits only intended or actual restraints on competition that affect the employer's product market, not the labor market. The decision held that union seizure of a company's plant during a violent strike and its refusal to release goods for shipment in interstate commerce were protected because the activity was designed solely to compel the company to accede to the union's demands.

Further articulation of labor's antitrust exemption was given by the Court the following year in *United States v Hutcheson* (1941) 312 US 219, which, dealing with an inter-union jurisdictional dispute, held striking, picketing, and boycotting immune. The Court specifically harmonized the Sherman, Clayton and Norris-LaGuardia Acts (Frankfurter, J., at 232):

So long as a union acts in its self-interest and does not combine with non-labor groups, the licit and the illicit under Section 20 [of the Clayton Act] are not to be distinguished by any judgment regarding the wisdom or unwisdom, the rightness or wrongness, the selfishness or unselfishness of the end of which the particular union activities are the means.

E. [§14.6] Twenty Years of Uncertainty

While *Hutcheson* seemed to offer a blanket exemption vis-a-vis union liability for activities defined in Section 20 of the Clayton Act (29 USC §52), *e.g.*, strikes, boycotts, and picketing, later decisions revealed great uncertainty. While the Court held in 1945 that a union acting alone does not violate the Sherman Act even if it maliciously forces an employer out of business by refusing to provide him with labor (*Hunt v Crumboch* (1945) 325 US 821), it also held that when a union combines with a non-labor group, its immunity may be lost. Thus, in *Allen Bradley Co. v Local 3, IBEW* (1945) 325 US 797, the Court held that hot-cargo agreements between a union and manufacturers and contractors to provide a completely sheltered market for electrical equipment produced in New York City violated the Sherman Act because they affected price and market control and were not limited to traditional terms and conditions of employment. Had the union acted without the cooperation of the contractors and manufacturers, its activities would have been exempt. 325 US at 810.

From 1945 to 1965 the scope of the exemption was subject to considerable doubt because neither the Court nor Congress clarified the elusive criteria articulated in *Apex*, *Hutcheson*, and *Allen Bradley*. Confusion was particularly evident in the following areas:

1. Some decisions turned on the insubstantial effect the union activity had on interstate commerce, following the *Apex* rationale. *E.g.*, *United States v Gold* (2d Cir 1940) 115 F2d 236.

2. Some courts focused on the legitimacy of the union objective whereas others required the absence of a specific intent to restrain competition. Compare *Hess v Petrillo* (7th Cir 1958) 259 F2d 735, *cert den* (1959) 359 US 954, with *United States v Hamilton Glass Co.* (ND Ill 1957) 155 F Supp 878, 882.

3. Courts were divided concerning whether *Allen Bradley* required the existence of a multi-employer conspiracy with a union or unions, or whether a union conspiracy with a single employer was sufficient to forfeit the antitrust exemption. Compare *United States v Hamilton Glass Co.*, *supra* (apparently required multi-employer conspiracy), with *Westlab Inc. v Freedomland, Inc.* (SD NY 1961) 198 F Supp 701 (court suggested that single-employer conspiracy with union sufficient).

4. *Allen Bradley* left unresolved the question whether the exemption was lost if employers actively opposed union demands before acquiescing under the threat of economic action by the union.

5. *Allen Bradley* and *Hutcheson* left open the question whether a collective bargaining agreement, standing alone, could operate to achieve a prohibited conspiracy. The *Allen Bradley* Court assumed that a collective bargaining agreement was not sufficient to establish an illegal conspiracy, but later decisions suggested that a collective bargaining agreement alone could manifest an illegal combination. Compare *Adams Dairy Co. v St. Louis Dairy Co.* (8th Cir 1958) 260 F2d 46, 53 (collective bargaining agreement insufficient) with *United States v Milk Drivers Union Local 471* (D Minn 1957) 153 F Supp 803 (collective bargaining agreement, standing alone, was sufficient).

F. The Pennington and Jewel Tea Decisions

1. Pennington

a. [§14.7] The Facts

In *United Mine Workers v Pennington* (1965) 381 US 657, the UMW Welfare and Retirement Fund sued Phillips Brothers Coal Company, a small mining operator, to recover royalty payments allegedly due under the 1950 National Bituminous Coal Wage Agreement, as amended. The agreement reflected a concurrence between the United Mine Workers and large coal operators that the industry's most critical problem was overproduction. The agreement represented the union's acquiescence to operator control over working hours and rapid mechanization of the mines in return for increased wages and welfare fund royalty payments. Phillips cross-claimed for treble damages under Sections 1 and 2 of the Sherman Act (15 USC §§1–2), alleging that:

1. The union had promised the large coal operators that it would impose the terms and conditions of the national agreement on Phillips and all other coal operators regardless of their ability to pay or the extent of their mechanization;

2. The large coal companies agreed not to lease coal lands to unorganized operators and not to buy or sell coal from or to such operators;

3. The large coal companies and the union successfully persuaded the Secretary of Labor to set a high minimum wage for companies selling coal to the Tennessee Valley Authority pursuant to the provisions of the Walsh-Healy Act, which made it difficult for smaller coal companies to compete in the TVA term contract market; and

4. Four major coal companies, two of which the UMW substantially controlled, participated in a price cutting campaign in the TVA spot market.

The jury found against the union and in favor of Phillips. The Sixth Circuit affirmed, ruling that the union was not exempt from antitrust liability. The Supreme Court reversed in divided opinions. While affirming the Sixth Circuit's holding that the union was not immune from antitrust prosecution, the Supreme Court remanded to the district court because the jury had not been instructed that the joint efforts of the union and large coal operators to influence public officials in the setting of high minimum wage rates did not constitute antitrust violations.

b. [§14.8] The Opinion of Justices White, Brennan, and Warren

Mr. Justice White, authoring the opinion of the Court and joined by Justice Brennan and Chief Justice Warren, articulated the following reasons for finding no antitrust immunity:

1. Unions may lose their exemption from the Sherman Act when they combine with non-labor groups;

2. Immunity is not conferred merely because the combination is expressed in a collective bargaining agreement;

3. Immunity is not conferred merely because the means for effecting the purpose of the conspiracy was an agreement on wages or hours;

4. Union self-interest will not confer immunity if the restraint on the product market is "direct" and the benefit to labor only "indirect";

5. The showing that the union was a party to the large coal companies' collusive bidding arrangement, which was intended to drive the smaller coal companies from the TVA spot market, destroyed the union's immunity;

6. The national labor policy requiring unit-by-unit bargaining prohibits unions, pursuant to a conspiracy to eliminate competitors, from agreeing with one set of employers to impose a certain wage scale on other employers, even though a union is free to impose previously-negotiated wage terms on other employers absent a conspiracy;

7. An employer's refusal to bargain until its competitors have done so is illegal;

8. Permitting an employer to demand that a union impose a similar contract on its competitors impedes collective bargaining; and

9. The agreement violated the fundamental antitrust policy of assuring to economic units freedom from restraints against acting according to their own choice, *e.g.*, if labor were exempt here, it would be exempt under any discriminatory scheme designed to impose higher wages on competitors. In effect, such an exemption would allow unions to surrender their freedom of action with respect to their bargaining policies.

c. [§14.9] The Opinion of Justices Douglas, Black, and Clark

A concurring opinion was authored by Mr. Justice Douglas, who was joined by Justices Black and Clark. Justice Douglas interpreted Justice White's opinion as a reaffirmation of the *Allen Bradley* principles and asserted that any industry-wide agreement that contains provisions imposing a wage scale exceeding the financial ability of some companies constitutes prima facie evidence of an antitrust violation.

d. [§14.10] The Dissenting Opinion of Justices Goldberg, Harlan, and Stewart

Mr. Justice Goldberg authored an opinion in which he was joined by Justices Harlan and Stewart, and in which he dissented from *Pennington* and concurred in *Jewel Tea*. This decision is analyzed in §14.14.

2. Jewel Tea

a. [§14.11] The Facts

In *Local 189, AMC & BW v Jewel Tea Co.* (1965) 381 US 676, Jewel Tea brought a Sherman Act conspiracy action against the butchers' unions and a trade association of independent meat dealers based on a provision in a multi-employer, multi-union collective bargaining agreement that restricted the days and hours during which meat could be sold at retail markets in the Chicago area. Prior to filing the action, Jewel Tea had protested that the restriction was illegal but signed the agreement under the duress of a strike vote. Jewel Tea, a self-service food chain, contended that butchers were not required to be present at all hours during which meat was sold and that the marketing hours restriction unlawfully impeded the use of its property and deprived the public of the opportunity to shop for meat during the restricted hours.

The district court held that the complaint was not subject to dismissal on either an antitrust immunity theory or on an exclusive NLRB jurisdiction theory, but it could find no evidence of the alleged conspiracy. The district court did find that removal of the restrictive marketing hours provision would result either in longer hours and night work for the butchers, or that the butchers' work would be performed by unskilled employees, and on that basis ruled that the activity was within labor's exemption from the antitrust laws because the restriction had been imposed by the unions solely to protect their own interests concerning conditions of employment. The Seventh Circuit reversed without disturbing the district court's findings, concluding that the evidence had established a conspiracy in restraint of trade. *Jewel Tea Co. v Associated Food Retailers* (7th Cir 1964) 331 F2d 547. The Supreme Court reversed, holding that the NLRB did not have exclusive jurisdiction and that the unions' conduct fell within labor's antitrust exemption.

b. [§14.12] The Opinion of Justices White, Brennan, and Warren

Mr. Justice White, authoring the judgment of the Court and joined by Justice Brennan and Chief Justice Warren, articulated the following reasons for reversing:

1. The union's contention that the district court should have stayed its proceedings under the doctrine of primary jurisdiction pending an NLRB determination of whether the marketing hours restriction was a "term or condition of employment" was rejected because: (1) courts are experienced in making such determinations, (2) the NLRB does not "classify bargaining subjects in the abstract" (381 US at 687), and (3) the Court's holding in *Pennington* would not have required a determination of whether the marketing hours restriction involved a "term or condition of employment" had the district court found a union-employer conspiracy.

2. The marketing hours restriction was "so intimately related to wages, hours and working conditions" that it fell within labor's antitrust exemp-

tion. This "intimately related" test was satisfied by the district court's finding that without the hour restriction, job jurisdiction would be impaired or hours or workload would be substantially altered.

Justice White noted that while the district court found no evidence of a conspiracy, the union had entered into a combination with a non-labor group through the collective bargaining agreement with Jewel Tea, and further, that the union did not achieve immunity merely because the non-labor party was a single employer.

c. [§14.13] The Dissenting Opinion of Justices Douglas, Black, and Clark

Mr. Justice Douglas, joined by Justices Black and Clark, dissented, concluding that immunity must be denied on the authority of *Allen Bradley Co. v Local 3, IBEW* (1945) 325 US 797, *e.g.*, the multi-employer collective bargaining agreement constituted prima facie evidence of a conspiracy between employers and unions to impose the hour restriction on Jewel Tea by means of a strike threat. Further, the restriction placed an obvious restraint on the product market because it deprived Jewel Tea of the ability to use "convenience of shopping hours as a means of competition." 381 US at 736.

d. [§14.14] The Opinion of Justices Goldberg, Harlan, and Stewart

In a single opinion concurred in by Justices Harlan and Stewart, Mr. Justice Goldberg dissented from the Court's opinion in *Pennington* and concurred in its judgment in *Jewel Tea*. After reviewing the relevant labor legislation and the judicial history of labor's antitrust exemption, Justice Goldberg found a congressional purpose to "limit severely" the use of antitrust laws as a means for judicial intervention into collective bargaining. He then articulated a test whereby labor should be exempt from the application of antitrust laws pursuant to any collective bargaining activity concerning "mandatory" subjects of bargaining under the National Labor Relations Act. Any narrower test, Justice Goldberg argued, would have a chilling effect on the duty to bargain about mandatory subjects and would mean that "Congress intended to permit the parties to collective bargaining to wage industrial warfare but to prohibit them from peacefully settling their disputes." 381 US at 712.

3. [§14.15] *The Continuing Uncertainty of Labor's Antitrust Exemption*

The basic conflict between the policies of the labor and antitrust laws will almost always require some judicial balancing. Neither *Pennington* nor *Jewel Tea* resulted in opinions attracting a majority of the members of the Court, and none of the opinions provide criteria that can be used by counsel in advising clients with any degree of assurance that the advice will be vindicated if litigation arises. For a compelling critique of these decisions, including an analysis of the illusive criteria applied by the three groups of Justices, see *Labor's Antitrust Exemption After Pennington and Jewel Tea* (1966) 66 *Col L Rev* 742, 755–763. The following section attempts to articulate the most important factors that must be considered when evaluating whether certain conduct does or does not fall within labor's antitrust exemption.

III. Considerations in Determining Whether the Labor Exemption Applies—A Checklist

A. [§14.16] Does the Conduct Affect Commerce?

As in all federal antitrust cases, the conduct must substantially affect interstate commerce before the provisions of the federal antitrust laws are triggered. See, *e.g., Quality Limestone Products, Inc. v Teamsters Local 695* (ED Wis 1962) 207 F Supp 75 (jurisdictional test is whether conduct affects the interstate commerce of the business, not whether the business is engaged in interstate commerce); *Howard v Local 74, Wood, Wire & Metal Lathers* (ND Ill 1953) 118 F Supp 387, *rev'd sub nom United States v Employing Plasterers' Ass'n.* (1954) 374 US 186. *But see Gilmour v Lathers Local 74* (ED Ill 1963) 223 F Supp 236 (conspiracy had direct and substantial effects on interstate commerce even though it was restricted to a local area).

A local union-employer conspiracy that has the effect of curtailing the free flow of materials into a state generally will be held to affect commerce and restrain trade even though the materials involved are purchased locally and all interstate activity has ended at the time the restraint takes place. *E.g., United States v Employing Plasterers Ass'n.* (1954) 347 US 186. *But see United States v San Francisco Electrical Contractors Ass'n.* (ND Calif 1944) 57 F Supp 57 (conspiracy to standardize wages and material prices purchased locally was legal absent agreement not to work on equipment originating out of state).

B. [§14.17] Does a Labor Dispute Exist?

The Clayton and Norris-LaGuardia Acts do not immunize unions against application of the antitrust laws unless a "labor dispute" is found to exist. 29 USC §§104, 113; 15 USC §17, 29 USC §52; see, *e.g., Hunt v Crumboch* (1945) 325 US 821.

The Norris-LaGuardia Act defines a "labor dispute" as encompassing any controversy concerning terms or conditions of employment. 29 USC §113. Under the Clayton Act, such controversies include strikes, termination of employment, persuading others by peaceful means to strike or terminate their employment, peaceful assemblies, boycotting or refusing to employ any party to such a dispute, or the payment of strike benefits. 29 USC §52. The Norris-LaGuardia Act eliminated the prior Clayton Act requirement that an employer-employee relationship was a condition precedent to finding a labor dispute.

Before a labor dispute can be found to exist to confer antitrust immunity, union conduct usually must directly involve only a "labor" group, not a "non-labor" group. Generally, a labor group exists when the group performs work and functions that actually or potentially affect the wages, hours, and working conditions of union members, e.g., there must exist some form of economic inter-relationship between the labor group and union members, such as wage or job competition, which affects the union members. *American Federation of Musicians v Carroll* (1968) 391 US 99 (since orchestra leaders performed work and functions that actually or potentially affected union members' wages, hours, working conditions and job security, they constituted a labor group involved in a labor dispute).

While courts must cast their conclusions with respect to labor's antitrust exemption in terms of the existence or non-existence of a labor dispute, such characterization typically begs the question concerning the bases for such findings, and courts emphasize other matters.

C. [§14.18] Does the Dispute Concern the Terms or Conditions of Employment?

To establish immunity the labor dispute must also involve terms or conditions of employment. The Clayton Act defines the kinds of conduct generally considered to involve terms or conditions of employment. See §14.17. However, as with the determination of the existence or non-existence of a labor dispute, a finding that conduct involves terms or conditions of employment is usually question-begging.

D. [§14.19] Is the Union Acting Alone?

If the conduct flows from unilateral actions of a union, the union generally is immune from prosecution under the federal antitrust laws. It is when the union conspires with an employer or employer association that antitrust immunity may be destroyed notwithstanding the existence of a labor dispute. In *American Federation of Musicians v Carroll* (1968)

391 US 99, the union was held exempt because it acted unilaterally even though it insisted on (1) wage minimums for member musicians hired by orchestra leaders, (2) control over bookings and the use of a minimum number of musicians in orchestras, (3) territorial restrictions and establishment of musician quotas, (4) a closed shop, including coercion of orchestra leaders to join the union, and (5) forcing orchestra leaders to execute the standard contracts. In contrast, *Allen Bradley Co. v Local 3, IBEW* (1945) 325 US 797, involved a joint union-manufacturer-contractor conspiracy to monopolize the New York electrical market by boycotting nonunion and out-of-city goods. The conspiracy was held to violate the Sherman Act. Similarly, in *Gilmour v Lathers Local 74* (ED Ill 1963) 223 F Supp 236, a union conspiracy with an employers' association and union president to put an employer out of business was held to violate the Sherman Act.

Legal individual agreements have included union refusals to furnish workmen and the refusal of contractors to perform contracts with dealer-applicators (*Weir v Chicago Plastering Institute* (7th Cir 1959) 272 F2d 883), and union prohibitions on subcontracting of work (*United States v Employing Plasterers Ass'n.* (ND Ill 1956) 138 F Supp 546).

In the collective bargaining context, whether a union has acted alone may only be a matter of proof, making important a determination whether the employer has benefited from the union's efforts. In *American Federation of Musicians v Carroll*, it was not clear that the orchestra leaders benefited from the union's demands (except, of course, when the leader performed as a musician). In comparison, the New York electrical contractors were direct beneficiaries of the union "requests."

It is not easy to determine what "acting alone" means. Each collective bargaining agreement requires joint action. It may be more precise to ask whether the objective was a joint one or represents the union's demand reluctantly agreed to by the employer. The determination is further complicated in industries in which the same individual may divide his time between being an employer, an independent contractor, or an employee. See §14.20.

Unilateral union conduct commonly found not to violate the Sherman Act includes:

1. Jurisdictional dispute between two unions with resulting picketing and boycotting. *United States v Hutcheson* (1941) 312 US 219.

2. Strike threat by union to compel assignment of work to its members rather than to rival union's members. *Schatte v Theatrical Stage Employees* (9th Cir 1950) 182 F2d 158, *cert den* (1950) 340 US 827.

3. Primary and secondary boycotts by union to compel other employers, unions, and its own members to cease doing business with an employer to win contract demands. *Davis Pleating and Button Co. v California Sportswear & Dress Ass'n.* (SD Calif 1956) 145 F Supp 864.

4. Primary boycott by union by prohibiting its members from working for employers who refuse to agree to use only available union members. *Taylor v Horseshoers Local 7* (D Md 1963) 222 F Supp 812, *rev'd on other grounds* (4th Cir 1965) 353 F2d 593, *cert den* (1966) 384 US 969. *But see I.P.C. Distributors, Inc. v Chicago Moving Picture Machine Operators Local 110* (ND Ill 1955) 132 F Supp 294, in which the court refused to dismiss a complaint alleging a refusal by union members to project film in theatres with which the union had a closed-shop contract and with which a distributing company had contracts for distributing films.

5. Striking and picketing to secure more jobs for union members. *Gundersheimer's Inc. v Bakery & Confectionery Workers* (DC Cir 1941) 119 F2d 205.

6. Strike and picketing accompanied by violence. *United States v Gold* (2d Cir 1940) 115 F2d 236.

7. Strike threat to force discontinuing use of labor-saving equipment or to force employment of original number of workers. *United States v Hod Carriers* (1941) 313 US 539.

8. Operation of closed shops and preventing employment of qualified applicant. *Courant v International Photographers of Motion Picture Industry Local 659* (9th Cir 1949) 176 F2d 1000, *cert den* (1950) 338 US 943.

9. Attempt to secure industry-wide closed shop by efforts to reduce use of phonograph records, to prevent amateur radio programs and to require broadcasting companies to hire "standby" musicians. *United States v American Federation of Musicians* (1943) 318 US 741.

10. Union's financial assistance to newspaper in competition with struck newspaper and blacklisting by union of merchants advertising in the struck newspaper. *Scott Publishing Co. v Columbia Basin Publishers, Inc.* (9th Cir 1961) 293 F2d 15, *cert den* (1961) 368 US 940.

E. [§14.20] Is the Union Legitimate?

Antitrust immunity often turns on the legitimacy of the labor organization. This issue arises when the union members are independent contractors, when no employer-employee relationship exists, and when there is no economic relationship between the "union" and the employer. Questions that help to ascertain whether the union is legitimate include:

1. Are the union members independent contractors?

A union that solicits or accepts independent contractors as members may not be immune from the Sherman Act unless the union has a legitimate interest in undertaking the conduct in question. *Local 189, AMC & BW v Jewel Tea Co.* (1965) 381 US 676. In *Milk Wagon Drivers' Union Local 753 v Lake Valley Farm Products, Inc.* (1940) 311 US 91, the Court found the necessary interest when the union sought to protect its members from the imposition of non-union wages and working conditions. See also *Teamsters Local 24 v Oliver* (1959) 358 US 283. Whether members of a union are self-employed businessmen or employees is a question of fact. *United States v Teamsters Local 626* (DC Calif 1962) 1962 Trade Cases ¶70,285. See also *United States v Painters Local 829* (SD NY 1961) 27 FRD 499, holding summary judgment improper when the "employee" issue was raised.

2. Does an employer-employee relationship exist between the union members and the employer?

Although an employer-employee relationship between the union members and the employer group is not an absolute requirement for the existence of a labor dispute under the Norris-LaGuardia Act, if a true employer-employee relationship is lacking, the union members may be held to constitute independent contractors who are subject to the antitrust laws, or a court may find that the dispute is not one concerning terms or conditions of employment. Thus, in *United States v Olympia Provision & Baking Co.* (SD NY 1968) 282 F Supp 819, *aff'd per curiam sub nom Provision Salesmen & Distributors v United States* (1969) 393 US 480, the court found an unlawful price-fixing conspiracy between a union composed of frankfurter distributors and frankfurter manufacturers. The court found that the distributors were independent contractors, not employees of the manufacturers, that they had sought admission to the union for their own purposes, and that the union's activity was directed solely at competition and did not serve any legitimate labor objective. See also *Columbia River Packers Ass'n. v Hinton* (1942) 315 US 143 (attempt by food producers association to force canners to purchase only from it was not a labor dispute); *United States v Women's Sportswear Manufacturers Ass'n.* (1949) 336 US 460 (agreement between garment manufacturer and stitching contractors' association to fix prices and allocate work was not a labor dispute); *American Medical Association v United States* (1943) 317 US 519 (medical association's attempt to prevent full-time employment of doctors with group health association was not a labor dispute); *Taylor v Horseshoers Local 7* (4th Cir 1965) 353 F2d 593, *cert den* (1966) 384 US 969.

3. Does an economic relationship exist between the union and its members?

Unless an economic relationship exists between a union's regular members and its businessman members, such as job or wage competition, the businessman members will not gain immunity from the antitrust laws merely by joining the union. Thus, in *Teamsters Local 626, Los Angeles Meat & Provision Drivers Union v United States* (1962) 371 US 94, businessmen were held subject to the antitrust laws despite their having affiliated with a legitimate union and formed a subdivision of it. Similarly, an association whose charter restricts its object and purposes to those of a traditional labor organization does not automatically acquire antitrust immunity. *Gulf Coast Shrimpers and Oystermans Ass'n. v United States* (5th Cir 1956) 236 F2d 658, *cert den* (1956) 352 US 927.

F. [§14.21] Does the Conduct Involve an Agreement between a Union and an Employer or Employer Group?

A union's immunity from the antitrust laws is particularly in doubt when it acts in concert with employers or an employer group to suppress competition. See, for example, *United Mine Workers v Pennington* (1965) 381 US 657, which held that joint efforts to impose wage scales and funnel royalty payments to a welfare fund constituted an unlawful conspiracy to eliminate small coal mine operators, and *United Brotherhood of Carpenters v United States* (1947) 330 US 395, in which an agreement not to handle competitive lumber products was held unlawful.

G. [§14.22] Is the Primary Purpose of the Agreement to Restrain Trade?

At least one case indicates that if the effect of the suspect clause in the agreement is to restrain trade, federal antitrust laws can be violated even if the clause was adopted for a lawful labor objective, *e.g.*, preserving work for members. *Alpha Beta Food Markets, Inc. v AMC & BW* (Calif Super Ct 1956) 1956 Trade Cases ¶68,357, *aff'd* (1956) 147 CA2d 343, 305 P2d 163.

H. [§14.23] Is the Restraint Direct or Remote?

When the conduct constitutes only an incidental, indirect, or remote restraint on trade and it furthers a legitimate union interest, antitrust immunity will exist. *Local 189, AMC & BW v Jewel Tea Co.* (1965) 381 US 676. See also *United States v Hamilton Glass Co.* (ND Ill 1957) 155 F Supp 878 (wage increases granted under collective bargaining agreement have incidental or remote effect on trade); *Adams Dairy Co. v St. Louis Dairy Co.* (8th Cir 1958) 260 F2d 46 (contract providing for increased commission rates for milk drivers did not restrain trade even though it tended to affect retail milk prices).

I. [§14.24] Is the Purpose of the Conduct Legitimate?

Generally, if the conduct is closely related to wages, hours, or working conditions, immunity will exist. *Local 189, AMC & BW v Jewel Tea Co.* (1965) 381 US 676 held immune a restriction on hours of work which required limitations on the hours during which the employer could sell meat on the ground that the restrictions were intimately related to wages, hours, and working conditions. Similarly, *Cedar Crest Hats, Inc. v United Hatters, Cap and Millinery Workers* (5th Cir 1966) 362 F2d 322 held immune union-coerced retailers' agreements not to purchase goods produced by employers engaged in disputes with the union on the ground that the union-induced boycott was in furtherance of the legitimate objective of unionizing employees and promoting the sale of union-made goods, and *Great Atlantic & Pacific Tea Co. v AMC & BW* (ED Mo 1968) 57 Lab Cas ¶12,664 held immune contract clauses restricting the use of pre-packaged meats in food stores on the ground that their primary purpose was preservation of work performed by union employees.

Immunity may be lost, for example, when a union and contractors require standby pay and reglazing when competitive pre-glazed products are used, thereby affecting the market price of pre-glazed products. *United States v Hamilton Glass Co.* (ND Ill 1957) 155 F Supp 878 (union and contractors formed combination insulating both employer and employees from competition), or when union demands deal with requirements of independent businessmen concerning the extension of credit. *United States v Fish Smokers Trade Council, Inc.* (SD NY 1960) 183 F Supp 227 (demand affected business competition, not wages, hours, or working conditions).

J. [§14.25] Is the Union Acting as an Employer?

A union is not exempt from antitrust prosecution brought against a business wholly-owned by the union. *Streiffer v Seafarers Sea Chest Corp.* (ED La 1958) 162 F Supp 602. However, a union can lend selective financial support to the companies with which it has bargaining agreements. See, *e.g., Ramsey v United Mine Workers* (ED Tenn 1967) 265 F Supp 388, *aff'd* (6th Cir 1969) 416 F2d 655, *rev'd on other grounds* (1971) 39 Law Week 4245, in which the court held that union loans to and purchase of capital stock in two coal companies did not support the inference that the union conspired to direct or control the companies' policies in violation of the antitrust laws, and *Scott Publishing Co. v Columbia Basin Publishers, Inc.* (9th Cir 1961) 293 F2d 15, *cert den* (1961) 368 US 940, in which it was held that financial aid to a newspaper by a union on strike against the newspaper's competitor did not violate the antitrust laws because the aid was not intended to eliminate the struck newspaper, but to keep the other newspaper in operation.

K. [§14.26] Is the Object of the Conduct to Affect Competition in the Product Market?

If the object or effect of the conduct is to affect competition in the product rather than the labor market, so that the price of the product is directly affected by the conduct, antitrust immunity may be lost. See, *e.g.*, *United Mine Workers v Pennington* (1965) 381 US 657 and discussion, §§14.7–14.10. In *United States v Gasoline Retailers Ass'n.* (7th Cir 1961) 285 F2d 688, an agreement prohibiting price advertising and the giving of premiums with the objective of stabilizing prices, and which was maintained and enforced by a union and retailers' association, was held to constitute an illegal price-fixing agreement. See generally, *Labor's Antitrust Exemption After Pennington and Jewel Tea* (1966) 66 *Col L Rev* 742.

On occasion, a court must balance the antitrust policy of providing a product market free of restraints on competition other than supply and demand against the labor policy of allowing unions to bargain on an equal basis with management, which requires permitting unions to achieve a degree of monopoly in the labor market. See, *e.g.*, *Antitrust–Labor Law– Exemption of Union from Antitrust Laws is Lost When It Imposes Minimum Price Levels on a Member-Employer* (1967) 20 *Vand L Rev* 1329, 1333.

L. [§14.27] Is There Clear Proof That the Union Has Participated in the Illegal Conduct?

The Norris-LaGuardia Act requires "clear proof" that a union participated in, authorized, or ratified the illegal acts of its agents before it can be successfully prosecuted. 29 USC §106. The same rule applies to employers. *United Brotherhood of Carpenters v United States* (1947) 330 US 395. "Clear proof" has been defined to require "a substantial margin" of evidence, *e.g.*, more than a "mere preponderance" but less than proof "beyond a reasonable doubt." *Mine Workers v Gibbs* (1966) 383 US 715.

IV. State Law and Federal Preemption

A. [§14.28] Does the Conduct Violate State Law?

When advising whether proposed conduct constitutes a potential antitrust violation, the practitioner must review the state laws that will govern his client's activities. Generally, a party is more vulnerable to prosecution under state antitrust laws than federal antitrust laws because (1) a majority of states have no anti-injunction statutes, (2) those states that have anti-injunction laws generally proscribe a narrower range of enjoinable conduct than does the Norris-LaGuardia Act, (3) many state courts view their anti-injunction laws as procedural rather than substantive, so that state laws which proscribe picketing and strikes in violation of their antitrust laws remain enjoinable, and (4) the Supreme Court has upheld state injunctions against picketing in violation of state antitrust laws. See *Giboney v Empire Storage & Ice Co.* (1949) 336 US 490; *Mayer Bros. Poultry Farms v Meltzer* (NY App Div 1948) 80 NYS 2d 874.

B. [§14.29] Is the State Law Preempted by Federal Law?

State antitrust laws will be subject to federal preemption if the conduct affects interstate commerce and is prohibited or protected under the National Labor Relations Act, or if the conduct affects interstate commerce and conflicts with federal antitrust immunity granted to unions, or if the conduct involves a collective bargaining agreement sanctioned by federal law.

To determine whether state antitrust laws will be treated as preempted usually requires an analysis of the following considerations:

1. Does the conduct affect commerce and is it prohibited or protected by the National Labor Relations Act?

If the conduct substantially affects interstate commerce and if the conduct is proscribed or protected by the National Labor Relations Act, then it is immune from state regulation. *Weber v Anheuser-Busch, Inc.* (1955) 348 US 468; *United States v Bay Area Painters* (ND Calif 1943) 49 F Supp 733. However, conduct such as mass picketing, violence and threatened violence can be enjoined in state court pursuant to the state's police power. *Weber v Anheuser-Busch, Inc., supra,* which also held that a state court can award compensatory relief for conduct that violates both the National Labor Relations Act and state or common law if the remedy is unavailable under the Act and if it does not conflict with remedies available in NLRB proceedings. State courts are prone to construe the preemption doctrine strictly. See *Commonwealth v McHugh* (1950) 326 Mass 249, 93 NE2d 751; *Alfred M. Lewis, Inc. v Teamsters Local 542* (1958) 163 CA2d 771, 330 P2d 53.

The National Labor Relations Act regulates a wide range of employer and union activity. Generally, most conduct is subject to regulation, other than violence, mass picketing and threatened violence, provided that the NLRB's jurisdictional standards are met. Again, state courts are not prone to implement the federal preemption policy. See, *e.g., Alpha Beta Food Markets, Inc. v AMC & BW* (1956) 147 CA2d 343, 305 P2d 163, holding that when the primary purpose of a union contract clause was to restrain trade, the state court could declare the alleged contract clause illegal under state and federal antitrust laws despite the existence of NLRB unfair labor practice jurisdiction, federal court antitrust jurisdiction, and the fact that the disputed clause was adopted pursuant to a lawful labor objective, *i.e.,* maintaining work for union members.

2. Does the conduct involve a collective bargaining agreement sanctioned by federal law?

If the conduct proscribed by a state antitrust law is performed under the terms of a collective bargaining agreement negotiated under the aegis of the National Labor Relations Act, it cannot be enjoined in state court. *Teamsters Local 24 v Oliver* (1959) 358 US 283. Thus, an agreement negotiated and executed under the NLRA's mandatory bargaining provisions concerning mandatory subjects of bargaining cannot be nullified by state law.

C. [§14.30] Is the Conduct Prohibited by the Federal Antitrust Laws?

The mere fact that the conduct involves unfair labor practices within the exclusive jurisdiction of the NLRB does not prevent federal courts from prosecuting violations of the antitrust laws. *Jewel Tea Co. v AMC & BW* (7th Cir 1960) 274 F2d 217, *cert den* (1960) 362 US 936. However, hot-cargo agreements, which violate the NLRA, cannot be prosecuted under the antitrust laws. *E.g., Texas Millinery Co. v United Hatters, Cap and Millinery Workers* (ND Tex 1964) 229 F Supp 341, *aff'd on other grounds sub nom Cedar Crest Hats, Inc. v United Hatters, Cap and Millinery Workers* (5th Cir 1966) 362 F2d 322; *Galveston Truck Line Corp. v Ada Motor Lines, Inc.* (WD Okla 1958) 1958 Trade Cases ¶69,121; *Meier & Pohlmann Furniture Co. v Gibbons* (ED Mo 1953) 113 F Supp 409, *aff'd* (8th Cir 1956) 233 F2d 296, *cert den* (1956) 352 US 879.

Table of Statutes

(Statutes in bold face, Book Sections in light face.)

Table of Cases

Table of Cases

Table of Cases

Table of Cases

771

Table of Cases

Sterling Drug, Inc. v Benatar (1950) 99 Cal App 2d 393, §*3.34*

Stern Fish Co. v Century Seafoods, Inc. (ED Pa 1966) 254 F Supp 151, §*12.51*

Story Parchment Co. v Paterson Parchment Paper Co. (1931) 282 US 555, §*2.48*, §*12.35*, §*12.36*, §*13.41*

Streiffer v Seafarers Sea Chest Corp. (ED La 1958) 162 F Supp 602, §*14.25*

Structural Laminates, Inc. v Douglas Fir Plywood Ass'n. (D Ore 1966) 261 F Supp 154, *aff'd per curiam* (9th Cir 1968) 399 F2d 155, 156, *cert den* (1969) 393 US 1024, §*8.21*

Students Book Co. v Washington Law Book Co. (DC Cir 1955) 232 F2d 49, *cert den* (1956) 350 US 988, §*5.14*, §*5.18*

Subpoena Duces Tecum, In re (ND Calif 1948) 81 F Supp 418, §*10.31*

Suburban Propane Gas Corp. (1967) [1967–1970 Transfer Binder] FTC Dkt 8672, Trade Reg Rep ¶*17,965*, §*5.4*

Suckow Borax Mines Consol. v Borax Consol. (9th Cir 1950) 185 F2d 196, *cert den* (1951) 340 US 943, §*2.38*, §*2.44*

Sugar Institute, Inc. v United States (1936) 297 US 553, §*8.12*, §*8.23*, §*8.27*, §*8.31*

Sun Cosmetic Shoppe, Inc. v Elizabeth Arden Sales Corp. (2d Cir 1949) 178 F2d 150, §*12.36*

Sun Oil Co. v FTC (7th Cir 1965) 350 F2d 624, *cert den* (1966) 382 US 982, §*3.27*

Sun Theatre Corp. v RKO Radio Pictures, Inc. (7th Cir 1954) 213 F2d 284, §*2.43*, §*12.34*

Sun Valley Disposal Co. v Silver State Disposal Co. (9th Cir 1969) 420 F2d 341, §*2.12*, §*2.13*, §*2.47*, §*13.31*

Sunkist Growers, Inc. v Winckler & Smith Citrus Products Co. (1962) 370 US 19, §*2.8*, §*2.11*, §*12.66*

Sunshine Biscuits, Inc. v FTC (7th Cir 1962) 306 F2d 48, 51–52, *reversing* (1961) 59 FTC 674, 680, §*5.50*

Surprise Brassiere Co., Inc. (1966) [1965–1967 Transfer Binder] FTC Dkt 8584, Trade Reg Rep ¶*17,566*, *aff'd* (5th Cir 1969) 406 F2d 711, §*5.50*

Surprise Brassiere Co. v FTC (5th Cir 1969) 406 F2d 711, §*5.31*, §*5.32*, §*5.50*, §*12.31*

Susser v Carvel Corp. (2d Cir 1964) 332 F2d 505, §*3.8*

Susser v Carvel Corp. (2d Cir 1964) 332 F2d 505, 519–520, *cert dismissed* (1965) 381 US 125, §*2.32*, §*3.6*, §*3.15*, §*3.18*

Susser v Carvel Corp. (SD NY 1962) 206 F Supp 636, *aff'd* (2d Cir 1962) 332 F2d 505, §*3.13*

Swanee Paper Corp. v FTC (2d Cir 1961) 291 F2d 833, *cert den* (1962) 368 US 987, §*5.31*

Swift & Co. v United States (1905) 196 US 375, §*2.60*, §*2.61*, §*2.62*, §*8.26*

Swingline Inc. (1968) 3 Trade Reg Rep ¶¶*18,305*, *18,948*, §*4.14*

Swingline Inc. (1969) 3 Trade Reg Rep ¶*18,867* and ¶*18,948*, §*4.64*

Sylvania Electric Products, Inc. (1954) 51 FTC 282, §*5.45*

Syracuse Broadcasting Corp. v Newhouse (2d Cir 1963) 319 F2d 683, §*5.15*

Tag Mfrs. Institute v FTC (1st Cir 1949) 174 F2d 452, §*8.27*, §*8.31*

Tampa Electric Co. v Nashville Coal Co. (1961) 365 US 320, §*3.5*, §*3.7*, §*3.8*

Taylor v Horseshoers Local 7 (4th Cir 1965) 353 F2d 593, *cert den* (1966) 384 US 969, §*14.20*

Taylor v Horseshoers Local 7 (D Md 1963) 222 F Supp 812, *rev'd on other grounds* (4th Cir 1965) 353 F2d 593, *cert den* (1966) 384 US 969, §*14.19*

Teamsters Local 24 v Oliver (1959) 358 US 283, §*14.20*, §*14.29*

Teamsters Local 626, Los Angeles Meat & Provision Drivers Union v United States (1962) 371 US 94, §*14.20*

Texas Millinery Co. v United Hatters, Cap and Millinery Workers (ND Tex 1964) 229 F Supp 341, *aff'd on other grounds sub nom Cedar Crest Hats, Inc. v United Hatters, Cap and Millinery Workers* (5th Cir 1966) 362 F2d 322, §*14.30*

Table of Cases

779

United States v Western Pine Ass'n. (SD
Calif 1941) 1940–1943 Trade Cases
¶56,107, §111(g) Consent Decree, *§8.31*
United States v Wilson Sporting Goods Co.
(ND Ill 1968) 288 F Supp 543, *§4.14,
§4.23, §4.30, §4.34, §4.35, §4.39, §4.56,
§4.61*
United States v Wilson Sporting Goods Co.
(ND Ill 1968) 1968 Trade Cases ¶72,585,
§4.61
United States v Winslow (1913) 227 US
202, *§2.61, §2.62*
*United States v Women's Sportswear
Manufacturers Ass'n.* (1949) 336 US
460, *§14.20*
United States v World Journal Tribune, Inc.
(SD NY 1966) 1966 Trade Cases
¶71,925, *§4.14, §4.38*
United States v Yellow Cab Co. (1947) 332
US 218, *§2.11, §2.12, §2.13*
United States v Youngblood (2d Cir 1967)
379 F2d 365, *§13.91*
Universal-Rundle (1964) [1963–1965
Transfer Binder] FTC Dkt 8070, Trade
Reg Rep ¶16,948, *rev'd on other
grounds* (7th Cir 1965) 352 F2d 831,
rev'd on other grounds and remanded
(1967) 378 US 244, *§5.21*
Universal-Rundle Corp. v FTC (7th Cir
1967) 382 F2d 285, *§5.17*
Upjohn Co. v Carlton Drug Co. (SD NY
1966) 1966 Trade Cases ¶71,775, *§3.35*
Upjohn Co. v Vineland Discount Center (D
NJ 1964) 235 F Supp 191, *§3.35*
*U.S. Industries, Inc. v United States District
Court* (9th Cir 1965) 345 F2d 18, *cert
den* (1965) 382 US 814, *§10.23, §12.61,
§13.75*
Utah Pie Co. v Continental Baking Co.
(1967) 386 US 685, *§5.39, §12.21*
*Utah Public Service Comm'n. v El Paso
Natural Gas Co.* (1969) 395 US 464,
§4.62
*Utah v American Pipe and Construction
Co.*(CD Calif 1970) 1970 Trade Cases
¶73,143, *§12.4*

*Valley Plymouth v Studebaker-Packard
Corp.* (SD Calif 1963) 219 F Supp 608,
§5.16, §5.52
Van Dusen v Barrack (1964) 376 US 612,
§13.20
*Vanadium Corp. of America v Susquehanna
Corp.* (D Del 1962) 203 F Supp 686,
§4.14, §4.81
Vanity Fair Paper Mills, Inc. v FTC (2d Cir
1962) 311 F2d 480, *§5.31, §5.32*
Vermont v Cayuga Rock Salt Co. (D Me
1967) 276 F Supp 970, *§2.41*
Vines v General Outdoor Advertising Co.
(2d Cir 1948) 171 F2d 487, *§2.48*
Viviano Macaroni Co. (1968) FTC Dkt 8666,
3 Trade Reg Rep ¶18,246, *§5.26*
*Volasco Products Co. v Lloyd A. Fry
Roofing Co.* (6th Cir 1962) 308 F2d 383,
393–395, *cert den* (1963) 372 US 907,
§2.48, §2.58, §12.27, §13.26
*Volasco Products Co. v Lloyd A. Fry
Roofing Co.* (6th Cir 1965) 346 F2d 661,
cert den (1965) 382 US 904, *§5.39,
§12.9, §12.40*
Vornado v Corning Glass Works (3d Cir
1968) 388 F2d 11, *§3.35*

Walder v Paramount Publix Corp. (SD NY
1955) 132 F Supp 912, *§2.48*
Waldron v British Petroleum Co. (SD NY
1964) 231 F Supp 72, *§12.5, §13.26*
*Walker Distributing Co. v Lucky Lager
Brewing Co.* (9th Cir 1963) 323 F2d 1,
*§2.48, §2.64, §3.40, §12.27, §12.41, §12.44,
§12.46*
*Walker Process Equipment, Inc. v Food
Machinery & Chemical Corp.* (1965) 382
US 172, *§2.62, §2.64, §7.7, §12.30, §12.72*
*Washington Gas Light Co. v Virginia
Electric and Power Co.* (ED Va 1970)
309 F Supp 1119, *§12.20, §12.32*
*Washington Professional Basketball Corp. v
National Basketball Association* (SD NY
1956) 147 F Supp 154, *§13.26*
*Washington State Bowling Proprietors
Association v Pacific Lanes, Inc.* (9th Cir

Index

F

G

passing-on defense, §12.25
pleading and procedure, §12.42-12.50
proximate cause, §12.26
release,
    form of, §12.77
retaliation or revenge cases, §12.23
settlements, §12.74
vertical restriction cases, §12.19
protective orders and, §12.63
proximate cause, §12.26
public injury doctrine, §12.28
regulated industries, §12.68
release,
    form of, §12.77
releases and covenants not to sue, §12.81
rule of reason and, §12.29
service of process, §12.52
service of the complaint, §13.19
settlement by sale of the plaintiff's busi-
    ness, §12.84
settlements, §13.50
    form of settlement letter, §12.76
    joint tortfeasors, §12.74
    offset for, §12.82
standing and, §12.27, 13.23
statute of limitations, §12.12
    FTC, §6.10
statutory basis for suit, §13.22
stipulation and order for dismissal without
    prejudice,
    form of, §12.79
sufficiency of allegations, §13.33, 13.34
tax treatment of antitrust recoveries,
    §12.85
tie-in arrangements and, §12.32
unclean hands, §12.69
venue and, §12.51, 13.19
    transfer of, §13.20
violations of the antitrust laws,
    FTC judgments and, §12.62
    rule of reason and, §12.29
Procedure. See also Discovery; Jurisdiction;
    Statute of Limitations; Venue.
Procedure
affirmative defenses,
    private antitrust suits, §13.38
allegations of a prior government judge-
    ment, §13.27

answers,
    government civil suit, §13.57
antitrust complaint, §13.3
    responsive pleadings, §13.4
appeal to the commission, §13.12
appeal to the courts,
    FTC antitrust complaint, §13.13
appeal to the Supreme Court,
    government civil suits, §13.70
civil investigative demand, §10.24
complaint,
    form for,
        private antitrust suit, §12.42-12.50
    injury alleged,
        private antitrust suits, §13.36
    sufficiency of allegations,
        private antitrust suits, §13.33, 13.34
    title and demand for jury, §12.42
consent decrees,
    antitrust division, §11.15-11.18
counterclaims and cross-claims,
    private antitrust suits, §13.39
depositions,
    private antitrust suit, §13.45
Federal Trade Commission,
    Robinson-Patman Act, §5.4
hearing on antitrust complaint, §13.8
injunction,
    papers in support of,
        private antitrust suit, §12.40
interrogatories,
    forms of,
        private antitrust suit, §12.55-12.57
interrogatories and motions to produce,
    private antitrust suit, §13.44
interrogatories to identify defendants,
    §12.56
intervention in government suit,
    mergers, §4.79
machine records interrogatories,
    private antitrust suit, §12.57
mergers,
    intervention in government suit, §4.79
pleading,
    nolo contendere pleas, §11.9
patent-antitrust cases,
    generally, §7.25
pleading,
    forms, §12.42-12.50